"I am prepared to believe that the sense of romance in those of our brothers and sisters who incline toward love of their own sex is heightened to a more blazing pitch than in those who think of themselves as normal."
Laurence Olivier

"[Larry] would have slept with anyone."
Producer David Lewis

"Noël adored Larry, there is no other word for it."
Larry Cole, Noël Coward's intimate friend

"Her Ladyship is fucking bored with such formality and prefers to be known as Vivien Leigh."
Vivien Leigh, on what it's like being referred to as "Lady Olivier."

"If ever there was a flawed masterpiece, it was Vivien."
Her lover, actor Peter Finch

"I was barely out of my teens when Larry started fucking me."
Vivien Leigh

Indecisive Hamlet,
Doomed Ophelia
1937

Damn You, Scarlett O'Hara

The Private Lives of

Vivien Leigh and Laurence Olivier

In 1937, the most famous and gossiped-about actors in Europe en route from London's Waterloo Station to Denmark for their upcoming royal command performance of *Hamlet* at Kronberg Castle.

OTHER BOOKS BY DARWIN PORTER

BIOGRAPHIES

Humphrey Bogart, The Making of a Legend
Howard Hughes, Hell's Angel
Steve McQueen, King of Cool, Tales of a Lurid Life
Paul Newman, The Man Behind the Baby Blues
Merv Griffin, A Life in the Closet
Brando Unzipped
The Secret Life of Humphrey Bogart (© 2003)
Katharine the Great: Hepburn, Secrets of a Life Revealed
Jacko, His Rise and Fall (The Social and Sexual History of Michael Jackson)
And Forthcoming:
Frank Sinatra, The Boudoir Singer
The Kennedys, All the Gossip Unfit to Print
J. Edgar Hoover & Clyde Tolson:
(Investigating the Sexual Secrets of America's Most Famous Men & Women)

FILM CRITICISM

Fifty Years of Queer Cinema (500 of the Best GLBTQ Films Ever Made)
Blood Moon's Guides to Gay & Lesbian Film (Volumes One & Two)

NON-FICTION

Hollywood Babylon-It's Back!, and *Hollywood Babylon Strikes Again!*

NOVELS

Butterflies in Heat; Rhinestone Country;
Marika (a roman à clef based on the life of Marlene Dietrich*)*
Venus (a roman à clef based on the life of Anaïs Nin*);*
Razzle-Dazzle; Midnight in Savannah;
Blood Moon, The Erotic Thriller; Hollywood's Silent Closet

TRAVEL GUIDES

Many editions and many variations of ***The Frommer Guides***
to Europe, the Caribbean, California, Georgia, and The Carolinas

OTHER BOOKS BY ROY MOSELEY

Bette Davis, An Intimate Memoir
Evergreen, Victor Saville in His Own Words
Rex Harrison, The First Biography
My Stars and Other Friends
Roger Moore
'Ay Hamlet, What's Wrong with Scarlett Tonight?
(an Overview of Vivien Leigh, Laurence Olivier, & Joan Plowright)
and, co-authored with Charles Higham:
Cary Grant, The Lonely Heart,
Elizabeth and Philip, and
Princess Merle

DAMN YOU, SCARLETT O'HARA

THE PRIVATE LIVES OF VIVIEN LEIGH AND LAURENCE OLIVIER

A Hot, Startling, and Unauthorized Probe
of the Two Most Famous and Gossiped-About Actors
of the 20th Century, by

Darwin Porter
&
Roy Moseley

DAMN YOU, SCARLETT O'HARA
THE PRIVATE LIVES OF
VIVIEN LEIGH AND LAURENCE OLIVIER

Manufactured in the United States of America

ISBN 978-1-936003-15-0

Cover designs by Richard Leeds (Bigwigdesign.com)
Videography and Publicity Trailers by Piotr Kajstura
Special thanks to Photofest in New York City
The authors extend special acknowledgment and thanks to
Monica Dunn and Robert Uher for their invaluable help and support

Distributed in North America and Australia
through National Book Network (www.NBNbooks.com)
and in the UK through Turnaround (www.turnaround-uk.com)

1 2 3 4 5 6 7 8 9 10

THE AUTHORS DEDICATE THIS BOOK TO
DANFORTH PRINCE

WITH LOVING ACKNOWLEDGEMENTS TO RAIE AND RALPH.

AUTHORS' NOTE

In the pages ahead, a description of the source of each individual piece of information is positioned very close to the spot where that information actually appears. Also, within the pages ahead, direct quotations have been transcribed "as they were remembered" by the witnesses who originally heard the remarks. They're presented with the same nuances, and with the same phraseologies, that were used when those remarks were originally transmitted.

Vivien Leigh in her most memorable role as Scarlett O'Hara (1939)

"I knew that it would take death itself to free me of this cursed character."

Where Love Has Gone?

Passion's fire was a dying ember as Vivien and Larry were photographed arriving at
St-Martin-in-the-Fields Church in London (1958).

CHAPTER ONE

At the age of seventy-six, Dame Joan, the actress Joan Plowright, was asked about the private life of her sexually ambiguous late husband, Lord Laurence Olivier.

This straightforward woman, known for her honesty, sophistication, and common sense, responded, "If a man is touched by genius, he is not an ordinary person. He doesn't lead an ordinary life. He has extremes of behavior which you understand. You just find a way not to be swept overboard by his demons. You kind of stand apart. You continue your own work and your absorption in the family. And those other things finally don't matter."

Those demons were hovering over the modest house of a clergyman and his wife at 26 Wathen Road in the market town of Dorking, Surrey, 24 miles (38 km) from London.

The date that spring day was May 22, 1907. That morning a pregnant Agnes Olivier had walked in her well-manicured garden. Her roses were at their most beautiful. She even saw a meadowlark, viewing that as a good omen for the imminent birth of her child.

At the time Laurence Kerr Olivier entered the world, England was giving birth to some of its greatest actors—Ralph Richardson in 1902, John Gielgud in 1904, and Michael Redgrave in 1908, a year later than Olivier.

All these future great actors were born too young to face the trenches of World War I. The sexual indiscretions of their youth had passed before England entered the Second World War.

Each of these artists would grow up between the wars, having been born at the apogee of the Edwardian age. Queen Victoria had died, ending her long reign. Her son, a corpulent and debauched Edward VII, sat on the throne, ushering in an era of liberated sexuality and greater artistic freedom in the theater.

The baby boy born that day in Dorking, next door to a chimney sweeper's house, would bring English theater into the modern era as its greatest actor.

His private life would be one of such undying passion and turbulence that it would equal any character he played on the stage or screen, even Heathcliff himself.

When her husband, Gerard, finally climbed the steps to their bedroom, Agnes was cradling their newly born son in her protective arms, as if sensing those demons.

"I don't know what he's going to become in life," she told her husband. "No doubt some self-made genius. A great architect, perhaps. The prime minister of the realm. A novelist to define us in the 20th century the way Charles Dickens did for the Victorians. All I know is that when our son is buried at Westminster Abbey decades from now, trumpets will sound across London."

***

The latest addition to the Olivier family may have been embraced by his mother, but his father, Gerard Olivier, was indifferent to the newborn, a feeling he had that would last a lifetime.

Gerard was cooking some sausages in the kitchen when the doctor brought in the newborn infant. Wrapped in a blanket, he was handed to Gerard who held him only for a moment. He handed him back and returned to his bangers on the stove.

"No wonder he turned in disgust from me," Larry later recalled. "I must have been a sight, covered in blood and afterbirth, or whatever just born babies are covered in."

The addition to the family was christened Laurence at St. Martin's Church. He was named for Laurent Olivier, a Frenchman who lived in the 16th century, the earliest recorded name in the family tree. Laurent Olivier, a French Huguenot, was born in Nay, France, in the Pyrénées, close to the

Good-looking parents: The Reverend Gerard Kerr Olivier and his wife Agnes Louise Crookenden Olivier

mountainous border with Spain.

"I came from a distinguished family, but we were the poor relations," Larry said. "Father was the black sheep of the family."

Gerard seemed to want Larry as much as he did a third leg. Gerard and Agnes already had two other children—Sybille, born in 1901, and Gerard, Jr. named after his father when he was born in 1904. Gerard Sr. was called "Fahv" by his children.

Before he settled down to the quiet life of a clergyman, Gerard had shown a rebellious streak in Victorian England. He attended Merton College at Oxford but was "sent down" because of his wild drinking sprees and his tendency to run up huge debts which he had no intention of paying.

There was even a suggestion that he wanted to appear on the stage. In a fit of daring, he posed naked for his brother, Herbert Olivier, who wanted him to pose as Actaeon, the famous Theban hero who fell to the fatal wrath of Artemis. Herbert later became England's official painter during World War I.

Another brother, Sydney Olivier, became even more famous. He was the first to have the title of Lord Olivier. A Fabian, he was a friend of George Bernard Shaw, who compared Sydney's look to that of a Spanish grandee and also claimed that Olivier was "strongly sexed."

Queen Victoria would name Sydney Governor of Jamaica in an era when that colony was one of the richest in the British Empire. Later, in 1924, he became Secretary of India under Ramsay MacDonald's Labour administration.

Sydney was young Larry's favorite uncle. When they would later meet, Larry, then nine years old, asked Sydney if he often went to the theater, considering that he'd been a close friend of Shaw's and had written three plays himself. "Never," Sydney said. "I prefer the cinema. It's less taxing on the brain."

Gerard had married Agnes Louise Crookenden on April 30, 1898 in the twilight of Victoria's reign. She was the sister-in-law of the headmaster at the school where he taught.

He'd encountered her while teaching at Boxgrove, a private school for boys some 40 miles (65 km) outside London near Guildford. "I found her the brightest flower growing in Surrey's garden."

Apparently, the few remaining photographs of her do not do justice to her beauty. She had alabaster skin, thick chestnut colored hair, and a quick wit.

After their marriage, the couple established a private school but it attracted so few pupils it went bankrupt.

Agnes with Laurence

3

When their school failed and Gerard became a clergyman, Agnes lamented. "I never wanted to marry a clergyman. We'll starve to death."

At the age of two, Larry moved with his family to a larger house they called "East Dene." It was on the border of the thick forests of Box Hill and within a short walk of the Mole River.

"As a child growing into boyhood, I was a weakling, a shrimp," Larry later said. "By the time I was five, I was a weed, a horribly thin creature whose arms hung like wires from my shoulders. My arms and legs were knobby matchsticks."

"As I grew into boyhood, I think my father feared I wasn't going to develop into a man," Larry said. "Once he told me that there are children born into this world who are borderline cases—not quite a girl, but not a real man either. It made me real insecure. I fled to my mother's arms. I was a real Mummy's boy growing up."

Of her three children, Agnes clearly favored Larry. At family picnics she would let her long hair down and allow him to go to sleep on it.

In later life he spoke of her luminous brown eyes that had shown him such love during her short life. "There was always a mystery about her. It was something in her eyes. It was as if she were holding something back, never wanting anyone, even her loving son, to unlock the door to her secrets. She was a romantic at heart, trapped in an unromantic role as the wife of a clergyman."

Larry was terrified of his father but continued to love his Agnes. He virtually worshipped his older brother Dickie, also named Gerard Olivier.

In the expurgated version of Larry's biography, *Confessions of an Actor*, he claimed that he looked upon Dickie as "my own special hero throughout my entire boyhood."

"He could do no wrong in my eyes," Larry said. "Even if he did something bad, I took the blame for it and suffered the spanking. I couldn't stand the idea of Dickie experiencing pain."

Gerard made Agnes punish the children, although in most Edwardian homes that job usually fell to the father. Agnes detested the task but was forced to do it when Gerard ordered her to. She hated spanking Larry most of all.

"Dickie always gave me some special treat when mother paddled me—not him," Larry said. He remained indifferent to his father, but spent as much time as he could with Dickie, whom he called "Baba."

Laurence's older sister Sybille

4

"Dickie called me Kim," Larry said. "All of us had nicknames. Dickie was very masculine. His body developed much quicker than mine. After he took his bath, Dickie let me dry him off."

Larry's father, a priest in the High Anglican Church, knew the value of a shilling. "To save on the hot water bill, he took a hot bath, then let my brother bathe," Larry said. "I got in last. The water was cold and murky since we bathed only one time a week. There was a certain irony that one of my most famous scenes in films, was a depiction of me luxuriating in a fabulous Roman bath and being serviced, so to speak, by a succulent Tony Curtis."

In *Spartacus,* Larry was cast as the patrician Crassus, the richest Roman of them all.

It appears that Larry developed a schoolboy crush on his older brother. He washed out his underwear and even shared his sausages and thinly sliced chicken with Dickie when he saw that the family's lean rations weren't satisfying his brother's appetite.

Larry shared the same bed with Dickie. Their house was not heated properly in winter. Larry later confessed that he was introduced to sex by Dickie. He was going to write about this in his autobiography but was discouraged.

"I wanted to service Dickie and bring him pleasure," Larry claimed. "Bringing pleasure to him delighted me. Some days I couldn't wait for bedtime. I never knew what sort of pleasure he'd want but I was eager to deliver. Sometimes it caused me pain, but if Dickie enjoyed himself, I could endure any discomfort."

"Father Olivier," as he was called, walked along Dorking High Street in a cassock and a black shovel hat. Gerard never became the actor he wanted to be, but he brought his theatrical flair to his sermons.

His father's loud, resonant voice rang throughout his church, and he had a flamboyant manner in the pulpit, attracting far wider church attendance than the priest before him.

As he grew older, Larry aided his father, waving caskets of incense in the

(upper photo, center figure)
Laurence, aged seven

(lower photo,left to right) Sybille, Gerard, and Dickie Olivier

5

church. "I filled the air with sweet, mystical scents," Larry said, "even though I didn't know why I was doing that. Early on I showed a flair for the theatrical."

To add even more drama to the church services, Agnes would show up and play the piano while Larry sang inspirational songs in his soprano voice. "He sang like a bloody angel," she later said.

"If I had any real fault as a child," Larry said, "it was that I could not tell the truth. I just couldn't. I had to embellish any event, regardless of how humdrum, to make it more dramatic. I became the most convincing liar of my generation. What is acting but lying?"

In 1910, when Gerard came to feel that he was growing stagnant in Dorking, he impulsively moved his family to London, settling into Notting Hill, which was a slum at the time.

He'd accepted a position as a curate attached to St. James's Church, which was nothing but a tacky tin-roofed mission hut.

The Oliviers lived in a four-story terrace house at 86 Elgin Crescent for only a year before Gerard lost his position. The stern Victorian vicar, noting Gerard's flamboyant preaching style, suggested he might be happier in the Catholic Church. Gerard was forced to resign.

Eventually he moved his family to a terrace house at 22 Lupis Street in Pimlico in South London, across from the Church of Saviour's, where he would be preaching. Larry was five years old at the time. He would live at this Pimlico address for six years.

It was in Pimlico that Agnes discovered what the "true calling" of her son was to be. Even at the age of seven, he wanted to be an actor.

Baby Laurence

The discovery came one summer day when she entered his bedroom to see him standing on a wooden chest. The window curtains served as an imagined stage curtain. Her son was performing a recitation of Mark Antony's "Friends, Romans, countrymen" speech from Shakespeare's *Julius Caesar*.

Agnes shared what to her was an exciting new discovery with her husband. Even though he had wanted to be an actor himself, he received the news with great disdain.

He was not at all enthusiastic about his son entering the theater. "I gave up my dream. The boy can also give up his dream." He reminded her that in his father's day, actors by law in England were classified as "rogues and vagabonds."

"It was not the life I'd want a boy of mine to enter," Gerard said. "It's a wicked place for a young boy. There are a lot of vultures out there eager for his flesh. But, if it's important to the both of you, I will not stand in his way. Neither will I encourage my son to enter a field where heartbreak is inevitable."

As the weeks went by, Gerard softened his hard line. Once when Larry performed a scene from *Macbeth* for him, Gerard turned to Agnes and said, "The acorn doesn't fall far from the tree."

By August, Gerard was constructing a wooden stage in their backyard in which Larry could present shows for not only his family but tolerant neighbors, who assured Agnes that "the boy has a lot of talent. He'll make a great actor someday."

"I certainly don't want to raise another preacher man," Agnes said. "One clergyman in the family is enough."

Beginning in 1914, Larry entered a number of prep schools, where he spent more time crying than studying. At one point he was enrolled in the Francis Holland Church of England School for Girls, which accepted only a few boys.

Larry had turned nine years old. Like a stage mother, Agnes wanted to enroll him in the prestigious All Saints Choir School lying off Oxford Circus in London. Her older son Dickie was already a student there.

She was persistent and didn't back down after receiving three rejections from the school. Finally, because Dickie was such a good student and "had such a fine voice," the younger Olivier brother was at long last accepted.

His father had warned him about the "vultures" waiting to devour a young boy such as himself in the theater. What Gerard didn't know is that such vultures also were fathers in the churches, waiting to entrap innocent boys.

***

By 1916 Larry was enrolled in the choir school of All Saints, which stood on Margaret Street, near Oxford Circus, in the heart of the West End. It was in this district in the years to come that Larry would distinguish himself in the theater.

He eagerly looked forward to bonding with

A developing thespian: Laurence, at 12, plays a matador

Dickie, but found that his brother had changed. As Dickie grew older, he preferred the company of classmates his own age. As for intimacy, Dickie told Larry that he had found an older woman in Marylebone who liked to entertain him while her husband was at work.

In spite of his earlier rejections, Larry was thrilled to be enrolled at one of the major Anglo-Catholic churches in London, a school known for its musical reputation.

Instead of Dickie, Larry attracted the attention of Geoffrey Heald, whom the students called "Father Heald." Many of the choir boys were afraid of Father Heald. He seemed to have a bad reputation, and the boys gossiped among themselves and warned each other to try to avoid being locked in the same room with him.

Larry had no such fears. He basked in the glow of Father Heald's approval and soon became known as the "teacher's pet."

The other boys figured out what was going on and privately mocked Larry. Two of them had been molested by Father Heald and had spread the word to the other boys.

"Father Heald's sermons became theatrical performances, very dramatic," Larry recalled. "My own father in the pulpit had a flair for the dramatic, but he paled in comparison to the high drama of Father Heald. Every Sunday it was as if Father Heald was staging, say, *A Midsummer Night's Dream*, with him playing all the parts. He kept his congregation spellbound."

"He was given to dramatic outbursts," Larry said. "He also brought humor to his sermons, when most other priests were of the fire-and-brimstone type. Instead of appearing in a black robe, he often came out in flaming scarlet, or 'Cardinal purple.' One time he was a vision in delicate Belgian lace with red shoes that had a very high heel. He seemed to take as his role models some of the more flamboyant queens in the Vatican."

Pre-teen Laurence

Father Heald asked Larry to carry the chain-suspended thurible, swinging it in a broad arc to fill the church with pillows of incense, sometimes so strong it made the more delicate members of the congregation reach for their smelling salts.

Larry, in later life, of course, would be helmed by some of the finest directors in the world, but Father Heald became the most influential person to fill Larry with a love of the theater. He confessed that instead of becoming a priest, he would have preferred going onto the stage, echoing a wish of Larry's own father.

It is not known when the relationship between Father Heald and Larry became sexual. But it did. Father Heald was just one in thousands of priests who were drawn to the church and its availability of young choir boys. It appears that Father Heald was the man who introduced Larry to sodomy, which had not been part of his relationship with Dickie.

To a few trusted friends over the years, including John Gielgud and Noël Coward, Larry spoke openly about his sexual involvement with the priest. Apparently, he did not view himself as a victim of the older man, but welcomed his advances. Dickie may have been aware of what was happening to his younger brother, but never interfered.

Having no friends at school, and Dickie with no more time for him, Larry moved more and more into Father Heald's orbit. The priest was either rehearsing him or helping him with his studies, perhaps acting as his counselor. The father always had some reason to be alone with the impressionable young boy. Often Larry returned to his dormitory bed at midnight, when "lights out" had been declared at nine in the evening.

At Christmas in 1916 Larry appeared as a policeman in a school play. But by the Christmas of the following year, he was cast by Father Heald as Brutus in a production of *Julius Caesar*. He would play opposite Dickie, who was cast as Caesar.

"I was introduced to William Shakespeare," Larry said, "and we would become bedfellows for life."

Among the distinguished guests watching Olivier's stage debut was the great Ellen Terry, aunt of John Gielgud.

The leading Shakespearean actor in Britain, Terry, like Larry himself, began acting in the Bard's works when she too was but a child. At the end of the performance, Terry told Father Heald "that young Laurence Olivier is already a great actor." Terry was accompanied to the play by the formidable Sybil Thorndike.

Father Heald conveyed Ellen Terry's praise to his protégé.

"Just who is Ellen Terry?" Larry asked.

"She's only the most famous actress in the world," Father Heald told Larry.

"Of all the compliments and critical evaluations I received in my life, none was as important to me as hers," Larry said. "After *Julius Caesar*, I decided to spend the rest of my days upon the wicked stage."

In 1918 Gerard became rector of St. Michael's Church

Teenaged Laurence

9

at Letchworth, in Hertfordshire, which lay 30 miles (48 km) north of London. His Queen Anne house in the old village stood near a church from the twelfth century. Letchworth itself was one of the new Edwardian garden cities laid out in 1903.

Larry was so successful as Brutus that Father Heald cast him in the role of Maria—"the smallest wren of nine"—in Shakespeare's *Twelfth Night*. Father Heald enjoyed dressing Larry up as a girl, supervising all his scenes, his makeup, and wardrobe.

Before he went back to school in 1920 and on his final visit to Agnes, she said: "Darling, Larry, no matter what your father says, be an actor—a great actor. For me!"

In March of 1920, when Larry was twelve years old, Father Heald brought him the "worst news of my young life up to that point. My mother, my beloved mother Agnes had died of a brain tumor. She was not even fifty years old. Father Heald asked me if I still wanted to go on stage and sing my solo, *Benedictus*."

"I told him I did," Larry said. "I sang my heart out, trying to be a brave soul. After the curtain went down, I cried and cried and cried some more. On most occasions Father Heald, after a visit with me in his private quarters, sent

Larry at 13
cast as Katharina in
Taming of the Shrew

me back to my dormitory. But on that particular night, he held me in his arms in his bed all night long."

In the days and weeks ahead, I came to realize that Father Heald was in love with me," Larry later recalled. "At first I thought it was just for the sex but I came to understand that he loved me."

Larry later wrote, "My heaven, my hope, my entire world, ended the day Mummy died when I was twelve."

After his mother's death, Larry wandered over to Chelsea Bridge. For two hours he stood there, wanting to drown himself in the Thames but lacking the courage.

Since 1918, Gerard had been living at the rectory in Old Letchworth. But the funeral for Agnes was held at Church Crookham in Hampshire.

Larry sang at his mother's funeral. "I don't think I ever sang with such a pure voice. It could be heard to the far end of the graveyard. It was my way of expressing my grief over my mother's unfinished life."

Back at school, Larry was morbid and didn't want contact with anybody, even Father Heald, for many weeks. But the priest in time counseled him and brought him the comfort he'd missed from Agnes.

He was so successful as Maria that Father Heald also cast him as Katharina in *The Taming of the Shrew* in a Christmas play in 1920, Larry's final year at All Saints.

Father Heald cast himself as Petruchio. He later said, "I had a strong role but that dear boy, Larry, stole the show. He was the prettiest Katharina in Christendom, with his earrings, large striped hat, and dark, rather fetching wig."

The plot, of course, revolved around Petruchio, a gentleman of Verona, and the head-strong, obdurate Katharina. Petruchio tempers her with various psychological torments until she becomes his obedient bride.

As Katharina, Larry was praised for his performance as the "bold, black-eyed hussy badly in need of taming."

After Larry's performance, Sybil Thorndike claimed, "That's the best Katharina I ever saw." She would later, most generously, extend a helping hand to the struggling young actor.

Larry's older sister, Sybille, married only a year after her mother's death, the bond lasting less than 10 months, during which time she engaged in an affair with a more attractive partner. When he learned of this, Gerard denounced his own daughter from the pulpit, condemning her adultery. Neither Sybille nor Larry ever forgave their father for that.

***

In the autumn of 1921, at the age of 14, Larry enrolled in St. Edward's School at Oxford. St. Edward's had been founded in 1863, and the students called it "Teddy's."

Gerard sent him to St. Edward's because the sons of clergymen had to pay only a modest 114 pounds a year, which could have been twice as much at more prestigious academies such as Radley, where Dickie was sent.

At St. Edward's he was assigned to the choir and performed as a soloist. Instead of acclaim, his soprano voice brought ridicule.

Larry's years at St. Edwards

St. Edward's, now a co-educational boarding school in North Oxford

11

during the early 1920s were the most shameful of his life. Even decades later, he could not speak of that time without tears welling in his eyes.

When he arrived there, he still had a puny physique, and his movements were gangly, unlike the practiced performer of precision he eventually became on the stage.

He was also girlish, even effeminate. The bullies at the school took note of that. In the tradition of British boys' schools of the time, young Larry was selected to become their sex slave.

In later life, he told Noël Coward, "I was their bitch in the terminology of prisoners who select the most effeminate or beautiful boy in prison to sodomize repeatedly."

Most of the boys mocked him. He became known as "that little shit Olivier." Unfortunately, a pretty boy also attracted the attention of sadistic prefects. "My bare butt was paddled so many times by these repressed homosexuals that it remained stinging and rosy red so much I could hardly sit down. Some of the prefects had me lie down bare-ass on top of their laps. I could feel their erections as they beat me. Often they made me scream."

When Larry was due for a caning, some of the other boys gathered in the quad outside the chamber to listen to his shrieks.

"I used to masturbate listening to Olivier's screams of pain and terror," said one of his classmates. "That little flirt could really scream, almost like an opera star. We figured that the schoolmasters were getting their rocks off, so why not us?"

"Prefects were allowed to paddle their juniors," Larry said. "The smaller ones of us also had to 'fag' for the other boys—do their laundry, polish their shoes, make their morning toast, and even run errands for them."

The boys were just coming into their sexuality and needed a release. Larry quickly became their target. "I was there for the taking. After one of the older boys raped me, he demanded that we repeat that every afternoon. A few weeks later, he invited all the other boys who wanted to rape me too. Such attacks on younger, pretty boys were an old tradition in certain British schools."

"I was ostracized by the other boys," Larry later wrote. "The boys called me a flirt who sang like an angel. I was so pretty I brought out the worst in certain males. My manner was florid and I was girlish and a bit sissy."

"After my first rape, I never fought off my attackers but willingly submitted, doing whatever they wanted me to do," Larry claimed. "I gave in because I knew they would overpower me and possibly injure me if I refused."

In later years, Larry admitted to certain dear friends like Noël Coward that, "I fell in love with one of the boys, a blond-haired Greek god. He was more sensitive than the others and gave me pleasure too. When he'd finish his business, he always kissed me long and passionately and thanked me for the joy I provided. Not since Dickie, had I ever responded to a young man like that."

One time, a master at St. Edward's discovered a note sent to Larry. Many of the older boys wrote love notes to him at the time. This one read: "Adonis, I dream of you each night. Let's slip away so we can be together, and I can show my love for you. I will love you forever." After the discovery of this note, the young man who wrote it was "sent down" [i.e., expelled] from St. Edward's.

At St. Edward's, Larry was cast as Puck in another Shakespearean role, this time in *A Midsummer Night's Dream*. Larry detested the role, calling it "dismally wretched."

"I went wild in the part," he later recalled.

The audience loved his over-the-top performance, although critics took a dim note, one claiming that "Shakespeare has seldom been more ill-served."

Unknown to Larry at the time of his performance, Gerard was sitting in the audience with Isobel Buchanan Ronaldson. Larry's father had met her on a missionary cruise to the British colony of Jamaica. She was to become the second Mrs. Gerard Olivier.

Gerard had gone to Jamaica at the invitation of his brother Sydney, who was the governor.

Three weeks after his performance as Puck, in January of 1924, Larry said he faced "the second saddest day of my life. My first was in burying Mummy. I had to go to Waterloo Station to tell Dickie goodbye. He was off to India for nine years to work on a rubber plantation. He kissed me on the lips. I knew our intimacy was gone, perhaps forever, and we would go on to others. For my father, it was also painful. Dickie had always been his favorite, and he faced the prospect of perhaps never seeing his first son ever again."

Larry and Gerard returned to Letchworth that night for their ritual bath. Gerard was still saving on hot water. Larry waited patiently as his father submerged himself. When he was finished, a nude Larry got into the tub.

"I asked Fahv when I could go to India to follow Dickie," Larry recalled.

Drying himself off, Gerard told him, "Don't be such a fool. You're not going to India. You're going on the stage in London."

"I was astonished," Larry recalled. "At first he didn't want me to become an actor. But somehow, perhaps as a promise to Mummy, he'd come to terms with it."

***

"I grew up to become a hopeless romantic, reaching for more than I could attain, often coming up empty-handed. Darjeeling is one of the most romantic

13

places in the world. *That's where I was born. My first memory is of the wafting aromas of the black tea coming from the nearby gardens.*

"My mother, Gertrude, believed in the Indian superstition that if a mother gazed at the Kanchenjunga, a beautiful child would be born to her. I was never sure I was that beautiful. After all, the opening line in Margaret Mitchell's Gone With the Wind *clearly states: 'Scarlett O'Hara was not beautiful but men seldom realized it when caught by her charm. . . .'*

"We fled to the mountain breezes of Darjeeling during the summer heat of Calcutta," Vivian said. *"There I could sit for years watching the majesty of the Kangchenjunga Mountains at both sunrise and sunset. The natives called these mountains 'The Five Treasures of Snow,' claiming that each of the five peaks represents a repository of God. In one he kept his gold, in another his gems, and so forth. Kangchenjunga didn't look like a mountain range to me, but a gigantic white wall hanging down from the sky.*

"The Indian Amah who looked after me told me that one day a handsome prince would descend from these mountains. He'd be escorted by snow leopards. My prince would take me away into the snowy sky and make me his beautiful princess. All my gowns would be made of spun gold, and my prince and I would live happily ever after.

"I continued to believe in that dream even after my life turned into a nightmare."

—Vivien Leigh

Ernest Richard Hartley

In 1905, Ernest Richard Hartley, age twenty, escaped the stifling life of rural Yorkshire. With tales of Rudyard Kipling dancing in his head, he took a slow boat to India in his search for riches and adventure.

He joined hundreds of other young Englishmen back in the time of the British Raj, when the mysteries of India were waiting to be unlocked. Although he might have dreamed of joining the hunt for the wild tiger, he took a boring clerk's job in the smothering heat of the Calcutta offices of Piggott Chapman & Co.

Reared in an uptight Victorian environment, he was shocked when he first

14

walked the streets of Calcutta. The stench was overpowering. Some of the locals defecated in the streets, and he was besieged by begging lepers.

He escaped that tawdry world into the drawing rooms of the white English with their cricket matches, polo games, and dinner parties, attended by turbaned servants.

He even became a member of the Royal Theatre and appeared on stage, as his secret dream had once been to be an actor, which was not a respectable profession for a young man of breeding.

Back home for a visit to Bridlington, Yorkshire in 1911, he was viewed as somewhat of a catch by the young women of the area. One woman claimed he brought with him "the charm, the mystery, and the romance of Arabian Nights."

Ernest spurned her that night at a ball when he met Gertrude Robinson Yackjee. He later said, "She had dancing eyes, skin like alabaster, and a fragile beauty that made her look like some goddess that appeared in the garden only on a midsummer's night." Perhaps he borrowed the last expression from Shakespeare.

Most women of her time might have shunned actors, but she found the prospect of returning to India with an actor/businessman intriguing. She had fantasies of living in grand palaces and being waited upon by a retinue of servants, which they could not afford in England.

"I swept her off her feet," Ernest later claimed. "Maybe it was my suntan or the jodhpurs I wore. She could not resist me. From the moment I saw her walking across the ballroom, I knew I had to have her. She was the most beautiful woman I'd ever seen."

Many people who knew Gertrude, and later in life, Vivien Leigh made the astonishing claim that Gertrude was even more beautiful than Vivien at her peak.

Gertrude married Ernest on April 9, 1912 at the Catholic Church of Our Lady of Victories on Kensington High Street in London.

The origins of Vivian's mother remain obscure. Some have claimed that, like her husband, she'd been born in Yorkshire. Others say that she was born in Darjeeling, India, and that her true surname was Yackjee, a Parsi-Indian name. Those who knew her in India claimed that she might have been Armenian.

Gertrude Yackjee Hartley
with daughter Vivian, aged two

15

On her passport, her name is listed as "Gertrude Jackjee," not Yackjee. Darjeeling is also listed as her place of birth on December 5, 1888.

If Gertrude were born part Indian, that would explain why she concealed her origins. In the imperial era, both purebred Indians and the ruling British class looked down on "half castes." In that respect, Gertrude's life evoked the film star, Merle Oberon, who one day would co-star with Laurence Olivier in *Wuthering Heights*. For years Oberon concealed that she was Eurasian.

Both the bride and groom were soon on a ship to India, sailing with George V and Queen Mary, who had come to see the gem of the British Empire.

As they sailed into the Bay of Bombay, with all its fireworks, Gertrude later wrote, "It was a magical place."

Once on ground, however, she was horrified by the stench, the garbage, and the endless beggars. In a carriage of emerald green and scarlet, she was whisked away from Victoria Station to her home in the upper-class suburb of Alipore.

Even on Ernest's modest salary, they enjoyed luxury which included a chauffeured automobile and three servants.

Gertrude set about to plant an English garden. One summer, when the Hartleys could take no more monsoons and the oppressive heat, they joined their neighbors and headed for the foothills of the Himalayas.

Already pregnant, Gertrude would remain in the "enchanting garden" of Darjeeling until her child's birth, which was anticipated in November.

Joining her in Darjeeling, having

16

"commuted" from Calcutta for the birth, Ernest later romantically claimed that his daughter was born "just as the sun was setting, turning the snow-capped peaks of Kanchenjunga a lustrous gold. The whole house and garden were bathed in a pink glow when I heard the little cries of Vivian Mary Hartley."

Little did he know that with a different name Vivien (with an e) Leigh would become one of the world's most fabled actresses.

Life in Calcutta wasn't always idyllic for the Hartleys, as Ernest had a roving eye and enjoyed numerous mistresses among the wives of other Britishers. At some point, or so it is believed, Gertrude cut off her sexual favors, leaving Ernest to more or less lead a life as a bachelor. However, he adored his beautiful baby girl.

In 1914, and now back in England, the Hartleys found their homeland at war. Ernest joined the Indian Cavalry and was sent for training with the Allied forces in Mesopotamia.

Gertrude and Vivian followed him "half way across the world," living in a rented house in the bleak hilltown of Mussooree.

From there, they followed Ernest to Bangalore in southern India. Once they got there, Gertrude and Vivian saw little of Ernest.

It was in the little English military town of Ootacamund that the future Scarlett O'Hara made her stage debut. She was three years old when asked to appear as "Little Bo Peep."

The audience was chatting when Vivian made her appearance. She

Two views of three-year-old Vivian Hartley playing "Little Bo Peep" in a school play in Calcutta.

stamped her shepherdess' crook for attention, announcing, "I won't sing. I'll recite."

In Vivian's second public performance, she was cast as a lion in the Biblical story of Daniel in the Lion's Den. Perhaps taking Method acting too far, Vivian viciously bit her mother's porcelain white leg, causing her to scream out in pain.

At the end of the war the Hartleys returned to Calcutta where Ernest became a senior partner in his firm. Their lifestyle had become decidedly upperclass.

Both parents were horrified at the idea of sending their daughter to a school in India. "She must return to England," Ernest told his wife. They settled on the Convent of the Sacred Heart at Roehampton, a backwater of London.

Vivian was born a Catholic, a religion her mother practiced with devotion.

In spite of the presence on board of her parents, Vivian felt lonely and desolate as she sailed back to England on the ship, *City of Baronda*. "I felt I was being sent into exile," she would recall. "When not seasick, I read the works of Charles Kingsley, pretty tough going for a girl of my age. I did it to punish myself, I guess."

Four and a half decades would go by before she'd make a triumphant return to India.

***

(top photo) Vivian in India, age six

(lower photo) Vivian, the only child of an affluent insider within the British Raj, maneuvers in a world well-accessorized with servants

One evening in the late 1930s, at a party given by Noël Coward in London's Belgravia district, Vivien Leigh asked her host a question. "Can you imagine it, darling? *Moi*, of all people, sent off to a convent. I think I must have corrupted every girl at that school."

"My parents dumped me at the Convent of the Sacred Heart. It was nearly eight years before I was paroled. I went two years before I saw Mummy again. It was much longer before I was reunited with my errant father, who seemed intent on seducing every beautiful woman in India."

The Rev. Mother Ashton Case had been a beauty at one time, and could have had almost any man she wanted. But she chose to become "the bride of Christ."

"Imagine never getting fucked," Vivien said to Coward. "That would be particularly difficult for you, wouldn't it, dear heart? As for me, I couldn't wait to get out of that convent and find some handsome young man to deflower me."

At the age of 6 1/2, Vivian was the youngest girl ever enrolled at the convent. "I arrived with a calico kitten, an adorable little thing." She recalled, "The Rev. Mother took pity on me and let me keep the kitten, even though it was against the rules."

"Thank God I brought along eight pair of warm woolen stockings from the Highlands. I needed them. That damn convent wasn't heated in those days. I don't think any building was heated in England back then unless it had a fireplace. It was bone-chilling cold."

Vivian often remained by herself at the convent, not mingling with the other girls, some of whom she "found just too damn devoted. I was never interested in religion all that much."

Born in 1911, Maureen O'Sullivan, the Irish beauty, was two years older than Vivian.

"After knowing her only two weeks, Maureen became my best friend," Vivian said. "Once we had a contest for the prettiest girl in the school, rather unusual for a convent. I won. Maureen came in second. That put a strain on our friendship but she recovered."

One day Vivian told Maureen that, "I'm going to grow up to become a great actress, but on the stage—not in films."

Interviewed years later, O'Sullivan recalled that young Vivian seemed rather disdainful of Hollywood in those days. "Imagine her surprise when I not only went to Hollywood but became Jane Parker in the movies, the aristocrat who falls for jungle boy Johnny Weissmuller in all those Tarzan movies."

"One night when I encountered a drunken Vivien Leigh at a party for David Niven in Hollywood, she made fun of me for playing

Viv, as an early teenager, far from her parents, in boarding school

19

Jane to Tarzan, but in a loving way, not a mocking way," O'Sullivan said. "I told her that if she ever got a chance to see what Weissmuller had under that loincloth, she'd be swinging through the trees with that jungle boy, too. Vivien laughed hilariously, and we resumed our old friendship."

Although she became famous as a screen *ingénue* of the 1930s, O'Sullivan is remembered today for giving birth to a daughter, Mia Farrow.

The convent presented some stage productions where Vivian was introduced to the works of Shakespeare, appearing as Fairy Mustardseed in *A Midsummer Night's Dream* and as Miranda in *The Tempest*.

Vivian detested mathematics but "adored" history and literature. As she confided to O'Sullivan, "one day I'll appear on stage as Cleopatra. She's the most interesting woman who ever lived. Perhaps I'll also get around to appearing in a play as Eleanor of Aquitaine."

When Vivian attended a performance of *Where the Rainbow Ends*, she was mesmerized by the swan-like grace of the dancers. That very evening she decided to train for the ballet. After several weeks of lessons, she lost interest. "I don't want to spend my life on my toes—maybe on my back."

Even at such a young age, she had a wicked wit. She also learned to play the cello, the violin, and the piano. "I was what you might say 'artistically inclined.'"

On holidays Vivian was allowed to visit the museums and galleries of London. She was even allowed to attend a stage show.

Maureen O'Sullivan with Johnny Weissmuller

Called *Round in Fifty*, it starred George Robey, appearing at the London Hippodrome. She was taken to the show by Gertrude, who visited England every summer to have a reunion with her daughter. Vivian went to see his performance six times.

During one scene, Vivian was particularly enthralled when Robey—known as the "Prime Minister of Mirth" —came out in full drag, dressing as "The Queen of Hearts." She laughed hilariously when Robey asked his audience to "kindly temper your hilarity with a modicum of reserve." In a touch of irony, Robey one day would appear as the dying Falstaff in Laurence Olivier's film version of Shakespeare's *Henry V.*

20

Weeks later, at a resort in the Lake District of England, Vivian by chance found that Robey was a fellow guest. She told him, "You are the delight of my life and the curse of my elders."

Robey was so enchanted by Vivian that he very quietly sang to her, "If You Were the Only Girl in the World," which was his signature song. The actor gave her six autographed photographs, one for each time she had attended his performance.

On rare occasions she went to see a silent movie. "I developed a big crush on Douglas Fairbanks Sr. when I saw him in *Robin Hood*," she recalled. But it was the stage that enthralled her, particularly when she saw a professional production of *Hamlet* at Stratford-upon-Avon.

A fellow student at the convent, Patsy Quinn (later Viscountess Lambert), wrote a description of Vivian at the time: "She is so tiny, so delicately made. She has wonderful large blue eyes and chestnut wavy hair nearly to her waist, along with a tiny *retroussé* nose. Hers is the only complexion I have seen that really *was* like a peach, almost downy as a peach is."

O'Sullivan claimed that, "I was jealous of Vivian's beauty because the other girls constantly told me how much prettier she was than I was. She was not a classic beauty, and had imperfections, perhaps a mouth that was too tiny for her face. Her concern was the size of her hands and feet. She took to wearing gloves at an early age to cover this defect. She overcame beauty's flaws by being absolutely luminous. When she entered a room, she almost glowed."

It was while they were still at the convent that both Quinn and O'Sullivan observed what in time became Vivian's descent into mental instability. "Viv could be the sweetest, nicest person at the convent," Pat Quinn later claimed. "No one had such a charming personality. But at times she could strike out at you, seemingly without provocation. At those times, she'd retreat into one of her darkest moods and would stay there for a long time. She adored her cat but would shoo her away. I'd go and get milk for the cat to keep her from starving. Viv frightened me. She was like a female Dr. Jekyll and a Mrs. Hyde. Then, like a spring flower bursting open, she'd emerge the next day like the dearest, most gracious and effervescent personality you could ever imagine."

Vaudevillian
George Robey

"If bad thoughts come to you, put extra heavy salt on your rhubarb," the Rev. Mother told Vivian.

On holidays, Gertrude took Vivian on a number of Continental trips, including the French Riviera.

In 1926, Ernest arrived back in England and invit-

21

ed his daughter for a vacation in Ireland, where she even went fishing with him. She told him of her dream of becoming a stage actress.

"My greatest desire," she told him, "is to go back to India with you. We'll appear on the stage together, perhaps in a production with you as Romeo and me as Juliet."

"I don't think that is an appropriate stage play for a father and daughter to perform," he said. "At some point we have to abandon our dreams, or perhaps make our dream a mere hobby. The theater is only a momentary escape for me. On Monday morning, I have to return to the real world."

Gertrude had gone to Ireland with them, but didn't accompany them on the fishing trip, preferring to stay with friends.

During the trip with her father, Vivian became acquainted with John Lambert Thomson, a beloved figure in the lives of both her mother and father. "Tommy," as both Gertrude and Ernest called him, was a confirmed bachelor.

Vivian suspected that Tommy was Gertrude's lover. He was known to have accompanied Gertrude to the Continent when Ernest was back in India. Gertrude sent Vivian postcards from such cities as Paris, signed "with love from Mummy & Tommy."

Sometimes Tommy, Gertrude, and Ernest traveled as a threesome, sharing suites together, which led to speculation. A *ménage à trois* was suggested.

"In those days, it took someone like Noël Coward to understand the sophistication of that arrangement," said Elisabeth Thomson, Tommy's favorite niece. "My uncle had a wife but didn't have a wife. And of course, Ernest had all those mistresses back in India."

In their rented Irish fishing hut, Vivian remembered that Tommy cooked the most marvelous fish dinners for them in the cabin overlooking a blue lake. "I slept on a sofa in the small living room. Father and Tommy shared the little bedroom. I noticed that they also preferred to take their baths together in this big claw-footed tub. At the time, I just assumed that was what grown men did together, perhaps to save on hot water. I'm sure they tried to keep their voices down, knowing I was in the next room, but even at that age I knew the sounds of passion when I heard them."

Even more shocking were the stories that circulated for years that Tommy enjoyed an "inappropriate relationship" with young Vivian. If such a rumor were true, it may have begun in Lugano where Gertrude underwent an operation, presumably gynecological. She was bleeding and in acute agony. Tommy was assigned the care and feeding of Vivian.

"From what I heard, he took that job very seriously," said Elisabeth. "Even though still a girl, Vivian was too old to sleep in bed with a grown man."

Years later friends in London queried Vivian about these rumors. She dismissed them almost like a future Scarlett O'Hara saying, "Fiddle-dee-dee."

At this point the truth will never be known, unless Tommy's secret diary surfaces. In some respects, Vivian's encounters with Tommy could be compared to the sexual involvement of young Larry and Father Heald.

As the Twenties came to an end, Vivian began "The Grand Tour" of the Continent. In those days, this was a pastime eagerly pursued by the upper-class British.

"When that tour and all those finishing schools ended for me, I returned to London," she said. "I was a fully grown woman though still a teenager."

In the movie, *Gone With the Wind*, Vivien the actress reflected on a line she had to deliver about her mother in the film. With great conviction, Vivien uttered the dialogue: "I always wanted to be like her, calm and kind. I certainly have turned out disappointingly."

"The same could be said of me," Vivien Leigh remembered. "Even though only a teenager, when I went to the Continent, I was determined to find a husband—or perhaps a husband and a lover on the side just like dear old Mummy. And if either my lover or my new husband looked like Ronald Colman, so much the better."

***

Larry was astonished when he returned home from St. Edward's and found that Gerard had married Isobel Buchanan Ronaldson without telling him. The wedding was on June 27, 1924, and Larry had not been invited. His father's bride was thirty-five years old, a decade younger than her groom.

After Agnes died, Gerard began to adhere strictly to the sect within the Anglo-Catholic High Church which at the time frowned severely on the idea of marriage for its priests.

When Gerard decided to remarry, he defied the earlier teachings he had endorsed during his tenure at St. Paul's Church in the seaside resort of Brighton. The Congregation there refused to tolerate a married priest, and became extremely upset with Gerard for going against the messages of his own sermons. The congregation's dissatisfaction about Gerard's second marriage made local headlines, the Brighton newspaper running a story about it entitled CUPID VS. CONGREGATION.

Forced to abandon the prestigious post in Brighton, Gerard and his new bride came to live in the more modest parish of Addington in Buckinghamshire.

Larry did not bond with Isobel, and seemed to resent her for trying to replace Agnes. The visit with his father was short.

Larry returned to London where he lived in a virtual box, really a small "bed-sitter" on Castellain Road in Maida Vale.

His great dream was to be accepted into the acting school of Elsie Fogerty, hailed as the greatest acting teacher in London at the time. In later years, Larry would claim, "Miss Fogerty taught me how to speak on the stage."

Fogerty was a rather ugly woman who dyed her petticoats magenta. She specialized in elocution.

When Larry met Fogerty, she was sixty years old but had performed on the stage when younger. "She wore the same plumed hat day after day," Larry recalled. "I think it was filled with the tail feathers of birds of prey. The long dress she wore was perhaps fashionable in 1898."

Nicknamed "Fogie," the actress turned teacher was called the result of "the mating of Queen Victoria with Mr. Punch," the latter the famous character in those Punch and Judy shows.

In June of 1924 Larry, age seventeen, was among four other wannabe actors auditioning for Fogerty's eccentric classes. One of his fellow students was George Coulouris, the Manchester-born son of a Greek merchant, who would become a distinguished actor in film and on stage. His most famous future role would be in Orson Welles' 1941 *Citizen Kane*, in which he played a J.P. Morgan-esque financier.

Through the help of his father, Larry won a meager scholarship to Elsie Fogerty's Central School of Speech Training and Dramatic Art in London at the imposing Royal Albert Hall. He also was given a starvation bursary, a meager allowance which came to only one pound a week.

That bursary was not really enough to pay for food. Later in life, Larry remembered going through a Lyons Corner House Restaurant near Paddington Station and stealing a roll not eaten on a table where diners had departed.

For his audition, Larry had delivered a speech from "Seven Ages of Man." When he said the line, "Jealous in honour and quick to quarrel," she told him it was not necessary to make fencing gestures.

Elsie Fogerty teaching an elocution class

The formidable Fogerty obviously didn't approve of much of what she saw auditioning before her. Larry's talent, mannerisms, and even his face were too raw at the time. She found some of his gestures on stage "effeminate" and suggested that he try for a more masculine performance.

On the first day she met him, Fogerty had placed her little finger on his upper forehead and ran it down along the bridge of his nose.

"You have an unruly mass of hair, from widow's peak to beetle brow," Fogerty chided him. "You'll have to do something about that."

Family friend Sybil Thorndike likened Larry's face to that of a gypsy's. "He had a dark, sullen quality to him, a brooding Heathcliff in the making. His one great quality was his eyes. They were the most expressive I've seen on any actor."

Fogerty's criticism of his facial features stuck with Larry for the rest of his life. Whenever he could, he tried to alter his features, especially his nose, using putty in *Romeo, Hamlet, Henry V*, and especially for his role as Crassus in *Spartacus*, the film. For *Macbeth*, he gave himself a broken nose; for *Richard III*, a snout.

Nonetheless, she told him, "I am impressed with you, though you have done nothing to impress me so far. You are a far better performer than your sister Sybille. As you know, she was a pupil of mine. I suggested to her that she should settle comfortably into a marriage and forget the theater, except to attend as a member of the audience."

At the time Larry linked his career to Fogerty, she was said to have the best elocution of any woman who had ever appeared on stage in the British Empire. Even professional actors hired her for private lessons, especially if they were performing a difficult role, usually Shakespeare. John Gielgud came to her to help him improve his speech. Behind her back, her students mocked her as "The Voice Beautiful."

Enrolled in class with Larry was Peggy Ashcroft. She joined him in a court scene from *The Merchant of Venice*. Larry was cast as Shylock, modeling his performance—or so he said—on his Uncle Sydney Olivier.

For years, his fellow students would remember his role as the deformed Caliban in *The Tempest*. Appearing coated in green slime, he took the author's description of Caliban too seriously—"a freckled whelp, hag-born, not honoured with a human shape."

Ashcroft, later Dame Peggy, was the same age as Larry. Larry bonded with her, and both of them discussed their dreams of becoming King and Queen of West End Theater. Ashcroft was on the dawn of fame when she would play Naemi in *Jew Süss* in 1929 and Desdemona opposite Paul Robeson's *Othello* two years later.

Larry remembered taking her out on a cou-

Peggy Ashcroft

ple of dates, but he really had no money to spend on young women, and perhaps not much desire to go out with them. He felt very awkward in the presence of a woman and often stuttered when he was alone with one of them.

Larry asked her out a third time, but she told him that she was seeing Rupert Hart-Davis, whom she married in 1929. In a way, as he later admitted, "I felt relieved because I didn't know where this so-called romance was going. Dating seemed like such a silly game anyway."

"I was not that impressed with Larry," Ashcroft later recalled. "I had no clue as to his future greatness. I think he wore clothes handed down from his brother Dickie, and they often looked dirty. He was a sad sight. In good weather, he carried his shoes and walked barefoot so he wouldn't wear out the leather. In winter he did not have a coat to beat off the wind, rain, and fog of London."

Dame Peggy said in later life that she might have seriously entertained a proposal from Larry—"I love the man dearly"—but he was too slow in approaching her. "I didn't want to be some precious porcelain doll locked away in some Victorian cabinet. I would have said yes but he never asked the question."

Most of the male students Fogerty attracted were homosexuals, some rather blatantly so. Although Father Heald still loomed somewhere in the background, Larry temporarily came under the "protection" of an actor and producer, Henry Oscar. Oscar became fascinated by Larry in 1924 and actively pursued him. For a short time, Larry moved in with Oscar.

Because of his momentary infatuation with Larry, the producer awarded him the small role of the Suliot Officer in his production of Alice Law's *Byron*, which opened at the Century Theatre in London in November of 1925.

Henry Oscar

This marked Larry's first appearance on a London stage. Oscar and the play soon disappeared.

Oscar and Larry would have an eventual reunion when they appeared together in *Fire Over England* (1937), a film which co-starred Vivien Leigh.

Years later, referring to Oscar, Vivien told Graham Payn and Noël Coward, "If I live long enough, I'll eventually get around to meeting all of Larry's male lovers."

Oscar later told his homosexual classmates that Larry did not have enough "fire in the belly" to become an actor. "But

26

he becomes a great actor in bed, pretending he enjoys what is being done to him when clearly he does not."

Another homosexual actor at school claimed that "Olivier could be had for the price of a hot meal on a cold January night."

Roger Halburn, who studied briefly with Larry, said, "He was completely out of his element among sophisticated people. Many of the women in Fogerty's class were not interested in the theater, but were using the school like a finishing school before they settled into the bucolic life with a husband at a country manse."

"Young Olivier was desperate to be liked," said Halburn, "almost embarrassingly so. His clothes did not fit him and they were worn. His shoes were new five years ago. He was still a teenager when I picked him up and took him back to my place to seduce him. I insisted he take a bath first. He didn't know grooming, and his manners were those of a country boy, but he'd been sodomized before. He knew just what to do, and I enjoyed him. I think he fell in love with me after the first night, but I had to put a stop to it. In those days I was what was known as a gay blade, and I liked to play the field. In a cast-off suit of mine, I dressed Larry up, took him to a barber, and invited him to be my escort at a number of wild parties."

At one cocaine party, Larry met Tallulah Bankhead and her lover, the honorable Napier George Henry Stuart Alington. She called him "Naps."

"I adore British men," Tallulah told Larry, kissing him very wetly and succulently on the mouth.

Under a mop of blond hair, Naps had a small delicate build. His most sensuous physicality was in his thick lips. He had a nervous habit of constantly licking the roof of his mouth, as if he were tasting honey.

Tallulah Bankhead...
"SHE, London"

Tallulah was outrageous, outspoken and uninhibited. "My dahling," she told Larry, "I got a letter the other day marked SHE, LONDON."

"That is indeed fame," he told her.

"If you could do something about those teeth, dahling, you could be quite beautiful," she said.

The host came out with the evening's supply of cocaine. "Let it snow!" Tallulah yelled to the party.

She took Larry's hand and directed him to a large coffee table where she taught him how to snort. "Dahling, why don't you come back to my flat tonight with Naps? We'll have a hell of a time. If you're a good boy, I'll let you fluff the hairs on my pussy. You'd like that, wouldn't you, you dear boy?"

"And don't forget my pleasure," Naps cautioned standing right behind Larry and placing his hand firmly on one of his buttocks. "I have to have my pleasures too."

"How could we ever forget a dahling man like you, Naps?" Tallulah said. She looked at Larry. "Let's have some fun tonight."

"I'm not sure," he said awkwardly.

"Dahling, I didn't invent three-ways," she said. "Ever since Edward sat on the throne, they've become very popular in England. How do you expect to make it in the theater if you don't know life?"

"I don't know . . ." he hesitated.

She grabbed his hand, "Come along, dahling, the night is young and so are we. London is madly gay, oh, so gay. And Tallulah rules the night."

He missed classes the following day. "I was devoured," he told Halburn. "Up until now, I did not know the human body had so many erogenous zones."

"I did more than take Larry to wild parties or provide a good hot meal for him," Halburn said. "He was desperate to go see the great John Barrymore perform in *Hamlet* at the Theatre Royal in Haymarket. I agreed to go with him and pay for his ticket."

On the way to the theater, the young men met Fay Compton, an English actress from a notable acting lineage. In theatrical circles, she is known for playing Ophelia opposite two celebrated Hamlets, John Barrymore and John Gielgud. In 1962, she would appear as Marya in Sir Laurence Olivier's production of *Uncle Vanya* at the Chichester Festival Theatre.

She warned Larry that at the performance of *Hamlet* that afternoon, "You'll see the most brilliant performance of *Hamlet,* or the most drunkard performance of *Hamlet.* With Jack, you never know until the curtain goes up."

Larry later recalled that seeing Barrymore perform *Hamlet* "changed my life forever. I think I didn't know what magic in the theater meant until I saw him leaping about the stage like an athlete. I almost had an orgasm when Barrymore recited the 'rogue and peasant slave' soliloquy. I learned the art of the soliloquy from Barrymore."

Because Halburn's father knew the stage manager, the young man escorted Larry backstage to meet The Great Profile.

Barrymore welcomed the boys into his dressing room where he stood attired shirtless in a pair of green tights. He was drinking a glass of whisky after the curtain had gone down.

Welcoming the boys and offering them a drink, Barrymore suddenly yanked a thick sock from his crotch. "I always stuff my crotch, especially during ladies' matinees. It increases attendance in the theater." Noticing the shock on Larry's face, Barrymore said, "The theater, dear boy, is all about illusion."

Barrymore was also casual about nudity, especially when well wishers came backstage after the show to greet him. If a visitor happened to walk in on him undressed, he always said, "There's far more to me than a Great Profile, as you have ample evidence to see for yourself."

Rumor had it that when he stayed in the Berkshire village of Cookham, which lies beside the River Thames, he walked along the High Street of Cookham Village, entirely nude, memorizing his lines from *Hamlet.*

After they left Barrymore's dressing room, Larry complained to Halburn. "Fogerty is always criticizing me for my flashing gestures. Well, I must inform her that John Barrymore's performance was filled with flashing gestures."

"Don't you know that lesbians like Fogerty don't like men with flashing gestures?" asked Halburn.

***

The next few days were among the darkest in Larry's young life. He completely lost confidence in himself. Seeing Barrymore perform in *Hamlet* had at first enthralled him. But later, Barrymore's performance came to haunt him. He felt he could never master the role like Barrymore had—in fact, he feared he lacked any talent at all. He could dream about becoming a great actor, but he began to feel his fantasy and ambition did not match his actual ability on the stage.

As he would later confide to his future friend, a young Roy Moseley, "I actually contemplated suicide." In a London tube station, he considered throwing himself in front of an oncoming train. He finally came to his senses at the last minute and didn't do it. Later, he felt that this irrational thought came from not having eaten for the previous three days.

The next day, when his allowance came in, and he had had a proper meal at the Lyons Corner House, he banished such dark thoughts and his hope for his future in the theater returned.

Occasionally when someone would invite him, Larry went to see the flickers, most of which were American imports. Although

John Barrymore *playing* Hamlet in 1922

29

his future wife, Vivien herself, had developed a screen crush on Douglas Fairbanks Sr., Larry was enthralled by the confident sexuality and male beauty of Ronald Colman, especially after he saw him perform on screen in *The White Sister* with Lillian Gish.

Like Larry himself, Colman had been born in Surrey. Larry wanted one day to appear in a film himself. "I want to make myself up to look just like Colman, who, as a matter of fact, has the most beautiful speaking voice in the British Empire."

"For a while, Larry tried to grow a mustache, just like Colman's but was not successful at the time," Halburn said. "That would come later."

Ralph Richardson signed up for Fogerty's classes, and he became her most prized pupil, male or female. She predicted that Richardson would go far in the theater. But she had doubts about Larry. "He's got a long way to go yet before he becomes a serious actor. He might drop out and join one of the trades."

(top photo) Olivier in his early 20s

(lower photo) His competition: Ronald Colman in the 1920s

After he left school, Larry drifted in and out of fly-by-night plays in the West End of London or else minor roles in classical dramas in provincial repertory.

One reviewer summed it up. "Lawrence *(sic)* Olivier is a minor actor in a minor play, which should close sooner than later."

Desperate for money, he took whatever role was offered, regardless of how meager. "It's all a blur now," Larry later recalled, "a medley of bishops, lords, officers, guards, and scribes."

In the summer of 1925, he made his first major professional stage appearance at the Brighton Hippodrome.

He was appearing in a short sketch called *Unfailing Instinct*, which had been configured as a curtain raiser for a large-scale production of Arthur Ridley's new play, *The Ghost Train*, starring Ruby Miller.

When Larry had not a shilling in his trousers and not a bite to eat all day except for an apple he'd stolen, he returned to his garret to find a telegram waiting. CALL CENTURY THEATRE PART TO OFFER LENA ASHWELL PLAYERS.

A woman in her late fifties, Ashwell was both an actress and producer whose stated purpose

30

was "to bring Shakespeare to the masses." She had her underpaid troupe perform in everything from the Deptford Baths to Battersea Town Hall. Larry's pay was two pounds, 10 shillings a week, which was barely a livable wage.

Ashwell's husband was Sir Henry Simpson, the royal obstetrician. He would be the surgeon who was present at the birth of Queen Elizabeth II. Her husband indulged Ashwell in her noble theater endeavors and often provided the financing.

"She was a woman before her time," Larry recalled. "She had intelligence and most of all a spirit willing to accept challenges. She could have invented the slogan, 'the show must go on.'"

The Lena Ashwell Players performed Shakespeare in provincial towns. Ashwell cast Larry as Antonio in *The Tempest* and as Flavius in *Julius Caesar*. In the drab towns in which they played, there was often no dressing room. The actors had to change in toilets. Larry dubbed them "The Lavatory Players."

In addition to his giggling, Larry was a practical joker on stage. He still hadn't taken the theater seriously. In one performance of *Julius Caesar* he had to take down some Roman wreaths pinned to a black velvet backcloth. Behind this the female members of the cast were dressing. Larry deliberately ripped the curtain to expose their bare pink bottoms to the audience, which brought a great laugh.

After a stern lecture, Ashwell forgave him for that. She could not forgive one performance of Larry's at Englefield Green where she had orchestrated yet another production of *Julius Caesar*. Philip Leaver, playing one of the Tribunes, lost his pantaloon while delivering his "Knew you not Pompey?" speech.

Cast as Flavius, Larry burst into hysterical and uncontrollable laughter and finally had to flee "the streets of Rome" to hide behind the curtains. This unprofessional display could not be forgiven by Ashwell. "She sacked me that night."

Larry had vowed never to turn to family friends such as Sybil Thorndike for help in advancing his career. But desperate for work after getting fired by Ashwell, he called on this imposing woman who had heard of his "frivolous behavior" in the theater. Before agreeing to help him, she gave him a stern lecture about how he owed it to the audience to be serious in serious roles. "*Julius Caesar*, my dear boy, is not a schoolgirl comedy."

Her husband, Lewis Casson, listened patiently,

former luminary of the British theatre: Lena Ashwell

31

silently evaluating young Larry.

Casson then delivered a presumptuous demand that Larry had to give up "that Tallulah Bankhead crowd he'd been running around with. No more snow parties. No more the little dandies and fops trying to get into your trousers. I refuse to hire someone in my troupe who associates with the likes of these degenerates. The legitimate theater must not tolerate these dilettantes."

Although it was a tremendous infringement on his personal freedom, considering the low salary and menial job, Larry amazingly accepted the draconian offer. "Does my father know about the life I've been leading?" Larry asked.

He was mortified when Casson told him that Gerard had heard many stories. "He's very disappointed in you. He never figured you for that kind of boy. He told me, 'Those vultures I'd warned him about in the theater are apparently devouring my son.'"

Thorndike later said, "We heard that the dear boy was up to incorrigible things. That Tallulah Bankhead and others had a big mouth. My husband told me that the next thing we could expect was Larry moving in with Noël Coward. I personally have worked with many homosexuals, but I didn't think Larry was the kind of young man who should be sucked into their world and used by them like a prostitute a man would pick up along the 'Dilly. The next thing I feared would be Larry turning into a rent boy between jobs in the theater."

Through Casson's intervention, Larry was offered a walk-on part in *Henry VIII*, the last legitimate theatrical performance at the old Empire Theatre on Leicester Square in the heart of London. After that, the landmark became a cinema and a showcase for MGM films.

(Dame) Sybil Thorndike and Lewis Casson in 1954

Thorndike and Casson were the stars of the play along with a beautiful actress, Angela Baddeley.

Both Casson and Thorndike became two of the most pivotal figures in Larry's life. He got to know them very well, and they were both sympathetic and understanding of Larry's many quirks.

At the time he met Casson, the theatrical director was deeply troubled about his past. During World War I, he'd been Britain's Secretary of Chemical Warfare Committee. "I will never escape the horror of what I've done," he told Larry. "For the rest of my life I will have this horrible guilt for having involved myself in the production of poisonous gases."

32

Henry VIII rotated performances with Percy Shelley's verse play, *The Cenci*, in which Larry, "young as a sprig," played an old servant. Larry's part in *The Cenci* went unnoticed but a fifteen-year-old actor, Jack Hawkins, got all the critical attention.

Thorndike said that Larry would always harbor a jealousy of Hawkins, who would marry Jessica Tandy in 1932. Larry learned that in 1923 Hawkins and a young Noël Coward had appeared together in the same production, *Where the Rainbow Ends*, at the Holborn Empire. The two young men were seen together about town.

Larry's jealousy was particularly sharpened when the drama critic of *The Evening News* in 1933 wrote that Hawkins was "the most indubitable of matinee idols," predicting that he would outstrip the talents of his contemporaries, including Laurence Olivier, Ralph Richardson, and John Gielgud.

Larry forever remained critical of Hawkins, both as an actor and in his very closeted private life. The producers of *Victim*, the first major film about homosexuality in Britain, approached Hawkins to play the role of a gay barrister. He turned it down. "The role might conflict with my masculine image," he said.

When Larry heard this, he said, "What Hawkins fears is that that role might prevent him from achieving knighthood."

After that, Larry, too, was offered the role in *Victim*. But he also turned it down as "far too daring—a film ten years ahead of its time." The role eventually went to Dirk Bogarde.

Larry became very close to Thorndike and Casson during the time they worked together, and would remain friends for life.

"I think that Larry became a serious actor working with my husband," Thorndike claimed. "Of course, I'm not a total innocent. I know on many a night he slipped away to those flats in Belgravia or Mayfair where the world of The Third Sex prevailed. But I'd rather not think about that."

Because they helped him when he most needed it, Larry would later refer to Thorndike and Casson as "my second parents." One day he'd end up directing Dame Sybil with Marilyn Monroe in *The Prince and the Showgirl*.

In addition to the walk-on part in *Henry VIII*, Larry was designated as assistant stage manager, a position known in English theatrical circles as "general dog's body," for some odd reason. Larry's job involved keeping unruly members of the audience quiet and ringing down the curtain at play's end. He was accused of being a little too zealous in quieting some members of the audience, who took offense at being told to shut up.

At first, he rang down the curtain at the right time. But three nights after Christmas of 1925, he pulled the curtain down three minutes before the play's climax. This brought a strong rebuke from Casson, who threatened to fire him.

Over the years, Larry had developed a series of crushes on boys. But he didn't really fall in love until he met Angela Baddeley, who was playing Anne Boleyn in *Henry VIII*. "He fell under her spell," Thorndike recalled.

Remembered today mainly for her role as Mrs. Bridges in the period drama, *Upstairs, Downstairs*, Baddeley would have a long and distinguished career, spanning six decades, on the stage. As an actress, however, she would never achieve the fame of her younger sister, actress Hermione Baddeley. Angela was appearing on stage at the Old Vic before she was ten. Critics called her the "consummate little actress."

Even though she'd married Stephen Thomas and had a daughter, Baddeley didn't seem to be devoted to him. Larry was uncertain of the status of the marriage. For all he knew, she had divorced Thomas.

Backstage she was extremely flirtatious. "She practically felt me up, and was always touching, feeling—no, not there," Larry said. "She rubbed her delicate hand across my cheek time and time again. She was a lovely woman back in those days, and she made me very excited."

Actor Carol Reed, who would later become a famous director, also was in love with Baddeley. Like Larry, he was a fellow spear-carrier, one of the knights holding up the train of Queen Katharine of Aragon, as played by Thorndike.

Reed and Olivier had many senseless arguments over Baddeley. Sometimes Thorndike would intervene. "Shut up, you two, and get about your business on stage or off."

Apparently, Reed was left with no hard feelings about Larry in their joint pursuit of Baddeley. In years to come, he would consider casting him as the lead in his 1949 classic, *The Third Man*, the part eventually going to Joseph Cotten.

Angela Baddeley in 1922

"I think Angela Baddeley aroused Olivier's masculine nature, his more heterosexual side," Thorndike said. "Of course, Angela was not available, but she did arouse a passion in Larry, even if that passion was misdirected. At least it became conceivable that he could be a man and not a bottom boy for some old sod."

"Angela had developed the habit of kissing young men on the mouth," Casson said. "This theatrical conceit was just coming into vogue at the time. Later it would permeate the theater with men kissing men, or whatever. Larry misunderstood her intentions. She also had this habit of speaking to him about three inches from his lips. Naturally, he responded like any red-blooded male and grabbed her, kissing her passionately. But she broke from his embrace and rushed out on stage to face the audience. Slowly very slowly, Larry began to realize that she was merely an outrageous flirt and meant absolutely nothing by intimacy. Angela was what men call a prick-teaser."

Baddeley may have come on strong to young men, but her heart belonged to Glen Byam Shaw, an actor and theater director who would become her husband in 1929.

A strapping six-footer, Shaw was just as handsome as Larry, maybe even more so. Instead of fighting Reed for Baddeley's affection, Larry now came to size up Shaw as his newest competition. The actress seemed to want to make Larry jealous by hugging and kissing Shaw every time Larry came around.

Larry did not take Shaw's love for Baddeley too seriously, knowing that the young man was the lover of the homosexual poet Siegfried Sassoon.

Sassoon arrived at the theater one night with Shaw to watch Baddeley perform. Both men came backstage when the curtain went down, ostensibly to pay homage to Baddeley.

While Shaw kissed her and congratulated her, the dashing poet turned his back to the embracing couple and smiled at Larry.

Larry had read his early poems, many of which overflowed with Romantic dilettantish sweetness, and he'd read many news stories about Sassoon's exploits on the Western Front during World War I.

The author had a strong sense of his masculinity and was exceedingly good looking, but not a pretty boy. His face looked like it had been created by a sculptor, with expressive eyes that seemed to burn through your skin. In London's homosexual circles, it was claimed that he had "the most sensuous lips God ever gave to a mortal man."

Larry was mesmerized by him and could hardly speak. Sassoon leaned in close to Larry and whispered in his ear, "I'll be here tomorrow at the close of curtain," he said. "Be here!" It was more of a military command than a request.

Larry found himself trembling. As Larry would relate to some of his homosexual friends in the future, "Many young men in the theater, those inclined in a certain way, have a forceful personality enter their lives unexpectedly and almost overnight. The Americans have an expression for it. They say, 'Blow in my ear, and I'll follow you any-

Seigfried Sassoon

35

where.' For me, Siegfried Sassoon was that kind of man."

Larry later confessed, "Siegfried came into my life and never really left it, although for years we never saw each other. The summer of 1967 was perhaps the saddest of my life. I lost both my beloved Vivien and Siegfried that dreadful summer."

When Siegfried walked backstage on that long-ago night, Larry had been in one of his darkest periods of despair. He'd actually fallen in love with Baddeley and had been spurned.

He also wasn't prepared to spend the long and arduous years in the theater that Thorndike told him was necessary for achieving success. He wanted his big break to come now while he was young and could enjoy it.

He also felt that he'd lived too long without love. He didn't trust women. Baddeley seemed the perfect example of the fickle nature of woman. He also didn't look forward to a lifetime of being the plaything of older men who would drop him when he aged.

He was searching for a different type of love—"a love among equals"— preferably but not necessarily with someone of his own age.

"I am hungry for fame, fortune, and, yes, love," Larry wrote Elsie Fogerty, who had become his friend and would remain so until her death in 1945.

Just when Larry thought he would find no real career in the theater and no lover to call his own, Sassoon emerged backstage. Suddenly, Larry felt he had a reason to live and would no longer flirt with suicide.

Luck came in pairs. A notice arrived the following day that he'd been invited for an interview with the Birmingham Repertory Theatre.

He told Thorndike, "I'm about to embark on Act I of my life. Up to now, it was just a minor amusement, a little sketch that goes on before the curtain is raised on the big show of the evening."

CHAPTER TWO

At this point in her young life, Vivian's knowledge of sex was extremely limited. Even though Gertrude's beloved Tommy may have fondled the girl, and may have kissed her excessively, those acts were more accurately defined as inappropriate behavior than sex.

At school in Roehampton with Maureen O'Sullivan, Vivian had speculated about the male genitalia. At that time, supposedly neither girl had ever seen a nude male, much less a man with an erection. Men were a puzzle to them, but an intriguing mystery.

"We used to get excited when a man would come to Roehampton," O'Sullivan claimed. "The girls would get together and whisper. We knew men were forbidden fruit, but we were anxious to bite into the apple to see what it was like. Vivian and I were told that men were vicious creatures who committed unspeakable acts on women, especially young girls. We never understood that. If men were such horrors, why did most women seem to be pursuing them? Vivian and I definitely decided that we weren't being told the truth about these creatures."

There may have been two or three "certified lesbians" among the older girls at the convent, and at least two of the sisters were suspect. When the lights were out, some of the girls engaged in sex play, but everything was kept secret and forbidden.

"Vivian told me that she couldn't wait to get deflowered by a man, although she felt a young boy might be a better candidate to introduce her to the thrills and mysteries of sex," O'Sullivan claimed. "Vivian and I made up for lost time after we left the convent."

Ernest Hartley had been so successful as a senior partner in the Piggott, Chapman and Co., in India, that he told Gertrude and Vivian that he was a wealthy man. He lived in a paradise of belief that the family fortune would only grow bigger in the years ahead. Like most investors of the world, he did not anticipate the financial reverses that would befall his family in only a year in the wake of the Wall Street Crash in New York in 1929.

In September of 1928, Ernest decided that the convent at Roehampton was far too restrictive for his daughter. He wanted "the finishing touches" of her education to be applied to her on the Continent, where he hoped that she would become fluent in French, Italian, and German.

The next four years of Vivian's life, as she embarked on the Grand Tour of the Continent, remain relatively obscure and have stumped her biographers. However, in bits and pieces from what little she's said over the years, plus snippets of gossip from schoolgirl friends, a portrait has emerged, however sketchy.

It is not a "warts-and-all" portrait, but more like an unfinished sketch left on an artist's easel. This period of her life marked the end of her girlhood and her emergence as a woman, albeit still a late teenager.

It was a hot summer day on July 7, 1927, when Ernest arrived at Roehampton to take away his daughter. She was only thirteen, but already was showing signs of developing into a beautiful woman.

"I was shocked by the transformation in her," Ernest later said. "My darling little 'mouse'—or should I call her my little wren?—had almost grown up overnight and blossomed into this exquisite creature."

Aboard a boat crossing the English Channel, the Hartleys arrived at the French sea resort of Dinard during high season. Ernest had rented a villa for them with its own private beach.

Since the 1800s, Dinard had been popular with wealthy British families who built magnificent villas along the coast. Vivian arrived just as the resort was starting to lose its prestige, falling to the Côte d'Azur.

While in Dinard, Vivian would spend endless hours strolling the beaches, taking in the beauty of the water, but also watching the people. She'd never seen "so many naked people before," as she claimed. In those days, the French wore far less on the beach than the more prim and proper English did. She couldn't help but notice that men revealed a "mound" in their bathing suits, whereas women showed nothing.

With school chums at the convent school. Vivian is at far right

Vivian was shown where Lawrence of Arabia had lived as a small child, and she dreamed that one day he'd come for her on a great white stallion and take her away. She selected as her favorite spot on the beach the exact place where Pablo Picasso had once anchored to paint.

For these walks along the sea, Vivian dressed as provocatively as Gertrude would allow. Although she was far from buxom, she began to attract both vacationing

English boys and local French boys, even some older men.

Later in life, Vivien Leigh would say, "Isn't it every grown man's fancy to seduce a thirteen-year-old virgin?"

Ernest told Gertrude that he thought their daughter was "boy crazy. That's all she talks about—what boys she saw on the beach today and what they said to her."

Her body was wraithlike, but Vivian was in good health. She never seemed to need much sleep. Long before her parents woke up, she was out wandering the shoreline by herself.

At night she noticed the growing tensions between Ernest and Gertrude. Up until now, she hadn't realized that their marriage was in deep trouble. She'd hear their arguments late into the evening, and learned that at one time in Calcutta, Gertrude had invited all of Ernest's mistresses, escorted by their husbands, to a dinner party at their villa.

Sometimes, however, Vivian would retreat into her room as she went into what Gertrude called "one of her dark moods." At such times, she'd refuse to come down for dinner. Gertrude ordered one of the servants to leave a tray outside Vivian's bedroom door, but it was often found untouched the following morning.

Her parents did not see any signs of mental illness in these periods of withdrawal. Ernest dismissed them as growing pains.

As the first autumn breezes blew in from England across the Channel, Ernest and Gertrude decided to leave Vivian at another convent school in Dinard, before they made their way to the more fashionable Biarritz, in southwestern France, on the Bay of Biscay. In the southwest, the weather was milder in the winter, and the summer lasted until late October.

Unlike Roehampton, Vivian did not like the convent school at Dinard—nor the girls who were enrolled there. As an older student, she was no longer the teacher's pet. All the lessons were in French, and she had not mastered even the most basic French. She worked hard and seemed determined to master at least conversational French before the term ended.

Her only breaks came when her parents met her in Paris during the school holidays and would take her to the theater. She had grown more and more fascinated by the stage. While Ernest squirmed in his seat during these performances, and Gertrude waited patiently for the curtain to fall, Vivian studied the action carefully with a surgeon's eye and strained to hear every line of French dialogue.

She was thrilled when summer came and her parents met her at the Ritz Hotel in Paris where they enjoyed a week of shopping and theater-going before heading for Biarritz for the summer. At that time, it was one of the most fashionable resorts in the world.

Except for Paris, Vivian found Biarritz the most glamorous place she'd ever visited. It had become renowned in 1854 when Empress Eugénie (wife of Napoléon III) built a palace on the beach. In time, Queen Victoria, Edward VII, and Alfonso XIII of Spain became frequent visitors.

Some days, Vivian walked all seven miles of the beaches. In letters sent to her schoolmates back in Roehampton, she claimed that the boys of Biarritz were far more beautiful than those of Dinard. She'd always write at the end of her notes, "Please don't forget me."

The bathing suits in Biarritz were far more revealing than those at the north coast beach resorts. She was particularly intrigued with young Basque men. "I know it's silly to make such a claim, but they are perhaps the sexiest men in the world," she wrote back to a classmate in the convent. "Englishmen in bathing attire look pasty white. These Basques are golden boys. They have sleek black hair, luscious brown eyes, and they flaunt their sexuality in their bathing attire."

In Biarritz, Ernest purchased for Vivian what she later called "the most revealing bathing suit in the world." He also bought three flapper dresses for her. "I looked like a young Zelda Fitzgerald, who was always getting written about in the newspapers with her husband F. Scott Fitzgerald, the novelist," Vivian later said.

In September, Ernest and Gertrude drove Vivian to the capital of the Italian Riviera, the old city of San Remo, opening onto the Ligurian Sea. Monte Carlo and Nice were just across the French border. Once there, they enrolled their daughter in the Convent of the Sacred Heart, hoping she'd become proficient in Italian.

Although she knew some of her classmates from Roehampton, an affiliate school, Vivian was very unhappy at the convent. Nearing fifteen, she felt constrained by the harsh nuns and their rigid rules. "I was not convent material," said Vivien Leigh later in life. "Neither was young Vivian Hartley."

She later claimed that there was more sex going on inside the convent school than outside. "Nuns with nuns, nuns with schoolgirls, and priests with nuns, maybe even priests with priests for all I knew," Vivian told her mother.

Vivian lost interest in school and did not take to the Italian language the way she did with French. She clashed frequently with the Reverend Mother, who wrote Ernest and Gertrude that their daughter's behavior was "reprehensible."

Boys had been accessible to Vivian in France, but not in San Remo. The girls were heavily segregated. "Boys were viewed like some horrid disease we might catch," Vivian said. "Later on, I realized that 'disease' was pregnancy. Even so, two girls dropped out of the convent that year because they became pregnant, and the Catholic Church opposed abortion."

In another part of the world, six lavish parties were thrown in Calcutta to say farewell to the Hartleys, who departed on March 2, 1929.

Vivian welcomed the arrival of summer which she spent with Gertrude and Ernest in Galway in Ireland. Her Roehampton schoolmate, Patsy Quinn, traveled westward from England to visit. Often they read plays together, dividing up the roles between them.

By September, Vivian was delighted to be transferred to a fashionable school in Auteuil on the outskirts of Paris. She always considered Paris a magical city, and it would be at her doorstep whenever she could escape from school.

On September 27, 1929 she was welcomed by Mlle. Manilève to her finishing school at the Villa Sainte-Monique. The French school mistress taught Vivian French literature and sharpened her skills with the French language. Mlle. Manilève was the first woman to achieve a baccalauréat in France.

Vivian's favorite teacher was Mlle. Antoine, who had been a performer at the Comédie-Française in Paris, one of the few state theaters at the time in France. Mlle. Antoine imbued Vivian with a love of the theater that would never leave her. She took three of the school's students, including Vivian, to Paris to see a play by Molière performed at the legendary theater.

Unlike the convent schools, the school in Auteuil allowed its young pupils to wear makeup. Whether they attended mass or church was up to each individual girl. Vivian chose to sleep in on Sunday morning.

She seemed almost blissfully unaware of "Black Tuesday" on October 29, 1929, when share prices on the New York Stock Exchange collapsed. Only vaguely did she realize that the Wall Street crash would have a great impact on her own life and the family fortune. From that point on, the Hartleys had to curtail their lifestyle, but still continued living well when compared to many others in their former position.

Gertrude became interested in promoting beauty products as a means of adding to their income, and was rather successful at it.

Vivian later said that her time spent in Auteuil was the happiest of her life so far, but she supplied no details. She was up to some sort of mystery. A friend of the Hartleys reported that Vivian had been spotted at a theater in Paris accompanied by an older man. She was

Two views of a blossoming beauty on holiday in the pre-crash prosperity of the mid-1920s

41

dressed in designer clothes with a plunging *décolletage* and wore heavy make-up.

This alarmed the Hartleys who suspected that Vivian had found "a patron," since they provided only a meager budget for her living expenses beyond the school tuition—not enough to buy expensive clothes.

When the alarmed Hartleys came to Paris to collect Vivian, she refused to tell them where she'd gotten the money to purchase such expensive items.

Ernest told Gertrude, "Our daughter's virginity has been taken—I just know it. Without our being aware, she has grown up while we were away from her."

***

To break up whatever liaisons Vivian had formed, the Hartleys took her to Germany, enrolling her in a school near the spa resort of Bad Reichenhall, close to the Austrian border.

Throughout France and Switzerland, Vivian had argued bitterly with her parents for having removed her from the scene in Paris. "I'm not a child," she screamed at them. "I'm a young woman. I demand to be treated as such."

The Bad Reichenhall school was run by the Baron and Baroness von Roeder, who would be her "parents" for four school terms, which came to an end in the late spring of 1931.

Contrary to her expectations, Vivian liked the German school. "Mostly I liked the boys, two in particular," she later said. "Both were blond Bavarians, very muscular. They'd grown up climbing mountains and enjoying the Alps."

The actual events of her life in Bad Reichenhall grow murky at this point. Her young beaux apparently took her on occasion to the neighboring city of Salzburg in Austria where she "fell in love" with Mozart.

On these occasions, Vivian reportedly shared a room with both young German men, who appeared to have been in love with each other as well as with Vivian. One of her school girlfriends later claimed, "Vivian Hartley was definitely involved in what the French called a *ménage à trois*."

It was a very different and more mature Vivian who greeted her parents at Kitzbühel, a famous ski resort in the Tyrol region of Austria, for a Christmas vacation. She seemed more self-assured, and both parents were struck by her astonishing beauty. She had a delicate look about her, but her green eyes also expressed a steely determination.

On her first day on the slopes, she encountered Leni Riefenstahl, accompanied by two handsome young men. The Austrians seemed in awe of her.

That night at their hotel, Riefenstahl had arranged for the guests to see one of her latest films, *Der heilige berg* (The Holy Mountain). In time, of course, the beautiful, athletic German would become Hitler's favorite filmmaker.

Vivian could only dream that one day, like Riefenstahl, she'd be surrounded by adoring fans.

After only the third day of their vacation, Gertrude complained to Ernest, "Our daughter has become a tramp. She flirts with every boy she sees. I found her kissing the Austrian waiter from room service who brought our breakfast trays."

On the slopes Vivian met a handsome young ski instructor, who became a regular escort of hers at *après-ski*. Vivian demanded the privilege of being allowed to date, and Ernest and Gertrude finally gave in, realizing that if they didn't, their daughter would slip behind their backs and date the young man anyway.

Ernest, however, warned the skier that their daughter was still a virgin, and that he planned to keep her that way. Perhaps the ski instructor only smiled and agreed, because it is believed that he and Vivian were already having a sexual relationship. She came and went from his room.

Back at Bad Reichenhall when the school term came to an end, Gertrude arrived to retrieve Vivian. It was the spring of 1931. Vivian had turned seventeen and was speaking German.

Vivian's knowledge of languages learned on the Continent helped her career as an actress. Vivien Leigh often dubbed her own films in French and German. She dubbed *Lady Hamilton* (the French version) and supplied the Italian for her role as Karen Stone in *The Roman Spring of Mrs. Stone*.

Vivian surmised that Gertrude and Ernest were still together, but leading somewhat separate lives. They appeared to stay married for appearance's sake.

Gertrude treated Vivian to a holiday in Munich where they attended opera every night. Vivian was particularly fascinated by Wagner's *Parsifal*.

After their holiday, Vivian said goodbye to Germany, a country she'd come to love. For a while, she corresponded with the two young men who'd been her beaux, but when they joined the Nazi army they stopped writing her.

Sailing across the English Channel, Vivian and Gertrude headed for London where they'd have a reunion with Ernest. With school behind her, she wanted to start living life as a young woman without parents telling her what to do.

Leni Riefenstahl

***

Back in London, Vivian still clung to some vague dream of becoming an actress. That ambition became all the more vivid when she went to see *A Connecticut Yankee* at the cinema in the Haymarket in the center of London. She almost screamed in shock when she saw Maureen O'Sullivan appear on the screen.

She'd lost touch with her former schoolmate and had no idea that she'd gone to Hollywood. Of course, the movie belonged to its star, that homespun philosopher, Will Rogers, but O'Sullivan was featured.

At the end of the film, Vivian rushed back to the hotel where she was staying with Ernest and Gertrude. She demanded that they enroll her at once in the newly opened Royal Academy of Dramatic Art. She knew the family finances were in bad shape, but she demanded this expense from her parents anyway. After endless nagging, Ernest finally gave in to her.

Before her term at the academy began in May, Vivian accompanied her parents to Teighmouth in England's West Country, where Ernest had rented a bungalow. Devon was a lot cheaper than London.

Ernest was friends with Geoffrey Martin, an associate at Piggott Chapman. He offered the Hartleys the comfortable bungalow, which lay close to where he lived with his wife and four daughters, Hilary, Dulcie, Clare, and Mills.

For a while in February of 1931, Gertrude and Ernest shared the bungalow with her lover, Tommy. Vivian was assigned a small room in the back. After Ernest lost his fortune in the Stock Market, Gertrude had become the main source of income for the family. Soon, when she returned to Biarritz to oversee her cosmetic business, Tommy went with her.

Ernest stayed in Devon for only a short while, returning to London to pursue his fading finances. That left Vivian alone in the bungalow, although the family promised to take care of her until her return to London.

One afternoon, Clare Mills invited Vivian to attend the Dartmoor Draghounds parade down High Street in the quaint village of Holcombe.

As she stood on the sidelines with Clare, Vivian noticed a handsome young man on horseback coming down the street. She smiled her sweetest smile at him, and he saluted her striking beauty.

After he'd passed on, Clare turned to her. "Isn't he the handsomest thing you've ever seen on horseback? Can you believe that only this afternoon, my sister, Dulcie, turned down his proposal of marriage?"

"He's the man of my dreams," Vivian said.

"He's probably not interested," Clare said. "Dulcie broke his heart. He'll need time to recover."

"I'll mend his heart," she said with a fierce determination. "That man, whatever his name is, is the one I've chosen to marry."

***

Larry may have embarked on a relationship with Siegfried Sassoon as a means of making Glen Byam Shaw jealous. It may have been no more than petty revenge against Shaw for stealing the affections of Angela Baddeley, "the only woman I've ever loved." But after three nights with Sassoon, Larry almost forgot about both Shaw and Baddeley.

Born to a Catholic mother and a Jewish father, Sassoon had no German blood in him, as most people assumed because of his first name. His mother, Theresa Sassoon, named her son Siegfried because of her predilection for Wagner operas.

Sassoon enthralled Larry with tales of his exploits in World War I, when he'd been commissioned into the 3rd Battalion of the Royal Welsh Fusiliers as a second lieutenant in 1915. During that time he became a close friend of the writer Robert Graves (1895-1985). Graves, of course, was the celebrated English poet, novelist, and translator who produced some 140 works during his lifetime, including innovative interpretations of the Greek myths.

Because of the horrible bloodshed he'd witnessed during the war, Sassoon lost the romanticism of his early poetry and began to write war verse in all its grim details—rotting corpses, mangled limbs, even the suicide of soldiers.

On the Western Front, Sassoon behaved like the future movie hero, Rambo. At one point he single-handedly captured an entire German trench on the Hindenburg Line. As a company commander, he led night raids on the Kaiser's troops and directed bombing patrols. His fellow soldiers called him "Mad Jack" because of his near-suicidal exploits on the battlefield. This bravery won him Britain's Military Cross in the summer of 1916.

At the time Larry became involved with him, Sassoon had become a pacifist and attacked war. For a time, Sassoon, as he related to Larry, had suffered shell shock and was confined to a war hospital near Edinburgh.

Sassoon introduced Larry to poetry and writing with which he was unfamiliar. "He opened my mind," Larry later claimed. At the time he first met Larry, Sassoon was deep at work on his three-volume fictionalized autobiography.

In time, Sassoon would share his early memories of Larry with such theatrical notables as Ivor Novello and Noël Coward. "When I first met young Larry, he was like an unfinished portrait. He was very impressionable and could easily fall under the spell of a stronger personality. He almost needed to be told what to do. He hadn't become his own man yet. He could be dominated like a woman—in fact, I think that is what he wanted. He later became a great man, but that piece of work took a long time in creation."

One night at a dinner party at the home of Robert Graves on the island of Majorca, Sassoon spoke openly of his homosexual involvements. He did not believe in living in the closet. He freely admitted to having affairs with, among others, the German aristocrat Prince Philipp of Hesse, the writer Beverley Nichols, and the effete aristocrat, the Hon. Stephen Tennant.

"Of the many men who have passed through my life, Larry was the most trusting, the most giving," Sassoon claimed. "Of all the men I've loved, he was the one who desperately needed affection. He needed a strong male figure in his life, one who loved him. From what I gathered, his father never gave him love. Somehow a mother's love was not enough for Larry. He wanted a manly love and masculine approval. He made a big mistake with me. He fell hopelessly, desperately in love with me. He didn't understand that I did not believe in fidelity. I have never believed that one person should virtually 'own' another. I can provide love, even great love, to the person I'm with. But when a new day comes, I may be experiencing that same great love with another human being. I refuse to make my love exclusive. I fear Larry learned that very painfully one night when he came to my flat—I'd given him the key—and he caught me in . . . What shall I say? A compromising position with Ivor Novello."

Sassoon would later claim that "the shock on Larry's face when he caught me with my trousers down, so to speak, should have been preserved on film. No actor in the British theater ever expressed betrayal with such a painful look. It would haunt me forever, though. It did not lead to my mending my whoring ways. Larry may have thought that our relationship ended that night. But, remember, he was young in his knowledge of human relationships."

"Over the course of a long friendship with another man, one must expect such betrayals along the way. He may have thought so that night, but my relationship with Larry was far from over. Not only that, but his relationship with that stunning beauty, Ivor Novello, had only begun."

After fleeing from Sassoon's flat, Larry packed his one suitcase and took the train to Birmingham, where he had set up a meeting with Barry Jackson, who directed Britain's finest provincial theater, The Birmingham "Rep."

Sybil Thorndike had recommended that Jackson "take Larry under your wing and do something with him." Out of great respect for Thorndike, Jackson agreed to shepherd this undisciplined and relatively inexperienced actor. Jackson already enjoyed a reputation for discovering some of the major stars of the British stage.

***

When he arrived in Birmingham, Larry found out he'd been misled. He wasn't asked to join the repertory company immediately, but went through a trial period that lasted for several months.

Barry Jackson, head of the Birmingham Repertory Theater, was called "a stage-struck millionaire." As the heir of the Maypole Dairies, Jackson did not enter the theater to make money, but for the love of the stage.

Larry's first assignment would be to return to London to appear in a religious drama, *The Marvellous History of Saint Bernard*, which starred Robert Harris and Gwen Ffrangcon-Davies.

At the time Harris was known "for bringing Shakespeare to life." He would later make his Broadway debut in Noël Coward's *Easy Virtue*.

Larry was already familiar with Gwen Ffrangcon-Davies. In 1924, he'd seen her play Juliet opposite John Gielgud. In 1942 she would star as Lady Macbeth opposite Gielgud. Born in 1891, dead in 1992, the actress became one of the few centenarians of the British theater. At the age of one hundred, she was created a Dame Commander of the British Empire.

Gwen later said, "I was absolutely shocked in the years to come to hear Olivier described as the greatest actor on the English stage. From my watching him work, even though he was still young and inexperienced, I saw no such promise in him."

Under Jackson's direction, Larry began what he'd call "my compulsive quest for versatility."

In Jackson, Larry would find a drama coach far more formidable than Fogerty. He was dedicated to excellence in the theater, and he tolerated no nonsense, often mocking and humiliating Larry in front of other cast members. Larry later referred to it as "tough love."

"I played in melodramas; I appeared in the occasional classic; I did thrillers, romantic comedies—all of them are but a blur in my mind today," Larry said in later life. "In fact, at the time, I was considering writing Dickie and asking him to get me a job on that rubber plantation in India. At one point I planned to abandon the theater forever."

He later claimed that he felt he was succeeding when one woman saw him in one play one week, and as a different character in another play the following week. She turned to her husband, "Sure that can't be the same young man we saw last week. He looks so different. He's aged somewhat terribly. Perhaps drinks a lot."

His role in the St. Bernard play brought Larry back to London to appear in the small role of a minstrel at the

Two views of Gwen Ffrangcon-Davies

ROUND THE NEXT CORNER

An intensely personal
autobiography
that also throws
much light on
London theatrical life
in the twenties & thirties

DENYS BLAKELOCK
GOLLANCZ

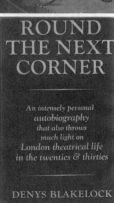

Kingsway Theatre. His salary of six pounds, ten shillings weekly was the highest he'd ever been paid in the theater.

Lawrence Ollivier (sic) was listed on the program.

The St. Bernard play was by Henri Ghéon, a fashionable French religious dramatist. A High Anglican himself, Larry pronounced it "a beautiful parable play." He was also assigned to understudy for the play's star, Robert Harris. But he was soon demoted to "second understudy." Instead of being jealous of Denys Blakelock, who'd replaced him as first understudy, Larry forgave the young actor and started leaving the theater every night after curtain for "some adventure," as Blakelock later recalled it.

When Blakelock took Larry home to meet his mother and father, almost like a prospective groom introducing his bride-to-be to his parents, Mrs. Blakelock found Larry "a very *plain* young man."

"He was pale, with an unmanageable mass of thick, black hair, and a gap between his two front teeth," Blakelock said. "His suit was ill fitting. But he had square shoulders and long straight legs that were to stand him in such good stead as a romantic actor in the days ahead."

Larry was drawn into the complex web of Blakelock. At first they seemed to have a lot in common. Both actors were the sons of clergymen. Blakelock offered friendship but more than that. A homosexual, he demanded sex from Larry, even though Larry later admitted that "I'm not really attracted to him all that much."

In the rather pretentious way Larry had of talking, he spoke of his friendship with Denys. "Having lived through my earliest days with a desperate wish to be liked unanswered, I embraced this unaccustomed happiness with an innocent young gratitude that I often think must have given Denys, who was a few years my senior, some embarrassment in those early days."

Sybil Thorndike entertained Blakelock and Larry at her summer cottage, St. Joan, named after her memorable 1924 performance. "They were staying in a small cottage

(upper photos) Two views of Denys Blakelock in his 20s

(lower photo) his 1967 autobiography

48

near mine. I invited them for dinner. They seemed madly in love with each other at the time, although I could be wrong about that. They sat on my living room sofa and held hands, which I found very romantic."

Blakelock later admitted to Noël Coward, "I think I first fell for Larry back at All Saints when he appeared as Katharina in *The Taming of the Shrew*. Even though he was dressed as a woman, I found him compelling. But I didn't go backstage to meet him at that time."

Blakelock would later pen his memoirs, *Round the Next Corner*. In his first draft, he wrote of his homosexual liaisons with Olivier, even though he promised his friend he'd be very discreet.

In his own memoirs, Larry too wrote four chapters about his homosexual liaisons, but at the request of family removed them immediately prior to publication. In Blakelock's case, it was his publisher who had the homosexual references removed for fear of libel, since some of the participants were still alive at the time.

Blakelock wrote in his autobiography, "Larry came out of that season of *Henry VIII* and *The Cenci* throbbing with desire to make something of himself in the West End." To his homosexual friends, Blakelock said, "He was throbbing with desire all right."

The St. Bernard play was interrupted by the worst general strike in the history of Britain. To help break the strike, Larry worked as a gateman on London's Underground. He later regretted his role in causing the underpaid laborers to lose their demands.

After London, it was time for summer theater, and Larry was sent at once to take the role of a minor actor in *The Barber and the Cow*, a so-called Welsh comedy by D.T. Davies, who should have known better.

He arrived in the tacky resort of Clacton-on-Sea, in Essex, southeastern England. Ironically, three of England's greatest actors would appear in this horrible little non-comedy with some of the worst dialogue ever heard on the stage. They were Cedric Hardwicke, Ralph Richardson, and Larry himself. All three, of course, would be cast as "knights-in-waiting."

Richardson and Larry formed one of the great friendships in the English theater but got off to a bad start. "The damn fellow is after my wife," Richardson complained to Hardwicke. Larry countered, "Richardson feels superior to the rest of us mere mortals."

Hardwicke admitted that Larry was lusting for Richardson's wife, but predicted that he'd get over that and go on to become one of England's great actors, "But at the moment he's bloody noisy and lacking in subtlety."

Larry had developed another one of his schoolboy crushes on Richardson's wife, the actress Muriel Hewitt. However, his feelings weren't as intense as his feelings for Angela Baddeley. Soon Larry was calling Muriel

"Kit."

"All the young actors fall for Kit," Larry told Hardwicke. "But I think she is forever faithful to Ralph, although God knows why. I'm so much more beautiful than Ralph."

Richardson told Barry Jackson, "I don't think this cocky young pup full of fire and energy can take Kit from me. She needs a real man, which she has in me. Personally I consider men like Larry between the sexes, neither here nor there. They live in twilight."

Richardson came to this conclusion after he witnessed the arrival of Siegfried Sassoon. He came to the seaside resort and confronted Larry at the end of his performance after the curtain went down. Sassoon virtually commanded Larry to resume their love affair, a romance that would have to be shared with others. In spite of Larry's protests, he finally gave in to Sassoon and disappeared into the night with him.

When Larry realized that Kit was beyond his reach, he developed a platonic relationship with her that would last throughout the fourteen years she suffered from encephalitis, a malady that led to her death in 1942. Besides, Larry was maintaining ongoing romances with both Blakelock and Sassoon, and each of those young men was very demanding.

Before the end of the Clapton run, Richardson concluded that Larry was a practicing homosexual and, therefore, could be no threat to his marriage. Feeling more relaxed with him, he invited Larry to join Kit and him in his new Morris Cowley to drive to the next town and the next theater.

Near summer's end, Jackson assigned Larry the role of Richard Coaker, a lovesick young farmer in *The Farmer's Wife*. Richardson himself had played the lead eighteen months before. Eden Phillpotts had first presented his play during World War I, and the old chestnut had been running somewhere ever since. This style of drawing room comedy was called "love among the teapots."

For six months, Larry was trapped in this vehicle, and he got to know his own country for the first time, even going to Scotland, a land to which he would return many times in his future. Somewhere along the way—details are missing—an amazing transformation occurred in his physical appearance.

Blakelock hadn't seen Larry in three months but caught up with him in Brighton to resume their affair. He later claimed, "Larry looked good enough to eat, which I proceeded to do. What a tasty cream pie. He had somehow got his hair to part the right way. He'd had his hairline plucked to get rid of that low forehead, and he had the gaps between his front teeth filled by some dentist. His eyebrows were trimmed and straightened, and he was beautifully and rather gaily dressed—no more castoff suits from the Olivier family."

When Richardson, too, had a reunion with Larry, he was amazed at the change in him. "Larry had gone through an astonishing transformation—born again if you like. That is not unusual. Many actors between the ages of eighteen and twenty-two go through much the same."

"When I first met Larry, his face didn't match his body," Richardson said. "He had a wild bush of hair in those days which looked like it needed washing. He had very bushy eyebrows that you might find on a worker in Limehouse. His nose protruded from his face like it wanted to take flight. His teeth were irregular. He must have had a lot of work done later on. His body was very delicate, almost fragile. His chest was sunken, and he was virtually skin and bones."

"At one time he parted his hair in the middle which was very unbecoming," Richardson said. "His lower lip was full but he had a thin upper lip. He tried to disguise this defect by putting on too much lipstick on stage. He was extremely fond of lipstick and wore it long after the curtain had been drawn. When reminded that it was still coated on his mouth, he'd apologize, 'Oh, I forgot to wash my face.'"

"Then, as if some magic fairy godmother waved her wand, Larry turned into a most beautiful man, the kind certain British gents like to sodomize," Richardson said. "He became matinee idol material. He was a most succulent specimen of manhood. He'd developed enough flesh on his legs to fill out green tights."

As writer Melvyn Bragg put it, "Stage front, tailored like a swell, glistening with the very latest line in handsome maleness, he presented his new self—*Beau* Olivier."

He began to exercise in gyms to build up his chest and arm muscles. "In case I have to appear half naked in some production," he told Barry Jackson.

When Larry came to London to resume his affair with Sassoon, he called on Gwen Ffrangcon-Davies, unaware that she'd not been impressed with him. She told him, "You look absolutely, positively ravishing. If you can ever tear yourself away from Siegfried Sassoon, girls will really go for you."

Of course, she was aware that those in-the-know people in the London theater gossiped about Larry's homosexual liaisons. Once she gave him some advice. "If you want to create a more manly image, earning thousands of female fans, you may have to take a wife to prove your

Larry getting buff

heterosexual credentials."

"I don't want to do that," Larry said.

"But at some point in the future you might," Gwen said. "My advice is to marry a lesbian. That way you and she could carry on with your fun while enjoying the respectability that only a marriage can bring. Incidentally, I'm a lesbian myself if you're interested."

Larry turned her down. Gwen did not take her own advice and lived openly with her life-long friend and companion, the actress Marda Vanne. Vanne met Larry when she appeared at the Old Vic with him in 1938 in a production of *The King of Nowhere*.

Gwen and Marda Vanne became a notorious female couple. "Scrappy" Vanne, as she was called, was a South African actress who found fame in London. She was born to Sir Willem and Lady van Hulsteyn, and was briefly married to Johannes Gerhardes Strijdom, who was prime minister of South Africa from 1954 to 1958.

When the two women tried to bring "the traditions of a faltering English stage to the culture-starved people of South Africa," they invited Larry to join their troupe. Preoccupied with World War II, and his various projects, he politely turned them down.

Larry officially joined the Birmingham Rep in 1927, appearing in varied roles which included playing Tony Lumpkin in *She Stoops to Conquer*. In dark makeup and a ridiculous wig, Larry bounded onto the stage in this Goldsmith play. He later recalled, "It was a romp for me."

He transformed himself for the title role in Chekhov's *Uncle Vanya*, where he, a nineteen-year-old, had to impersonate a character in his forties. Uncle Vanya, that "incarnation of futility," became one of Larry's first major roles.

Even more challenging was his role of Parolles in the modern-day production of *All's Well That Ends Well*. Larry's character was described by critic J.C.

Marda ("Scrappy")
Vanne in 1921

Trewin as "an amiable, too smart young man, a sommelier's scourge."

He was particularly nervous on opening night because he'd been told that George Bernard Shaw was in one of the front seats to see one of his favorite plays.

Backstage, Shaw praised Larry for his performance, but not as effusively as had Shaw's friend, Ellen Terry. Privately the playwright told Jackson, "This young Olivier squirt could become one of Britain's best actors, but first he'd got to decide which sex he wants to be."

Up to his old tricks, Larry tried to upstage a veteran like Meville Cooper when they appeared in Eden Phillpotts' *Something to Talk About*, another so-called comedy. Appearing as a rich young man with a monocle and an Oxbridge accent, Larry invented a line to get a laugh.

Summoned before Jackson's producer, W.G. Fay, the next day, Larry was told: "We're not running an East End Music Hall around here. I have a right to fire you for not following the script, but I'm giving you one more chance."

At long last, Larry got a romantic lead appearing on September 3, 1927 in John Drinkwater's *Bird in Hand*, opposite his "former love," Peggy Ashcroft.

While visiting a friend's apartment with Ashcroft, Larry claimed he almost came close to proposing. But when their host excused himself, and when he heard the chain toilet flushing, the romantic mood was broken.

Completing the fall 1927 season in Birmingham, Larry appeared in his first American play, Elmer Rice's *The Adding Machine*. Rice's play satirized the regimentation of man in the age of the machine.

From January to May of 1928, Larry returned to London to appear in a series of plays for the Birmingham Rep at the Royal Court Theatre.

In Birmingham, Larry had tried to imitate an American accent for his star part in *The Adding Machine*. He wasn't really sure what an American accent sounded like. He attended a lot of American movies, but all of them were silent back in those days.

In his repeat of the role in London, he feared that actual Americans might be in the audience and would no doubt be critical of his attempt to play a Yankee.

Denys Blakelock had been cast as the son of the American actress, Clare Eames, in *The Silver Cord* at London's St. Martin's Theatre. When Blakelock introduced Larry to the actress, she agreed to help him with his American accent for *The Adding Machine*. When the play opened, London critics hailed his "Americanese."

Eames was very generous in giving of her time to Larry, and she may have found him physically appealing. "Few stars agree to take on a pupil for no motive other than kindness of the heart," Blakelock said.

During their lessons in American diction, Larry noticed that Eames frequently excused herself. From the bathroom, he heard coughing sounds.

Before meeting Larry, she'd appeared as both Lady Macbeth and Hedda Gabler. Larry was right about her health. He went to visit her in a London hospital shortly before her untimely death on November 8, 1930.

Until her death, Eames was married to Sidney Howard, the American playwright and screenwriter. Larry met him at the London hospital when both men had gone there to call on the ailing Eames. Their meeting was only a handshake and a brief chat, but they would eventually develop a famous link through Scarlett O'Hara.

Howard would be awarded a posthumous Oscar for his screenplay of

Gone With the Wind in 1940. Only that past August he'd been crushed to death by a runaway tractor.

Larry continued to be sexually involved with Blakelock, but it hardly resembled love on either of their parts, although their relationship would drag on for years. Privately, Blakelock admitted to friends, "We turned to each other for sexual relief and companionship. It was never that romantic." Sassoon continued to pop in and out of Larry's life unless he was otherwise engaged.

His "American voice coach," the noted actress Clare Eames, had only praise for Larry. She told Blakelock, "He looks down at me with the eyes of a conqueror. You're a very lucky man to see him after the curtain falls. I should be so lucky. I think he's just beginning to be aware of his dynamic power as an actor."

After hearing about this exciting actor, Ivor Novello attended a performance of *The Adding Machine*. He did not go backstage but left a note with the door manager to deliver to Larry in his dressing room: I SIMPLY ADORED YOUR PERFORMANCE. PLEASE CALL ME LATE SATURDAY MORNING. OF COURSE, YOU'VE FORGIVEN ME FOR OUR INAPPROPRIATE FIRST MEETING. LOVE, IVOR NOVELLO.

Larry apparently was stunned at the invitation from "the most beautiful man in Britain," and planned to make that call exactly at eleven on Saturday morning. Obviously he didn't want Sassoon to know about this, and he also didn't want to make Blakelock hysterically jealous either.

***

Impulsively Barry Jackson decided to bring a modern dress version of *Macbeth* to the London stage, casting Larry as Malcolm. For his appearance, Larry was outfitted in a gray flannel suit with a charcoal felt hat.

Ivor Novello

From the beginning, Jackson had his doubts but bravely or else stupidly forged ahead. At the conclusion of its opening night performance, he knew *Macbeth* had been a disaster. He even came out at curtain call, telling the audience, "Experiments do have their failures."

In spite of the dismal play, Larry was singled out for praise by some critics, who were probably desperately trying to find something good to say about this play. *The Times* concluded that, "The modern *Macbeth* wasn't illuminated but overwhelmed."

Sitting in the audience on opening night was the great English actress, Jessica Tandy, who was only two years younger than Olivier. She had only praise for Larry's Malcolm. In 1947 on Broadway, he returned the favor, calling her performance as Blanche DuBois in Tennessee Williams' *A Streetcar Named Desire* one of "my greatest nights in the theater, here or abroad."

"Back when we were young, I thought Larry as an actor had enormous potential based on his performance of Malcolm in *Macbeth*," Tandy recalled decades later. "I had the same feeling about Marlon Brando in *Streetcar*. In 1947 on Broadway, both actors came to my dressing room at the same time. Instead of paying homage to me, they argued as to which one was a greater actor than the other one. Marlon would argue that Larry was greater, but Larry countered that Marlon was far greater on the stage than he was."

Based on his performance in *Macbeth*, Jackson cast Larry as Martullus in a revival of George Bernard Shaw's *Back to Methuselah*. Jackson had already produced this play with unconvincing results in 1923, but thought it would be more appreciated by the audience he'd find in London.

Even Shaw had his doubts, as some of his critics had called Methuselah his worst drama. Before Jackson risked his money on the play, Shaw wired him, "Mr. Jackson, are your wife and children provided for?"

Larry found himself working with Richardson, who no longer regarded him as "frivolous and immature." On many a night during the run, Larry cemented his friendship with Richardson at their local pub until it closed. Then Larry would be off in the night to visit Sassoon or Blakelock, or someone else who had caught his fancy in those days.

Also cast in the play was Gwen Ffrangcon-Davies, whose disdain for Larry had turned to admiration. She would always recall the "March of the Children" sequence. "I was lifted out of an egg by Laurence Olivier and Ralph Richardson, both playing young boys," she said.

***

Exactly at eleven that Saturday morning, Larry placed a call to Ivor Novello. Although he is almost forgotten today, Novello was even more famous than Noël Coward at the time. He'd been a silent movie star and Coward's rival. Of him, Coward said, "There are two perfect things in the world— my mind and Novello's profile."

Novello had become a household word when at the age of twenty-one he wrote Britain's popular

Jessica Tandy

55

wartime song, "Keep the Home Fires Burning." The song became the unofficial anthem of the Allies during World War I and made Novello a millionaire. At the time Larry met Novello, he had already seduced everybody from a young Winston Churchill to the Prince of Wales, the future King Edward VIII.

Over dinner that night, Larry agreed with the public assessment that Novello was England's answer to the late Rudolph Valentino in Hollywood. When Larry met the star, he was already thirty-six years old, but looked much younger.

Larry was immediately won over by Novello's charm. "I see no reason why we can't share Siegfried," Novello proposed. "When he's away from us, we can have each other."

"An intriguing but frightening suggestion," Larry responded.

Although Larry had concentrated almost entirely on the theater, Novello intrigued him that night with the prospect of pursuing a film career. Novello had already made *The South Sea Bubble* (1928), his last silent film. He told Larry that "pictures are learning to talk, and filmmakers will need trained stage voices like yours. You're also a beauty, so you'll look gorgeous on camera."

"Looking gorgeous on camera is something you know a lot about," Larry said.

"Compliments like that will win my heart," Novello told him.

Back at Novello's flat, the star continued to hold out bait before Larry, suggesting that if "we become intimate friends, I might speed up your entry into films or even the theater. Whatever you do, don't get mixed up with Noël Coward. He'll use and abuse you, then toss you aside like yesterday's cup of tea. Have you met the dear man?"

"Never," Larry said. "I've heard a lot about him. The thought of him intimidates me."

On Novello's coffee table, Larry noticed a copy of two novels by Edgar Rice Burroughs. "I'm surprised by your reading material," he said, noting the jungle books. "Tarzan, the ape man and Ivor Novello don't seem to go together."

"The nearest I've ever been to a jungle was when I dressed up in a leopard skin outfit and descended on this fancy dress party at Royal Albert Hall with Fay Compton." It may never happen but there's a suggestion I might be asked to write the script for a Tarzan movie. Why the producers would turn to me is beyond imagination, but there's something in the wind."

As unlikely as it seemed, Novello did write the first of the Tarzan movies to star Johnny Weissmuller opposite Maureen O'Sullivan, Vivian's school friend, playing Jane.

Over their third drink, Novello went so far as to promise an introduction

56

to Greta Garbo. "She's going to be making talkies in spite of her accent, and she'll need a strong leading man with a voice—not that pathetic John Gilbert, with whom she was involved. Greta Garbo and Laurence Olivier starring in . . . perhaps *Camille*. I can just see both of your names on the marquee."

"Ivor Novello doesn't need to hold out career promises to seduce me," Larry finally said. "All you have to do is come and sit beside me."

"I think I knew that all along, but I meant every word I said," Novello told him.

Larry was very close to remembering every line Novello spoke to him, so he could repeat everything said to Blakelock tomorrow.

"Why don't we skip all this talk of the theater and speak of love?" Novello paused. "But you're shaking."

"I'm nervous," Larry said. "Siegfried Sassoon is a tough act to follow."

"Before going into my bedroom, I must play something for you," Novello said. "It will make you less nervous." He sat down at his living room piano and played Isolde's *Liebestod*. When he arose, he saw tears running down Larry's face.

"Come to me, my dear boy," Novello said, reaching out for him. "I will kiss away those tears or else turn them into tears of joy."

And so he did.

***

A month before his twenty-first birthday, Larry was offered the most difficult acting assignment of his life, the title role of Alfred Lord Tennyson's *Harold*. Jackson chose Larry over another much-admired actor, John Gielgud.

Tennyson's neglected 19th-century verse drama, *Harold*, was based on the last Saxon king of England.

Larry had to memorize three thousand lines of dialogue and was on stage at all times. Although older than Larry, Richardson was cast as his younger brother. Larry would later call the role of Harold "unactable," noting that even such a legendary thespian as Henry Irving couldn't pull off the role.

For his role as the lead, Larry was paid twenty pounds a week. "I had never seen that much money at one time in my life. I felt rich. Every night when I went on stage to say, 'Oh, Tostig, Tostig, what art thou doing here?' I thought of the new suit and new pair of shoes I could buy."

An admirer like J.C. Trewin found that Larry could "spark off Saxon fire," but critic John Ervine claimed that "his faults are those of inexperience rather than of ineffectiveness."

To conclude the season in London, Jackson chose to present a modern dress version of Shakespeare's *The Taming of the Shrew*. At All Saints, Larry had played Katharina, but in the London production he had only a small part playing "The Lord" in a dinner jacket. Appearing again with Larry, Richardson as Tranio walked off with the show and the best notices playing a Cockney chauffeur in a morning coat and silk hat.

"It was highway robbery," Larry said, when he read the reviews. From that day forth, Larry and Richardson would often compete for the same choice roles, but managed to keep their friendship intact through it all.

***

Actress Jane Welsh, who entered the world in 1905 in the city of Bristol, always appears at the top of the list of Larry's lovers, yet she remains a somewhat shadowy figure in his life. Two years older than Larry, she played a pivotal role in his maturation into a man.

Those researchers who compile lists of celebrity seductions long ago concluded that it was this "lovely English lassie"—as one reviewer put it—who won the prize of Larry's virginity, at least with a female. Technically speaking, he'd lost his virginity a long time ago to men.

In the summer of 1927, Larry met Welsh and worked with her in the Birmingham Rep, at one point appearing as her uncle in a play. That summer, Welsh—amid the heat, pollution, and grime of Birmingham—found Larry "very courtly in manner."

Although Welsh never made it as a big star like some of her contemporaries, she was a trouper, having been on the stage since the age of ten. She amused Larry with stories of her early days.

"Once in Sheffield, when I was carrying a theatrical basket as a prop, two ladies stopped me to ask what time the jumble sale began. I played in drafty church halls and dressed in smelly toilets. One time one of the male members of the audience came in and took a horse piss while I was in my bloomers stuffing my brassiere."

She was immediately attracted to Larry. To a lesser degree, he returned her affection. He told Barry Jackson, "Jane is not the type of woman who devours a man. She seems more sensitive and understanding and realizes that an actor can't always perform privately as well as he does on the stage. On stage, he's playing a character. Off stage, he has to be himself, and that is somewhat difficult for some of us to pull off."

Jane Welsh

Welsh, who would live a long life, dying in

London in 2001, was a strong young woman with a determination to succeed in the theater. She also had a very nourishing side, which Larry always needed in a woman. She claimed that when she first met him, he was "an astonishing mixture of boy and man. I wanted both to love him and mother him." It appears that she succeeded in both goals.

Until he met Jane, claimed Sybil Thorndike, all of Larry's involvements with women were mere schoolboy crushes.

"Larry drove Jane to visit me at my country home in Kent, 'St. Joan,' and I treated the couple with the same respect I had shown Denys Blakelock and Larry," Thorndike said. "When one enters the theater, one must get used to both homosexual and bisexual liaisons. That has never been a problem for me—perhaps for my husband, but not for me."

With Welsh, the schoolboy crush turned into a genuine, even intense romance. In speaking of his momentary love for Welsh, Larry asked Richardson, "Have you ever picked a wildflower in the spring meadows of Devon and taken it home? Unlike the greenhouse, cultivated rose, that wildflower does not live long."

News spread among the actors and actresses of the Birmingham Rep, most of whom thought Larry was strictly homosexual. "He's finally fucked a woman!" Barry Jackson proclaimed with a certain pride in his discovery.

From the little bits and pieces she said over the years, Welsh and Larry did not score a sexual bull's eye on their first night together. "Larry just didn't know what to do," Welsh told Angela Baddeley at the Strand Theatre when they appeared together in 1932.

"It took a little doing, but we finally got the plumbing up and running," Welsh said. "Even so, I don't think Larry will ever become one of the great Romeos off stage. Much of his virility is confined to the stage, not the boudoir. In private, he expects the woman to take the lead. He should marry only strong, determined women who can direct him. Just like an actor, he needs direction."

The white heat involvement of that smoggy summer in Birmingham dissipated as the first of the autumn winds swept over England. Both Welsh and Larry were offered a two-week vacation.

She wanted him to spend it with her in England, but he preferred to go to France with Siegfried Sassoon. The poet-author wanted to revisit some of the battlefields of World War I where he had shown such heroism.

He was also tentatively working on a play about the grim realities he'd confronted during the war, and he wanted Larry to star in the autobiographical play of himself. Larry was fascinated by the idea of playing Sassoon on stage.

Larry and Welsh officially broke off but would get back together again, at least when both of them were working in London. By the time Larry was appearing in London in *Harold*, he had reconciled with Welsh, albeit for a short time.

Near the end of the run of *Harold*, Larry expected another star role. Instead Jackson demoted him, so to speak, by giving him a small role in his modern-day version of *The Taming of the Shrew*.

"Before he opened in *Shrew*, we went to see Ronald Colman starring in *Beau Geste*," Welsh said. "Larry was mesmerized by the star. Over drinks that night in a pub, he told me he planned to become the next Ronald Colman. I thought Colman was rather superficial, a suave charmer but not much else, but Larry took him as a role model. Physically I think he tried to reshape his appearance to resemble Colman's, and he did to an extent. He looked like Ronald Colman's little brother."

"One night in London when we were having dinner in Soho, a lady stopped by our table," Welsh said. "'Mr. Colman,' she said to Larry, 'May I have your autograph, please?' Larry signed 'Ronald Colman' with a flourish. Actually Larry looked so much younger than Colman who was born in 1891."

Larry later told Welsh that he'd gone back to see Colman emote in the 1926 film six more times. The silent film was based on the novel by P. C. Wren. The movie in 1939 would be reshot in a virtual scene-for-scene remake, this time starring Gary Cooper and Ray Milland. It was the story of three devoted brothers serving in the French Foreign Legion in North Africa and battling raiding Arabs and a sadistic martinet commander.

"On opening night of *Shrew*," Welsh said, "Larry played it just like Colman personified. In fact, some members of the audience thought the real Ronald Colman was appearing in a cameo. Larry was a dead-ringer, right down to the pencil-thin mustache, the slicked back hair, and the syrupy voice. I couldn't tell if Larry was playing it straight or doing a Colman parody. Whatever, he grabbed the attention of the audience and in some ways became the most memorable performer in the play, in spite of his small time on stage."

It was in *The Taming of the Shrew* that Larry showed off his new Ronald Colman mustache to Richardson. He'd heard that producers were about to cast *Beau Geste* as a play.

When Richardson had a reunion with Larry backstage, he was stunned by the new facial hair.

"What's that?" he asked.

"My mustache," Larry said.

"Looks painted on."

"It is," Larry admitted.

In late May when *Shrew* closed, Welsh invited Larry to sign up for one of Jackson's summer tour circuits. "We could appear in plays together and live together in some rented room somewhere," she said. The tour was slated for June and July, playing in such seaside resorts as Brighton.

At first Larry agreed to join, but then abruptly turned her down one night. "I want to stay in London," he told her. "I want to continue to work on the London stage. I'm going to find a role suited for me."

"He left that night," Welsh said. "I won't say I was exactly heartbroken, but I was terribly disappointed. England was a much smaller place in those days, and I knew our paths would cross in the future."

She was right.

Fast forward to London's Strand Theatre. The year was 1932. Ironically, Welsh was cast opposite Larry's former love, Angela Baddeley, in *The Night of the Garter*.

In their shared dressing room, both Baddeley and Welsh were shocked to open the door to discover not only Larry, but his escort, Noël Coward.

Backstage, Larry said, "Noël, I want you to meet my two former loves, Angela Baddeley and Jane Welsh."

A bit of a provocateur, Baddeley asked, "Larry, is this your new love?"

Coward answered for Larry. "I am every beautiful, bright thing's new love, and I plan to play that role until I'm late in my fifties. Then I guess I'll have to switch to rent boys or settle down with a true love."

Looking at his two former female loves, Larry said, "When the heart is young, it feels the pangs of love until it comes to despise love."

"What playwright did you steal that from?" Coward asked with a wicked gleam. "Come along, dear boy, the night is young and so are we, at least for a few more summers."

When the men, arm in arm, had departed, Baddeley asked Welsh, "Do you think dear Larry is lost to the heterosexual world?"

"He is married to Jill Esmond," Welsh said.

"That's what I mean," Baddeley chimed in. "Do you think he's lost to the heterosexual world?"

Back in 1928 and out of work, but only temporarily, Larry waited for a call from Jackson which came in June. The director wanted Larry to appear at the Royalty Theatre in London to take over the romantic lead in John Drinkwater's *Bird in Hand*.

The juvenile role he already knew, having appeared in it in Birmingham. Now he was set to play Gerald Arnwood, the

Noël Coward

squire's son who proposes marriage to the innkeeper's daughter.

For the production in Birminghamn, Peggy Ashcroft had come up from London to play the female lead. But now she was busy, appearing as Desdemona to Paul Robeson's *Othello*. A new actress had to be substituted.

At the Royalty Theatre, Larry went backstage to meet his leading lady. Having appeared in the play before, he felt confident, especially after receiving so much praise from his contemporaries for his "new look."

Jackson was waiting for him. He grabbed Larry's arm. "Come along," he said, "We're running late." He knocked on the dressing room door of his new young star.

In a few seconds, the door was thrown open by a handsome—not beautiful—dark-haired young woman.

"Miss Jill Esmond, meet Mr. Laurence Olivier," Jackson said. "I'll leave the two of you alone to get acquainted."

That introduction became a historic moment in the annals of British theater.

Jill Esmond in the early 1930s

CHAPTER THREE

Jill Esmond came from theater nobility. Her mother, Eva Moore, was a famous actress of her day, having starred on both the stage and in silent pictures. In 1938 she would appear in a film with Larry himself, *The Divorce of Lady X*.

She had been married to Henry Vernon Esmond, the English actor and playwright who died in 1922. Jill's parents had often toured in England, acting in plays he'd written, usually light-hearted romances and comedies, which were a favorite of Queen Mary (wife of George V). Nine of Henry Esmond's plays were produced on Broadway between 1899 and 1907, the biggest success being *Eliza Comes to Stay*, which opened in 1913.

Before his death from acute alcoholism in Paris, Eva's husband had accumulated a small fortune from his plays. The money allowed his wife and daughter to live in a style and grace Larry had never known.

He'd had dinner with Jill and Eva in their London residence, a mock-Tudor maisonette in Whitehead's Grove in the Chelsea district. The evening had gone so well Eva invited him to her country home, "Apple Porch," on a Berkshire hill overlooking the distant Thames.

It was the most luxurious house he'd ever visited, with a grass tennis court, a croquet lawn, flower beds, a vegetable and herb garden outside the kitchen, and even a cottage for the gardener.

Burning with ambition, and with the trained eye of a hustler eager to get ahead, Larry focused his attention on Jill. He told his confidants, including Blakelock, that there was much for him to gain by marrying into a well-connected theatrical family.

At first, Jill was suspicious of Larry's motives in pursuing her. She told her mother, "Larry wants to advance himself in the theater. Almost from the first week on our appearing together, he started claiming that he loved me. I doubt that. If Larry loves anybody, it is himself. He has raw ambition."

"But, darling, that's what it takes to succeed in the theater," Eva claimed.

After knowing Jill for only ten days, Larry proposed marriage. She turned him down. "For whatever reasons you have, I think you're in love with the idea of marriage—not with me," Jill said. "Besides, you need to grow up a bit. Girls mature faster than men. I am already a woman, but you're still an impetuous boy."

If Larry were crestfallen, he didn't show it, and he continued to pursue her in spite of rejections. Eva liked him more than Jill did. She told her daughter, "If I were twenty or so years younger, I'd go for him myself. With a lot of training, we could present him at court one day."

Jill was twenty years old, just one year younger than Larry.

She'd decided to become an actress like her mother. At the age of fourteen, she made her stage debut playing Wendy to Gladys Cooper's *Peter Pan*. Jill had starred with Eva in a West End play, *Mary, Mary Quite Contrary*, and she had attracted the attention of critics when playing a young suicide in *Outward Bound*.

A graduate of the Royal Academy of Dramatic Art, Jill, though younger, was far more experienced as an actor than Larry was.

In his memoirs, Larry downplayed his wife's sexual allure, awkwardly admitting that she was "not dazzlingly attractive but would most certainly do excellent well for a wife." He also admitted that he wasn't likely to do any better at his age, considering his undistinguished career in the theater so far.

"He went about pursuing marriage to Esmond with the same cold calculation he pursued his career," said Noël Coward years later.

Larry's new friend, Ivor Novello, had been a long-time friend of Eva and Jill. Eva was delighted that Novello and Larry knew each other, and invited them to Apple Porch for the weekend, where they shared the tiny upstairs bedroom.

West End legend Eva Moore with her husband, Henry Vernon Esmond

If Eva or Jill knew what was going on between the two young men at night, and perhaps they did, neither woman said anything.

Jill maintained her own private relationships with various girlfriends, and urged Larry to pursue his own relationships. "After all," she told him, "we can't be together all the time—that would be smothering. And Ivor, of course, is absolutely, divinely delicious, even more so than Noël Coward."

"You know him, too?" Larry asked.

"My dear boy, I make it a point to

know everyone important in London theatrical circles. You should follow my example."

"I'd love to be introduced to Noël Coward," he said.

"I'll mention you to him," she said. "I'm sure he'd adore meeting a pretty boy like you."

During the run of *Bird in Hand*, Larry spent a total of five weekends—accompanied by Novello—with Eva and Jill in Berkshire. He called and asked if he could visit the sixth weekend, but Eva claimed the "guest room was occupied by a family friend."

She was mysterious, not identifying the guest. However, she invited Larry the following weekend. "See if Ivor is free. I love to see the two of you walking in the garden. I'm sure Jill will agree with me that you and Ivor are the two most beautiful men in England."

Larry called Novello, planning to spend the weekend with him, but found that he'd left London without telling anybody where he was going. It was not until Larry's lonely weekend had passed that Novello called him late Monday afternoon. He did not tell Larry where he'd been, and Larry was too polite to ask. However, he did extend an invitation to Larry for a gathering scheduled for the following weekend at the Berkshire home of Eva and Jill.

That Friday night, Novello and Larry arrived at the Berkshire cottage for dinner with Eva and Jill. The following Saturday morning, Larry complained of a headache and didn't join the house party for a drive into nearby Windsor.

After reading a play in the Esmond library, he began to explore. On Eva's desk, he spotted a photograph. It looked recently taken. He was shocked to see Novello in the picture, with his arm around Glen Byam Shaw. He decided not to say anything when Novello returned.

Back in London Monday afternoon, Larry called his confidant, Denys Blakelock. "Can you believe this bloke? This creature. This Glen Byam Shaw. How cheeky of him! First, Siegfried Sassoon. Then he steals Angela Baddeley from my clutches. Now I find out he's taken up with Ivor. You're next on this little whore's list."

"I've already had him," Blakelock said nonchalantly. He paused. "I've got an idea. Instead of moaning like a jealous lover, why don't you take up with Glen yourself—see what the excitement is all about."

"Don't dare me," Larry threatened. "I might just do that if an opportunity arises."

"I dare you!"

Larry Olivier with Jill Esmond
in the early 1930s

***

Over a period of three months, Larry had proposed marriage to Jill three times, and had been rejected each time. Still, he persisted and still their close friendship continued, although he'd never kissed her, or so he claimed to his friends. Novello referred to Larry's marriage proposals to Jill as "an amusing conceit," whatever that meant.

Eva had her own reasons for encouraging her daughter to have a liaison with Larry. Already, word was spreading that Jill was a lesbian. Eva feared such rumors would seriously damage Jill's chance to develop into a romantic heroine both on the stage and in the newly arrived talking pictures.

Hearing about the squalor Larry lived in in London, Eva invited him to occupy the guest room in her own home.

Larry moved into the Esmond family's London townhouse, occupying a room on the top floor that had been earmarked for the maid. He continued to visit the Berkshire house on weekends, unless Sassoon had other plans for him. Blakelock remained his confidant and lover.

On stage in the West End, Jill played passionate love scenes with Larry, but at home she treated him like a boarder. He noticed that she had no other man in her life. But her free evenings weren't spent with him, but with a gaggle of young women. Larry was never invited to join in these soirées to the West End clubs.

One night before the curtain rose on *Bird in Hand*, the actors backstage were buzzing with excitement that Basil Dean would be in the audience that night. Dean, the most prominent and influential producer in the West End, had recently announced in the newspapers that, "I'm looking for a dashing young

actor, perhaps a relative unknown, to play the lead in my stage production of *Beau Geste*. It could become a career maker for the right kind of actor. *Beau Geste* certainly did all right for Ronald Colman on the screen."

Larry told Jill, "I'm going out there tonight to give the performance of my lifetime."

"You're only twenty-one," Jill said. "What lifetime?"

As the curtain went down, even the usually skeptical Jill congratulated Larry on his performance.

Basil Dean

But Dean did not come backstage to congratulate him, as Larry had expected. He was greatly

66

disappointed. Jill found him crying in his dressing room.

Still dreaming of getting cast in the London stage version of *Beau Geste*, Larry knew that *Bird in Hand* would soon be closing. Producers wanted to open it on Broadway, with Jill heading the cast. But the New York backers had someone else in mind for the romantic lead. Larry was not invited to join the cast.

When he complained to Jill about their upcoming separation, she shocked him. "I think it will be good to let time and distance come between us. Perhaps you'll get over this silly crush you have on me."

As he complained later to Blakelock, "Those were not the most encouraging words I wanted to hear."

"Cut out this nonsense!" Blakelock lectured him. "When will you two face the truth? She's a lesbian; you're a homosexual. Deal with it."

"But homosexuality is illegal," Larry protested. "Do you want me to become a notorious figure like Oscar Wilde?"

"Why not use Noël Coward as your role model?" Blakelock asked. "He seems to be doing just fine in the theater. By the way, have you fucked Glen Byam Shaw yet?"

"Not yet, but I plan to get around to that little whore sooner than later," Larry said. "I might have him fall in love with me."

Bird in Hand was closing. There were no job prospects in the theater. Jill was leaving for New York. Novello had just appeared in the film version of *The Return of the Rat* for Gainsborough Studios in 1928, his successful sequel to *The Rat* in 1925. He was busily preparing another film, *Symphony in Two Flats*, for Gainsborough for a 1930 release. More importantly he was weighing an offer from Paramount to make films in Hollywood. Although Noël Coward was rising rapidly in theatrical circles, Larry had not yet met him.

"Everybody seems to be doing well except me," Larry said. "I have just joined the ranks of the unemployed. That elusive bitch, Stardom, never comes knocking on my door."

He was right about that. Stardom had not come calling. But one night, Novello invited Larry to a party in Mayfair. It was for men only, an elite gathering of notable homosexuals in the theater. Larry eagerly accepted the invitation, thinking Coward would be there.

The moment Novello arrived at the party, he deserted Larry, telling him, "I've got to work the room. Mingle, dear boy, mingle."

Instead of mingling, Larry stood alone in the corner, nursing his drink.

As he looked up, one of the guests was approaching him with his hand out. "Good evening, I'm James Whale. You must be that divine star of *Bird in Hand*, Laurence Olivier."

At the time Larry met the English film and theater director, Whale was yet to make some of his biggest films, such as *Frankenstein* in 1931 or *The Invisible Man* in 1933.

Whale learned that he had a talent for producing shows while housed in the Holzminden Prison Camp, having been captured by the Germans. He was held there for two years, during which time he produced shows for the guards and fellow prisoners.

In London in 1928, he was offered the chance to direct two private performances of R.C. Sherriff's then-unknown play, *Journey's End*.

Journey's End—"a slice of life—horribly abnormal life," as labeled by George Bernard Shaw—was considered not suitable because it had no leading lady. When Sherriff published his autobiography in 1968, he called it *No Leading Lady*.

He worked in an insurance office as a clerk. However, from 1915 to 1918, he'd been a captain in the 9th East Surrey Regiment in World War I, serving at Vimy and Loos until he was severely wounded near Ypres.

That experience led to his writing *Journey's End*.

James Curtis, Whale's biographer, claimed that the play "managed to coalesce, at the right time and in the right manner, the impressions of a whole generation of men who were in the war and who had found it impossible, through words or deeds, to adequately express to their friends and families what the trenches had been like."

Before he left the party that night, Whale gave Larry the script to *Journey's End* and asked him if he could read it overnight, as he was running out of time to cast the lead.

The following morning, Whale eagerly called Larry and asked if he'd read the play. Rising early for his morning tea, Larry indeed had read the play, disliking it intensely. Whale asked Larry his opinion of the drama. "Too morbid—there's no audience for this play," Larry said. "The British are tired of war and don't want to be reminded."

Even though Whale offered Larry the lead role of Captain Stanhope, he continued to refuse. Whale later admitted to his long-time lover, the producer David Lewis, "I had two motives in wanting to cast Olivier. One, to give him the role; two, to unbutton his trousers for a little fun."

That evening Larry showed the script to Novello, who urged him to take the role. "It's not only a great part, but the perfect showcase for you to audition for *Beau Geste*, Dean's next big thing. I know Basil Dean, and I'll see that he gets to see you perform. That fluff you played in *Bird in Hand*, which Dean saw, hardly qualified you for the lead in *Beau Geste*. *Journey's End* is the perfect vehicle."

Convinced that the more mature Novello was right, Larry called Whale the next day to accept the part.

"You're just in time," Whale said. "I was about to offer the role to Maurice Evans. When it comes to beauty, he can't hold a candle to you—not even a match. He's a good actor, though. I'll let him play the secondary role of Raleigh."

Evans was one of the best-known actors in England for his interpretations of Shakespearean characters. Regrettably, today he is better known to TV audiences for playing Samantha's father in the hit sitcom *Bewitched*.

In adherence to local regulations at the time, mainstream London theaters were locked and shuttered every Sunday. A private membership theater society, however, such as the Incorporated Stage Society, managed to avoid those restrictions, and could mount private performances of plays on Sunday.

Because of that, *Journey's End* was featured twice every Sunday during its run, when larger theaters went dark.

For appearing in *Journey's End*, Larry was offered five pounds—"a miserable fiver," as he put it. For that, he had to endure three weeks of rehearsals for just two performances.

All during rehearsals, Larry failed to see what a powerful drama he was starring in. "There's nothing but meals in it," he complained to Whale.

"Food was about all we could think about in Flanders during my time in prison," Whale countered.

After each of the first two nights of rehearsals, Whale asked Larry to go "pubbing" with him, and after rehearsal on the third night, Whale invited Larry for a sleepover at his apartment. Larry willingly agreed.

Years later, the producer David Lewis, longtime lover of Whale, said, "Larry would have slept

That's Showbiz:

Three views of Shakespearan actor and Samantha's father in *Bewitched*, Maurice Evans

69

with anyone."

Whale became quite enamored with Larry, but the affection was not mutual. "This was an early example of Larry on the casting couch," Lewis said. "Women were put on the casting couch. Why not men? Why not Larry? He was overly ambitious to succeed in the theater, which has a hell of a lot of homosexual directors and producers eager to seduce a pretty boy."

It was ironic that Larry shared a dressing room with Maurice Evans, with whom he was in a neck-and-neck race to get cast as the lead in the upcoming *Beau Geste*. "At least Basil Dean can see both actors on stage at the same time," Whale said.

"Evans and I both knew what was at stake," Larry recalled. "As we undressed in front of each other, he was checking me out and I was sizing up the competition."

The budget for *Journey's End* was practically nonexistent. For his on-stage costume, playwright Sherriff had to lend Larry his tunic, revolver, holster, and Sam Browne belt.

For its Sunday night performance at London's Apollo Theatre, Basil Dean sat in the third row, hawk-eyeing every movement on stage. Dean had not gone backstage after he'd seen Larry in *Bird in Hand*. But he grandly marched backstage when the curtain went down on *Journey's End*, which had received a standing ovation.

Barging into the room Larry shared with Evans, Dean ordered Evans out. "I was painfully embarrassed for Evans," Larry recalled. "He grabbed a towel, his Army officer's breeches, and a winter undervest, his face covered in grease. He made the only wretched exit of his life."

After Evans had gone, Dean turned to Larry. "You are my *Beau Geste*."

Siegfried Sassoon was in the audience that night and seemed jealous of the success of *Journey's End*. In bed he told Larry, "I discovered post-war disillusionment. This shitty insurance salesman is stealing my thunder. I'm sorry you agreed to perform in his stupid play. It is for idiots."

Also sitting in the audience that same Sunday night was Maurice Browne, a producer who, along with his friends, would bring *Journey's End* to London's Savoy Theater where it ran for two years. Whale offered Larry the lead but he turned it down for *Beau Geste*. He also took the opportunity to spurn any more casting couch sessions

Director James Whale (*left*) and
Journey's End star Colin Clive

with Whale.

Whale later said, "Larry made a big mistake, career-wise. He should have stuck with *Journey's End* instead of doing that God damn Ronald Colman impersonation in *Beau Geste*."

Journey's End became one of the greatest of all dramas to come out of World War I. Filling in for Larry was another bisexual actor, Colin Clive, who also ended up on Whale's casting couch. Clive became Whale's new boyfriend.

Perhaps as revenge, Maurice Evans sent Larry a telegram when Clive opened in the West End. "I'm prejudiced but I rather thought Colin made a much better Stanhope than you. Sorry, old chap."

Journey's End with Clive opened on January 21, 1929 and was an immediate hit. The play was on its way to New York and around the world, and, of course, headed to a Hollywood film studio.

Larry hoped that he'd be asked to play Captain Stanhope in the film version of *Journey's End* but instead, the part went to Clive. Later Larry said, "The experience taught me never to lust after a part that genuinely belonged to another actor. Such lust can succeed in doing nothing but eat at you and make you miserable."

Whale would later cast Clive in *Frankenstein* and *Bride of Frankenstein*.

One night in London, Larry told a group of homosexual theater friends, "Just think, if I had let Whale continue to bugger me, I could have become Dr. Frankenstein on the screen."

As for the playwright, Sherriff, he would become one of the most notable scripters in Hollywood, turning out such heralded fare as *The Invisible Man* (1933), *Goodbye, Mr. Chips* (1933), *The Four Feathers* (1939), and *Lady Hamilton* (in the United States, *That Hamilton Woman*). Released in 1941, Sherriff's *Hamilton* screenplay would costar Laurence Olivier and Vivien Leigh.

Like Larry with Jill Esmond, Clive would enter into a lavender marriage with Jeanne de Casalis, a lesbian born in Africa of British parents. During the course of his Hollywood career, he would, much to Larry's envy, appear with such leading ladies as Bette Davis and Katharine Hepburn. But at the young age of 37, Clive would die in 1937 of chronic alcoholism and tuberculosis. His ashes, resting in the basement of a Hollywood funeral parlor, went unclaimed for forty years.

Madeleine Carroll

***

71

Basil Dean was the martinet of all West End producers, bullying his cast members, both male and female. Like a military commander, he even drilled the actors playing soldiers, ordering them to march and sing martial songs.

Calling *Beau Geste* "a mighty Wurlitzer of a production," Dean hired a cast of 120 actors, and featured Madeleine Carroll and Marie Lohr in the female roles.

An older actress, Australian-born Marie Lohr had made a name for herself by appearing in several plays by George Bernard Shaw, who was her friend. She'd made her first appearance on the stage in 1894 at the age of four.

The beautiful, blonde British actress, Madeleine Carroll, was on the dawn of film stardom when she appeared in *Beau Geste*. In 1935, she would attract the attention of Alfred Hitchcock and become the prototype of the director's icy, remote blondes, as evoked by Grace Kelly in the years to come.

Carroll was the first British beauty to be offered a major Hollywood film contract, paving the way for Greer Garson, Deborah Kerr, and Julie Andrews. In 1938 Carroll's salary was the highest of any actress in Hollywood, as she took in $250,000 that year.

She pursued Larry during the rehearsals for *Beau Geste*, but he spurned her overtures. "I have been called the most beautiful woman in the world by some astute members of the press," Carroll said. "How can any man turn me down unless he's something less than a man? My suspicions about Olivier are confirmed by his rejection of me. He claims he's heartsick over Jill Esmond in New York. How can any man who calls himself a man be heartsick over a lesbian? I'm a real woman."

In *Beau Geste*, Larry modeled himself after not only Ronald Colman but Douglas Fairbanks Sr. as a swashbuckling hero. Larry hoped the play would establish him as a big star and matinee hero. Regrettably it would not. "I merely brushed by Dame Fame when I appeared in *Beau Geste*," he said. "But the bitch passed me by."

On January 30, 1929, the overblown stage version of *Beau Geste* opened at His Majesty's Theatre in London.

The dramatic high point of the play involved a funeral wherein the body of the character Larry played would be cremated on a pyre. The director had elaborately devised an onstage protected area where fireproofing would (at least theoretically) contain the blaze. But during the climax of the play's first performance, as the flames shot upward, the stage manager panicked and quickly drew shut the theater's asbestos curtain. By the time the actors came out in front of the curtain to take their bows, the audience had fled from the theater.

One theater critic asked, "Who does Basil Dean think he is? Cecil B. DeMille?" The critic went on to assert that elaborate sets and unnecessary stage gadgetry detracted from any human drama going on.

In spite of the dismal box office, Larry was bolstered by occasional good notices. James Agate wrote, "Mr. Olivier gets out of bad parts all the charm there is in them." But then he added, "Olivier made *Geste* an ass but not a commanding ass."

Larry's stage rival, Jack Hawkins, playing a younger brother, got better reviews. One critic called him "an actor with a future."

"What am I?" Larry protested. "An actor with a past, an actor who missed out on the chance of a lifetime by not playing the lead in *Journey's End*."

Another critic, Charles Morgan, claimed that "Laurence Olivier is overwhelmed by the slickness of his part and by the weight of the stage trappings."

To make him even more upset, Hawkins obtained permission to leave the cast of *Beau Geste* and head for New York to appear in *Journey's End*, which was also a hit on Broadway.

Still appearing on Broadway in *Bird in Hand*, Jill had not written in several weeks. But Ivor Novello learned that Hawkins was taking Jill around to the speakeasies after curtain time.

Larry felt angry, betrayed, and hurt, as he entered one of the deepest despairs of his young life. Nothing seemed to be going right for him. Most evenings after work, he wanted to be alone.

After nine appearances on the London stage, he felt his theatrical career had stumbled and fallen. More failures lay ahead.

***

Showing poor judgment, even disastrous judgment, over *Journey's End*, Larry embarked on what he called "my series of seven flops." He savored whatever good critical appraisal he could. Often he'd take a bad review of the play in which he appeared and underline with red pencil any line that suggested he might have some talent for the stage.

He'd tried so hard to get cast in *Beau Geste*, and he'd worked even harder during the actual short run of the play. "I wanted it to matter," he said. "I wanted my part in it to matter. When it closed, it was a bitter disappointment to me. I was wounded, and it would take a long time for that wound to heal. More disappointments were on the way for me."

In spite of Larry's failure in *Beau Geste*, Basil Dean took another chance on him and cast him as the lead in *The Circle of Chalk*, his latest extravaganza. The backdrop for this classical zaju play in five acts was the Yuan Dynasty (1259-1368).

Larry was cast as Prince Pao, who falls under the spell of a teahouse girl who'd been sold into sexual slavery. He did his own makeup, complimenting himself on "my cunningly slanted eyes."

As he was to tell his future friend, Noël Coward, "At least I got to appear in a gorgeous red silk robe, the kind you're so fond of wearing at all hours of the day and night."

Los Angeles-born Anna May Wong, the silent screen star, was cast opposite him. She was half-American, half-Chinese. She'd launched her screen career back in 1919 with the notorious Nazimova, with whom she'd had an affair. Larry nicknamed her Tiger Lily from her appearance in a 1924 silent screen version of *Peter Pan*. Wong had come to London hoping to revitalize her fading screen career. On screen, Wong had become the stereotype of an exotic Eastern lady of mystery.

She was not impressed with Larry, primarily because she objected to Western men playing Oriental roles.

The Circle of Chalk opened on March 14, 1929 at London's New Theatre, running for forty-eight performances, all of which were sparsely attended.

London audiences were familiar with Wong's face from her silent movies. But when she opened her mouth to speak, there was a ripple of giggles in the opening night audience. She spoke in a kind of squeaky Americanese, or, as one critic put it, "Her face is a lotus flower of Peking; her voice the nasal pipe of Broadway."

Larry didn't fare much better. "My costume had been designed for an actor seventy-five pounds heavier than myself. Suffering from laryngitis, I was forced to speak in a bloated *Chinoiserie*. Oh, yes, one of the actors fell into the orchestra pit on opening night."

Fearing opening night, Larry had gone to a doctor who dropped nitrate of silver down his vocal chords. This chemical was believed to have been beneficial for victims of laryngitis, despite the risk that it would damage the throat. After submitting to the treatments, Larry made his entrance singing, "I'm As Weak As Any Woman." He warbled the words in a high pitched falsetto that brought laughter throughout the theater.

At the end of the run, Wong told him, "Appearing in *The Circle of Chalk* will set us up for our next gig, the unemployment line."

Amazingly, he kept finding work, winning a lead in a play by Philip Barry called *Paris Bound*. It had already been made into an American movie starring Ann Harding and Fredric March. In some ways, the plot evoked Larry's future marriage to Jill.

The leads in the play, Herbert Marshall and Edna Best, had recently been married for real. In

Anna May Wong

74

the drama, they also go through the rituals of a church wedding, but agree to an open marriage where each of them will have the freedom to become romantically involved with others. Larry played Harding's off-the-record beau, with whom she has an affair.

On a visit to Marshall's dressing room, he was shocked to see that the actor had a wooden leg. He'd lost it on the battlefields of World War I. That was kept a secret from his public throughout most of his career, in which he played romantic leads opposite Bette Davis, Marlene Dietrich, and Greta Garbo.

Like Larry himself, Edna Best was soon to become a film star and is best remembered today for her role as the mother in the original 1934 film version of Alfred Hitchcock's *The Man Who Knew Too Much*.

Paris Bound opened at London's Lyric Theatre on April 30, 1929, and ran for only thirty-one performances, playing to mainly empty houses.

Larry later admitted he gave "one of my worst performances—I was very depressed at the time. I was on the outs with Jill and that life I lived in the shadows was going nowhere."

Marshall blamed Larry for the failure of *Paris Bound*. "It could have done better if Olivier had appeared alive on stage. He moped about, forgot his lines. He was totally undisciplined as an actor, almost shockingly so. I could not believe that such a tart would one day be hailed as England's greatest actor, even the greatest actor in the world. He seemed more interested in a string of homosexual friends, perhaps lovers, who came backstage to greet him every night during our short run. A lot of man-on-man kissing backstage."

Critic St. John Ervine had generally been kind to Larry. But in *Paris Bound*, even he lost his patience. "*Paris Bound* is too much for Mr. Laurence Olivier and too much for us; and in the last act when several of the characters began to be simultaneously bright, while Mr. Olivier played the final passages of the ballet on the piano, endurance almost came to an end."

Larry followed with yet another flop when he was cast as John Hardy in *The Stranger Within*, which opened on June 20, 1929 and ran for fifty-three performances at London's Garrick Theatre.

Larry didn't bring the slightest charisma to the role, in the opinion of London critics of the day. Nor did the play's male lead, Roland Culver. This former Royal Air Force pilot became known for his portrayals of impeccable English gentlemen not given to displays of emotion.

Like so many British actors of his day with trained voices, Culver would head for Hollywood to break into the Talkies. Although Culver played numerous lords and colonels in films, one reviewer claimed, "It would take a very practiced cinema-going eye to notice the difference he made as he made his way through about ninety films."

Playing with Culver and Larry in *The Stranger Within* was Olga Lindo, who would also appear in about thirty movies beginning in 1931.

Noticing the large size of Larry's name on the theater marquee outside, she bitchily said, "If I saw your name on a theater marquee, I would not go inside. You've hardly created an image for which the public would want to pay even a shilling."

Years later he got his revenge on Lindo. When asked about working with her, he said, "I have no memory of appearing on stage with her. You no doubt have confused me with Ivor Novello or some other actor."

Culver summed up Larry's year of discontent. "There was the problem of Jill Esmond, the regret of having turned down *Journey's End*. But there were other demons too, notably his lack of direction about where he was going. Acting in flop after flop that year enabled him to realize that he had a huge talent but was wasting it. He was unable to fully exploit it in the conventional theater. I reminded him that a young John Gielgud was making a name for himself as a Shakespearean specialist."

"That seemed to pique his interest," Culver said. "Larry even accepted my invitation to go see Johnny Gielgud in a Shakespeare production. He resisted at first, telling me that 'I have little tolerance for homosexuals in the theater.' Everyone in the cast knew about Larry's secret life, so he was just posturing. Larry expected to laugh at Gielgud's effeminate performance on stage, but instead found the young actor to be eloquent and full of grace."

"Yes, it's true, Johnny was feminine, but not effeminate," Culver said. "He managed to combine both his masculine and feminine side, something Larry would learn to do later on. Up to then, Larry had suppressed his feminine side on stage. He didn't want to be mocked. I think seeing Johnny perform profoundly changed Larry, but it would take some time before that change would manifest itself."

After the closing of *The Stranger Within*, there was no immediate acting job on the horizon. "I guess I've appeared in one West End flop too many," Larry told Denys Blakelock.

An unexpected call came in from Frank Vosper, the playwright and actor who was starring in his hit play *Murder on the Second Floor*. He invited Larry to see his performance as a detective novelist who imagines that the guests at his mother's inn are involved in various nefarious deeds.

Larry wasn't all that impressed with the role of Hugh Bromilow, as interpreted by Vosper, but went backstage to falsely congratulate him. To his surprise, he met a New York producer, A. H. (Al) Woods, who was talking to Vosper.

The British actor told Larry that he didn't want to accept Woods' offer of starring in the play in New York. "You know how ghastly Americans can be,"

Vosper said. Noting Woods, he quickly interjected, "present company except-ed, as always."

Woods pitched Larry an offer of a ten-week guarantee on Broadway at five-hundred dollars a week. On the spot, Larry agreed to appear in *Murder on the Second Floor*, mainly because it meant a reunion with Jill, who was still appearing in *Bird in Hand*.

"You should be lucky that your plays open and close so quickly," she had written to Larry. "This stinker will run forever. The Americans eat it up."

As Larry later so eloquently put it, "In the West my pleasure lay." For some impulsive reason, he decided not to alert Jill that he was on his way for his first visit to America.

Before leaving London, he spent considerable time with Vosper, learning the role. He desperately wanted to go over with an American audience. He later profusely thanked Vosper for giving him this break on Broadway.

In March of 1937, Larry was saddened to hear that his former patron had drowned after falling from the transatlantic liner *SS Paris*. The death was eventually ruled accidental, but caused extensive media speculation that he was actually murdered.

"I will always believe that Frank was pushed overboard," Larry said. "He was murdered. He was always writing about murder, even adapting a play from a short story by Agatha Christie. It just has to be murder in poor Frank's case. I know it in my heart, but that's not enough to convince a jury."

Heading to New York to perform in *Murder on the Second Floor*, Larry sailed on Cunard's *Aquitania*. Ironically, his fellow shipmate was Richard Bird, who was also heading to New York to take over the role of Captain Stanhope in *Journey's End*, which Larry had foolishly turned down but later coveted.

"I tried to pick his brain for tips about how to play Stanhope," Bird said. "But all I got from Larry was, 'Well, I kept putting my right foot up on a beer crate.'"

Intrigue with Esmond (*shown in left photo with Laurence*) and the present and previous wives of Humphrey Bogart: *(center)* Mary Philips and *(right)* Helen Menken

A Liverpudlian, Bird was a minor actor and director of stage and screen who appeared in films mainly in the 1930s and 40s. His wife, Joyce Barbour, of Birmingham, was also a minor actress who would appear on TV screens in the 1960s in various Television Playhouse episodes.

Also on board was Phyllis Konstam, who was sailing to America to appear as Larry's leading lady in *Murder on the Second Floor*. She and Larry became friends, but most of her attention was devoted to a young tennis star she had met on board.

He was Bunny Austin, a champion tennis player who had worked the courts with the likes of Charlie Chaplin. He was a friend of Daphne du Maurier, and had received invitations from everybody from Queen Mary to President Franklin D. Roosevelt. When she married him in 1931, they became a celebrated couple of their day, enjoying fame similar to today's David and Victoria Beckham.

Barbour later remembered Larry as "strikingly handsome but surprisingly inexperienced. We tried to teach him bridge. He was hopeless. He wore a white flannel suit all the time he was aboard. All the single girls flirted with him. He seemed immune to their charms and talked about Jill all the time. I feared he had no self-confidence at all, and that Broadway would devour him. I didn't think Jill Esmond was the kind of woman to instill confidence in any man."

***

Still without notifying Jill, Larry arrived in New York and checked into Manhattan's Algonquin Hotel, where all the major British stars stayed. In London, Tallulah Bankhead had sung its praises to him.

Larry was hesitant to call Jill because rumors had reached him that she was seen around town with another performer, the London-born actor Roland Young, who was also having an affair with Humphrey Bogart's second wife, Mary Philips, a stage actress.

Ironically, Jill herself was often seen in the company of another actress, Helen Menken, who had been Bogie's first wife.

"Rather incestuous," Larry said when he heard the latest gossip from Broadway. "What does this Humphrey Bogart think about this?"

Jill had abandoned Jack Hawkins as her escort but was sometimes seen with Donald Krolik, a Jewish stockbroker. "When Larry heard of this, he was very, very upset," said Blakelock. "He was worried about his own manhood. He'd heard that Jewish men have larger penises than Gentile men, and he was afraid he wouldn't measure up—that is, if he ever got around to bedding Jill."

At the Algonquin, Larry learned that Jill was staying at the Bristol Hotel.

He didn't want to go there but decided to surprise her in her dressing room after curtain call at the Ethel Barrymore Theatre.

The stage manager knew who he was and let him in. Larry would later say, "That night was the first time we'd really kissed . . . I mean, really, really kissed. I was delighted that she was glad to see me."

When Larry and Jill emerged from her dressing room, the entire cast applauded. News of their romance had crossed the ocean, and New York welcomed them as a couple in love.

In the afternoon, when she didn't have a performance, Jill became his official guide to New York, taking him on the Staten Island Ferry, visiting museums, and most definitely letting him take in all the skyscrapers which utterly fascinated him. When asked by a reporter if she were engaged to Larry, Jill said, "unofficially."

In addition to basement speakeasies, Tony's, a bar popular with actors, became their favorite hangout.

Larry claimed he felt like a New Yorker when Jill bought him a hot dog from a street vendor.

During rehearsals for *Murder on the Second Floor*, he proposed to her one more time.

This time she surprised him by accepting his offer aboard the Staten Island Ferry as it returned to Manhattan at five o'clock one morning. "We were both bathed in the pink light of dawn, as the sun rose over Brooklyn, a strange, scary place inhabited by ruffians which I was afraid to visit," he said.

Even though she accepted the proposal, she imposed conditions, warning him of the dangers of two actors getting married. She claimed that any day now she might be offered a Hollywood contract and would no doubt leave for the West Coast to star in movies once *Bird in Hand* finished its road tour beginning in Chicago.

Larry wanted to tour with her, assuming his former role in *Bird in Hand,* but he was prevented from doing so by the rules of Actors Equity, the American stage performers' union, which would not allow him to work again on an American stage until March of 1930. Since no Hollywood talent scouts had approached him during the run of *Murder on the Second Floor*, he decided he'd have to return to England to seek work on the stage in London.

Ethel Barrymore

She had more conditions, however, and they were rather draconian. "Ours will not be a traditional marriage," she said, evoking the heroine of his London play, *Paris Bound*. "I don't believe that when a man marries a

79

woman he is immediately entitled to conjugal rights. You have to earn those rights, and it may take months, even years, if necessary."

He was anxious to begin sexual relations with a woman, although terrified of the prospect. Nonetheless, he gave in to her demands. The next day he accompanied her to Tiffany's where he bought her an engagement ring with pounds earned on the London stage. She in turn gave him a stunning cigarette case in three shades of gold—green, orange, and bright shiny yellow.

That night they celebrated over a lavish dinner at "21," one of New York's finest restaurants. When it came time to pay the bill, Larry discovered that he'd left his wallet back at the Algonquin when he'd dropped by his room to dress for dinner.

She had only ten dollars in her purse. Instead of washing dishes, as was the custom in those days for those who could not pay, he left the cigarette case as a deposit. Arriving at the restaurant on the following day at lunch time, Larry retrieved it after settling the bill.

Murder on the Second Floor opened at the Eltinge Theatre on September 11, 1929 to dismal reviews. About the only good review Larry got, if it could be called that, was one critic who claimed that every now and then Larry bore "an alarming suggestion of Alfred Lunt." The play would run for only five weeks and did lackluster business, the same as his London flops. "Yet another disaster and this one across the pond," a despondent Larry told Jill.

One night, the *grande dame* of the theater, Ethel Barrymore, came to see Larry perform. "Young man," she told him in his dressing room at the end of the play. "You're as gorgeous as Tallulah told me you were. So you have beauty on your side, always good for a stage actor. But your gestures are obvious, never subtle. The audience always knows what you're going to do before you do it. This hand on the brow to indicate distress, *please*!"

"When you have a long speech, don't bore the audience," she said. "Breathe in unusual places when the audience least expects it. For God's sake, make yourself a fascinating character. People come to the theater to be surprised. They do not expect to see the ordinary."

"Miss Barrymore, I'll take your words to heart."

And so he did throughout the rest of his stage career.

During the run of *Murder on the Second Floor*, Al Woods, the producer who had brought Larry to New York, had a chance to observe the relationship of Larry and Jill from an up close-and-personal point of view. He concluded that at this point in their engagement, neither Jill nor Larry had admitted to each other that they were bisexual.

"Jill was very open with me about her lesbianism," Woods claimed. "I knew she was involved with Helen Menken, a notorious lesbian who, even though married to Bogart, had carried on affairs with both Tallulah Bankhead and Louise Brooks. Jill was dreaming of going to Hollywood. She confided in me that as soon as she got there, 'I'm going to seduce Joan Crawford.' She had this crush on Crawford, who was bisexual too."

"Larry looked calf-eyed as he followed Jill around like a lovesick fool," Woods said. "She was a very bossy lady—Larry had nicknamed her The Colonel. She gave him career advice. 'You'd be all wrong to attempt Romeo right now. You'd be laughed off the stage.' Some of her appraisals were devastating to him, wounding him. I think there was a little S&M in their relationship. In some ways, she reminded me of a stern schoolteacher, with Larry acting like her unruly pupil who needed strong discipline."

"During his stay in New York, Larry impressed nobody I introduced him to," Woods said. "He was so shy that he appeared rude to the people he met. He was very reserved, very distrustful. He seemed to hang on to Jill like he was a small child and she was his unforgiving mother. In London I had been told that he was a known homosexual. His devotion to Jill seemed to contradict that, unless he was bisexual. Even though seemingly devoted to her, I felt he wanted a mother, not a woman. He told me that his mother had died when he was very young, and apparently in Jill he was hoping to replace mama."

"Jill bossed Larry around," Woods said. "She went to see his performance in *Murder on the Second Floor* and gave him a devastating critique that reduced him to tears. I would have slapped her face, but he took it. Even though Jill and Larry were about the same age, she was much more mature and knew a hell of a lot more about stage acting than he did. I didn't give their marriage a chance. To tell the truth, I thought there would be no wedding. When Jill was off on some evenings with her lady friends, Larry was seeing this well-built blond stud from Jacksonville, Florida. I'd hired him as a stagehand. All the homosexual guys in the production were after him, but I think Larry won the prize."

According to his contract, Larry was to get paid for another five weeks of work after *Murder on the Second Floor* closed. "I think Al Woods was hoping I'd get killed in heavy traffic along Sixth Avenue," Larry said. He decided to stay in New York for another five weeks, viewing it as a well-paid vacation.

"Jill and I enjoyed the last of the boom days before the great Wall Street crash in October of 1929," Larry recalled.

He wrote to Denys Blakelock back in London. "I fear that any day now Jill will demand that I begin the sexual duties of our relationship. But, so far, she has not given me the slightest indication that she is willing to rush into that part of our lives together. I can be thankful for that."

Larry recalled that "it was one of the saddest days of my life when I said good-bye to Jill" in the New York harbor. Unlike his sail to New York, he'd been booked on the *Lacastria*, a small and less desirable vessel among

Cunard's fleet. He was headed for Southampton. "My cabin was so small there was room for only a bed. None of Cunard's big girls for me to sail this time."

After Larry left New York, Jill resumed her tour of the speakeasies, often with a woman and a male escort serving as a "beard."

Back in London, Larry faced the gloom of a worldwide economic depression. "An aura of despair hangs over London like one of those Jack the Ripper fogs," he wrote back to Jill.

***

In London, Ralph Richardson had lent his flat to Larry, while Richardson himself was appearing on Broadway in a successful play. For the first two weeks, Larry pounded the pavement looking for work, along with literally hundreds of other out-of-work actors. Finding nothing, he decided to have a family reunion.

He journeyed to Addington in Buckinghamshire to stay at the vicarage with Gerard Olivier and his second wife, Isobel Buchanan Ronaldson. It had taken Larry a long time to warm to his stepmother, but on his latest visit he bonded with her, calling her "Ibo." She called him "Kim."

Gerard was the tyrant he always was, but Ibo had softened his rough edges. During Larry's visit, Gerard warned him he should seek another line of work in view of his many dismal failures on the stage. "You'll soon have a wife to support, and Jill Esmond can't remain a young thing on the stage forever. She's not good enough to drift into older character parts like Sybil Thorndike."

Larry sensed trouble in his father's marriage. During a long walk in the countryside, Larry found out what was wrong. At the time, Gerard was sixty-five, his wife ten years her husband's junior. "My father was still full of beans," as Larry put it. "But Ibo had sworn off sex."

"She just doesn't want it any more," Gerald told his son.

On his third day back, Larry learned more sad news from Ibo. His father had kept it from him, but his sister Sybille was in a mental hospital in north London. She'd married a schoolteacher, Gerard Day, and the couple had given birth to a baby daughter.

One night, Day had awakened to the sounds of their baby crying. He rushed into the nursery where he found Sybille trying to smother their daughter. "She's completely lost her mind," Ibo said. "That why we had to have her committed."

Larry journeyed to London where he visited Sybille at the asylum. He found her dancing in the hospital gardens. The caretakers let her do that every day. The doctors told Larry that she begged them to let her dance, and they had decided it was good therapy for her. Later Larry tried to talk to his mentally unstable sister. Most of the time she babbled nonsense.

But very coherently she asked him to give her baby daughter away—"perhaps to some nice couple you meet on the street." He left the hospital in tears.

That night at Richardson's flat, he wrote Jill a long and passionate letter, pouring out his grief. She cabled back as soon as she received the letter.

LARRY, DARLING,
THIS IS YOUR PROBLEM—NOT MINE.
JILL

She then wrote her mother, expressing her fears about marrying Larry.

Do you think insanity runs in the family? What if we have children—perish the thought. Our son or daughter might be born stark, raving mad.
With love,
Jill

When Larry got her cable, he called Denys Blakelock. "I'm beginning to think that Miss Jill Esmond is a cold-hearted bitch."

"Honey," Blakelock said, "I could have told you that all along. Come over to my flat. I'll comfort you like no woman can."

The cold message he'd received from Esmond made him want to have a reunion with his real family. He felt he'd been neglecting them during his pursuit of a career in the theater.

Larry rushed back to Buckinghamshire for a reunion with his brother Dickie, on leave from that tea plantation in India, which he had come to despise.

Dickie shook his hand without an embrace and was rather formal to Larry. Their intimacy as boys seemed a distant memory. Dickie not only wanted to erase their shared past, but his most recent history in India as well. He absolutely refused to talk about the tea plantation. Larry wondered what had happened to him in India.

To compound matters, Dickie showed no interest in Larry's attempt to make it big on the London stage. Dickie viewed acting in a theater like a phase a young man goes through, perhaps appearing in dramas in college.

"To say that my reunion with Dickie was a failure is to put it mildly," he wrote Jill, forgiving her for her indifference about Sybille. "I am so very disappointed to see how the passage of time can change a person. I wanted him back in my life as before. Obviously that will not be the case. He has moved on."

She wrote back a simple note, "Shouldn't any young man move on from his boyhood? Isn't that what life is all about?"

His father and stepmother lived long enough for Larry to see each of them decline. Gerard seemed to grow weaker every year and died about the time of the German invasion of Poland in 1939, the event that plunged England into war.

Ibo would live for another twenty years after Gerard. She spent the last of those years in awful pain and confined to various hospitals. On Larry's last visit to her, she could speak out of only one corner of her mouth. She took his hand and, with pleading eyes, begged him, "Please tell the doctors to let me go."

***

Money to produce plays anywhere in England was drying up. Larry feared unemployment and financially did not appear ready for marriage, unless he planned to live off Jill and her mother, Eva, a dismal prospect to him.

Many plays announced for the 1929-30 winter season never even went into rehearsals. London was filled with out-of-work actors. Since many of them were well built and good-looking young men, male prostitution flourished. A few directors and producers recommended such a role for Larry when he went to them seeking an acting job. He turned down such offers. "I'm not that desperate yet," he told Blakelock.

Just when he was about to give up, a surprise offer came in for him to star in Frank Harvey's soggy spiritual melodrama, *The Last Enemy*. Larry later said the play "was poised between Heaven and Hampstead."

He was cast in the lead role of Jerry Warrender, a shell-shocked pilot on leave during World War I. He sounded like a schoolboy when he wrote "Jilli,"

as he was now calling his intended bride. "Oh, Gosh, oh Golly, I'm so lucky. In a lovely play. Great part. Good back-up cast. But I feel guilty working when so many other actors are looking for a job in the theater."

"*The Last Enemy* brought me friendly and timely establishment as a leading character juvenile," he later said.

Harvey, the scion of an Anglo-French marriage, was known mainly as a playwright, whose career flourished in Australia as an actor, producer, and writer.

The director of *The Last Enemy* was Tom Walls. As Larry remembered, Tom spent more time at the race track than he did in helming his stellar cast of talented actors.

Jazz Age nightlife mogul Texas Guinan

84

"We more or less directed ourselves," Larry recalled.

He was cast with first-rate performers, all forgotten names today—O.B. Clarence, Nicholas Hennen, Frank Lawton, and Athene Seyler.

Born in 1889, Seyler told him that the only plays worth performing were those by Shakespeare, George Bernard Shaw, and Oscar Wilde. "Try to avoid anything else," she cautioned. She didn't take her own advice and began making films in 1935, becoming known for playing slightly dotty old ladies. Later in life, when Larry challenged her about lowering her standards, she said, "Even an actress gets hungry from time to time."

The Last Enemy opened on December 19, 1929, at London's Fortune Theatre where it would run for ninety-seven performances.

Cast as a member of the Royal Flying Corps, Larry did not draw large audiences. Perhaps it was too bleak a drama for Londoners facing Christmas in 1929 with long unemployment lines.

Critic Ivor Brown of *The Observer* admired Larry's performance, claiming that he was known for delivering solid acting in ill-fated plays. "May *The Last Enemy* be Olivier's lucky break," he wrote. "At any rate, his time will come."

Larry sent the review to Jill, with the note: "There's hope for your husband-to-be. One day I'll be bringing home the bacon."

***

Larry's love affair with his bride-to-be was conducted through irregular letters. When *Bird in Hand* opened in Chicago, Jill claimed she was having wild adventures.

From Chicago, she wrote of gang wars, cops chasing crooks with machine guns, and bathtub gin. "I'm spending wild nights with Texas Guinan, The Queen of the Night. She sees that I'm hauled around the city in an emerald green limousine. She truly fancies me. Al Capone has repeatedly raped me, almost nightly. Queer Christmas in Chicago. Queer people. The women wear diamonds on their arms."

In another note, she claimed "the people in Chicago are outrageous. I went to a party last night. The host ordered all the guests to take off their clothes. Men fell on top of me from all sides. I danced the night away. All you have to do is have a white face, full red lips, long earrings, and a sad expression and men think you're marvellous."

Her wild notes made Larry nervous. He wrote, "I feel you may be snatched from me at any minute, and I'll be powerless to stop whatever force is taking you from me. My demons, those same demons who haunted my miserable childhood, are back. I'm miserable. I can't escape them! What kind of man am I? Am I really a man at all? I don't know."

Based on her letters to Eva, Jill was obviously having serious doubts about having agreed to marry him.

To Eva, Jill expressed her serious concerns about Larry's lack of maturity. Eva responded by touting Larry's goodness and essential charm. "The man is a bar of gold," Eva claimed. Then she added an enigmatic postscript. "Of course, the bar of gold must be melted down to be useful."

After an absence from England of nine months, she wrote that she would return to London before mid-January of 1930. But that time came and went and still no Jill.

Her next postcard was from Nassau in The Bahamas where she claimed, "I'm having the time of my life." She didn't say with whom, and he didn't dare ask.

Suddenly, without warning, evocative of his own surprise arrival in New York, she notified him that she'd landed in Southampton and was boarding the train to London.

Eva, his future mother-in-law, and Larry met her at Victoria Station. She embraced Eva so warmly it was almost hysterical. She was more reserved when she hugged and kissed Larry. He could not help but notice that her greeting to him was less passionate than when he'd arrived in New York.

She had changed, and he wasn't certain just how. Always a mature, sensible young woman, she seemed even more so after her experiences in America. It was only an assumption, but she appeared to be suffering from a broken heart, perhaps in a relationship with a woman which had ended in disaster.

Jill had arrived just in time to catch the final performance of *The Last Enemy*. Rushing backstage to greet him after the curtain fell, she shocked him by not commenting on his performance. Even if he didn't expect praise, he anticipated a critique of some sort.

Instead she announced that she was taking over for the departing actress Kay Hammond, who had been appearing in a successful West End play called *Nine Till Six*. "The play's already a success," Jill said, "and I just know I'll do better in it than that Hammond bitch."

Larry would later tell his friends, "When you're contemplating marriage to an actress, a man must expect that his male ego will take a little battering."

He was even more shocked by Jill's comments in the press. She was interviewed about her upcoming marriage to Larry, because at the time she was a bigger star than he was.

Over breakfast in London he picked up a paper to read an article by Jill herself. It was headlined WHAT I THINK OF MARRIAGE.

"If ever the man I married behaved decently towards me, or I towards him, only because it was laid down in an unwritten marriage contract, I should feel it was high time we parted. Not that I expect married life to be one long romantic dream. It is impossible that the first careless rapture should last forever. And luckily, too, for nobody could ensure such a mental condition for long."

As an early advocate of women's liberation, she suggested that women were equal partners of men, not their playthings. She also claimed that women were the intellectual equals of men and did not exist to provide domestic comforts for men, including cooking, housecleaning, laundry, or whatever.

She continued to give interviews, as if publicly staking out her position before her marriage to Larry. "I should certainly have secrets and friends unknown to a husband of mine, and I should sometimes have a holiday from him as well as from work."

Since she was making far more money in the theater than Larry, she also claimed that she saw no problem with the wife being a better wage-earner than her husband. "The tradition of the husband as the chief breadwinner is quaint and old-fashioned. It does not belong in the modern Britain of 1930."

Perhaps to salvage his male ego after Jill's comments, which he called "emasculating," he wrote to Ralph Richardson. *Jill may be riding high today. But there are many who have told me that I will become a bigger name in the theatre than she ever was, maybe one of the biggest names of all time, with the one exception of your majestic self, dear boy.*

Love, Larry."

***

The start of the New Year of 1930 for Larry would mark an eight-month absence from the theater except for an unpaid starring role in John Van Druten's *After All*, which opened at London's Art Theatre on March 30 and ran for only nine performances.

After All was Van Druten's synthetically sentimental family melodrama. Larry had encountered this homosexual playwright before, and Van Druten still had seduction on his mind, but Larry evaded his clutches.

What made *After All* especially memorable for Larry was his female costars, Elissa Landi and Cathleen Nesbitt. Larry was especially intrigued with Landi, because he'd heard through

Cathleen Nesbitt *(left)* and Elissa Landi

87

the theatrical grapevine that she'd had an affair with Jill.

The chic, attractive Landi was, with a little bit of a stretch, the pretender to the throne of Austria and Hungary.

She was said to be the secret (i.e., illegitimate) granddaughter of "Sissi," the Empress Elizabeth of Austria, the beautiful but strong-willed Bavarian-born wife of Franz Josef, the monarch of the Austro-Hungarian empire who presided over its demise. After a brief affair with Humphrey Bogart, he had nicknamed her "Empress of Austria" and the label had stuck.

Landi preferred to be introduced simply as "Countess," a title assumed from her mother's second marriage to an Italian nobleman, Count Carlo Zanardi-Landi. The actress was not only beautiful but bright and quick-witted and had even written novels.

In theatrical circles, she was called "double-gaited," having been through affairs with other actresses such as Myrna Loy, who was called Miss Gillette "because she shaves on both sides." Landi was well connected socially in Hollywood and was often entertained by press baron William Randolph Hearst and his mistress, the actress Marion Davies. Landi was also on the dawn of an affair with Katharine Hepburn in Hollywood.

Larry was much impressed with the other female costar of the play, Cathleen Nesbitt.

In time, Larry would get to know nearly all of the great English actresses. A case in point was his working with Nesbitt, who was born in 1888, and would survive until 1982, enjoying a career that spanned more than eighty years, one of the longest in show business history.

Making her stage debut in 1910, she became the love of English poet Rupert Brooke in 1912, who wrote great love sonnets to her. They were engaged to be married when he died during WWI.

Although Larry didn't see that much of her, she often called him with amusing tidbits about the progress, or lack thereof, of her career over the years. "Larry," dear boy," she said, "I'm playing Cary Grant's grandmother in *An Affair to Remember* (1957), although I'm only sixteen years older than the boy. Good work if you can get it." When she made *French Connection II* (1975), she called again. "Dear boy, I'm cast as an elderly drug addict."

She would often ring off with a pungent remark. "Dear boy, first you married plain, then you married the most beautiful creature on earth, and now you're back to plain again." She was referring, of course, to Larry's third wife, Joan Plowright.

It appears that during the rehearsal period for *After All*, Larry had a brief fling with Landi. He wasn't that attracted to her physically, although he found her fascinating. They would later become friends in Hollywood. In some psychologically murky way, he wanted to seduce one of Jill's female conquests.

After their weekend fling, Landi confided to Van Druten that "Larry is rather inexperienced around women."

"At least you succeeded in seducing him, which is something I haven't been able to do," Van Druten said. "I find him most attractive. As for me, I prefer inexperienced young men in bed, instead of those who perform like a trained male prostitute."

Larry experienced a temporary break in his friendship with Denys Blakelock. One night in Blakelock's flat, Larry bluntly told him, "I suggested to John Van Druten that you be cast as one of the leads in *After All*. But he said, 'Denys is a very good actor but he hasn't got star quality.'"

The wounded actor didn't speak to Larry for three months.

Larry's performance in *After All* drew praise from the critic for *The Times*. "The delicate contrasts with the dexterous sketches of character are continually delightful. Of these contrasts, the utmost is made by Mr. Olivier."

With nowhere to go following curtains for *After All*, Larry was thrilled to receive a call from Tallulah Bankhead. She wanted to meet with him to discuss his costarring with her in an upcoming West End play.

As her closest friend, the actress Estelle Winwood once said, "Tallulah wanted to play *Hamlet* and be taken seriously as an actress." Since Tallulah couldn't play *Hamlet*, she settled for a revival of Alexandre Dumas *fils* 1849 *La Dame aux Camélias*, known in English, of course, as *Camille*.

In her rented flat, Larry was astonished to learn that she wanted to revive *Camille* with him cast as her young lover, Armand. At the time, the play was considered scandalous in Britain.

"Darling, we will make magic on the stage," Tallulah assured him.

Larry did not take Tallulah seriously as an actress, and had once dismissed her "as more of a lingerie act." She'd become notorious for undressing on stage of front of her screaming "gallery girls" in the balconies. These were mostly low-paid shop girls who had made Tallulah a cult figure.

That night he found out that she could talk seriously and didn't always go for the cheap laugh or joke.

Almost all of her London plays had been produced by Americans, and this was causing great resentment in the West End. "I've become the symbol of the American invasion into the London theater, and the newspapers are very cruel to me. *Theatre World* just ran an attack on me. When the press is not attacking my career, they are criticizing my private life, which is not any of their God damn business. I would certainly be attacked if an American actor were cast as Armand. I turned to you because I consider you the quintessential British stage actor. As far as I'm concerned, you *are* Armand, darling. Of course, I don't have the final word on casting, Nigel Playfair makes those decisions."

"I'm honored and flattered that you've chosen me," Larry said.

"Let the negotiations begin," she said.

Before he left and after a few drinks, she invited him for a sleepover. He declined, claiming he had a rendezvous with Jill Esmond.

"Oh, *that* one," she said. "She hasn't sucked my cock yet. Has she sucked yours?"

"No," he answered in embarrassment, "We haven't moved to that part of our relationship."

"Too bad," Tallulah said. "I hear she gives great head. As for me, I always choke going down on a man. As for muffing it with a woman, I feel I'm being smothered."

When Larry shared the news about his good casting fortune with Eva and Jill, Eva became adamant. "I absolutely refuse to allow you to work with that creature. I saw how she ruined Tam's life."

Eva was referring to Tallulah's affair with the actor Hugh Williams, who became a major film star in British cinema of the 1930s.

Even though he was married to the actress Gwynne Whitby, Tallulah pursued him mercilessly, and they had a torrid affair during their star roles in *The Gold Diggers*. It almost broke up Williams' marriage.

"Everybody thought this American woman's pursuit of Tam shameless," Eva claimed. "If you appear with her in *Camille*, I'm sure she'll figure some way for you to break off your engagement to Jill."

Larry was utterly confused. He was desperate to play Armand, but he didn't want to harm his burgeoning friendship with his future mother-in-law or jeopardize his engagement to Jill. Fate intervened for him.

A few nights later Tallulah called Larry to meet her at her flat. "There will be a surprise guest."

Larry just assumed that the surprise guest was going to be Nigel Playfair, a pre-eminent yet elusive theatrical figure in the West End, who had been announced to direct Tallulah in *Camille*.

Glen Byam Shaw with
Angela Baddeley

As he knocked on the door to her flat, Larry was still undecided about what to do. He'd even considered breaking off his engagement to Jill, if Eva were going to interfere in his career choices. His career meant far more to him than a marriage.

Once inside Tallulah's flat and to Larry's amazement, he found himself shaking hands with Glen Byam Shaw, who had just married Angela Baddeley, Larry's first serious love.

Even while pouring Larry a drink, Tallulah made the announcement. "Playfair doesn't want me to use you,

90

darling," Tallulah said to Larry. "He wants to cast Glen here as Armand."

The two rival actors stood looking at each other in embarrassment, perhaps resenting Tallulah for bringing them together in the same room.

Larry did not respond directly, but congratulated Shaw on his marriage to Baddeley. "She's a fine girl," he said.

Tallulah stood between them. "I brought you boys together to erase any hard feelings," she said. "That's the way of the theater. You win some, lose others. Who knows? You two gents might work together time and time again. No need for a feud. Every actor takes a choice role from another. Now I want you boys to kiss and make up."

Shaw and Larry stood awkwardly facing each other. Neither one of them moved.

She turned to Shaw. "To the victor, go the spoils. You're on, kid."

Shaw moved awkwardly toward Larry. Instead of a kiss on the cheek, he kissed him softly but sensuously on the mouth. As Larry was later to tell Denys Blakelock, when they'd resumed speaking, "I found the kiss very erotic. I began to see Glen in a different light. I decided that Angela was a very lucky girl. For that one brief moment, I wanted to put Glen in my pocket and take him home."

It was two o'clock in the morning, and both Shaw and Larry were amused by Tallulah's endless stories, including a detailed description of John Barrymore's cock when erect.

In contrast, Shaw seemed a sensitive, caring individual. He had nothing but praise for Larry's stage work, and Larry was deeply flattered. "You'd make a far better Armand than I ever can," he graciously told Larry. "But I need the gig. I hope you understand."

"I was considering dropping out," Larry said. "My future mother-in-law, Eva Moore, doesn't trust me with Tallulah."

"That bitch!" Tallulah said. "Get me another bourbon, darling, and go easy on the branch water."

By three o'clock that morning, she invited both of the inebriated actors into her all-pink bedroom. Larry wanted to decline the invitation. What decided it for him was when Glen reached for his hand, guiding him on his way to a forbidden pleasure.

Larry had virtually been instructed to seduce Shaw by none other than Denys Blakelock. This seemed like a golden opportunity.

By 3:30 that morning, Tallulah had passed out and was snoring. As Larry told Blakelock, "Glen made love to me until we both fled from Tallulah's boudoir shortly before dawn. I truly liked him. Maybe more than like. Now I know firsthand why Angela chose him over me. He's a great lover, satisfying in every way. He's not aggressive and hard driving but tenderly seduces you.

We've begun a relationship. I want to be with him again. Siegfried Sassoon wants to take both of us to Devon for a holiday. I think all of us will have a very good time."

"That Siegfried," Blakelock said. "He knows that two pretty boys in bed are better than one."

***

Most of Larry's contemporaries in the British theaters shunned movie-making. Ivor Novello was not one of them, and he urged Larry to consider talking pictures between engagements on the London stage. "Films are the art medium of the future more than the stage," Novello said. He was very convincing, and he knew what he was talking about, having appeared in films himself.

When a movie role was offered, Larry eagerly accepted it. "It's a new frontier for me. I'm not a snob when it comes to film. What's the real reason I'm going into the movies? I desperately need the money. I'm about to get married."

Two views of Lilian Harvey

In the wake of the closing of *After All*, Jill drove Larry to Croydon Airport, London's only airport in 1930. He'd been booked on a flight to Berlin where he was to star in his first motion picture.

"Good luck, darling," Jill said. "I wish I could go with you. Right now I belong to the stage."

"Soon you'll be Mrs. Laurence Olivier."

For her final words to him, she said, "That's okay on a dinner invitation to our intimate friends, but I much prefer to remain Jill Esmond. I've worked too long and hard to make that name mean something to just abandon it for a man's name."

"Your wish, my command," he said, giving her a final kiss before dashing for his first flight to Germany.

After refueling stops in Rotterdam and Hannover, Larry flew into Berlin, where he was driven to Neubabelsberg Studios where he'd signed a contract with UFA. He was to do the English language version of Curt Goetz's play, *Hokuspokus*. For six weeks of work, Larry received three-hundred English pounds.

Larry had accepted the role without seeing any script. In Berlin, he learned that the English language version was to be entitled *The Temporary Widow*, later changed to *Murder for Sale* in America.

The female star of both the English and German versions was the celebrated Lilian Harvey, who was cast as a woman accused of murdering her husband. Larry played an artist who fakes his death in order to inflate the value of his paintings.

Willy Fritsch, the star of the German version, had appeared in a number of movies with Harvey since 1928. To welcome Larry to Berlin, he'd thrown a small party on the set. Here Larry met the other costars of the German version of the film, including Gustaf Gründgens, one of Germany's most famous actors of the 20th century, and Oskar Homolka, an Austrian film and theater actor with a strong accent, stocky appearance, and bushy eyebrows.

Co-starring with him as the male lead in the English version was Felix Aylmer, a Wiltshire-born actor who'd been a member of the Oxford University drama society. He became one of Larry's best friends and would work with him in the film version of *Hamlet* (1948).

Athole Stewart was another British actor. He was born in Lehighton Buzzard in England in 1879. Larry had many long talks with him because both of them were on the verge of launching film careers, and Larry had a number of reservations about that.

In Berlin, Larry was introduced to the star of the picture, Harvey. "She was the most fascinating leading lady I've ever worked with," Larry later recalled. "Before or since, including appearances with all of my three actress wives."

Although born in London of English parents, Harvey had been trapped in Germany during World War I and had learned the language. She'd become a leading silent film star at UFA, the major German movie production company. When films were silent, she'd risen to international superstardom, enjoying great popularity in Europe and America as well. Harvey's directors had included Billy Wilder and Erich Pommer.

Some Olivier biographers were aware of Larry's fling in Berlin with Harvey, but identified her only as "a dancer." She was far more than that, of course, and was in fact Germany's biggest star during the Weimar era, dwarfing the fame of Marlene Dietrich.

Although Larry's fling with Harvey ended at the completion of their Anglo-German movie, and Larry would go back to London to marry Jill, he and Harvey stayed in touch, especially when Hollywood beckoned to her in 1932. Her career at Fox had been brief, and she returned to Germany, only to find UFA under the control of Josef Goebbels, for whom she developed an immediate distaste.

She was not a Nazi and moved to Hungary where she hired Jews to work on her estate, pending their escape from Nazi-occupied territories. She also rescued Pink Triangle victims, such as the gay choreographer Jens Keith.

Escaping from Hungary, she drove to the south of France in 1939 where she entertained French troops, made French films, and worked as a volunteer in a leper colony.

When the Nazis invaded France, Harvey fled, as Goebbels had put her on his "hit list." The British Embassy secured for her a seat on the last flight out of Paris headed for London before the Nazi soldiers paraded down the Champs Elysées.

During the war, she turned down a role with Humphrey Bogart and Ingrid Bergman in *Casablanca*, but recorded anti-Nazi broadcasts for the Americans and toured the United States in Noël Coward's *Blithe Spirit*

After the war, she returned to Germany where she was viewed as a traitor, although she had never held a German passport. The Germans resented her getting war reparations because the Nazis had seized all her properties in Europe in 1939. *Der Stern* did a vicious article on Harvey, entitled *Sunset Boulevard auf Deutsch*.

Harvey survived at her Villa Asmodée on the French Riviera, living in exile until her death in 1968. Every year on her birthday, January 19, she received a card from Larry. Whether he meant it or not, he always wrote the same message.

Dearest, dear one, Lilian,
You remain my one true love and a reminder of what might have been. God certainly had a talent for creating exceptional women, of which you remain the stellar example. There was Cleopatra. Helen of Troy. Eleanor of Aquitaine. And then there is Lilian Harvey.
Love, Larry."

***

Greta Keller (left) and Conrad Veidt

Back in Berlin, Harvey liked to retire at around ten o'clock "for my beauty sleep" before facing the cameras early in the morning on the set of *The Temporary Widow*. But Larry was young and "wanted to sow some wild oats," he later claimed.

For his partner of the night, he became acquainted with Greta Keller, who was also appearing in a supporting role in the film in Berlin. She was a chanteuse of renown, and had just ended a lesbian affair with Marlene Dietrich, who had departed for Hollywood. Marlene and Greta had met in Vienna, when Greta was the star of a show called *Broadway*, with Marlene in a supporting role.

"Later, Larry wrote that while in Berlin he attended an opera every night," Greta said. "To my knowledge, he did not. It was still the era of the cabaret when Larry arrived in Berlin. Hitler hadn't taken over yet. It was a time of great decadence and debauchery. Larry wanted to explore the seedy glamour of Berlin's notorious night life. My dear friend, Conrad Veidt, and I set out to corrupt Larry completely. In time, as I would later tell Noël Coward in London, we viewed time lodged in Berlin as a *chiaroscuro* of Larry's coming of age. A great bachelor party for him before going back to England to marry Jill Esmond."

Veidt himself was a homosexual, and Greta was bisexual, so the trio set out to visit the dens of Berlin to seek sexual conquests. In later years, Veidt would share some of these memories of Larry's nights in Berlin with Vivien Leigh when the actors appeared in *Dark Journey* in 1937. Veidt, of course, would later immortalize himself in Bogie's *Casablanca*.

Greta and Veidt were fond of transvestite clubs, and they took Larry to several. "One night Larry went home with the club's most stunning beauty," Greta said. "The next day at work he told me that he discovered that Hildegarde—her stage name—was really a man, but I'm sure he already knew that. Another time, Conrad took Larry to a house of male prostitution, said to house some of the most beautiful men in Berlin. Larry and Conrad made their picks for the evening. Larry told me that he didn't know male houses of prostitution existed in Europe, at least not since Roman times."

Greta quickly became Larry's intimate friend. He told her, "I'm heading into a marriage that has all the makings of a disaster."

"Then why go through with it?" she asked.

"I can't stop myself," he told her. "I feel compelled to go on. I'm afraid not to. My demons have haunted me since childhood, and they are moving me forward, even though I know the marriage is wrong."

Greta assumed that Larry hoped to escape from the shadow of his bisexuality by entering into a marriage. "He seemed to think marriage was the cure for homosexuality," Greta said. "You have to remember during his days in Berlin that Larry was a very young, inexperienced, and naïve young man. He was less so when he departed from Conrad and me."

While in Berlin, Larry told Greta that "I want to go everywhere and experience everything. Berlin is not London."

"I went wild," he later confessed to Denys Blakelock.

Before returning to England, Larry took a two-week vacation. In the company of Felix Aylmer, one of the stars of *The Temporary Widow*, he headed for a lakeside vacation. In his autobiography, he claimed he also went on holiday with "one or two others."

"Larry was being very discreet," Greta said. "Those one or two others were actually Conrad Veidt and myself."

On his secret vacation, Larry decided to deal with what he called "some mechanical problems with my plumbing." As he'd matured into manhood, he'd developed a severe case of phimosis, whereby his foreskin was so tight it was too painful to retract. He could have intercourse but it was not the pleasure he imagined it to be.

"Through Greta, I arranged to visit a Swiss doctor near our hotel," he wrote to Denys Blakelock. "He was an expert in such matters. She advised me, and I agreed, to be clipped just like a little Jewish boy sent to a rabbi. That's not all. In Germany, one half of my scrotum became swollen, actually blocked. An operation was required."

After the operation, one of his testicles became sterile, although the other one was active, as his fathering of children in the future proved.

As Larry so dramatically put it, in words passed on to his future son, Tarquin, "I went to my honeymoon bed with my orb and scepter not in working order but in a kind of post-operative pain."

He was not being totally honest. Perhaps he was using his operation to delay his duties as a husband. Before his marriage, he entered into a torrid affair where, to judge from the outcome, his "plumbing" had been restored as never before.

***

As Larry flew back from Germany to London, his wedding day was set for July 25, 1930. The prospect obviously loomed large in his mind. He wired Jill and Eva the time of his arrival at Croydon, expecting either or both of them to meet him. He'd already written Denys Blakelock, Ivor Novello, and Siegfried Sassoon with the details of his return from the Continent.

Perhaps it was his vanity, but he more or less expected an array of friends who might have turned out to welcome the conquering hero and UFA star.

Instead, a lone figure in a raincoat to protect himself from the sudden storm emerged on the airfield to greet him.

As the man walked toward him, he saw it was Glen Byam Shaw. Larry rushed to meet and embrace him.

Looking around at the passengers disembarking, Shaw said, "Let's drive away from here so I can kiss you and welcome you home properly. You dear, dear boy. I miss you so much I've been half out of my mind."

"What a glorious thing to say to welcome me back to England." Rather facetiously he said, "I conquered UFA and turned down their offer to become Germany's biggest star. I just refuse to act in German. What a difficult language."

Both had safely retreated into Shaw's car, as the clouds burst open, providing a curtain of privacy for them as passengers and airport personnel scattered for shelter.

"I've fallen in love with you," Shaw said, peppering Larry with kisses. "You belong to me now."

"But what about dear Angela?"

"What we have together she need never know about," Shaw said. "The love between two men is purer than anything that could exist between a man and a woman."

"That sounds like a line straight from Siegfried Sassoon," Larry said.

"So what?" Shaw said. "That doesn't make it any less true. Now I want to get going. I've got this place where we can hide away for the night. It's down in Rye. No one will ever find us there."

"But what about Jill?" he protested.

"She can wait. You can always tell her your flight was delayed until the following day . . . or days."

"So I can," he said. "I'll cable her."

"Besides, she's seeing this Hollywood producer who's in town," Shaw said. "She's thrilled not at the prospect of marrying you but of getting a Hollywood contract."

"Sounds like I'm losing her before I even marry her," Larry said.

"There's one more thing," Shaw said, peering ahead to keep on the road. The visibility in the pouring rain was bad. "This note. Jill gave it to me to give to you."

Larry took the concealed note and slowly opened it. The stationery was perfumed, the paper colored lavender.

Dear boy, please come by my home on June 18 at ten o'clock in the morning for breakfast in bed. I saw you in Paris Bound and thought you were delectable—so imposing, so handsome. That is all fine and good, because the role I've written for you calls for a devastatingly handsome man, and I've picked you for the part. Your beauty is astonishing. On stage, only my wit can equal that beauty of yours. Perhaps we'll become known in London as The Beauty and the Brains. I do not mean to be condescending. I'm told

you're a very bright lad, clever enough to accept my invitation with all its implications, both professional and personal. I count the moments until you will arrive in my bedroom to dazzle me with your male charm. Kisses, kisses, and more kisses on the way. Love, love, love from your devoted servant,
Noël Coward."

"Who's it from?" Shaw asked.

"Oh, nobody important," Larry said. "Some star-struck fan."

"I get a few letters like that too," Shaw said. "I don't bother to answer them. Are you going to reply?"

"Only if I can find the time," he said nonchalantly. "The important thing is that we're running away together."

As Larry would relate to Denys Blakelock later, "I was afraid Glen would hear my heart beating. I don't think I've ever been so excited in my life. It was wonderful being with Glen again, but the prospect of being summoned to Noël Coward's bedroom was the most important invitation I'd ever received. Even then, without meeting him, I knew he was going to make me a star. I was prepared to give him whatever he wanted from me."

***

Over the years, Larry was discreet in what he said or wrote about Glen Byam Shaw, only going so far as to call him "my intimate friend" in a letter to Elsa Lanchester in 1968.

No one knows for sure what happened between Shaw and Larry at the Mermaid Hotel in Rye. Larry cabled Jill that he was delayed in Hannover and that it would be four days before he could get a plane to Croydon Airport in London.

During those idyllic nights at The Mermaid in a small room with crooked beams, Larry got to know Shaw as he had almost no other person in the world, certainly not Jill. With Jill it was all about concealment; with Shaw, he could be openly himself, as he could with few other people, not even Denys Blacklock.

Years later, when asked about such lovers as Shaw, Blakelock, actor Henry Ainley, Noël Coward, Danny Kaye, and Richard Burton, among others, Lord Laurence Olivier replied obliquely. "I am prepared to believe that the sense of romance in those of our brothers and sisters who incline toward love of their own sex is heightened to a more blazing pitch than in those who think of themselves as normal."

Perhaps Larry was thinking of that long ago extended weekend he spent in the arms of Shaw back in Rye.

What is known is that Shaw during this time confessed to him his difficulties in playing opposite Tallulah Bankhead in *Camille*.

"There is no chemistry between us," Shaw said, "on or off the stage. We're just not making it. Maybe you should have taken the role. Tallulah Bankhead's not for me. I'll tell you who's for me. One Laurence Olivier, my kind of guy."

"Let's seal it with a kiss," Larry said.

After breaking away for air, Shaw said, "Bankhead says I'm ethereal looking."

"I rarely agree with Miss Bankhead, but this time I do," Larry said.

"How would you describe me?" Shaw asked.

"A strapping six-footer who packs a concealed weapon of infinite pleasure to those who come to worship it."

"I like that."

Although some Bankhead biographers have suggested that Shaw "serviced" Tallulah during the run of *Camille*, she denied it when the question came up during her road tour of *Crazy October* in 1958.

"It's an absolute lie, darling," she said. "Glen Byam Shaw had nothing left for me after he'd serviced Larry Olivier. He also had a wife, Angela Baddeley, to service. Perhaps her sister, Hermione, too. That is one horny bitch, that Hermione. Poor Shaw also had to service Siegfried Sassoon. That boy must have eaten his Wheaties every morning."

It was a very lackluster reunion Larry had with Jill, who seemed to be dreaming of Hollywood more than of him.

The following day back in London, Shaw confessed to him, "It's not the same making love to Angela. After making love with her, the intensity is gone from our relationship. With you, the champagne is always flowing and it's an eternal Saturday night. With Angela I was thinking what my next gig is going to be after Bankhead heads back to America."

"What about Siegfried?" Larry asked.

"He wants to go away with us and share a bedroom," Shaw said. "But I don't know."

When it came time for Sassoon to go away with both Shaw and Larry, Sassoon apparently was disappointed. The poet was given the free run of a country house in Kent when the owner, a friend of his, went to the continent for a week.

After the holiday was over, Sassoon told both Larry and Shaw, "I came to believe that three's a crowd. There was a lot of action going on, but not aimed in my direction. In the future, I plan to see each of you dear boys, but separately. Each of you seemed to forget that I'm the star of the show. I don't like my supporting players putting on a sideshow of their own. It was fun to watch for a while, but ultimately unsatisfying for me."

***

Before his fateful meeting with Noël Coward, two quickie films loomed on Larry's immediate horizon.

The British Quota Act had decreed that a proportion of British-made films had to be shown amid the flood of imports arriving from Hollywood. To meet this quota, an array of British films were turned out in the early 1930s, although with exceptions most of them were quickies and just as quickly forgotten.

Back in London, Larry tried to make as much money as he could and agreed to shoot *Too Many Crooks* in only four nights, for which he was paid sixty pounds. "I shall never forget the horror of sitting down at one o'clock in the morning to a meal of boiled mutton, boiled potatoes, and watery cabbage, tinned fruit and custard," he wrote in his autobiography.

Too Many Crooks, released in 1930, ran for only forty minutes with Larry listed as the star. It was a British crime comedy directed by George King, who was making his debut as a film director. He'd actually studied to be a doctor. He would have a rather undistinguished career, making lightweight comedies, romances, and thrillers. In later years Larry dismissed King as "the man who introduced Diana Dors to the movie-going public." He was referring to the 1947 *The Shop at Sly Corner*, which introduced the bombshell who later became known as "Britain's answer to Marilyn Monroe."

Too Many Crooks was the story of a man who tries to rob his own safe on the same night a professional burglar attempts to break into it. Dorothy Boyd, the female costar, had appeared in silent films since 1926 and would make a number of lackluster talkies before fading from the screen shortly after the outbreak of WWII.

Charles Laughton with Elsa Lanchester

The film was shot at Twickenham Studios outside London where Larry met Laurence Evans, with whom he'd engage in a personal friendship and a business relationship that would span six decades.

"*Too Many Crooks* opened and closed so quickly nobody knew it existed," Larry said. "I asked my friends not to go see it, an unnecessary request."

Ignoring Larry's request, Denys Blakelock went to see it anyway. He later claimed that he was surprised at the sound of Larry's voice. "It seemed to me that he wished to acquire a mid-Atlantic style of speech, something that was neither British nor American, but a compromise that would be acceptable on both sides of the ocean."

Larry was then cast in *Potiphar's Wife* (1931). The 79-minute film, directed by Maurice Elvey, starred Nora Swinburne as Lady Diana Bromford, a spiteful, young noblewoman married to a prominent lord. In the film, she attempts to ruin the life of a highly principled chauffeur (Larry in the role of Straker), who spurns her philandering advances.

For American distribution in 1932, *Potiphar's Wife* was retitled *Her Strange Desire.*

On seeing the film, Roger Lewis, the chief book critic for *Punch*, wrote of "the softness and delicacy of Larry's skin. There's no blood circulating in it. His eyes are made up like a girl's, and his moustache is the narrowest black wisp, but there's no mistaking his masculinity, nor his dignity."

Lewis was even more colorful in describing Nora Swindburne's role as Lady Diana, "a bejeweled cat-lady vamp that survived from the silent-movie era and was inspired by such pseudo-biblical bitches as Salome, Delilah, and Bathsheba."

The critic went on to say that Swinburne played her role like "those other pyrogenic vamps who ignited the silver nitrate, Theda Bara, say, or Gloria Swanson, who swept in from a Beardsley drawing or a Conder painting."

Larry's chief memory of appearing in *Potiphar's Wife* was of meeting Elsa Lanchester, who played (of all things) a French maid, Therese. Although horribly miscast—Lanchester was about as French as roast beef and Yorkshire pudding—she captivated Larry. Her eyes popped and her voice quavered on camera, making her vibrantly batty. He found her enchanting and would become her friend for life. He'd later meet her homosexual husband, Charles Laughton, who would become his acquaintance for life.

***

As his marriage ceremony to Jill loomed, his bride-to-be invited him for a stroll along the moonlit Thames near Eva's home. He was anticipating a romantic evening. But Jill had looked too sincere for that. Rather bluntly, she confessed, "I don't love you. I love another."

He demanded to know who it was, and she refused to tell him. He suspected that it was another woman. In spite of Jill's honest confession, Larry amazingly kept his plan to marry her. Knowing how wrong the marriage was for the both of them, he still asked her to go through with it. She reluctantly agreed.

Jill's true love the night of her confession has never been accurately pin-pointed. Over the years the rumor was that the object of her affection was none other than Elissa Landi, whom Larry had already seduced.

Going places: Larry Olivier with Jill Esmond, early 1930s

Chapter Four

In Japanese red silk pajamas, Noël Coward was enjoying his second "cuppa" of the morning when Larry was shown into his bedroom for their first meeting. It would be the first of many times Larry would be ushered into that bedroom.

The meeting of Laurence Olivier and Noël Coward would be a milestone in the history of the British theater. Regrettably, no camera was there to record it. The events that took place that bright morning can only be resurrected through bits and pieces of second-hand information from a hundred memoirs, published or otherwise.

Some seven years older than Larry, Coward had been writing and acting in plays, even producing them, since he was twelve years old.

"You divine creature," Coward said upon encountering Larry in the flesh. "Come and stand before me in the morning light. I'm sure that the real Adonis looked better in the golden light of day than at night. Looking at you on this particular day, I feel very much like Aphrodite. Perhaps it was something the maid put in my tea."

"Good morning, Mr. Coward," Larry stammered. He later recalled, "It was like meeting the King of England. I was very nervous."

"You can call me Noël," he said. "Yes, we might as well get familiar right away. You are going to play Victor in my new play, *Private Lives*. The play will make you a star. You're going to star with Gertie and me."

The playwright, of course, was referring to his great and dear friend, Gertrude Lawrence.

Coward had written *Private Lives* in just four days. He was recovering from the flu, which he privately told friends he had caught in a male bordello in Shanghai.

"Go home, read the play, and come back tomorrow morning at the same time," Coward said. "Your breakfast will be waiting."

Larry agreed and after profuse thanks departed from Coward's boudoir, eager to return.

Private Lives, still performed in the 21st century, would become Coward's greatest theatrical triumph. The plot concerns a divorced couple who meet on their honeymoons with new spouses, only to realize they are still in love with each other.

Coward, of course, had cast himself in the male lead opposite Gertrude Lawrence as his divorced wife.

Larry had far less enthusiasm when he came by in the morning. He didn't like the role of Victor in the play, and he was prepared to tell Coward so.

Larry audaciously asked if he could play the male lead. Coward burst into mocking laughter. "My darling boy, don't forget I am the star. Your day will come, I can assure you."

Coward was in bed, having breakfast like the day before, except this time his Japanese silk pajamas were dragon green.

Larry astonished Coward by telling him if he could not play the lead, he

would not accept the minor role of Victor. "At this point in my career, I'm used to star parts. My days at the Birmingham Rep are over. If you'll forgive me, the role of Victor is very weak. He's a dull bore. And, if you'll continue to forgive me, I would say that the role of Victor is underwritten."

Anger flashed across Coward's face. "How cheeky of you, darling. You can find no better offer in London. You're getting married to Jill and you need the money."

"My role is that of a muted second fiddle," Larry complained.

"Yes, yes, yes, Sybil and Victor are mere puppets, little better than ninepins," Coward said. "I deliberately wrote them as wooden. They are there only to be repeatedly knocked down and stood up again."

Larry looked crestfallen. Coward was mocking the very role he wanted him to perform.

"Here is the point," Coward said. "Victor is a bore, a prig. But he has to be handsome enough and challenging enough for a smart woman like Amanda to have married him in the first place. Only an exciting actor can play a bore on stage

(top photo) Larry working out
(lower photo) Manflesh connoisseur
Noël Coward

104

effectively."

Coward had to be very persuasive to get Larry to agree to play one of "the minor spouses," the role of Victor, Gertrude Lawrence's new husband in the play. To sweeten the deal, Coward promised him fifty pounds a week, which was a good theatrical salary in the early 1930s in London.

"I will hear no more of your silly nonsense," Coward said. "You're playing Victor—and that's that. Rehearsals start in a fortnight. Now let's get down to some other more urgent business."

The story may be apocryphal, but Coward allegedly said to Larry, "I hope I'm not being too personal, but are you the type of gentleman who takes it up the bum?"

"I have been known to indulge in that form of pleasure," Larry reportedly said. "Those boys at Oxford are a randy bunch."

"Fine, fine," Coward said, placing his breakfast tray on a night table. "The time has come for the unveiling. Sometimes the unveiling is more exciting than the act itself. In your case, I think both the unveiling and the action itself will be a standing ovation."

"I'm afraid I don't understand," Larry said, growing increasingly nervous.

"I detest having to speak in plain English," Coward said. "It's so very unromantic." In a harsh voice he ordered Larry "to take off all your garments and crawl into bed with me."

"Everything?" Larry asked, stunned by the request. "My underwear too?"

"Everything," Coward commanded. "It's already been established that you do take it up the bum."

Larry giggled and stripped down for action, as he moved toward Coward's bed. The playwright extended an assuring hand to a very nervous young actor.

As Larry crawled in under Coward's fine linen sheets, it would mark the beginning of countless seductions over the years between Coward and himself.

"I heard all about it the next day," said Gertrude Lawrence. "Noël told me everything. It was the launch of one of the great romances of the theater. Noël simply adored the boy from the bridge of his nose to the tip of his big toe. No part of Larry's anatomy was overlooked. Of that I'm certain."

In his future memoirs, Larry was obviously referring to Coward when he wrote "of the one male with whom some sexual dalliance had not been loathsome for me to contemplate."

One reviewer called Larry's confessional, "overblown and elliptical. What he meant to say was, 'I had a jolly good time having sex with Noël.'"

In spite of his true nature and desires, and in spite of his many sexual affairs with men, Larry was still deeply troubled by homosexuality, perhaps because of his religious upbringing. "I felt that the homosexual act would be a step darkly destructive to my soul," he wrote. "I was firm in my conviction that heterosexuality was romantically beautiful, immensely pleasurable, and rewarding in contentment."

At least that's what he wrote. What he actually did in life was another matter. His sexual desire obviously overcame what religious morality he had left when he met Coward.

As the weeks of *Private Lives* went by, Coward urged Larry to assume a public persona and stick to it. "You must create an image for yourself. My deliberately cultivated image is to appear on stage in an elegant dressing gown, smoking a cigarette in a long holder and saying, 'Darling, how wonderful!'"

"I understand that," Larry said. "But what kind of image can I cultivate?"

"I'll need days to think about that," Coward said. "Unfortunately, you can't show your most stunning asset upon the wicked stage."

"Exactly what is that?" Larry asked.

"Your bum," Coward said. "It would take a Michelangelo, and even he would need the pinkish glow of a Florentine dawn, to sculpt buttocks such as yours."

Coward was more than just a lover to Larry, "a source of forbidden pleasure," he told Denys Blakelock. "He is my mentor and friend."

Coward also taught Larry how to behave socially and took him to some of the major gatherings of the London glitterati at the time.

Through Coward, Larry learned about chic luncheons at The Ivy, a restaurant much frequented by the theatrical elite.

Larry also learned how to engage in sophisticated chatter at cocktail gatherings and upscale supper parties. "You can never live too well, dear boy," Coward told Larry. "When you live well, people want to know you."

"They almost became thought of as a couple," Sybil Thorndike said. "Many invitations to Coward contained a postscript. 'By all means, bring that divine boy, Larry Olivier.'"

Two views of *grande dame* Sybil Thorndike *(upper photo)* playing Saint Joan in 1924 *(lower photo)* On air for the BBC in 1932

Except for the plays and sonnets of Shakespeare, Larry, in Coward's view, was not well read. "On reading matter, start with the Brontës, move on to Arnold Bennett, and then, for sheer wickedness, W. Somerset Maugham, that old sod."

Larry was always generous about crediting Coward for changing his life around. "He took hold of me and made me think. He made me use my silly little brain. He taxed me with his sharpness and shrewdness and, yes, his brilliance. He used to point out when I was talking nonsense. Nobody else had done that before."

No man, before or since, would ever have the impact on Larry's personal life and his career that Coward had. Years later Coward would say to him, "Other lovers have come and gone, but it was always you and me, even after passion's well ran dry."

***

The dreaded wedding of Jill Esmond and Laurence Olivier moved forward with a speed of its own, although both parties had road-blocking reservations about entering into such a union. Only Eva Moore and "Ibo," Larry's stepmother, seemed to want the marriage to take place. Among Larry's friends, Siegfried Sassoon, Glen Byam Shaw, and even Ivor Novello were adamantly opposed to the wedding, joining a chorus already led by Coward.

Eva Moore came into conflict with Larry's father, Gerard. She wanted her daughter's wedding to take place in the Chapel Royal, Savoy, in London. Eva herself had been married there.

As a conservative Anglican, Gerard was horrified at Eva's choice. The Chapel Royal had become notorious in the 1700s as a place where marriages without banns (public announcements of an impending marriage) were conducted, sometimes with contested results. In *Brideshead Revisited,* Evelyn Waugh referred to it as "the place where previously divorced couples got married in those days—a pokey little place."

The theatrical impresario Richard D'Oyly Carte, the ostentatious and flamboyant entrepreneur who had developed the nearby Savoy Hotel and the Savoy Theatre, had been married there in 1888. In the early 1940s, most of its stained glass windows would be destroyed during the London Blitz.

Defiantly, Gerard vetoed Eva's choice for the wedding venue, asserting that his reputation would be tainted "by conducting the sacrament of marriage at a place that catered to divorced couples."

Eva was deeply distressed by this, but opted nonetheless to respect the wishes of her daughter's future father-in-law.

On the afternoon before his wedding, Ibo, Gerard's new wife, wrote Larry a "Kim darling" letter. She preferred to call him by his childhood nickname.

> *"You said the other day, that you were both feeling such strangers to one another—that is just how it is—you are strangers until that wonderful service—afterwards you are just a complete one! Larry darling it's just beautiful and every day you will, please God, find that oneness becoming bigger and bigger.*
> *Be very gentle with her, darling, but be the leader."*

Ibo's wish for Jill and Larry never came true.

At no point did Larry ever become the leader in the marriage—quite the opposite.

As Coward wryly observed, "Jill always donned the trousers. Larry, of course, looked better without them."

For his best man, Larry selected Denys Blakelock. The two men slept together the night before the wedding. Years later Larry claimed that "Blakelock's hands strayed that night, but I decided I couldn't do it, and that was that. I had to reject him, and I felt sorry about that."

To his homosexual friends in London, Blakelock gave a very different account. "On the night before his wedding to Jill Esmond, I buggered him until dawn's early light."

That was an obvious exaggeration, but it appears that Larry erased his pre-wedding jitters in the comforting arms of Blakelock, with whom

Portraits of the Olivier/Esmond wedding
Star power and British theatricality meet High Society

he'd enjoyed such intimacy for months.

The wedding took place on July 25, 1930, with Father Mackay officiating at All Saints, the school that held so many memories, both good and bad, for Larry–including the scene of his earlier molestation by Father Geoffrey Heald.

Jill and Larry argued about extending an invitation to Jack Hawkins, her former beau. Larry was still jealous of the actor. Acting as an independent woman, Esmond invited Hawkins over Larry's protestations.

Invited to the wedding, Coward came into the bedroom where Larry was getting dressed, ostensibly to check out Larry's appearance. But Coward had another reason. Very privately he told Larry his opinion of the wedding. "It is ill advised. The marriage is doomed from the start. I've known Jill for years. She's a lesbian. Of course, if you're doing it for appearance's sake, then I understand."

Larry's former co-star, Nora Swinburne, also showed up. She'd long ago changed her dim view of Larry, and the two thespians had become friends. Other formally dressed friends arrived, notably Ralph Richardson, Sybil Thorndike, and Gladys Cooper, even the cricket-loving C. Aubrey Smith. Larry felt compelled to invite Ivor Novello and seated him on the opposite side of the church, far removed from Novello's rival, Coward.

The most spectacular gift, a string of exquisite black pearls, was sent to Jill from the theater-loving Princess Marie-Louise of Schleswig-Holstein, granddaughter of Queen Victoria. Larry presented his bride an octagonal bloodstone ring. It was a gift he could ill afford at the time, but she would wear it for the rest of her life.

Eva had organized a lavish reception at Whitehead's Grove, and Lady Fripp, a close friend of hers, offered Larry and Jill her country house at Lulworth Cove in Dorset.

In his autobiography, Larry painfully described their honeymoon night, if it could be called that.

> We had been most kindly lent a lovely house by Lady Fripp, whose generous inclinations did not stop there; no doubt with the kindest intentions in the world, she left us also her two sweet, but agonizingly embarrassed, grown-up, single, young daughters as hostesses for the occasion. This made a signal addition to the bride and groom's already mounting embarrassment . . .The two sweet Fripp girls served us supper and toyed with something on their own plates as well. None of us was capable of dealing with the degree of agonized shyness that was reached at the end of that meal. Finally, Jill and I both dived at something of the order of 'Well, now . . . er . . . Perhaps it's time we went up to our room and . . . er . . . unpacked?'

I have never been able to think of that slightly pagan festivity referred to as the honeymoon as anything but disastrous, and I am sure that Jill has always felt the same. After some hesitant efforts to accomplish something we hoped would pass for foreplay—my own efforts, I knew, would not pass muster in a third floor back room in Lisle Street, and all that would rest in my bride's memory would be an endurance test—at last we turned away from each other.

They moved into a house at 13 Roland Gardens (London SW7), which Eva had sparsely decorated for them. When Coward arrived the next day, he said, "Eva was so cheap. She could have given you a sofa for your living room. I'm getting a new one but my old one is in great shape. I used it as a sort of casting couch but it's not stained. I'll send it over tomorrow."

Coward talked until four o'clock in the morning, discussing future plans not only for his own career, but for theirs.

After staggering upstairs with fatigue, Larry headed for Jill's boudoir. "Pack it up, mate," she scolded him. "The room next door is for you. You know I've had a headache all day that nearly killed me."

When he pleaded with her, she dismissed him. "I've heard all of your rot I want to hear for one day. You and Noël sometimes make me sick. He was practically salivating over you all night, and you were lapping it up like a puppy with fresh milk. I need to be alone. The star of this family needs her beauty sleep."

The next day he called Coward. "The glories of a marriage aren't what I had imagined them to be. I think you're right. Heterosexuality is vastly over-rated."

"Come over at once, dear boy," Coward said. "You will be my Delta of Venus, and I will not remove myself from you until you've given at least two offerings to the gods."

***

For the role of Sybil in *Private Lives*, Coward had cast the actress Adrianne Allen, wife of Raymond Massey. Along with Gertrude Lawrence, Larry and Coward went in a taxi to Allen's house on Wilton Crescent in London for a run-through rehearsal. Massey was not present.

After rehearsal, Lawrence had another engagement and departed early. After telling Allen good-bye, Coward and Larry walked to the nearest pub.

Over a beer, Larry told Coward, "I adore Gertie, but frankly I can't stand Allen. I know I'm being unreasonable, and she's done nothing for me to hate her. But I just despise her. Maybe it's the way she parts her hair. But it's more than that. There is something wrong with a woman who would let Raymond Massey fuck her. Put yourself in Allen's place. How would you like buggery with Massey?"

"The thought is utterly appalling," Coward said.

The first opening of *Private Lives* was at the King's Theatre in Edinburgh on August 18, 1930.

All four stars—Lawrence, Coward, Allen, and Larry—boarded the London North-Eastern Pullman heading for Edinburgh.

On the train, Allen noted the "incredible, almost playful, intimacy" between Coward and Larry. "They behaved almost like two schoolboys falling in love."

With Allen and Lawrence, Larry and Coward ate at a table in the dining car. At the end of the meal, the waiter brought out a crystal bowl of chocolate mousse. A dollop fell onto the tablecloth, missing Larry's plate. As the waiter left, Larry lifted up the mousse with his dessert spoon and tossed it at Coward, scoring a bull's eye.

Wiping his face with a napkin, Coward then took his dessert spoon and lodged a missile, hitting Larry in the face. The war was on.

"By the end of it, the boys had gone through the mousse on our table and even taken mousse from the bowls of the other guests in the compartment," Allen claimed. "The diners were not amused. But Larry and Noël were rolling in the aisles with laughter."

"The boys turned our trip to Scotland into a Mack Sennett custard pie comedy," Allen said.

"After three months in Coward's bedroom, Larry was a changed man," said Ralph Richardson who had lunch with him at The Ivy in London after a period of several months. "He was elegantly dressed, very well groomed, like a visiting movie star from Hollywood. Of course, it helped to have a pair of schnauzers on leash walking the streets of the West End."

From Edinburgh, *Private Lives* moved on to Manchester before its opening in London. Every seat was sold out, but Larry still didn't like the part of Victor. In his hotel suite at Manchester's Midland Hotel, he gave an unfortunate interview, one that would inevitably infuriate Coward. "I

Two views of *Private Lives:*

(top photo) Olivier with Coward
(lower photo) Coward romancing Gertrude Lawrence

hate the part I'm playing now," he told a reporter. "Victor Prynne is a most hateful character."

When the article ran in the Manchester newspaper, it gave Larry's name as "Lawrence Olivier." That was not too surprising, since Larry was relatively unknown at the time.

However, that doesn't explain why seven years later, Coward referred to him as "Lawrence" when he published *Present Indicative*, his first volume of memoirs.

In *Private Lives*, Larry had a tendency to giggle on stage.

Although sleeping with him at night, Coward could be a stern taskmaster during the day. "I'm going to do everything in my power to make you giggle and corpse at every performance until I break you of this habit," he told Larry. "If nine months of that treatment does not knock this amateurish smear off your beautiful face, then you'd really better start brushing up on some other trade. Then, when I finish with you, Gertrude will start."

At the new Phoenix Theatre on Charing Cross Road in London, *Private Lives* opened on September 24, 1930. Crowds virtually besieged the box office wanting tickets for the show's limited run.

Backstage, on opening night, Coward grabbed Larry in a tight embrace. "It's a hit." In front of the cast, Coward gave Larry a succulent kiss on the mouth. "Kiddo, you're in your first triumph in the West End."

"The experience was almost like a sexual thrill," Larry later said. "I'd never been in a West End success before. I felt exhilarated. I wanted to follow *Private Lives* with bigger and bigger hits, but in better parts than Victor, of course."

In London, critic James Agate wrote, "Mr. Laurence Olivier and Miss Adrianne Allen handsomely pretend to absence of brains and breeding."

Called dazzling, even amoral, *Private Lives* was a smash for Coward and Lawrence. Larry envied their acclaim, and continued to complain about the weak role of Victor, enough so that he began to bore Coward. "I fear the public will think I'm like that prig you wrote as a role for me."

"Then get arrested raping a twelve-year-old boy and make your image more scandalous," Coward advised, not concealing his impatience with Larry.

Private Lives could have run for a year in London, but Coward had grown tired of it and wanted new territory to conquer, specifically Broadway in New York where he arranged for his play to be booked into the Times Square Theatre.

Allen couldn't go to New York with *Private Lives*. She was pregnant. Larry recommended Jill for the role, and Coward agreed. That way, Jill and Larry wouldn't have to face a long separation at the very beginning of their marriage. At least that was the point that Larry made to Coward when he was touting Jill for the role of Sybil.

"All right, Jill has the part," Coward said. He gave Larry a cynical, very skeptical look. "You and Jill are married? That's news to me."

***

The most difficult goodbye involved abandoning the arms of Glen Byam Shaw, who had grown almost obsessively attached to Larry. On his part, Larry interpreted Shaw's passion for him as a crush that would soon fade away.

Shaw was crying when Larry left him in London in early January of 1931, taking the train to Southampton for his ocean crossing to America.

"I just know you're not coming back to me," Shaw said. "Hollywood will discover you, and you'll be gone forever."

"That's nonsense," Larry said. "I'll come back to you. I'll write every other day."

Later that night, Shaw told Sassoon, "With Larry, I'll always be a some-time thing, and I have to accept that."

Larry's prediction that Shaw's crush on him would soon fade eventually came true, but it would take five years to dissipate.

His goodbye to Shaw unfolded in private, but his departure with Jill for Southampton from Waterloo Station was public enough to have the press snap their pictures. Once they reached Southampton, Mr. and Mrs. Laurence Olivier, a married couple in name only, boarded a ship for a return voyage to New York to appear on stage in *Private Lives* with Noël Coward and Gertrude Lawrence, who would attract all the thunder in the press.

In Manhattan, Jill and Larry moved into a furnished apartment at 34 East 57th Street.

In spite of his closeness to Jill, Larry's marriage to her had never been consummated. His own sexual "plumbing" had been repaired. Their only son, Tarquin Olivier, in his memoirs *My Father Laurence Olivier*, in referencing the awkward honeymoon of his parents, claimed, "The reason was that some-thing gynaecological was wrong and interfered with their love-making."

Evoking its success in London, *Private Lives* became a hit in New York, although Broadway critics found the script weak. Critic John Mason Brown singled Larry out, claiming "he did nicely enough in a part Mr. Coward had forgotten to write."

Nearly all critics agreed that Jill and Larry were "straightman and straight-woman for that road show called 'Noël & Gertie.'"

Over morning coffee, Jill laughed when a columnist in the *New York Journal-American* identified her as "the wife of Mr. Olivia." He was not amused.

113

During the day, when not attending one of Coward's celebrity lunches, both Jill and Larry made separate screen tests for RKO, Fox, and Paramount. Jill was getting more approval from agents than Larry did for his screen tests, where he appeared rather wooden. In a letter back home to Eva, Jill wrote that the agents for RKO "found me the eighth wonder of the world."

At one formal party in New York, Jill and Larry met Alfred Lunt and Lynn Fontanne, whom he called "the god and goddess of the acting world." He'd first seen them in 1929 when they'd starred in *Caprice*, a play at London's St. James's Theatre.

Lunt and Fontanne would become Larry's lifelong friends.

Larry and Jill met not only Lunt and Fontanne, but they were seen dining in the Broadway area one night with a fellow British actor, Charlie Chaplin. He urged both of them to pursue a career in Hollywood films. "Unlike me,"

he told them, "many of my fellow Hollywood stars are laughed at when their squeaky voices are recorded by a sound technician. Of course, there are many long waits and boring technical aspects to making a film, but the financial rewards are far greater than the theater, especially those stage salaries paid in London."

"We are living the swish life," Larry wrote to Eva Moore back in London. "I feel guilty on the way to the stage door to pass many unemployed actors selling apples."

One night after the curtains went down on Broadway, a Hollywood agent came backstage. In Larry's shared dressing room with Jill, the agent offered both of them contracts on the West Coast. For Jill, it was a dream come true.

RKO filed the best offer for Jill, agreeing to put her under contract for about $900 a week, which was the best money she'd ever made. Her last London stage salary had been only eight pounds a week, roughly $40 in U.S. currency at that time.

(*Upper photo*)
Alfred Lunt with Lynn Fontanne
(lower photo)
Chaplin, the Tramp

Jill got her Hollywood contract, but so did Larry. RKO presented him with a contract calling for a salary of $1,000 a week for two pictures. If those movies were successful, an option called for him to make two more films at $1,400 a week.

Larry wavered back and forth. At one

moment, he wanted to head West and conquer Hollywood. Within the hour, he was making plans to return to the London stage.

Later that night, Larry told Jill, "It's a dreadful idea. Hollywood will destroy any serious ambition we might have entertained for the London stage. I urge you to turn down the offer. I know I'm turning it down."

Somehow Jill managed to persuade Larry to take the deal and head to California with her. "Otherwise," she warned him, "our marriage might come to an end. Back in London, you'll face temptations. I know I will in Hollywood."

Actually Jill at the time was merely holding out the promise that she'd be a wife to him. During the run of *Private Lives*, both she and Larry were free to spend the night away from their apartment, with no questions asked the next day.

When Coward heard of Larry's offer to work in films, he mocked "*Hahllee-wood.*" He accused Larry of having no artistic integrity like Ralph Richardson and John Gielgud. "Do you want to become a second-rate Ivor Novello, who will be forgotten by 1935? If you get on that train to Hollywood, you will have cheapened your name in the theater."

When Louis B. Mayer at Metro-Goldwyn-Mayer acquired the film rights to *Private Lives*, he cast Norma Shearer and Robert Montgomery in the Coward/Lawrence roles. Reginald Denny took over Larry's lackluster role of Victor, Una Merkel the role of Sybil.

Backstage in New York, during one of the final performances of *Private Lives*, Coward briefly introduced Larry and Jill to Hollywood's most widely celebrated young married couple, Joan Crawford and Douglas Fairbanks Jr.

Jill was excited at meeting her screen idol, Crawford. When the Fairbanks/Crawford couple departed, there were a lot of kisses and promises to get together on the coast when Larry and Jill came to Hollywood.

After the New York run of *Private Lives* closed on April 25, 1931, Coward invited Jill and Larry to join him for a brief holiday in Nassau in The Bahamas. Several stories have emerged from that vacation to show the extreme intimacy of this theatrical trio.

The manager of their hotel in Nassau reported that he entered their suite to make arrangements for a dinner party Coward was hosting that evening for friends. He claimed that he found Larry, Jill, and Coward on their sun terrace, all

Larry in Nassau,
early 1930s

115

three of them completely nude. Seeing him, Coward looked up, claiming, "A tan is more attractive when it's all over; otherwise, you get a pasty white spot around your private areas."

Some tonsorial worked occurred in Nassau, with Coward serving as Larry's below-the-stomach barber. Earlier that day, Coward had picked up a strapping black waiter in the dining room of their hotel. He had ordered the young man to seize Larry and hold him down. While the Bahamian did that, Coward with a pair of scissors cut off a lot of Larry's pubic hair. "Your bush is far too much for even a whore with an oversized cunt," Coward told the struggling Larry. "A neat trim is in order. Besides, it will make your dickie look much bigger."

When Jill later appeared on the terrace to witness the source of the commotion, Coward proudly displayed the result of his barber's trim. "Don't you think Larry looks better with less pubic hair?"

"Yes, much better to have some of that hair trimmed off," she said matter-of-factly before disappearing back into her suite where she was reading a book.

Coward took several nude pictures of Larry around the swimming pool. During the holiday, Larry shared Coward's bedroom, Jill sleeping alone in her own bedroom. She obviously had to know at this point that her new husband was carrying on an affair with their playwright.

Back in New York after their holiday in The Bahamas, Jill didn't feel well. A doctor discovered she had an ovarian cyst the size of an orange. Not only that, but two days later, she developed acute appendicitis. She was rushed to the hospital. Perhaps that ovarian cyst was that gynecological problem Tarquin was referring to in his memoirs.

Larry, cruising, in the early 1930s

Both operations were successful, but left her in an extremely weakened condition. "Her skin looks like sticky white paste," Larry told Coward, who had yet to visit her in the hospital.

Jill's recovery was uncertain, and she still needed the care of a hospital. Feeling she was in safe hands within the New York Hospital where she was registered, Larry paid her a final visit to confirm with her that he was taking that evening's night train to Los Angeles via Chicago.

He'd spent his final night in New York with Coward, but just before the departure of his train, Larry phoned him with a final goodbye and with news about what had transpired with Jill at the hospital. "She had not been able to urinate for four days. Just as I was squeezing her in a final embrace, her water broke. I was drenched in piss."

"It's called golden showers, dear boy," Coward said. "Some people are into that."

Larry spent most of his time on the train staring vacantly out the window at the vastness of the American continent. When not doing that, he read a script called *The Sphinx Has Spoken*. Larry was to have the second lead after Adolphe Menjou in an all-star cast that included the sultry, notorious Lili Damita and the great Erich von Stroheim.

***

In Hollywood, a pre-arranged meeting had been set up with a realtor, who drove him at once to a three-bedroom house with a panoramic view from the top of the aptly named Look-Out Mountain. When Larry found oranges and lemons growing in the back yard, he said, "I'll take it. My wife, Jill, will love it. The view is spectacular."

As soon as a phone was installed the following day, it rang within two hours. He had given his number to no one but was just getting ready to make calls to both Jill and RKO.

Picking up the phone, he anticipated it would be the phone company itself. But he was surprised at the melodious male voice at the other end.

"This is Douglas Fairbanks, Junior that is," came that voice. "Billie and I want to be the first to welcome you to Hollywood."

He was referring, of course, to his wife, Joan Crawford.

"My God, I'm honored," Larry said. "I hope you're the real thing and not some so-called friend playing a practical joke on me. The Prince of Hollywood himself calling me, along with his emerging Princess about to take over MGM."

"With your permission, we'll be right over," Fairbanks said. "Billie has already prepared lunch for you. Don't bother to give us your address. We already know it. As for the phone number, I know this gal who works there. She can get me any number in Hollywood I ask for."

"I'm starving," Larry said, "but mostly hungry to see the two of you, the most glamorous couple in Hollywood. I can't believe how dazzling you two looked when you came backstage to say hello to Jill and me in New York."

"Since we met you, Billie and I have been dying to get to know you and Jill better," Fairbanks said. "I hope she's with you."

"Jill will be out here soon," Larry promised. "Right now I'm leading the bachelor life."

117

"No need to be lonely, not when I'm around," Fairbanks said. "Billie and I have already decided that you and Jill are going to become our new best friends."

"I always heard things are speeded up in Hollywood," Larry said.

"That's very true," Fairbanks said. "Out here we even have to race through our sexual affairs and don't have time to savor them."

"Come on over," Larry said, "I'll be standing at the front door holding it open."

***

Because Ernest Hartley had fared so badly during the Depression that began with the New York Stock Market crash in 1929, and rippled across Europe after that, he, along with his wife, Gertrude, and their very bored daughter, Vivian, had moved for the winter into a West Country home near Teighmouth. There, the living was relatively comfortable, slow, and reasonable in price. Vivian eagerly anticipated the big social event of the season.

The South Devon Hunt Ball of 1932 was the big event of the season, taking place at the Two Bridges Hotel located near the Torquay Pier. Vivian had spent hours getting ready for the event

The ball was in full swing when a stunningly dressed Vivian Hartley made her spectacular entrance. Dressed in an emerald green gown that set off her cat-green eyes, she was still a teenager but attracted the attention of the room. There were whispers, "Who is that girl?"

Herbert Leigh Holman, a thirty-one-year-old barrister-at-law at London's Middle Temple, walked toward her. He was the man she'd seen on horseback riding through town and had vowed to marry. He didn't wait for anyone to introduce him to this magnificent young woman, but came up to her and presented himself.

Up close, she found him even more handsome than on horseback. With his blond curly hair and clear eyes, he reminded her of the actor Leslie Howard. She'd recently developed a crush on the London-born actor, whom she'd seen in *Outward Bound* (1930). As Holman spoke to Vivian, she recognized in him a cultivated sensitivity that seemed to belong to a bygone era.

"We came here in a two-seater Alvis," Vivian told Leigh between dances. "Along the way, we suffered a puncture. Fortunately, a kindly man came along and changed our tire. Girls are so helpless without a man around."

He was not a good dancer, but Vivian told him, "you have such grace on the floor that I thought you must have trained for the ballet."

He laughed at her exaggerated compliment. "My darling mother didn't raise a ballet dancer. No, not that. Not ever that! Ballet, what nonsense. But you said it so convincingly. What an actress. You must have had the lead in all your school plays."

"An occasional role," she said demurely, feeling this was the wrong moment to tell him of her desire to go on the stage.

As the orchestra sounded the notes of a Viennese waltz, Holman asked her to dance once again. As Vivian was to relate later that night to her hostess, Clare Martin, "I fell in love with him as we were dancing the waltz. It was the way he held me, the way he looked into my eyes. With his eyes, he told me I was the most important girl in the world, perhaps the only girl in the world."

"But he's a grown man," she protested. "In his thirties if he's a day."

"It doesn't matter to me," Vivian said. "I like a man of maturity and refined manners. I'll bring youth to our relationship. It's true, he's a bit stuffy. But I'll liven him up. In fact, ever since the ball, I've been in a trance. He's all that I can think about. I can't wait for him to take me in his arms and kiss me."

The very next afternoon, with the understanding that Vivian and her parents would be there, Leigh came to have tea with the Martin family, friends of both Leigh and the Hartleys. Dulcie, one of the Martin daughters, had recently turned down Leigh's offer of marriage, and opted to go shopping instead of being present for his arrival.

When tea was over and

The Holman-Hartley courtship and wedding

119

the appropriate social niceties had been observed, Leigh invited Vivian for a walk along the lanes of Devon. "I know the most beautiful lane there is. It should be photographed for a calendar."

The lane was as beautiful as he'd promised. She asked probing questions, as she knew little about the man she'd chosen to marry. She did find out that his father was also a barrister, and that her future husband had been educated at Harrow and Jesus College at Cambridge.

At the end of the walk, he stopped yards from the Martin home.

"I hope I can make you forget all about that Dulcie," Vivian said. "She's a sweet girl, but. . . ."

"Don't say anything," Leigh said. "Dulcie's a very sweet girl but she was not ready for marriage. I proposed to her, but it was an impulsive decision and I later regretted it."

"Do you still love her?" Vivian asked.

"I never did love her," Leigh said. "I thought it was about time I got married and settled down."

"I don't think a man or a woman should ever marry someone they don't love. Do you agree?"

"I agree completely," he said. "I know that now. I didn't know that when I proposed to Dulcie."

At the door to the Martin home, he kissed her lightly on the cheek.

"I hope you don't plan to make yourself a stranger around here," she said. She was playing the coquette, an early rehearsal for her immortality when she was cast as Scarlett O'Hara in *Gone With the Wind*.

"Not at all," he said. "I want to invite you to join a friend of mine from Cambridge, Hamish Hamilton. You can watch us team up with some friends down from Cambridge. We're having a squash match."

That night Vivian complained to her hostess, Clare Martin, "I hate squash matches, but I'll go. I won't look at that silly old game. I'll have my eyes trained at all times on Leigh."

Since their days at Cambridge, Hamish Hamilton, a publisher, had been Leigh's close friend. Hamilton was called "Jamie." On meeting Vivian at the squash match, he told her, "Your beau is a great athlete but a very bad barrister."

Years later, Hamilton remembered meeting Vivian. She was "a vision of beauty far lovelier with her eyebrows unplucked before the theatre people got ahold of her."

After the squash match, Leigh walked her home again. He came every day to see her, the squash matches giving way to quiet dinners.

After a particularly romantic dinner, he walked her down the lane to her doorstep. Up to that point, he'd given her nothing but kisses on the cheek.

When he attempted to do that again, she took control and kissed him succulently on the lips. From that night on, their intimacy deepened.

As she told Clare, "I get carried away when I'm with him and want to extend our love-making much farther, but Leigh says some things have to be postponed until marriage. I wish he wasn't such a gentleman. I want him now."

Leigh and Vivian found a secluded bench along their favorite primrose path in Devon, where they would sit for hours and talk. "Vivian looks at me with a childlike expression that appears to be so innocent," Leigh wrote to a friend, Oswald Frewen, who was called "the indefatigable diarist of his own life and times."

"But I have cause to wonder," Leigh wrote in his letter. "Those eyes are also extending an invitation. Marriage is not out of the question. But I don't love her . . . yet."

Each time she went out with Leigh, she learned more about him and asked many questions.

He had been born on November 3, 1900 and was the third son of barrister Herbert Holman.

In college, Leigh had been a champion rower and a key player on the Thames Rowing Club at Henley-on-Thames. Graduating in 1921, he'd received his B.A.

Over their final dinner in Devon, Leigh delivered the bad news. He had to return to London the following morning for work.

That night he spent a much longer time kissing her good-bye, and both of them made promises to meet in London very soon.

The following morning, Vivian begged Gertrude to allow her to return to London in advance of the debut of her acting classes at the Academy.

Her mother steadfastly refused, and insisted that Vivian go instead to Bridlington to stay with the Hartley grandparents, who were aging and in bad health. "Your presence will be a beacon of light and hope for them."

For six weeks, Vivian was trapped "in this wretched place." Her grandparents were loving and kind but boring, and they retired to bed at eight o'clock every night. Vivian had discovered Colette and she read a lot. She

Vivian Hartley's role model, Lillie Langtry, playing Lady Macbeth

121

even took up knitting, making a red sweater for Leigh, a man who had never worn anything red in his life.

It was also during this time that Vivian read the biography of Lillie Langtry, the actress. As a result, she became even more deeply inspired in her plans for a life on the stage. "Of course, as she wrote her friend, Patsy Quinn, "I'll have to figure out how to work that into a marriage."

The highlight of her day involved writing a long letter to Leigh in London. Even though he had a busy schedule at Middle Temple, he answered every one of her letters. Over the weeks he changed his sign-off from "fondly" to "with love."

At one point, not meaning it, Vivian wrote Leigh that she was considering running away to London to be with him—or else she'd kill herself. "The sea is too cold for drowning, and I couldn't face all the blood of a knife. Perhaps it will just be my grandmother's old gas oven."

On March 1, 1932, Vivian returned to London, and Leigh met her at Victoria Station, locking her in a tight embrace. She'd arrived in time for him to escort her to the Pegasus Ball.

She'd begged Gertrude to let her stay in Leigh's bachelor flat, assuring her mother that "Leigh is a perfect gentleman," but Gertrude refused.

Instead, Vivian stayed with Jay Wilson, an elderly and respectable male friend of the family. She was furious that Ernest and Gertrude wouldn't let her go live with Leigh. She claimed that it is "absolutely useless for parents today to try and restrict their offspring or attempt to run their lives."

In London Vivian would often spend her evenings with both Leigh and his friend, Hamilton. They even went out on dates together. Since Leigh didn't like to dance that much, in spite of his dancing at the hunt ball, he often sat and watched Vivian and Hamilton on the floor. Their favorite dance floor was at the old Berkeley Hotel opposite the Ritz.

"It was clear to me that there was little love involved," Hamilton later claimed. "Vivian wanted to escape from Gertrude's clutches, and Leigh feared the loss of his bachelor freedom if he took a wife."

As Leigh moved closer and closer to proposing marriage, he told Hamilton, "I still don't love her, but I try to, I really do. I find her utterly fascinating, and perhaps in a marriage fascination is better than love."

RADA
Gower Street Entrance, London WC1

***

When Vivian informed Leigh that she was enrolled at the new Royal Academy of Dramatic Art (RADA), he did not take her ambition to become an actress seriously, viewing the Academy as no more than a finishing school. "She did not seem to have the drive or ambition to become an actress," Leigh later claimed. "Also, her voice was a bit thin for the theater."

After her classes at the Academy and after he'd finished his duties at Middle Temple for the day, Leigh and Vivian met and spent their evenings together, usually over a quiet dinner. They were getting to know each other.

At the Academy, her trial run as an actress revolved around the role of Starveling in *Midsummer Night's Dream*. For this part, she blacked out her front teeth to get bigger laughs. She followed that by playing Rosalind in *As You Like It*. Her Shakespeare teacher, Ethel Carrington, was impressed with both performances, but felt her voice would have to be trained a lot more. "It's too high pitched," she told Vivian.

Although Gertrude disapproved, Leigh and Vivian took a number of short motor trips together, mainly to see his friend Oswald Frewen, who was first cousin to Winston Churchill.

Brede Place, Frewen's home in Sussex, dated from 1350. Leigh's friend was the most fascinating man she'd ever met. In contrast to Frewen, Leigh was positively "the dullest thing ever" to Vivian.

Frewen's friends included Rudyard Kipling and, at one time, Henry James, when he lived in Rye. Vivian begged Frewen one afternoon to drive over to see Kipling, because she claimed that his novel, *Kim*, set in India "is my all-time, all-time favorite."

True to his word, Frewen did drive her one day to have tea with Kipling. Leigh preferred to stay at Brede Place, working around the homestead.

Frewen drove Vivian there in his baby Austin, the same vehicle he'd driven across the Sahara Desert with his eighty-year-old mother. The press had referred to Frewen's Austin as "the most disreputable car in England."

Born in Bombay, India, Kipling had won the Nobel Prize for Literature in 1907. Over tea, the author and Vivian shared their mutual fascination of India. Later he took her on a tour of his house, Batesman, which dated from 1634 when it was constructed in East Sussex.

That night she told Leigh, "It had no bathroom, no running water, and no elec-

Rudyard Kipling in his study at Batesman

123

tricity. It's the way to live. I hope you purchase a country place like that for us one day."

In later life, the actress Vivien Leigh would defend Kipling when older editions of his books were being removed from British libraries because the covers had a left-facing swastika.

On the covers, the swastika was depicted with an elephant carrying a lotus flower in its trunk. Some Englishmen accused Kipling of being a Nazi sympathizer. Vivien explained that the swastika symbol was based on the Indian sun symbol, conferring good luck and well being on a person.

In fairness to Kipling, he was a staunch defender of the British empire, and Vivien knew he was not a Nazi. As early as 1935, when much of the world slept, he'd warned his countrymen of the rising dangers of Hitler's Nazi Party.

On her second afternoon at Brede Place, Vivian was exhausted and chose not to join Leigh and Frewen for a long country walk. During their time together, Leigh confided his grave concerns about entering into a marriage with Vivian. "She seems to become more impetuous every day now that I've gotten to know her better. I used to think she was more demure and more willing to give in to a man's wishes."

Two weeks later, Leigh wrote Frewen another letter. "Vivian is not only beautiful but intelligent. She is not some silly girl who, like her friend, Maureen O'Sullivan, wanted to rush off to Hollywood and become a movie star. Vivian is far too sensible for that. She would make a good wife and would, with her charm, make a great hostess which would help me with my clients. She's essentially a homebody who would be a great mother if we decide to have offspring."

To show their different states of mind, Vivien Leigh, writing years later in *What Success Has Taught Me*, said, "I was under nineteen when I married, and not quite twenty when my daughter was born. I felt too young to be the mother of a child, and very lacking in the qualities of restfulness and serenity which a mother should have."

"Marry the girl," Frewen said to Leigh, "or else I will."

Back in London. Leigh went to Mappin & Webb to purchase an engagement ring with a green stone for thirty-five pounds. Vivian thought the ring was beautiful, but was shocked that he'd bought it at a cutlery store instead of from a reputable jeweler.

Nonetheless, she rushed to show it to Gertrude the following day. Her mother withdrew in horror from the ring.

"You must return it at once," Gertrude told her daughter. "Green is unlucky. It will doom your upcoming marriage."

The next day Leigh graciously returned the ring, replacing it with a small diamond engagement band instead.

On Vivian's second visit to Brede Place, she met Frewen's sister, Clare Sheridan, the sculptress who was known primarily for creating busts of famous sitters and writing diaries of her worldly travels. She had broken with her cousin, Churchill, over her support of the Russian revolution. Before that, she had done two busts of her first cousin, which are exhibited today at Blenheim Palace and in Churchill's estate at Chartwell.

Sheridan was the first major British woman to travel to Russia in the summer of 1920, where she'd gotten Lenin to pose for a bust, even though he was rather busy. Trotsky also posed for her and took time out to have an affair with her.

Sheridan published *Mayfair to Moscow* in 1921, which became a notorious diary because of its support of what she called "my darling Bolsheviks."

Sheridan and Vivian became "confidantes for life." She even told Vivian of her affair with Charlie Chaplin who had also posed for a bust for her. "Charlie has a definite feminine streak in him—oh, I'd say about sixty percent woman, twenty percent man, and the rest unknown even to himself." In spite of the low male percentage Sheridan gave the comedian, she and Chaplin nonetheless were lovers."

Like Frewen himself, Vivian found Sheridan the most fascinating woman she'd ever met. She asked Vivian to pose for a bust, and Vivian agreed but apparently Sheridan never got around to sculpting Vivian. She invited Vivian to visit her North Africa home near Biskra, an oasis town in French Algeria, but Vivian didn't find the time to do that either, although she later regretted that she hadn't gone.

Sheridan and Vivian remained in touch throughout their lives, as Vivian avidly followed her friend's ups and downs in life. As Sheridan's biographer, Anita Leslie, put it, "Sheridan was imperious (if often penniless), restless, reckless, and liable to pop up anytime, anywhere, and anyone—often trailing ominous whiffs of scandal behind her—infuriating, rude, lovable, brave, and vulnerable."

Vivian horrified Leigh when she told him, "I want to build the blocks of my life using Clare Sheridan as my role model."

Gertrude feared that Leigh and Vivian would not be compatible. "You're a very high spirited

Two views of Clare Sheridan *(top)* her 1920 portrait by Sir Oswald Birley

girl," she told Vivian. "Leigh likes to spend hours alone with his briefs. You like to go to the theater. He finds it boring and you have to go with girl friends. You have not told him how committed you are to becoming an actress. You might one day be called away to Hollywood like your friend Maureen O'Sullivan. Do you honestly think Leigh will give everything up and follow you? I don't think so."

Almost like the future heroine, Scarlett O'Hara, that Vivien Leigh would play on the screen, Vivian seemed to brush aside such concerns, as if she'd think about it tomorrow.

Sophia Holman, Leigh's stern mother, objected strenuously to her son's plans to marry Vivian. "They are not our kind," she warned. She'd heard scandalous stories about both Ernest and Gertrude. "He's had many mistresses, Indian harlots no doubt. And Gertrude keeps this lover, this so-called Tommy on a leash. I heard only the other day that she and this Tommy creature have run away together to Biarritz. And what is her husband doing all this time? The last I heard he's off to Scotland. Who's keeping him company up there?"

She was referring to John Lambert Thompson, so beloved by both Ernest and Gertrude.

Overriding grave parental concerns, the wedding took place on December 20, 1932 at St. James, a Roman Catholic church on Spanish Place. Patsy Quinn was Vivian's maid of honor, showing up in peach satin with puffy sleeves.

Vivian was a stunning beauty as she walked down the aisle on Ernest's arm. She later recalled "I was shaking like a leaf." Dressed in white satin, she had placed a crocheted white Juliet cap on her head. In the morning light her face was like white porcelain. The cap made her look like she was no more than fourteen years old.

Mrs. Leigh Holman
née Vivian Hartley
later, Vivien Leigh

She appeared much older when she changed clothes for her honeymoon, slipping into a metallic blue suit with a silver fox fur. When Gertrude saw her take off her diamond wedding band to show friends, she went into a panic. "By your doing that, you've doomed your marriage. To do what you did is very unlucky. I should have warned you."

For their honeymoon, Vivian lured Leigh back to the Continent, revisiting many of her former haunts, such as Kitzbühel in Austria and Bad Reichenhall in Germany. These places looked different through his more provincial eyes. After a stopover in Salzburg, she wrote Clare Sheridan,

"My new husband has made love to me. He is so kind and gentle with me, perhaps too much so. He proceeds to do his husbandly duties in an efficient way. In other words, he does his duty. But where is the passion? Shouldn't honeymooners have passion? If there is no passion on the honeymoon, what will marriage be like?"

When she returned to London to settle into his bachelor flat at Eyre Court in St. John's Wood, she found out.

Their rooms were small, and he had a maid who performed all the duties, even preparing his supper for the evening. All Vivian had to do was heat it up.

Sometimes there were parties in the country, but most weekends she stayed at home while he prepared briefs. She read plays and dreamed.

He had persuaded her to give up her studies at the Academy before he married her, and now she resented him for that.

"Leigh is gone all day, and I feel desperately alone," Vivian wrote Clare Sheridan. "There is nothing for me to do here. When I complained to Leigh, he put me in charge of his wardrobe like some valet."

And then one day her luck changed.

She was taken to meet Alwyn Boot, Leigh's cousin and the daughter of Sir Jesse Boot, who had founded Boot's Chemists, with branches all over England. Alwyn and Vivian bonded and became fast friends almost overnight.

Through her connections, Alwyn promised she would arrange to have Vivian presented at court.

At last Vivian had something to live for, and she furiously went to work, preparing for her court appearance. She later recalled, "There was no opening night that I worked harder for than my first appearance at court."

Over Leigh's objections, she spent lavishly on a gown she had designed by a French couturier in Mayfair. She demanded ostrich feathers for her hair, and paid for lessons in social etiquette. She was taught how to hold herself as she walked, how to curtsy, and most of all what to do with her hands. Fortunately, "my paws," as she called them, would be concealed in white silk gloves. The day before her appearance, she went to a stylist, also in Mayfair, who swept her hair back so that her entire face would show.

Royal protocol:
King George V and Queen Mary

"It is your loveliest feature and should be on full exhibit," her hairdresser told her.

On "my greatest day" [her words],

127

June 13, 1933, she was thrilled but also disappointed. Leigh's latest case was held over for another day in court, and he could not be her escort. She would have to appear before the king and queen alone.

Arriving at court, she was awed by the pomp and circumstance of it all, the scarlet uniforms of the attendants with their gold braid and white plumed hats. The mountains of flowers gave off an intoxicating smell.

King George V and Queen Mary sat regally under a durbar canopy they had acquired on their trip to India in 1911, when the Hartleys had witnessed their arrival.

As Vivian glided forth, an orchestra was playing soft music by Mozart. Her gown was made of peach-colored taffeta which crackled, giving off a soft sound that seemed part of Mozart's music. She wore white pearls Ernest had given her years ago in India.

Loud enough for the court to hear her, Queen Mary said, "What a lovely child!"

Vivian's day had been made. She was a success and later that night would reenact every precious moment with Leigh.

As she had regally walked through the palace courtyard to a black chauffeur-driven limousine that awaited her, she made a vow. The vehicle itself might look like a funeral hearse, but she wasn't going to die. That very evening she was going to confront Leigh and tell him that she planned to re-enter the Academy.

That night, after she'd regaled him with the palace scenario, she summoned her courage to confront him. "I was only six years old when I told Maureen O'Sullivan that I was going to become a great actress. I will not abandon my dream. I must fulfill my destiny."

"Destiny, is it?" he asked in shock. "I really believe you're bloody serious about appearing on the stage."

With a determination that a future screen Scarlett O'Hara would have when vowing never to go hungry again, Vivian told her new husband, "I have never been more bloody serious in my life!"

***

Communications czar
David Sarnoff

David Sarnoff was the virtual communications czar of America, the founder of the National Broadcasting Company (NBC) and for most of his career, the CEO of the Radio Corporation of America (RCA). Widely referred to as "The General," he had also formed the film company,

RKO. One night he went to see Jill and Larry performing in *Private Lives* on Broadway. He later claimed that "the faggot Coward wrote lousy parts for both of them, but the kids stand out, especially Olivier, who plays the latent homosexual."

At the time, Sarnoff almost stood alone in seeing Larry's role in *Private Lives* as a latent homosexual, although dozens of critics of the future agreed with his assessment.

"Sign them up," Sarnoff instructed his staff. "For all I know Esmond and Oliver [sic] will be the next Lunt and Fontanne."

In his writings, Larry has admitted that when he arrived "cocksure" in Hollywood in 1930 at the age of twenty-three, he was "very snooty about moving pictures. I went for the money and the chance of fame."

The Talkies had arrived, and in Hollywood, producers and directors wanted actors who could speak the English language. Many silent screen stars could not, and directors developed an obsession about using actors from the London stage. "I was sure I could outtalk anyone," Larry claimed. "Hollywood viewed me as RKO's answer to Ronald Colman, although Colman had hardly gone away and didn't really need to be replaced."

On reflection years later, Larry took a dim view of his performances in his first Hollywood films. "I could talk all right, but my performances were precious, lacking vitality, charmless."

Larry's newcomer lunch with Joan Crawford and her husband, Douglas Fairbanks Jr., had stretched out for five hours. Both of these stars seemed eager for his friendship, especially Fairbanks. Feeling alone in Hollywood, with Jill still in a hospital back in New York, Larry eagerly responded to this dazzling couple who had swept into his life so sud-

Three views of Larry and Douglas Fairbanks, Jr.

(top photo) Yachting off Catalina Island

129

denly after only a brief introduction backstage on Broadway.

Son of the swashbuckling Douglas Fairbanks Sr., and stepson of the former queen of Hollywood, Mary Pickford, the suave and sophisticated Fairbanks Jr. was Hollywood royalty. After their lunch for three that day, Fairbanks invited Larry to a private *tête-à-tête* dinner for two so they could talk and get acquainted with each other.

Dinner was scheduled for eight o'clock, but at three that afternoon a delivery man from a florist brought a single red rose to Larry's home. He would later claim it "was the world's most beautiful red rose." During their courtship, a single red rose, equally beautiful, arrived every afternoon.

As Larry got to know Fairbanks intimately, he came to realize how painful it had been living in the shadow of the most famous swashbuckler of the era, Douglas Fairbanks Sr., who had reigned in silent pictures as the virtual King of Hollywood.

"Dad told me that one swashbuckler in the family was enough," Fairbanks said. "He did not want me to go into pictures. When I was a kid, I didn't like baseball. Dad called me 'foppish' and feared he was raising a homosexual until I started dating and having affairs with all sorts of women. That led to my getting hooked up with Billie. Billie I can tolerate, but when she becomes Joan Crawford around the house, it's a bit much. I told her her ideal man would be a skilled butler during the day and a stud in bed after midnight with a twelve-inch dick."

"My father told me I'm a 'smudge' against him, and he's cut me out of his will," Fairbanks said. "I started taking film work because I was short of cash." On his first night away from Crawford, Fairbanks also confessed to Larry, "My marriage is collapsing. We're seeing other people on the side."

After their dinner together, Larry began calling Fairbanks "Douggie."

In the days ahead, and especially the nights, Fairbanks and Larry began to see each other at the rate of four or five times a week. Crawford was rarely included.

Fairbanks confessed to Larry and a few intimates that "Billie's fierce ambition kills my manhood."

"I don't find anything wrong with your manhood," Larry assured him.

A favorite hangout of Larry and Fairbanks was the Russian Club in Hollywood, which was run by expatriate White Russians who had fled Lenin. One performer, an Egyptian Cossack, provided Fairbanks and Larry with "Happy Dust," as he called cocaine.

In his memoirs, Fairbanks said he and Larry snorted cocaine which caused Larry to retch, just as Raymond Massey walked into the men's room to discover them.

Fairbanks' suggestion was that this was their first time for the white powder, but actually Larry had indulged in the drug with Tallulah Bankhead in London years before.

When Fairbanks invited Larry to swim nude with Crawford and him in their pool, Larry later claimed, "Her eyes are big as saucers, and her geometry closely resembles that of the Venus de Milo."

Crawford later told her gay pal, William Haines, "We'd all had a little too much vodka that afternoon. As they were lying nude on two lounges, I offered to perform fellatio, a word you taught me, on them and take measurements, but Larry refused."

"Perhaps Larry feared his sword would not equal a swashbuckling Fairbanks," Haines said.

"I bet if you made the same offer to those two boys, each of them would eagerly accept," she said.

"Cranberry, you know my sword-swallowing technique is known all over Hollywood."

Back in New York, Jill took more than six weeks to recover from her extensive surgery. She missed out on what was to have been her first film, the role going to another actress.

Her absence gave Larry enough time to consolidate his affair with Fairbanks. He later learned that when Crawford was not with her husband, she was in the arms of Clark Gable, who was rapidly emerging as a big star.

When Jill did arrive in Hollywood, Crawford befriended her. They became instant friends, although both Larry and Fairbanks suspected that there was much more going on than mere friendship.

Likewise, the sexually hip Crawford seemed perfectly aware of the growing intimacy between Larry and her husband. To her closest pal, William

Anglo-American glamor during a transatlantic crossing *(left to right)*
Jill Esmond, Douglas Fairbanks Jr., Joan Crawford, Laurence Olivier

131

Haines, she confessed, "While Olivier is away getting butt-fucked by my husband, I'm entertaining Jill Esmond. You must meet her, darling gal."

A surprise offer came in from MGM for Larry and Jill to repeat their stage roles in the screen version of *Private Lives* with Norma Shearer and Robert Montgomery. Both Larry and Jill turned it down. "I can't see myself as Sybil on the screen," Jill said. "Besides, I'm the same type as Shearer."

Jill had a valid point. She'd already made a film for Alfred Hitchcock, released in 1930, which had been based on John Galsworthy's play, *The Skin Game*. It had starred the lovely actor Edmund Gwenn, along with Helen Haye, whose name was always confused with the more famous Helen Hayes. Every reviewer pointed out the similarity of Jill's face and manner to Norma Shearer, at the time the virtual Queen of MGM, though Greta Garbo was closing in.

Both Larry and Jill grew impatient waiting for RKO to assign them a role in a film. Finally, an offer, more like a command since he was under contract, came in for Larry.

Director Victor Schertzinger told Larry that shooting would begin that Monday on his first movie for RKO. The script he'd been given, *The Sphinx Has Spoken*, had been retitled *Friends and Lovers*.

Although it had a first-rate cast, it was a mere 58-minute "programmer," and Larry was disappointed with his role of Lt. Ned Nichols.

The lead was played by Adolphe Menjou, with Lili Damita cast as the female star. Back-up support was provided by the imperial Erich von Stroheim.

"The cast, apart from its eminence, was wretchedly ill-assorted," Larry said. "So my first Hollywood picture died the death of a dog." *Variety* found Larry "extremely personable," but referred to him as Maurice [sic] Olivier. *Picturegoer* spelled Larry's name right but called him "precious" [code word for gay back then].

A modern critic who'd seen a copy of *Friends and Lovers* claimed Larry was "slender, high-voiced, and so camp he's almost feline."

Friends and Lovers, an adventure romance set in India, would go on to lose $260,000 at the box office.

Menjou struck Larry as "the false epitome of knavish, continental charm, but he was the best dressed man in Hollywood, known for his waxy black mustache. He would go on to be voted America's best dressed man nine years in a row."

He spent most of his private time with Larry claiming he owned one hundred suits and asserting that he hated Franklin D. Roosevelt.

Schertzinger was a violinist and a former symphonic conductor, who was known for getting along with everybody, even the difficult Menjou and the imperial von Stroheim.

Stroheim told Larry, "I should be directing this movie. I am still the greatest director in Hollywood."

True to character, Stroheim wore a black patch over one eye and a monocle over the other, but he kept reversing them.

When Larry, in years to come, saw *Sunset Blvd.*, a film starring Gloria Swanson, in London, he was captivated by Stroheim, as cast in the butler role. "It occurred to me that he was very much like that in real life, the fallen giant of the silent era, dazed by his fall," Larry said.

Schertzinger thought Larry as a screen actor was a disaster. "He'd look right into the camera in the middle of the scene," the director charged. "He brought all his broad stage mannerisms to screen acting, including exaggerated expressions which we'd stopped using when movies learned to talk. I saw no future for him in Hollywood."

There was a certain irony in Larry meeting Walter Byron, who played Count Nikolai in *Friends and Lovers*. This handsome actor had been hailed as "Hollywood's new John Gilbert." He'd landed the male role of the year when he was cast as the German prince opposite Gloria Swanson's shy little Irish girl from the convent in *Queen Kelly*.

"Swanson promised me I stood to be the next great male star of Hollywood," Byron told Larry. "Imagine my disappointment when Swanson and Joseph Kennedy pulled the plug on Erich von Stroheim. The film will never be finished."

"A lot of films here at RKO are not being finished," Larry said. "I heard that bankers from the East arrive daily to pull the plug, as you say, on film projects."

"I still have hope," Byron said. "Gloria still wants me to be her leading man in a film she's partially financing herself. It'll be shot in England and called *Perfect Understanding*."

Ironically, Swanson would later offer that lead role to Larry, not Byron.

Larry was charmed by the beautiful French actress, Lili Damita. The fan magazines were touting her as "the new Garbo." She was struggling through *Friends and Lovers*. She'd launched herself in silent pictures, and to everyone's dismay, her heavy French accent did not record well on sound tracks for

Two views of Lili Damita *(upper photo)* modeling jewelry

(lower photo) with then-husband, Errol Flynn

"talkies."

Larry agreed to help her with her lines, since she admired his "beautiful English-speaking voice."

At her home, he encountered a sensual woman with a fiery, dynamic personality, though she was rather petite in statute. She was relatively young, but carried an air of worldly sophistication about her.

At night she dressed only in blue. "If monkeys can have blue asses, I can have blue tits." That was a favorite line of hers.

Damita may have been reared in convents in Portugal and Spain, but she'd obviously chosen not to become a nun. She'd once been married to the tempestuous Hollywood director Michael Curtiz and had had numerous affairs, including one with King Alfonso XIII of Spain. In Berlin, she'd had an affair with Marlene Dietrich.

On his first date with Damita, who was between husbands, Larry invited her to the Russian Club. He'd never met a woman as outspoken as Damita. She never censored what came out of her beautiful mouth. "I fuck better than any other woman in Hollywood," she said.

At first dazed at her comment, he quickly recovered. "I imagine the competition out here is rough."

"I must tell you I have a desire for cunnilingus," she said. "Gary Cooper was no good at it. Unlike Frenchmen, British men don't seem very good at it either. Perhaps you are an exception."

"If not an exception, then an eager pupil," he said. "I'm sure Marlene Dietrich would be a fine teacher."

"Why Marlene?" she asked. "You don't need her. You have Lili Damita."

"It appears that I do," he said.

Larry admitted to Fairbanks and another close friend, Laurence Evans, that he was having an affair with Damita. "I have to get female company somewhere," he said. "I don't get it at home. Jill has not granted conjugal rights as of yet."

After their tryst came to an end when the movie was wrapped, Larry and Damita would remain casual friends, mainly running into each other at parties.

His interest in her would be greatly renewed when she married that dashing newcomer swashbuckler Errol Flynn in 1935.

In the meantime, Fairbanks Jr. and Larry became two of the biggest hellraisers in Hollywood. "We were the wildest of the wild boys in those bad old, good old days," Larry claimed.

***

Fairbanks and Larry joined a secret club formed by Bankhead. It was

134

called "The Tallulah Club," and was open only to bisexuals. Jill Esmond and Joan Crawford did not join.

Members in the club could recognize other members by the way they dressed. Tallulah ordained that some part of a member's wardrobe, if only a tie on a man, should contain the colors of lavender, scarlet, and pink.

The club, whose formation was proposed one drunken night by Tallulah, existed for about two months, until the inside joke ended, and so-called members reverted to their regular wardrobes.

Tallulah, on occasion, accompanied Larry and Fairbanks to one of the "pansy clubs," in Los Angeles that featured drag acts. Sometimes they were joined by Marlene Dietrich, with whom Fairbanks would later have an affair.

**

While Larry was turning out "my bad movies," Jill was faring slightly better in Hollywood. Director Guthrie McClintic asked her to play an ingénue opposite Ivor Novello and Ruth Chatterton, who was cast as a woman of dubious virtue, in the 1931 film adaptation of *Once a Lady,* formerly a successful play. Up until then, Jill had seemed unaware of the closeness of Novello and her husband. But when Larry started visiting the set every day, she obviously had to realize how close they'd become, although Noël Coward was threatening the Novello/Olivier liaison.

Coward, who regarded Larry as "my discovery," seemed to resent all attention paid to Novello, which he felt should be directed at him.

Director McClintic was the husband of the reigning American stage diva of her era Katharine Cornell. The director and his wife, "Kit," as he called her, would in the future become close friends of Vivien Leigh and Larry Olivier, staying with them at their home, Notley Abbey.

McClintic was a homosexual and Cornell was a lesbian. Jointly, they had entered into a "lavender marriage," somewhat like Larry and Jill.

In *Once a Lady*, Jill was afraid of being overshadowed on the screen by Chatterton, who at the time was hailed as the finest actress in Hollywood.

Chatterton told Jill, "Instead of being Hollywood's leading actress, I would much prefer being America's number one aviatrix." In time she would fly alone across the United States several times, making her a rival of Amelia Earhart.

Given her next script, *The Eternal Feminine* (1931), Jill had little faith in the film. She was cast in the third lead after Guy Newall and Doria March.

At one point in his career, Newall was feted as "Britain's finest actor." But Jill quickly assured Larry that he had assumed that position now, although she was rather premature in her judgment when she told him this. Canadian-born

Doria March began and ended her film career so fast no one noticed her.

Ladies of the Jury, released in 1932, found Jill co-starring with Edna May Oliver. Oliver played a society matron selected as a juror in the trial of an ex-chorus girl, Yvette Gordon, as played by Jill.

Both Larry and Jill were amused by Oliver, who would go on to make a career in the 1930s of playing tart-tongued spinsters. She was a direct descendant of the sixth American president, John Quincy Adams.

Jill had higher hopes for *State's Attorney*, released in 1932, starring John Barrymore and Helen Twelvetrees. Larry seemed to resent his wife being cast opposite Barrymore. "I'm sure I'd have far more to learn from Barrymore than you."

Jill found Brooklyn-born Twelvetrees had come to Hollywood to replace the silent screen stars who could not make the transition to talkies. "I'm going to devote my career, you darling girl, to playing suffering women fighting for the love of the wrong men," Twelvetrees told Jill. Both women would be pushed aside at RKO to make way for the newly arrived Katharine Hepburn.

Larry visited the set of *State's Attorney,* ostensibly to have lunch with Jill, but he secretly wanted to meet Barrymore once again.

When Larry showed up on the set, Barrymore was feuding with the director, George Archainbaud. Born in Paris, Archainbaud had been directing films since 1917. He knew more about how motion pictures were made than Barrymore, but the two often blasted each other in front of the crew.

Barrymore was obviously drunk yet not speaking in a slurred speech. He was being chastised for failure to learn his lines that day, and he had the same response to that that he did on many other such occasions.

"My memory is full of beauty——take Hamlet's soliloquies, for instance, certainly the Queen Mab speech," Barrymore said. "Let us not forget the King Magnus monologue or most of the sonnets. Do you expect me to clutter up all that with this horseshit?" He tossed the script for *State's Attorney* back at Archainbaud.

When introduced by Jill, Barrymore gave no indication that he'd previously met Larry in London.

In his dressing room, Barrymore shook Larry's hand, as if meeting him for the first time. "I'm John Barrymore. Who are you?"

"Laurence Olivier, I'm an actor."

"Oh, yes, dear fellow, the husband of Jill Esmond. Why did you marry a lesbian? Are you a homosexual?"

"Sometimes," Larry said.

"At least you admit it," Barrymore said. "I hate people who lie about who they are. Did you come here to suck my cock? All you young British actors like Ivor Novello want to suck my cock. Perhaps they hope that with my

136

semen floating around in their gut, it will put fire in their belly when they go on stage."

"I didn't come here to do that," Larry said, "although I'm sure it would be one of life's greatest pleasures. I came to pay tribute to you. I saw your *Hamlet* in London. You are the greatest."

"In that case, let's have a drink, and you can tell me what a marvelous actor I am. I like to be introduced as America's foremost actor. It saves the necessity of further effort. You will also tell me your dreams, your hopes, for a career in the theater."

"I'd be honored to share my meager goals," Larry said.

"Don't be so modest," Barrymore said, as he started to undress. "Take off all your clothes. I insist young actors do that. That way, when they talk to me they tend to tell the truth and not embellish. Without clothes, one must tell the naked truth. Don't you agree?"

"I have never considered that before," Larry said, removing his shirt and then unbuttoning his trousers. "I'm willing to see if that is the case."

"Good, we'll get naked together and perhaps have a libation. Drink always tastes better in the bright noonday sun of California instead of past midnight when you've had so much you can't feel it. Don't you agree?"

"I agree with everything you say, Mr. Barrymore," Larry said.

After removing his trousers, Barrymore said, "I'd offer you my cock, but I don't think I can get a rise out of it today. You see, I started drinking at six o'clock this morning."

That evening, Larry dined out on his second encounter with Barrymore.

The next week Jill

(top photo) Jill Esmond in 1931
(lower photos) Ricardo Cortez *(left)* and
Helen Twelvetrees

137

showed Larry the script of her next gig. Larry read it, finding it a star vehicle for Helen Twelvetrees, with whom Jill would appear again. The film was called *Is My Face Red?*, and it was released in 1932.

Both Twelvetrees and Jill were cast opposite the dashing Ricardo Cortez, who came on strong to Jill. "I have a husband who takes care of all my needs," Jill lied to Cortez.

Until she learned better, Jill thought Cortez was Mexican. He was actually a Viennese Jew who grew up in New York. He'd come to Hollywood to replace Rudolph Valentino, and the studio decided to change his name from Jacob Krantz to Ricardo Cortez and promote him as a Latin lover.

When Jill met him, he was recovering from the death of his wife, the silent film actress, Alma Rubens. Cortez had already starred as Sam Spade in the

1931 version of *The Maltese Falcon*. The actor had been billed over Greta Garbo when they'd been cast in *Torrent* (1926).

As for Twelvetrees, Jill later told Larry that "Helen has the saddest eyes I've ever seen on a woman. Her psyche is so fragile you fear it won't make it through the night." Jill almost predicted the star's death by suicide on February 13, 1958, following an overdose on drugs.

Before that, in 1949, when Larry was directing the London stage version of *A Streetcar Named Desire*, Jill suggested that he cast Twelvetrees as Blanche DuBois. Larry turned Jill's suggestion down, casting Vivien Leigh into the role instead.

After the release of all these movies starring Jill, some people at other studios began referring to Larry as "Mr. Esmond."

To put an added burden on their careers and married life, Eva Moore also arrived in Hollywood. She'd contracted to play character roles in MGM's *But the Flesh Is Weak* and in Universal's *The Old Dark House*, both released in 1932.

(top photo) Larry's mother-in-law, Eva Moore, a player in *The Old Dark House*

Eva had come to Hollywood to play the supporting role of Lady Florence Ridgway in *But the Flesh Is Weak*, a comedy/drama by Ivor Novello, who had also written the original play. His film had an all-star cast of Robert Montgomery, Nora Gregor, Edward Everett Horton, C. Aubrey Smith, and Nils Asther. It was the story of a father and son who live on the generosity of rich women.

Eva and Novello had remained friends after her daughter's marriage to Larry. She'd obviously known about her son-in-law's involvement with Novello before his marriage, because some of that affair had been conducted at her country home in Berkshire.

It is not known if Eva knew that Larry had reclined on the casting couch of James Whale, who had cast Eva in her upcoming film, *The Old Dark House*. Like her previous picture, *The Old Dark House* also had an all-star cast that included Boris Karloff, Melvyn Douglas, Charles Laughton, Lilian Bond, Raymond Massey, and Gloria Stuart. This sinister movie foreshadowed Whale's even more bizarrely camp, *Bride of Frankenstein*. "In my role I rant about laughter and sin," Eva told Larry.

The Old Dark House is significant in that it marked Laughton's first American film. Larry visited Eva on the set and asked Whale if he could also visit Laughton in his dressing room. Larry didn't want to knock, unannounced, on Laughton's door without having cleared it with the star in advance.

Whale agreed to check with Laughton, but returned shortly and told him that Laughton had scribbled a note to Larry.

"Sorry, old chap," Laughton wrote, "it's always good to talk to a fellow Britisher, but I'm too busy learning my lines."

"I can entertain you in my bungalow," Whale said.

"Sorry, old chap," Larry said, imitating Laughton, "but I've got to get back to my own set."

***

One of Larry's favorite film stars in silent pictures was Pola Negri. She was famous for her "staged" romances with Charlie Chaplin and Rudolph Valentino, but privately she also sought women out as well for romantic liaisons.

Negri wanted Larry to be her leading man in a picture later entitled *A Woman Commands*. He was called to record a

Two views of Pola Negri
(lower photo) as Queen Draga in
A Woman Commands

139

screen test with Negri, who was trying to regain the popularity she had previously enjoyed in silents, but finding it a losing battle.

After his brief exposure to her, he changed his opinion of her and vowed "never to see another Pola Negri movie—not that I think there will be many of those," he told Fairbanks.

"She was a carnivore," Larry claimed. "When we did our love scene together, she secretly fondled my genitals. I'd never seen a professional actress pull such a stunt. She's a real ham on camera, still acting in that exaggerated silent screen manner. Not only that, but she's fat. Her days as a sex siren on the screen are over. Negri convinced me that I'll never be able to work with one of those so-called vamps of the silent screen."

Unknown to Larry, Gloria Swanson was lurking in his immediate future.

In this film, Negri was cast as Queen Draga, the late 19th-century wife of King Alexander of Serbia. Larry was commissioned for the role of the queen's lover and conspirator to the throne. In a final scene, he was to be tossed out a window, clinging to the sill until his fingers where crushed with rifle butts.

By three o'clock that afternoon, he was running a high fever and fainted on the set. The studio doctor came to see him and ordered an ambulance. In the hospital, it was discovered that he had yellow jaundice. He would not be released for five weeks and had to notify Negri that he was off the picture.

Basil Rathbone replaced Larry in *A Woman Commands*. Negri found Rathbone too stiff and unromantic, and was saddened by the loss of Larry.

During his confinement in the hospital, Fairbanks visited Larry's bedside at least three times a week, bringing Crawford on occasion. Sometimes Jill would skip a whole week without a visit.

While in the hospital, Larry read an item in the press, claiming that he had come to Hollywood "in the hopes of knocking Ronald Colman off his perch as England's champion movie leading man." Larry wrote Colman a note to apologize.

Colman responded with a phone call welcoming Larry to Hollywood and calling him "old boy." After Larry was released from the hospital, Colman invited Larry, along with Jill, to meet his wife Benita.

The tradition continued for years, Jill being eventually replaced by Vivien Leigh who arrived on Larry's arm for these intimate dinners between two English couples.

Larry knew some of the British actors working in Hollywood in the early 1930s. "They kept me from being homesick," he said. "Almost every last one of them was anti-Semitic but they sucked up to the Jewish studio heads, including Louis B. Mayer who was a vile creature."

Larry formed a major bond with Colman, but he also socialized with Hollywood's growing British colony, many of whom he already knew from theatrical circles in England. Some of the more prominent members included Herbert Marshall, Nigel Bruce, Cedric Hardwicke, Ray Milland, Claude Rains, Cary Grant, C. Aubrey Smith, and even George Arliss, the aristocratic star who gave voice to *Disraeli* (1929).

Larry's affair with Fairbanks continued after his health improved, and Larry did not feel as lonely once he'd formed relationships with his fellow countrymen. As a wife, Jill remained respectful and even kind to him, but she was not really a spouse, at least in the traditional sense.

Perhaps to bring her marriage more into focus, she suggested a brief vacation with him on Catalina Island. There she felt "we can be locked away from Hollywood and the rest of the world."

On the island, Larry rented a speed boat, which Jill demanded that he drive at full throttle.

At night they retired early and slept together. As Larry later revealed to his friends, including Fairbanks, "we kissed and fondled," but apparently there was no penetration.

One night while dining at a seafood restaurant, they met a young homosexual filmmaker, who was doing location shooting on Catalina. Larry conceived of an idea which met with Jill's approval.

For two hundred dollars, he asked the filmmaker to shoot footage of him naked. "I want to be filmed walking, sitting down, running, diving, whatever. Directors have complained that I'm too stiff on the screen. I want to be completely free of clothing so I can carefully observe my body movements in all sorts of positions. I think seeing how I perform naked will somehow liberate me."

It is not known who the cameraman was or what

Dropping trou: Two views of Larry, nude, in California early to mid-1930s

became of the footage, although it is rumored to have been purchased by a wealthy collector in Santa Barbara who had fallen in love with a picture of Larry.

***

After his brief vacation, Larry returned to Hollywood, where he learned that he'd been cast as a lead in *The Yellow Ticket*, a heavy-handed Czarist melodrama. The story line of *The Yellow Ticket* ever so slightly evoked the opera *Tosca*.

The picture was a tired recycle. Not only had it been a play but it had been brought to the screen twice—first in 1916 with Clara Kimball Young and later in 1918 with Fannie Ward.

Larry played a British journalist who goes to 1913 Russia to write about social conditions. Once there he meets and falls in love with Elissa Landi, playing a Jewish girl victimized by the secret police. The role of the Czarist secret police chief was interpreted by a lustful Lionel Barrymore.

In England, the play had been called *The Yellow Passport* and had starred John Barrymore. Now Lionel had assumed his younger brother's role.

Larry was lent by RKO to Fox to play the English journalist entangled with Landi.

In spite of their aborted fling in London, Larry referred to Landi as "my sweet friend." Apparently, he wasn't jealous of the attention she was paying to his wife.

However, Larry told Fairbanks that there was no mention ever made of Jill when he talked to Landi. "But I knew what was going on between those two," he claimed.

William Pratt
(aka Boris Karloff)

Jill was about to suffer a loss on two fronts. She would not only lose Landi but also a coveted role to an actress about to arrive in Hollywood from New York. Her name was Katharine Hepburn.

A strong director, Raoul Walsh, helmed Larry through *The Yellow Ticket*. Reportedly, he detested Larry and wanted to send him back to England. He favored co-stars Barrymore and Landi.

Walsh wore a patch over his eye, claiming that an "errant jackrabbit" jumped through his windshield as he was driving his car in the desert.

142

"Walsh's main direction to me was to have makeup apply large dabs of Brilliantine," Larry said.

Larry came up and shook the hand of actor William Pratt. "How do you like Hollywood, old boy?" Larry asked him.

"I'm going to stick around for a while," he said. "And, do you mind, it's not William Pratt. I've changed it to Boris Karloff."

"Yes, Eva told me that when I visited the set of *The Old Dark House* to see my mother-in-law," Larry said. "Sorry I didn't encounter you that day."

Karloff's career would get the blast-off in 1931 when James Whale cast him as "the monster" in Universal's production of *Frankenstein.*

The Yellow Ticket produced disappointing results at the box office. *Photoplay* defined the melodrama as "moth eaten." Critics had only faint praise for Lionel Barrymore and Elissa Landi. Larry's performance was slammed by reviewers.

***

Back in Hollywood, Larry had high hopes for his third picture, which he hoped would make Hollywood forget about his first two screen failures. He was cast in *Westward Passage*, scheduled for a 1932 release, and he was teamed with the beautiful, elegant, and very blonde Ann Harding.

In *Westward Passage*, Larry played "a selfish, self-centered, conceited, egotistical, and brash character," which did little to advance his film career. The plot involved a failed marriage between a noble but naïve young woman and an impoverished writer. They divorce, she remarries, and decades later, during a chance reunion, they fall in love again. Larry later claimed, "Ann taught me more about movie making than any director. She really promoted me. Although she's a fine looking lady, I think she's the type who would be more interested in Jill than me. I don't have the right equipment. Not for dear angelic Ann. Although she usually appeared on screen as a prim and proper lady, she had a wicked sense of humor. When I asked her if she were a true blonde, she said she'd prove it to me

(top photo) Ann Harding
(bottom) ZaSu Pitts

143

if she knew me better."

The Russia-born director, Robert Milton, had previously directed *Outward Bound* (1930). Its plot, an allegory involving suicide, love, and death, had been inspired by Sutton Vane's 1923 play about illicit lovers who had each, at earlier points in their lives, attempted suicide, and who now find themselves as passengers aboard a mysterious ocean liner sailing in a fog, without lights or a crew, to an unknown destination.

One day during lunch with Larry, Milton told him that he should try to get cast with Bette Davis, a graduate of his acting school in New York. "She's going to become the queen of Hollywood. You could become her king."

"I'll think about it," Larry said.

(top photo) Raoul Walsh
(lower photo) Robert
Montgomery in the 1930s

He enjoyed working with the character actress ZaSu Pitts, and got to meet "a star of tomorrow" Bonita Granville, who played a nine-year-old in the film. Granville said, "I was the only one in the cast who got his name right. I called him O-liv-ee-ay. Everyone else called him Larry Oliver."

When *Westward Passage* opened in 1932, it bombed, costing RKO $250,000. Larry had become *persona non grata* at the studio.

Near the end of his life, Larry was asked if Hollywood had made a mistake in failing to recognize his acting genius in the early 1930s.

"Not at all," he said. "I was a twerp."

After a wrap was called on *Westward Passage*, Larry flew to Mexico, where he hooked up with his "Douggie," as he continued to call Fairbanks, and Robert Montgomery. They were on a fishing holiday, and Larry wanted to join them.

At the Ensenada Airport, Larry was arrested by two Mexican policemen who put him in jail when he could not come up with a 1,000 peso fine. Five hours later Fairbanks appeared with Montgomery, explaining it was all a practical joke.

The charge was that he did not have a proper Mexican visa to enter the country. Actually, the arresting officers were right in holding him. He'd left Hollywood so quickly he hadn't done the border-crossing paperwork.

Montgomery and Larry bonded at first until they got to know each other. Since Larry wanted to be alone with Fairbanks, he began to resent Montgomery's intrusion as an unwanted third party.

On their small fishing craft, Larry and Fairbanks shared a small cabin, with Montgomery taking an even smaller cabin next to them. At night Fairbanks and Larry, though often drunk, had to keep the noise level down so Montgomery wouldn't hear what they were doing.

Details are sparse but apparently one night Montgomery accidentally discovered them making love. A homophobe, he denounced them as faggots.

He ordered the two-member Mexican crew to take him back to shore. Back in Hollywood, he spread the news, and word traveled quickly along the grapevine. Soon *tout* Hollywood was talking about Fairbanks and Larry.

In those days, the Hollywood press did not print such accusations, but opinions about Fairbanks changed quickly. Before Montgomery spread his story, Fairbanks had been known as a womanizing actor in pursuit of beautiful women. Now Hollywood gossip claimed he also pursued beautiful men such as Larry.

When the director Raoul Walsh heard the rumor, he said, "My God, what do you expect? He's an Englishman. They all do that, or at least talk, walk, and act like they do."

When a woman at a party confronted Crawford about her husband's infidelity and his possible bisexuality, the actress said, "You think I give a rat's piss about that? Get out of my way."

***

Back in Hollywood, when Fairbanks invited both Jill and Larry to dinner, he talked mostly about the break-up of his relationship with Crawford, but he also sensed their dismay about their Hollywood careers.

"Frankly, I think Larry was jealous of Jill in those days," Fairbanks later recalled. "Not that her career was creating brush fires, but she was better known. Let's face it: Actors and actresses who marry each other can expect jealousy. Billie and I were jealous of each other's careers." He was referring, of course, to Crawford. Putting in a dig, he said, "Of course, she was lying down on more casting couches than I was."

Although both Jill and Larry were on RKO's payroll, there were long weeks when neither of them had anything to do but go to Hollywood parties and enjoy secret affairs on the side. Offers came in for Larry for roles on the London stage, but because of his contractual obligations to RKO, he was forced to ignore them.

"Let's face it," Jill told him during the Christmas season of 1931, "the year was a total failure."

"We're wasting our time in Hollywood, and I want out," Larry said. "The only thing worth sticking around for is Douggie."

When Larry asked her to return to London with him to save their marriage, he realized that Jill was still dreaming of a movie career. "I gave up a most promising career on the stage in the West End to come to Hollywood with you. It was a big sacrifice for me. Now I'm asking you to make a sacrifice for me. Come back to London."

She adamantly told him that she planned to remain in Hollywood. Rumor had it that David O. Selznick was going to cast her as Sydney Fairfield in the successful hit, *A Bill of Divorcement*. "This is the role that will make me a star."

Larry's former producer, Basil Dean, had produced *A Bill of Divorcement* as a play in London where it was a big hit. Jill felt the part "almost belongs to me," and she was eager to work again with its male star, John Barrymore.

Other stars also wanted the part, including Norma Shearer, hoping to get released from MGM. Irene Dunne coveted the role, as did the former child star, Anita Louise.

But when at last the call came in from Selznick's office, it was not for Jill but for Larry.

When Selznick worked at Paramount, he had turned thumbs down on Jill and Larry, but after he migrated to RKO to beef up their sagging finances, he appeared ready to take a second look at Jill.

Myron Selznick, brother of David O. Selznick, became Jill's movie agent. Such a profession hardly existed at the time. He also agreed to be Larry's agent as well, although he got no work for his new client.

Myron was delegated with the unhappy responsibility of telling Larry that RKO did not plan to renew his contract. So the day that Larry went to David's office, he was already in the know about what fate had befallen him.

Larry asked Myron if any other studios were interested in signing him. "Paramount showed some interest in New York."

"I hate to be blunt, but no other studio wants you," Myron said. "A guy over at Paramount told me that the best way to lose

(left figure) Producer David O. Selznick and his brother Myron

146

money was to put Olivier in a film."

"I see," Larry said. "They want my wife, perhaps, but not her husband. Well, tell them to go fuck themselves. I don't need them. I want to return to London anyway."

David Selznick's office requested that Larry come in at three in the afternoon for a chat. He dreaded this confrontation, as he had already learned from Myron what was about to happen to him.

Getting fired during the Depression of the early 1930s was painful. Even stars who were retained had to accept severe pay cuts. Myron had told Jill that she'd be offered a seven-year contract at $750 per week, a cut from her previous salary. For Larry, there was the unemployment line.

When Larry arrived at Selznick's office, the producer was late. What happened next is the matter of some dispute. Larry later claimed that the secretary allowed him to wait inside Selznick's office, something against the producer's policy.

While waiting for David Selznick, Larry said he'd done some snooping and discovered a projected contract that would sign Katharine Hepburn at $1,500 a week, twice what he planned to pay Jill for renewing her contract. Larry had heard a rumor that George Cukor was lobbying to have Hepburn star in *A Bill of Divorcement*.

When Selznick came into the office, he lectured Larry on how disappointed RKO was with his film work. "Your wife has a chance to become a star, and perhaps you do too. But you've got to give it more. You're a mannequin on the screen. When Schertzinger told you to tone down your stage mannerisms, he didn't mean for you to become a zombie."

Selznick had two reasons to meet with Larry. First, he wanted to deliver the bombshell that Larry's contract would not be renewed. He also wanted to talk over the implications of Jill signing a seven-year contract with RKO.

Selznick wondered if Jill signing that long-term contract would doom Larry's marriage. The producer had called his brother, Myron, to express his concerns about Larry and Jill. With no firm deal yet set for Jill, Selznick dismissed Larry. "We have no more pictures for you at RKO," he told him before taking a call from Louis B. Mayer.

Katharine Hepburn and David Manners in *A Bill of Divorcement*

Crestfallen, Larry left Selznick's office and made his way off the RKO lot. Years later Larry recalled, "I felt like Norman Maine in *A Star Is Born*. My star was falling as Jill's was rising."

That night Larry told an angry Jill that "Selznick is just toying with you. He plans to give the role to Katharine Hepburn. I have already seen the signed contract. She's got the Sydney role in *A Bill of Divorcement*."

"I don't believe you," Jill told him. "You're doing that to deliberately sabotage my film career. You don't want me to become a bigger star than you. Your male ego can't stand for that."

He barged out of the house, not able to listen to any more of her allegations.

Jill may have been right. Apparently, Larry had lied to her. He could not have seen such a contract between Selznick and Hepburn at the end of 1931. Hepburn did not sign for *A Bill of Divorcement* until the summer of 1932.

Both Larry and Jill were back in London when they heard that Hepburn had been cast in the role of Sydney, launching herself into one of the screen's greatest careers.

Eva blamed Larry for her daughter's failure in Hollywood.

It appears in hindsight that Larry did deliberately attempt to sabotage Jill's chance to play the lead in *A Bill of Divorcement*. On the other hand, Jill probably would not have gotten the role anyway, considering Cukor's powerful pushing of Hepburn with Selznick.

Larry faced a moment of truth in December 23, 1931, in downtown Los Angeles while he was doing some Christmas shopping. He went alone to see *King Lear* performed by the visiting Stratford-upon-Avon Festival Troupe, starring Randle Ayrton.

Later that night Larry told Fairbanks, "I want to go back on the stage. I want to become the greatest actor of all time. When they write the history of acting in England, David Garrick's name will appear, of course. But so will that of Laurence Olivier. That's Laurence with a U."

CHAPTER FIVE

As 1932 deepened, Jill Esmond finally capitulated and agreed with Larry that David O. Selznick had shifted his interest onto Katharine Hepburn, not her. As Larry put it, "Jill decided to plump for wifely rather than artistic duties."

Both of them reflected on their failed careers in Hollywood as the *Santa Fe* train crossed the great American plain to Chicago. There they transferred to the *Twentieth Century* for the final overland lap into New York.

Work awaited them, a film role for Jill at UFA in Berlin and a co-starring role with the fast-fading Gloria Swanson for Larry in London.

Larry was not to make another movie in Hollywood until *Wuthering Heights* in 1939, although there would be one more failed attempt to become a Hollywood star before that.

In New York, Jill and Larry stood on the deck of their ship, the *Bremen,* watching the spectacular arrival of Joan Crawford and Douglas Fairbanks Jr., their sailing partners. Mayor Jimmy Walker had commissioned eight motorcycle policemen to escort them to the pier, where at least three hundred fans mobbed them.

Crawford made a startling statement in that it was so public, but the world was a lot more naïve then. "The idea that we should travel together was hatched by Douglas and Larry. Looking back, I think they were both men who loved women, but the full-time company of just women didn't seem to satisfy them. They enjoyed the friendship of other men and the physical activity."

The marriage between Crawford and her handsome young husband was almost over.

Jill stayed in Crawford's stateroom, whereas Fairbanks "bunked" (as he called it) with Larry. However, the two couples dined together at night, creating much interest among the fellow passengers.

Louis B. Mayer had urged Crawford and Fairbanks to take the trip abroad, the press hailing it as a "second honeymoon." It was anything but. Mayer's real reason to bring the couple together was to separate Crawford from her growing romantic attachment to Clark Gable.

One drunken night when Crawford stood with Larry on the bridge, she confessed that, "I can't conceive of my life without Clark. But he's tied down right now. It may be a long time before he's free. We have no other choice but to engage in a drawn-out, dangerous affair." Before she kissed Larry good night, she thanked him for taking care of her husband's sexual needs while at sea.

"Perhaps I should thank you for handling Jill so very well," he said.

To deflect the press from suggesting any involvement with Jill, Crawford later referred to her first trip abroad sailing with Larry and Jill. "She would not have been my choice of companion," Crawford said. "She seemed unfriendly to me. Maybe I seemed unfriendly to her."

(upper photo) Crawford and Gable in love
(lower photos) high-drama Olivier
vs. high-drama Crawford. Who's the greater thesp?

"Esmond and I had two romantic, passionate relationships with two gorgeous men," Crawford claimed. "Those two were quite a duo."

Even though Crawford had not mastered the King's English yet, she was also trying to learn Spanish and French—and failing miserably.

Larry never became overly fond of Crawford. "She was always on, always performing," he said. "She wouldn't even play ping-pong on the afterdeck with us. 'My nails, darling,' she said. 'My nails. I must protect them at all cost.'"

"It was during our cruise east that Larry developed the greatest impersonation act of Billie before or after," Fairbanks said. "Most impersonators go for the obvious—Bette Davis, Mae West, or Marlene Dietrich, never Joan Crawford. But Larry had her mannerisms and speech down perfect. He never per-

150

formed in front of Billie, but he was the toast at certain London parties impersonating Billie, especially her appearance as Sadie Thompson in *Rain*."

"On our final day at sea, we were standing on the upper deck—Jill, Larry, Billie, and myself," Fairbanks said. "It was about nine in the evening. The northern lights were still pinkish. It was Larry who shouted, 'Look, it's dear little England! It's home.' I turned to embrace him and found tears streaming down his cheeks."

As the *Bremen* arrived in Southampton, Noël Coward was on hand to take Larry, Jill, Crawford, and Fairbanks to London, and to fill them in on the latest London gossip. He also wanted to hear "everything about Hollywood that's unfit to print."

Jill and Larry visited Fairbanks and Crawford at their suite at the old Berkeley Hotel in London. But throughout most of their stay, "Hollywood's most romantic couple" was fully engaged making personal appearances.

Fans reached a point of hysteria when Coward accompanied Crawford and Fairbanks to his hit show, *Calvalcade*, which was playing in the Theatre Royal, Drury Lane. On the way into the theater, Crawford's coat was pulled off her back.

Bobbies carried Crawford into the theater. When she and Fairbanks appeared within the Royal Box, the entire audience rose to applaud. "I felt like the Queen of England," she later told Larry.

Back in London, Larry's friends pretended they hadn't had an opportunity to see his Hollywood films. Actually, most of them had seen them but didn't want to criticize Larry. His enemies had viewed them, however, and many of them had filed devastating critiques in the newspapers.

When Eva Moore finally arrived back in England from her own stint in Hollywood, she said, right in front of Larry, "Oh, Jill, darling, you can act Larry right off the screen. The camera loves you." When she turned to Larry, she told him, "You look so thin on the screen. Now that you're back in England, you should eat more roast beef and Yorkshire pudding."

(upper photo) Ivor Novello

(lower photo) America's sweethearts, Joan Crawford with Douglas Fairbanks, Jr.

Jill stayed with Eva in Berkshire, but Larry slipped off to join Ivor Novello at Redroofs, his countryside home near Maidenhead. Crawford and Fairbanks were the guests of honor. Novello asked Larry to share his boudoir and had arranged for Fairbanks and Crawford to share the master bedroom. Privately, Fairbanks asked for a separate room. "No need, old boy," Novello said. "For company, you can join Larry and me."

The following week, Coward invited Fairbanks and Crawford to his rambling house, Goldenhurst, in Kent. Larry and Jill were also invited. Jill turned down the invitation, which pleased Coward, who got to sleep with Larry.

When Crawford and Fairbanks returned to Hollywood, she told pals such as William Haines, "The Olivier/Esmond marriage is all but over." Oddly enough, that was what Jill and Larry said about them.

After the excitement of the Crawford/Fairbanks visit to London, Larry went with Jill to see the opening of *Thirteen Women* (1932), a psychological thriller Jill had made for David O. Selznick before leaving Hollywood. Today, the film is viewed as a "cult classic."

It had an all-star cast led by Myrna Loy, Florence Eldridge, Irene Dunne, and Ricardo Cortez, with whom Jill had already made a film. George Archainbaud, who had directed Jill in *State's Attorney*, had been assigned to helm the project. This odd precode Hollywood movie plays out today like a harbinger of the slasher films of the 1970s. Incidentally, Myrna Loy is the murderous fiend, Dunne the "scream queen."

The film achieved notoriety when one of the supporting players, Peg Entwistle, committed suicide two days after the film's release. She jumped off the Hollywood

MEANWHILE, AS REGARDS *JILL'S* DRAMAS IN HOLLYWOOD.....
(photos, left, top to bottom)
1. Trailer poster for *Thirteen Women*
2 Peg Entwistle and   3. the site of her suicide
4. *Thirteen Women*'s star, Myrna Loy, and one of its supporting players   5. Jill Esmond,

sign on Mount Lee in Los Angeles, a sign which at the time spelled "Hollywoodland." Her death became a legend that has grown in fame and symbolism over the years.

Although Larry had nothing but praise for Jill's role in *Thirteen Women*, he privately told Coward and others, "Jill lacks a certain magic on the screen. So do I, of course. I really think the kind of movie stardom she's dreaming of will elude her."

Jill's own son, Tarquinn Olivier, in years to come, would point out both her good qualities and her flaws on the screen. "She had a well-modulated voice," he said, "a fine well-bred face, but she still moved in a roly-poly way and lacked elegance."

In spite of his many other sexual and emotional involvements, Larry managed to see Glen Byam Shaw any chance he got. As for Shaw, absence had indeed made his heart grow fonder for Larry. Shaw claimed that his marriage to Angela Baddeley is "just not enough. Something is always missing, and you are the missing part."

Larry was flattered by Shaw's attention, and continued to be sucked into his world. At no point, according to friends, did Larry feel that he was "really, really in love with Glen." He admitted to Blakelock, however, that he enjoyed sex with Shaw.

"As personalities, we are very compatible," Larry said. "Even though I enjoy his devotion and his love-making, I will await the day when our relationship will segué from an affair into an enduring friendship. He shares his dreams with me. Instead of being an actor, he wants to direct."

That dream would come true. Between 1957 and 1959, Shaw was the director of the Shakespeare Memorial Theatre in Stratford-upon-Avon, among many other director roles.

On the night before he was scheduled to meet Gloria Swanson, Larry was warned by Shaw, "I had my Tallulah Bankhead. Now you must face an even more devouring creature. There's good reason she's known as the Wicked Witch of the West."

***

When Eva heard that Larry had signed to appear opposite Gloria Swanson in *Perfect Understanding*, she said, "The poor creature, a no-neck monster. She moves in front of the camera like it was 1924 and she's doing pantomime for retards. Her voice is monotonic. She will only embarrass herself in talking pictures. Good luck with *that one*."

When Larry first encountered Swanson, he came face to face with a woman in crisis. After the failure of her recent talkies, Joseph Schenck had

cancelled her contract. Because of her marriage to Michael Farmer, a British citizen, she became a U.K. citizen by marriage. Legally she could form a film production company in England.

Originally she wanted Farmer to star opposite her in *Perfect Understanding*, but he tested so wooden in front of the camera that the film's director, Cyril Gardner, advised her to drop him. Swanson insisted that he remain in the picture but in a minor role.

She was also having marital troubles. In August of 1931, she'd married Farmer, although her divorce from James Henri La Bailly de la Falaise, the Marquis de la Coudraye, had not been completely finalized, making the actress a bigamist. She was forced to remarry Farmer legally later on when she was already four months pregnant with Michelle Bridget Farmer, who was born in 1932.

Noël Coward, who had had a brief homosexual fling with Farmer, had introduced Swanson to her next husband.

"I talk to Cyril, but I can't abide facing him," Swanson said. Gardner's face had been disfigured by a skin infection, and he was forced to switch from acting in films to directing them."

Michael Powell, Swanson's co-writer, would go on to greater glory as a director (*49th Parallel*, *The Red Shoes*).

At first Larry had high hopes for the movie, bragging to Eva, "This film is going to make me the biggest star in cinema." He also claimed that Swanson planned to make him her screen lover in a number of romantic movies. "She told me we're going to become a screen team, and millions of fans will flock to see my handsome face and her classic beauty and chic couture."

Assuming that movie stardom was around

the corner, Larry and Jill moved to a house on fashionable Cheyne Walk in Chelsea, overlooking the Thames. Artists J.M. W. Turner and James McNeill Whistler had each previously lived in the house. Jill later told friends, "All Larry does is talk about movie stardom and Gloria Swanson. He's always been contemptuous of movie acting before. I think he's fallen under Swanson's spell and been bitten by the Hollywood bug."

Swanson was thirty-three when she came together with Larry, who was only twenty-five. He looked so young in his test with Swanson that she insisted that he sport a mustache, even a fake one.

Also cast in *Perfect Understanding* was Nora Swinburne, Larry's friend. She was an acute observer of what was going on behind the scenes during the filming. She later claimed that Farmer was "pathologically jealous of Larry. He hawk-eyed Larry and Gloria at every turn, and became filled with rage when they had an intimate scene together. Perhaps to seek revenge, Gloria seduced Larry one afternoon when Farmer had to go to a doctor because of a big sore that had appeared on his penis. He accused Gloria in front of everybody of giving him syphilis but that turned out not to be the case."

It was during a sexual tryst with Swanson that Larry, when fondling her breast, discovered a lump. At least that's what she told the director, Cyril Gardner. She also said she'd have to have it removed "but I can't face that right now." She later did have the lump removed, and it turned out to be benign.

Soon after the cast and film crew moved to Cannes for location shooting, Larry was involved in an automobile accident, which meant he had to spend three days in a French court before he was finally cleared.

When the money ran out, Larry recalled that Swanson had to sell her stock in United Artists for $200,000 to finish the picture.

The weak plot concerned a couple from British high society who endure various, relatively meaningless perils before arriving at the film's happy ending. The proceedings were arch, the plot (co-written by Swanson herself) soapy.

On the day *Perfect Understanding* opened in the United States, Franklin D. Roosevelt had, in response to a nationwide fiscal crisis, declared an emergency bank holiday. The movie's New York premiere produced an audience of ten people, mostly loyal Swanson fans who remembered her from her screen vamp days in the 20s. Farmer's "petrified" performance in front of the camera only hastened the end of her marriage.

After a critic from *Variety* sat through *Perfect Understanding*, he commented on Larry's rail-thin physique. "When Olivier removes his shirt in the bright light of Cannes, he shrinks sadly in romantic suggestion and never quite recovers the glamor."

After Swanson made a triumphant comeback in the 1950 film *Sunset Blvd.*, Larry saw her interpretation of Norma Desmond. He said, "William Holden was far luckier than I was. Swanson and I once made a film together. It was called *Perfect Understanding*. Misunderstanding would have been the better title. It was, in fact, the worst film ever made."

When Larry invited Glen Byam Shaw to see *Perfect Understanding*, his lover told him, "The characters could have been based on you and Jill. You two seem to have a perfect understanding to pursue romance outside of marriage. Speaking of that, I wouldn't mind some romance from you this very afternoon."

"Curtain going up," Larry said.

***

In Berlin, Jill had been cast in the English-language version of *F.P.1*, the plot concerning a permanent air station floating in the middle of the Atlantic Ocean. The script was science fiction, created after Charles Lindbergh's transatlantic flight to Paris. It was written by Curt Siodmak, best known as the creator of *The Wolf Man*. Jill found the plot riddled with holes but was glad for the paycheck.

The star of the movie was Conrad Veidt, who had befriended Larry during his own Berlin film work and had gone on vacation with him. Jill was eager to learn from Veidt what Larry had been up to at the time, but Veidt remained discreet and told her nothing.

The German-language version of *F.P.1* was Peter Lorre's last film in Berlin before WWII. He would later go to America and greater glory.

In Berlin, Jill met Greta Keller, at the time, one of Germany's most

Peter Lorre

sought-after cabaret singers, who had also befriended Larry when he had worked in Berlin for UFA.

One night, between acts in a cabaret, a slightly drunken Jill confessed to Greta that she'd never been penetrated, either by her husband or by any other man. She claimed that Larry had attempted penetration, but she'd screamed in pain.

Suggesting to her that something was seriously wrong, Greta set up an appointment for her to visit a urologist and sex expert in Berlin. Ironically, Greta had been with Larry when he discovered he had problems with what he called

156

"my sexual plumbing."

After a two-hour visit, Jill reported to Greta on the doctor's theories about her frigidity. The German doctor discovered she was suffering *vaginismus*, a conditioned reflex of the pubococcygeus muscle, causing the muscles in the vagina to tense suddenly, making vaginal penetration during sexual intercourse extremely difficult if not impossible, and incredibly painful.

The doctor told Jill that he suspected that Jill's *vaginismus* was the result of some early trauma in life. He pointedly asked her if any man had ever attempted to rape her. She denied it. But he suggested she may have some form of repressed memory and that she should visit a psychiatrist colleague of his in London.

Jill wrote down the name of the psychiatrist. But once back in London, she could not tolerate the idea of going to a psychiatrist to talk over such a personal matter. She decided to postpone a visit, promising herself every week that she was going to call and make an appointment. But the weeks drifted by and she took no action.

***

After Larry's new home with Jill on Cheyne Walk had been redecorated, he invited Coward for dinner. Coward was later to mock the décor as "Hollywood-on-the-Thames." He also told others that "Larry has delusions of grandeur."

Larry told him that a "sweet old puss" had placed tapestries on the walls and hung massive white silk curtains, with lots of fluffy pillows—some of them heart-shaped—on the sofas, which were covered in flowery cabbage rose patterns.

After dinner, Jill said she had to retire early and invited Coward up to look at their seven-foot-wide bed, which was positioned beneath a skylight. The room had once been used as James Whistler's studio. Coward was later shown Larry's smaller bedroom, which was actually a guest room.

Returning to the downstairs area, Larry invited Coward out to his little private courtyard for a chat. Once there, he told Coward that he and Jill had spent all their savings on purchasing and redecorating the house. "I need money," Larry said.

Coward came up with a solution. Gertrude Lawrence had been looking for a leading man to appear with her in a romantic sex comedy on film called *No Funny Business*. "Both Gertie and I agree you'd be perfect for the juvenile male lead, dear boy," Coward said.

"Who do I have to sleep with to get the part?" Larry asked.

"Never ask the obvious," Coward said.

It can be assumed that Jill's seven-foot-wide bed in Chelsea remained empty while Larry cavorted around the West End, with continuing male-on-male affairs with Coward, Shaw, and the odd homosexual encounter here and there.

In *No Funny Business* (1933), both Larry and Jill played supporting roles within the orbit of the great Gertrude Lawrence in this United Artists-British Picture film. Both John Stafford and Victor Hanbury were co-directors in this stagy farce, which was later reviewed as an inferior imitation of something that might have been better written by Noël Coward.

No Funny Business would be the only film Larry ever made with Jill, but he made no comment about it in either of his autobiographies. Both Jill and Larry played employees of an agency which provided professional co-respondents (supposedly, someone who has been sexually intimate with one of the members of a collapsing marriage) for couples wanting a divorce. Unknown to each other, both are sent to the Cote d'Azur as co-respondents, respectfully, for Yvonne (Gertrude Lawrence) and Edward Kane (Edmond Breon). *The New York Times* suggested that *No Funny Business* deserved some sort of booby prize.

During the filming, Larry told Shaw, "It's one of my fucky-fuck roles. Noël should sue for plagiarism. It's a rip-off of *Private Lives*."

After working with Jill and Larry on *No Funny Business*, Victor Hanbury, the co-director said, "I felt their marriage would not make it through 1933. They were very competitive on the set, each one trying to out-act the other. There was a lot of clenched teeth spatting. Larry went through the movie like an unruly school boy. He was still contemptuous of film acting, whereas Jill

Gertrude Lawrence

was giving it her all. She had many open battles with Larry, at one point accusing him of upstaging her."

"You ruined my chance in Hollywood," she shouted one afternoon at Larry in front of the crew. "Now you're trying to fuck up this picture for me."

Larry took Shaw, who still called him "my beloved," to a screening of *No Funny Business*. Shaw later recalled, "Larry cried after seeing himself on the screen. 'I'm just a vapid foil for Gertie,' he told me."

Some reviewers noted that Larry and Jill, though married, showed no on-screen chemistry in their scenes together.

"Gertie" Lawrence might have left a greater

158

screen legacy had she accepted the tentative offer to play Margo Channing in the 1950 *All About Eve* after Claudette Colbert was forced to withdraw because of a back injury. Of course, the part went to Bette Davis who gave, arguably, her greatest film performance.

When work ended on the lackluster *No Funny Business*, which was aptly titled, Larry was offered a role that would return him to the stages of the West End.

Despite its off-putting title, *The Rats of Norway* was a serious play that intrigued Larry, who agreed to appear in it. Set in a boys' preparatory school in Newcastle-on-Tyne, the play is about loyalty, and it drips with nostalgia for times gone by.

He did not have the star part, but enjoyed working with his friends Raymond Massey and Gladys Cooper, whose stage work he'd admired since he was a late teenager.

In Keith Winter's play, Larry played Steven Berlinger, an idealistic young schoolmaster corrupted by his elders.

Harold Hobson of *The Sunday Times* claimed that Larry's performance was a "*coup de foudre*, a thunderclap!"

On opening night, Larry told Coward, "I'm an actor again."

The play is significant as a milestone in Larry's career for two reasons. He received rave notices after a series of dismal film reviews, and he took as his temporary mistress Helen Spencer, his leading lady, who would also become his lifelong friend.

Not a lot is known about the Olivier/Spencer fling. Years later, when Vivien Leigh was married to Larry and had given birth to a daughter, Suzanne, fathered by Leigh Holman, Vivien called on Spencer, which came as a complete surprise to the actress.

She later wrote a letter to Larry, complaining about Vivien. "She doesn't care a bugger about her child," Spencer charged. "She spent her entire time with me wondering whether you were fucking someone else or not. Vivien has a rather shallow outlook on that question. I suppose that when a girl has fucked a bit herself she finds it difficult to understand constancy."

Simultaneous with Larry's appearance in *The Rats of Norway*, he seems to have had a brief affair with actress Annie Rooney. The night she attended *The Rats of Norway*, she didn't come backstage because she didn't want to encounter Jill. Rooney did leave Larry a note, however. "If a mistress can send love to a wife, give yours my love!"

That's about the only clue left of her fling with Larry, although Ralph Richardson dined with them at the Ivy and just assumed from their actions they were having an affair. "Lovely girl," he later wrote.

Although Richardson was not always privy to Larry's homosexual liaisons, he felt that he kept abreast of "the odd mistress here and there." Richardson dated Larry's affair with Rooney to the period just right before he left again for Hollywood after swearing "I will never set foot there again."

***

From California, Larry's agent, Myron Selznick, cabled him in London that MGM wanted to put him under contract, signing him for one thousand dollars a week, with a forty-week guarantee.

Larry rejected the offer, but Myron cabled again. HAVE ONE PICTURE PROPOSITION LEADING MAN OPPOSITE GARBO. GREAT PART STARTING IN TWO WEEKS. ANSWER IMMEDIATELY.

"That is an offer I cannot refuse," Larry told Shaw, who agreed with him.

"I'll miss you something terrible," Shaw told him, "But this is the role that could make you a big-time Hollywood star. You certainly have the looks for it."

Larry upped the ante, demanding $1,500 a week. He also asked his agent to "look out for a picture for Jill."

Amazingly, after first reading the cable and agreeing to the terms as early as the end of May, 1933, it was only on June 27 that Larry cabled Myron, "What will the picture be about?" Myron did not answer the question, only telling him that the engagement should last until around September 8.

Myron wanted Larry to relay his complete body size measurements for early costume making. Larry responded, giving his waist at thirty, hips at thirty-eight, and chest also at thirty-eight among other measurements.

His agent responded that MGM wanted far more detailed measurements. In anger, Larry wrote a cable, "I've given you all my measurements except my cock size. Do you want that too?"

The woman at the cable office in London refused to send the message.

Garbo had seen the best of Larry's three Hollywood films, *Westward Passage*, and had been impressed with his acting and his appearance. She was intrigued by Larry's slight resemblance to her discarded lover John Gilbert.

"Olivier misunderstood our intentions from the beginning," claimed Rouben Mamoulian, the director of *Queen Christina*. "He was called to Hollywood for a test, not necessarily to be cast in the role. Originally, I wanted John Barrymore, and he was eager to do the part. But then I decided he was too old. Of course, Olivier's test would have to be with Garbo. The young Englishman was very inexperienced, and I had to see if he could stand up against the enormous screen presence of Greta Garbo. When the camera was turned on him, Olivier thought he was actually performing the role, not testing."

Finally, Larry learned that he was to play Don Antonio, the Spanish ambassador who captivates Queen Christina of Sweden and precipitates her abdication.

Gladys Cooper, co-producer of *The Rats of Norway*, released Larry from his contract before the end of the play's run. His role of the schoolmaster was transferred to Louis Hayward. Like Larry, this South African-born actor was urbane and suave.

He was also bisexual, and Larry later expressed regret that there was no time to get acquainted with him. In time, Hayward would also go to Hollywood to splash about in the swashbuckling genre, although he never became a threat to Errol Flynn.

Jill agreed to accompany Larry to Hollywood to give his chance for a film career another try. When they arrived at Waterloo Station, seemingly half of London's press corps had shown up. News that Garbo had selected one of their own as her new leading man caused Larry to be treated like a national hero. Jill herself was more or less ignored. They boarded the train for Southampton where they would sail on a Cunard vessel to New York harbor once again. From there, they would travel by train across North America to Los Angeles.

They arrived in California on July 23, 1933, and checked into a bungalow at the Garden of Allah Hotel. The bellhop told them that Tallulah Bankhead had occupied this same bungalow. According to the bellhop, Tallulah had written FUCK ME in lipstick on the bathroom mirror before departing.

In Hollywood, Larry renewed his affair with Fairbanks, whom he found living separately from Crawford. Larry's friendship with "Douggie" was just as alive and vital as it had been before.

Jill also operated like a free agent at night. Joan Crawford no longer wanted to see her, and perhaps Elissa Landi had already launched her affair with Katharine Hepburn and was not available either. From what he gathered, Jill was seeing a lot of Fifi D'Orsay, that spit-curled faux-Parisienne who had also caught the roving eye of Greta Garbo.

On the first day Larry reported for work on the set of *Queen Christina*, he learned that Garbo had already rejected four actors for the role of Don Antonio. Those rejects had included Ricardo Cortez, with whom Jill had worked before, along with Fredric March, Nils Asther, and Franchot Tone.

Born in Tbilisi, Georgia, which had been ruled during his childhood by Imperial Russia, the director,

Fifi D'Orsay

161

Rouben Mamoulian, had scored a big success in 1931 for Paramount with the release of *Dr. Jekyll and Mr. Hyde*, starring Fredric March.

On the set of *Queen Christina*, Mamoulian greeted Larry warmly, vigorously shaking his hand. But his first words were puzzling and could be interpreted many ways. "I think that anybody—and I'm not exaggerating—is capable of giving one hell of a good performance."

Later, Larry wrote of his traumatic experience with Garbo:

"I realized in the first two weeks with ever-increasing apprehension that I was not by any means making the best of myself; something was stopping me. I was too nervous and scared of my leading lady. I knew I was lightweight for her and nowhere near her stature, and began to feel more and more certain that I was for the chop. I made up my mind that I must make

a big effort to get along with her and find some way to get on friendlier terms.

Before work had started one morning, I found her sitting on an old chest on the set. I went boldly up to her and said the three or four sentences that I had made up and practiced; but no utterance came from her. I began to flounder and grab at anything that came into my head; some sayings of Will Rogers, of Noël—anybody—anything at all, until I came to a wretched end and stopped, pale and panting. After a breathless pause, she slid herself off the chest sideways saying, 'Oh, vell, life's a pain, anyway.' I knew then that the end was not far off."

In his Don Antonio costume, Larry confronted Garbo the following morning for the actual test. Hidden behind dark glasses, her enigmatic face did not seem to take in his features. Presumably no eye contact was made, although he couldn't be sure. She wore lounging pajamas and smoked a cigarette. This time she spoke first. "I do not like to rehearse."

"I understand we are to play a love scene this morning," he said awkwardly, his voice pitched too high.

Greta Garbo *(upper photo)* as Queen Christina of Sweden, and *(lower photo)* in repose

"I especially do not like to play love scenes with some of the leading men Mayer assigns me," she said. "As I told Nils Asther, I don't know where your mouth has been the night before. Entertaining some sailor no doubt."

He didn't know if she were making some veiled reference to his affair with Douglas Fairbanks Jr., which was widely gossiped about at the time.

Back in London, he would tell what happened next to Coward, Shaw, Blakelock, and even Ralph Richardson.

"Mamoulian, the Boy Wonder of Hollywood, told me I was to come forward, grasp Garbo's slender body—tenderly, that is—and look into her eyes. With those gestures, I was to awaken passion in her. Imagine assigned to awaken passion in the Sphinx, who really wasn't into men that much. I gave it my everything. But when I touched Garbo, she was as frigid as Jill. I tried the scene again and again and again, with Mamoulian yelling at me, which caused a passion to arouse in me, but not for Garbo. I wanted to punch him out. As hard as I tried, I got no response from Garbo. With another woman, I might have gotten an erection. With Garbo, my penis shrunk two inches."

Finally, in frustration, Mamoulian tossed the script for *Queen Christina* on the floor. "Is there anyone for god's sake—man or *woman*—she will warm to?" He said that within earshot of Garbo.

As she stormed off the set, one of the technicians gave a belated answer to the director's question. "John Gilbert," he shouted to Garbo's departing back.

The following morning, the film's producer, Walter Wanger, had the unpleasant task of firing Larry. Wanger wanted to make it as painless as possible for Larry. "We're crazy about you here at Metro and want to put you under contract. Personally, I thought you came off great in the screen test for *Christina*, but Garbo doesn't agree. As a consolation prize, we want to sign you to a contract and begin your film career at MGM by playing Romeo to Norma Shearer's Juliet."

"Isn't she a bit long in the tooth for Juliet?" Larry asked. "No, I don't want a Metro contract. But I do want to get paid for my involvement in the *Christina* project."

"Oh, yes, of course," Wanger said. "Get on to money."

At the time, Larry had an odd point of view, claiming that "Shakespeare cannot be put on film—only on the stage." Leslie Howard did not agree and took the role of Romeo.

Garbo finally decided she wanted to

John Gilbert with Greta Garbo in
Queen Christina

bring John Gilbert back to the screen. Louis B. Mayer, MGM's chief, hated Gilbert, who had once punched him in the face. But Mayer gave in to Garbo's wishes because of her clout at the box office.

The reporters had a feeding frenzy over Larry's firing and Gilbert's comeback. One journalist claimed that Larry had stood helplessly by as Gilbert was fitted into Larry's former costume. Before the camera, according to a "quote" from Larry, "Gilbert brought warmth and love into Garbo's eyes which I found only veiled and cold." This was fiction. Larry never said that and was long gone when Gilbert arrived on the set.

After his firing and with two weeks free before he was to go to New York, Larry invited Jill on a vacation to Hawaii. They checked into the Royal Hawaiian Hotel, on Oahu's Waikiki Beach, with money provided by MGM.

The next day Larry broke his big toe in a water sports accident. Three nights later when he felt better, he continued in his attempts to seduce Jill. He failed to arouse passion in her, just as he'd failed to arouse on-screen passion in Garbo.

Larry was not entirely disappointed when he learned that *Queen Christina* had flopped at the box office in December of 1933. Depression America wanted to escape with Shirley Temple, not Garbo. News spread along the Hollywood grapevine that Garbo might retire at any moment.

After Larry and Jill returned to Los Angeles from Hawaii, they boarded a train for Chicago and later another train for New York. Both Jill and Larry had signed to perform in a play for producer Jed Harris. It was called *The Green Bay Tree* and carried a theme of homosexuality, a concept which until then was almost unknown as the subject of a Broadway play.

Another disaster awaited him.

***

Two weeks after her honeymoon, Vivian rejoined her fellow actors at the Royal Academy of Dramatic Art (RADA). At the end of the term, she was cast in a big production of George Bernard Shaw's *St. Joan*.

Vivian played a warrior maid in chain mail and hinged armor. It marked her last appearance on the RADA stage.

When she checked out of the Academy for the second time, she was four months pregnant. Since she didn't want to be removed from the cast, she never told officials at RADA that she was with child.

When Vivian learned that she was pregnant in February of 1933, she was horrified. Her greatest fear was that a child would destroy her chances of a career in the theater.

When Leigh Holman heard the news, he was delighted, perhaps thinking

164

Vivian would now settle into the role of housewife and mother that he so desired from her. Leigh could hardly contain his enthusiasm. He knew that his mother, Sophia Holman, was ill and would perhaps die soon. He took Vivian to her bedside to tell her the good news. Sophia had not really accepted the marriage, feeling that Vivian was "too flighty." The dying woman was relieved to know that a child was on the way. "This is the stability you've been hoping for in your marriage," she told Leigh.

With a baby on the way, Leigh decided in July of 1933 that he and Vivian needed larger quarters. They found a narrow-fronted Queen Anne house that was "utterly charming and most fashionable." Vivian was enthralled to learn that the great Lynn Fontanne had lived here when she was appearing on the London stage.

"I felt it was a good omen," Vivian said, "but only in my wildest fantasies did I expect to become the next Lynn Fontanne."

The house was later destroyed in the blitz over London in 1940.

They moved to this more spacious address at 6 Little Stanhope Street in Mayfair. Even though pregnant, Vivian set about redecorating it, and often went to antiquarian markets to pick up antiques at very affordable prices. "If there was a valuable antique at a flea market," Leigh said, "Vivian knew how to ferret it out. She could bargain like a fishmonger's wife."

The birth of Suzanne Holman on October 12, 1933 at the Rahere Nursing Home on Bulstrode Street was so painful Vivian told Leigh, "I will never have another child." In her diary, without further explanation, she wrote a cryptically short phrase, "I had a baby."

When Patsy Quinn came to visit, Vivian told her, "The baby was premature. I thought it was going to kill me coming out. I think God got it all wrong. He should make men have the children."

"A real live, shitting, vomiting, belching, smelly baby is not my idea of a good time," she told Quinn. "I find the whole birth thing a messy, bloody affair. It's something animals do. I guess we should keep it up for the preservation of the species. But I think the role of birthing babies should be left up to breeders."

It was ironic that she should say that, espe-

Two views of Mrs. Leigh Holman with her daughter Suzanne

165

cially using the words "birthing babies," as it presaged one of the world's most famous movie scenes in the forthcoming *Gone With the Wind* that lay in her future.

During a physical examination at Rahere, Vivian's doctor discovered a small tubercular patch on her lungs. "Nothing serious, right now," the doctor said, "but it's something to watch."

Vivian made it clear to Leigh that, "I will not be some nanny, some breast-feeding nursemaid. It was never my plan to be a housewife, scrubbing shit off the toilet bowl. I never planned to stand over pots and pans cooking Bubble & Squeak for the rest of my life."

Wanting to please her, he hired a professional nanny, a cook, and even a maid for her.

Because of complications from the birth, Vivian's doctor had kept her in the hospital for three weeks. Leigh visited her every day after his work at Middle Temple. Without giving him an opportunity to tell her his opinion, she announced that, "I'm going back on the stage as soon as my body recovers. It is horrible what some revolting old semen can do to a woman's beautiful body."

In an interview the following month, Vivian was much kinder. She praised her husband's "tolerance and unselfishness" in allowing her to continue to pursue a career in the theater.

"I need excitement and joy in my life," Vivian wrote to her friend Clare Sheridan. "You had Charlie Chaplin. I'm married to a barrister. He is deeply kind and wise, but do I dare tell the truth? My darling Leigh is a bore!!!!!!! Love, Vivian"

Back in the game:
Fashionable Viv

In another more frantic letter, Vivian wrote Sheridan: "Help me! I've got to escape. God never intended for me to be trapped in a bourgeois marriage. In India, Gertrude promised me that a dashing young prince on a white horse would come for me and take me away to live in his magical kingdom. Where, oh where, is my shining knight?"

While Leigh was at his law offices, Vivian arranged a session with a society photographer in Mayfair. He had a large collection of gowns and frocks which could be fitted to her body, at least for a photograph. He took a portfolio of nearly one hundred shots of her, of which she selected fifteen.

Later, she had these photographs of herself circulated around to various casting agencies in London, with the help of her friends from RADA.

Within three weeks, she got "a bite," as she called it.

The director, Albert de Courville, found her "most photogenic" and sent for her. When he met her in person, he asked her if she'd play one of the Mayfair-type debs at a posh girls' school. The picture was to star Cicely Courtneidge, a leading stage comedienne of her day. Vivian eagerly accepted the offer.

Gainsborough Pictures would contact her about when to report to work. In the meantime, Vivian spent most nights "out with the girls," as she said, attending plays and going to *après*-theater parties. She even went to night clubs with other aspiring actresses from RADA, including Helen Terry, Beryl Samson, and Gillian Maud.

These young women believed that public appearances in chic dress at the right places would lead to their discovery by directors and producers.

Often it was three o'clock in the morning when Vivian arrived home. Leigh never demanded to know where she had been all night. He arose early to work in his small library on his briefs. Vivian was still asleep when he left home.

Often Gertrude came over in the afternoon to give the nanny a break in looking after Suzanne.

On a weekend visit to Owen Frewen, Leigh complained, "I feel my marriage to Vivian is slipping through my fingers."

Frewen took a fairly neutral position because of his friendship with Leigh, but his sister, Clare Sheridan advised, "A woman's career must come before her obligations to husband and child. If we don't take that position, how can we be free of the bondage men have held us in for years?"

In an attempt to save his marriage, Leigh invited Vivian on a cruise to the Baltic, and she gladly accepted. He told her, "It will be our second honeymoon. They visited Gothenburg on the west coast of Sweden and later sailed to Elsinore on the northeast coast of Zealand, in Denmark, where the actress Vivien Leigh and Laurence Olivier would appear in an Old Vic production of *Hamlet* in 1937.

A telegram was waiting for Vivian when the cruise came into port in Copenhagen to the south. Vivian was asked to report to work "at once" on the film, *Things Are Looking Up*.

In spite of Leigh's pleadings with her, she cut short her trip. "I hate to leave you, darling," she said at the train station where she planned to cross Denmark, arriving on the west coast of Jutland where a ferry would take her on to England.

Once in London, she learned, to her dismay, that shooting on the film had been delayed for three weeks.

Even though Vivian may have felt guilt about abandoning her husband in Denmark, he was the one filled with remorse when he returned to London. "I should not have tried to stand in the way of your career. I know how important it is to you."

She gracefully accepted his apology.

Finally, shooting on the picture had begun. Vivian arose at five o'clock to prepare herself, leaving their Mayfair home to drive in her small two-seater to Lime Grove Studios.

Dressed as a school girl once again, with white gym shoes and white stockings, Vivian was driven in a van to Cobham Hall, a country house in Kent that the filmmakers had defined, at least temporarily, as a school.

She was disappointed to find out she had only one line of dialogue. The name of her character was called in the script, "The Girl Who Puts Her Tongue Out." In front of the cameras, she delivered her first-ever dialogue on film. "If you are not made headmistress, I shan't come back next term."

Between takes, Vivian practiced making faces in the mirror. She learned to raise one eyebrow, which became a famous mannerism of hers, seen in her portrayals of both Scarlett O'Hara and Blanche DuBois.

For her work on the film, Vivian was paid 30 shillings a day. *Things Are Looking Up* was not released until April of 1935. It came and went from movie houses quickly.

Vivian was not dismayed by the smallness of her part. She became all the more determined to land a better role next time, even though she didn't have an agent. Night after night, Leigh arrived home from the law courts to find a note on the kitchen table: "Darling Leigh, the maid left your supper in the oven."

Beryl Samon, Vivian's friend, encountered Ivor Novello at a theater party in the summer of 1934. Novello had just filmed *Autumn Crocus* with Fay Compton and Jack Hawkins. Samon had once worked with Novello on a stage production, and she introduced the famous actor to Vivian. Only three nights before, Novello had slept with Larry.

Novello was stunned by Vivian's exceptional beauty. On the spot he held out the promise of getting her cast in a play. "Even if you can't act, you can get by on your looks alone. It pays four pounds a week."

Her answer stunned Novello. "I can get two pounds a day working in films."

"Then I don't think we can use you," Novello said, turning his back on her. In spite of this temporary setback, Vivian and Novello would become friends in the future.

Samon scolded Vivian. "When you're trying to break in, you should accept what's offered at any price."

"Maybe I should throw myself on the casting couch," Vivian said.

"Don't bother in his case," Samon said. "Novello has a steady lover and likes to seduce young actors on the side."

"My husband told me I should get an agent, a man to look after my interests and to bargain for me," Vivian said.

"I have someone in mind," Samon said. "John Gliddon. He's just setting up an agency and is interested in signing up new talent. If you agree, I'll set up an appointment."

Samon had worked with Gliddon on a play called *The Gay Lord Quex*. The next morning she called Gliddon, who agreed to meet Vivian at a café in Mayfair.

She arrived fifteen minutes early so she could carefully arrange herself. Exactly at three, Gliddon appeared on the sidewalk.

Although Vivian wore a wide-brimmed hat, the agent seemed to know who she was at once.

"You are the most enchanting creature in the British Isles," he said to her. "I'm John Gliddon, and you must be Vivian Hartley. We'll certainly have to work on changing that name."

"I can also be billed as Vivian Holman," she said.

"No, we have to come up with something better than that," he said, sitting down opposite her. "I intend to become a star maker in my new agency. Why should America be the only star-making factory in the world?" He pointedly asked her what she'd done before.

"A two-day job as an extra with one line of dialogue," she said frankly.

"In the future only leading roles for you," he said.

"You are a man after my heart," she said.

"I predict that your name within a matter of months will become a household word in London. That is, the new name I'm assigning to you."

Vivian became outrageously flirtatious, evoking the future opening scene when she portrayed Scarlett O'Hara in *Gone With the Wind*. "I really like the way you sweet talk an innocent girl like me," she said. Then her facial expression changed drastically as she tried to imitate a Soho tart. "I can be had for the asking."

(upper photo) the dreaded Jed Harris

(lower photo) The Green Bay Tree, Broadway, 1933. *(left to right)* Jill Esmond, Leo G. Carroll, and Laurence Olivier

***

Broadway producer Jed Harris was said to have "charmed the daylights out of us" when he got both Larry and Jill to agree to star in his controversial play, *The Green Bay Tree*, on Broadway.

The Green Bay Tree was about a struggle for control of a beautiful young man, as played by Larry. Lined up for battle are his dominating guardian, who is in love with him, his nearly deranged father, and his ingenuous fiancée.

When Harris acquired the rights to Mordaunt Shairp's *The Green Bay Tree*, Noël Coward had urged him to cast Larry in the lead in the New York production, although Harris had not been impressed with Larry's lackluster role in *Private Lives*. Surprisingly, Harris agreed.

"The play calls for two classy British queers," Harris told his staff. "That's why I'm bringing in James Dale and Laurence Olivier, but I'm going to tell them not to swish around the stage so much."

Before Harris appeared on the 1980 *Dick Cavett Show*, he discussed Larry with the talk show host. Privately he said, "I thought he was one of those typical British fags like Coward and Gielgud. I got that impression from his performance in *Private Lives*. Then I found out he was married to Jill Esmond. Then I found out she was a lesbian, so I went back to thinking Olivier was a fag. Still do."

Harris was a brutal director and looked for a scapegoat in every one of his productions, often a handsome young man. Larry became his latest victim.

Harris also acquired the rights to *The Lake*, in which he would star Katharine Hepburn in her most disastrous stage appearance. Harris decided to direct both *The Lake* and *The Green Bay Tree* ("after all, nobody directs better than I do," he said).

That Harris charm didn't last long. During rehearsals for the play, Harris, in Larry's words, "transformed himself into the most hurtful, arrogant, venomous little fiend that anyone could meet."

On the first day of rehearsals, Harris told Larry, "You are playing a male whore. You let your guardian, Dulcimer, pump your ass. You suck his dick. Remember that."

Away from Larry, Harris told his cast, "Olivier's ambition is vulgar. He wants to be another Ronald Colman with a little mustache. He has no mind whatsoever. What he has is an immense network of nervous antennae that go out in a thousand different directions."

In the play's London production the homosexuality had been very explicit. But Harris wanted to soften it for Broadway. For example, Leonora (as played by Jill) tells Larry, "I suppose someday I shall see you walking down

170

Piccadilly with painted cheeks." That line was removed from the Broadway opening.

In an amazing interview with Michael Munn, the biographer, Larry made an astonishing statement. "After *Queen Christina*, I went through the indignity of being raped by a New York stage director." He made this comment in 1979.

When Munn queried him about the rape, Larry quickly explained, "Emotionally, dear boy."

Larry was obviously referring to Jed Harris, though not naming him. Those familiar with the notorious life of Harris thought that Larry was literally telling the truth in his first statement. It is entirely possible that Larry was actually raped by the charismatic but rather sinister Yale dropout and former press agent who became the terror of Broadway.

"The Harris legend threw a shadow over Broadway that endured for fifty years, and no one escaped from it," said Harold Clurman at the home of off-Broadway producer Lucille Lortel one night. "If Harris suspected that an actor was homosexual or bisexual, he often interviewed him in his office while Harris was seated and completely nude."

"He had such power on Broadway that many eager actors submitted to his demands, even though against their wishes," Clurman maintained. "Harris claimed that he forced Archie Leach, later Cary Grant, to perform fellatio on him in his office. He also bragged that he raped a hysterically sobbing and drunk James Cagney one night in the men's toilet of his office. Cagney was a tough guy on screen, not off screen."

"I think that Harris did force Olivier to submit to sodomy, perhaps in an attempt to show him who's boss," Clurman claimed. "Olivier was a fairly weak character in those days and was dominated by Jill Esmond. The actors Harris assaulted could have resisted and put up a fight, but few of them did. Harris had the power to ruin their careers in show business."

"Harris practiced the most brutal form of casting couch auditions ever in the history of Broadway," Clurman said. "He preferred sex with women, and had a string of actress mistresses over the years, including Margaret Sullavan, Henry Fonda's wife. I think he sodomized young actors to break their spirit and to dominate them as a director. Who knows? He was a very sick individual."

One afternoon, Larry almost bolted from the play. He later claimed, "I hate Harris so, I have to get rid of all my impulses to murder him."

The Green Bay Tree opened at the Cort Theatre on Broadway on October 20, 1933, and it did a thriving business at the box office.

On opening night, as Larry waited to go on stage, Harris came up to him. His last words to Larry were, "Goodbye, I hope I never see you again."

Larry would later get his revenge on Harris when he modeled his stage and film portrayal of Shakespeare's monstrous *Richard III* on the producer. "He was the most venal person I had ever met," Larry later told a reporter. "I based my make-up and my performance on this swine."

Whereas *The Green Bay Tree* became a sellout at the Cort Theatre, Hepburn's *The Lake* bombed.

After his own play closed, Larry would never speak to Harris again.

In spite of Larry's disdain for Harris, Harold Clurman claimed, "Harris, in spite of his brutal methods, actually made Olivier a Broadway star for the first time."

Hepburn came backstage to congratulate Larry on his performance, pointedly ignoring Jill. There was still bitterness on Jill's part over losing out on the role in *A Bill of Divorcement*.

"My God, Larry, you were brilliant," Hepburn said. "What an extraordinary emotional performance. Unlike mine in *The Lake,* where I was ridiculed off the stage."

"I was put in an emotional stew pot by Jed Harris himself," Larry told her. "You've worked with him. You know what an actor must endure."

"Jed Harris will burn in hell," Hepburn said. "The most fiery chamber."

James Dale thought Hugh Williams in the London production was better than Larry on Broadway. "Larry's character was a limp, wet, lackadaisical, rather effeminate lad," Dale said. "I understand that Larry didn't like himself in the part."

For the most part, Larry's performance met with critical approval. Writing in the *Pittsburgh Press*, Florence Fisher Parry claimed: "In the horrifying scene where he is beaten into slavish submission by his benefactor's abnormal attraction for him, Olivier's acting becomes not acting, but an exhibition of emotional collapse so painful to witness that the eyes of the audience are torn away."

Harris later told Hepburn and others, "This play is really about Noël Coward and Jill Esmond struggling for the body and soul of young Olivier."

The Green Bay Tree closed in March of 1934, and Larry was delighted. He told Jill, "I know it's wrong for an actor to wish a play in which he's starring to close, but in this case I want out of here."

Noël Coward arrived in New York, and one of the first orders of his night was to arrange a private supper with Larry. He was said to have written the hit song, "Mad About the Boy," with Larry in mind.

His intimate relationship with Larry resumed, although Larry was hardly the entire focus of Coward's sexual life.

He'd become lovers with John Chapman Wilson, whom he affectionately called "Jack." Wilson had been a New York stockbroker but had become one of the major figures in Coward's life, both as a lover and a business partner.

Along with Wilson, Coward wanted to produce and direct a London version of S.N. Behrman's play *Biography*, an American comedy of manners which had already been a hit on Broadway.

Coward offered the male lead to Larry, who eagerly accepted, delighted to be returning to London with a job in hand.

"I've been away from the West End stage for a year, one of the most painful times of my life," Larry told Coward. "It will be so good to go back home."

"I failed in Hollywood, but it was a failure of the soul on Broadway, even though the play was a hit," Larry said. "During the ocean crossing, I counted the days until I would see the coast of dear old England."

As he'd later tell his sister Sybille when he got back to London, "I've never hated playing any part so much in my life."

***

Back in London, Larry went into rehearsals with Ina Claire, the American actress noted for her marriage to John Gilbert from 1929 to 1931. The play was Coward's first venture into a theatrical production with his lover Jack Wilson.

Larry found Claire a delight to work with. Both of them shared their mutual hatred of Jed Harris. She called him a sadistic son-of-a-bitch.

"He didn't rape me," she said, perhaps shocking him with her knowledge of Harris's attack on him.

"He wasn't able to rape anyone when I finished with him," Claire said. "He attacked my acting in *The Gaoler's Wrench* so much I could take it no more. I surprised him with my right hook. He fell on the floor, a perfect target for the toe of my stiletto heels. I landed a bull's eye in his much-overworked testicles before storming out of the theater."

Although American audiences had flocked to see her perform in *Biography* on Broadway, she was nervous about appearing again in the West End. She had last been seen in London two decades before, starring in *The Belle of Bond Street*.

Larry was cast as the priggish Richard Kurt, a fanatically idealistic magazine editor who tries to goad Claire, a celebrated painter, into writing a tell-all autobiography.

Back in London, headquartered at their home in Chelsea, Jill and Larry virtually led separate lives. Whenever he was not occupied with Coward, Larry was spending many an evening with Glen Byam Shaw. Jill was involved in another play, *Men in White*, which, as it eventually turned out, had a more

173

successful run than Larry's *Biography*.

Biography opened at the Globe Theatre on April 24, 1934 and ran for only forty-five performances. After the first week, Coward asked the cast to go on half pay because of the poor box office.

Ivor Brown, writing in *The Observer*, said that "Olivier did as well as any actor could to hold our interest in this boor." Other critics praised Larry's New York accent, evocative of Jed Harris's speech, but found his role more of an impersonation than acting.

Larry later claimed that *Biography* was the first flop for Claire—"unless you count her marriage to John Gilbert, which was an unkind, empty gesture on his part, taking advantage of a young female's flattered fascination simply in order to snap his fingers at her as he paraded her in front of Garbo."

***

In the early summer of 1934, Ralph Richardson heard that *Biography* was closing, and he approached Larry to fill in for him in the role of the Earl of Bothwell in *Queen of Scots*. A droll character actor, Richardson knew how wrong he was for the role of the romantic, athletic, dashing Bothwell.

The play was directed by John Gielgud, who had seen Larry perform in *Journey's End* and thought he'd be ideal for the role. Larry also had the back-

Two views of a young John Gielgud

ing of the star of the show, Gwen Ffrangçon-Davies, who had worked with Larry during their days at the Birmingham Rep.

At first, Larry expressed grave reservations about Gielgud, yet was intrigued with the challenge of being directed by him.

"I think your temperament suits Gielgud's more than mine does, although I've come to admire his talent," Richardson said. "He is a brilliant sort of butterfly, not my type at all. He has a voice of lyrical beauty and that unquenchable charm he inherited from Ellen Terry, his great aunt. In the course of one season he played Romeo, Antonio, Oberon, Richard II, Orlando, Macbeth, and Hamlet. His clothes are extravagant, his conversation flippant, and he overdirects, but the role of Earl of Bothwell could mark a turning point in your career."

After only briefly pondering the role, Larry said, "I'll go for it."

"Only one warning," Richardson said. "Gielgud is known for performing fellatio on the handsome young men in his cast. You don't have to get fully naked—just drop your trousers."

"That's no problem for me," Larry said. "Gielgud is just following standard casting procedures in the British theater."

Gielgud was only thirty when he met the twenty-seven-year-old Larry, but Gielgud as Larry's mentor appeared far older. At the time Larry came together with Gielgud, the actor was known as "the young meteor" of the Old Vic.

The coming together of Gielgud with Larry was one of the milestones in the British theater. When they met, Gielgud, the older actor, was already an established Shakespearean actor. Larry was not.

"I took responsibility for launching the turbulent Gielgud-Olivier relationship," said Richardson. "It would be characterized by bitter rivalries, incredible support, jealousies over mutual boyfriends, up and downs. But through all their pettiness, a greatness emerged. They became the two leading actors of the London stage, except for yours truly, of course."

"Our relationship did not catch fire with *Queen of Scots*," Gielgud later said. "That conflagration was yet to come."

"Beginning with *Queen of Scots*," Larry said, "people already started comparing me to Gielgud. I detested that. We were as different as we could possibly be on the stage."

Rehearsing Larry fourteen hours a day, Gielgud found himself physically attracted to his young star.

When queried by the press, Gielgud was kind in his appraisal of Larry, citing his "attention to detail, complete assurance in his conception of character; athleticism, power, and originality."

Privately, Gielgud was less enthusiastic with Larry's talent. He told Gwen, his female star, "Young Olivier promises more than he delivers on stage. But he's strikingly handsome, and beauty always goes over big in show business."

This was Larry's first historic costume role, the first of many, and he was so proud of his embroidered cloak that he even wore it for walks in the Berkshire countryside. In eccentric England, passers-by pretended not to notice anything unusual about his wardrobe.

Queen of Scots was written by Gordon Daviot, who had scored a major success with another play, *Richard of Bordeaux*. That play had elevated Gielgud into the star supreme of the London theater, but he was not to have such luck with *Queen of Scots*, which Gielgud called "only a moderate success."

One reason Larry wanted to do the play was that it also starred Glen Byam Shaw, with whom Larry continued in a very intimate relationship.

Larry read Daviot's description of Lord Bothwell in the play—"red haired, well built with vitality radiating from him."

"I can do that," he told Gielgud. "A little dye will turn my hair red."

After plotting the murder of Lord Darnley, Bothwell, of course, became the Scottish queen's third husband.

Larry and Shaw formed a drinking club called The Bothwell Club as a vehicle for socializing and pub-crawling after their rehearsals were over for the evening. For a third member, they invited the Scottish actor Campbell Gullan. Larry even designed a tie for the club members in stripes of "passionate purple, blood red, murky black, whisky yellow, and spring green."

Even after Gullan died in 1939, Shaw and Larry continued their club membership, honoring the custom of wearing the club tie on the day before each other's first nights.

Even though his marriage to Jill was coming to an end, Larry seemed fun-loving and gregarious with the cast, especially in those drinking sprees with Shaw, who still adored Larry.

"The closeness of Shaw and Larry aroused jealousy in Johnny G," Gwen said. "I truly think that our dear director wanted Larry to become his boyfriend. Several times in front of the cast, he planted wet kisses on Larry's lips, ostensibly congratulating him for pulling off a scene so beautifully."

A young, aspirant actor, James Mason, was also cast in *Queen of Scots*. Two years younger than Larry, this Yorkshire-born actor appeared in what he called "a clever double," both as the Earl of Arran, the hysterical young suitor of Mary, as well as a French valet to Larry's Lord Bothwell.

"Sometimes Mason was invited into Larry's dressing room for one of the after-work drinking parties," Gwen said. "The two actors circled each other like cocks about to fight in the ring. My money was on Larry. I thought Mason too prissy and precious ever to make it as a matinee idol. How wrong I was."

Shaw claimed that Larry was beginning to get a bit pretentious, showing up backstage with a ring-tailed lemur captured in the rain forests of Madagascar. "Larry called his mascot Tony," Shaw said. "If the little devil jumped up in your arms it was sure to urinate."

Details are lacking, but Shaw later claimed that Gielgud "got his man," referring to Larry. The director lived up to his reputation of fellating young actors. Though limited and one-sided, Larry's sexual trysts with Gielgud aroused jealousy and tension between Shaw and Larry.

Larry finally managed to convince Shaw that Gielgud basically used him as a "rent boy" and that there was no sexual passion on Larry's part at all. Gielgud was hardly Larry's idea of a sexual partner.

As in the case of director James Whale, Larry had shown that he was willing to indulge in sex with certain men such as Noël Coward who may not have been his ideal physical specimen.

"Larry loves me," Shaw confided to Denys Blakelock and others. "He uses Coward and Gielgud for career advancement."

"That's a completely accepted way to get ahead in the British theater, especially if you're gorgeous," Blakelock said.

On opening night, Larry made a spectacular entrance as Bothwell, appearing in high leather boots and sporting a reddish goatee.

"He looked absolutely glorious," Gwen said. "Every woman in the audience wanted him—and a lot of the men too."

James Agate of the *Sunday Times* found that Larry provided a well-executed portrait but was a little too light, "especially in the voice which has the tennis club, will-you-serve-first-partner-or-shall-I ring about it." This normally articulate critic actually wrote that.

One reviewer noted Olivier's swashbuckling style and suggested that he'd been inspired by Douglas Fairbanks Sr.—"more Hollywood than Holyrood."

Another critic wrote that Larry played Bothwell "with the Hollywood mannerisms of Clark Gable."

"The play might have run longer, but that August, London experienced one of its most bloody heat waves," Larry said. "The inside of a theater auditorium felt like the Sahara, and here we were performing in costumes more suited to Scotland in the dead of winter."

Undaunted by his loss of $30,000 on *Biography*, Coward plunged into another production, an American play, *The Royal Family* by Edna Ferber and George S. Kaufman, which Coward would produce and direct.

To avoid confusing British audiences with the actual royal family, he changed the title to *Theatre Royal*. This rollicking satire was based on America's most famous acting family, the Barrymores.

Coward had already agreed to cast Brian Aherne in the role of the pyrotechnic John Barrymore character. Coward decided to move up his original fall opening to help recover his losses, which meant that he needed an actor to fill in for Aherne until the star became available. Throughout the course of that summer, Aherne was already committed to work in America.

At the New Theatre, Larry went on every night as the Earl of Bothwell, but quickly became bored with the role.

When he heard that he might get temporary work portraying John Barrymore before Aherne turned up in London, he was thrilled with the possibility. "There's no actor in London who could play John Barrymore like I could," he told Shaw.

From his dressing room, he called Coward. In front of Shaw, he said, "Noël, you sweet, dear thing, this is John Barrymore, the young man of your

Brian Aherne

177

dreams. Drop whatever you're doing. I'm coming over right away. Please be waiting for me in your boudoir. I'll start taking off my clothes in the entrance hall. By the time I've mounted the steps, I'll be as naked as God made me by the time I enter your bedroom."

***

Before Larry left Coward's home that night, he told him, "Damn it! No one but me. The part is mine!"

"And so it is, dear boy," Coward said.

Brian Aherne had been detained in Hollywood because his picture for MGM, *What Every Woman Knows*, fell way behind schedule. For 100 pounds a week, Larry was offered the John Barrymore role for the play's preview performances in Edinburgh, Glasgow, and Manchester.

"Even though in the summer of 1934 I was still idiotically skinny, I thought of myself as a kind of Tarzan since I performed so athletically on the stage," Larry later recalled.

Evoking his athleticism of the Bothwell role, Larry imitated Douglas Fairbanks Sr., especially in the stunts he performed, including a leap from a balcony. In time he was to become notorious for these dangerous stunts. *Theatre Royal* even featured a duel fought on stage.

Coward's partner, Jack Wilson, said, "London theater audiences saw a new Larry up there on the stage. He'd become obsessed with the part. No longer was he impersonating a character, as he'd been accused of before. He

became the character. He suggested glamour, but also virility and lusciousness. He put *balls* into the part. Noël never had such a splendid time directing another actor."

Larry was cast with Marie Tempest, who played a role based on Ethel Barrymore. When she saw the play in New York, Miss Barrymore threatened to sue.

Born in 1864, Tempest was both a singer and actress and had become famous in late Victorian light opera and Edwardian musical comedies. Her career spanned 55 years, and she would become a Dame Commander of the British Empire in 1937.

In *Theatre Royal*, Larry also worked with Madge Titheradge who was born into a theatrical family in Melbourne, Australia. She'd made her London stage debut at fifteen, was known for her

(Dame) Marie Tempest in 1935

beauty, her likeness posted on many a postcard or cigarette ad.

Tempest was a complete autocrat in the theater, chastising any actor who did not perform to her liking. Somehow she developed a soft spot for Larry, but not for others. One night Larry caught Madge Titheradge sobbing in her dressing room. When he asked her what was the matter, Titheradge claimed, "Dame Marie hit me with her walking stick." Previously, Marie Tempest had accused Titheradge of upstaging her.

It was in the Glasgow previews that Aherne, fresh from MGM in Hollywood, turned up to witness Larry's performance. Before the performance began, he went backstage with Coward to meet the fellow cast members. Coward introduced him first to Larry. Aherne thanked him "for filling in for me." Larry promptly excused himself, an evasion which Aherne interpreted as an insult.

The other leading actors in the cast—Mary Merrall, George Zucco, and Titheradge—were polite but distant to Aherne. The star of the show, Marie Tempest, was downright hostile. She told Aherne that she would refuse to rehearse with him.

Sitting out front with Coward, Aherne was dazzled by Larry's spectacular performance. "He was marvelous, and I was deeply impressed," Aherne later said. "I was terrified and feared I would be unable to make all those leaps and jumps without breaking both of my legs. I left the theater with serious doubts that I could fill Olivier's boots."

Five nights later, perhaps the result of a secret intervention between Coward and his friend, Katharine Cornell in New York, Aherne's dilemma was solved. Cornell cabled Aherne that she wanted him for the role of Mercutio in her upcoming production of *Romeo and Juliet*. Basil Rathbone had already been cast as Romeo.

Aherne called Coward and asked to be excused from his contract for *Theatre Royal*, and Coward was relieved to let him go, since he wanted to keep Larry in the role.

The New York cast of *Romeo and Juliet* became perhaps the most prestigious of the year, as it also featured Edith Evans as the Nurse and Orson Welles as Tybalt. The bisexual Aherne had another reason he was glad to return to New York. Also in the cast was a little-known but stunningly handsome actor named Tyrone Power. After knowing each other for only two nights, Aherne and Power launched a torrid affair.

Theatre Royal opened at the Lyric Theatre in

Madge Titheradge

London on October 23, 1934. The reviews, mostly focusing on Larry's *tour de force* interpretation of John Barrymore, were raves.

Larry was cited for "satiric braggadocio," as he appeared on stage applying greasepaint and powder before a dressing room mirror, putting on a fur coat with a scarlet red scarf, or donning a snap brim hat with olive and russet tweeds.

James Agate wrote that Larry's performance was "hair raising—lifesize and lifelike, which is not necessarily the same thing."

"The play is one long swashbuckler, with twirling moustaches," wrote one critic. "Olivier plays a wild screen lover with all the women in the world at his feet, giving the best performance of his career."

In the opening night audience sat John Gielgud, who later praised Larry's marvelous use of physical technique and his mastery of timing. "Both were breathtaking and widened my own perception of my own art," Gielgud said. "It definitely had an influence on my future work. Larry claimed that seeing me at the Old Vic had a great influence on him. In playing Tony Cavendish, the name that the playwright used for the character inspired by John Barrymore, he paid back his debt to me."

Gielgud went backstage to congratulate Larry, but had to wait in a long line of screaming young women who wanted their programs autographed, or something else, mostly something else.

When Gielgud finally got in to see Larry, he found him freshly showered and wearing a red satin dressing gown, a gift from Noël Coward. He was sipping Scotch and puffing on a cigarette with a holder. "He had finally become what I could never be," Gielgud later said. "A matinee idol."

Even though Gielgud was lavish in his praise of Larry, privately he told friends, "I began to see Larry as my rival for supremacy on the British stage. I felt because of his youth and beauty, combined with his incredible virility on stage, he might surpass me. In future performances, I decided to let out my sails, give it my all. I did not want Larry to overtake me."

During the run of the play, two young men from Oxford who had repeatedly sodomized the "weak and feminine" Olivier came backstage to pay belated respects. Noting his virility and physicality on the stage, one of his former classmates told him, "You're more man than I'll ever be. I hope you can kindly forgive a stupid schoolboy's brutality."

Larry responded with graciousness. Perhaps to shock the young man, he hugged and kissed him on the mouth. "I enjoyed every minute of it."

When the young man hurried off, Larry turned to Shaw and burst into laughter. "Lesson Number One in how to handle your rapist."

During the run of *Theatre Royal*, Larry was asked by Princess Alice, granddaughter of Queen Victoria, to give a charity performance as Captain

Stanhope in *Journey's End*, which was now a famous play around the world. He graciously accepted and received raves in the London press. Larry had always regretted dropping out of *Journey's End,* and starring in it again made him realize anew what a grand theatrical opportunity he'd missed.

In the dueling scene of *Theatre Royal*, two weeks into the run, an accident happened. Larry's rapier flew from his hand and struck Tempest's ample bosom. This brought a telegram of warning from Coward, his producer. "Remember, Larry sweet. Marie Tempest needs her feet."

Coward had also warned Larry not "to break your padded legs." Larry took no notice. After two months of daring stunts, he finally broke his ankle leaping from that balcony. Since the accident occurred at the end of the second act, an understudy had to take over to finish the play, much to the disappointment of the audience.

Caught playing bridge backstage, Larry's understudy, Valentine Dyall, rushed for his makeup and finished the third act for Larry.

Since Larry had to drop out of the play and be confined to bed, he was replaced by Robert Douglas.

Even without Larry in the cast, the play managed to attract audiences for a six-month engagement, allowing producer/director Coward to recoup the financial loss he'd suffered during his previous production of *Biography*.

Larry was confined to bed in his house in Chelsea for two weeks before he was able to move about in a wheelchair.

Helen Spencer, his former mistress, wrote Larry that she wanted to come to his aid, but she suspected that Jill would resent her presence. "I suppose you are already surrounded by ministering blondes," Spencer said.

No blondes, but Larry was administered to by Sofka Zinovieff, a White Russian refugee who hired out as a secretary. She'd been born in Moscow as Princess Sophia Dolgorouky but after the revolution had fallen on bad days. Jill hired her through a service called Universal Aunts, and she stayed with Larry, working for him as his secretary even after his divorce from Jill. For some reason, she left his employment shortly after the beginning of World War II in 1939.

Amazingly, a play called *Ringmaster* came to Larry's attention. It called for him to play the role of a formerly fashionable actor who is in a wheelchair.

"Type casting, mate," Jill Esmond told him. "Go for it. It's the husband's job to keep bread on the table."

***

Unknown to Larry, the newly christened and stunningly beautiful actress named "Vivien Leigh" had invited her friend Patsy Quinn to go with her on opening night to see *Theatre Royal*. Her husband, Leigh, had turned down her invitation to be her escort.

She'd heard "absolutely marvelous things" about Larry's role as the flamboyant John Barrymore, his character disguised behind the stage name of Tony Cavendish.

She sat mesmerized throughout the performance. When the curtain went down, she was almost in a trance. Finally, she pulled herself together to leave. Before standing up, she turned to Quinn. "That's the man I'm going to marry."

"But he's already married," Quinn said. "To Jill Esmond. And the last time I checked you were Mrs. Leigh Holman with a daughter waiting for you back home."

"That doesn't matter," Vivien said. "I will still marry him one day. You'll see."

Larry Olivier in the early 1930s
with Joan Crawford on the set of *Dancing Lady*

Chapter Six

Although confined to a wheelchair, Larry had high hopes for *The Ringmaster*, a play by Keith Winter he'd acquired the rights to for an opening scheduled for London's Shaftesbury Theatre on March 11, 1935. Pre-London tryouts were conducted in both Oxford and Birmingham.

Cast as Peter Hammond, Larry played a crotchety meddler who finds amusement by disrupting the lives of the guests at a Devon country house hotel. Raymond Massey directed him, and Jill appeared as his long-suffering wife.

Eva Moore warned Jill not to accept the role. "Since Larry is also the producer, it suggests nepotism. Audiences don't like that. It's the equivalent of a director casting his daughter or wife as a female lead."

"First, I don't have another job in the West End," Jill said. "Or anywhere else. Larry insists that I play his wife. And I will."

Eva, however, was pleased when Larry cast her longtime friend, Dame May Whitty, in the play. Larry also rounded up one of the most talented casts in England, including Nigel Patrick, Cathleen Nesbitt, and Colin Keith-Johnston.

Larry had only disdain for Massey's acting ability, although they remained friends. He thought even less of Massey as a director. "I should take over the job myself," he told Eva and Jill.

The Observer noted that "Mr. Laurence Olivier, as the dark, ferocious Hammond, continually lit his part with baleful flashes, and easily had the house cheering with his ultimate contortions on the floor."

Other critics weren't so kind, Ivor Brown complaining of Larry's delivery which he pronounced "unintelligible." He asked, "Where is the melodious voice of John Gielgud now that we need him?" James Agate also claimed that, "It was a continual strain to hear Olivier."

Regrettably, the play lasted for only eight performances.

On his final night, Larry was wheeled out for a curtain call speech. "We as characters have unfortunately died tonight. But we hope that brief though our appearances have been, we will live in your memories."

Members of the audience called out, "Don't take it off!" But the play closed the following morning when future audiences lined up at the box office to get their money back.

"This is very embarrassing for me," Larry told both his wife and mother-in-law. "I'm being treated as a celebrity. Even Sir James Barrie invited me for lunch. I've had cocktails with Sir Gerald du Maurier. Now I must live down this latest fiasco."

"I lost money as well as prestige by starring in this play," Larry later said. "I had mistakenly thought it was a great play with a great role for me. Months later I came to my senses. It was badly written."

Some observers maintained that Larry had completely recovered from his broken ankle when he performed in *The Ringmaster*, but effectively used the wheelchair as a prop. "For an actor who was incapacitated, Olivier managed to go through agonized contortions to bring down the final curtain to roaring applause," said the stage manager. "I think he was up to speed with his injury but was faking it."

Just when he was feeling "washed up," "a failure," and "a miserable lout," Larry received two calls, one from the famous British film producer, Alexander Korda.

The other was from Maurice Browne, still counting his money from his successful production of *Journey's End*. He had purchased a comedy for the West End. "It'll put you right back up there on the top, old boy," Browne predicted to Larry.

***

Alexander Korda

The producer, Alexander Korda, who would play roles in both the lives of Vivien Leigh and Larry Olivier, was known on both sides of the Atlantic. He was the British equivalent of a ruthless, flamboyant studio boss like Louis B. Mayer or Darryl F. Zanuck. A man of immense charm, he could also turn violently on people.

Korda was a boy from the *puszta* in Hungary who made good and he was also a star maker. Even Sir Winston Churchill secretly wrote film scripts for him. Korda would eventually marry one of the fabled beauties of his day, Merle

Oberon.

Korda immediately cast Larry in *Conquest of the Air*, a partially drama- tized documentary tracing man's effort to fly, spanning the years between 57 A.D. and the 1930s. Larry appeared only in a brief cameo.

Winston Churchill was a consultant on *Conquest of the Air*.

In *Conquest of the Air*, Larry was cast as Vincent Lunardi, the first aerial traveler in England, who, in 1784, floated bravely over the skies of London in a balloon.

Although Larry did little more than stand confidently beside a studio's prop balloon, Korda was impressed. "I think you will become one of Britain's great screen actors," he told Larry. "I will see that that happens."

Alexander hired his brother, Zoltan, a former Hungarian cavalry officer, to do some of the directing. For various reasons, the film was shelved for five years until 1940. The movie did nothing for Larry's career, and critics weren't enthusiastic, one of them referring to it as "a bit scrappy."

As part of its final 1940 release, *Conquest* included some sword-rattling which was appropriate propaganda for the opening months of World War II.

The most provocative review of *Conquest of the Air* came years later when Roger Lewis wrote *The Real Life of Laurence Olivier*. He called Larry's performance as Lunardi "all frills and foppishness—and innuendo: the ascent into the sky is an erotic experience, a thrill. Olivier, in periwig and beauty spots, is a giggling god. His high-pitched, fast-paced enunciating toys with effeminacy, but it also contains a kind of sigh, a kind of groan, that's sexual."

Korda gave Larry a much more substantial role in the 1935 *Moscow Nights* (released in America by United Artists in 1936 as *I Stand Condemned*). It was an English-language adaptation of a 1934 French-made original, and was directed by Anthony Asquith, the co-scripter.

Larry played a wounded officer, Captain Ignatoff, who falls in love with Natasha (Penelope Dudley- Ward). He was cast as a dashing, mustachioed officer rescuing a damsel in distress.

Moscow Nights was Larry's second picture under his new contract with Korda. The setting of this roman- tic spy thriller was Russia during World War I.

The movie also starred Harry Baur, the grand old man of French cinema, and marked the debut of Anthony Quayle. Quayle, a Lancashire-born actor, would go on to have a distinguished career in London and on Broadway. In private, he shared his philosophy of life with Larry. "If life doesn't have that little bit of danger, you'd better create it."

THE
CONQUEST
OF THE AIR

An ALEXANDER KORDA
PRODUCTION

In spite of some good reviews, the film bombed at the box office. Larry later said that the script and even the title, *Nuits Muscovites,* sounded better in French.

Larry's leading lady, Penelope Dudley-Ward, as noted by many reviewers, was one of the dullest actresses ever to step onto a British stage. One London critic claimed, "She always looks like she should be at Croydon, waiting to board a Hanley-Paige for India, not playing a nurse named Natasha." When she married Sir Carol Reed, she abruptly—her critics said "mercifully"—retired from the stage.

Larry and the film's director, Anthony Asquith, got along fabulously. After the first day, Olivier became "Larry," and Anthony Asquith was called "Puffin," a nickname bestowed by his mother who thought he resembled one.

In time, Asquith became one of the most successful British directors on the international scene, along with Sir David Lean and Sir Carol Reed.

Sometimes Larry and Asquith would have an argument. Larry complained that the director was having makeup apply too much lip rouge. "I look like a sodomite's dream boy," Larry claimed.

"A director is entitled to live out his sexual fantasies on camera," Asquith told Larry.

Larry and Asquith would develop a relationship that would last for years. Both Dudley-Ward and Quayle claimed that "Larry & Puffin" had a brief fling during the filming of *Moscow Nights.*

The director's most successful post-war film was Oscar Wilde's *The Importance of Being Earnest* (1952). There was a certain irony here. Anthony's father, H.H. Asquith, while serving as Home Secretary (1892-1895), had ordered Wilde's arrest for homosexuality. His subsequent sentence to the Reading Gaol, of course, destroyed the great playwright personally and stifled gay culture in England throughout most of the 20th century. The irony is that "Puffin" himself, the youngest Asquith son, was himself gay.

Asquith directed Richard Burton and Elizabeth Taylor in Terence Rattigan's *The V.I.Ps* (1963) based on an incident in Larry's life.

Prior to Asquith's death in London in 1968, he'd been designated as director of the screen adaptation of Morris West's best-selling Cold-

(top) director Anthony Asquith and *(bottom)* Anthony Quayle

War novel *The Shoes of the Fishermen* (1968) to star Larry and Anthony Quinn. But Asquith had to tell Larry, "I can't do it. I'm dying of cancer."

But for a while in 1935 until the dismal box office returns came in, Larry was flying high in more ways than one. He was not only taking flying lessons, but reading *Film Pictorial*, which claimed that "With *Moscow Nights* is born a new English film star."

When the movie opened in New York, John T. McManus of *The New York Times* was not enchanted, finding Larry's portrayal "clipped and flippant" and noting that his "voice cracked a couple of times just when folks were expecting great things in the way of diction to complete his resemblance to Ronald Colman."

One critic felt that Larry didn't look like Ronald Colman but more like Sir Anthony Eden.

***

Larry's next play was *Golden Arrow*, in which he was cast as Richard Harben, a young English politician. He was not only going to star in it, but produce it along with Maurice Browne. *Golden Arrow* was written by the novelist Sylvia Thompson in collaboration with Victor Cunard.

Golden Arrow was viewed as "modish" for its time as it was the story of an unmarried couple living together. From the beginning, Browne had serious reservations about the play that he himself had discovered, finding "the script frothy and the pace much too slow."

Larry needed a leading lady, and the search was on. By chance, Thompson, the co-scripter, discovered an "enchantingly beautiful young Irish lassie" while dining out in London one night.

Unknown to anyone at the time, the novelist had discovered the future screen legend Greer Garson.

Thompson introduced herself to Greer and

(left photo) Actor Ronald Colman in the 1930s

(right photo-- Does he look like Larry?) 1931 view of Conservative politician Anthony Eden (British Foreign Secretary 1935-1955, and Prime Minister 1955-1957)

learned that she was an actress, having made her professional debut at the Birmingham Rep. An audition was arranged for the following morning, at which time Greer met twenty-seven-year-old Larry, the play's director and star.

Thompson and Larry were immediately won over by Greer's audition, but Browne was turned off. "She doesn't attract me sexually," Browne said in front of the young actress.

She later shot back. "What a strange man. He wears one earring and has whips hanging on his wall. I fear I'm far too young and wholesome for the likes of him."

Within days Browne withdrew as co-producer, and Larry decided to go it alone, proud of the theatrical proclamation LAURENCE OLIVIER PRESENTS.

He became temporarily enchanted with the self-styled "Irish colleen," even after his discovery that she had actually been born in London. In later years, he recalled, "Greer, bless her, could bring believability into some dangerously hokey material, as all those war-time films of hers for MGM proved."

She immediately fell under Larry's spell. "What a handsome and talented man he is," she said. "He both intrigues me and inspires me."

They began to meet after rehearsals, often having a late supper at the Ivy. He warned her against a Hollywood career, claiming the stage was the proper vehicle for her talent. "Hollywood devoured me," he told her. "It'll do the same for you."

"Larry convinced me that Hollywood was Babylon-on-the-Pacific," Greer said. "A citadel of make-believe and meretricious values."

Their relationship became sexual, Larry preferring to spend his nights 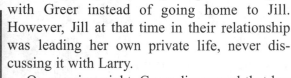 with Greer instead of going home to Jill. However, Jill at that time in their relationship was leading her own private life, never discussing it with Larry.

On opening night, Greer discovered that her gown was missing from her dressing room. In panic, she appealed to Larry. He tossed her a pair of his own pajamas, suggesting that she play the scene for comedy.

Slipping into the pajamas, she made her appearance on the stage and proved to be a hit. The pajamas scene was kept in for the short run of the play, which opened at the Whitehall

Greer Garson

Theatre in London on May 30, 1935, running for

nineteen performances.

Larry's long-time friend, Denys Blakelock, was cast in a secondary role. He later wrote, "*Golden Arrow*, though witty and entertaining, was very light-weight and did not give Larry much chance to stretch his imaginative powers."

In a speech on opening night, Larry came out to greet the audience. "It is a pleasure to introduce to you Greer Garson who is—I won't only say promising—but already a very polished actress, who tonight is making her London debut. You will, I am sure, be seeing a great deal of her."

Writing in the *Sunday Times*, James Agate sarcastically said that the curtain speech was "the only worthwhile thing Olivier had said on stage all evening."

Larry's romance with Greer lasted only until the end of the production. She did not heed his warnings about Hollywood, and fell into Louis B. Mayer's net during his annual "roundup" in Europe seeking stars abroad. He assigned her to her first picture, *Goodbye, Mr. Chips*. At the same time he also signed another actress, Hedwig Keisler, whose name he changed to Hedy Lamarr.

In later years, Greer recalled, "I was really starting to fall in love with Larry, and he with me. I knew his marriage to Jill Esmond was falling apart. I actually fantasized about becoming the second Mrs. Laurence Olivier. But another young actress was about to appear in Larry's life. Miss Vivien Leigh."

Blakelock recalled that at two o'clock one morning, Larry uttered a familiar lament. "I'm washed up. I'll never make it in film or on the stage. I'm a failure in my marriage and in my love affairs. Greer and I are through."

"What about me?" Blakelock asked. He later recalled, "Larry could be terribly blunt. He said, 'You and I are also washed up. As much as it hurts me to tell you this, I've outgrown you.'"

After failures on both stage and screen, Larry found himself unemployed, even though he'd become a theatrical celebrity. It was the summer of 1935. Jill was rehearsing a play called *The Black Eye*.

"I'm the one with the black eye," he complained to her.

During the course of one of his most despondent afternoons, the phone rang. He recognized the voice on the other end at once. It was his rival John Gielgud.

That call would change his life.

Coral Browne

***

189

As an actress, stardom for Vivien was on the horizon, but before she reached that pinnacle, "I had to pay some dues," she later recalled.

Once again the chance arose for her to appear with Ivor Novello in a play called *Murder in Mayfair*. The leading lady was Fay Compton, and Vivien would have only one line. "Oh, what a lovely dress!"

Her competition for the role was Coral Browne, who would later marry actor Vincent Price. Although Coral and Vivien both started out as *protégées* of the same agent, John Gliddon, and potential rivals, they later became "bosom buddies."

Director Leontine Sagan gave Vivien the role. But after watching Novello late one morning going through a scene, Vivien suggested to Sagan that, "Larry Olivier could do this role so much better."

When news of that reached Novello, he exploded in fury. Unknown to Vivien, Novello and Larry had ended the intimate part of their relationship. At the time, Novello had protested, "No man walks out on Ivor Novello."

"I'll be the first," Larry told him.

Vivien's unfavorable comparison of Novello to Olivier would have been wrong at any time, but coming as it did in the wake of a break-up, it was more than the temperamental actor could tolerate. "I was chucked out," Vivien said.

At night Leigh Holman sat at home with his daughter, Suzanne, while Gliddon escorted Vivien to the leading nightclubs and restaurants of that time.

Gliddon's belief was that for Vivien to be noticed, she had to be spotted nightly on the see-and-be-seen circuit, whose stops included, among others, the Ivy Restaurant, the Ritz Hotel, the Savoy Grill, and the Colony Club. Gliddon could ill afford these swanky places, but he destroyed his budget and took Vivien anyway because he had such high hopes for her.

Despite her clothes allotment of 200 pounds a year, she seemed to appear in a different outfit every night. Clever in the use of accessories, she often disguised the fact that she was wearing the same dress.

One night over dinner Vivien confided in Gliddon that Gertrude, her mother, had made a big promise to her when she was a little girl growing up in India. "Mother promised me that one day a Prince Charming on a white horse would ride into my life. My darling Leigh, the poor dear, can never be my prince charming. It has to be someone like the Prince of Wales. But I hear he is involved. Ivor Novello is handsome enough, but he's treated me poorly. Noël Coward is not handsome enough. Besides, Ivor and Noël are homosexuals. It has to be Laurence Olivier. He is dashing on stage with his slim hips encased in those tight black trousers. He is a romantic figure on stage, a prince among players. He will soon be mine. I admire his talent but he also arouses a feeling of sexual desire."

"But for security you have Leigh waiting for you at home," Gliddon said.

"Olivier is a little bit out of your league. For sex, I will introduce you to John Buckmaster. He's the son of Gladys Cooper."

One night while dining at the Ivy, Vivien spotted Leslie Howard, the movie star upon whom she'd long harbored a crush. She insisted that Gliddon escort her over to Howard's table and introduce her. "I had on this perfume I called Rape. But Leslie didn't, at least on the night we were introduced. That would come much later in our lives."

Although seemingly entranced with Vivien, Howard had a date that night and didn't want to shower too much attention on her. He did point Gliddon in the right direction, which led to a meeting with John Payne (not the famous movie star, of course), who ran a casting agency for B-film quickies being churned out in Britain.

Payne was impressed with Vivien's beauty and successfully recommended her for two leading female roles in *The Village Squire* and *Gentleman's Agreement*.

The Village Squire (1935) was a comedy about how an itinerant movie actor comes to a small village and transforms a squire's local stage production of *Macbeth*, and also falls in love with his daughter.

The star of the picture was veteran actor David Horne, a former Grenadier Guards officer who was born in Sussex in 1898.

Reginald Denham, in his apartment in New York shortly before his death, said, "I was honored to direct Vivien in the first film where she had star billing. But, in truth, I did not realize her potential. She was beautiful but seemed like any number of lovely British girls at the time. She was so very insecure."

For her role in *The Village Squire*, Vivien earned five guineas a day.

She immediately followed *The Village Squire* with another picture, *Gentleman's Agreement* for release in 1935. This movie, of course, is not to be confused with the Gregory Peck Oscar-winning film of 1947 with the same title.

Director George Pearson cast her as a typist in this story that focuses on two men who trade places. A rich man becomes poor to discover the joy of the simple life, and a poor man becomes rich. David Horne was also the star of *Gentleman's Agreement*.

He claimed to one interviewer that "acting brought out passions in Vivien like lava from an exploding volcano. Once that lava started to flow, it could

Viv in *The Village Squire* (1935)

191

never be put back into the crater of the volcano."

After completing his film with Vivien, Horne was cast in a play called *The Green Sash*, a 15th-century costume drama. It was produced and directed by Matthew Forsyth. When the role of Giusta, the leading lady, suddenly became available, Horne recommended to Forsyth that he cast Vivien.

Based on her first two movies, Forsyth cast Vivien in this romantic stage play with a setting in Florence. The salary was five pounds a week.

The Green Sash opened on February 25, 1935. "I am sure I was not good in the part," Vivien later claimed. "It was a long one and far too difficult for anyone as inexperienced as I was."

The Green Sash ran for only two weeks. That delighted Leigh, who felt that his wife should come back home and resume her family life. "I can see the handwriting on the wall," Leigh told Vivien. "The theatrical world is no place for you. Perhaps a brief moment on the stage and then oblivion."

The playbill for *The Green Sash* had erroneously stated that Vivien had appeared on stage at the *Comédie Française* in Paris. Her performance was praised by Charles Morgan, a critic for the *London Times*, who wrote of her "precision and lightness."

The review caught the attention of stage director Basil Dean, who had previously cast Larry in *Beau Geste*. Dean arranged an interview with her and her agent John Gliddon.

(top) J.B. Priestley and *(bottom)* Gracie Fields

Dean was struck by her beauty and immediately cast her in his upcoming film, *Look Up and Laugh*, a musical starring Gracie Fields, with screenplay by J.B. Priestley. For her appearance, Vivien was offered a salary of three hundred pounds.

Although almost forgotten today, J.B. Priestley was one of England's last great writers, belonging to a generation of authors who contemplated both science and philosophy in their literary output.

Fields was the highest paid actress in Britain in the 1930s; her Northern, working-class girl character was a favorite with audiences "between the wars."

In *Look Up and Laugh,* Vivien played the daughter of a mean tycoon (Alfred Drayton).

In the film, a "gutsy lass," Gracie, rallies fellow stall-holders at Birkenhead Market to prevent its takeover and demolition by a department store chain.

Virtually neglecting Leigh and Suzanne, Vivien rose at 6:30 every morning in time to make up and reach the studio, even if her presence wasn't required until late afternoon.

Dean turned out to be a tyrant, mocking her inexperience and performance on camera. "It's a swan!" he called out in front of the entire cast and crew, ridiculing her long neck. Often Dean drove Vivien off the set in tears.

"Don't worry, love," Gracie Fields told her. "You've got something."

Look Up and Laugh, opening in London on August 4, 1935, was reissued in 1942, one of the darkest years of World War II in London.

Vivien's meager exposure in film and on the stage led to a call from the offices of Alexander Korda for an interview about becoming one of his contract players. A taxi deposited Vivien, with Gliddon, at the offices of London Films on Grosvenor Street in Mayfair.

Vivien was all too aware that it was Korda who had given her girlfriend, Maureen O'Sullivan, her first starring role in *The Princess and the Plumber*, opposite Charles Farrell.

Vivien and Gliddon had to wait three hours in Korda's outer office, his schedule dominated by the director Anthony Asquith. Vivien sneered at the director when he emerged from Korda's office. She had no way of knowing, of course, that he was involved at the time in a fling with her future husband.

On Gliddon's arm, Vivien was escorted into the chambers of Korda, still basking in the glow of the critical acclaim and the box office success of *The Private Life of Henry VIII*, which had starred Charles Laughton in a role that had won him the Best Actor Oscar in 1933.

During his brief interview with Vivien, Korda was absolutely noncommittal, asking her about films she liked, questions about her family, and her marital status, what her ambitions as an actress were.

Vivien left his swank offices elated. She told Gliddon, "The contract with Korda is all but signed."

But when Korda called Gliddon the next day, he told her agent, "Miss Leigh is exquisitely beautiful, even charming. But she does not have star appeal like my contract players Merle Oberon or Wendy Barrie. I can spot a star a mile away. Miss Leigh will never be a star. Trust me on this one. Perhaps she should return to home and hearth, with her husband and daughter."

"Your client is merely an English rose," Korda told him. "Now take Merle Oberon. She's exotic. She fires the public imagination."

On hearing of Korda's rejection, Vivien was bitterly disappointed. She stayed home with Leigh and Suzanne for a whole week, but was often so depressed she did not come down to have dinner with her husband and daughter.

However, when Gliddon called with a dinner invitation at the Savoy Grill, she eagerly accepted. "We're not giving up this easily," he told her. "It's back to the see-and-be-seen circuit."

In those days the theatrical elite dined at only a few choice spots. It was inevitable that you'd encounter a certain star if you showed up frequently enough.

As Vivien was served a platter of mussels at the Savoy, she looked over to spot a familiar couple in a secluded nook. It was Larry Olivier dining with Jill Esmond.

"That's my future husband," she whispered to a stunned Gliddon. "I'm going to marry him. But, first, you've got to introduce us."

Gliddon knew Larry but was reluctant to barge over to the couple. But when she wanted something, Vivien could be very persistent.

The introduction was far too casual for her. Larry gave her only a passing nod, but Jill was warm and friendly, supplying most of the brief chatter.

Back at table, Vivien in a soft voice, claimed, "He was sexually attracted to me. A woman knows these things."

"He didn't appear to be," Gliddon said.

"For God's sake, don't you understand," she protested. "He's an actor. He didn't want to be caught panting for me in front of his wife."

For the rest of the supper, all Vivien could do was talk about Larry, describing how magnificent he was, how beautiful he looked, how sexy he appeared in his immaculately tailored clothes. "He arouses a grand passion in me both as an actress and as a woman. I could find fulfillment as his mistress, something I never found with Leigh."

"My darling Vivien," Gliddon said. "You are one hot-to-trot actress. You remember I promised an introduction to John Buckmaster. He's very handsome too. Since every man or woman in London is pursuing Olivier, I don't think you have a chance. But John will fall in love with you at first sight."

***

Jill Esmond seemingly never had any objection to Larry's affairs with men. She considered them non-threatening. However, when news reached her of her husband's affair with the beautiful, red-haired Greer Garson, she felt threatened as never before. She compared her own looks unfavorably to those of the perky, vivacious Garson.

Jill also was aware that many other beautiful women in London were signaling their availability to Larry, and she felt she had to make their relationship vital as a man and wife, something she'd never seen fit to do beginning on her wedding night.

At long last, she took the advice of that doctor in Berlin who had examined her. Very surreptitiously without Larry knowing it, she booked appointments for three sessions a week with a London psychiatrist in his darkened offices in Mayfair.

She approached his office with all the cloak-and-dagger mystery of a woman conducting an adulterous affair.

Slowly, very slowly, she began to reveal her innermost secrets, beginning with her powerful sexual attraction to women. She presented her dilemma to the psychiatrist, claiming that she'd come around to accepting the fact that she was a lesbian, and perhaps had always been one.

But she also wanted to continue to be Mrs. Laurence Olivier, feeling that he was on his way to becoming one of the great actors of the English stage, and perhaps even a film star one day, in spite of his early failures on the screen.

After endless probing, the psychiatrist finally tapped into the root of Jill's fear of penetration by a male. The condition is known as *vaginismus* (often anglicized as vaginism). Technically, the condition affects a woman's ability to engage in any form of vaginal penetration. The PC muscle, as it is called, causes the vagina to tense suddenly, making intercourse painful or in some cases impossible. A vaginismic woman does not consciously control the spasms. The reflex is often compared to the response of an eye shutting when an object comes toward it. The severity of *vaginismus* in women varies great-ly. After a gynecological examination, the doctor pronounced Jill's case as one of the most severe he'd ever seen.

In the course of his sessions with Jill, it was revealed that her father, H.V. Esmond, had repeatedly raped her when she was a pre-teen. This apparently set off a traumatic response in her and a fear of all men, even Larry.

Jill finally brought Eva into her innermost life, revealing to her secrets she'd never shared with anyone. As regards her privacy, that was a mistake for Jill.

When Eva was appearing in a small role in *The Divorce of Lady X* (1938), Eva, horrified and distraught, shared some of these revelations with Larry, hoping to win his sympathy and perhaps keep him married to her daughter.

Larry was so disconcerted that he revealed these dark secrets to both Noël Coward and Vivien. Somehow, through some link somewhere, Jill's condition was eventually made known in theatrical circles and became a source of gos-sip.

Vivien doesn't appear to have been the source of this scandal—perhaps it was Coward who indulged, on occasion, in indiscreet gossip. Jill knew that her mother had betrayed her when a loud and drunken Tallulah Bankhead once encountered her, provocatively, at a party. "Unlike you, Esmond, I don't suf-fer from your condition. In fact, I was known in Alabama as 'Legs Apart Tallu.'"

One of the reasons prompting Jill to confront her condition involved

Larry's increased insistence in wanting to father a child. Both Larry and Eva had been urging Jill to become pregnant. Eva, apparently, was not completely aware of Jill's physical condition.

But as Jill's sessions with the psychiatrist continued, she finally brought both Eva and Larry into her struggles and physical challenges. Each of them was most sympathetic.

The subject of Jill's *vaginismus* has not completely escaped all biographers of the past.

Eva was also aware of "Larry's straying eyes with both men and women."

When Jill told her she wanted to preserve her marriage, Eva urged her daughter "to trap Larry with a pregnant wife. He's a loving, gentle man. He would never desert a pregnant wife."

Jill and Larry began to explore a complicated sexual relationship, which Larry once hinted at with an interviewer. He suggested that he became the female in the relationship, with Jill in the male role. It has even been speculated, though there is no definite proof, that Jill repeatedly penetrated Larry with a dildo to bring some sexual gratification to him.

It was said that they engaged in "sexual games" of some sort in the months that led to the birth of their only child, a son, Simon Tarquin Olivier, who was born at 11:30am on August 21, 1936.

But by that time, as Larry told Ralph Richardson, "My desire for a child has passed. It is no longer a top priority. I have other interests, both professional and personal." By personal, it can only be assumed that he meant the entrance of Vivien into his troubled life.

It is not known how Larry overcame Jill's condition to achieve penetration, leading to her impregnation. It's been suggested that some drug was administered to her to cause her to relax into almost a coma-like state. When Larry confided to Glen Byam Shaw, among others, that "fucking Jill was like seducing a corpse," a comatose state on Jill's part was suggested by that statement.

As their marriage was collapsing, Jill and Larry amazingly started having sex. "I hope I don't get arrested for necrophilia," Larry told Shaw, again suggesting that Jill might have been drugged when having sex with her errant husband.

As she opened more closed doors to her forbidden past, and as her old demons surfaced, she became more belligerent with Larry. Sometimes she became irrational and made false accusations, suspecting that he was having sex with every handsome man and every beautiful woman with whom he was seen.

Even when Jill informed Larry that she was pregnant with his child, he privately told his most intimate friends, including Shaw and Noël Coward, "I still plan to divorce her. I can't go on with this charade of a marriage."

***

John Gliddon accurately predicted that Vivien would be sexually attracted to the dashingly handsome John Buckmaster, who had inherited some of the beauty passed on to him by his mother, Gladys Cooper, a friend of Larry's.

The mentally unstable Buckmaster, in the words of one writer, "was one of the many doomed gentlemen moths attracted to this particular flame," meaning Vivien, of course.

Ironically, Buckmaster was the stepbrother of Jack Merivale, another handsome actor with whom Vivien would engage in a long and turbulent affair in the years to come after Larry divorced her.

Soon Buckmaster replaced Gliddon as Vivien's escort, allowing her agent to stay home and save his money, as he'd been lavishing hard-earned pounds taking her to all the hot spots in London.

Vivien made a grand entrance on the arm of Buckmaster, as he escorted her into the Café Royal, former haunt of Oscar Wilde. He also took her frequently to Quaglino's, where on occasion he performed in sketches he'd conceived himself.

One night for his one-man show at Quaglino's, he'd written a pastiche composed of place names from the historical plays of Shakespeare. The highlight of the performance was when he demonstrated what a man could do with a piece of string. His act ended when he faked hanging himself with that piece of string.

Vivien was nervous when Buckmaster asked her to spend a weekend with his formidable mother. Her son seemed to adore Gladys Cooper but, like Vivien, was in awe of her at the same time.

Everyone, including Larry, had an opinion of her. Larry found her "one of the great hurdlers of the British theater in the 20th century." W. Somerset Maugham suggested she was a "woman without evils." Sybil

The formidable Gladys Cooper and *(lower photo)* her emotionally unstable son, Vivien's lover, John Buckmaster

197

Thorndike found her "a darling girl."

Vivien, in contrast, suggested she was "the Serpent of the Nile" because of her objection to her son flaunting an adulterous relationship with a married woman in front of the world.

Cooper had started out as a Gaiety Girl, singing and dancing her way through frothy London musicals. She did a stint as a World War I pin-up girl but ended up as a Dame Commander of the Order of the British Empire, her career spanning two world wars and two continents.

Cooper was enchanted, perhaps even a bit jealous, of Vivien's striking beauty. Whenever she could, she preferred private moments with Vivien so she could press an agenda. During the course of their weekend together, she urged Vivien to divorce Leigh Holman, "a man you obviously don't love, and marry John." She also revealed that her son "becomes a bit unhinged at times. He needs a strong woman in his life, and you look like a very determined young lady. I don't believe in suffering through loveless marriages like you seem to have."

Vivien remained noncommittal on that subject, but managed to steer the conversation around to Larry. She was aware that Cooper had starred with him in the play, *The Rats of Norway*. She asked a question that was burning into her mind, "What is Larry really like?"

"A very confused young man," Cooper said. "Handsome enough, of course, but unpredictable. He has so many conflicting emotions. He can fall in and out of love like a hot noonday sun that can suddenly turn chilly by three o'clock in the afternoon. I think he may struggle all his life deciding just what his sexual proclivities are."

If Vivien was shocked, she apparently did not let Cooper know, but, as far as it is known, this may be the first time she discussed her future husband's bisexuality with someone of authority.

"I always like the unpredictable in men such as your son," Vivien said. "God only knows how mercurial he is. If I have any criticism of my husband, it's how predictable he is. At two minutes after six every morning, he brushes his teeth. Not at six o'clock, not at 6:03, but at 6:02. He always has the same breakfast—slightly fried eggs, two strips of bacon, one piece of cold toast. He likes his tea at room temperature. I have never seen him, even on a rainy day, in shoes that weren't polished brightly."

During their affair, Buckmaster was seen so frequently with Vivien that a "romantic couple" picture of the two of them appeared in *Sketch*, a society magazine. She was identified as Miss Vivien Leigh, and no mention was made of her marriage to Leigh Holman. This obviously caused Leigh great embarrassment among his friends, but he apparently never confronted Vivien about this indiscretion.

There were times during their whirlwind romance that Vivien thought she was falling in love with Buckmaster. He had a rakish charm and a swashbuckling physique that in time would evoke the screen image of Errol Flynn. "He was a hell of a lot of fun," she said.

One night, in their finest clothes, he suggested that they run down the Haymarket in pouring rain. Both of them caught colds.

"I take after my father, not my mother," he told her. He was referring to Herbert Buckmaster, who had founded "Buck," an exclusive St. James's Club for gentlemen.

One night, as it seemed inevitable, Buckmaster was dining with Vivien at the Savoy Grill when she spotted Jill and Larry also dining. They sat in a far corner of the room and seemed engaged in an intense dialogue.

Vivien was aware that Buckmaster knew both Jill and Larry because of his link through Gladys Cooper.

At first Buckmaster turned down Vivien's request to go over and present her once again to the Oliviers. But she was so persistent that he rose to his feet, "Well, come along then; otherwise, I'll have no peace for the rest of the night."

Vivien seemed a bit awkward when she extended her hand to Larry. If he were attracted to her, he concealed it, returning to his succulent beef steak. Jill was exceptionally gracious but also slightly dismissive, as if Vivien and Buckmaster had intruded upon a very private conversation that she was eager to return to.

Buckmaster and Vivien returned to their table where, naturally, they talked about the Oliviers. "What a silly little creature this Olivier looks without his lip covering. I thought he'd go throughout his career imitating Ronald Colman. But now he's clean shaven."

Vivien immediately defended him. "I think he looks adorable. The sort of man I'd like to be married to."

"What a fickle bitch!" he said. "Now I know where I stand. For saying that, you won't get the Rooster tonight." That was John's pet name for his penis.

That was merely a threat he would not carry out.

After their respective dinners, by coincidence, Jill, Larry, Buckmaster, and Vivien each found themselves under the canopy of the Savoy Hotel waiting for the doorman to put them into a taxi. As Buckmaster was kissing Jill on both cheeks, Vivien extended her hand once again to Larry, and told him how privileged she was to have seen him again at the Savoy. She gazed dreamily into his eyes.

In contrast to the casual greeting at his table in the grill, he seemed enchanted with her while Jill was distracted with Buckmaster. Without checking with Jill, Larry impulsively invited Buckmaster and Vivien for a weekend at Dower House near Maidenhead in Kent. That was the country house that he and Jill had recently rented. It is not known at this point if Larry even knew that Vivien was a married woman. Leigh Holman was left out of the invitation, although that omission would be rectified in the weeks ahead.

In a taxi back to Buckmaster's lodgings, Vivien told him, "Larry has the most expressive eyes I've seen on any man."

"That may be so," Buckmaster said, "but I have a larger penis. I've seen him nude in his dressing room."

Months later, when Vivien encountered Maureen O'Sullivan, she said, "John was the first affair I had after marrying Leigh. She added an ominous note. "It will not be my last. Leigh and I now maintain separate bedrooms."

***

In mid-October of 1935, London braced for the theatrical sensation of the season, John Gielgud's upcoming production of Shakespeare's *Romeo and Juliet*. Two rival actors, Gielgud and Larry, would alternate the roles of Romeo and Mercutio.

London newspapers viewed the production as a "duel" between Larry and Gielgud for acting supremacy in the West End.

Opening at the New Theatre, *Romeo and Juliet* would run for 186 performances, closing March 28, 1936.

But this famous production almost never reached the stage.

Hailed as England's greatest Shakespearean actor, Gielgud was nearing thirty and realized that this might be his last chance to play Romeo, a role he loved. He was also enthralled at the chance to play both Romeo and Mercutio during the run of the play, alternating the roles to show his versatility.

Larry was not Gielgud's first choice. He'd gone first to Robert Donat, only to learn he was planning his own production of *Romeo and Juliet*. Donat declined, fearing that Gielgud might overshadow him when they alternated roles. Donat had become the toast of English cinema with his classic performance in Alfred Hitchcock's *The Thirty Nine Steps*.

In the early stages of Gielgud's production, he was unaware that both Ivor Novello and Larry were each considering mounting their own productions of *Romeo and Juliet*.

Larry's original (and later, much-altered) plan involved casting Jill as Juliet opposite his Romeo. Although she felt confident in her ability to

Robert Donat

play the role of Juliet—"after all, if that bitch Norma Shearer can play her, so can I"—she expressed her belief that her husband was completely wrong for Romeo. "You'd be laughed off the stage," she taunted him.

When she realized that he was adamant, and absolutely refused to budge, she reluctantly began rehearsing the play at their home in Chelsea.

Both Jill and Larry were stunned when the offer to appear with Gielgud came in. Larry wanted to do it, but Jill was opposed. "Gielgud would make mince meat of you."

A bitter fight ensued, and Larry stormed off, disappearing for ten days. When he came home he did not explain where he'd been. It is believed that he was with Glen Byam Shaw.

With only three weeks to rehearse before opening night, Gielgud clashed with Larry over his interpretation of the role of Romeo. Larry preferred a more realistic approach to the character, whereas Gielgud wanted to drain every ounce of blood from Shakespeare's poetry. Larry saw Romeo "as a sixteen-year-old boy rough around the edges, a boy with conkers in his pants."

He stubbornly resisted Gielgud's direction. Although the older actor pleaded and cajoled, Larry refused to change his interpretation of Romeo.

Gielgud was shocked when Larry told him, "You have to play Romeo as if he has a permanent erection. He wants to get into Juliet's knickers."

In despair, two days before opening night, Gielgud walked off the stage. "Do it however you bloody want to. Shakespeare's poetry be damned." He told the cast, "I fear the dear boy is substituting impetuosity for elegance."

Right from the beginning, neither Gielgud nor Larry had any disagreement over the way Peggy Ashcroft was playing Juliet. Even in rehearsal, she delivered brilliant performances. The cast soon learned that she and Larry were engaged in a backstage affair, not uncommon on Broadway or in West End productions. They were merely resuming a relationship "that might have been" years ago, but which had been abruptly cut off.

Stylistically different rivals in the Battle of the Romeos John Gielgud *(top photo)* and Larry both circa 1935.

201

Larry, in his always oblique way of writing, more or less confessed to the affair in his autobiography. "It is not surprising that those playing Romeo and Juliet are supposed to present a more stirring partnership if they develop the same passion between themselves as that which they are emulating; some believe that Shakespeare's magic depends on it."

"The affair seemed to be conducted in Peggy's dressing room," said Edith Evans, cast as the Nurse. "I should know. I had the dressing room next to hers. The walls were very thin."

Jill accused Larry of having an affair with Ashcroft, although he denied it. His affair put a strain on their already troubled marriage.

One afternoon, Larry complained to Ashcroft that his legs were far too skinny for green tights. With the help of wardrobe, she arranged for his legs to be padded, which caused Larry to have a splendid figure as Romeo.

Two hours before curtain on opening night, Gielgud told Ashcroft, "Larry is a trifle too coarse in the role, I fear. The Bard might turn over in his grave if he should come to hear Larry tonight."

On opening night Larry made his entrance on the stage and was called "every inch an Italian Renaissance prince straight out of the Uffizi." One writer found Larry "all flashing eyes and fire-and-brimstone."

As Gielgud had predicted, Larry's Romeo on opening night produced a backlash. One critic claimed, "Olivier plays Romeo as if he were riding on a motor bike." Larry called the assault on his acting "the sledge hammer of opprobrium."

After the devastating reviews, Larry escaped for the night to the home of Glen Byam Shaw in Putney and took a long walk with him in the country. Shaw had been cast in the production as Benvolio Montague, Romeo's cousin.

When Larry returned to London that night, he told Gielgud that he was quitting the cast and that his understudy could go on as Romeo. He suggested that Shaw knew all the lines and might give a more classical performance. Gielgud turned down his resignation. "Put on your makeup and get into those green tights. And pad those skinny legs."

"You're one to talk, you of the knock-kneed class."

In defense of his Romeo years later, Larry revealed that Gielgud's boyfriend—"of the time and the moment—came backstage and personally told him that he preferred my Romeo to Johnny's Romeo, because I was more realistic than his boyfriend."

After Larry's devastating reviews were being used to wrap fish and chips, praise was belatedly heaped upon Larry's performance as Romeo.

Jill did not like his Romeo, but Eva, his mother-in-law, did. She wrote: "Larry, darling, your Romeo gave me the greatest joy. I've seen lots, but never one who *was* youth and really in love, and never had one, till now, made me cry."

Writing in *The Observer*, St. John Irvine differed from most critics. "I have seen few sights so moving as the spectacle of Mr. Olivier's Romeo. Shakespeare's eyes would have shone had he seen this Romeo, young and ardent and full of clumsy grace."

Larry's future employer, Alexander Korda, told the *London Daily Telegraph*: "I have never seen anything like this in the theater. If anything, Larry Olivier transcends Shakespeare in giving a true glimpse into the soul of a man. In fact, I'm going to ask him to bring Shakespeare to the screen. Or perhaps not."

Future friend, the director Tyrone Guthrie, praised Larry's interpretation of Romeo, finding it "virile and full of life. Muscularity took the place of Shakespeare's lyric poetry."

When the time came for Gielgud to open as Romeo, he was highly praised by London theater critics for his classical performance. James Agate, however, found that his Romeo "never warmed to Juliet until she's cold."

Alec Guinness attended two performances to see both actors as Romeo. He later said, "We admired John greatly but were not so keen on Larry. He seemed a bit cheap and vulgar, striving after effects and making nonsense of the verse."

In the end, Larry would win the Battle of the Romeos. Future actors would follow the trail he blazed more than the lyrical portrait Gielgud presented on that long-ago night.

As Mercutio, Larry scored a hit with both the public and the London critics, especially in his scene with Edith Evans as the Nurse.

Evans stole the scene every time she walked on stage. In the words of W.A. Darlington, Evans was "as earthy as a potato, as slow as a cart-horse, and as cunning as a badger."

Uttering "A sail, a sail, a sail," Larry as the dashing cavalier Mercutio, partially lifted Evans's voluminous skirt with his sword's point.

This formidable woman, who said she was born "intoxicated—a raving lump of a girl"—went on to become one of the greatest English actresses of the 20th century. Her biographer, Bryan Forbes, claimed that Dame Edith "knocked the balance of the play into a cocked hat with her now definitive Nurse."

Larry would never again appear on stage with Gielgud. As late as 1986, Larry said Gielgud "is still harking back now and again at how terrible I was as Romeo. Surely you don't have to harbor unpleasant thoughts about people for forty-five

Welsh playwright/actor
Emlyn Williams

years."

Larry may have felt he was a failure as an actor. But as a dashing man with a decaying marriage, he was eagerly sought out by both women and homosexual men.

The Welsh playwright, Emlyn Williams had romantic designs on Larry and attended five productions of *Romeo and Juliet*, with seduction on his mind.

Vivien one night came backstage to congratulate Larry. She caught Larry as he and Williams were going to a late-night party in Mayfair. "I have such admiration for your work on the stage," she told him. "I saw *Ringmaster* two times. But your Romeo tops all of them. You have defined Romeo for the ages."

Larry might have lingered longer had it not been for Williams, who linked his arm with Larry's and practically propelled him to the stage door.

With John Buckmaster at her side, Vivien impulsively kissed Larry on the shoulder.

It would be the beginning of thousands of more intimate kisses to come.

***

Producer Sydney Carroll was searching for a beautiful but talented young actress for a key role in his upcoming costume play, *The Mask of Virtue*. Set in the days of Louis XV, *The Mask of Virtue* was adapted from Denis Diderot's story, *Jacques le Fataliste*. The premiere of the play was scheduled at the Ambassadors Theatre in London on May 15, 1935, a date that was kept.

The more experienced members of the play had already been cast—Jeanne de Casalis as Madame de Pomperaye, Frank Cellier as the randy Marquis d'Arcy, and Viola Tree (Lady Tree) as Madame Duquesnoy.

The role left uncast was that of Henriette Duquesnoy, a prostitute masquerading as a paragon of innocence. Carroll had already approached four actresses and offered them the role. Peggy Ashcroft, Anna Neagle, Jane Baxter, and Diana Churchill each had other commitments.

Jeanne De Casalis

Carroll remembered spotting Vivien one night at the Ivy dining with John Gliddon. After being turned down by the other actresses, he called Gliddon and set up an audition for Vivien.

The following day at the audition, Vivien remembered that, "I was shaking from head to foot with fright." Carroll was impressed and offered her the role that afternoon.

Later, in a bit of self-advertisement, he said, "I took a big chance. But I just knew she was the one. A lot of other people claimed they discovered Vivien, but I was the one. I have a great knowledge of palmistry, and Vivien reluctantly let me read her hands. She was ashamed of what she called 'my paws.' After that reading, I decided the role was hers."

Vivien bonded with Jeanne de Casalis, the play's star, who found her "as friendly and irresponsible as a kitten."

De Casalis told Vivien, "You may know that I'm married to Colin Clive, but I haven't seen *Frankenstein* since 1931." She was referring to the English actor who is best remembered for the 1931 movie.

It became apparent during the course of the play that De Casalis had lesbian designs on the young Vivien. Protected under the umbrella of a "lavender marriage" to Clive, De Casalis was known in the 1930s for developing a series of crushes on comely young actresses.

This African-born British actress was the daughter of a father who was one of the largest corset retailers in the British Isles. She was equally at home on the stage or in front of a camera, having made her first movie, *Zero*, in 1928.

Carroll claimed that De Casalis had only a "passing crush" on Vivien and nothing really came of it.

During the run of the play, she was always at Vivien's side, embracing her and sharing her suggestions as a more experienced actress than Vivien.

"Vivien may have interpreted this older woman's embrace of her as that of a loving mother instead of a woman of prey who had sexual designs on her," Carroll said. "We have no way of knowing."

Antony Beauchamp, who took publicity photographs of Vivien, said that De Casalis "hovered over her like a mother hen, adjusting her hair and costumes. But I doubt if this older lesbian ever got her hooks into Vivien."

Viola Tree said that she thought that it would take a far more aggressive woman to seduce Vivien. "I was certain that at some point in her future, Vivien would perhaps relate to someone of her own sex. But with Jeanne, Vivien needed more of a mother than a female lover."

Lady Tree later said, "In the course of Vivien's career, many ladies who like ladies fell for Vivien, as did many men who like men fell for Larry."

Lady Tree told Vivien that she was the real author who wrote *The Dancers* in 1923. "Tallulah Bankhead made her London debut in my play. We opened at the Wyndham's Theatre. Of course, I used a pen name. I wrote it with Gerald du Maurier. Our nom de plume was 'Hubert Parsons.' Tallulah seduced both Gerald and me during the first week's run of the play."

Later in her life, Vivien admitted that all during rehearsals, "I was an ass on stage and expected to get fired at any minute."

Leaving Suzanne one night with her nanny, Leigh showed up at rehearsals. He asked the director, Maxwell Wray, when his wife was "going to get this acting bug, which is really a stinging bee, out of her bonnet."

"Maybe never," Wray bluntly informed Leigh. "Get used to it. When this play opens, Vivien, in spite of her thin voice and limited range, will become an overnight star."

On opening night, May 15, 1935, at the Ambassadors Theatre, Vivien became an overnight sensation, the toast of London. "The fact that I was young and unknown caught the imagination of the audience. The roar of applause when the final curtain fell told me that the miracle had happened. I had arrived. *I was a star*!"

Leigh extended a rare invitation to Vivien to come dancing with him at the Florida Nightclub, which at the time was the trendiest in London. They left the club shortly before four in the morning, heading for Fleet Street to read the reviews. The headlines echoed the approval of the critics:

YOUNG ACTRESS IN TRIUMPH
FAME-IN-A-NIGHT GIRL ACTRESS IS A DISCOVERY
NEW STAR TO WIN ALL LONDON

Vivien Leigh in
The Mask of Virtue

For the most part, the reviews were sensational, although some critics wrote about her beauty more than her limited talent. She was called a star of tomorrow. The critics suggested that she would one day become as legendary as Eleonora Duse, Sarah Bernhardt, or Elisabeth Bergner.

On the following night, when Carroll escorted Vivien into the Savoy Grill for a late night supper, virtually the entire room of diners stood up and applauded the newly discovered star.

"From this night on, and for the rest of my life, I know that whenever I enter a room in the future all eyes will turn and look at me. The thought scares me to death."

"The price of stardom," Carroll told her.

As soon as he could, Larry went to watch Vivien perform in *The Mask of Virtue*, wanting to see what all the excitement was about. "Apart from her looks, which were magical," he said, "she possessed beautiful poise; her neck looked almost too fragile to support her head and bore it with a sense of surprise, and something of the pride of the master juggler who can make a brilliant maneuver appear almost accidental. She also had something else: an attraction of the most perturbing nature I have ever encountered. It may have been the strangely touching spark of dignity in her that enslaved the ardent legion of her admirers."

Larry went backstage and congratulated Vivien on her brilliant perform- ance, kissing her gently on both cheeks. He extended a specific invitation to Vivien and John Buckmaster to visit Jill and him at Dower House on Sunday and Monday, when the play was closed down. Vivien eagerly accepted.

She was very discreet in recalling that weekend, claiming, "And so we went [meaning Buckmaster] and played football. I remember Larry roaring around one minute and then unaccountably falling fast asleep under the piano the next."

With both Jill and Buckmaster watching their every move, there was little time for flirtation, much less romance. However, Larry did manage to encounter her privately one morning when he came down for tea and found her sitting in his garden. His wife and Vivien's beau were still asleep.

She later shared with Diana Churchill what Larry had said to her:

"When one is in a marriage where there is no love," he said, "one is forced to slip surreptitiously in between another man's sheets. And when one partner is not particularly romantic, and the other partner lives for romance, one must seek it elsewhere. Wouldn't you say?"

"I couldn't agree more," she told him. "Lovers down through the ages have found a way. Hopefully, not a solution as drastic as Romeo and Juliet."

"That would be too drastic," he said, "now wouldn't it?"

"Far too drastic," she said.

"There is always the furtive life," he said, "the lying life."

"There is always that, and I must say it appeals to my sense of drama as an actress. Perhaps at heart we are just two drama queens, or, in your case, a drama king."

"Thanks for amending the gender," he said.

"By the way, if Peggy Ashcroft ever tires of playing Juliet, I'd love to take over the role from her."

"You'd make the perfect Juliet," he assured her.

"But only to your Romeo."

Before she left Dower House, Larry invited Vivien to a luncheon sched- uled for the following Wednesday at the Ivy. She was eager to meet with him alone even if in a public restaurant. To her disappointment, she arrived to find him at table with John Gielgud. He would later become her dear friend, but at that particular moment she wished he had dined elsewhere. "You, darling, darling girl," Gielgud said, rising from the table to kiss her hand. "I just adored your performance in *The Mask of Virtue*. Splendid, splendid indeed."

When Gielgud later excused himself to go to the gent's toilet, she said, "Did you invite him as protection? I don't bite."

"I'm the shy type," he said. "Besides, Johnny makes a good beard. What if Buckmaster and Jill learned that we were dining alone at the Ivy?"

"What if?" she said, raising one eyebrow.

During the run of the play, a parade of Larry's on-again, off-again lovers came backstage to greet Vivien and congratulate her, perhaps as a means of collecting first-hand fodder for later dissemination. Among others, she met Douglas Fairbanks Jr. and Noël Coward.

Cecil Beaton, who would become her close friend, came back and asked her if he could photograph her for *Vogue*. Privately, he wrote, "Beautiful nose, lips, violet eyes, long neck, heart-shaped face. But does it add up to beauty?"

When Beaton's photographs of fashionable Vivien appeared in *Vogue*, the caption read: "She is slim and luminous. And she can get away with her taste in clothes which runs to heavy, almost barbaric jewellery, leopard skins, and queer colours . . . and is like a Persian gazelle in the dark studio forest."

On *Mask of Virtue's* opening night, Korda had arrived late at the theater but caught Vivien in the closing scenes. He barged backstage and walked into her dressing room without knocking. "Even a Hungarian can make a mistake," he told her, explaining why he'd misjudged her during their first interview.

Right on the spot, he wanted to sign her to make films for him. "Have Gliddon come in tomorrow morning," he told her.

Gliddon not only showed up the next day, but was a tough negotiator. It was six months before Vivien agreed to sign a five-year contract, allowing her to work on the stage six months out of every year. It was announced in the newspapers that Vivien had signed a contract for Korda for 50,000 pounds, the equivalent of a million pounds today. What the newspapers didn't say was that it was a five-year "bondage contract."

At the Ambassadors Theatre, *The Mask of Virtue* might have had a longer run, but Carroll unwisely moved it into the St. James's Theatre, which was much larger. Vivien's voice could not be heard in the back rows or the upper balconies. On most nights the cavernous theater was only half filled. The play closed in London, and Vivien went on tour with it.

Back in London at the end of the tour, Vivien found to her shock and dismay that there were no immediate job offers. Korda had not developed a film project for her.

She was still a media event and continued to give interviews. In one, she posed on the sofa of her home with daughter Suzanne. "I just know she will grow up to become an actress like me," Vivien said. She expounded on how it was possible to have a successful career and be a full-time mother at the same time.

When the press left, Suzanne's nanny complained that she was an obstinate child. Vivien called her "a silly old bitch," and blamed her for spoiling Suzanne.

Vivien showed no interest in motherhood. "Stars do not have time to breed children," she said, "much less look after them."

Finally, Leigh and Vivien found the perfect nanny in Daisy Goquel, who would keep house for Leigh until the end of his life.

Between roles, Vivien endorsed Matita, a skin cream for which she was paid 15 guineas. She posed for billboards advertising magazines such as *Britannia and Eve*. Her 200-pound allotment for clothes from Leigh was not enough. She modeled clothes for Victor Stiebel, a South African couturier, who let her then purchase the wardrobe at a greatly discounted price.

She hoped Korda would cast her as Roxanne opposite Charles Laughton in *Cyrano de Bergerac*. "He's a fine actor but a hideous creature," she told Gliddon. "For the life of me, I don't understand how a handsome young actor can maintain an erection to insert into that slobbery mouth of his. Oh, but he can dominate a stage or screen. I'll say that for the old sod."

Buckmaster accompanied Vivien to her screen test with Laughton. "I need to protect you from that monster," he told her.

"From what I hear, I must protect you from Laughton," she said.

"'Tis true," he said. "Every time he sees me, he begs me to let him suck my cock."

The test did not go well between Laughton and her. He told her her hair would have to be dyed blonde. She resisted that, claiming she could wear a blonde wig instead.

"No," he protested. "I want everything to be authentic in this production."

"A dyed blonde is not authentic," she shot back.

Laughton later told Korda, "There are actresses, and then there is Miss Vivien Leigh."

She also dreamed of following Leslie Howard, on whom she still had a crush, to the United States. She wanted to appear as Ophelia on Broadway with him in his production of *Hamlet*.

"Maybe I'll finally get him to seduce me," she told Gliddon. "He seems to seduce every other beautiful actress on either side of the Atlantic."

When Gliddon made her intentions known, Howard had already cast another actress, Pamela Stanley.

Considering the reception of Howard's *Hamlet* on Broadway, Vivien later was glad she wasn't chosen. Stanley, born in Cheshire, had appeared as Queen Victoria in *Victoria Regina* at the Gate Theatre in London in 1935.

Critic James Agate had also seen Helen Hayes starring as the Queen. He wrote: "Unfortunately, I found Hayes' portrayal of Queen Victoria like a blazing sun, and I am so blinded by the dazzling performance of Helen Hayes that I literally cannot see Pamela Stanley."

On Broadway, Gielgud had just ended a successful run of *Hamlet*, and the critics weren't impressed with another *Hamlet,* this time with Howard and Stanley, so their play closed after only thirty-nine performances.

As one job after another fell through for her, Vivien became despondent. "One day I'm the toast of the West End. The next day I'm sitting around waiting for the bloody phone to ring."

She called Gliddon. "Get me a star role and soon, matey," she said in her best Cockney accent. "I'm going back on the party circuit. I need to let London know that Miss Vivien Leigh is still around."

She was a vibrant, sexual woman. Since her needs weren't being satisfied by Leigh, she seemed to have very few compunctions about cheating on her husband. "I have no guilt about such things," she told Patsy Quinn.

"Leigh and I are no longer man and wife," she confessed to Buckmaster. "He's like a wonderful older brother to me. The white heat of a romance burns out very quickly. Nature did not intend for a man or a woman to be monogamous. I feel it's perfectly all right to have an off-the-record affair outside of marriage."

Buckmaster's half-sister, Sally Hardy, later claimed, "Vivien was the love of John's life, and the only man, according to my mother, Gladys Cooper, that Leigh didn't mind Vivien dating."

Buckmaster wasn't the only man Vivien dated. She took up with two oarsmen from the class of 1921. John Fremantle (later Lord Cottesloe) rowed for Trinity, and David Collet rowed for Jesus College, both at Oxford. Vivien recalled Fremantle had "twinkling eyes but wasn't as handsome as John Buckmaster. Collet might not be the handsomest man in London, but he is the best dressed." Vivien was spotted dancing with these "fun dates" at such clubs as the 400.

An actress and fashion model, Eve Phillips, became Vivien's close friend and confidante for a time. She later revealed that Vivien had "borrowed" her London flat for two assignations—one with Alexander Korda himself, the other with a "married actor."

Vivien obviously wasn't physically attracted to Korda, but perhaps used the producer presumably for career advancement. Although Korda had Merle Oberon lurking in the background, he continued, like Darryl F. Zanuck in Hollywood, to seduce "starlets" he had under contract.

If Phillips is to be believed, Vivien's fling with Korda lasted no more than three weeks. She did not name who the "married actor" was, and it was generally assumed she was referring to Larry.

John Gliddon, Vivien's loyal agent, disputed the claim that Vivien had an affair with her producer. Of course, he could have been protecting her professional reputation, a task which somehow Vivien had extended into a part of his job.

Vincent Korda, Alexander's brother, was a close associate of Merle Oberon, and he too had a reason to dispute the claim that Vivien had conducted an affair with his more famous brother. Vincent was one of filmdom's great art directors. During his distinguished career, he won an Oscar for his work on *The Thief of Bagdad* (1940), and he gave *That Hamilton Woman* (1941) its scenic look.

In contrast, Vivien's friends and confidants, the sister/brother team of Clare Sheridan and Oswald Frewen, claimed that Vivien admitted to the affair with Korda.

Years later, actor Stewart Granger was talking with Vivien about the casting couch which applied both to men and women. She claimed that both she and Larry had lain on the casting couch for certain producers and directors.

Surely she didn't mean David O. Selznick. She must have been suggesting Alexander Korda, although she didn't name him. Who else could it have been? Perhaps Victor Saville, Basil Dean, Erich Pommer, or Sydney Carroll, but each of these candidates appears unlikely. Most biographers name Korda as the primary suspect.

All such seductions had to happen before 1939. After that year, both Vivien and Larry were too big as stars to "audition" themselves on any producer's casting couch.

Korda promised Vivien the female lead in Victor Seastrom's *Under the Red Robe*, a film going into production. At the last minute, he cast the French actress, Annabella, instead. He explained to Vivien, "There is French money in the film, and I had to do it."

Co-starring with Annabella were veteran actors Conrad Veidt and Raymond Massey. Vivien had wanted to work with both of them. Korda promised that he'd soon star her in a movie with Veidt. He kept his word when he cast her in *Dark Journey* in 1931.

Annabella would soon divorce Jean Murat to marry Tyrone Power, a future lover of Larry's.

On losing the role to Annabella, Vivien turned to Glen Byam Shaw, and he held her tenderly as she sobbed her disappointment.

It had been assumed that it was Larry who was that "married actor" having an affair with Vivien in the flat of Eve Phillips. Quite possibly it was Shaw himself. The married actor was also Larry's lover. Whether Vivien knew that at the time isn't known. As a bisexual man, Shaw seems to have been equally attracted to Vivien.

He'd become acquainted with her when he and John Gielgud were directing Shakespeare's *Richard II* for the Oxford Dramatic Society, with an opening set for February 17, 1936. Gielgud wanted to cast Vivien in the role of the queen.

Already cast as Richard II was Michael Rennie, a tall, smoothly handsome actor with a fine authoritative speaking voice. "I have to be careful as an actor and not get trapped in stodgy costume dramas," Rennie told Vivien. To judge from his future films, this Yorkshire-born actor didn't follow his own advice.

She agreed to audition, and Gielgud praised her performance highly, claiming that "all the young men at Oxford would fall madly in love with her."

Shaw later admitted that Gielgud's prophecy came true, and Shaw himself fell under her spell during rehearsals for *Richard II*.

Of all the beaux who wooed Vivien at Oxford, at least those who escaped the clutches of John Gielgud, Hugh Martin made the best claim. "I once took a bath with Vivien Leigh," he told his panting classmates. They were jealous of Martin and accused him of lying. Actually he was telling the truth. Hugh was the son of Geoffrey Martin, who had been Ernest Hartley's friend and business partner. Vivien and Hugh had shared a bath in India when both of them were two years old.

"That gave me a head start over some of the other boys who were queuing up to ask Vivien to lunch . . . or whatever," Hugh said. "I half-jokingly, half-seriously asked Vivien to share a bath with me again. I told her that a certain part of my anatomy had grown to an impressive size. She laughed in that charming little way she had and kissed me gently on the lips. 'The pleasure would be great, I am certain,' she said. 'If only I weren't so busy learning this damn part.'"

Shaw later issued a public statement about Vivien.

She was wonderful to work with. She was tremendously serious, sensitive, eager for direction, punctual and professional and gave me great encouragement and help throughout the rehearsals. No leading lady could have been more generous in her attitude to an inexperienced producer and it was the start of a friendship that was always very precious to me.

When *Richard II* opened, the reviewer from *The Times* stabbed Vivien in the heart. "Miss Vivien Leigh makes a pretty figure of the pathetic queen, but she has yet to make herself at ease with Shakespearean verse."

Years later, when Shaw was no longer close to the Oliviers, he proposed a tell-all memoir, shopping it around, sending it to a publisher in London. In New York, he submitted the manuscript to Bertha Klausner, a leading literary agent. In his proposal, he "outed" Larry as a bisexual and also claimed to have had an affair with Vivien some time late in 1935, spilling over into the early winter of 1936.

He claimed that he was attracted to Vivien, but also "deflowered" her as an "act of petty revenge and jealousy" because Larry talked about her beauty day and night. "I got to her before Larry did, and that infuriated him."

Of course, how Shaw could deflower a married woman and the mother of a child wasn't explained. The British publisher rejected the manuscript. Klausner sent it to about ten major publishers, including Random House, and each of them rejected it also.

At the time, it was tolerable, albeit saucy, to write about a heterosexual seduction of Vivien Leigh, but the bisexual outing of a major star like Larry Olivier was far ahead of its time. Later, of course, such revelations would become commonplace in book publishing.

***

While waiting for work, Vivien studied vocal techniques with Larry's former teacher, Elsie Fogerty, of the Central School of Speech Training and Dramatic Art. She loved hearing Fogerty talk about Larry in his early days, as she knew virtually nothing about his life as a young boy and aspirant actor.

A strange coincidence occurred one Saturday afternoon in Soho in 1936. Vivien had no classes that day, and Leigh had invited her to the Ivy, since she was always talking about dining there with various people. By chance Leigh and Vivien encountered Jill Esmond and Larry, who also happened to be lunching at the Ivy. The two couples nodded politely and exchanged pleasantries.

Observing all this was the French actor, Jean-Pierre Aumont, who had recently made a film in England. He was dining with an English actor, Tony Bushell.

As Vivien was seated, Aumont turned to Bushell and said, "This is the most ravishing creature that can be imagined; immense eyes that pass from melancholy to the most ironic vivacity, a little insolent nose, and an oval face lengthened by a frail neck."

As he continued to watch her, he noticed that she wasn't paying attention to her older companion. At frequent intervals, she kept glancing at the dark, romantic-looking young man who sat at

Jean-Pierre Aumont

213

table with a blonde-haired woman. Aumont told Bushell, "The young woman and that man sitting at the other table are madly in love with each other."

"Oh, you Frenchman," Bushell said. "You see love everywhere. That beautiful woman is the actress Vivien Leigh. She is dining with her husband, Leigh Holman. The handsome young man at the other table is Laurence Olivier dining with his wife, Jill Esmond. She's also an actress."

"So, the couples are married," Aumont said. "It doesn't matter. I know love when I see it. Miss Leigh is obviously in love with Mr. Olivier."

On the way to the powder room about twenty minutes later, Vivien passed by Aumont's table and smiled at the handsome French actor. Their eyes met. Little could either of them know that in the years to come they'd be starring together on Broadway. Not only that, but they'd become lovers.

In another ironic touch, Bushell himself would become a lover of Larry's and would, in time, work in close association with him on such future productions as *Hamlet* (1948), and *Richard III* (1955).

At the time Aumont spotted Vivien and Larry at the Ivy, they had not become lovers. "They were circling each other," said Vivien's producer, Sydney Carroll. "He came to see her when I cast her as Anne Boleyn in my production of *Henry VIII* in Regent's Park. "When Larry came back to congratulate Vivien after the show, I could tell by the way he held her hand and looked longingly into her eyes that he was falling in love. She was like a schoolgirl with a crush when in his presence."

It was a soggy June for outdoor theater in London, and Vivien came down with a bad case of influenza. "I called Larry and told him the bad news. He used that as an excuse to visit her home while Leigh was at work. Of course, having Larry see her in her sick bed was hardly Vivien's idea of a romantic encounter."

A maid showed Larry upstairs to Vivien's bedroom where she was attended by her mother, Gertrude. Vivien looked pale and thin, and she was smoking incessantly, using a long ebony cigarette holder. Between puffs, she was coughing slightly.

"Oh, Mr. Olivier," Gertrude said, "Perhaps you can get her to stop smoking. Those cigarettes will kill her."

"Mother doesn't understand," Vivien said. "You're an artist. You'll understand. I have anxiety attacks."

Larry walked over to her bed, removed the ebony holder from her hand, and crushed the cigarette out in an ashtray on her nightstand. He looked down at her lovingly before turning to Gertrude. "What Vivien needs is a good strong man in her life."

***

So far, when it came to casting roles in plays with him, Vivien had struck out with Ivor Novello. But once she became a star in her own right, the handsome matinee idol wanted to star with her in his latest play, *The Happy Hypocrite*, a Clemence Dane adaptation of Sir Max Beerbohm's novella about the transfiguring power of love.

Vivien took the script with her to read as she and Leigh celebrated Christmas at the stately old Lygon Arms Hotel in the historic wool-trading market town of Broadway, deep in the Cotswolds. Her husband found her distracted, more interested in the play than in him. At Christmas dinner, she merely toyed with her food. Suzanne had been left behind in London with her nanny.

Instead of attempting to rekindle their romance, Vivien discussed legal matters with her barrister husband. According to her contract, Korda could call her to work on a film at any minute. Producer Sydney Carroll was another problem. He had the option to star her in a play, although he had no project for her at the time. Leigh had a solution. He advised Vivien to buy her way out of the contract with Carroll, and he agreed to negotiate the deal. By the following week, he managed to get Carroll to agree to a sixty-five pound termination payout. Vivien was free of Carroll.

To Vivien's regret, *The Happy Hypocrite* was postponed for a few weeks, during which time Novello invited Vivien for a weekend at his country home, Redroofs. Before leaving, she confessed to her friend, Clare Sheridan, "If he were not homosexual, I think I could

Three views of *The Happy Hypocrite:*

(top photo) Vivien, Ivor Novello, & Isabel Jeans
(middle photo) Ivor Novello holding one of his masks
(lower photo) Isabel Jeans

Easy Virtue

Isabel Jeans

Three views of Isabel Jeans

fall for Mr. Novello. He surely is the most beautiful man in England, other than Larry, of course. When he was but a boy, a young Winston Churchill seduced Ivor. That's how powerful the boy's attraction was. Imagine: a nose that's regal, eyes large and luminous, and those lashes. But Ivor prefers Larry to little ol' me. Alas, why do all the beautiful men of England tend to be homosexual, or at least bisexual?"

Vivien arrived at Redroofs, believing that Novello was a secret bisexual. He made a point that she was not to arrive with an escort. To her disappointment, she discovered that Novello's fellow houseguest that weekend was the playwright, Terence Rattigan.

Although they were later to play major roles in each other's lives, Rattigan and Vivien did not start off liking each other. "I thought she had the most beautiful face I'd ever seen on a woman," Rattigan said. "But was that enough? She had a vague crush on Ivor, even though it would bear no fruit. It seemed that Ivor found me highly desirable. I found that out on the first night there, when he invited me to share his bedchamber and spent the rest of the night making love to me. Vivien slept alone. But I suspected a woman that beautiful didn't sleep alone on most nights."

Novello called Vivien again a few weeks later to schedule rehearsals for *The Happy Hypocrite*. During her first meeting with other members of the cast, she renewed her friendship with Viola Tree (Lady Tree), with whom she'd recently appeared in *The Mask of Virtue*.

It was Tree who introduced her to the stunningly beautiful Isabel Jeans, another member of the cast. Vivien was already familiar with the career of the older star, who had been born in 1891, twenty-two years before Vivien, but who looked almost the same age.

216

Jeans was hailed as one of the most beautiful actresses ever to grace the British stage. She had been famously but turbulently married to Claude Rains from 1913 to 1915. During that marriage, she separated from him three times but reunited twice.

Rains divorced her in a sensational trial, accusing her of adultery after she miscarried with Gilbert Wakefield's baby. In court, in front of the press, she admitted to the adultery and would later marry Wakefield.

When Hitchcock was directing Rains in *Notorious* (1946), starring Cary Grant and Ingrid Bergman, Rains told him that his divorce from Jeans could easily have been even more scandalous than it was. He claimed that he'd returned to their shared home early one afternoon and caught his wife in bed with a young actress.

Hitchcock's response to this revelation was somewhat bizarre. He told Rains that he wished the Production Code could be rewritten, claiming that he'd always wanted to make a movie about two lesbians. "Your former wife and Judith Anderson would be perfect casting."

Hitchcock had cast Jeans, a former leading lady in Harley Granville Barker's Theatre Company, in two of his silent movies. Released in 1927, *Downhill* was based on a play *Down Hill*, with a slightly different spelling. It had been penned by Ivor Novello and the noted British actress and acting coach Constance Collier, writing jointly under the *nom de plume* of "David L'Estrange." Both Novello and Jeans had starred in *Downhill*.

Jeans had starred with Novello in *The Rat* (1925), also written by "David L'Estrange," and she had followed that with *The Triumph of the Rat* (1925). Novello and Jeans even starred together in *The Return of the Rat* (1928). All of these Novello/Jeans silent movies were made for Gainsborough, the British film company that was the U.K.'s answer to RKO.

Hitchcock had liked Jeans' acting so much he'd also cast her in *Easy Virtue* (1928), another silent film based on a play by Noël Coward. Jeans played the persecuted victim of

(top photo)
Vivien Leigh as Jenny Mere in
The Happy Hypocrite

(lower photo) Satirist and social commentator Sir Max Beerbohm

217

social hypocrisy who twice makes headlines in divorce proceedings, an acting role which echoed her own scandalous divorce thirteen years before from Rains.

During rehearsals and out-of-town tryouts in Manchester, Newmarket, and Southport, Vivien played endless card games with Jeans and later retired to the same bed in a hotel. They became inseparable, and rumors of an affair spread quickly throughout the cast.

Ironically, at the time Vivien and Jeans came together, she had been offered a role in the American movie *Tovarich* (1937). In a secondary part, Jeans would later take the role of Hermonde Dupont, the leads going to Claudette Colbert, Charles Boyer, and Basil Rathbone. *Tovarich*, of course, would also be Vivien's musical hit on Broadway in 1963. Its plot involved White Russian royals who flee the Revolution and who are subsequently reduced to working as servants.

On the road tour in England for *The Happy Hypocrite*, "Vivien's card games became obsessive," said Clemence Dane, a popular woman author of her day. "She couldn't wait for the curtain to go down at night, and she played to win."

"There's the devil in Jenny's cards," Vivien would shout when she won. The stage character she was playing was named Jenny Mere, and the role called for her to sing, which petrified her.

Max Beerbohm (1872-1956) showed up one day and introduced himself to Vivien, who was enchanted with this essayist, parodist, drama critic, and caricaturist. He hoped to see what Novello was doing to his original story, and he also wanted to join his wife, Florence Kahn, whom he had married in 1910. She had a minor role in *The Happy Hypocrite* as Lady Gloster.

Vivien invited both Beerbohm and Florence to join Jeans and herself in their card games.

Lord David Cecil, in his biography of Sir Max Beerbohm, defined the subject of his book as "an artificial pastoral in the Regency mode, told in delicately flippant tones and in which, if Max does indulge in a romantic feeling, it is quickly to deflate it with common sense."

From seeing Max and Florence together, Vivien assumed that it was, as speculation had it, a *mariage blanc*. Evelyn Waugh told friends that Beerbohm was a "non-active homosexual."

Vivien bonded with Beerbohm and became his friend. Years later, during her marriage to Larry, the couple visited him in his "exile" in Rapallo, Italy.

Beerbohm later claimed that Isabel Jeans moved in on Vivien at a weak moment. "She was trapped into that marriage with Leigh Holman, who had grown like an old professor before his time. She had her hat set for Olivier, but those hopes were dashed when she heard that Olivier had impregnated his lesbian wife."

"At times, Vivien seemed half crazed with despair during our play," Novello told Denys Blakelock. "Jeans seized the opportunity and offered her comforting bosom. One thing led to another, and of that I'm certain. They went everywhere—breakfast together, bed together. I even heard from a hotel maid that they bubble-bathed together. I am certain they made love, perhaps a first for Vivien, although I don't know about some of those girls' schools she went to."

"I think it wasn't so much physical attraction that drove her to Jeans, but it was the love, support, and comfort an older woman offered," Novello said. "Of course, Jeans was one of our island's greatest English roses in full bloom. Any man—dare say, any woman?—would find that one hard to turn down. She was also the epitome of charm and grace."

One night when the cast had a night off, Novello invited them to a touring version of Lillian Gish's *The Old Maid*, a play that had debuted on Broadway in 1936, and which was now making scattered appearances in the U.K. "The cast laughed at the overacting, but Jeans and Vivien cried," Novello said.

Of course, all was not idyllic between the two actresses. In Manchester, Jeans got better reviews than Vivien. "I told Clemence Dane that if she inserts any more bits for Isabel's La Gambogi character, I shall insist on two more scenes, a dance, and another song," Vivien said.

She may have slept every night with Jeans, but somehow she managed to slip in a brief fling with actor Carl Harbord, who was cast in the play as Mercury. Years later, after Vivien had divorced Larry, Harbord complained to John Merivale, who was Vivien's lover at the time. "During my affair with Vivien, she spent all the time I was making love to her talking about Olivier."

(top photo) Autoportrait of Angus McBean, by Angus McBean

(lower photo) In 1985, the British Postal Service issued stamps honoring the British film industry. Included was a stamp with an Angus McBean photograph of Vivien Leigh

When Jeans found out about the brief fling between Harbord and Vivien, she became furious. Vivien refused to be possessed by anybody. Right in the presence of Novello, she informed Jeans that, "Lesbian love is a mere diversion, a momentary stopover, on my road to a far greater horizon."

Other actors who worked with Jeans in the years ahead claimed that she was very frank and upfront about her former affair with Vivien. Denys Blakelock, appeared with Jeans in the highly successful play, Oscar Wilde's *Lady Windermere's Fan* (1945-46). "She told me about the affair," Blakelock claimed.

For both Blakelock and Jeans, *Lady Windermere's Fan* arguably was the highlight of their respective careers. The play opened for the 1945-46 season at London's Theatre Royal in the Haymarket. John Gielgud was the director, Cecil Beaton the designer. In British theater legend, that production lives on as the greatest version of Wilde's play ever presented.

Coral Browne, who was married to actor Vincent Price at one time, and who was a close friend of Vivien's, said that Jeans admitted to the affair with Vivien when Browne and Jeans appeared together in the 1966 revival of *Lady Windermere's Fan*.

When the road tryouts were over and *The Happy Hypocrite* opened in London at His Majesty's Theatre on April 8, 1936, Vivien's world underwent rapid change. So did her relationship with Jeans.

***

During the rehearsals for *The Happy Hypocrite*, Novello introduced Vivien to a young man who would play a pivotal role in her life. He was the photographer Angus McBean.

"The moment I saw her, I fell in love with her," he later said. "Her beauty is for the ages."

Almost immediately she became his favorite model, and he became her official photographer for life.

Born in South Wales in 1904, McBean worked as a maker of theatrical props. From John Gielgud, he received a commission to create the medieval scenery for his celebrated production of *Richard of Bordeaux*. "I not only got paid," McBean later said, "but received a number of blow-jobs from Gielgud."

His "patron," Gielgud, brought McBean to the attention of Ivor Novello, who was so impressed with his work that he granted him a commission in 1936 to create masks for his play *The Happy Hypocrite*.

Novello was so pleased with the masks to be worn in the play that he hired McBean to take a set of production photographs as well.

After their first week together, Vivien told McBean, "I want you to photograph me in every stage production of mine until the day I die."

Although that might have been uttered as a vague promise at the time, it became a life-long commitment on the part of McBean.

A single image of Vivien, shot in 1938, was sent to Hollywood to David O. Selznick, who was conducting a nationwide search to find a suitable actress to play Scarlett O'Hara.

Vivien, and later Larry, remained loyal friends of McBean during his turbulent years surrounding World War II. In 1942, McBean was tried in Bath on a charge of "criminal acts of homosexuality" and sentenced to four years in prison—"twice as long as Oscar Wilde's sentence," said McBean. He was released in the autumn of 1944.

After prison, McBean slowly recovered his career, with Larry and Vivien championing him. McBean photographed celebrity visitors arriving in London who ranged from Marlene Dietrich to Elizabeth Taylor. His photographs of a young Audrey Hepburn led to a screen test for the future star.

Three weeks before her death, Vivien posed for McBean for a final time. The following day, she wrote him a note:

"My darling Angus, through your surrealistic photographic images of me, you made me a greater actress than I will ever be on stage. Though Larry and I are not together any more, we remain wedded in our joint love for you. I am certain that someday, far, far into the future, when you ascend to Heaven, God will make you his official photographer. It saddens me at times how England has treated some of its greatest artists, but you have triumphed over your enemies. Heaps of love on you, you dear, dear man. Vivien."

After the nightfall of McBean's 86th birthday, death knocked on his door. Sir Cecil Beaton hailed him as "England's greatest photographer." Lord Snowdon declared him a genius.

The photographer had lived to see his 1938 photograph of Vivien used in 1985 on a stamp for the Royal Mail. For McBean this was a kind of apotheosis from the government that had so wrongly imprisoned him in 1942, when Britain had more pressing concerns at the time, including staving off a Nazi invasion of its homeland.

Ivor Novello also ended up in jail in 1944, but on a very different charge. He was arrested for misuse of petrol tokens and was sentenced to eight months in prison, serving only four. He was driving from theater to theater around the country. When a fellow thespian offered him her unused petrol tokens, he gladly accepted, an action that defied British law at the time.

***

When *The Happy Hypocrite* arrived in London, it was Beerbohm who spread the word that "Isabel Jeans and Vivien are having an affair." He didn't condemn it. At his club, he said, "the idea of two women doing it together, an act regarded as 'impossible' by Queen Victoria, actually is quite titillating to my jaded senses."

Upon Vivien's return to London, she quickly reverted back to the heterosexual life. Her thoughts were monopolized by Larry. "Poor Isabel lost out," Novello said. "I guess it was inevitable."

Although Vivien and Jeans lost touch, Jeans would live until 1985, dying at the age of ninety-three, a faded beauty of yesterday. Upon her death, *The Times* called her "one of the aristocracy of British players."

When asked about Jeans in 1962, Vivien said, "She was strikingly beautiful, designed to play chic, sophisticated, worldly roles."

Before the opening night in London of *The Happy Hypocrite*, Vivien was aware that many women in the audience, and dozens of homosexuals, came to see Novello play because of his male beauty. But in *The Happy Hypocrite*, he wore hideous masks throughout most of the production.

"Why would you want to obscure the most famous profile on the English stage?" Vivien asked him.

"Well, duckie, it's like this," Novello said. "I won't always have this maddeningly perfect profile, and I will want to act. So I'm merely preparing my fans for that dreadful day when they will no longer be able to feast on my male beauty."

As Vivien predicted, the audiences who came to bask in Novello's beauty were disappointed when he appeared on stage looking fat and bloated, absolutely dissolute.

The Happy Hypocrite opened on April 8, 1936 at His Majesty's Theatre. Reviews were mixed, and the run would be short. As "a star on the rise," Vivien generated some polite press and an occasional barb. She ended up taking home 332 pounds for her work on the show.

Elisabeth Bergner
Vivien Leigh used this great
actress as a role model.

James Agate, who had been critical of Vivien's performance in *The Mask of Virtue*, wrote that in the role of Jenny "she might have stepped out of a poem by Tom Moore."

Opening night was memorable, as much of *tout* London turned out, including Larry accompanied by Jill who was six months pregnant. The couple came backstage to congratulate Vivien. Larry embraced both his former lover, Novello, and his future lover, Vivien, warmly.

"Vivien kept staring at Jill's big belly as if she viewed it as a personal threat to her future plans for Larry," Novello recalled.

When Vivien had visited the Oliviers at Dower House, Larry had told her, "We just know Jill is giving birth to a son. I'm going to name him Tarquin."

"How quaint," Vivien had said, barely concealing the sarcasm in her voice.

When she encountered Jill again backstage at the theater, she said in a slightly mocking tone, "And how's little Tarquin coming along? Starting to kick around a bit?"

After the Oliviers had left, Vivien told Novello, "That lesbian bitch doesn't want to have a kid. She got herself pregnant just to hold onto Larry. That's the only reason. I know that. Some women will stop at nothing to keep a man."

Feeling bitchy that night, Novello said, "and some women will stop at nothing to get another woman's man."

She turned on him in anger. "You've already had him, you poof. Now it's my turn." She turned and walked away.

Vivien's momentary flare-up with Novello hardly lasted a night. They became life-long friends. "He was like a rock for me when I needed him," she claimed years later. "He stood by me in the good times and especially the bad times when I sought refuge with him at Redroofs or even in Jamaica."

***

"I don't believe that the plays of Shakespeare can ever be adapted for the screen," Larry had told producer Walter Wanger before fleeing Hollywood after his failure there. He also made another prophecy: "I will never spend another night in this so-called Tinseltown. It can destroy a real actor. No more Hollywood, and no Shakespeare on the screen. No, never! I swear it on the grave of my beloved mother."

The Austrian actress, Elisabeth Bergner, had gone to see Larry's performance in Gielgud's production of *Romeo and Juliet*. She was most impressed, turning to her husband, the producer-director Dr. Paul Czinner. "I have found my partner to play Orlando in *As You Like It*." That was the first film they planned to shoot after fleeing

Two views of Henry Ainley

from Hitler's Nazi Germany in 1933.

A leading lady on the stage in Germany and Austria, Bergner had launched her theatrical career in Zurich in 1919. In time, she became the favorite actress of Max Reinhardt, the celebrated German stage director.

Writer/actress Mary Orr used Bergner's *persona* as inspiration during her crafting of the character of Margo Channing in her piece for *Cosmopolitan* magazine called *The Wisdom of Eve*. When Orr's much-altered script eventually reached the screen, it was entitled *All About Eve* and starred Bette Davis.

Dr. Czinner offered Larry 600 pounds a week for a thirteen-week shoot, which was the best acting salary he'd ever drawn. Since he needed the money, he decided to change his mind about bringing Shakespeare to the screen, although he still had many reservations.

He told the press, "I hope I can do something with Orlando, something reasonably intelligent. No one can play with Bergner without learning something from her."

He was happily surprised to be working with Henry Ainley, cast as the exiled Duke. Unknown to almost anyone at the time, he and Ainley had been on-again, off-again lovers since 1930.

It was Jill herself who had first alerted Larry to the brilliance of Ainley's acting back in 1930 when he appeared at London's Haymarket Theatre in *Hamlet*. Larry was in Germany making a film at the time.

Born in 1879, Ainley was one of the greatest actors on the British stage. "Shakespeare's speeches just ripple from his tongue," Jill wrote Larry. "But I should think you'd make a better Hamlet. You'd be as good as Ainley—no, even better because you could bring youth to the role. Ainley first appeared on the stage in the last months of Queen Victoria's reign, so he's getting a little long in the tooth for *Hamlet*."

Back in London, Larry was eager to see Ainley perform and even to meet him. He learned that one of his greatest moments on stage was in 1926 when he'd starred as *Macbeth* for Sybil Thorndike's company. He called her and arranged for her to introduce him to Ainley.

Larry was twenty-three when he first met Ainley backstage. He told Jill at the time that he was "awed" being in the presence of such a great actor. From all reports, Ainley was mesmerized by Larry, who looked far younger than his years.

Apparently, a sexual relationship between Ainley and Larry began within the week. Ainley was married and had a son, so he was most discreet.

But Noël Coward soon learned of this strange liaison between an older man and a young boy. He called Ainley "an old sod," and feared that the Ainley/Olivier affair would turn into a master/slave relationship. Coward knew many young actors who had been seduced by Ainley. "He likes to dominate a young man in bed, or so I hear," Coward told his friends. "I think there is some element of pain involved in the sexual act. Poor Larry."

When he starred in the 1960 release of the film *Spartacus*, Larry told director Stanley Kubrick that he used Ainley for his inspiration in the famous and controversial homosexual scene with Tony Curtis. As an older Crassus, Larry's character tries to seduce his young, handsome, and near-naked slave.

"I understand Curtis's role better than I do my own," he told Kubrick. Enigmatically, Larry said, "It's a scene taken from my own life." He was no doubt suggesting that he had somewhat of a master/slave relationship with Ainley. There appears no other relationship in his life that would merit such a comparison.

Denys Blakelock, Larry's confidant, was very clearly made aware of the relationship. The actor later claimed that Ainley held some spell over Larry "that's hard to describe and understand. It's a bit sick, or so I would gather."

After Larry died, more than a dozen love letters appeared, each written by Ainley to Larry. Larry's letters to Ainley apparently have been destroyed.

Most of the letters are pornographic or near-pornographic. They are overtly homosexual in content.

In one letter to Larry, Ainley claimed that, "I lie awake at night, tossing and turning and dreaming of you. How Jill must hate me for taking you away from her."

He ends his letter by telling Larry that, "I should like to run my fingers through your hair. Your sweet little kitten, Henrietta."

Ainley was known for writing sexually provocative letters to his close homosexual friends. In those days when the homosexual act was criminal in Britain, men who loved men found a sexual outlet in writing privately to each other, expressing secret desires.

One such letter of Ainley's has surfaced. It was written on November 11, 1932 and mailed to a Ralph Raleigh in Exeter, the cathedral city of Devon.

In the letter, Ainley wrote:

"Ah, sweet beauty, I always say as I encounter the pink rosebud of a beautiful young man. What a thrill to devour it as I push my face forward into this Garden of Delights. It's like a journey into a scented valley between those down-covered buttocks. The grandest treasure that the young actor I've fallen in love with can give me, an older man, is his virgin bum. Surely you will agree, you wicked old gal you. Love, Henrietta."

Could Ainley in this letter to a friend have meant Larry? It certainly fits into the time frame when Ainley was showing his greatest passion for Larry.

Czinner had hired J.M. Barrie (author of *Peter Pan*) to write the screen treatment for *As You Like It*. At one point, Shakespeare's play had not been seen on the stage for an entire century.

On the set of *As You Like It*, Ainley warmly embraced Larry—whom he called "Harrikin"—and kissed him long and hard on the lips. By this point in his life, Larry seemed to have escaped from whatever sexual bondage Ainley might have forced on him.

As You Like It was to be Ainley's final film, as he was in ill health. He had asked Larry to use his influence to get his son, Richard Ainley, cast in the film as Sylvius, and Larry had come through for him.

When Ainley's final scenes were shot, Larry did not want to be alone with him, so Ainley was forced to say his good-bye in front of the cast and a visitor to the set, Glen Byam Shaw.

"On the last day of my life, I will be thinking of you," Ainley told Larry. "Would that we could have been boys together growing up in the last years of Victoria's day. If only we could turn back time." In front of everyone, he kissed and hugged Larry.

After Ainley had gone, Larry told Shaw and others, "One day in Henry's dressing room, I asked him to deliver the 'Friends, Romans, Countrymen' line. He did so, making the jars on his dressing table vibrate. He had the greatest voice ever heard in the British theater. If I have any criticism of him at all, it is that he is more interested in the sound of his voice than he is in the words being uttered."

Larry's praise, such as it was, was reserved for Ainley, not Bergner. He disliked her intensely, and she regarded him with disdain, claiming, "He was not charming or friendly to work with. He could be inspirational, but he treated us both—me and my husband—as foreigners."

In his memoirs, *On Acting*, Larry wrote, "My performance in *As You Like It* looked eccentric, playing to a Rosalind with a German accent, whose impersonation of a boy hardly attempted to deceive the audience; but they loved what she did. I made my humble most of Orlando, but the circumstances were too much charged against me. The director's flock of sheep ran away with the film."

The score for *As You Like It* was by William Walton, who was to become Larry's long-time musical collaborator on such movies as *Hamlet*, *Henry V*, and *Richard III*.

Actor John Laurie played Orlando's brother Oliver, and would go on to co-star with Larry in three Shakespeare films that Larry himself would direct.

As a trivia note, *As You Like It* was Larry's only on-screen Shakespeare performance not nominated for an Oscar.

Upon its opening, *As You Like It* was a failure, although it enjoys a vogue among cultists today. Annuska Riedlmayer called Bergner a "poor woman's

226

Garbo and ever giddy." She found Larry "young, pretty, and very athletic, but his athleticism is the only life in the picture."

Larry had trained with professional wrestlers for his camera-ready wrestling scenes in this movie, which was his first film appearance, hardly his last, in a work by Shakespeare.

Ainley's passion for Larry continued long after he'd cut off any sexual connection. While he was filming *Wuthering Heights* in Hollywood, Ainley wrote him a love letter addressing him as "My Blessed and Most Dear Larry." In yet another letter, he called him "Lorenzo Mio."

In one of his strangest communications, he wrote: "Darling, Christ. You are a lousy pansy. Don't you ever dare write to me again. The Brute who is keeping me found your letters, and beat me unmercifully. O I did enjoy it! Love, Diana."

When Ainley learned of Vivien's entrance into Larry's life, he wrote a "Lorenzo Mio" letter, claiming "You call me names but I do love you. I am stale. A wanton. I wish to God I were. I would wear fur undies, and I would be a tease!"

In this same letter, perhaps the last he ever wrote to Larry, Ainley said: "I have a few more years from which lonely height I see so clearly. Fate ordained that you and Vivien should possess this beauty. Let not the past mar by thought your well won peace and glory. Shine! Like the angels you both arc. H.A. Bastard."

Ainley died on October 13, 1945, but by then Larry had closed the door to that particular chapter of his past and didn't want anyone to comment on it or ask him questions about his former friend.

In Larry's next film, he would work with an actress much more to his liking, Miss Vivien Leigh, who'd be making her first screen appearance "with the love of my life."

228

CHAPTER SEVEN

Larry, meeting with Ralph Richardson and writer J.B. Priestley, decided to pool two thousand pounds of their own money to present a play, curiously entitled *Bees on the Boatdeck*. "With Ralph and me as the stars, script by Priestley, how can we lose?" he said to Jill. "It's a cinch to become a hit."

"Don't be so sure," she warned him. "Audiences are a fickle lot."

Jill was right. The play, a satire on contemporary England, opened on May 5, 1936 at the Lyric Theatre, closing on June 6 after thirty-seven performances.

During the run, Vivien, escorted by Ivor Novello, came to see the play. They went backstage to congratulate Larry, who kissed his former lover (Novello) and his future lover (Vivien).

James Agate gave Larry a bad review, claiming that in his role as Second Officer on a ship he evoked "a young man behind the counter of a bank."

Larry was beginning to develop a pattern in his career. After a failure on the stage, he'd rush into a film, a medium which he still did not respect.

Ever since Alexander Korda had enjoyed such success with Charles Laughton in *The Private Life of Henry VIII*, he'd wanted to bring the story of Henry VIII's daughter, Elizabeth Tudor, to the screen.

It was *Fire Over England*. Scheduled for a 1937 release, it was based on a popular novel by A.E.W. Mason. Korda hired Clemence Dane to adapt the script for the screen, although he wasn't completely pleased with her final result.

To portray Elizabeth I, he cast the rather plain but extremely talented Flora Robson. For the young romantic lead, the bilingual (English and Spanish-speaking) sea officer (Michael Ingolby), he signed Larry. For his lover, Cynthia, one of the queen's ladies-in-waiting, he chose Vivien. On hearing she'd been hired, Vivien said, "At long last I'm going to make love to Larry, at least on the screen."

On the first day at the studio at Denham, Vivien encountered Larry, politely telling him that it was an honor to be working with him.

"We'll probably end up fighting," he predicted. "Actors always get sick of each other when making a movie together."

"Not in all cases," she said rather provocatively. "Sometimes they fall in love."

Erich Pommer, one of the great directors of German cinema, was hired to produce *Fire Over England*. He had met Larry before when he was filming in Berlin. Larry introduced him to Vivien. "An English rose," Pommer said. "Of course, we have many beautiful girls in Germany too."

When Larry tried to engage him in talk about Hitler, he declined. "We are here to relive on screen the glories of the Elizabethan Age, not discuss European politics of today."

Fire Over England
(top photo) Tamara Desni
(bottom photo) its producer,
Erich Pommer

Korda had informed Larry that he had planned to cast him in *Knight Without Armour*, starring opposite Marlene Dietrich. But Robert Donat, suffering from chronic asthma, insisted on doing the role with the help of cocaine lozenges.

"You mean Donat rescued me from the clutches of Dietrich," Larry said to Korda. "I fear I'm not man enough for that one."

"Were it not for Donat," Larry told Jill, "I would right now be the highest paid male star in films in England. That Donat really pulls in the big paychecks, which keep eluding me."

Within two days, Larry had met the cast of *Fire Over England*, most of whom he already knew.

He was reunited with James Mason, who had not yet become a big star. Mason recalled, "Mine, as can be seen, was a vitally important role, but after one day's and one night's shooting it was all over." Korda did not even give Mason screen credit. But years later, when *Fire Over England* was re-issued and Mason had become a big-time movie star, he was given star billing in the ads, ranking up there with Vivien and Larry.

Tamara Desni was cast as Elena, one of the ladies of the Spanish court, her beautiful head emerging from a ruff like a flower in full bloom.

Filming started on July 15, 1936. Larry found himself working again with Raymond

230

Massey, cast as King Philip of Spain, and Leslie Banks, playing the Earl of Leicester. Robert Newton was cast as Don Pedro.

Both Vivien and Larry admired Leslie Banks, a Liverpudlian who in 1912 and 1913 had toured with Jill's parents, Henry V. Esmond and Eva Moore, throughout the United States and Canada. During the first World War, he served with the Essex Regiment and suffered injuries that scarred one side of his face, leaving him partially paralyzed. That, however, did not ruin his acting career.

When playing comedy or romance, he turned only the good side of his face to the camera. When he wanted to show menace in drama or tragedy, he revealed his whole face.

Along with Errol Flynn, Newton became one of the most popular actors among male juvenile audiences in Britain in the 1940s. Drummer Keith Moon later cited Newton as "my role model."

Newton would go on to play Horatio to Larry's *Hamlet* at the Old Vic. Larry would also cast Newton as "Ancient Pistol" in his 1944 film, *Henry V.*

He would later immortalize himself in his portrayal of the feverish-eyed Long John Silver, coming up with the phrase "Arrgh, matey," in the Walt Disney version of *Treasure Island* (1950). He is credited with inventing the stereotypical "pirate voice," which he claimed he created by exaggerating the accent of the country people of his native Dorset.

Vivien and Larry both admired and liked working with him, and were sorry to see his film career cut short by chronic alcoholism, which ultimately led to his death from a heart attack.

The actual launch of the affair between Vivien and Larry, which became one of the most romantic liaisons in the history of the theater or the cinema, is much disputed by biographers. Some place the date quite later. However, the American director of the film, William K. Howard, later claimed, "Larry and Viv became lovers while making my movie."

Massey watched the affair unfold before his eyes and later said, "I felt sorry for Jill. I think she was unaware of what was going on. I feared that Larry and Vivien were doomed lovers like Romeo and Juliet."

James Wong Howe, the cameraman, recalled,

(top photo) Raymond Massey

(mlddle and lower photos) Leslie Banks alone and with Larry and Viv on the set of *21 Days*

231

"All the cast thought Larry and Vivien were madly in love. They did not socialize with the rest of the cast. When not needed on set, they disappeared into Vivien's dressing room."

Three days later, when Vivien was back at work, Howard spotted Larry emerging from her dressing room late one afternoon.

"I know you like to do your own stunts," the director said. "But you should let me use a double. You look completely spent."

"It's not the stunts," Larry told him. "It's Vivien. It's every day—two, three times. She's bloody wearing me out."

From this comment, we can assume that Larry, very early into his relationship, learned of Vivien's voracious sexual drive, which would be accelerated in the years ahead during her frequent manic-depressive episodes.

"Her sexual energy would increase alarmingly," said her biographer Michelangelo Capua. "Although her body was delicate, and she almost looked as if she were made of porcelain, Vivien had an incredible erotic power over all of her men, a strength that she physically had to exercise on a daily basis through sex."

Vivien might have drained Larry's energy, a complaint that would rise constantly during the early years of her marriage to him, but she recalled their times together quite differently in an interview with journalist Godfrey Winn at Tickerage in the 1960s.

I don't think I have ever lived quite as intensely ever since. I don't remember sleeping, ever, only every precious moment that we spent together. We were so young. I mean all of us were so young. Like those who went to the war and didn't come back. I trusted everyone and I imagined, like the very young always do, that everything lasts forever."

In elaborate Elizabethan costumes which invariably included mammoth ruffs framing her head and face, Robson looked like she'd sprouted gigantic insect wings. Her screen presence was so formidable that Korda knew that she was stealing the picture from Larry and Vivien, cast as the young lovers.

In the film Vivien and Larry seemed to be playing an English court version of Romeo and Juliet, stealing kisses as they dart along the dank

Flora Robson
as the Virgin Queen

232

corridors of the palace.

When the picture came out, Graham Greene, writing in the *Spectator*, claimed that "Elizabeth Tudor would never have allowed 'so much cuddling and kissing in her presence.'"

Flora Robson had a comment about that. "Not only on-screen, but off-screen as well."

Robson later said, "You'd be a fool not to see that Larry Olivier and Vivien were falling in love. Unlike Jill, who was more or less the boss of the family, Vivien worshipped Larry, hanging onto his every pronouncement. It was a new experience for him. He'd been dominated by his wife and many of the men in his life. Now he was the man, and he seemed to relish the role."

Vivien herself wrote of the beginning of her affair with Larry.

It was during the making of Fire Over England *that Larry and I fell in love. Alex Korda was like a father to us—we went to him with every little problem we had. We usually left convinced that he had solved it—or that we'd got our way, even when we hadn't. Well, one day we went to him and said, "Alex, we must tell you our great secret—we're in love and we're going to be married." He smiled and said, "Don't be silly—everybody knows that. I've known that for weeks and weeks.*

Korda was investing a lot of money in *Fire Over England*, and he feared that a scandal breaking out in the newspapers would lead to a boycott of the film. After all, Larry was a married man with a baby son, and Vivien was a married woman with a young girl waiting at home for the mother who never seemed to show up. Korda asked them to discontinue their affair until the end of production.

Both Vivien and Larry agreed, but did not really comply with Korda's wishes. Larry did end his visits to Vivien's dressing room during the day, but he was seen with her at night—attending the theater, going to the ballet, dining at the Savoy Grill or the Ivy.

He told Howard, "I really should give her up. But I don't want to. God

Leigh and Olivier as Elizabethan lovers in *Fire Over England*

knows I must give her up. Yet somehow I can't bring myself to do it."

Larry had his own version of the emotional tides sweeping through them. "This thing was as fatefully irresistible for us as for any couple from Silegmund and Sieglinde to Windsor and Simpson. It sometimes felt almost like an illness, but the remedy was unthinkable; only an early Christian martyr could have faced it. Virtue seemed to work upside-down; love was like an angel, guilt was a dark fiend."

Larry also told Raymond Massey, "I am consumed with guilt. I'm putting an end to it. My thing with Vivien has been a wild infatuation I've lost control. Vivien is the warrior queen, not Flora Robson. Hard to resist. I've got to force myself to go back to Jill and be a husband to her, a father when our baby is born." It was a commitment that he did not keep.

During the shoot, Korda brought Winston Churchill, at the time a member of Parliament, to the set. He was especially interested in the script for *Fire Over England*. He met privately with Larry and Vivien, telling them of his grave concerns that "I fear that England, within a matter of months, will be at war with Hitler's Germany."

"I read A.E. Mason's novel, and I hope Clemence Dane will be true to the story," Churchill said. "Perhaps a man should have written it, as we seem to know more about waging war. I would have written it for Korda if I'd had the time."

"It shows how a proud little England, with its strong queen, stood up and faced the mighty forces of the great Spanish Armada," Churchill said. "If it's done right, I think your movie will be propaganda for us, showing how we stood up against tyranny."

This was the first of many encounters that Vivien and Larry would have with the future prime minister of England. In time, Vivien would become his favorite female movie star.

Winston Churchill:
A film industry
scriptwriter?

One night, Charles Laughton and Elsa Lanchester encountered Larry and Vivien in the lobby of Claridge's Hotel. Laughton and Larry did not like each other, although Lanchester was gracious to both of them.

Larry couldn't resist a dig. "Is it true, Laughton, old chap, that your father ran a B&B in Scarborough and got you your first job in London? Washing dishes at Claridge's?"

"Yes, and it was with these dish-pan hands that I clutched my first Oscar, the first of many no doubt. Oscar has a great ass on him, wouldn't you say?"

On another occasion, the formidable Marie Tempest,

who had starred with Larry in *Theatre Royal,* was visiting relatives in a room at the Savoy Hotel. To her surprise, she saw Vivien and Larry emerging from a hotel room at six o'clock in the morning. The couple rushed past her without speaking.

During the shooting of *Fire Over England,* Simon Tarquin Olivier was born on August 21, 1936. On the set, Korda, Vivien, and the cast drank a toast to "Tark," Larry's nickname for his newly born son.

Larry had rushed to his home in Chelsea. Racing up the steps two at a time, he entered the bedroom where Jill was holding their child.

As he bent over to kiss her, she said, "I recognize the scent of Vivien's perfume. She told me she calls it Rape."

He stumbled awkwardly before finally saying, "We have just played a love scene on the set."

At the time of Tarquin's birth, Leigh was sailing in Sweden on a vacation. Posing as a family friend, Vivien called on Jill, hoping to see the baby. The next day Vivien wrote Leigh:

> *"Jill had her baby & I saw it last night. It is really very attractive and very big but not fat. Larry said it is like Edward G. Robinson which is a little cruel. He has already started reciting Shakespeare to it. I will be busy for the next five weeks shooting* Dark Journey. *I suggest you extend your vacation because I won't be at home very much. Miss you terribly. Love, Viv."*

When Larry's sister, Sybille, heard of the birth, she said, "My brother's intense desire to have a family has faded, and he is immersed in other things."

At their Cheyne Walk home, Jill and Larry organized a christening for Tarquin, inviting his godfather, Noël Coward, along with such illustrious guests as Sybil Thorndike and Ralph Richardson. After the formalities, the event evolved into a lavish cocktail party. Jill remained upstairs in bed, and Larry was thirty minutes late for his own party.

Suddenly, he appeared at the door with a beautiful young woman dressed in red slacks, shocking for the time, since all the women were formally dressed. She was recognized at once as Vivien Leigh.

Building the props (in this case, a hollow replica of a Spanish galleon) for *Fire Over England*

She disappeared before entering the party. Larry followed her. When he came back, he worked the room, shaking hands or kissing some of the guests like Coward. On Larry's cheek was the trace of a lipstick kiss.

While Leigh was still sailing the Baltic, Vivien came down with a severe sore throat. When her friend, Oswald Frewen, came to London he dropped by her home to visit her. "I found Larry Olivier there, being her nurse, perhaps a lot more," he wrote the next day to his sister, Clare Sheridan.

Larry shocked Vivien by announcing that he and Jill were going off on a vacation to Capri. "Jill thinks in sunny Italy, we can repair the damage to our marriage."

Although horrified of that possibility, Vivien kissed him goodbye. But even before he'd left London, an idea was percolating in her mind. She did not want Larry to save his marriage, and she planned to see to it that he did not.

She poured out her hysteria to Korda, sobbing in his arms. "Let him go," Korda advised her. "He owes it to Jill and his newborn son."

Through teary eyes she looked at him with a steely determination. "Jill Esmond is history. I will become Mrs. Laurence Olivier."

When *Fire Over England* opened in London, it was a huge success. Londoners, possibly fearing another invasion from the continent, this time from the Nazis, flocked to see how "little old England" had withstood an invasion in its past.

"The picture stands head and shoulders above any historical drama yet made in this country, and it has had few rivals from other countries, including Hollywood," boasted Lionel Collier, critic for *Picturegoer*.

Adolf Hitler
But why was he such a fan?

Foster Hirsch penned an amusing view of Larry's performance. "As his country's saviour, Olivier leaps on and off ships and balconies, engages in brisk swordplay; courts an aristocratic Spanish lady in addition to making love to Vivien Leigh's lady-in-waiting; masquerades as a spy in the Spanish court; and sings a song about wooing. The character is almost never seen in repose. Olivier, however, doesn't have the graceful exuberance of Fairbanks or the easy charm of Errol Flynn that the material needs. Many times throughout the action, after he's completed a daring mission or while he's receiving counsel from the queen, his character must kneel, and Olivier slumps down on one knee as he scowls in evident discontent. 'Not again, surely?' he seems to be saying to himself."

236

Ironically, the greatest fan of *Fire Over England* was one Adolf Hitler, who perhaps did not understand the implications of the movie. When his storm-troopers overtook Prague, a general acquired a copy of *Fire Over England* and took it back to Berlin.

Josef Goebbels arranged for a showing in the presence of Hitler. The Nazi dictator was so impressed with the film that he demanded four additional showings. He asked Goebbels, "Do you think Elizabeth I was actually as ugly as Flora Robson?"

The United States did not take to the film as well as England. Fans were unfamiliar with the stars except for Raymond Massey.

In one scene, Larry was depicted weeping over the ashes of his father, who had been burned at the stake by the Spanish Inquisition. Movie-goers laughed in New York and Hollywood. Korda ordered the scene to be cut before more screenings.

Edward H. Griffith, the Hollywood director, arrived in London, claiming that the position of the screen's most romantic actor was now vacant. "Fredric March," he told reporters, "I don't think so. Leslie Howard is a possibility, but an odd bet. He's also not a spring chicken any more. My own nomination is Laurence Olivier. He got a false start, but should he want to return to films, the day is his."

In 1986, when a journalist came to interview Larry, he found him watching a rerun of *Fire Over England* on the TV screen. He had tears in his eyes. Looking up at the reporter, he said, "That, dear boy, is true love. It was the real thing. It's so sad that it lasts for such a short while, like a flower that blossoms at night but wilts at dawn's light."

***

Long after everyone recorded the passions that raged between Vivien and Larry during the making of *Fire Over England*, a different insight has emerged.

"One day a very strange occurrence took place," said James Wong Howe, the cinema photographer. "Vivien wasn't needed on the set for four days, as we were shooting sea battles. Larry showed up on the arm of this beautiful actress, who turned out to be Ann Todd. They disappeared for hours in his dressing room. Because I saw him with another woman, I did not realize the extent of his love for Vivien at the time. I'd heard that he was a homosexual, but he looked very heterosexual on the set of *Fire Over England*. Very heterosexual indeed."

Larry had met Todd years ago at the Central School in London. She was two years younger than him. It is not known when Larry's affair with Todd began. John Gielgud recalled seeing them lunching at the Ivy some time in 1935, long before he took Vivien to the restaurant. In Larry's diary, it was revealed that he'd had a rendezvous with Todd the day before the christening of Tarquin, although he was also deeply involved with Vivien at the time.

Tamara Desni, who had a supporting role in *Fire Over England*, while retired and living in France, admitted that she allowed Larry and Todd to use her flat during their love affair.

Born in Berlin, Desni appeared in German films before starring in the hit musical, *White Horse Inn*, which ran for 500 performances at the London Coliseum in 1931.

Desni was a close friend of Todd's. One day on the set, Vivien without warning slapped Desni so hard she almost injured her. Desni ran sobbing from the set.

It had been an afternoon of exasperation, and Vivien had seemed out of control all day. She might have been in love with Larry, but she was also infuriated with him for some petty reason long forgotten. No one knew why she'd turned with such fury on Desni. It was not like Vivien to show such unprovoked violence.

Howe later revealed that he'd told Vivien that when she was away, Larry had brought Todd to his dressing room three days in a row. Vivien was aware of Desni's friendship with Todd, and seemed to blame Desni for the incident.

When Desni came back onto the set for a scene with Larry, Vivien apologized profusely for her outburst and attack. After that, the two actresses avoided each other.

Todd was able to get Desni cast in her next picture, *The Squeaker* (1937), the title later changed to *Murder on Diamond Row*.

"Ice Queen" Ann Todd

When Vivien was told of this casting, she mockingly said, "The picture should be called *The Kraut and the Whore*," a reference to Desni and Todd, respectively.

The full details of Todd's affair with Larry are not known. What is known is that they did meet in secret during most of the late 1930s and early 1940s. Ralph Richardson, who worked with Todd on *The Sound Barrier* (1952), said that Todd more or less confirmed that she and Larry had been lovers, even after his marriage to Vivien.

Todd was known to have had a number of affairs, including with Gregory Peck when they shot *The Paradine Case* in 1948, and again with

238

Ray Milland when they'd starred in *One Woman's Story* (1949). Todd had married film director David Lean in 1949, so her affair with Milland occurred around this same time.

Her biggest affair, and the picture for which she is most known today, took place with James Mason when they made *The Seventh Veil* (1945).

Larry on some level was still seeing Todd in 1954 when he helped her in her interpretation of Lady Macbeth at the Old Vic.

On screen, Todd was unsympathetic—somber, even sullen, her face a mask. One critic wrote: "Is Ann Todd made of ice? I mean, did someone create her, place her in a freezer, and when she thawed out it was found she was devoid of all emotions. She was as icy as icy gets. I can see why she, arguably, was the most popular British actor of her generation in the 1940s, but there is such a depth of coolness in her eyes that it makes me feel frozen just looking at her."

A slightly jealous Glen Byam Shaw once asked Larry, "What do you see in Miss Deep Freeze?"

Larry smiled enigmatically. "I can thaw her out."

Decades later, in 1989 in London, at Larry's funeral, Todd showed up heavily veiled. Throughout the ceremony, she could be heard sobbing.

***

Before leaving for Italy on vacation, Vivien rushed through a film for Alexander Korda. *Dark Journey* was directed by Victor Saville, a founding father of British filmmaking. Originally, he'd wanted Miriam Hopkins for the lead in this spy drama set in Stockholm in 1918.

Vivien played a spy, Madeleine Godard, working for the British allies. She was cast opposite Conrad Veidt, who was known to both Jill and Larry. In her role, Vivien, as a spy working secretly for the British, was masquerading as a shopkeeper, traveling the continent selling clothes. This was a cover, as she furtively bore coded messages, which were sewn, along with secret maps, into the patterns of her dresses. In an unlikely scenario, Veidt, with his usual "liquid villainy," played a secret agent on the opposite side who falls in love with Vivien's character.

On the first day of shooting, Veidt told her that Korda had signed a contract with him but was having "a hell of a time finding roles suitable for me. Originally, he wanted us to play lovers in *Fire Over England*. But at the last minute, Korda decided that Larry is far more romantic than I am. Surely you'd know that better than I would."

"I'm not so sure," she said. "After all, you spent time with him at a Bavarian spa."

"My memory grows dim," Veidt said enigmatically.

"I understand that Korda sees *Dark Journey* and the two of us in it as star-crossed lovers like *Romeo and Juliet*," she said.

"A bit of a stretch, wouldn't you say?" asked Veidt.

Vivien and her director worked beautifully together. Critics were somewhat confused by the convoluted plot, and Vivien herself admitted she didn't understand what was happening at certain points in the film. *Dark Journey* was re-issued in 1953 under the title of *The Anxious Years*.

On the set of *Dark Journey*, Vivien developed a friendship with Ursula Jeans, cast as Gertrude in the film.

At the time of her meeting with Vivien, Ursula herself had fallen in love with Welsh-born Shakespearean actor and RAF pilot Roger Livesey. She would marry him in 1937 and stay wed until her death. Ursula had a brother, Desmond Jeans, a boxer and an actor, who had previously married Livesey's sister, Maggie.

Right from the beginning, Vivien and Ursula found they had much in common. Each of them had been born in India to British parents and each had been educated for at least a period of their youths in London.

Ursula also knew both Larry and Jill, as she'd acted with them during the Shakespeare Birthday Festival at the Old Vic in London in 1937. Tyrone Guthrie had frequently been her director.

Before the release of *Dark Journey*, Veidt saw the ads announcing the film's imminent arrival. In those ads, Korda had placed Vivien's name above his. Veidt stormed into Korda's office and demanded that the ads be redone. Korda ushered him out, and Veidt never spoke to the producer again.

In the aftermath of *Dark Journey*'s premiere, *The New York Times* hailed Vivien as England's most charming screen actress, and cited Veidt as "that bulwark of villainy."

***

Roger Livesey

Instead of rushing her into another picture, Vivien persuaded Korda to let her, like Larry, go on a holiday too. She was completely exhausted and emotionally drained from her affair with Larry. The possibility that she might lose him forever overwhelmed her, and she spent three days in bed.

Not comprehending what was wrong with her, Leigh urged that she go on a motor holiday throughout the countryside of France with him.

But at the last minute, he couldn't leave his chambers at Middle Temple and arranged for his friend, Oswald Frewen, to accompany Vivien instead.

"I hear Sicily is wonderful at this time of year," Vivien told Frewen, who set out to explore southern Italy with her.

Frewen had always been sexually attracted to Vivien, and his restraint was put to the test when Vivien asked him to share her bed. "I cannot stand to be alone in a hotel room by myself in a strange country."

Before setting out with Vivien, Frewen told his sister, Clare Sheridan, "Vivien is a sex kitten, we both know that, and she likes to be scratched. But I couldn't do that to Leigh, my dear friend, I just couldn't."

In his diary, he wrote, "She was so natural that sex didn't obtrude, and I was never once conscious of a defensive action on her part." After a brief stopover in Taormina, where they stayed at the landmark Palazzo San Domenico, they visited the volcanic Mount Etna before Vivien cut short their plans. She announced to Frewen that she wanted to visit Capri.

From Naples, they took a boat to Capri and arrived at the Hotel Quisisana. To Frewen's surprise, they encountered Jill and Larry who were vacationing there. The couple did not know that Vivien was arriving.

In his diary, Frewen wrote of "a joint passionate embrace" among Jill, Larry, and Vivien, which may have been more theatrical than sincere.

Frewen was assigned a room on one side of the Oliviers, with Vivien on the

Views of a holiday in Capri for a dysfunctional threesome: Jill Esmond, her husband, Larry, and their tagalong friend, Vivien Leigh

photos by Oswald Frewen

other side. The rooms had connecting doors, which were kept open, the quartet coming and going from one room to another, using it like a suite. "It was communal living, very intimate," Frewen said. "We often saw each other naked."

On the day of Vivien's departure for Rome with Frewen, Jill left the suite for early morning tea in the courtyard. Vivien stayed behind for some last-minute packing. Larry, too, made some excuse to stay behind.

Frewen could clearly overhear their voices in the next room as the door was open. "I will never, never let you leave me," she said to Larry.

"I could never tear myself away from you again," Larry told her.

Frewen's suspicions were confirmed: They were lovers. He later revealed that his first thought was the devastating impact this would have on Leigh. After watching Larry and Vivien together, Jill, too, must know that they were falling in love. Frewen surmised that it was obvious, as in Capri, Larry and Vivien had hardly managed to keep their hands off each other.

In Rome, over a dinner in a remote trattoria opening onto a Renaissance square, Vivien admitted to Frewen what was going on. "Larry told me that in Capri he had a chance to compare Jill and me together. He said his heart made the choice for him. I am the one he loves. He's divorcing Jill, not that it was much of a marriage anyway. He's going to let her keep Tark. Of course, I will have to tell Leigh. I'll let him keep Suzanne, because he just adores our daughter. Leigh as a barrister can arrange his own divorce."

"Don't rush back to London and be impetuous," Frewen urged her. "Capri is a very romantic place. Both of you may have been swept away by your emotions."

While Vivien and Frewen were exploring the glory that used to be Rome, Jill and Larry were fighting in Naples. Vivien was the subject that led to a violent eruption between them, when Larry called his wife "a Victorian prude." Jill countered that Larry was "a two-timing bastard, dishonoring me, bringing shame to your son."

Abruptly cutting short their holiday, they flew back to London in silence. Before they did, Larry had put in a secret call to Vivien who was asleep in her bed at the Grand Hotel.

"It's all over but the divorce," he confessed to Vivien. At this point in their relationship, she was unaware as to how wavering Larry could be in his emotions.

On the phone, he made an impulsive decision. "I have this grand idea," he told her. "Let Frewen fly back to London by himself. I'll put Jill on the next plane. Get ready in the morning to return to Capri and join me in that albergo. I'll reserve the honeymoon suite even though we're not married."

"Yes, yes, yes, my darling," she told him. "It'll be the beginning of our life together. I will notify Leigh in London."

Before ten o'clock the next morning, Frewen had "talked some sense into both Larry and Vivien," he later recalled. He warned her that running off with Larry might not only jeopardize her own promising career, but would definitely threaten Larry's growing fan base.

Finally she caved in to Frewen's advice. "The poor dear wiped tears all the way back to London," he claimed. "She behaved like a schoolgirl who's been told she can't run off with her teenage boyfriend."

Somehow Gertrude had been made aware of the emotional turbulence Vivien was experiencing because of her affair with Larry. She came to see her daughter the very next day after Vivien had arrived in London. She asked pointed questions. "Why have you no sexual desire for your husband anymore? Why do you have no maternal love for your daughter? And why have you turned your back on your Catholic upbringing? Don't you have guilt?"

"I'm bloody weighed down with fucking guilt," Vivien shouted at her mother before fleeing from the living room and heading upstairs.

Gertrude followed her into the bedroom, where Vivien told her, "There is only one guilt I have, and that is I can't live without Larry. Therefore, I have to take him away from Jill and Tark."

"You're a wicked woman," her mother told her.

Vivien looked at her with such a steely, cold expression it shocked Gertrude, who later said she would carry Vivien's look to her grave. "If only you knew how wicked."

"Her words chilled me to the bone," Gertrude later said.

Another mother also weighed in. Leaving London at once upon her return, Jill fled to the comforting arms of Eva. "She told me that Larry was going to leave her for Vivien," Eva recalled. "I had suspected that for some time. I told her she had the perfect arrangement with Larry, and she should fight to hold on to it. Their marriage was the ideal beard for other indiscretions left unmentioned."

To Eva's surprise, Jill continued to entertain Vivien. Sometimes Jill would meet her for an intimate luncheon. At other times, Jill invited Larry and Vivien for a cozy dinner for just the three of them.

"When I'm alone with Vivien, I know she's picking my brain to learn all she can about Larry," Jill confessed to Eva and to her friends. "She wants to know what kind of books Larry likes to read. What are his favorite foods. What habits can he not tolerate in other people—that sort of stuff."

"They're falling in love right before my eyes," Jill told Eva. "There's nothing I can do to stop it."

When Gertrude came to call on Vivien again, she seemed to have accepted that she didn't plan to give Larry up. "Stay married to Leigh and be a mother to your daughter. Have an affair with Larry on the side. These moments of passion such as yours have a way of burning out quickly, like a candle left in a holder overnight. When it's over you can go back to your husband."

Her words angered Vivien, who at that time and place was planning on spending the rest of her life with Larry.

"Thanks for the advice, mother," Vivien said to her. "That's the kind of advice I'd expect from a woman who's lived your kind of life. By the way, darling, just how is that dear boy Tommy?"

***

Back in London, Vivien learned more about the impulsive young man she'd given her heart to. In many ways, he was still very much a stranger to her. In southern Italy, he was willing to run away with her, leaving Jill and Leigh behind. Once he returned to London, however, Larry and Jill seemed to have had some sort of reconciliation, as Jill desperately wanted to hold onto Larry and save her deteriorating marriage.

Jill's clinging to Larry was not done with any particular great love or devotion to him. She was convinced that it was necessary to keep up the appearance of a respectable marriage for the sake of their careers and for Tarquin.

It is believed that at this time both Jill and Larry admitted to each other that they were bisexuals. She told him that she did not mind him pursuing handsome young men on the side or even having an occasional fling with one of his female co-stars. She also revealed to him that she was ninety-five percent lesbian, but promised to be very discreet about her affairs, never flaunting them in front of him.

"It is very important that we maintain our marriage and put up a respectable front to the world," she said.

Finally, with the approval of Eva, who'd coached her, Jill brought up the subject of Tarquin. "He needs both a loving mother and a father. We owe it to him to save our marriage. And think of Leigh. If Vivien left him, he might kill himself. He's absolutely devoted to her. Besides, Vivien is given to sudden, dark moods, from what I hear. She's very flighty. She could ruin your life. I'm sure she'll know many men. You are but a station on her trip to somewhere else."

In an attempt to save her marriage, Jill paid a surprise call on Vivien for afternoon tea at her home while Leigh was at work.

Once seated comfortably, Jill stared long and hard at Vivien. "My divorcing Larry is out of the question," she bluntly stated even before she'd had a sip of tea. "I suggest that the two of you have your little affair and then go back to your spouses where you belong."

"We belong where our heart is," Vivien said. "The heart wants what the heart wants—there's no changing that."

"Life is about nothing if not change," Jill cautioned her. "Believe you me, life with Larry will be all about pain. *Hamlet* is the perfect role for him. He's a troubled soul who can't make up his mind from day to day what he wants. You don't understand. On your wedding night, he's likely to run off with a handsome waiter."

"I can change that," Vivien said.

"He'll never change," Jill said. "Larry is about duplicity. He can be swayed, even overwhelmed, on a moment's notice by some strong personality who can move in on him in a minute. I'm sure he's passionate when he's with you, but he can put that aside and plunge recklessly into another involvement the very next afternoon. I should know."

"Both Larry and I, of course, are creatures of impulse," Vivien said.

"If you divorce Leigh and Larry divorces me and marries you, such a union will not last," Jill said. "Larry likes to play roles both on and off the stage. Right now he's caught up in some *Romeo and Juliet* fantasy with you. You must recognize your affair with him for what it is. It's play-acting. There is no reality here."

"Then we'll live the fantasy," Vivien said, "as we rush down that road to hell. Both of us have artistic souls. We are dramatists, not just on the stage but in our private lives. We'll feed off each other like some devouring vultures."

"What a ghastly image," Jill said, slamming down her teacup. "Let's drop this talk and turn our attention instead to that sherry trifle your maid just brought in. I see that you and I can resolve nothing over tea. You must understand. I don't hate you for what you're doing to Larry's life, or to your own. I'm going to make you an amazing offer, that of friendship."

"You want to remain friends with me?" Vivien asked, not concealing her astonishment.

"For some reason I do," Jill said. "I like you, as strange as that sounds. I can even understand Larry for choosing you. If you'd been of a certain nature and inclination, I might have chosen you for myself. Now I need to dig into my trifle. I'm meeting Eva for dinner where I'm going to report every word of our conversation."

***

At first Vivien seemed to reject Jill's warnings, but eventually came to accept them. A week later she wrote her a note, which Jill later gave to Eva who preserved it as a souvenir.

"Jill, darling,

I feel your offer of friendship was genuine, and I accept it in spite of the embarrassing circumstances we find ourselves in. You know Larry far better than I do. I am only discovering him. But now I have a secret to share with you. I am very much like Larry. We are both artists on the grand scale. Our ambition to expand our range as actors knows no boundaries. Our appetites for new experiences are insatiable. Deep in my heart, I know that Larry will never settle for just one woman . . . or one man as the case may be. But we can still have wonderful, passionate moments together, and so few people in life are granted even that. I feel in bondage to Leigh. I want to escape, to experience life. I feel that Larry has the key to unlock my prison cell. I will give him the freedom to discover himself as a man and an artist. You can offer freedom, Jill, but as you yourself confessed you cannot arouse passion. Larry needs passion in his life. Please do not deny him the very thing his soul desperately needs. Otherwise, without his freedom, without the passion, his artistic soul will die and there will go Britain's greatest actor.

Love, Vivien."

***

Oswald Frewen started out as Leigh's friend, and so he remained. In time, he became Vivien's friend. After their meeting in Capri, "Larry won my heart," Frewen said. "I wanted to be loyal and loving to all three of my dear ones."

Whenever Larry and Frewen met in London, Frewen urged Larry once again not to leave Jill and not to break up Leigh's marriage. Frewen recorded his impression of his last dinner with Larry in London before heading back home.

"I made all the obvious demurrers, & Larry accepted them all as true, but he also said he had been alarmingly loose before he married Jill. He feared that with his terrific temperament, he was afraid of becoming loose again, & that the only partner in the world who could keep him steady was Viv. I said, 'If she should fail, & statistics are against you, you will have wrecked her, & that is a very serious matter.' He said if this did crash he would despair of himself & let himself go to the devil, & then, on the other side, said that Viv anyhow could never continue to live with Leigh, so

246

unsuited were their tastes & temperaments, & if it was not him it would be someone else. As a last shot I told him frankly that I didn't expect the passion of two people of his age & Viv's to endure, & begged him to give themselves at least a year before doing anything irrevocable, & indeed he said he would."

After much obvious "stewing," as Larry called it, he invited Frewen for lunch in London a few days later. It sounded urgent, so Frewen drove up.

Over a beer at table, Larry handed Frewen a note he asked to be delivered to Vivien at home. "Now's a good time," he said. "Leigh had to go back to Paris on business."

After lunch and a bear hug with Larry, Frewen called Vivien and asked to come over. When he arrived, he found her sitting alone in her living room. Suzanne had gone for a walk with her nanny in a neighboring park.

Once the pleasantries were over, Frewen handed Vivien the note from Larry. "It was burning a hole in my pocket, and I had to get rid of it," he said.

In front of him, Vivien carefully read the note and seemed to read it once again, maybe more, before clutching it to her heart. She rose slowly to her feet. "I don't feel well," she announced. "I'm going upstairs to bed. Please stay with me and hold me tonight like you did in Italy. I need you with me."

That night he asked the nanny to sleep over and look after Suzanne. He asked her to prepare Vivien a light supper. For the last three hours, he had not intruded on her. He carried the tray into her bedroom and found her resting on the bed.

"Food is the last thing I want," she said. "Put it over there." She reached into her gown and produced the note. "Read it!" She said those words like they were a command.

He read the note:

"Vivien, my darling, my precious one.
I cannot see you any more, except under social conditions—you with Leigh, me with Jill. I'm going back to home and hearth, and my faithful Jill and my dear son, Tark. My heart is bleeding tonight as I write this, but I know I've made the right choice. Time spent with you, loving you, caring for you, will remain in my heart as the most glorious moments I've ever spent on this Earth with another human being. You are, without a doubt, the single most beautiful woman in England. You will know many more Romeos in your future, and I envy those very fortunate men. Sometimes the greatest pleasure in life is to dream and imagine what might have been.
Your devoted servant forever more,
Larry."

In her bathroom later that night, Frewen prepared for bed, borrowing Leigh's pajamas. When he came back into the bedroom, he discovered that she'd gone to sleep. He slipped in beside her and drifted off himself.

He didn't know how much time had passed but it was deep into the night when he felt a sudden movement. She was straddling him. Sounding like some harridan on a Soho square, she called out in a voice not her own: "Fuck me! You've always wanted to. Here's your chance, matey. I'll show Mr. Olivier that I'm still desirable to a man."

Frewen later confessed to Clare Sheridan that he could no longer restrain

himself. "My God, here she was, the most beautiful woman in England. Nude in bed, demanding that I service her. I'm a mortal man. Even though Leigh was my best friend, I was out of my mind with lust. She practically demanded I rape her. I attacked her. Had we stayed a few more nights that time in Rome, I'm sure it would have happened sooner."

After sexual intercourse, he drifted off into a deep coma and she lay down beside him. He didn't know how long he slept, but he was awakened by the ringing of the doorbell downstairs. The noise disturbed Suzanne in the back room, and he heard her crying.

He looked around but Vivien was nowhere to

Two views of Oswald Frewen (upper photo) in naval uniform (lower photo) with his sister, sculptress Clare Sheridan riding in the sidecar of her motorcycle, "Satanella"

be seen. He opened the door and was greeted by a rainstorm. Standing only in her panties and a brassiere, Vivien was soaking wet, held in a firm grip by a London bobby who had placed a rubber raincoat around her shoulders.

"Is this your wife?" the policeman asked. Vivien was sobbing hysterically.

"Yes, officer, I was looking everywhere for her," Frewen said. "She's distraught. She just heard her mother died, and she became hysterical. I had no idea she'd run out on the streets."

He possessively reached for her, as the policeman retrieved his raincoat. Frewen took off his robe and placed it

248

around Vivien, who was shivering. "I'll take care of her, officer, and thank you." He quickly shut the door before facing any more inquiries.

The next afternoon, Frewen in Sussex told Sheridan, "Our dear, sweet Vivien, whom we adore, is a much more complex woman than I'd ever imagined. Leigh has never said anything about this. Maybe he doesn't even know."

"What in hell are you talking about?" Sheridan asked.

"Vivien has a split personality, a regular Dr. Jekyll and Mr. Hyde. I've just spent the most extraordinary night with her. She went bonkers when she got that note from Larry."

"You're making too much of it," Sheridan said. "She'll be all right. She was just overreacting, undone by the loss of Olivier—that's all. You don't understand women, you never did. Viv is an actress, a woman of deep emotions. She's lost the love of her life. As time goes by, she'll recover from it and go on. When Charlie Chaplin left me, I thought I'd commit suicide. But I didn't and went on with my life. Trust me. Viv will do the same. She's much stronger than she looks. She'll rebound."

***

Tyrone Guthrie was the first cousin of American actor Tyrone Power (Larry's future lover). An Anglo-Irish man, Guthrie in time would become one of the leading impresarios of the theater, presenting the plays of Shakespeare. His biographer, James Forsyth, hailed him as "anti-Broadway, anti-West End, but the most important British-born theatre director of his time."

Guthrie called Larry one morning and asked if he could drive out to Eva's country home in Berkshire and have a little talk with him.

Once there, Guthrie proposed that instead of making 500 pounds a week in films, Larry settle for 25 pounds a week for a season starring in Shakespeare's plays.

Without much hesitation, Larry agreed, especially when Guthrie proposed presenting the four-hour version of *Hamlet* instead of the usual 2½ hour play. "The Bard deserves no less than a full presentation," Guthrie said.

He found Guthrie fascinating. He was a giant of a man but spoke in a light voice. At the time he met Larry, Guthrie was known

Sir Tyrone Guthrie

for staging inventive, witty, and very theatrical productions.

Larry shared his fear of tackling Shakespeare after his disastrous reviews from *Romeo and Juliet*. But Guthrie was most assuring. "A season of Shakespeare will turn you into the actor you want to be." To challenge him, Guthrie asked, "Do you want matinee idolatry, stardom in Hollywood, or acclaim as the greatest actor on the British stage? The decision is yours."

After three hours of negotiations, Larry finally caved in, proclaiming, "I was destined to play it. I'm living Hamlet in real life—a violent, immature love for Vivien and a much more natural love for Jill. My love for her is subdued, less involving, and lacking the kind of passion that can drive a man wild."

Before the sun set over Windsor Castle, the deal was agreed upon. Larry had yet to meet Lilian Baylis, the doyenne of the Old Vic. Critic Ivor Brown called her an "odd little Empressario, with her fire of faith, her queer face, her spluttering speeches, and her vanities of cap and gown."

She addressed people completely without pretension, as when she told Queen Mary, following a matinee, "Hurry home, dearie, you've got to give the king his tea."

Baylis was noted for being the stingiest woman in the British theater. The closing line of her prayers was, "Oh, God, send me a good actor—and cheap."

Still lingering in the twilight glow of the Victorian era, Baylis shocked Larry when she said, "Are you pure, dear boy? Mind you, I am not narrow-minded, but I won't have anything going on in the wings. The stories I could tell you about what Gielgud and Laughton did backstage." She stared at him through the pince-nez on her very prominent nose.

He assured her that, "I am pure as the newly fallen snow on the Yorkshire moor. Unsullied by man or beast, faithful to the one and only woman I've ever known, Jill Esmond, my beloved wife."

Rehearsals began for *Hamlet*. Peggy Ashcroft had been cast as Ophelia, but she had to bow out at the last minute because of prior commitments, and was replaced by Cherry Cottrell.

To understand the complicated character of Hamlet, both Larry and Guthrie called on Professor Ernest Jones, the noted psychiatrist. A Freudian, he had recently published a book that claimed that Hamlet had an Oedipus complex and was almost incestuously in love with his mother.

Larry became convinced and decided to play the role according to the dictates of Dr. Jones. Guthrie agreed with him. Surprisingly, this Oedipus fixation went largely unnoticed by both the audience and critics, who failed to take note of the implications even with the lascivious kissing of his mother in one scene.

Henry Ainley, a master Shakespearean actor himself and Larry's longtime lover, praised his performance. Even though his guidelines were followed, Dr. Jones was disappointed in the performance. "Mr. Olivier is temperamentally not right for the role of Hamlet. He is personally what we call 'manic' and so finds it hard to play a melancholic part."

Larry worked with cast member Michael Redgrave, beginning a long and troubled relationship with the actor. Cast as Laertes, Redgrave had to stage a duel with Larry. On three different occasions, Redgrave played the scene so realistically that Larry got nicked and had to be bandaged.

"The bloody, jealous fool is trying to kill me so he can take over the role of Hamlet himself," Larry told Guthrie.

However, Larry was most gracious on the night of January 30, 1937, when he appeared before the curtains at the end of the performance. "Ladies and gentlemen, tonight a great actress has been born. Laertes has a daughter."

He was correct in his assessment. Vanessa Redgrave was born that night.

Redgrave, a young member of the cast, told Alec Guinness, another young member of the cast, that Larry "is not sufficiently subtle in the role of Hamlet."

In contrast, Redgrave praised Gielgud's Hamlet, failing to mention that he was in love with "Johnny G" at the time.

During rehearsals, Guthrie suggested to Redgrave that he and Larry would be competing for the same parts in their future.

Guinness was known for his attraction to handsome young actors. At first he'd been mesmerized by Larry's male beauty and charm. Apparently, as later privately reported by Guthrie, Guinness made a pass at Larry that was not intercepted. That was a beginning of Guinness' life-long animosity toward Larry.

Over the years he made catty remarks about Larry. He told friends, "As an actor I want to be the opposite of Olivier. He is merely an actor. He's technically brilliant, but humanly shallow. That's not me."

Hamlet premiered at the Old Vic on January 5, 1937, and Larry shockingly portrayed the melancholy Dane as the complete opposite of Gielgud's more elegant, yet detached, performance. Larry's *Hamlet* brought lust to the stage, as he pranced around as an athlete, impulsively

(upper photo) Sir Alec Guinness
(lower photo) Sir Michael Redgrave

251

royal.

Such a performance did not amuse James Agate, who wrote: "Mr. Olivier does not speak poetry badly, he simply does not speak it at all." Another critic suggested that Larry should learn there's more to acting than gymnastics.

In spite of such attacks from critics, the theater-going public adored the play and lined up to fill the house every night. But even as Larry was taking his tenth curtain call, Redgrave told Guinness: "Olivier is a very bad Hamlet, too assertive, too resolute."

Larry's favorite critical appraisal came from Ivor Brown in *The Observer*. He claimed that Larry returned a virility to Shakespeare that had "been out of fashion for a generation."

The critic, Kenneth Tynan, a future lover of Larry's, revealed that Larry had once told him that his portrayal of Hamlet was directed entirely at Vivien, who was in the opening night audience.

"With all its physical virility and acrobatic flash, it was his way of wooing her. And she confirmed it. She told me later on that she went to see at least half the performances, just so that she could be near Larry during a time when she was supposed to be staying away from him. Larry's performance was his long-distance Valentine to her."

On opening night, Vivien almost didn't recognize Larry when he first emerged on stage as Hamlet under his crown of thorns and with "an absolutely frightening beard and mustache." Perhaps the unkindest cut of all came from Guthrie himself in his 1972 autobiography, *A Life in the Theatre*. He wrote, "Offstage, Olivier was not notably handsome or striking, but with makeup he could achieve a flashing Italianate, rather saturnine, but fascinating appearance. He had, if anything, too strong an instinct for the sort of theatrical effect which is striking and memorable."

***

Vivien's next film was *Storm in a Teacup*, a satire on European dictators. Based on the German play, *Sturm im Wasserglas* by Bruno Frank, it was adapted for the screen by James Bridie. The story was inspired by a dog tax levy in Germany, but the setting for the English-language film was changed to Scotland.

The producer and director was Birmingham-born Victor Saville, a founding father of British cinema who had graduated from the silent screen to talkies.

Vivien's co-star was Rex Harrison, or "Sexy Rexy," as he was called

252

because of his reputation as a lady killer. The term was apt, as in the course of his life, women would commit suicide over him.

For the most part, Vivien and Saville had a smooth working relationship. She balked at only one scene where she was asked to fall on her buttocks. "I am a distinguished British actress," she told Saville, "not some cheap comedienne. I do not do scenes falling on my ass."

Although Vivien for the most part was the personification of a lady, she had taken to interjecting the word "fucking" into almost everything she said. She used fucking instead of bloody. It was a habit she'd picked up from Larry, who at the time was also overusing the word. "It came as a surprise to me to hear fucking emerge every minute or so from such a beautiful mouth," Saville said. "I figured she'd grow out of it."

During the shoot, Harrison admitted to falling in love with his leading lady, which was not unusual for him, even though he was married at the time to Collette Thomas, with whom he had a son, actor Noël Harrison.

Rex later wrote: "All she wanted to do was talk about Larry, and so I went along with that, gazing on that beautiful face with an uphopeful ardour. I loved Vivien. Although we never as much as held hands, I cannot say my love was platonic. It was more exciting than that."

What Harrison wrote and what he actually did in private were two different things. In some respects, he was the most devious of British actors, covering up his many indiscretions, including the suicide of his mistress, the actress Carole Landis, in 1948.

Rex began driving Vivien home at night after the day's shooting was finished. Sometimes it was midnight before he delivered her to Leigh's doorstep where her daughter had long since gone to bed.

Vivien was happy to be working with Ursula Jeans once again. In *Storm in a Teacup,* her friend had been cast as Lisbet Skirving, a contender for Vivien's screen father. Ursula and Vivien shared long talks about the possibility of England going to war against Germany. Both of them agreed if such an event occurred, they

(top photo) producer Victor Saville on the set of *Kim* with Errol Flynn

(lower photo): "Sexy Rexy" Harrison

253

would sign up for employment as ambulance drivers as part of their war effort.

"Vivien was going through a difficult period and was cut off from Olivier at the time," Jeans said. "She later told me that Harrison was such a cad. He moved in on her at a vulnerable moment. He told her that instead of going back home to Jill, as he'd promised Vivien, Larry was conducting a torrid affair with Ann Todd. Not only that, but Harrison told Vivien that Larry planned to divorce Jill and marry Todd. Vivien was so heartbroken she was almost suicidal. Harrison to the rescue. He offered her much 'comfort' time and time again, and she fell for his line."

Two views of *Storm in a Teacup* with Rex Harrison and Vivien Leigh

In later years, perhaps to justify his own behavior with a vulnerable Vivien, Harrison, in the presence of friends, often debunked the grand romance of Vivien and Larry.

"What all these writers, chronicling the great romance of the 20th century, the coming together of Vivien Leigh and Laurence Olivier, don't understand is that even at the peak of their romance they were having affairs with other people."

"It's true, they had a very passionate relationship," Harrison claimed. "I don't want to take that away from them. But their love affair was not exclusive. As time went by, they demanded loyalty from each other, not fidelity. Both of them were a bit crazy in that regard, but who am I to talk? I've been known to wander down the primrose path from time to time myself."

Larry later found out that Harrison had moved in on Vivien during the filming of *Storm in a Teacup*. He was furious at Harrison, and friends of both men noted the "submerged hostilities" that existed for years between the rival actors.

One of Harrison's biographers, Patrick Garland, claimed that "Rex and Sir Laurence, who were similar in many ways as men—egocentric, supremely gifted, insecure, envious, deeply attractive to women—actually disliked one another a very great deal."

As the years went by, Vivien tried to heal the rift between the two men and sometimes invited Harrison and his partner of the moment to be their weekend guest at their country home, Notley Abbey.

"Larry put up a brave front and was a gracious host to Harrison," Tyrone Guthrie said. "But once Larry told me, 'I detest the man. He's a liar. He's also a homophobe, even though I once walked in on him when he had his tongue halfway down a young actor's throat. He always hated me for discovering that.'"

Since Harrison had accepted invitations to Notley Abbey, Larry assumed that the rift between them had healed. He sent Harrison the script for the play *Dance of Death*, asking him to star in it opposite himself. Harrison wrote back: "*Dance of Death*. Only on your grave, dear boy."

When *Storm in a Teacup* was released, critics hailed Harrison and Vivien as England's answer to the American screen team of Myrna Loy and William Powell, and recommended that the pair be cast again in another movie.

The Spectator was overly lavish in its praise, calling *Storm in a Teacup* "the first genuinely British comedy to appear from an English studio. It may well be the best English film to date."

As a Christmas present, Saville handed Vivien a very thick novel. Taking it from him, she said, "It's so big I can hardly lift it. What is it about?"

Recovering from a ski injury in *(top photo)* Kitzbühel, Austria, Vivien Leigh "discovers" GWTW.

"The American Civil War," he said.

"Oh, goody, goody," she said mockingly. "What role do I get to play? Robert E. Lee, no doubt. Or maybe Mrs. Abraham Lincoln."

"Neither," he said. "There's a fabulous role in it for you. You'd make the perfect Scarlett O'Hara, the heroine of the novel. She spends most of the book lusting after another woman's husband."

"*Touchée!*" she said.

After the film was wrapped, Leigh invited Vivien to spend the Christmas holidays with him at Kitzbühel in Austria, where she'd once fallen in love with a ski instructor. Over New Year's she injured her knee so badly she was confined to bed.

Trapped in her suite while Leigh was out skiing, she picked up the big novel Saville had given her as

255

a present. For the first time she noticed the title, *Gone With the Wind*.

"Very evocative," she said. Turning to the first page of Margaret Mitchell's saga, Vivien was immediately enchanted by the heroine, Miss Scarlett O'Hara.

***

Larry came back into Vivien's life but was very restrained. What brought them together again was the news from Alexander Korda that he had cast them in *Twenty-One Days* (1937), which was released in the United States as *Twenty-One Days Together*.

Accompanied by Leigh, Vivien attended a party honoring Jill and Larry. Again in the company of Leigh, Jill, and Larry, Vivien even drove to see Frewen at his Sussex homestead. After that, the two couples journeyed by car to the town of Rye where they stayed for the weekend at the Old Flushing Inn.

Larry remembered Leigh as "a dull man, dry, cerebral, without sparkle." He later changed his opinion. "He was highly intelligent, clever, but not exciting or outwardly romantic." In time, he would grow to like Leigh very much.

Of course, Jill at this point was completely aware of her husband's affair with Vivien. Surprisingly, Leigh, who was not a stupid man, was not privy to the relationship.

"Everybody was being very English about it," Frewen said, "when they came to see me. Larry and Viv did not mention a word about their past indiscretions. Nor did they give any clue as to what was going on."

Back in London, Frewen remembered hosting a dinner just for Vivien and Jill, without Larry, at the Moulin d'Or, which attracted a theatrical crowd.

When Korda met with both Larry and Vivien, he asked them, "How can *The First and the Last* lose?" That had been his original title for *Twenty-One Days*.

"Based on a play by John Galsworthy. Screenplay by Graham Greene. Basil Dean as the director. Leslie Banks in the third lead? A surefire box office hit."

After each of them read the script, neither Vivien nor Larry were sure the movie would be a hit. But they eagerly agreed to do it because they wanted to be together, and the movie provided the excuse they needed to conceal their resumed affair.

Larry was cast in *The First and the Last* as a ne'er-do-well younger brother of Leslie Banks, who played a distinguished London barrister. The script calls for Larry to fall in love with Vivien, cast as a Russian refugee. Unknown to Larry, she has a secret, older husband. After a struggle with the blackmailing husband, Larry kills him accidentally. The plot thickens.

David Niven, who became a close friend of Larry and Vivien, later claimed, "They were fucking between each take on the set of *Twenty-One Days*. Larry may have ended his relationship with Vivien, but he sure as hell resumed it quickly enough."

Basil Dean still had no great love for either Larry or Vivien, and his animosity toward Vivien had remained unchanged. In his diary, he wrote that he had serious doubts about casting her because of her obvious lack of experience, "but Korda was adamant."

"They were a pain in the ass to work with," Dean later said. "They didn't take the film seriously. They were always laughing and giggling on the set. It was very disconcerting. I had worked with them before, and never wanted to see them again. I found both of them completely unprofessional. Vivien was acting like a silly schoolgirl. Dare I say it? So was Larry. He could be very effeminate when caught off guard."

During the making of *Twenty-One Days*, Korda himself came on the set and directed some scenes from the film when Dean's battle with his two stars grew so tense they could not continue filming.

Vivien felt her life changed when she received through the Royal Mail an envelope bearing the letterhead of the Old Vic. It read: THE DANISH AUTHORITIES WOULD VERY MUCH LIKE IT IF YOU COULD PLAY OPHELIA, AND WE, TOO, WOULD BE DELIGHTED."

She ran to Larry to learn the details, finding out that they'd been asked to give a command performance, for presentation to audiences which included members of the royal family of Denmark, of *Hamlet* at Kronberg Castle in Elsinore, Denmark.

Larry was to reprise his role as Hamlet, with Vivien starring opposite him. "I cannot believe this. My dream has come true. I wonder who arranged for me to play Ophelia."

"I wonder," Larry said.

Guthrie did not think Vivien had the voice or the experience to be an effective Ophelia. He and Larry quarreled. Larry promised to work with her on her voice, but Guthrie was not convinced. "No, I want Jill."

"Then you don't have me," Larry said. "I don't need the role. I'm already making a film for Korda. Count me out. Get yourself another Hamlet—perhaps John Gielgud. He's more your type."

"Who else can I come up with at this last moment?" Guthrie said. "Alec Guinness."

"Okay, cast him," Larry said. "His Hamlet will be booed off the stage by all those in the audience."

Finally Guthrie caved in and cast Vivien. He dreaded making the call to inform Jill.

Cherry Cottrell, who had faithfully interpreted the Ophelia opposite Larry's Freudian interpretation of Hamlet at the Old Vic, was furious when she learned that she had not been invited to Elsinore to reprise the role. "Give me a sword," she said. "I'll turn Olivier into a eunuch."

It was Korda who adapted the shooting schedule of *Twenty-One Days* that allowed Vivien and Larry to escape to Denmark to perform in *Hamlet*.

A week would go by, with production shut down, while Larry and Vivien performed *Hamlet* for four nights in Denmark.

For the American market, the movie's title was changed to *21 Days Together*, and Vivien was given top billing.

Shot in England in 1937, *21 Days* was not released in America until 1940. Korda referred to it as "a disaster."

When they returned to London and shot the final scenes of *Twenty-One Days*, Korda arranged a press party aboard a vessel sailing the Thames.

Much to the regret of Korda, Vivien spent all her time talking to the press about the upcoming filming of *Gone With the Wind*. "I desperately want to play Scarlett O'Hara," she told Caroline Lejeune of *The Observer*. "I have never been so gripped by any book in my life. It's the finest novel I've ever read. What a grand film it will make."

"I have read about half the book," Lejeune said. Noticing Larry standing beside Vivien, she added, "I think Larry here would make a divine Rhett Butler."

"Not a chance," Larry said. "No way."

"Larry won't be Rhett Butler," Vivien said. "I see Robert Taylor as my Rhett. I fancy him. He's almost as handsome as Larry. I will be Scarlett O'Hara. Wait and see."

When Korda saw the final cut of *Twenty-One Days*, he told Basil Dean. "You've fucked up this picture. Now I know why Vivien didn't want to promote it on that press boat. The picture is a disaster. I'm shelving it indefinitely. If released, it will destroy the careers of my stars."

Korda followed through on his threat. He released *Twenty-One Days* only after Larry had scored a big hit as Heathcliff in *Wuthering Heights* and Vivien had won an Oscar for her portrayal of Scarlett O'Hara in *Gone With the Wind*.

Upon the film's release, the *Sunday Express* summed up the plot. "In a fit of temper Olivier kills Vivien's caddish husband and runs desperately to his brother for advice. Vivien and Olivier start life anew."

In New York, when the film opened at a seedy little cinema, Vivien and Larry disguised themselves and slipped in after the credits had come on the screen. But they left in disgust before the movie was half over.

When Leigh in London attended the film, he objected to the plot. "I don't like it when Larry kills Vivien's husband."

***

Invited by the Danish government as the wife of Larry, Jill flew to Copenhagen with Larry and Vivien, although the loving couple clearly did not welcome her presence. En route Vivien learned that Tyrone Guthrie had not wanted her to play Ophelia.

Sitting beside Jill on the plane, Guthrie noticed Larry and Vivien huddled together in a seat up front. "I'm so sorry that Vivien replaced you as Ophelia."

"It looks like I've been replaced by Vivien in more ways than one," Jill said.

Never seen by Shakespeare, Kronberg Castle was the setting for *Hamlet*, and the Danish Tourist Board convinced the Old Vic to present the play without financial compensation to celebrate the Silver Jubilee of King Christian X.

After a brief stay at the Hotel d'Angleterre in Copenhagen, the cast and crew were driven to Elsinore. Larry found Kronberg Castle "more like a Hans Christian Andersen fantasy than the bleak castle the Bard wrote about, with its fortified towers and ghost-stalked battlements."

Jill and Larry shared a bedroom at the nearby Marienlist Hotel, with Vivien sleeping alone. As Guthrie recalled, "Her door was always open for Larry to come calling at any time of the day or night when he could slip away from Jill."

Michael Redgrave could not make the trip to Copenhagen, so Anthony Quayle took over his role, cast as Laertes, brother of Ophelia. Alec Guinness, cast as Osric, did make the trip.

As the understudy for Larry, he resented having to keep Jill entertained "while Larry stayed back at the hotel fucking Vivien."

Quayle turned critic in assessing Vivien's performance. "I remember how beautiful she looked, and I remember how far her talent fell short of her beauty."

"There is so much added pressure with Jill watching my every move with Vivien as Hamlet," Larry told Guthrie. "Imagine acting with my mistress in the presence of my wife."

He later wrote, "Vivien and I could not keep from touching each other, making love almost within Jill's vision. The welding closeness tripped the obvious decision, and two marriages were severed."

Rehearsals in the courtyard of Kronberg were interrupted by frequent rainstorms and the forever sound of steam hammers in an adjacent shipyard.

It has been suggested by some that Larry entered into a marriage with Vivien totally unaware of her "states," as she continued to call them. That is not true. Once when they were staging their movements outdoors when the sun came out, she turned on him. He saw a screeching harridan of a woman, not his beautiful goddess.

"Who do you think you are?" she shouted at him in front of the cast. "You're not man enough to play Hamlet. Alec Guinness or even Michael Redgrave could do it better. I hate you."

Without warning, she rushed toward him and began flaying his face with her delicate arms. Guthrie intervened and subdued her with the help of a stage manager. She was carried out of the courtyard.

Larry explained to Jill. "Viv went bonkers today. She attacked me. A fit of some kind. It was very strange."

The next day, Vivien appeared before cast and crew staring blankly into space. She was letter perfect in her delivery that night.

After a rehearsal, Larry downed a stiff aquavit and approached her dressing room. He recalled that she was "utterly charming, her old self again. She didn't explain what happened,

Something is rotten in Kronberg Castle *(lower photo)*
(upper photos) Larry (playing Hamlet) and Viv (Ophelia)

260

and she didn't apologize. I wondered at the time if she even remembered what had taken place the previous afternoon."

On opening night June 2, 1937, the worst storm in twenty-three years forced the cast to perform on the ballroom stage of the Hotel Marienlist. In the front row seated near his father, Christian X, was Crown Prince Frederik (later, King Frederik IX), whose feet were thrust out in front of him, practically tripping Larry at several points. The play drew an audience of 2,000.

Ironically, in July of 1939, Gielgud, only weeks before the launch of World War II, also appeared at Elsinore, and the Copenhagen press hailed him as "the world's best Hamlet."

***

From Copenhagen, Larry, Jill, and Vivien flew back to London. By that Thursday night, Vivien informed Leigh that she was leaving him. On Friday, Jill heard the news that Larry was moving out and would in the future be living with Vivien.

Hamlet marked the end of Vivien's marriage to Leigh. Back in London she told him, "Our marriage is over. You are a very nice man, but I don't love you. However, I want to keep your friendship, and I'd like to visit my daughter whenever you allow it."

He pleaded with her to reconsider and not end their marriage. "Your infatuation with Larry could be just a passing thing. Jill told me many stories about Larry. Are you aware that he is a bisexual? If you want a man who puts on makeup every night, including a slight coating of lipstick, and who has lain for other men, then that is your dreadful choice. I understand that he's a good actor, and one day may be a great actor, but plays are not my favorite pastime. I prefer to be anchored in reality, not lost in some fantasy created by some sod of a playwright."

"Larry's past is behind him, and he's ready to start life anew with me," she said. "He fell in with that Noël Coward crowd. Let's face it: Most British actors are homosexuals or at least pass through a homosexual period when they are young. Larry wants to settle down with me. I can keep him on the straight and narrow path."

"I wouldn't be so sure, my dear," Leigh said. "I think I know a little more about human nature than you do. It's hard for a tiger to change his stripes."

In a letter to Gertrude, Leigh tried to explain what had happened to their marriage.

When she left me for Larry she told me that after a month she would write me to say whether it was final. I got that letter & it was the only one from

*her I have ever destroyed. I felt utterly hopeless but I did not badger &
beseech her to change her mind & had I done so I would only have got
something equivalent to no flowers or cable on a first night. Since then of
course we have got so much from each other's friendship, and friendship
was the only possible basis on which we could get anything.*

The usually strong Gertrude, who was acting as Suzanne's mother, called
Vivien in hysterics from Scotland. She had gone there to nurse Tommy. He
was suffering from throat cancer and could no longer speak.

He would in time die at the Royal Hotel in Campbeltown, on the Kintyre
Peninsula, on September 30, 1938. A few hours later, Gertrude called Vivien,
sobbing into the phone. "Tommy is the only man I've ever loved," she confessed.

In the wake of Tommy's death, old resentments arose. Apparently, Vivien
blamed Gertrude for bringing Tommy into her family life. She had buried the
more sordid aspects of her own inappropriate relationship with Tommy when
she was a young girl, although she confided to certain friends, "I think Tommy
wanted to seduce all of us—Gertrude, my father, and myself."

Without confronting her mother as to what Tommy had done to her, she
turned on her in other ways. She accused Gertrude of trying to make Suzanne
love her more than she loved her own mother. At one outrageous point, she
said, "Now that Tommy is gone, I guess you'll be making love to Leigh."

Gertrude begged Vivien to see a psychiatrist, but she refused. Her condition back then was called "manic depressive."

Vivien often insulted Larry's friends and had to apologize and send flowers the next day, along with a note of apology. Some of these friends claimed,
"She's a cruel bitch."

Rex Harrison disagreed. "I don't think she was that. A lot of people even
thought she was stark raving mad at times. I prefer to think she had periods
when her demons took over. She was getting no help from anyone, certainly
not from Larry. He didn't seem to know what to do."

Gielgud always was her champion, defending her after some of her cru-
elest attacks on people. "I always knew that the horror would subside and
dear, sweet, charming Vivien would emerge intact from the rubble. Even when
she attacked me, calling me all sorts of vile names, I was never angered by her.
I knew it wasn't the real Vivien talking. It was her illness."

To John Gielgud, Larry confessed, "The turmoil in my private life is causing me to be a better actor on stage. It is stirring up emotions in me I didn't
know existed. I'm releasing and exploring those emotions as never before."

"My, dear boy, you'll overtake me yet unless I can find some way of stopping you."

"You never will because you'll never really fall in love," Larry told him. "I don't mean to put you down, and I know you will have many lovers, but your true love is Johnny G. himself."

"Truer words were never said, except for that old refrain, 'I won't come in your mouth.'"

Suddenly, Vivien was faced with a new emergency. She had to find a suitable home to set up housekeeping with Larry. She was both filled with excitement and fear. One day a real estate agent led her to Durham Cottage at 4 Christchurch Street in Chelsea. That night Larry arrived to inspect the house, and fell in love with it at once. He signed the lease the next day under his own name.

Back in London, Larry and Vivien secretly lived together, waiting until the house he'd purchased for them in Chelsea could be renovated.

When he could no longer stand the loneliness, Leigh wrote Vivien, asking her to come back. Very politely she responded, telling him that the marriage was over. "I am never coming back as your wife, only as your good friend. Thank you for taking such good care of Suzanne."

***

Larry was reluctant to appear opposite Merle Oberon in *The Divorce of Lady X*. He told Vivien, "Korda obviously will see to it that the film is thrown in the direction of his lady love." Korda and Oberon were having a torrid affair at the time.

"And Ralph Richardson will steal every scene," Larry said. "Not only that but the 'divorce' in the title comes too close to home. I'll be playing a barrister, reminding me of the man I'm cuckolding." At that point, Larry lived in fear that Leigh might name him as co-respondent in Vivien's upcoming divorce from him. Nightly he poured out these fears and frustrations to Vivien when he came home to Durham Cottage.

Concerned with her own problems, Vivien told him, "I'll think about it tomorrow," borrowing a line from Scarlett O'Hara in Mitchell's novel.

In the film, playing the role of a young bar-

(lower photo)
Merle Oberon with Larry in
The Divorce of Lady X

263

rister, Larry is trapped inadvertently in a romantic web of mistaken identity.

The Divorce of Lady X, a United Artists release in 1938, was actually a remake of another Korda film, *Counsel's Opinion*, based on the Gilbert Wakefield play of the same name. Many critics found the original better than the remake.

Larry's movie was a piece of fluff, and of so little importance to his career that he ignored it in his autobiography. He filmed it at the same time Vivien was starring in *A Yank at Oxford*.

On the set Larry found Oberon very self-centered, even self-enchanted. She seemed overly concerned with the lighting and how she photographed, factors of more urgent concern to her, it seemed, than the role she was playing.

In spite of such self-involvement, he got on reasonably well with her, his future co-star in *Wuthering Heights*. Their artistic battles lay in the future. However, during the filming she constantly accused him of spraying spittle and saliva into her face when he delivered face-to-face dialogue with her.

It was most irritating to Larry that Korda and Oberon did not arrive on set until around 12:30 every afternoon. They slept late, breaking for lunch at 3:30pm. Filming began again in the very late afternoon, lasting until eleven most nights.

When Larry heard that "Queenie" (the nickname for Oberon) finally married Korda, in 1939, he said, "I'm not surprised. Merle is the type of actress who marries the head of the studio."

Lady X, that drawing room comedy of manners, was one of those "It Happened Last Night" or "It Didn't Happen Last Night" films. Other than looking good, Larry shone only in a misogynistic speech where he found a rather mature voice.

Merle Oberon Becomes Lady Korda. Oberon and Alexander Korda in 1942 after a ceremony at Buckingham Palace where the king granted him knighthood.

He came off well within the format of his first Technicolor film—in fact, many moviegoers found his close-ups "more beautiful" than those of Oberon, an opinion that infuriated her.

The most astute of critics awarded the picture to Richardson, who performed with a deft comic touch, making Larry's screen acting appear too stagey.

Actress Binnie Barnes had appeared in both versions of the film, its original and its remake. In the earlier film she'd appeared as Leslie. In *The Divorce of Lady X*, she was cast as Lady Mere.

There was no magic between Larry and his Indiana-born director, Tim Whelan. They were just two professionals engaged in their job. Whelan had begun his career in Hollywood working with Harold Lloyd, who had ranked alongside Charlie Chaplin and Buster Keaton as the leading comedians of the silent film era. Whelan had moved his family to England, where he was making his mark as a director.

A future star, Michael Rennie, appeared briefly in an uncredited part. Larry worked again with Morton Selten, cast in the film as Oberon's grandfather. In *Fire Over England*, he'd played Lord Burleigh. (Selten was alleged to have been the illegitimate son of King Edward VII.)

Film Weekly found Larry in "unusually good form" and claimed that he "gives what is his best screen performance yet." Frank S. Nugent of *The New York Times* wrote Larry "has an engaged inability to defend masculine integrity against the feminine foe."

One critic used F-words to describe Oberon and Larry. When Oberon starred in *Wuthering Heights*, the critic claimed she was "still the fluffy Leslie Steele," her character from *The Divorce of Lady X*. As for Larry, the critic judged his performance "too fizzed-up."

Another critic suggested that had *The Divorce of Lady X* been made in America, it would have starred Kay Francis, Cary Grant, and William Powell."

***

Larry wasn't the only actor getting film roles. So was his mistress. *A Yank at Oxford* was Metro-Goldwyn-Mayer's first British-made film under Hollywood supervision. The film was shot during the summer and autumn of 1937 in England, with some early sequences filmed in Hollywood.

Vivien was very disappointed in her status as the film's fourth lead when John Gliddon gave her the script. "The part of Elsa Craddock is all wrong for me," she told Gliddon the next day. She'd been cast as the horny wife of a "fusty" bookseller in the film. She bikes around Oxford all day pursuing male undergraduates.

But once she learned that Robert Taylor was going to play the American at Oxford, she changed her mind. "My God, don't you see?" she asked Gliddon. "This is my big break. I'm almost certain that he'll be Rhett Butler in *Gone With the Wind*. This will be like a big screen test for me."

"I'm not so sure," Gliddon warned her. "Louis B. Mayer didn't even want to cast you in *A Yank at Oxford*."

"Hell with that fucking Louis B. Mayer," she said. "It's David O. Selznick who will make the choice of Scarlett. I'll sleep with him if I have to, although

he's a bit repulsive."

Shot on location, *A Yank at Oxford* was produced by Michael Balcon and directed by Jack Conway. An amazing array of top writers had worked on the screenplay, including George Oppenheimer, Herman J. Mankiewicz, C.S. Forester, John Van Druten, Christopher Isherwood, and even F. Scott Fitzgerald.

All of the sequences involving Lionel Barrymore, playing Taylor's father, were filmed in Hollywood.

Conway, the Minnesota-born director, had once been an actor himself, starring in one of the earliest movies ever filmed in Hollywood, *Her Indian Hero* in 1912. Vivien told O'Sullivan, "He lacks a certain sense of fantasy so needed, at least for the theater."

A Yank at Oxford was the first film in which Vivien demonstrated what screenwriter Gavin Lambert described afterward as "a mixture of exquisite control and passionate excess."

Vivien was amazed the following day when she learned that her former schoolgirl friend, Maureen O'Sullivan, had been assigned the film's female lead. Privately Vivien was jealous at how fast O'Sullivan had become a star in Hollywood, especially after appearing in all those Tarzan movies with Johnny Weissmuller. O'Sullivan had also scored successes in such prestigious pictures as *The Thin Man*, *David Copperfield*, and *The Barretts of Wimpole*

A Yank at Oxford
(middle photo) Vivien in fourth billing as a predatory coquette
(bottom photo) Leigh, Maureen O'Sullivan, and Robert Taylor promoting "The Roving Romances of a Two-Fisted American"

Street.

Married to John Farrow, she was also a successful mother. To an increasing degree, in stark contrast to O'Sullivan, Vivien seemed to feel she was an awful mother to Suzanne. Not only that, but she was living with a married man "in sin."

A Yank at Oxford was the first of the roles which "roughed up" the screen image of Taylor. Trying to escape from his reputation as a "pretty boy," Taylor played a cocky American athlete who falls for a British coquette, as played by Vivien.

When she met Taylor, she found him even handsomer and more charming than he was on the screen. She walked right up to him and kissed him on both cheeks. "Rhett Butler, meet your Scarlett O'Hara."

"I'm delighted to meet you, Scarlett," he said. Stunned by her beauty, he said, "You look more like Scarlett than any woman I've seen. I'm not sure I'll be your Rhett Butler. When I last heard, Selznick was considering casting my dear friend, Barbara Stanwyck, and Humphrey Bogart."

"That idea is so absurd that I'm sure Mr. Selznick will soon abandon it. I didn't mean, of course, to trash Miss Stanwyck's talent."

"Even *I* think Barbara's wrong for Scarlett," Taylor said. "I told her she'd do better as a gun moll from Brooklyn. After that, I got my face royally slapped."

Vivien linked her arm with Taylor. "Come on, you gorgeous creature, and let's have a cuppa."

"I'm trying to get away from that gorgeous image," Taylor said. "When I did *Gorgeous Hussy* with Crawford, the press asked which was the gorgeous one. I'm cultivating a more masculine image."

"Rhett Butler will do that for you," she said. "He's the most masculine man I've ever read about in a novel."

That night they met for dinner. "I've been reading your press about your arrival in England," Vivien said. "Not since William the Conqueror arrived on our shores has there been such commo-

(top photo) Maureen O'Sullivan
(lower photo) Robert Taylor

tion."

"Newspaper reporters exaggerate," he said.

"Of course, they do," she said. "But 5,000 young girls greeting the *Berengaria* when it docked in Southampton. In London I heard that you flicked a cigarette butt from your balcony at Claridge's, and thirteen people were injured in the rush to reclaim it as a souvenir. That's star power."

Never in a previous play or in a film had Vivien showed such mental insta- bility. Michael Balcon, the director of MGM's British production, immediate- ly insulted Vivien when he told her, "I don't want you to slow down produc- tion by falling in love with our star [a reference to Taylor]. I know you have this thing of falling for your leading man," a reference, of course, to Larry.

Vivien's new friend, Ursula Jeans, arrived on the set to spend two or three days with Vivien, who had sent for her. Jeans found Vivien engaged in an off- screen fling with Taylor.

"I know all those homosexual rumors about him, but he's a real man," she confided in Jeans.

"Are you sleeping with this pretty boy?" Jeans asked. "I don't blame you. I'd jump at the chance myself."

"You don't understand," Vivien said. "It's not one of those leading man/leading lady romances. It's almost certain that he'll play Rhett Butler or so I heard. When we're not working on *A Yank in Oxford*, we're testing out our sexual chemistry with each other. If our private love scenes could be put on tape, I'm sure Selznick would sign a contract with us immediately."

A Yank in Oxford was the first American movie to be made at MGM's new studio in Denham, near London. Taylor rented a small cottage in the village of High Wycombe. According to O'Sullivan, Vivien could be seen coming and going from that cottage.

"Can you imagine this man?" she asked Jeans. "He likes to go for long walks with me in the fog and rain. When I met him, he was a confirmed cof- fee drinker. Seven, eight cups a day. Now he's a confirmed tea drinker, and eagerly looks forward to having tea with me in my dressing room at four o'clock every afternoon."

"I'm sure you offer tea," Jeans said jokingly. "And you're the cupcakes."

"Something like that," Vivien said. "There's no future with Bob. I'm madly in love with Larry. Besides, Bob calls Stanwyck in Hollywood nearly every day, begging her to marry him. It's wonderful when a man and woman like us can enjoy each other's company with no strings attached. I think I'm developing into a modern woman, just like my mother."

One night when she slept over in Bob's cottage, she reported to O'Sullivan the next day. Her friend wanted to know all the details.

"Bob has this dreadful habit of bathing in ice every morning, and he invited me to join him. I declined. He claims the ice toughens him for those out-door racing scenes he performs. By the way, did you know a man shrinks quite a bit in a cold bath filled with ice?"

"I've never witnessed that myself," O'Sullivan said. "But I imagine it would be true."

After the release of the film, Vivien read all the headlines in the world press, which had discovered that "pretty boy Bob" had hair on his chest.

The news made world headlines—ROBERT TAYLOR BARES CHEST TO PROVE HE-NESS? Even in Paris, the French press proclaimed MON DIEU QUEL HOMME!

"I discovered the hair on that beautiful chest long before the world did," Vivien said. "And quite a mat it was."

It has never been fully explained, but Vivien began to become irrational during filming of *Yank*. The story made the rounds among the Oxford under-graduates that Vivien one night in a park performed fellatio on five of the young students. When she heard of this, Vivien adamantly denied it, but the tellers of this tale insisted that it was true.

"She was completely out of control at times," O'Sullivan in Hollywood claimed years later. "She was stubborn, willful, refusing to perform in the way the director ordered, calling people names on the set."

She threw her biggest fit when the director, Conway, asked her to wear a leopard-skin collar to suggest she was a bit whorish as she bicycled around Oxford, picking up young men. "I'm a lady," she shouted at Conway. "No lady would wear that. Only a whore would wear such things."

"But Vivien you're playing a slut," Conway protested. "You're a lady in real life."

"You're lying," Vivian shouted at Conway. "I know you're lying. You believe all those vile rumors spread

Two views of *A Yank at Oxford*
(top) O'Sullivan, Taylor, and Leigh
(bottom) Taylor and O'Sullivan

269

about me." She ran from the set and refused to shoot the scene until the following day.

But just a few days after that, she practically quit working on the picture because of a dispute with MGM accountants as to who would pay for her shoes.

Korda's office got wind of some of Vivien's behavior on set, and the producer sent Gliddon a warning. "Miss Leigh's behavior is incomprehensible and inexcusable. It is making things very difficult for us. Please tell her she must behave herself in the future. If not, we shall have to reconsider taking up her option when it next falls due."

Korda didn't explain to Gliddon what reports he'd received from Michael Balcon to suggest exactly what Vivien had done.

One writer in the future would point out that Vivien's role in *A Yank at Oxford* was a harbinger of her Scarlett O'Hara in depicting a headstrong young girl and Blanche DuBois in evoking nymphomania. One line in *Yank*, when Vivien encounters Taylor, reads: "I'm drawn like this to strangers." That evokes "I have always depended on the kindness of strangers" in *A Streetcar Named Desire*.

When actress Eve Phillips, a sometimes confidante of Vivien's, saw *A Yank at Oxford*, she said, "When Viv was playing Elsa Craddock, she was, in fact, doing an elaborate screen test for Scarlett O'Hara. She was saucy and sexy as Elsa, just like the heroine of the Margaret Mitchell novel. She was a kind of English version of Scarlett O'Hara."

Her seduction of Robert Taylor might not have been for pure lust. O'Sullivan suspected that he was part of her long-range plan to win the role of Scarlett O'Hara for herself, with Taylor playing Rhett.

"Bob was just Vivien's faraway casting couch," O'Sullivan said. "She didn't like sex with him that much. She complained to me that his dick was too small. Vivien's purpose was accomplished. When Taylor returned to Hollywood, he met with Selznick and told him that Vivien was 'just the gal' to play the high-spirited Scarlett. As an added note, Taylor said, "I keep getting tons of letters every day from fans who just insist that I play Rhett Butler."

When Vivien came back to London, Gliddon went over to Durham Cottage and told her that Korda was threatening not to renew her contract.

He later claimed, "She went berserk. She flew into me, beating me with her fists. For such a delicate creature, she packed a punch. When she decided that wasn't enough, she scratched my face severely. The voice that came from deep within her was like no voice I'd heard from her before. She was the devil. She looked at me with utter contempt. The coldest eyes I'd ever seen. Then she proceeded to kick me out of her house."

"I thought it was over between us," Gliddon said. "But the next day when she called it was all sweetness and light, the Vivien I had known and loved. It was as if the night before had never happened. She made no mention of it. The next afternoon when I had lunch with her, she looked shocked to see my face scratched badly. 'What happened?' she asked me."

"Some trade I picked up at the Dilly roughed me up a bit," Gliddon told her.

Some reports have Vivien remembering what she did and apologizing, but Gliddon maintained the version he gave is what actually happened.

***

Back in London, Larry prepared for the role of Sir Toby Belch in Shakespeare's *Twelfth Night*, set for an opening on February 23, 1937 at the Old Vic. Larry played the high-spirited Sir Toby as a comic buffoon, and Jill appeared opposite him as Maria, a servant girl in the Belch household.

When Vivien learned that Larry and Guthrie had cast Jill in *Twelfth Night*, it provoked a row with Larry. She accused him of thinking that Jill was a more accomplished actress on stage than she was. "Who am I?" Vivien shouted at him. "Some woman to be used like a Saturday night whore?"

Filled with fury, she raged at him, but he managed to subdue her.

Jessica Tandy, who had admired Larry early in his career, was also in the cast, playing Viola. She said that Larry "had all the physical attributes of a romantic juvenile, and he had the time of his life playing Sir Toby."

In *Twelfth Night*, Larry appeared with Alec Guinness, who'd been cast as Sir Toby's companion, Sir Andrew Aguecheek. On stage, even in rehearsals, Larry and Guinness competed for which of them could get the most laughs. After two days of fierce one-upmanship, Larry said to Guthrie, "I have developed a supreme distaste for the charms, or lack thereof, of one Mr. Guinness."

Guinness told Guthrie, "Mr. Olivier is a man to be wary of. He doesn't upstage fellow actors, he merely overwhelms them." Unfortunately, Guinness would share somewhat that same sentiment decades later when he addressed an audience of mourners at Larry's memorial service in Westminster Abbey.

John Gliddon took Vivien to see Larry perform in *Twelfth Night* at the Old Vic, where she squirmed in her seat and seemed uncomfortable watching Jill star opposite Larry.

At the end of the performance, and before going backstage to congratulate them, she told Gliddon: "I should be playing opposite Larry and not trapped in this *Bats in the Belfry* crap you got me into."

Larry's boisterous interpretation of Sir Toby did not go over well with the critics. One reviewer wrote: "Mr. Olivier shows more and more a tendency to distance himself from Shakespeare's intentions and to impose his own views upon the Bard's character and text. In *Twelfth Night* he has gone too far. The audience tends to laugh at Mr. Olivier rather than Sir Toby."

Larry followed *Twelfth Night* with Shakespeare's *Henry V*, which opened at the Old Vic on April 6, 1937.

***

As a pacifist, Larry always detested *Henry V* as a play, calling the character a "glorification of heroic warfare." However, Guthrie persuaded Larry that it would be a fitting choice to occur simultaneously with the 1937 coronation of King George VI.

Larry was leery of the militaristic aura of the play. Like much of England, he wanted his country to stay out of a war with Germany. But both Guthrie and Ralph Richardson urged Larry "to go into battle."

Guthrie asked Larry to give a "buccaneerish performance," which he ultimately did. "I finally have come to embody English nationalism," Larry said after a week of rehearsals.

He exhibited stellar talent in his interpretation of *Henry V*, a production that included Jessica Tandy as Katherine and also Anthony Quayle in a pivotal role.

Critics appreciated Larry's more subdued interpretation of *Henry V*. "It is by far his best handling of a major character in Shakespeare," wrote one reviewer.

On opening night Larry was immensely flattered when his nemesis, Charles Laughton, came backstage and shouted at him, "*You are England!*"

***

Vivien was also performing in plays in the West End, though none as distinguished as Larry's Shakespeare repertoire. She was disappointed that all Gliddon could come up with for her was *Because We Must*, which opened at Wyndham's Theatre on February 5, 1937.

Vivien had been assigned a small, lackluster role in this comedy, produced and directed by Norman Marshall. She played a character called Pamela Golding-ffrench.

After only two days of rehearsals, Vivien stormed into Gliddon's office. She was in another one of her "states."

Although she didn't attack him physically, she accused him of "being an incompetent, a total failure." She even accused him of deliberately sabotaging her career.

"You don't want me to be cast as Scarlett because you know you'll lose me as a client. Who will you be left with? Deborah Kerr. You'll go far with *that one*."

The next day she sent a loving note and a bunch of flowers to Gliddon, asking for his forgiveness.

Because We Must did not attract much critical acclaim or much of an audience. The biggest event on opening night was when Vivien handed out a copy of *Gone With the Wind* to each member of the cast.

Another play, *Bats in the Belfry*, was presented by Sydney Carroll, who always claimed, "I discovered Vivien Leigh."

Cast as Jessica Morton, Vivien opened this play at the Ambassadors Theatre in London on March 11, 1937. It was another so-called comedy that called for the actors to improvise parts of the text while teasing and taunting each other.

At the end of its short run, she complained to Gliddon, "My career is on a downward spiral."

Even though they feuded constantly, Gertrude continued to be a fixture in Vivien's life. She still remained shocked at her daughter's desertion of Leigh, whom she liked and admired. "Vivien's Catholic upbringing was a vaccine that didn't take," Gertrude said.

Vivien continued to turn to Gertrude when she entered one of her "states," as she plunged into irrational behavior and total despair.

Many observers felt that these emotional and mental collapses often didn't occur until later in Vivien's life, but there had been previous manifestations as early as when Vivien was growing up.

Gertrude never understood Vivien's emotional distress. "She's just a temperamental girl, always was," Gertrude told Larry. "Actresses are always temperamental. You, of all people, should know that. You've known so many of them. All of Vivien's nerves are on the surface of her skin. She finds the role of celebrity hard to live with. I read that Greta Garbo has the same problem." One afternoon Gertrude told Larry, "Vivien can be so dear, but at times she must cause you grief."

"She does, more times than I would wish," Larry said. "But it is such rapturous torment."

Feeling despondent with her plays, Vivien was eager to see her friend Oswald Frewen again. He had been in Marseilles when her separation from Leigh had occurred. In his diary he quoted Vivien in a letter to him. "It was a week of nightmares for Larry and me and torture for the others. I feel completely sapped."

Frewen ultimately forgave Vivien for leaving his dear friend, Leigh. He did not think she should marry Larry, and he began to have serious fears about her mental stability once she cut herself loose from old Leigh's helmsmanship.

In his diary, he pondered her move. "Vivien has brain and a heart, but not ethical upbringing and instead an overdose of temperament. Can she remain unsubmerged? Will her intellect and heart fade out?"

Back in London, Frewen called first on Leigh, later claiming that "he'd aged seven or eight years since Vivien left him."

On a sad note, Frewen reported that Leigh every night laid out Vivien's dressing robe and nightgown. "They'll be waiting for her when she returns," he told Frewen. "She'll come back to me one day. I must wait and be patient."

That same evening, Frewen visited Larry and Vivien, finding them "as much in love as ever, but they are not having an easy time."

Rather enigmatically, he wrote: "I'm not at all sure that the wave of promiscuity has not passed its peak and that they aren't finding a backwash."

By "promiscuity," Frewen could be referring to the desertion of their families by Larry and Vivien. Clare Sheridan, Frewen's sister, had a different interpretation.

"My brother told me that he had some serious private talks with Viv in London," Sheridan claimed. "Oswald learned that when Viv goes into one of her 'stages,' she becomes sexually aggressive and falls for whatever temptation is in front of her. I don't mean that she loves Larry any the less, but at times he doesn't satisfy all her sexual needs when she goes into one of her spells. Apparently, Viv is not able to restrain herself and often embarks on a very dangerous course."

"Oswald has also heard that Larry is still carrying on, at least sporadically, with Glen Byam Shaw and Noël Coward," Sheridan said. "Obviously these men offer Larry something Viv cannot. My brother has even suggested that Viv has admitted to a small streak of lesbianism. When Oswald and Viv were holidaying in Rome, they met this beautiful young Italian actress. Viv had even suggested that they take her back to their hotel and share. Then Viv smiled that delicate little smile of hers as if to suggest she were merely joking."

"Oswald thinks a potential marriage between Viv and Larry is doomed," Sheridan continued. "I disagree. I think the relationship will last because they feed off each other like vultures. They are the two of the greatest dramatists in England. They can't confine drama to the stage, but must create it in their private lives. If things are too quiet, I really believe they would stir up trouble, especially Viv. They may stay bonded with each other for years to come long after passion's flames have died out."

As England moved closer to war, Vivien and Larry became aware of changes going on in the lives of those around them. When Frewen came to call on them in London, she was shocked to learn that he was shipping off to

Gibraltar to join the Royal Navy. She had depended on him so that she felt deprived to see him go. She would not see him again until 1941, one of the darkest days of World War II.

During the course of a final visit with Larry and Vivien, Frewen found both of them "agitating about gas-masks and gas precautions."

Later on Larry's patio, when Frewen could speak privately with him, he found Larry "in a *To Be Or Not To Be*" frame of mind. Should he enlist in the British armed forces or go to Hollywood and become a movie star?"

"In her parting words to me," Frewen said, "Vivien warned me she may not be in England when I return. She told me, 'I'm going to Hollywood to play Scarlett O'Hara in *Gone With the Wind.*'"

***

When a break came in their careers, and each had a short time to slip away for a holiday, Vivien proposed that Larry and she go to the French Riviera "before some irresistible offer comes in and fucks up our plans."

On holiday in France, they stayed at both the Colombe d'Or in St.-Paul-de-Vence and at the Calanque d'Or at Le Dramond-Plage in Var.

Also showing up in the area was Peggy Ashcroft. Larry met with her. He told her, "My private life and my conscience are constantly at war with each other. I believe I perform best when I'm torn apart inside, my guts in a tight grip."

He was delighted to be with Glen Byam Shaw again. He was on holiday with his wife, Angela Baddeley, Larry's long-ago flame. Larry and Shaw sneaked off to private coves along the Riviera where they could swim in the nude. Later, Shaw complained to the worldly, sophisticated Ashcroft, "When Viv finishes with Larry, she doesn't leave much left over for me."

On vacation, Vivien immersed herself in the long novel, *Gone With the Wind*, which she'd already read three times. More and more, she came to identify with the personality of Scarlett.

"While Scarlett wasn't the most easy-going type, neither am I," she told Robert Carroll in an interview for a magazine, *Motion Picture*. If I've made up my mind to do something, I can't be persuaded out of it. When Scarlett wanted something from life, she schemed about how to get it. That was her trouble. I just plunge ahead without thinking."

"Scarlett was a fascinating person whatever she did," Vivien said, "but she was never a good person. She was too pretty, too self-centered. But one thing about her was admirable. Her courage. She had more than I'll ever have."

"There's one thing wrong with Mitchell's book," Vivien said to Larry. "At the opening she wrote, "Scarlett O'Hara was not beautiful . . .""

"That would hardly describe you," Larry said.

When Peggy Ashcroft arrived to have dinner with Vivien and Larry, Vivien spent most of the evening talking about Mitchell's heroine.

Upon leaving, Ashcroft said, "Good luck in your endeavors to play Scarlett. I haven't read the book, nor do I plan to, but I hear it's a great role."

"Mitchell must have had me in mind when she created the character of Scarlett," Vivien said. "It's about a charming, vivacious young woman who will stop at nothing, nor have the slightest pang of conscience, at loving another woman's husband."

"Sounds like type-casting to me," Ashcroft said with a smirk.

While on the Riviera, Vivien received a letter from Maureen O'Sullivan. "Have you heard about casting in *Gone With the Wind*?" O'Sullivan wrote. "Perhaps you have. Everybody else seems to know. It's all but certain I will play Melanie. Melvyn Douglas will be cast as Ashley Wilkes. It seems that Joan Crawford has locked up the role of Scarlett and thrown away the key. Love, Maureen."

She added a footnote: "Now it can be told. When you went back for two nights in London, I too tried to seduce Robert Taylor. He turned me down. I later heard he ran off with an undergraduate student—male that is—at Oxford."

Unknown to O'Sullivan, and even to Larry, Vivien months before had Gliddon submit her name to David O. Selznick, asking if she'd be considered for the role.

On February 3, 1937, Selznick responded to Gliddon, advising him that, "I do not have any interest in Miss Vivien Leigh at the moment." He added a footnote, "However, I do plan to see *Fire Over England*."

In spite of the formidable competition for the role, including Tallulah Bankhead, Paulette Goddard, Bette Davis, Jean Arthur, and Katharine Hepburn, Vivien became even more determined to get the role for herself. And although Selznick had already rejected her, she told Gliddon, "As God is my witness, I will play Scarlett O'Hara in *Gone With the Wind*."

Dame Peggy Ashcroft at twilight time

***

While on holiday, Larry and Vivien learned that John Gielgud and Hugh (Binkie) Beaumont were sharing a vacation house together in the South of France. Larry and Vivien dined with them, but found their main interest was in sampling the beautiful olive-skinned young men along the Riviera.

As Vivien had more or less predicted, film offers came in for them even while they were on vacation. The most astonishing for Vivien was from Cecil B. DeMille himself, asking Vivien if she'd star in *Union Pacific*, opposite Joel McCrea, for a salary of $2,000 a week, with a seven-week guarantee.

The script was a brawling saga about building the first transcontinental railroad, the part calling for Vivien to speak with an Irish brogue.

Vivien was tempted, because Larry suggested that he, too, might give Hollywood another try. If she took the role, she'd be in Hollywood at the same time he was. But if she accepted, and the role of Scarlett became available, she might not be free to take it.

She sent a telegram to Gliddon demanding virtually impossible financial terms that DeMille was certain to reject. He not only rejected Vivien, but didn't respond to Gliddon's counter offer.

The female lead in *Union Pacific* went to Barbara Stanwyck, who was urged by none other than Robert Taylor to take the role.

Gliddon was horrified that Vivien had turned down DeMille's offer, and he feared that his usefulness to her was near an end. On the Riviera she wrote him a "Dear John" letter.

In it, she noted that his option on her talents, signed November 29, 1934, was coming to an end on June 30, 1938. Their professional relationship was all but over. Of course, she thanked him graciously for all his efforts on her behalf.

While still on vacation, Larry received the most startling offer of all, a telegram from the offices of Samuel Goldwyn in Hollywood.

What almost was,
but never happened:
VIVIEN LEIGH in *Union Pacific*

ARE YOU INTERESTED GOLDWYN IDEA FOR SEPTEMBER FIRST FOR VIVIEN YOURSELF AND MERLE OBERON IN WUTHERING HEIGHTS STOP ANSWER AS SOON AS POSSIBLE STOP.

Both Vivien and Larry were taken by surprise. "Personally, I think Samuel Goldwyn and Emily Brontë are strange bedfellows," he told Vivien.

Neither Vivien nor Larry were enthusiastic about Goldwyn's offer. Larry was a study in contrasts, tempted by Hollywood, yet repulsed by it because of his earlier failures there.

Vivien was horrified to learn that Oberon had been cast in the lead role as Cathy. "Then what are they offering me?" she asked Larry. "It's obviously the role of Isabella. I will not return to Hollywood to play a fourth lead to Miss Princess." She was referring, of course, to Oberon.

After her holiday in France, Vivien returned to London determined to find a Hollywood agent to promote her candidacy for the role of Scarlett. Larry already had an agent, Myron Selznick, David's brother. Through various manipulations, Vivien got Myron to become her agent as well as Larry's.

Vivien and Larry learned that William Wyler, the future director of *Wuthering Heights,* was in London. He asked to meet with them at their cottage, and they invited him over. Both Larry and Vivien had seen Wyler's movie, *Jezebel,* starring Bette Davis, and were impressed.

When Wyler came to visit their Chelsea home, Vivien and Larry learned that it was Bette Davis herself who had lobbied to star in *Wuthering Heights.* She was hoping to be cast in the role of Cathy on a loan-out from Jack Warner. When Goldwyn decided to go ahead with the production, he threw Davis under the bus and opted for Oberon instead.

At Durham Cottage, Vivien seemed more interested in picking Wyler's brain about the casting for *Gone With the Wind* than she was in hearing about *Wuthering Heights.*

Wyler was very frank with Larry, admitting that three actors had already been tested for the role of Heathcliff—Ronald Colman, Douglas Fairbanks Jr., and Robert Newton. Goldwyn had rejected every one of them.

Wyler had heard that Larry had a "grudge" against motion pictures. Larry denied that, in fact, claimed that only next week he'd be appearing in a movie with Ralph Richardson called *Q Planes.*

In fact, it was on the set of *Q Planes* that Larry put a question to Richardson. "Ralphie, be an angel and give me your best shot like a friend. Should I go to Hollywood and play Heathcliff? Wyler's goosing me into it."

Richardson's reply was brief. "Yes. Lot of Fame. Good."

Before Wyler returned to Hollywood, Larry had strongly urged him to persuade Goldwyn to let Vivien play Cathy. But once he returned to California, Wyler wired Larry that he'd met with Goldwyn, who was adamant about retaining Oberon. The director telegraphed him, "You're still our number one choice for Heathcliff. As for Vivien, it's Isabella or nothing."

"Then it'll be nothing," Vivien said, refusing to change her mind.

One day Larry came home between a matinee and evening performance at the Old Vic. He encountered Angus McBean and Vivien dressed as her fantasy version of a Southern belle.

"My God," Larry said, "you look like a tart. What's going on here?"

"I'm having Angus take these pictures of me dressed as Scarlett O'Hara. I am going to grab that role."

"No, you're not," he shot back. "It was just announced in *The Times* today that Selznick is signing Norma Shearer for the role."

Vivien took to her bed for three days, and Larry could offer her no comfort. She denounced him and told him she didn't want to see him ever again.

But when he arrived less than a week later with a copy of *The Times*, he was allowed in. Norma Shearer had bowed out of the role, based on thousands of her fans urging her not to play the role of a Southern bitch. The casting of Scarlett was a wide-open field again.

To celebrate Larry's thirty-first birthday on May 22, Vivien invited four dozen guests to Durham Cottage, and even hired a jazz combo to play in their conservatory. Even though not united in marriage, Larry announced to her guests that, "We have become wedded on the stage and will be performing in four plays in summer, including *Othello* and *King Lear* as well as *Hamlet* and *Macbeth*."

Of course, Hollywood and their subsequent international fame would interfere with those plans.

For most of the evening, Vivien was arguably the most gracious hostess in London. But as the evening wore on, her mood changed. She insulted John Gielgud, who was her friend and loyal supporter, calling him an "old sod." She called Sybil Thorndike "a frumpy bitch with no talent."

Suddenly she rushed toward the stairs, ordering all

Q Planes
(middle photo) Ralph Richardson
(bottom) Valerie Hobson with Laurence Olivier

279

of her guests to leave their home.

The next morning, she called Gliddon, even though she'd more or less dismissed him. She had invited him to the party.

"I have been in one of my states," she told Gliddon. "Please, dear John, tell me who I insulted last night so I can send apology notes and flowers."

***

Larry's next film, *Q Planes*, co-starring his old friend, Ralph Richardson, was a pre-war spy story about a quirky British Secret Service agent who discovers an enemy plot to use secret weapons to steal experimental planes. Larry liked his part of a dashing young test pilot, and worked smoothly with Irving Asher, an American producer on his first assignment in England.

The female lead was played by Valerie Hobson, a beautiful Irish-born actress who, nonetheless, looked quintessentially English and very elegant. At the time she came together with Larry, she had not yet married her first husband, the producer Anthony Havelock-Allan.

Hobson told Richardson, "I find Larry overwhelmingly attractive. I know he's involved with Vivien, but if he moves in on me, I don't think I could say no."

It is not known for certain if Hobson had a brief fling with Larry, although she appears on nearly every list of Larry's suspected lovers, flings, and romances.

Richardson, who vicariously tried to keep score of Larry's female conquests, told director Asher that he thought Larry and Hobson were "slipping off for naughties." But there is no confirmation of that.

Larry seemed excessively fond of Hobson, and they may very well have had an off-camera romance. What is known is that he encountered her again in the years ahead.

He was especially proud of her when she stood by her second husband, John Profumo, whom she'd married in 1954.

Profumo became Secretary of State for War in the cabinet of Prime Minister Harold Macmillan. His affair with a "model," Christine Keeler, the reputed mistress of an alleged Russian spy, caused his downfall and forced his resignation. Profumo was caught lying to the House of Commons when he was questioned about this tryst.

After his resignation, Profumo worked as a volunteer cleaning toilets at Toynbee Hall, a charity based in the East End of London. By 1976, his reputation was redeemed, and he was honored at Buckingham Palace for his charity work. In 1995, at the 70th birthday of then-Prime Minister Margaret Thatcher, Profumo even sat next to the Queen.

Valerie, too, later in her life turned to charity work, helping mentally retarded children and lepers.

Years later Larry told Richardson, "I should have married Valerie. She's a saint."

"Oh, dear boy," Richardson said. "What joy is there for a man who marries a saint?"

***

Larry rushed into a production of *Macbeth*, slated for an opening at the Old Vic on November 26, 1937. "It was a time in my life when I went all out for Shakespeare," Larry told Ralph Richardson. "I began to dream that I was the Bard at night."

Vivien wanted to play Lady Macbeth opposite Larry but the French director, Michael St. Denis, cast Judith Anderson instead. "At least I know that castrating lesbian will not steal your heart from me," Vivien said to Larry.

"One day, and I promise you this faithfully, you will be my Lady Macbeth on stage," Larry responded.

In an unrelated coincidence, just before *Macbeth* opened, Lilian Baylis, the grand old dame of the Old Vic, took ill and died. She had left instructions that "the show must go on, regardless of what happens to me."

Before opening night Larry had greatly altered his face. For *Macbeth*, he padded his gums, making his lips protrude. Coming by for rehearsals, Vivien saw him and told him, "You look like Genghis Khan with that fantastic eye makeup. And why did you raise your cheekbones."

Even on opening night, Vivien still found Larry's makeup disturbing. In her critique, she said, "You hear Macbeth's first line, then Larry's make-up comes on, then Banquo comes on, then Larry comes on."

Later that night she'd say to him, "That makeup was a bit much, matey."

It wasn't just his makeup, or even the role of Macbeth itself. Larry had other insecurities. News that he was living with Vivien had become somewhat of a national scandal. He feared he'd be booed from the gallery. But when Queen Elizabeth, wife of King George VI, honored him with her pres-

Larry's *Q Planes* co-star, Valerie Hobson, with her scandal-soaked husband, John Profumo

281

ence on opening night, he was reassured.

Before going on to face the queen and an audience likely to be highly critical, Larry told the director, "I've put on my chain mail jockstrap, and I'm hoping for the best."

During their shared past, Larry's performances had been almost universally praised by Vivien, but she wasn't certain about his portrayal of Macbeth under St. Denis' highly stylized direction.

Larry's confidence was shattered when Noël Coward on opening night came backstage laughing.

"Noël was unnecessarily cruel to Larry that night," Vivien said. "It seemed uncharacteristic of him."

One critic found Larry's performance "fine indeed for a young man, but it would have been twice as good if he were twice as old."

Larry himself referred to his performance in *Macbeth* as "not an unparalleled success."

***

(top photo) Dame Judith Anderson
(bottom) Lilian Baylis, manager of London's Old
Vic Theatre from 1912-1937

He arranged for Vivien to join the Old Vic, and she was featured with Ralph Richardson in Shakespeare's *A Midsummer Night's Dream* which opened in December of 1937.

Because of Larry's intervention, the play's director, Tyrone Guthrie, began to re-evaluate Vivien's talent when he cast her as Titania in the Christmas production of Shakespeare's fantasy.

John Mills, who became such a good friend of Larry and Vivien, was cast as Puck.

Playing Oberon, Robert Helpmann came more intimately into her life during the rehearsals. Later she'd claim, "He is among my most cherished ones."

Helpmann had first met Vivien when he'd gone backstage to congratulate her on her performance in *The Mask of Virtue*.

He didn't think "she was as good as her notices, but her looks were ravishing," he later said.

A friendship developed

between the two of them after she told him, "I've seen you dance. You have beautiful legs."

"We used to meet after plays or at a party," Helpmann said. "Quite slowly we drew close. Like so many other men, I fell in love with her. She had a superb sense of humour, and a great deal of character—not at all the frail little thing she appeared to be."

When Helpmann described falling in love with Vivien, we can assume it was platonic, given his sexual proclivities.

Emerging from Australia, Helpmann was a very flamboyant personality and wore makeup both on and off the stage. That didn't prevent his honorary designation by the British monarch as a "Knights Bachelor" in 1968. For some, he evoked the performer Joel Grey in the musical *Cabaret*.

He was described as "strange, haunting, and rather frightening" in the press. Even his obituary in *The Times* of London called him "a homosexual of the proselytizing kind."

For thirty-six years, he lived in a virtual married state with the handsome, bright, Michael Benthall, and never quite recovered from his death in 1974.

Growing up in Adelaide, Helpmann practiced dance, learning the moves of a girl because his dance teacher had no prior experience teaching boys. At home he dressed up in his mother's clothes. Over the years he liked to surround himself with famous names, not only Vivien and Larry, but the likes of Margot Fonteyn and Katharine Hepburn, among countless others.

He went on to become the principal dancer at the Sadlers Wells Ballet from 1933 to 1950. Helpmann was called "a giant in seven-league boots," striding from ballet to opera, from the stage into film roles. He was a dancer and choreographer first and foremost, but also an actor, director, and producer.

When Vivien introduced Helpmann to Larry, he did not at first like him. "He has the sting of a wasp, the gossipy tongue of a magpie, and the wit of a malicious Noël Coward on a bad hair day," said Larry. But in time Helpmann and Larry bonded.

Their initial introduction had turned Larry off. "My greatest achievement in life will be in pulling those green tights off you," Helpmann said.

Larry had just been performing on stage. "That will never happen," Larry predicted.

Vivien Leigh as Titania in
A Midsummer Night's Dream

283

"I'm very persistent in pursuing what I want," Helpmann claimed. "I specialize in catching men in a moment of weakness."

A Midsummer Night's Dream opened at the Old Vic on December 27, 1937. On January 12, 1938, it was performed in front of the royal princesses, Elizabeth and Margaret Rose, aged 12 and 7, respectively. It was the first time they'd ever seen a live performance of a play by Shakespeare.

The princesses were enthralled by the stunning sets designed by Oliver Messel, all muslin fairy-wings and chaplets of coral roses. "It was magic," Guthrie later proclaimed.

Later in her life, Margaret would commission Messel as decorator for her private homes in, among other places, Mustique, in the Grenadines. Elizabeth was so intrigued by "how the fairies flew," that she leaned over the balcony and nearly fell into the orchestra pit. A security guard rescued her at the last moment.

In the Royal Retiring Room, Helpmann and Vivien were presented to the

 royal princesses. They curtsied but when they rose up, Vivien caught her elaborate headdress of gilded twigs and ferns in Helpmann's silver antlers. They became interlocked. With much embarrassment, they did an elaborate *pas de deux*, exiting backwards until they were out of sight of royal eyes. The princesses were seen giggling with each other.

One critic claimed that "Helpmann glides into imagined invisibility."

Oswald Frewen had come to see the play before he'd joined the Royal Navy. He had a different point of view. "I saw a lot of Victorian fairies prancing and mincing about the stage."

***

On February 8, 1938, Larry as Iago performed in *Othello* for an opening night audience at the Old Vic, the play running for 35 performances.

It was a play he would return to again and again in his life, including other performances in the 1960s.

Australian dancer and choreographer Robert Helpmann performing as Satan with the Vic-Wells Ballet in 1933

Director Tyrone Guthrie cast Richardson as the Moor. Before rehearsals began, Guthrie,

284

along with Larry, visited Dr. Ernest Jones, the biographer of Sigmund Freud. The doctor convinced both Guthrie and Larry that Shakespeare intended for the character of Iago to be subconsciously in love with Othello and he, therefore, had to destroy him. "That is the clue to the plot. Iago's jealousy of Othello is not because he is in love with Desdemona, but because he possesses a subconscious affection for the Moor, the homosexual foundation of which he didn't understand."

Going back to the Old Vic, Guthrie and Larry decided to keep this revelation from Richardson. However, in rehearsals, Larry in his enthusiasm got carried away. Impulsively, he threw his arms around Richardson and succulently kissed him on the lips. Taken by surprise, Richardson backed away. "There, there, now dear boy, good boy."

At one point Larry, in a scene beside Richardson, simulated an orgasm on stage, but no one seemed to understand what he was doing. Before opening night, Richardson told Larry to subdue the homosexual overtone of the play, suggesting that Iago hated Othello because he was black and his superior.

Larry's performance in *Othello* didn't please most of his critics, including James Bridie, who protested in the *New Statesman* that "Olivier's Iago had a diseased and perverted sexual makeup."

Privately Guthrie gave him a review, calling the performance of both Richardson and Larry a "ghastly, boring hash."

Before Larry tackled Shakespeare again, he cooperated with the Old Vic in an experiment. He interrupted the Bard with a modern, avant-garde comedy, James Bridie's *The King of Nowhere*. It was a strange and obvious political commentary about a mentally ill actor who escapes from an asylum and becomes the leader of a neo-fascist party trying to save Britain and reform the world. The public's attention was focused at the time on Munich and Neville Chamberlain's quest "for peace in our time," and the Bridie play failed.

In the wake of its failure, the Old Vic quickly called on the Bard again, announcing that Larry would star in *Coriolanus*, which opened on April 19, 1938 at the Old Vic, running for thirty-five performances. *Coriolanus* was one of the Bard's least produced plays.

Sybil Thorndike's husband, Lewis Casson, produced the play, and Larry was generally pleased to be working with his mentor from his debut days of so long ago.

Casson decided to cast Sybil Thorndike, Larry's "surrogate mother," in the role of Volumnia, where she would give her usual magnificent performance.

For the role, Larry once again became almost too daringly athletic on stage, delivering a head-over-heels triple tumble down the staircase, dying in front of the footlights.

In response, Casson severely lectured Larry, claiming, "You've wandered too far into realistic, modern acting." The director preferred a more classical approach to Shakespeare.

For the role, Larry overly made up his face, as noted by critic James Agate. "He robbed his face of much of its character and seriously reduced his range of expression. He buried his face beneath loam and plaster."

Most critics believed that Larry delivered "a great performance," perhaps because of Casson's direction. He'd toned down a lot of Larry's impetuosity.

Critic J.C. Trewin defined Larry's Coriolanus as "a pillar of fire on a plinth of marble."

Vivien went to see *Coriolanus*, accompanied by Ivor Novello. As the curtain came down, she turned to Novello, "I thought Larry delivered the performance of his career. His voice was deeper, his appearance more masculine on stage than I've ever seen him. What do you think?"

Novello looked at her sternly. "I'm jealous."

***

Once again Vivien found herself making a film. Called *St. Martin's Lane* in the U.K., it was released in America as *Sidewalks of London*. Cast and crew were familiar to her; her co-stars were Charles Laughton and Rex Harrison, her producer Erich Pommer, her director Tim Whelan, and the scriptwriter Clemence Dane.

The great producer, Pommer, who had already turned out such German classics as *Metropolis (*1927), and other UFA films, had become a refugee from Nazi Germany.

Laughton, never Vivien's greatest fan, came up and greeted her. "My wife, that darling ol' gal, Elsa Lanchester, had originally been cast in your role. But when Alexander Korda's money came aboard, Elsa got dumped."

Vivien detested Laughton. She snapped back, "Maybe Elsa one day will wise up and dump you, too."

Meeting up with Harrison again, she asked him, "How did anyone think a lady like me could play a Cockney street entertainer and common thief?"

"You were meant to play only a queen, perhaps a princess," Harrison told her.

He was still in love with Vivien, as he proclaimed to anyone interested, but he wasn't so lucky in his second film with her. "I've moved on," she told him, kissing him lightly on the lips. "But you were great fun."

Having heard of Vivien's brief fling with Harrison, Larry turned up on the set rather frequently, especially if Vivien had any intimate scenes with Harrison. When Larry did appear, and providing Vivien wasn't needed on the set, he disappeared with her to her dressing room, arousing jealousy and envy in Harrison.

Harrison told Pommer, "I'm a far better lover than Olivier."

The producer looked startled. "But how would you know that? There's only one person in the world who could have told you that—and that's Vivien herself. And I can't believe she'd say such a thing."

"Are you calling me a liar?" Harrison asked. He turned and walked away.

Both Harrison and Vivien were united in their dislike of Laughton. She called his performance "gluttonous," and Harrison claimed, "I don't want Laughton to come within ten feet of me. I've rejected all of his advances, but I know some of the members of the crew have benefitted from his services. Laughton, you know, has a reputation as London's King of Fellatio."

"I don't know what I'll do with that information," she said. "I find that his face resembles the back side of an elephant."

On the set, Vivien had a reunion with Tyrone Guthrie, who had directed Larry so many times. In a small role, he was making a rare screen appearance.

At the film's release in England, Vivien got mostly rave notices, critics calling her "gutsy" and "fetching." More and more she was being labeled England's most charming female performer.

St. Martin's Lane would be Vivien's last film in England before going to Hollywood to make *Gone With the Wind*. The movie would not have its premiere in New York until 1940, after England had already gone to war.

| Vivien Leigh with Charles Laughton in *St. Martin's Lane/Sidewalks of London* (1938) | Vivien Leigh with Rex Harrison in a publicity shot for *Storm in a Teacup* |

Both Vivien and Larry wanted a quicker divorce from Jill and Leigh than their spouses were willing to grant them. In desperation, Larry and Vivien went to see Harry Nathan, a barrister who had been a solicitor for Britain's liberal former Prime Minister (in office from 1916 to 1922), Lloyd George.

Harry, later Lord Nathan, advised both of them to "cool your heels." Before meeting with them, he'd learned that Jill's lawyers were "dragging their feet" in coming up with a settlement, thinking that Larry, an impulsive man, might change his mind.

Nathan reminded Vivien that Leigh was an ardent Catholic. "We have this religious thing to deal with as well," he said. Before Vivien and Larry departed, Nathan urged both of them "to be patient—let nature take its course."

On leaving his office, Vivien denounced Nathan "as a ridiculous little man." She seemed to explode in fury after saying that. When Larry calmed her down, he told her, "The little gnome does make sense in a way."

On March 2, 1938, Vivien wrote Leigh, almost pleading with him to grant her a divorce. In her note, she told him that "my feelings for Larry will not change."

Both Jill and Leigh remained adamant in their refusal to grant their errant spouses a divorce. "Let Larry have his fling," Jill told Leigh. "He's had so many of them. I'm still confident he'll come home to Tark and me when he comes to his senses."

As time went on, Vivien began to portray Jill and Leigh as villains in her divorce drama, especially when she entered into one of her "states."

"They are becoming so mean and hateful," Vivien said, almost sounding like Scarlett O'Hara before the film was even made. She told this to Noël Coward whom she encountered at a party. "They are forcing Larry and me to live in a state of adultery. They're just being selfish."

"Perhaps, my dear," Coward said. "Although Victoria is rotting in her crypt, even as we speak, the public might not see it that way. They could easily see you and Larry as villains of the drama. Go carefully into that good night, my beloved."

Vivien wrote Leigh on July 19, 1938:

Leigh, you will know how hard it is to write this letter. Although I am very very happy, I do want to know, Leigh, if you are well & feeling happier, as I do wish & hope with all my heart you are.

You know that I have seen Suzanne several times & if, that, if any way is troubling you for your own self or hers do tell me, as I would like to do anything that you think best.

However painful it may seem at the moment, Leigh, I do feel that this is the right thing to have happened for you & me, & I hope that perhaps later we can still be friends, inspite of whatever has come between us. I do pray that it may turn out well, dearest Leigh,
Vivien

Despite the content of her letter, Leigh continued to believe that Vivien's infatuation with Larry would not endure. Larry and Vivien would be forced to live together in adultery for three more years before Jill and Leigh granted the long-awaited divorces. "Jill is plotting to use me as a meal ticket for life," Larry told Vivien.

As she had hoped, Leigh, in spite of their differences, did bond into a friendship, settling into an older brother, younger sister type of relationship. In spite of what had transpired between them, they still liked each other.

There had never been any grand sexual passion between them. As Vivien had once told Maureen O'Sullivan, "Leigh's sexual drive, even at the height of our marriage, burned on a very low flame—perhaps once a month. I'm a woman who likes it at least twice a day."

"You vixen," O'Sullivan said half jokingly.

When Vivien visited Leigh on October 3, 1938, he said that little Suzanne at breakfast had told him that when he died, there would be no one to look after her.

Vivien reassured him that she would take care of their daughter in case something ever happened to him. Whether opportune or not, she took the occasion to continue to press him for a divorce. Before leaving, she thanked him for "being both a mother and father" to little Suzanne.

By now, Vivien and Larry had lived together for many months, and, like most other couples, tensions flared, especially when Vivien went into one of her moods. One week she didn't even speak to him for four days, and he didn't know the reason why. When she came out of her black despair, she chose not to reveal to him what had set her off.

They sometimes fought over their famous neighbors in Chelsea. Vivien claimed that their maid had seen Larry emerging one afternoon from the home of Valerie Hobson who lived nearby. Larry counter-charged that Vivien was seen going into Rex Harrison's townhouse one afternoon before coming home to him.

One night, Harrison remembered Vivien and Larry inviting some of their famous neighbors in for food and poker. Distinguished guests included film director David Lean and actor John Mills. Glen Byam Shaw was a late arrival. Vivien decided that she wanted to be "queen for a night," so she didn't invite any other women.

"Larry retired around midnight, but Vivien urged us to stay," Harrison said. "When the party started to break up around four o'clock—everybody was exhausted—Vivien threw a fit when we headed for the door. She called many of us names. I'd never seen her like this, but would many times again in the future. I began to suspect some sort of mental disorder, because on most occasions she was the most gracious of all London hostesses. The next day she sent us notes of apology. Of course, we forgave her. She was our beloved Viv. Actually, some of the names she called us were dead accurate."

Shaw saw signs that Larry had begun to tire of Vivien's slavish devotion to him.

"At first she worshipped him and praised every single thing he did, even if it was letting a fart," Shaw said. "But Larry was far too sophisticated a man to fall for that act forever. After a life with Jill, who could be very critical, Vivien's adoration at first was a welcome relief."

"Having a cooing lovebird around the house all the time is not my fantasy of the perfect life," he told Shaw.

Many of Larry's disagreements with Vivien centered on Hollywood. Instead of starring in *Wuthering Heights*, he still wanted to launch another season of Shakespeare plays at the Old Vic, with her starring in the female parts.

"I don't want to be one of Shakespeare's whores," she bluntly told him. "I'd rather go to Hollywood and become an American movie star, launching myself as Scarlett O'Hara."

As tempting as the offers were, Larry still wanted to stay in London with her. But she finally convinced him to play Heathcliff. "It's the role of a lifetime. You're the only actor in the world who can play Heathcliff. The film could immortalize you long after your stage plays are forgotten."

That was perhaps all the inducement he needed to hear. The next day he sent a telegram to Myron Selznick. "Tell Sam Goldwyn I'm his Heathcliff."

***

While waiting for David O. Selznick to make up his mind about the casting of Scarlett O'Hara, Vivien agreed to do another play. It was *Serena Blandish*, adapted by S.N. Behrman from an Enid Bagnold novel, *A Lady of Quality*. At first Larry was going to direct it, but later gave up that duty to Esme Percy. The premiere was set for September 13, 1938 at the small Gate Theatre in London.

Vivien was reunited once again with her friend Jeanne de Casalis, who was cast as Countess Flor di Folio.

When a dashingly handsome young actor, Stewart Granger, heard that Larry was going to direct Vivien in a play, he hurried over to the Gate. He'd

290

just learned from an actor friend that the role of Lord Ivor Cream had not been cast.

In New York in 1989, at a private dinner party hosted by 1940s movie star Ruth Warrick, Granger spoke candidly to such notables as dancer Tamara Geva (ex-wife of choreographer George Balanchine), author Stanley Mills Haggart, and off-Broadway producer Lucille Lortel. He regretted that he had not been even more candid in his memoirs, *Sparks Fly Upward.* "If I'd told everything, I would have had a bestseller," he lamented.

Haggart goaded him into some revelations he'd left out.

"I might as well confess," Granger said. "What does it matter now? I'll be dead soon anyway. Someone has to tell the bloody truth about what was going on back then." Among other revelations, he spoke of his coming together with Larry and Vivien.

"When I met Larry at the Gate for the first time, I came face to face with my idol," Granger confessed. "He was the cause of my giving some pretty devastatingly bad performances in Rep. I imitated him, and I was no Laurence Olivier."

"I thought Larry was the most virile, inventive, beautiful actor in the theater," Granger recalled. The bisexual actor privately told his friends, "I fell in love with Larry that day, although I'd have to wait quite a while before seducing him. Even as he interviewed me, I did all I could to suppress an erection."

"When Larry introduced me to his beloved Vivien, I thought she was the most beautiful woman I'd ever seen," Granger said. "Ravishing, really. My erection had gone down but rose up again in all its impressive might when I met Vivien. I was always horny in those days. My friends called me Everready."

"Larry directed me through a scene with Vivien, and I was absolutely awful," Granger claimed. "Horrid. But both Vivien and Larry seemed dazzled by my good looks, or so I assumed at the time. When I left the theater, I had the role. Larry even gave me a succulent kiss on the lips before I departed. Conveniently Vivien had returned to her dressing room."

There was one problem. Granger was under contract to Basil Dean for twenty-five pounds a week. He wanted Dean to release him so he could accept a role that paid only three pounds a week at the Gate.

"To work with Larry and Vivien, I would have given my left nut," Granger said. "No, not that. Too many people get off on it."

John Gliddon was Granger's agent. "You're about to be married, and you want to work for peanuts," Gliddon said to him. "My clients will drive me into the poorhouse." Nonetheless, he went with Granger to persuade Dean to release him from his contract.

Even though he'd fallen madly in love with both Vivien and Larry,

Granger still went ahead with his plans to marry Elspeth March. "I was marrying her, but I had no intention of being faithful," he later recalled. "If I wanted a wedding, it would be to marry both Vivien and Larry in a joint ceremony. That was illegal in Britain. The day will come, though."

Granger even invited Vivien and Larry to his wedding, where the actor learned that Larry was about to depart for Hollywood.

Granger remembered Vivien looking "incandescent—so wonderful and so in love with Larry, but capable of giving me a side glance. At my wedding, of all places, Larry hugged me in a tight embrace, and I moved so that he could have an encounter with my most glorious but yet hidden asset. It was obvious we were both physically attracted to each other."

Jeanne de Casalis was also invited to the wedding. She told the director, Esme Percy, "At least Vivien knows what the bride is getting on her honeymoon. She's already tested out Granger." She had walked in on Vivien in her dressing room to discover Granger's tongue halfway down her throat. A jealous De Casalis just assumed that Granger's affair with Vivien had already begun.

Granger had boasted to Percy that he planned to seduce Vivien before the end of the play's run. Granger also made Gliddon aware of this. Discreetly, Granger failed to elaborate about his intention of seducing Larry. "Let's face it, I can have any woman I want in the UK, even the Queen of England, I would imagine."

"Remember, you're soon getting married," Percy cautioned him.

"Isn't a man entitled to a little fun before marriage?" Granger said, "before settling down?" He added as an afterthought. "Not that I plan to be faithful. When God gave me what he gave me, he meant for me to spread around the goodies."

"Conceited bastard, aren't you?" Percy said.

After Granger's wedding, and after impatient waiting, a chance to be alone with Vivien was emerging.

"Larry had signed to do *Wuthering Heights*. The foolish but beautiful young man was actually leaving me alone with Vivien. Before kissing me good-bye, he told me to take care of Vivien for him. I wanted to tell him that I was man enough for the both of them, but I refrained. Larry would have to wait. Vivien lay in my immediate future."

Stewart Granger

***

292

On November 5, 1938, Vivien's 25th birthday, she drove Larry from London to Southampton for his morning departure on the *Normandie* for New York.

In Larry's stateroom, and to her surprise, she found that he would be sailing to New York with Noël Coward.

Vivien had enough time to stay briefly for an on-board pre-departure party for which Coward had ordered champagne for guests who included Herbert Wilcox, Anna Neagle, and Monty Banks.

Coward delivered the champagne toast to Larry. "To Heathcliff," he said.

Larry suddenly reversed the toast. "To Scarlett O'Hara," he said, tipping his glass to Vivien. The room joined in.

After kisses to everybody, Vivien stepped out into the hallway for her most passionate embrace with Larry. The two lovers didn't know how long they'd be separated.

Vivien headed off the ship with a heavy heart.

Cole Lesley, Coward's biographer, wrote: "Larry and Noël—still great cronies since *Private Lives*—were as happy as bird-dogs" as they set sail together for New York.

Anna Neagle later said, "Vivien looked very distressed to learn that Larry was blissfully sailing away with darling Noël. When we went to powder our noses, she told me that she planned to get even with him. She also wondered why Larry hadn't told her about Noël before now. 'Larry is so devious,' Vivien said to me."

As Vivien was about to disembark, she stepped aside to make way for a late-arriving passenger. She was shocked to discover it was Leslie Howard, who was also sailing to New York.

"I know you," he said. "You're Vivien Leigh."

"It's an honor to see you again."

"I'm going to Hollywood," he said. "I've reluctantly agreed to play Ashley Wilkes in a movie called *Gone With the Wind*. It's almost certain."

Impulsively, she blurted out, "I'll let you in on a secret. Selznick has already cast me as Scarlett O'Hara. I'll be joining you soon."

He looked astonished and wanted to ask her so much more, but two attendants quickly escorted her down the gangplank as the *Normandie* was about to sail.

She stood on the pier, looking back at the ship. She so very much wanted to sail on that vessel with her signed contract from Selznick. Mortified that she'd so blatantly lied to Howard, she rushed toward her Ford. She'd have to get back to London in time for curtain.

At the Gate, Granger noted that Vivien was still shaking and almost in tears as she waited for her cue. He held her close and comforted her.

In spite of her pain, Vivien, at least in Granger's view, delivered her most magnificent performance that night. As the curtain came down, he asked her to join him for a light supper.

"I don't want to be alone tonight," she said.

Supper at the Café Royal, where Vivien was besieged by autograph hounds, was followed by an invitation to his flat. Fortunately, his bride-to-be was in Oxford that night.

"I fear I was an opportunist, a cad of the worst sort," he'd recall to Percy the next day. "I took advantage of her. But, before any of that happened, I had to sit through two hours of chatter about what a magnificent creature Larry was, as if I hadn't figured that out for myself."

"We spent the night in my bed," Granger said. "I held her for a long time. She wept. I comforted. Shortly before dawn I woke up. She was sleeping beside me. In the very early light she looked more beautiful than ever. I could-n't resist. I'm not a total gentleman in such matters. I moved onto her and plunged ahead. Before she completely came around and realized what was happening, we were both too far gone. She's a most passionate young lady. But the end was unfortunate and a bit of a letdown. At what I called 'the moment of truth,' she screamed: LARRY, LARRY."

CHAPTER EIGHT

"Catherine Earnshaw, may you not rest so long as I live on! I killed you. Haunt me, then! Haunt your murderer! I know that ghosts have wandered on Earth. Be with me always. Take any form, drive me mad, only do not leave me in this dark alone where I cannot find you. I cannot live without my life. I cannot die without my soul!"

—Heathcliff

In November of 1938, When Larry arrived in Hollywood once again, he checked into the Beverly Hills Hotel, taking a room for eight dollars a night. His first call was from his agent, Myron Selznick, the well-connected brother of David O. Selznick, producer of *Gone With the Wind*.

"There must be a God in Heaven, or somewhere," Myron told him. "Luck is on your side. Merle Oberon, who, incidentally, is also my client, has bolted from her lead role in *Wuthering Heights*. Samuel Goldwyn wants you to call London on his dime and ask Vivien if she's available for the role of Cathy, and whether she'd be able to fly to Hollywood at a moment's notice to take over the role."

In catering to this request, Larry ran up the most expensive phone bill of his life during his presentation to Vivien in London of this fast-breaking news.

During their first dinner together, Douglas Fairbanks Jr. gave Larry some of the details about his previous screen test for the role of Heathcliff, and revealed that he wasn't jealous of Larry for winning the part. "I would have been awful in it."

"If you want a good laugh, see *my* test," he told Larry. "Merle wanted to play opposite me, but Goldwyn just couldn't see me shoving horseshit out of a stable. He told me I belonged at a glamorous Hollywood cocktail party, wearing a tux."

"Larry was a happy fool that night," said Fairbanks. "All he could talk about was Vivien, Vivien, Vivien. Finally, I put down my drink and told him I needed equal time."

"Who are you in love with?" Larry asked, "other than the odd wife. Not

Joan Crawford any more. Let me guess."

"You're going to be surprised," Fairbanks said. "I mean, really surprised. She's bigger than Rin Tin Tin ever was."

"Let me guess," Larry said. "Greta Garbo. You've melted her ice."

"As big as Garbo, though on the box office poison list right now."

"That could be only one actress," Larry said. "I know it couldn't be Katharine Hepburn. Bette Davis is not box office poison. That leaves only Marlene Dietrich."

"You've got it!" Fairbanks said. "Finally."

"You do go in for Grade A flesh," Larry said. "Since you like guys, too, are others on your future list—say, Robert Taylor, Tyrone Power, and Errol Flynn?"

(lower photo)
Heathcliff (Olivier) broods

"All of the above," Fairbanks said.

By Monday morning Larry's dream was dashed. Myron called and told him that Oberon and Goldwyn had made up, and that the actress was back in the picture. Larry remembered, "I felt my heart collapse. Even worse, I had to call Vivien and tell her. I knew how disappointed she'd be. When I'd reached her in London on Saturday morning, she had danced a jig of joy. She told me I'd be fucking her real soon."

"But when I called again, somehow she already knew the bad news," Larry told Fairbanks. "She took it with the courage she so often possesses. 'Win some, lose some,' she told me. 'I lost the part of Cathy Earnshaw, but I will not lose the role of Scarlett O'Hara. I count the days until I'm in your arms again, my darling.'"

Fairbanks reported that his weekend had been equally disastrous. "When Marlene went shopping, I had nothing to do, so I was at her writing desk. I opened a drawer for a pen and discovered a series of love letters. They were from that German writer, Erich Maria Remarque, who wrote *All Quiet on the Western Front*. They were half in German, half in English, but I got the point. He was fucking Marlene. When she came home, I flew into a jealous rage and struck her. She kicked me out of her house. It's over."

Larry leaned back and sighed. "Passionate white heat love lasts but just a short time," he said reflectively. "I wonder how long Vivien and I will feel this way about each other. For all I know, she's in the arms of someone else right now."

"Speaking of that," Fairbanks said. "How about it? For old time's sake."

"Yes," Larry said, "for old time's sake."

***

Wuthering Heights, Emily Brontë's (1818-1848) tale of jealousy, tragic love, and revenge, had first been published in 1847 under the *nom de plume* of Ellis Bell. She didn't want the reading public to know she was a woman. It would be the only novel she'd ever write, and is today rated as one of the ten greatest novels of all time.

In 1920, it had been brought to the screen in a British adaptation starring Colette Brettel and Milton Rosmer.

Filed under "Believe It Or Not," producer Walter Wanger had originally optioned the script for Sylvia Sidney and Charles Boyer, the latter of which would have been the worst miscasting call of 1939.

Wanger's second choice for the role of Cathy was Katharine Hepburn, but when she was labeled "box office poison," he backed away. Finally, Samuel Goldwyn purchased the script from Wanger, even though he wasn't entirely sure that he wanted to produce it. "Too God damn grim," he said.

Goldwyn didn't like the title of *Wuthering Heights*. His story department came up with such alternative titles as *The Wild Heart*, *Dark Laughter*, and *Bring Me the World*. But eventually, Goldwyn was convinced that the Brontë novel was a classic and that the title should stand.

The incident that eventually convinced him to stick with the original title was a question asked by Jock Lawrence. "Do you really think the title of *Little*

Players in the adaptation of a gothic novel to the silver screen *(top to bottom)*

Author Emily Brontë, Studio mogul Samuel Goldwyn, Director William Wyler, and screen diva Merle Oberon

Women should have been changed to *Katy Wins Her Man?*" Even so, Goldwyn always referred to the film as "*Withering Heights.*"

When Goldwyn hired William Wyler as the director, he learned that Wyler would actually have preferred Robert Newton as the film's romantic lead. "Newton has the strength and power that Olivier lacks," Wyler said. "Olivier has unavoidable weakness. Even he admitted to me that Newton would make a better Heathcliff."

As a means of bringing cinematic life to the Gothic novel, Goldwyn hired

two of the best screenwriters in the business, Charles MacArthur and Ben Hecht, to adapt Brontë's novel. The two men kept in much of Brontë's original dialogue. Not trusting the script, Goldwyn also brought in John Huston to sharpen the language, but Huston told Goldwyn that the script was perfect the way it was.

Hecht had seen Larry in *21 Days* and championed him for the role. He wrote Wyler, "I saw Lawrence *(sic)* Olivier on the screen last night, and thought him one of the most magnificent actors I have ever seen. He could recite Heathcliff sitting on a barrel of herring and break your heart."

After ensuring that he'd hired topnotch writers, Goldwyn cast one of the most brilliant lineups of actors of any film in 1939, equaled only by the cast of *Gone With the Wind.* Geraldine Fitzgerald was cast as Isabella, the role Vivien had turned down. On the set, Larry had a reunion with Flora Robson, with whom he'd starred in *Fire Over England.* In a dialogue with her, Larry quipped, "I see that Goldwyn's gold has also lured you to Hollywood."

Trapped by convention and in the throes of love:

Two scenes from *Wuthering Heights* of Laurence Olivier with Geraldine Fitzgerald

"With a war coming on," Robson said, "a lady like me can use a shilling or two in the bank."

Other members of the cast included Donald Crisp, Hugh Williams, Leo G. Carroll, Miles Mander, and Cecil Kellaway. Gregg Toland would later be praised for his brilliant cinematography.

Both Wyler and Goldwyn wanted *Wuthering*

Heights to be as authentic as possible. They'd already sent cameramen to the Yorkshire moors for background shots.

One scene in which a doctor used a stethoscope ended up on the cutting room floor when it was discovered that such instruments were not in use before 1850.

In spite of his wanting both authenticity and an adherence to Brontë, Goldwyn impulsively switched the setting from 1801 to 1841 because "I don't like Oberon in Regency dress."

Rehearsals for *Wuthering Heights* began on the Monday morning of November 28, 1938.

Making the greatest classic movie of his career, and the film for which he is most remembered by fans today, Larry claimed that the actual work on the movie "was the most miserable time of my life."

Unusual for Hollywood, Wyler blocked out and staged these elaborate rehearsals before filming actually began. From the first day, he and Larry con-

flicted. He found his director inarticulate. At the end of a scene, he'd call out to Larry, "that's lousy." When Larry asked for guidance, he didn't get it.

After an astonishing forty takes on one scene, Larry in desperation came to Wyler. "I've done it calm. I've shouted. I've done it angry, sad, standing up, sitting down, fast, slow—how do you want me to do it?"

"Better," was all that Wyler said.

Larry later admitted to overacting in *Wuthering Heights*. A scene would often be interrupted by Wyler who asked: "Do you think you're at the Opera House in Manchester?"

Larry came to regard Wyler's dictates as "persecution" more than directing.

To add to his misery, Larry learned of his father's sudden death of a stroke in Sussex. At the time of his death, Gerard was sixty-nine years old.

To Larry's consternation, Wyler as director concentrated excessively on the role of Cathy, paying elaborate attention to Oberon at the sacrifice of Larry's character of Heathcliff. It seemed that everything Oberon did won approval from Wyler, and every scene that Larry performed as

(Top photo) Cathy (Merle Oberon) gets dressy onscreen with a dapper but still tormented Heathcliff

(lower photo) Dysfunctional off-screen trio: Oberon, Olivier, and Leigh between takes on the set of *Wuthering Heights.*

Heathcliff provoked a tirade of resentment from the director.

Wyler finally did give Larry some advice, which stuck in his brain. "Olivier, you can't 'perform' Heathcliff, you must be Heathcliff. There's a big difference. I want to see a real actor in front of the camera."

During the first weeks of filming, Wyler stripped away whatever security Larry had as an actor. On stage he was used to projecting emotions on a much broader range. On camera the most delicate shades of subtlety could be picked up by the camera, as he was soon to learn. "The camera is wicked," Larry said. "It can tell when an actor is being insincere. My greatest challenge was in having to make love to Merle Oberon, an actress I came to detest."

"Wyler was a marvelous sneerer and debunker, and he brought me down," Larry said. "I knew nothing of film acting or that I had to learn its technique. It took a long time and several degrees of Wyler's torture and sarcasm before I realized it."

Years later, when he looked back, Larry claimed, "working with Wyler on *Wuthering Heights* was a journey on the road to hell. But through this little dictator I learned to respect and understand the art of making motion pictures, which would serve me well in the years ahead."

"The only person who brought me joy on the set of *Wuthering Heights* was David Niven," Larry later claimed.

Niven had been cast as the third lead in the role of Edgar Linton, who marries Cathy in the film. He'd called the role of Edgar "an actor's nightmare," and didn't want the part. "It's the most God awful part ever written," he told Samuel Goldwyn, "and one of the most difficult for an actor to play." Even though he couldn't afford to, he opted to go on suspension.

But eventually, he was persuaded to take the role by Wyler himself. Actually, Niven didn't want to work with the director again either. He'd come

Smile for the camera, honey, we're in California, USA, and it's show-biz!

Merle Oberon with David Niven

to detest him when Wyler had directed him in *Dodsworth*. "The guy's a son of a bitch," Niven told Larry.

Eventually, Niven came abroad, and he bonded with Larry in their mutual hatred of Wyler.

Like Larry, Niven would also have trouble working with Oberon. He recalled that one of his biggest moments in the film is when he was supposed to lean over the corpse of Cathy, shedding tears. "In take after take, I just couldn't cry," he claimed. "The best I could come up with was some sort of squashed-up grimace."

The prop man, Irving Sindler, came to the

rescue, puffing menthol through a handkerchief into Niven's nose.

Bending over Oberon, Niven produced not tears but green slime from his nose which he shared with Oberon.

The "corpse" rose from the dead, shrieking, "Oh, shit! How horrid!" Then she ran screaming to her dressing room.

"Thank you for sharing your green goo with our star," Wyler told him. "You'll go far in motion pictures." He deleted the scene.

Larry fared even worse with Oberon than Niven. She apparently had planned to transform her working agenda with Larry into a lovefest.

Jerry Dale had been assigned to handle press for Larry during the shoot. He later claimed he knew "the real reason" for the feud that raged between Merle and Larry during the filming of *Wuthering Heights*.

"Let's be frank," he said. "Merle wanted to have an affair with Larry while Vivien Leigh was in London and Alexander Korda was also there. Back when she made *The Divorce of Lady X*, and even though Korda was in hot pursuit of her, Merle still made herself available to Larry. But he didn't take her up on that offer. Since Merle thought she was the most enchanting woman on the planet, Larry's rejection of her in favor of Vivien damaged her ego. But that gal could recover quickly."

"On the set of *Wuthering Heights*, with their respective mates far out of town, Merle made another play for Larry," according to Dale. "Her pitch to him was that Korda had once confessed to going to bed with Vivien. 'Let's pay them back,' she suggested to Larry. 'Sweet revenge.' But Larry was not buying that line. Once again he rejected her. This time, it was too much. After that second rejection, Larry got the Arctic chill from Merle. Vivien ended up with the handsome prince, and Merle got that old Hungarian goat Korda."

After the end of a typical day coping with Wyler, Larry was often exhausted, but occasionally he accepted an invitation to a dinner or party organized by one or another of the leading hostesses of Hollywood. One of them was Joan Crawford.

Crawford invited Larry to one of her chic dinners. After a perfect meal—the star always adored perfection—she announced she was showing a film clip for the amusement of her guests.

After everyone was seated, her butler presented Fairbanks' screen test for the role of Heathcliff. The star overacted like some silly fool on the silent screen. At the end of the clip, Crawford's guests burst into laughter. Crawford, of course, had been long divorced from Fairbanks, and she seemed to

Happier Times
Douglas Fairbanks, Jr.
with then-wife, Joan Crawford

301

take delight, some sort of petty revenge, at showcasing his wretched screen test as a means of ridiculing him. Never Crawford's greatest fan, Larry henceforth began liking her even less. Later in the evening, when she noticed Larry looking sullen, Crawford came over to him and asked why. "First, Douggie is a dear friend of mine, as you well know, and I hate to see people make fun of him. Also, as I watched that screen test, I said to myself, 'There but for the grace of God go I.' I fear I, too, will be laughed off the screen."

"Have no fear," she said. "I can already envision us on Oscar night. I'll be accepting the big boy for Scarlett O'Hara, and you'll be walking off with the prize for playing Heathcliff. Perhaps to celebrate our joint Oscars that night, we'll take them to bed with us and fuck our brains out."

"Perhaps," Larry said, sounding more than a little reluctant.

Picking up immediately on his reluctance, she shot back, "You'll find out that I'm much better in bed than Douggie is." She kissed him on the lips before walking away. He was overcome by her bad breath.

In spite of the parties and his many Hollywood invitations, Larry felt desperately alone. After retiring every night, "I cried myself to sleep," he later admitted.

He wrote Vivien nightly. In one particularly long letter, he asked a blunt question. "Are you playing with yourself or *anything*?"

He confessed to masturbating himself but then promised "not to do *anything* till I see you again." He claimed that when he did masturbate, "I am only thinking of my beloved."

***

Larry's first major clash with Oberon came during the filming of a love scene between Heathcliff and Cathy at Peniston Crag. "You're spitting on me again, like you did in Lady X," she told him. She withdrew from him and went to her dressing room to sterilize her face.

It is a long tradition in the theater for actors to get caught in the spray of a fellow actor's plosives. Larry had not yet learned that film acting didn't require such intensity of enunciation, and he was overprojecting—hence, the saliva spray.

When Oberon returned to the set with her sterilized face, they resumed their scene together. But minutes later, Oberon shrieked. "The asshole spat on me again." Once more, she fled from the set to her dressing room.

To her fleeing back, he screamed after her: "Why you little amateur bitch, you bloody whore. How dare you speak to me that way. What's a little spit between actors for Christ's sake? You're a bloody little idiot *Miss Queenie*."

For the sake of the picture, Wyler intervened, asking Larry to go to

302

Oberon's dressing room and apologize.

"Bloody hell!" Larry said. "I won't be insulted by that little half-caste Korda whore."

Reaching for his crutches, Larry hobbled out of the studio and headed back to his hotel. He'd come down "with the world's worst case of athlete's foot" and was also suffering from a leg injury.

Somehow, Wyler was able to lure both the feuding actors back onto the set the following morning. Suddenly, the inarticulate director found a voice. "Now let's go through that love scene again. I want the two of you to convey love's tenderest emotions. Remember the camera eye is all-seeing. If you fake it, the camera will catch you."

"As the director," I could also see the feud from Oberon's point of view. Here she was with David Niven and Laurence Olivier. As her former lover, Niven had walked out on her and told her to go to hell, and Olivier had spurned her advances. From the men's point of view, both Niven and Olivier, at least on screen, were supposed to love Korda's bitch, a self-centered, conceited, arrogant woman each of them loathed."

"Deep down," Larry said years later, "I think Oberon knew I held her in low regard, viewing her as a no-talent pick-up by Korda."

Added to Larry's enemy list, including Oberon and Wyler, was the producer himself, Samuel Goldwyn.

Goldwyn had a lot of his money riding on the success of *Wuthering Heights*, and he demanded to see the rushes at the end of every day, both the good and the bad. He was generally pleased with Oberon's performance, but highly critical of Larry's acting and appearance. In the first scenes he'd seen of Larry as Heathcliff, he said, "My God, the guy looks like an ape. His face is filthy."

"But he's playing a stable boy," Wyler pointed out to him.

"The limey bum looks like he's got horse-shit on his face," Goldwyn kvetched. "Women who go to movies want to see romantic leading men."

The next day, Goldwyn appeared on the set and came up to both Wyler and Larry, who was on crutches. "Willie," he said, putting his arm around the director, "if this actor goes on playing Heathcliff in this hammy way, I close up the picture. Will you look at this guy's ugly face? He's dirty, his performance is rotten—it's too stagey, it's nothing."

Goldwyn then turned his ire onto Larry,

Onscreen osculations with Oberon

Sprays of saliva, spittle, and slobber and behind-the-scenes venom that movie fans never saw

303

looking him up and down scornfully. "Remember, you don't have to act like Theda Bara."

"You're a great producer," Wyler told Goldwyn, simmering with anger. "But I'm the director. You will either leave the set or . . . or I will!"

Goldwyn slowly walked away without issuing any further commands.

***

When Larry saw the finished cut of *Wuthering Heights*, he was horrified

 by its final scene. As producer, Goldwyn had asserted his ego and overruled Wyler as director. "I don't want to look at a corpse at fadeout," Goldwyn growled.

Larry had gone to New York, and Oberon, with Korda, had returned to London. Goldwyn hired their stand-ins to re-shoot the closing scene. In the revised endings final moments, a ghostly Heathcliff and Cathy, hand in hand, are seen wandering the bleak moors forever.

After watching the scene, Larry said, "It goes to show what happens when a great director is overruled by a not-so-good producer."

Premiering in 1939, *Wuthering Heights* became one of the greatest films released in that year of great films—movies which included *Gone With the Wind*. Arguably, no other year in the history of Hollywood witnessed the production of such a plethora of magnificent movies.

Under a red-letter slogan which read THE MARK OF HELL IN HIS EYES, Larry's long-suffering face stared back at the American public from billboards across the country.

Strange bedfellows gushing over *Wuthering Heights*:

(top photos) The Brontë Society's logo and official portrait of Charlotte, Emily, and Anne Brontë.

(bottom photo): Gossip maven Hedda Hopper "Come here, you're mine."

In spite of Larry's own reservations about his performance, *Wuthering Heights* drew rave reviews. Even the highly literate Brontë Society, a West Yorkshire-based historical organization promoting itself as one of the oldest literary societies in the world, wrote Goldwyn that club members were completely satisfied. Even the acerbic and usually stern drama critic, Alexander Woollcott, cooed, "Sam has done right by our Emily."

Frank S. Nugent in *The New York Times* claimed that Larry "has Heathcliff's broad lowering brow, his scowl, the churlishness, the wild tenderness, the bearing, speech, and manner of the demon-possessed."

Graham Greene in *The New Statesman* posted a negative comment: "This Heathcliff would never have married for revenge. Mr. Olivier's nervous, breaking voice belongs to the balconies and Verona and romantic love."

Back in Hollywood, Hedda Hopper practically drooled in print after seeing *Wuthering Heights*. "When Laurence Olivier says, 'Come here, you're mine!,'" she wrote, "how gladly you'd go. And even suffer a third degree burn and love it when he puts his head on your arm."

Although *Wuthering Heights* drew crowds in big cities such as New York, it was not a grand success in other parts of the country. Perhaps its dark somberness and its sense of psychological tragedy were too heavy for appeal across the vast plains of an America about to be sucked into World War II. Finally, however, on its re-release after the War, *Wuthering Heights* made a profit for Goldwyn Studios.

Later, Wyler said, "I made an international star out of one Laurence Olivier. After *Wuthering Heights*, his power and prestige were at such a point that he could virtually dictate what film role he would play next. But the fucker wanted to return to the stage. You figure. Actors!"

In the immediate wake of the movie's release, the Hollywood Post Office had to hire extra staff because of the massive volume of fan mail pouring in for Larry.

"I did not want to become a romantic leading man of Hollywood in the 40s," Larry said. "Had I followed that course, I might have been on screen dancing around with Betty Grable or Rita Hayworth, and perhaps ended up in the ranks of such actors as Victor Mature and John Payne."

Author Foster Hirsch analyzed Larry's post-Heathcliff choices of the film roles he accepted: *Rebecca, Pride and Prejudice*, and *That Hamilton Woman*.

"He was determined to transcend stereotypes, so he chose heroes who were in some way flawed or unacceptable, whose appeal, in fact, was based on some character defect. The dark, romantic Olivier here was rigid, ironic, sinister; there was something threatening and almost otherworldly about him, and he seemed to belong in a particularly neurotic Gothic novel. Even in his brief matinée idol phase, then, Olivier avoided being merely charming or urbane; he was instead the isolated hero, the wounded prince, the man with a secret mission."

Hirsch, of course, was referring to Larry's roles of Max DeWinter (in *Rebecca*), Darcy (in *Pride and Prejudice)*, and, to a lesser extent, Admiral Nelson (in *That Hamilton Woman)*.

Since 1939 was viewed as the greatest year in the history of motion pictures, competition was at a historical high when the Academy Award released its roll call of nominees.

Best Actor nominees included Robert Donat for his role in *Goodbye, Mr. Chips,* Clark Gable for *Gone With the Wind,* Laurence Oliver for *Wuthering Heights,* Mickey Rooney for *Babes in Arms,* and James Stewart for *Mr. Smith Goes to Washington.* Nominees for Best Actress included Vivien Leigh for her role in *Gone With the Wind,* Bette Davis for *Dark Victory,* Irene Dunne for *Love Affair,* Greta Garbo for *Ninotchka,* and Greer Garson for *Goodbye, Mr. Chips.*

In what is often referred to as a "trial run" before the Academy Awards are presented, the New York Film Critics met in 1939 to vote on their selection for the year's best picture. The front-runners were *Gone With the Wind* and *Wuthering Heights.* Although GWTW was a heavy favorite, *Wuthering Heights,* in a surprise upset, was voted Best Picture of the Year.

Merle Oberon was a heavy Academy Award favorite as a nominee for her portrayal of Cathy in *Wuthering Heights.* But to the surprise of Hollywood, she failed to get nominated. According to her producer, Sam Goldwyn, she was "savagely furious" that she had not been nominated for the Best Actress Oscar.

For his role as Heathcliff, Larry lost the Oscar to Robert Donat for his role in *Goodbye, Mr. Chips. Wuthering Heights* lost to *Gone With the Wind* as Best Picture, and Geraldine Fitzgerald lost to Hattie McDaniel for playing the devoted Mammy in *Gone With the Wind.*

Although Thomas Mitchell gave an award-worthy performance as Scarlett O'Hara's father (Gerald O'Hara) in *Gone With the Wind,* he was actually nominated for Best Supporting Actor for his role in *Stagecoach* with John Wayne. In that film, Mitchell played a whiskey-soaked Doc Boone.

During the filming of *Wuthering Heights*, when relations among the dramatic leads, the film's director, and its producer had become particularly venomous, Larry was "virtually rescued from the ranks of the suicidal by the arrival from England of a fantastically beautiful, kitten-like creature, Miss Vivien Leigh," Niven said. "For one brief moment—actually much longer than that—I was tempted to take her away from Larry. After all, they weren't married, and my mate, Errol Flynn, had long ago convinced me that all's fair in love and war."

Wyler took a more cynical view. "Vivien Leigh, like Cathy with Heathcliff, flew in to suck the blood from my star."

Before Vivien, however, Larry had to deal with a very formidable Hollywood star, Miss Bette Davis.

During the filming of *Wuthering Heights*, Larry received about ten invitations a day to various parties and dinners, most of which he had to turn down. Missing Vivien, he was in a despondent mood and didn't want "to become a British exhibit in a Hollywood showcase," as he put it.

But when Bette Davis asked him to visit her at her home, he eagerly accepted. He and Vivien had both been enthralled by her performance in the film *Jezebel*, which they'd seen in London. Although he felt that Bette overacted in a lot of the film, he considered her a formidable screen presence. "A true bitch goddess," he told Vivien. "I bet Hank Fonda doesn't have any balls left after working with Bette."

Years later, in an interview with Whitney Stine, Bette said, "I met Olivier only once, but I always wanted to work with him. In the late thirties, he was the most handsome thing on earth, and it was the image of his sexiness that I dreamed about."

When Larry was shown into Bette's living room, she was clad in a magenta dress with a plunging *décolletage*. He came over to greet her on her sofa, where she extended her left hand. Her right hand held a glass of whiskey.

"It's an honor to be welcomed into the home of the greatest living actress in Hollywood's galaxy of stars," he said. "Forgive me, that came out a little more pretentious than I meant it."

"The honor is all mine, Mr. Olivier," she said. "I hear Oscar is waiting to go to bed with you."

"How very flattering," he said. "But that's mere gossip right now. By the way, I hear you gave the Academy Award statuette the name of Oscar."

"It reminded me of Ham's backside," she said.

"Ham?" he asked, puzzled. "What a strange name, and perhaps a deadly one for an actor."

"My darling husband, Harmon Oscar Nelson Jr." she said, "an ill-fated marriage that's being buried at Forest Lawn." She motioned for him to freshen her drink from a nearby bottle.

Like an English butler in a British movie, he elegantly poured whiskey into her glass.

"Have one yourself," she said. It was more of

Two views of Bette Davis *(lower photo)* As Elizabeth I emoting with Essex (Errol Flynn)

307

a command.

"Don't mind if I do," he said. "After a day with William Wyler, I could use more than one."

"I, of all the people in Hollywood, know exactly what you mean. Wyler and I go way back. The bastard first rejected me when I was an *ingénue* at Universal in '31."

"What a big mistake that was," he said, joining her on the sofa.

After ten minutes of informal chatter, she came right to the point. "I want to get down to business. First, I'd like to ask you a personal question, then proceed from there."

"I'll answer as best I can," he said.

"In a kissing scene on camera, do you believe that the leading man should stick his tongue halfway down the throat of his leading lady?"

"Please," he said, "I'm British. We British actors are very closed lipped in our on-camera smooches, perhaps off-camera as well."

"When I made *The Sisters* with Errol Flynn, he always stuck his tongue down my throat in kissing scenes," she said.

"Well, in the case of Mr. Flynn, I don't think any lady would object," he said. "He is the most beautiful male specimen on the screen today."

"I beg to differ," she said. "That honor belongs to you."

"If only that were so," he said. "Your claim is a debatable point, but I think most critics would agree that Flynn fills out a pair of green tights better than I do. I have a confession to make. I've been known to use a bit of leg padding to give me the right contour."

She looked at him with a smirk on her face. "I hope you don't have to use padding anywhere else."

He raised an eyebrow. "That is for the lucky few to find out." He cleared his throat. "I was told you have an offer to present to me. From the way our little talk was going, it seems it might be of a sexual nature. I have to warn you: I'm a married man and also have a mistress, whom I love very much."

"Have no fear," she said. "This is not my week for raping young British actors. I have another offer to make. Jack Warner has cast me in this big-budget ersatz-historical drama in Technicolor, no less. It's called *The Private Lives of Elizabeth and Essex*. Perhaps you know the blank verse play by Maxwell Anderson."

"I missed it, but I know that Lynn Fontanne and Alfred Lunt starred in it," he said.

"I told Jack Warner that if Flynn is cast as Essex, he'll be the fly in my ointment. He simply doesn't have the talent for the role. With Flynn, Anderson's blank verse would go down the drain. He would cheapen the role, turning it into a paperback novel. I want you to play Essex to my Elizabeth.

Would you consider it? Time is of the essence."

"Of course, I'd consider it," he said. "I feel an affinity for the Essex character. But I have other considerations—contracts, previous commitments. I'll have to get back to you on that."

The next day, Larry shared the details of his talk with Bette with Wyler and others.

"Did she invite you for a sleepover?" Wyler asked, sounding angry.

"Not in so many words," Larry said. "But it would have been mine for the asking."

"That's Bette all right," Wyler said, turning and walking away.

It was only later in the day when Larry discovered what might have sparked Wyler's flash of anger. Larry heard that Bette and Wyler were just coming down from a torrid affair.

That night Larry weighed his options, thinking he had a better chance going with Alfred Hitchcock who wanted him to play the lead in *Rebecca*. He sent Bette a telegram, thanking her for her offer but bowing out. In spite of Bette's objections, Flynn stayed in the picture as Essex.

Years later Bette did not seem resentful that Larry had spurned her offer, both professionally and personally. In an interview, she said, "My favorite actor with whom I never played, was Laurence Olivier. He was a great actor, and he was my dream man. Literally and figuratively, Larry was my fantasy lover, the perfect man, or at least I thought he would be. He was not only beautiful, but intelligent."

***

"Here was the last ever to be seen of knights and their ladies fair, of master and slave. Look for it only in books, for it is no more than a dream remembered, gone with the wind."

--from David Selznick's 1939 movie trailer for **Gone With the Wind**

***

In London, and desperately lonely for Larry, Vivien made an impulsive decision when a break came in her work. She was scheduled to play Titania in a West End theatrical production of *A Midsummer Night's Dream*. Faced with a three-week break in her schedule, days which straddled the Christmas holidays, she made arrangements to join Larry in Hollywood, a distance from London of 6,000 miles. To reach Larry would take six days for a transatlantic crossing by ship, and then a fifteen-hour flight to Los Angeles that would involve three separate stopovers for refueling.

Factoring in travel time, she'd have only five days with him in the California sunshine before being obligated to return to her commitments in the West End, but she decided that the staggering inconvenience would be worth it. Of course, if David O. Selznick had yet to cast Scarlett

Characters, a book, and a film that mourned the death of the much-romanticized Old South
(photos, above)
Vivien Leigh as Scarlett O'Hara and Clark Gable as Rhett Butler

310

O'Hara, she would suddenly be on the scene and available.

On the first day of sailing from Southampton on the *Majestic*, Vivien encountered Hamish Hamilton, the Scottish-American entrepreneur who, in 1931, had founded a literary publishing house that today, after many permutations, functions as a division of Penguin. Hamilton happened to be one of Leigh Holman's best and most long-standing friends, and a personal friend of some of the most visible British and American authors of his day. During Leigh's courtship of her, years previously, Leigh, Hamilton, and Vivien had shared many a fun day in Devon and many happy dancing soirées together in London.

On the transatlantic crossing, she tried to rekindle a friendship, but he rejected her. "I was horrified to learn of your desertion of Leigh," Hamilton told her. "He is my dear friend, and I can't imagine why you'd want to cause him such pain. To run off with Olivier. It's the talk of London."

"Oh, please Hamish," she said, "you must understand the ways of love."

He looked at her sternly. "Our friendship is over. For me, Vivien Leigh no longer exists."

On the third day of the sail, her smile won him over again, and he was seen dining with her that night.

Over dessert, she told him that right before leaving London, Leigh had allowed Suzanne to come and visit her for three days. "On the second day, she complained to me," Vivien said. "Suzanne said, 'Oh, this is so dull. I miss dad. I needed someone to box with.' The poor girl looked so desperately unhappy that I sent her back to Leigh."

Before leaving, Vivien's erstwhile and long-suffering agent, John Gliddon, still trying to hang onto her as a client, told her that he'd secured the lead role for her in a play called *Dream*, whose first rehearsal had been scheduled for December 15, 1938. and whose performances wouldn't interfere with her present commitment to *A Midsummer*

(top and middle photos) Margaret Mitchell (1900-1949) and her living quarters in Atlanta, now a museum *(lower photo)* Hamish Hamilton, portrait courtesy of the Thames Rowing Club

Night's Dream. She had assured Gliddon that she'd be back in time from California to begin rehearsals for *Dream*.

But as the *Majestic* glided into New York harbor, she told Hamilton that she was heading at once to Hollywood, not only to see Larry but to play Scarlett O'Hara.

"But I heard that Paulette Goddard has all but gotten the role locked up," Hamilton said.

"David O. Selznick hasn't seen me yet," she said.

Before she disembarked, he said, "I bet you ten pounds you won't get the part." Decades later, he mused, "I never paid her that ten pounds I owed her. I should have."

Disembarking on the piers of New York, Vivien, to her surprise, found out that she was enough of a celebrity to be greeted by members of the American press.

"Why are you in the States, Miss Leigh?" asked a reporter from the *Journal-American*.

"To see Laurence Olivier," she answered bluntly.

That news was printed in only two newspapers, but at the pier a press agent from Samuel Goldwyn's office warned her to be cautious. "Remember, Miss Leigh, we're not as sophisticated over here as you Londoners are. You'll find that the average American is a bit prudish. Remember, you and Mr. Olivier are not divorced."

"I don't need to be reminded," she snapped back at him, "and thank you very much."

Vivien and her luggage were bustled into a taxi heading for the airport. She caught the first plane to Los Angeles, her first flight ever. "It was pure terror for me. At the first refueling stop, I wanted to flee but stuck it out."

She couldn't sleep on the long flight and stayed awake practicing her "Scarlett expressions" in her makeup mirror, including a "Cheshire cat smile," as described by Margaret Mitchell in *Gone With the Wind*.

At the airport in Los Angeles, Larry was "crouched in the back of a car" a few feet from the airport entrance, so as not to be detected by the press.

Safely in the car with him, "we went at it like animals," she recalled to her friends. "I'd never missed anybody so much in my life. As he drove to the hotel, I couldn't wait and had to take it out and service him. He nearly crashed the car before we got to the hotel."

At the Beverly Hills Hotel, it was a night of passion until dawn. Sleep mercifully came to both of them.

She made an artfully feeble attempt to keep her presence in California secret, but Hedda Hopper broke the item the following morning in her widely read newspaper column. "The cute English vamp, Vivien Leigh, is in our midst, but not doing a picture. Her romantic interest seems to be Laurence Olivier in spite of the fact that some here are trying to link his name to Merle Oberon. Are we laughing, because Alex Korda is on the way over."

That night, Myron Selznick, who was not only Larry's agent, but had become Vivien's agent as well, invited them for dinner at Romanoff's.

Myron's list of clients was impressive—Katharine Hepburn, Paulette Goddard, Helen Hayes, Merle Oberon, Carole Lombard, Fred Astaire, Ginger Rogers, Fredric March, Henry Fonda, and Gary Cooper.

One writer had called Myron "a combination wailing wall, mine detector, espionage agent, drinking companion, occasional pimp, and available Father Confessor" to his famous clientele, including Vivien and Larry.

"Humphrey Bogart suddenly approached their table at Romanoff's. "What happened, Myron?" he asked. "All those stories that I was to play Rhett Butler."

"Better stick to Duke Mantee roles," Myron said. "You belong in gang battles on the streets of Chicago, not in Georgia fighting off the Yankees. Besides, Rhett Butler didn't lisp."

"Why don't all of you, and these two limeys here, go fuck yourself?" He walked away to join Mayo Methot, the other half of "The Battling Bogarts."

At table, Myron told them of his scheme. "Tonight, my brother, like some beefy Nero, is burning down Atlanta."

"What on earth do you mean?" Vivien asked.

Myron explained that David was under pressure to begin shooting *Gone With the Wind*, even without having cast a Scarlett O'Hara. He was going to set flames to some of the sets on the MGM lot—custom-built but flimsy relics from such films as *King Kong* and *David Copperfield*. "He will simulate the burning of Atlanta, with extras in horse-pulled carriages playing Scarlett, Rhett, and some other members of the cast. I want to present your gleaming face against the backdrop of those flames burning Atlanta. Now let's get going before David burns down Culver City."

(top photo) Humphrey Bogart as gangster Duke Mantee in *The Petrified Forest* (1936)

and *(lower photo)* David O. Selznick's "Burning of Atlanta"

As Vivien arrived on the set, oil was flowing through the pipes and jets of flames were leaping into the air. Dry wood was blazing like a blast furnace. Showers of sparks lit the night sky.

Myron, Larry, and Vivien were ushered to the platform where David O. Selznick, George Cukor, and three assistants were standing watching the "burning of Atlanta."

"You're late," David shouted at his brother. There was always a certain rivalry between the two brothers. "What kept you, Mr. Napoleon of agents?"

"Hey, genius, meet your Scarlett O'Hara," Myron said. He stepped back to present Vivien, ignoring Larry.

Not dressed in Victorian garb, as wrongly reported, Vivien actually wore a mink coat and a beige silk dress that emphasized her tiny waist. Her stunningly beautiful face was crowned by a little black hat that Chanel might have designed.

As the final fiery sets collapsed in the background, Vivien stood in front of David, his eyes red from smoke. The dying embers of the flames bathed her in pinkish glow.

Larry beamed with pride, and David said what was on Larry's mind. "She's the most beautiful woman I've ever seen."

David O. Selznick

She boldly confronted him. "Tonight at dinner, Myron told me that your inability to find a Scarlett O'Hara was the greatest failure of your career. Your search is over, even though you had to go through 1,400 young women to find me."

David Selznick later recalled that Vivien "stepped Phoenix-like from the dying embers of Atlanta. I took one look and knew that she was right. But I didn't want to be too impulsive. Only an hour before, I had been dead set on Paulette Goddard. But because so much was riding on this picture, I decided to go through proper procedures—readings, screen tests, the like."

After one final glance at the set where the flames by then had died down, David invited the party to his office for drinks. Vivien had a chance

314

to observe him more closely. A tall man with black curly hair, he was unattractive and shaggy in appearance. His face was somewhat hidden behind thick-lensed spectacles.

Since no final decision had been made, Selznick did not want Vivien to let her hopes rise too far up in the air. "To be truthful, Miss Leigh," he said cautiously, "I saw your performance in *A Yank in Oxford* with Bob Taylor. You seemed to be a little static, not sufficiently fiery enough for the role of Scarlett. Hopefully, if I give you the role of Scarlett, you'll play it with fire in your belly."

"Mr. Selznick, I've got enough fire in my belly tonight to burn down Atlanta again."

He laughed and finished his drink. Before telling her good night, he suggested she go into Cukor's office for a reading. He kissed her good night on the cheek.

Cukor, Larry, and Vivien entered the director's cluttered office.

The next morning Selznick wrote a letter to his wife, Irene Mayer Selznick, who was staying at the Sherry-Netherland Hotel in New York. "Shhhhh: Vivien Leigh is the Scarlett dark horse, and looked damned good."

Selznick later said that "Vivien Leigh was as Margaret Mitchell described her—the green eyes in the carefully sweet face, turbulent, lusty for life, distinctly at variance with her decorous manner."

It was one o'clock in the morning.

Vivien's reading for Cukor started off badly. She was nervous and tense. Finally, he told her, "Take your finger out of your ass and get on with it."

She laughed at the remark, and it broke the tension between them, and she gave an especially good reading of the scene where she confesses her love for Ashley Wilkes even though he is already betrothed to Melanie.

By the time she'd finished her reading, Cukor remembered that, "She was Rabelaisian, this exquisite creature who told outrageous jokes in that sweet little voice."

After the reading, Cukor graciously invited both Larry and Vivien to spend Christmas with him at his home. They eagerly accepted.

On the way back to the Beverly Hills Hotel, Vivien sighed and snuggled up against Larry even though he was steering the wheel in these early morning hours.

"All this waiting and hoping to play Scarlett," she said. "I'm tired. The trip from England, my red-hot reunion with you—it's been too much. I need to sleep for a year. I've decided I don't want to play Scarlett O'Hara after all, even assuming I get offered the part,

George Cukor

315

which I'm sure will not happen."

"You don't mean a word you're saying," he said. "You'd give your left nipple to play Scarlett." As an afterthought, he added, "and a lot more."

***

Before Vivien was due at the studio to make her first screen test for Cukor, Larry rehearsed her in the two scenes required—one with Mammy who was lacing a corset on her and another with Ashley Wilkes when she tells him, early in the course of the film, that she loves him just prior to his official announcement of his intention to marry Melanie.

Hattie McDaniel was cast in the role of Mammy. In Margaret Mitchell's words, she was "a huge old woman, with the small, shrewd eyes of an elephant. She was shining black, pure African, devoted to her last drop of blood to the O'Haras."

But Hattie was nobody's servant. Vivien found her utterly fascinating, a professional singer-songwriter, comedian, stage actress, radio performer, and, in time, a television star. She would become, in fact, the first black woman to sing on the radio in America. In time she would appear in 300 motion pictures before her untimely death in 1952.

(top photo) Mammy (Hattie McDaniel) prepares Scarlett for the barbecue
(middle photo) Ashley Wilkes (Leslie Howard) gets chivalrous with Scarlett
(bottom photo) On the eve of war, Ashley and Melanie (Olivia de Havilland) applaud Scarlett for her "sacrifice of love."

The competition to play Mammy had been almost as stiff as that for the role of Scarlett. Eleanor Roosevelt had even written Selznick, asking that he cast her own maid, Elizabeth McDuffie, in the role.

316

"I love the role of Mammy, and I hope you get to play Scarlett," Hattie told Vivien. "My own grandmother worked on a plantation not unlike Tara. My father had also been a slave who was set free by his master. Of course, Tallulah will be really pissed off. But no one would believe Tallulah as an innocent sixteen-year-old gal."

Vivien had heard stories that Hattie and Tallulah had had a brief fling, but was too polite to inquire about that, although vastly intrigued. It seemed so unlikely, but as she told Larry, "Any and all combinations of the sexes are possible in Hollywood. It's just like dear old London."

Vivien falsely assumed that Hattie was from Alabama or "one of those Confederate states," but learned that she too had to take lessons in Southern diction. "Honeychild, I was born in Wichita, Kansas, never you mind the year."

"They call me 'The Colored Sophie Tucker,'" Hattie told Vivien. "But you can call me 'Hi-Hat Hattie,' that's my nickname."

"The black folks don't want me to play a maid," Hattie said. "You know stereotypes. But like I told Mr. Selznick, why should I complain about making $1,000 a week playing a maid. If I didn't, I'd be making $7 a week."

During their screen test, Vivien saw Selznick as he darted into the studio. He kissed Vivien on the cheek and wished her luck with the test. He spoke to Hattie, telling her that he'd been deluged with mail from blacks across America, especially from the NAACP, "worrying about how Negroes will be pictured in *Gone With the Wind*. I have no desire to produce an anti-Negro film—rest assured of that. I'll see that in *Gone With the Wind*, Negroes will come out on the right side of the ledger."

"That's fine news to me," Hattie said. "We'll make the villains the Yankee dogs."

After Selznick left, Vivien was fitted into the corset. "It was still warm from the body heat of another actress."

Three views of
Hattie McDaniel

(top photo) early days in Wichita; *(middle photo)* as Scarlett O'Hara's Mammy; *(lower photo)* with gardenias, on Oscar night, 1940.

"Before you came in, I had to lace up Joan Bennett in the same corset," Hattie said.

During the actual shooting of *Gone With the Wind*, Gable also befriended Hattie. Both of them often played practical jokes on each other. Even off-camera, she called him "Mr. Rhett."

One day Vivien was watching as Hattie and Gable filmed a scene together. "What is that rustling noise I hear, Mammy?" Gable said on camera. When Hattie forgot the sequence and didn't exit on cue, Gable said, "What is that rustling noise I was supposed to hear if you had walked away, Mammy?" The crew burst into laughter.

When he saw the final cut of *Gone With the Wind*, Selznick fired off a memo to sign Hattie to a long term contract. "I think she is going to be hailed as the great Negro performer of the decade. I think she, and Olivia de Havilland as Melanie, are both going to be nominated for Oscars, even though Hattie is colored. Regrettably, they'll probably cancel each other out and give the Oscar to a runner-up."

In the early 1950s, when Hattie was dying of breast cancer, Vivien went to see her. Hattie described her dream of a funeral. "I desire a white casket and a white shroud," she said. "White gardenias in my hair and in my hands, together with a white gardenia blanket and a pillow of red roses."

When she was notified of Hattie's death, Vivien was "prostrate with grief," as Hattie had said of Scarlett in *Gone With the Wind*.

Vivien said she deplored the racism in America that ultimately denied Hattie her dream of being buried in The Hollywood Cemetery. Instead, her remains were interred at Rosedale Cemetery, where they lie today. Founded in 1884 in the West Adams district of Los Angeles, just southwest of downtown, it was the first cemetery in L.A. that was open to all races and creeds.

"She will always be my dear sweet Mammy, that sassy servant repeatedly scolding me and reminding me not to show bosom before three o'clock in the afternoon," Vivien said.

***

Cukor called Vivien the next day to schedule a screen test with Leslie Howard as Ashley Wilkes. The scene being developed was the one in which she declares her undying love for him at the Twelve Oaks Plantation without knowing that Rhett Butler is eavesdropping on the sofa. Vivien had long sustained a crush on the English actor, and was eager to be working with him.

"I think it was because my husband, Leigh Holman, resembled you that I married him," Vivien told him. "I figured if I couldn't have the real thing, then I had to make do with a stand-in for you."

"Coming from the most beautiful girl in the world, I'm flattered," he said.

Over lunch that day, Leslie confided in Vivien as if he'd known her for years. "I repeatedly turned down the role of Ashley Wilkes," he said. "I told Selznick I didn't have the slightest intention of playing another weak, watery character such as Ashley. I've played enough ineffectual characters already."

"What changed your mind" she asked, "other than money?"

"He told me I could direct Ingrid Bergman and myself in *Intermezzo* if I'd do *Gone With the Wind*. Actually, Selznick considered several other actors, Melvyn Douglas, Ray Milland, Jeffrey Lynn. Vincent Price tested for the role, but Selznick found him too effeminate. Now Selznick is stuck with me. I find Ashley a soft dullard, a total weakling. It's unbelievable why a strong-willed woman like Scarlett would prefer Ashley over Rhett Butler."

"I would prefer you to Rhett Butler," she told him.

"That's good to know," he said. "I guess you've heard of my reputation."

"Yes, I have," she said. "With the one exception of Bette Davis, you are said to have seduced all your leading ladies, including Tallulah Bankhead in *Her Cardboard Lover* in 1927 and Merle Oberon in *The Scarlet Pimpernel* in 1934."

"You really have been investigating my life, haven't you?" he said.

"Guilty."

"I get tons of fan letters claiming that I'm wrong for the role," he told her. "It seems most fans want Randolph Scott. I don't know if he'd make a better Ashley, but I hear he's a great cocksucker. Cary Grant must be one lucky Englishman."

Two days later, after he'd seen the results of his test with her, he called her. "Selznick has seen my first scene with you. You look terrific, fourteen if you're a day. I'm supposed to look like a twenty-seven-year-old but I photographed like I'm forty-five years old."

ONLY ONE OF THIS TRIO WAS A SOUTHERN BELLE: Fangs-out contenders for the role of Scarlett included: *(top to bottom)*

*Paulette Goddard,
Katharine Hepburn,
Tallulah Bankhead*

319

Howard had been born in 1893. "*Fiddle-dee-dee*," Vivien said. "We'll both look like young lovers in love on screen . . . or off, as the case may be."

"Talk a little more like that, and I think I'll fall in love," he said. "I'd like to take you out to dinner one night as soon as Larry Olivier heads out of town."

"Wouldn't your wife object?" she asked coyly. "Perhaps your mistresses will file a complaint."

"Of course, they'd object," he said. "But we don't have to call up Louella Parsons. The most fun in Hollywood occurs late at night when those old bag columnists have gone to bed."

***

Selznick sent Vivien's screen tests to John ("Jock") Whitney, his chief financial backer. The tests met with his approval. In a private phone conversation with Selznick, Whitney said, "I've had several of the Scarlett hopefuls, notably Paulette Goddard and Tallulah Bankhead. Sign Vivien Leigh. I'd like a chance at her too."

When word about the success of Vivien's screen tests leaked out, she became an official enemy of virtually every hopeful in "The Scarlett Sweepstakes." Myron Selznick said, "Vivien has moved into second place, hot on the heels of the lead runner, Paulette Goddard."

Katharine Hepburn desperately wanted to play Scarlett. She could no longer handle the suspense over casting. One afternoon she barged into Selznick's office. "This part was practically written for me," she told the startled producer in a strident New England voice. "I am Scarlett O'Hara."

He looked her up and down before saying, "I can't imagine Rhett Butler chasing you for ten years."

"Well," she said, deeply offended. "Maybe other people's view of sex appeal is different from yours. Ever hear of Howard Hughes?"

Although *Variety* was still reporting that Tallulah Bankhead had the role of Scarlett locked up, the flamboyant actress knew better. "I'm not going to play Scarlett O'Hara," she told *The New York Post*. "Of course, Scarlett is divine, but Cleopatra [a reference to her stage role] is much diviner, don't you think?"

In 1937, Tallulah starred on Broadway in *Antony and Cleopatra,* one of history's great camp performances on the Great White Way. In

Scriptwriter Sidney Howard

320

the words of one reviewer, "Tallulah Bankhead barged down the Nile last night—and it sank."

Actress Estelle Winwood (1883-1984), the English stage and film actress who moved to the U.S. in mid-career and who happened to be Tallulah's best friend, later revealed, "The loss of the role of Scarlett broke Tallulah's heart."

Marcella Rabin, personal assistant to David O. Selznick, said, "David never seriously considered Bankhead. If she'd attempted to play a young and relatively innocent girl, her homosexual fans would have laughed her off the screen."

Selznick did offer Tallulah the small but significant role of Belle Watling, the madam of the local bordello. Tallulah turned it down, claiming that the role was too small. "She would have been perfect running a Southern bordello and entertaining Rhett Butler," Selznick said.

In 1960, in Key West, Florida, Tallulah regretted not having accepted the role of Belle Watling. "I could have immortalized myself. *Gone With the Wind* will be shown 200 years from now when all my stage plays, even my triumphs, have truly gone with the wind."

Tallulah told Winwood, "I'll go to my grave convinced that I could have drawn cheers from General Beauregard and Robert E. Lee had I been permitted to wrestle on screen with Rhett Butler."

Earlier in the then-unresolved process of casting Belle Watling, Selznick had leaked to the press that Mae West was "all but signed" for the role, but that appears to have been merely a publicity stunt.

Louella Parsons became so certain that Goddard had snared the role of Scarlett that in print the columnist began referring to the actress as "Scarlett O'Goddard."

As late as December 20, 1938, Cukor was still choreographing screen tests with Goddard, perhaps because he'd falsely assured her that the role was hers.

"David had decided on me, or so he led me to believe," Goddard said years later. "I gave a tennis party to celebrate. I decided to invite Larry Olivier, the new star in town. He asked me if he could bring along a girlfriend, and, of course, I said yes. He showed up with Vivien Leigh, and the rest is Hollywood history."

Errol Flynn

***

As the casting dramas associated with who would play Scarlett O'Hara continued to occupy the nation's headlines, the script was being written by Sidney

321

Howard. He faced a daunting challenge of condensing the mammoth novel into a picture that might conceivably have run for a full twelve hours. In his first draft, Howard presented a script that would have lasted five and a half hours on the screen.

Selznick believed that Sidney Howard was a "sure fire bet" to adapt the novel. He'd won a Pulitzer Prize for Drama in 1925 for his scripting of the romantic Broadway drama, *They Knew What They Wanted*. Hired by Samuel Goldwyn to write screenplays, Howard was a veteran when Selznick hired him. Howard had already been nominated twice for an Oscar for his adaptation of the Sinclair Lewis novel, *Arrowsmith*, and again in 1936 for his writing *Dodsworth*, based on another Sinclair Lewis novel.

Not pleased with the final script—in fact, very disappointed—Selznick reached out to other writers, even the English playwright John Van Druten. Selznick also called in the talented Ben Hecht as a "play doctor," but no script satisfied him.

F. Scott Fitzgerald was hired to do rewrites. He wrote to his daughter that, "I feel no contempt for the novel but only a certain pity for those who consider it the supreme achievement of the human mind." When he was fired, his confidence as a writer was destroyed and he went on a drinking spree.

Ultimately, in desperation, Selznick would even bring Sidney Howard back for rewrites.

***

Selznick told the widow of John Gilbert, "We have buried the man who should have been cast as Rhett Butler in *Gone With the Wind*."

Even without having chosen an actress for the character of Scarlett O'Hara, Selznick continued to cast his film, making deft, almost perfect choices. In 1936, when she sold the movie rights to *Gone With the Wind* to David Selznick, Margaret Mitchell had cast her vote for Basil Rathbone to play Rhett Butler. Although many actors were considered, even Charles Boyer, the choice eventually narrowed to Errol Flynn, Clark Gable, and Gary Cooper. The latter two had no enthusiasm for the role.

(top photo) Clark Gable with his then-wife, Ria Langham
(bottom photo) Butterfly ("Prissy") McQueen

The offer from Jack Warner to lend Bette Davis and Errol Flynn to Selznick for the roles of Scarlett and Rhett had fallen through. But Flynn

322

still wanted to play Rhett, and indulged in some "plea bargaining" with Cukor.

In a private visit to Cukor at his home, Flynn promised the director that he could have him sexually throughout the months-long making of *Gone With the Wind*.

The director confided this to Katharine Hepburn, Vivien, and others. "I'm a man of mere flesh, and Flynn overcame my resistance," Cukor said. "After we'd done the dirty deed, I had to warn him that there still wasn't any guarantee that he would play Rhett."

Myron Selznick told Vivien that Gary Cooper had turned down the role of Rhett Butler. At a party when she encountered the lanky actor, Vivien pointedly asked him why. "I'm against it with a passion," Cooper said. "It's going to be the biggest flop in Hollywood history. I think Selznick and Mayer are going to con Gable into taking the role. Let him make a horse's ass of himself—not me."

"Oh, that's too bad," she said diplomatically in her most flirtatious voice. "I'm hoping to get cast as Scarlett O'Hara. With you as Rhett, I'd really look forward to playing love scenes with you."

"I may not be your Rhett on screen, but I sure as hell wouldn't mind playing Rhett to your Scarlett off screen."

"I'm flattered," she said. "Your reputation has preceded you."

"You mean all that Montana Mule crap?" he said. "Every word of it is true. You can find out for yourself any night you choose."

"That's an offer I plan to take you up on," she said.

It is not known if she ever carried through with her promise.

Cukor told Vivien and Larry that Gable had asserted that "public opinion decided that I was going to play Rhett Butler—and that was that."

What really solidified the deal for Gable was the $4,500-a-week salary. In the throes of a divorce from his second wife, Ria Langham, the Houston socialite, Gable needed some $300,000 "to buy the bitch off."

(top photo) Ellen O'Hara (Barbara O'Neil) and Gerald O'Hara (Thomas Mitchell) at home

(lower photo) Melanie (Olivia de Havilland) with Aunt Pittypat (Laura Hope Crews)

323

Louis B. Mayer agreed to advance the full $300,000 as a means of freeing his major star from the Texan's clutches. Gable was already living with Carole Lombard at the time. Mayer planned to deduct the advance against Gable's future earnings.

The third lead, that of Melanie, the demurely gracious soft-spoken belle who takes Ashley Wilkes from Scarlett, was also sought out by various actresses. Louis B. Mayer himself preferred Vivien's friend, Maureen O'Sullivan. Selznick also considered Anne Shirley, Priscilla Lane, Andrea Leeds, and Geraldine Fitzgerald.

Cukor leaned toward Joan Fontaine. "She would make a great Melanie," he told Selznick, who was not convinced.

When Fontaine was summoned into Cukor's office, she arrived with the mistaken belief that he was about to offer her the role of Scarlett O'Hara, which she had long coveted. She was shocked when the director offered her instead the secondary role of Melanie. Rising to her feet, she told him, "It's Scarlett or nothing. As for Melanie, I think my sister, Olivia, would make a perfect Melanie. The role is too soapy for me."

She was referring, of course, to Olivia de Havilland.

Later, Jack Warner told Olivia, "If you must be in the picture, and you know how I feel about that stinking script, then go for the role of Scarlett. Hell with this nerdy little Melanie shit."

"But I want to play Melanie," Olivia responded. "I understand her."

Backbiting for Beaux
Sibling Rivalry among the O'Hara Sisters

(left to right) Ellen O'Hara (Barbara O'Neil), facing her daughters:

Carreen (Ann Rutherford),
Scarlett (Vivien Leigh), and
Suellen (Evelyn Keyes)

"Okay, but it's your funeral," Warner told her.

Vivien was utterly fascinated by Butterfly McQueen, who had originally been a dancer before being cast as Prissy in *Gone With the Wind*. "I adore Prissy," Vivien told Hattie McDaniel. "But, let's face it, Butterfly is certifiably insane."

Years later when she encountered Vivien, Butterfly told her, "Everywhere I go, people mock my line, 'I don't know nuthin' 'bout birthin' babies! I'll never escape my image in *Gone With the Wind*."

"Wherever I go," Vivien said, "people call me Miss Scarlett."

"I still don't know nuthin' 'bout birthin' babies,' Butterfly said. "I've never married and don't intend to. What would I do with some ol' man sitting around the living room in his dirty underwear watching a football game while I'm on screen as some ethnic stereotype?"

Ona Munson won the role of Belle Watling. She'd first come to fame on Broadway, in the original production of *No, No Nanette*. She also introduced the classic, "You're the Cream in My Coffee" in the 1927 Broadway musical *Hold Everything*.

Born in Portland, Oregon, Munson had entered vaudeville at the age of fourteen. She'd made her first film playing opposite Edward G. Robinson in *Five Star Finale* (1931).

"I could not believe it," Munson said, "when Selznick cast me. I was the very opposite of the voluptuous Belle. I was freckled and had a slight build. I think it was my deep, throaty voice that won the role for me."

Cast as Scarlett's father, Gerald O'Hara, veteran actor Thomas Mitchell was undeniably Irish, stocky, and beady-eyed. One of the most talented and dependable character actors of Hollywood, he was the first actor to win an Oscar, an Emmy, and a Tony. His breakthrough role had been as the embezzler in Frank Capra's 1937 film *Lost Horizon*.

In time, his credits would read like a list of the greatest films of the 20th century, including *It's a Wonderful Life* in 1946 and, previously, *Stagecoach* in 1939.

While playing her father in *Gone With the Wind*, Mitchell honored Vivien by inviting her to become the only female member of his entourage of drinkers and raconteurs, which included John Barrymore, W.C. Fields, Roland Young, and Errol Flynn. Once, when she complimented Mitchell on his portrayal of her onscreen father who'd lost his mind in the Civil War, he told her, "A man looks bigger in the bathtub than he does in the ocean."

Barbara O'Neil was only twenty-eight years old when she was cast as Ellen, Scarlett's mother. Originally silent screen great Lillian Gish had been asked to do the role, and she later regretted turning it down.

Even though only three years older than Vivien, O'Neil pulled off the characterization. In the novel, Ellen had married at fifteen and given birth to Scarlett when she was only sixteen.

Right after making *Gone With the Wind*, O'Neil married the famous director, Josh Logan, but the union was brief. She never remarried and was rumored to be a lesbian. A striking, mature-looking brunette, she often played socialites with flair or

Barbara O'Neil (left) and
then-husband Josh Logan

neurotic, over-the-edge wives. She adored Vivien and later said, "I just wanted to adopt her and take her home in my pocket."

Billie Burke was originally considered for the role of Aunt Pittypat, but at fifty-four was considered too young. She opted instead to take the role of Glinda, "The Good Witch" in *The Wizard of Oz*, which was being filmed at the same time.

In one of film history's greatest over-the-top performances, the role of the silly Aunt Pittypat went to Laura Hope Crews, who was always having fainting spells and demanding her smelling salts.

She was already a friend of Clark Gable whom she'd met when he was selling ties in a department store. She always claimed that it was she who urged him to pursue a career in acting. She never married and once said, "Gable is the only man for me, and he never asked for my hand in marriage."

As a footnote in Hollywood history, Crews used her earnings from *Gone With the Wind* to purchase a colonial-style white mansion in Beverly Hills. Later Lana Turner and her daughter, Cheryl Crane, occupied the house, with Lana's lover, gangster Johnny Stompanato. He was stabbed to death either by Lana or Cheryl (a matter of some dispute even today). Ironically, at one time, Lana herself had been a candidate to play Scarlett.

Originally, Judy Garland was set to play Scarlett's sister, Carreen O'Hara, but was cast in *The Wizard of Oz* instead. The role went to Ann Rutherford, who had worked with actors such as John Wayne and Gene Autry and also with Mickey Rooney in the Andy Hardy series. When she asked Mayer if she could play Carreen, he told her, "It's a nothing part. You've been playing leads, and now my son-in-law wants to reduce you to a walk-on."

Regardless of how small the role, Rutherford wanted to be in *Gone With the Wind*, and as late as 2010 was still making appearances on behalf of this blockbuster.

The role of the bratty, petulant Suellen O'Hara, Scarlett's perpetually jealous sibling, went to Evelyn Keyes. The actress would later write a memoir called *Scarlett O'Hara's Younger Sister*. Her memories of Vivien were not pleasant. "In one scene in the movie she whacked me because I complained. And she didn't pull her punches. My cheek wore the imprint of Vivien's fingers for the rest of the afternoon. She had big hands."

(lower photo) Evelyn Keyes as Suellen, and

(top photo) her Hollywood memoirs

326

With thanks to the Harry Ransom Center at the University of Texas at Austin, we present the makeup stills for some of the characters we remember, with love and respect, from the cast of Gone With the Wind

Vivien Leigh (Scarlett O'Hara)

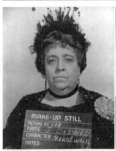

Jane Darwell
(Dolly Merriwether)

Laura Hope Crews
(Aunt Pittypat)

Eddie Anderson
(Uncle Peter)

Eric Linden (soldier
with a gangrened leg)

Isabel Jewell
(Emmy Slattery)

Victor Jory
(Jonas Wilkerson)

Ona Munson
(Belle Watling)

Barbara O'Neil (for the
death mask of Ellen O'Hara)

George Reeves and Fred Crane
(The Tarleton Twins)

Ann Rutherford
(Carreen O'Hara)

Ward Bond
(Tom, a Yankee Captain)

As an afterthought the next day, Keyes suggested to Vivien that she should become a professional boxer.

Other notable cast members included Eddie Anderson as Uncle Peter, Aunt Pittypat's favorite slave. He is best remembered as Jack Benny's side-kick, Rochester, on *The Jack Benny Show*. Jane Darwell played Dolly Merriweather, one of Aunt Pittypat's gossipy friends and a social arbiter of the crashing-to-an-end antebellum South. She later was cast as Ma Joad in *The Grapes of Wrath*. Victor Jory played the plantation's sleazy overseer, Jonas Wilkerson. Previously, he had appeared with such stars as Will Rogers and Janet Gaynor.

Mickey Kuhn, a well-respected staple among Hollywood child actors of the late 30s and early 40s, got to see Vivien in action in both *Gone With the Wind* (where he played Beau Wilkes, the son of Melanie and Ashley) and later, in *A Streetcar Named Desire*, where he was cast into a small role as a sailor. He later said that Vivien was "a magnificent, wonderful person. She may have had this terrible problem—I mean, her mental illness and all—but she worked very hard to hide it from the outside world."

As Vivien told Larry, "All the cast has been set, even the minor roles. When is Selznick going to announce the actress for the Scarlett O'Hara role? As we go to the countdown, I predict it's Goddard and me in a neck-to-neck race. I know she's fucked 'Mr. Moneybags,' Jock Whitney. For all I know, the bitch is giving Selznick a blow-job right now."

***

Arriving on the doorstep of George Cukor's home to celebrate Christmas Day, Vivien was apprehensive and nervous. She clung to Larry's arm.

Cukor came to the door to greet her, embracing her before kissing Larry on the cheek. "Welcome to Tara," he said, imitating Mammy in *Gone With the Wind*. He stood back and appraised her, "*Fiddle-dee-dee*, Miss Scarlett, you know you're not supposed to show bosom before three o'clock in the after-

Leslie Howard

noon."

She sensed something sinister in his jovial mood, fearing all this banter was but a prelude before he delivered devastating news.

Larry seemed to sense it, too. "Selznick has cast Scarlett, hasn't he?"

"It's the Goddard bitch, isn't it?" she asked.

"No, we're stuck with you, kid," Cukor said, ushering her into the house.

She practically danced a jig of joy, swirling around

328

Cukor and kissing Larry on the lips.

Standing right inside the door were Olivia de Havilland and Leslie Howard, waiting to greet her. "Oh, Melanie," Vivien cried out. "Oh, Ashley." She hugged both of them in a tight embrace. Larry stood behind her. She turned and kissed him in a desperate bid for reassurance. "Oh, Larry, how I wished you were playing Rhett. If there's a god in heaven, we must pray to him to keep us from fucking up this picture."

Cukor appeared and led her into his crowded living room where all the guests applauded her entrance. She bowed gracefully, playing her role of a queen being received into the inner bowels of *tout* Hollywood.

Almost like a receiving line, the guests lined up to greet her and congratulate her. Many of the guests, both male and female, kissed her.

Caught up in the party, her head spinning, Vivien years later could hardly recall the events of that afternoon. She was enthralled with the thrill of victory. But with that thrill also came a sense of panic. On two or three occasions, she found it difficult to breathe. She was so excited that her heart was pounding furiously.

As if sensing her anguish, the gay actor, William Haines, came up to her. "Howdy, Miss Scarlett," he said in a thick Southern accent, all faked. "Give your lovin' man a big sloppy wet one, and we'll flounce over to George's bar in our hoop skirts and lower his liquor supply."

An hour later, the Christmas party was interrupted by the sudden appearance of Greta Garbo. She was about the only actress in Hollywood who did not want to be Scarlett O'Hara.

After a few whispered words to Cukor, she immediately headed for Larry, taking him by the arm and leading him into Cukor's beautiful garden.

"It looks like Garbo is trying to seduce your boyfriend," a drunken Haines said. "She's decided to try a boy for a change."

"I just hope poor Larry knows what to do," Vivien said with a smirk. She walked away from him and stood by the open French doors, looking at Garbo and Larry

Three views of
Olivia De Havilland
*(photos above,
top to bottom)*

1. As modulated, modest Melanie in the antebellum South

2. As a star, with Vivien Leigh, early in the production of GWTW

3. "Cheesecake!"

standing close to one another in a distant part of the garden.

The writer, Garson Kanin, a close friend of Cukor's, came up to Vivien and introduced himself. Over the years, he gave several interviews about that day.

"Isn't Garbo the most stunning woman you've ever seen?" he asked her.

Those were not the words to say to a fuming Vivien. "There are those at this party who told me that I was the most exquisitely beautiful woman they'd

ever seen. Surely they were not lying."

Kanin quickly tried to recover. "Garbo is Old World beauty, the kind you see at twilight in a silent film. You represent the pinkish glow of dawn, lighting up a field of yellow roses just emerging into light."

"Frankly, I think Vivien was in a raging jealous fit that Garbo had upstaged her during her big moment," Kanin later said. "But when Garbo walks through a door, all eyes are on her. Vivien stood at the door with me and glared at Garbo and Olivier in the distance. She showed more emotion than she did as Scarlett O'Hara, furious that Ashley has chosen Melanie over her."

Garbo must have been gone with Larry for about an hour. When she came back into the living room, she kissed Cukor on the cheek and thanked him for inviting her. Then she left the party without meeting the other guests, including Vivien.

Two views of **Greta Garbo**
(top photo) as *Mata Hari* (1931)
and *(lower photo)* as *Queen Christina* (1933).

Ad slogans for the 1933 film defined her as "A 17th century maiden who loved with a 20th century madness."

Larry came back into the room and joined Kanin, Cukor, and Vivien, each eager for details about the face-to-face meeting of Larry with Garbo, whom he had not seen since she'd fired him from *Queen Christina*.

"First, off," Larry said, "I told the Swede I applauded her for having the good taste to get rid of me on that picture. I know now I wasn't up for it and could have seriously fucked up my career. I told her I have no bitterness for her, only admiration."

"She must have loved hearing that," Vivien said sarcastically. "I will never forgive the

Swedish cow for how she humiliated you. The nerve of her coming here today to confront you. On Christmas, no less."

"She was quite apologetic to me, actually," Larry said. "She blamed Irving Thalberg and Louis B. Mayer for firing me—not herself."

"Of course, she'd say that," Kanin chimed in.

"Vivien accused Olivier of behaving like a ninny once Garbo entered the room," Kanin later recalled.

"You were stumbling all over yourself, sucking up to her," Vivien said to Larry. "You were treating her as if she were the real Queen Christina."

"Garbo told me she wants me to star with her in an upcoming picture, and she hopes George here will direct it," Larry said.

All faces turned to Cukor. "I don't know about that. The way things are going on *Two-Faced Woman*, that picture might be Garbo's swan song. Now that her European markets are closed off to us because of the War Embargoes, her box office allure isn't what it used to be."

At the end of the party, Kanin agreed to drive Larry and Vivien back to where they were staying. "You could cut the tension between them with a knife," Kanin recalled. "She was spoiling for a fight. The press called them the most romantic couple in the world. They were anything but."

"Larry kept trying to calm her down," Kanin said. "He kept saying, 'Puss, Puss, now, now Puss.' I guess that was his nickname for her. Perhaps short for pussy."

"You were like a lovesick schoolboy around Garbo," Vivien shouted at Larry. "You're a rotten liar. I don't believe for a moment you told the real truth about what happened between you and Garbo."

"When I arrived, Vivien bounded out of the car and didn't even thank me for the ride," Kanin said. "Larry shook my hand and thanked me. I stood watching his back as he left to deal with her. I knew then that he would never really make her happy. I'm sure there would be high points in their life together, but always incredible lows, the lows becoming bigger than the highs as the years went by."

Garbo was not entirely bluffing when she spoke of one day starring in a movie with Larry. She tried for months to stage a comeback after the war, attempting to arrange a star role for herself in a movie based on the life of George Sand, with Larry playing opposite her. The project fell through when financing could not be arranged.

She would make one final stab at a comeback, when Luchino Visconti asked her to play the role of Queen Sofia of Naples in Marcel Proust's *Remembrance of Things Past*. She requested Larry for a role in the film along with Marlon Brando and Alain Delon. Production was scheduled to begin in France, but Visconti was not able to raise enough money to meet Garbo's demands. The project was called off, and Garbo's comeback would remain only a dream.

***

There were other Hollywood parties to attend before the year's end. Vivien and Larry were designated as the honored guests at one of Cukor's Sunday afternoon gatherings. Katharine Hepburn was also invited. "I still haven't forgiven her for taking the role of Scarlett O'Hara from me," Hepburn told Cukor.

Cukor retorted that "you should blame David Selznick for that. Come on over and meet Vivien. She'll be there with Larry. You'll love her."

Finally, Hepburn acquiesced. She'd met Larry before on Broadway when both of them had worked for the dreaded Jed Harris.

"At first, Kate, when she got to my party, circled Vivien like Indians around an armed camp of early settlers, waiting to move in for the kill," Cukor said. "But when the women started talking, they found they had much in common. It was the beginning of a life-long friendship, even though they would be up for some of the same roles in the future."

During the first fifteen minutes, however, that friendship got off to a rough start. When Larry excused himself to talk to Cukor, Hepburn found an opening. She was well aware that Vivien and Larry had been living together while married to others.

"You know, of course, that you're marrying a homosexual," Hepburn said. Normally, she wasn't that vicious but the loss of the Scarlett role had been painful.

Katharine Hepburn

(inset photo)
Vivien, outraged, as Scarlett O'Hara

"Oh, darling," Vivien said, seemingly not at all alarmed by Hepburn's warning. "You Americans are so silly about such things. In Britain, we know that all actors are homosexuals, some more than others. That's why we have such great theater."

As Hepburn later related to Cukor, "that remark coming from one so young made me enthralled with Vivien. It was not her fault that she was cast as Scarlett. Regrettably, of course, because I would have made a much better Scarlett."

Before the year's end, there was one

final party hosted by Myron Selznick at his Lake Arrowhead retreat, 90 miles east of Los Angeles. He'd asked his client, Merle Oberon, to compose the guest list and to function as the hostess. She willingly agreed, perhaps too willingly. Myron chartered a luxurious bus to pick up his weekend guests at various points within Los Angeles and then haul them collectively off to the lake.

When she boarded the bus, Vivien was shocked to see that Oberon had invited three losers in the Scarlett O'Hara sweepstakes, notably Paulette Goddard, Miriam Hopkins, and Joan Bennett.

"All we're missing is Bette Davis," Vivien whispered to Larry.

As Vivien passed her on her way to a seat, Goddard had deliberately engrossed herself in an intense conversation with their mutual friend David Niven.

At the back of the bus, Vivien discovered Errol Flynn hanging out with the jazz combo that Myron had hired to perform en route. She was literally mesmerized by him. As he spoke to her, after kissing her on the mouth, she found him devastatingly handsome and charming. Both of them expressed sorrow that he wouldn't be playing Rhett to her Scarlett.

Larry joined them, and Flynn kissed him on the mouth too, as succulently as he had Vivien.

Animated by the music from the jazz combo, the guests exchanged seats on the bus like musical chairs, each getting to talk to each other. Vivien remained in her seat but was engaged in dialogue by most of the other guests at one time or another before the bus finally reached Lake Arrowhead.

For a portion of the ride, Joan Bennett sat beside her and congratulated her on winning the role. "Cukor told me I was too highly polished and very socialite—more like a New York debutante than an Atlanta belle," Bennett said to Vivien. "Cukor also told me I was just too glib."

"You would have been marvelous," Vivien assured her.

Bitchery on the Bus
(aka, "Getting There Is Half the Fun")

(left to right), Joan Bennett, Miriam Hopkins, Paulette Goddard

Bennett said she was shocked to learn that Goddard had lost the role. "I thought she was a shoe-in. Look at the bitch up there, all tanned and beautiful. She's just gotten back from Bermuda where she was the house guest of Jock Whitney. He's Selznick's chief money man."

Miriam Hopkins also joined Vivien. In spite of her fiercely combative reputation, she seemed relatively kind. "I knew I'd lost out on the role long ago," Hopkins said, "even though I'm a daughter of the Old South. When I heard that you'd been cast, I nearly jumped for joy. Anybody, *but anybody*, other than Bette Davis."

On the bus, Vivien had been prepared not to like Hopkins, but ended up becoming friends with her and her husband, director Anatole Litvak. During their time on the West Coast, Vivien and Larry visited Hopkins on several occasions at their beach house. They were often joined by Ronald Colman and his wife, Benita.

Vivien was fascinated to watch Flynn jitterbugging in the aisle of the bus. "When Errol sat down beside me," Vivien later said to Larry, "he couldn't keep his hands off me."

"When he sat down beside me," Larry confided, "he couldn't keep his hands off me either. He told me I could come over to his place in the afternoon for a nude swim while you're at the studio playing Scarlett."

"Did you accept?" she asked.

"Of course, I did," he said. "What man or woman in their right mind would turn down an invitation from Errol Flynn?" Seeing the look of concern on her face, he told her, "Don't be too concerned. I told him to be discreet."

At the house party, Goddard was overheard telling friends, "I thought Vivien Leigh was rather mousey when I first met her. Perhaps she can play Scarlett O'Hara as a little brown wren. When she spoke in that delicate voice of hers, she didn't sound like a Southern belle to me. I was flabbergasted when David cast her in a fit of madness. Who is she anyway? Olivier's whore. She's completely untalented and wrong for the role. Charlie [a reference to Charlie Chaplin] agrees with me. He told me that Miss Leigh will ruin the movie, and that I could have won an Oscar as Scarlett."

***

In the cold light of a Monday morning, on January 16, 1939, the glow of receiving the role of Scarlett dimmed when she learned she was to be paid only $1,250 a week and had to sign a seven-year contract with Selznick. She was even more disappointed when she tallied up, learning that she would make only $25,000 at the end of the picture. She'd spend grueling months up to her neck in the most exhausting and demanding role she'd ever play until she came across Tennessee Williams' Blanche DuBois in *A Streetcar Named Desire*. "That's about what I'd be paid if I still worked in England," she told Cukor.

News that Vivien Leigh, a relatively unknown British actress, had been cast in the coveted role of Scarlett O'Hara was immediately flashed around the world. Myron had plotted for Vivien to sign the contract without letting Larry know. When he found out it included a seven-year commitment to David Selznick, he exploded in fury.

The next day he burst into Selznick's office to confront him. "I'm going to marry Vivien," he shouted at the producer. "You can't tie her up in such a long-term bondage contract."

"The deed is done," Selznick said. "How can you forget when I was head of RKO and wanted Jill for *A Bill of Divorcement*? You insisted that your wife return to London with you. Larry, don't be a shit twice."

He backed down and gave in to Selznick.

Selznick was very critical of Larry in an interview he gave in 1944. "Olivier tried in every possible way to prevent my casting of Vivien as Scarlett O'Hara. He claimed he was dead set against it. In England he'd just pretended to encourage her pursuit of the role. He didn't really want her to do it. Privately, he told me, 'Casting an English girl as a Southern heroine, that's absurd. Vivien will be ridiculed in the role, her fake accent mocked.' Frankly, I think Olivier was afraid that Vivien would become a bigger star than he was, that *Gone With the Wind* would end up competing against *Wuthering Heights*, which it did. Also, he was being selfish. He knew that if Vivien became a success, she wouldn't go back to England with him."

In Hollywood, Selznick was feverishly trying to generate as much press coverage as he could. He wired Margaret Mitchell in Atlanta that "I promise to make Scarlett O'Hara live as you described her in your brilliant book." He sent her a stunning photograph of Vivien at her most beautiful. The author sent back her approval with a note. "If Bette Davis was cast, audiences might confuse Jezebel with Scarlett."

Logos associated with the United Daughters of the Confederacy.

"Better an English gal (as Scarlett O'Hara) than a Yankee like Katharine Hepburn or Bette Davis."

Selznick also announced to the press that Vivien was married to a London barrister and was the devoted mother of a little girl. No mention was made, of course, of Larry.

The producer feared a backlash from the

Daughters of the Confederacy when they learned of the casting. But the president of the club told the press, "Better an English gal than a Yankee like Katharine Hepburn or Bette Davis. Of course, our favorite was Miss Tallulah Bankhead of Alabama."

"That fucking English bitch," Carole Lombard shouted at Clark Gable when she learned that she'd lost the role of Scarlett O'Hara to a twenty-five-year-old relatively unknown English actress. Lombard was hoping that she could play the lead along with Gable, her lover. "I heard from an unimpeachable authority that the cunt slept with David O. Selznick himself. I bet the limey whore even gave fatso rim jobs."

Until she died in a plane crash in 1942, Lombard would continue to refer

to Vivien as "that fucking English bitch who married Olivier, that cocksucker." Lombard was known, of course, for her potty mouth.

Mitchell didn't object to the casting of Vivien as Scarlett, but she had serious reservations about giving the role of Rhett Butler to Clark Gable.

Soon, Gable learned that Margaret Mitchell did not want him to play Rhett. Earlier she had nixed the idea of Norma Shearer as Scarlett—"too much dignity and not enough fire."

Without Kay Brown, Selznick's personal assistant, he might never have produced *Gone With the Wind.* It was she who discovered a then-unpublished manuscript about the American Civil War and brought it to her boss's attention. Based on her recommendation, Selznick optioned *Gone With the Wind.*

Kay also functioned as the agent who convinced Selznick, at RKO, to sign Larry to his first American contract. Among many other accomplishments, she urged Alfred Hitchcock to direct *Rebecca.* She was even instrumental in persuading Gable to appear in *Gone With the Wind* as Rhett Butler.

Born to the American purple, Brown had been launched in Hollywood by none other than Joseph Kennedy. She worked under him (emphasis on "under").

To Kay Brown, Margaret Mitchell wrote,

Players & Heavy Hitters:

(top photo) Kay Brown with financier Jock Whitney
(bottom photo)
Carole Lombard with Clark Gable

336

"Clark Gable is not our choice of Rhett here in the Old South. He doesn't look Southern or act Southern and in no way conforms to our notion of a Low Country Carolinian. In looks and in conduct Basil Rathbone has been the first choice in our area, with Fredric March and Ronald Colman running second and third."

"Is Mitchell out of her fucking mind?" Gable asked Selznick. "All those guys are pale-faced drawing room dandies, hardly the description of Rhett Butler."

"I completely agree with you," Selznick said. "Oh, my God, I can't believe my own ears. Here I am agreeing to something Clark Gable said."

Gable was infuriated the very next day when he read a review of *Gone With the Wind* that suggested that Rhett Butler was a secret homosexual. "Let's face it," the critic wrote, "Rhett Butler buys the latest Paris fashions for Scarlett and seems very sophisticated about Paris couture. He's also a fancy dresser, no doubt wearing perfumed underpanties when most of his downtrodden fellow Southerners are in tattered, lice-enriched clothing. In other words, a fancy dandy who I suspect secretly wanted Ashley Wilkes for himself. That's the real reason he's jealous of Scarlett. He seems to possess an intuitive understanding of the interests of women and is the perfect *confidante* for a woman. Although he's supposed to be a real man, his masculinity is threatened by Scarlett."

What really infuriated Gable was when Cukor read the article and facetiously told Gable that he should play Rhett as a homosexual—"perhaps raising your pinkie when you take a drink." Gable later claimed, "I almost struck Cukor in his cocksucking mouth that day."

Gable reported to work in an angry mood, itching for a fight with Selznick, who had sent nearly one hundred pages of instructions to him the previous night on how he was to play Rhett Butler.

To try to get him out of his bleak mood, Lombard had a parcel delivered to Gable's dressing room. It was a hand-knitted "cock-sock." Her card read, "Don't let it get cold. Bring it home hot for me."

Gable completely exploded when costume designer Walter Plunkett fitted him for his wardrobe as Rhett Butler. Rejecting every costume, Gable stormed into Selznick's office.

"These tight trousers make me look like a faggot," Gable told Selznick. "The collars are too tight. They make my neck look like a bull's. What about these fucking jackets? Far too short. The goddamn sleeves exaggerate my wrists and hands."

"Now, now Clark," Selznick said. "The costumes are authentic to the period. Wear them with your customary grace and style."

"While we're at it," Gable said, "What made you hire this pansy woman's

337

director? The queer will favor Scarlett and Melanie, and virtually overlook Rhett Butler in every scene. Cukor should go back to directing that lesbian cunt, Katharine Hepburn. If that Miss High-and-Mighty ever saw a man's dick, she would run screaming all the way back to Connecticut."

Cukor and Gable also fought over his accent, Cukor demanding a more pronounced pattern of Southern dipthongs. "You speak in a twang from some bog in Ohio," Cukor lambasted Gable.

"I'm speaking like Clark Gable," he said. "If you don't like it, fucker, I'll walk off the picture." Finally, Cukor gave in to Gable's demand and retained his normal speech patterns in his portrayal of Rhett Butler.

With what for the time was an astonishingly high budget, *Gone With the Wind* started shooting on January 23, 1939. The film would wrap on June 27, an exhausting six months that would lead to nervous breakdowns for some of the cast and crew.

***

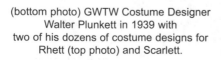

(bottom photo) GWTW Costume Designer Walter Plunkett in 1939 with two of his dozens of costume designs for Rhett (top photo) and Scarlett.

Meanwhile, Vivien was having her own troubles. Her main fear was that she was still under contract to Alexander Korda.

At a party at the home of Myron Selznick, she came face to face with the English producer and pleaded with him to release her to Selznick. At the time, Vivien was legally bound to an exclusive contract to make films for Korda.

"You're not right for the role of Scarlett O'Hara," Korda angrily told her. "If I owned the rights to *Gone With the Wind*, I would never have cast you. It'll ruin your promising career." He never explained why.

In spite of his reservations, the Hungarian agreed to order his attorneys to release Vivien so she could play Scarlett. "Thank you, thank you," she said, kissing him, "and please don't tell Selznick that I'm wrong for *Gone With the Wind*. I've fooled the sucker."

She wrote Leigh asking him to bring her up to date on all the news and expressed her fear about the war clouds looming over England. She told him that she feared for Suzanne's safety in the event of war, and wondered if he'd agree to allow her to go to Canada or America for the duration of the war. She once again pressed him for a divorce and warned him that she might be in the States for many months shooting *Gone With the Wind*.

As she became entrenched in Hollywood, there were other pressing matters left unattended in London.

The time had come to make the final split from her London agent, John Gliddon. She cabled Gliddon that a deal was being worked out between Selznick and Korda. "YOU WILL PARTICIPATE IN THE KORDA SET-UP ONLY," she cabled. That meant that Gliddon was being left out of her contract with Selznick and the earnings from *Gone With the Wind*. He was angry at her and bitterly disappointed, because he took credit for having launched her career.

After mulling it over, he finally agreed to break from her if he were paid 2,700 pounds in three equal yearly installments, "this figure being the minimum amount of my loss."

Amazingly, Vivien turned down this sweetheart rescue. In an earlier era, Gliddon had adored Vivien and had worked ceaselessly to build up her image as a star, paying the cost out of his meager earnings. "Now she's gone Hollywood and thrown me under a double-decker bus."

Back in Hollywood, William Price, the actor husband of actress Maureen O'Hara, worked with Vivien on her Southern accent. He found her a bright pupil quick and eager to learn. He recalled, "Vivien was a bawdy little thing and hot as a firecracker, and lovely to look at. Can't understand why Larry Olivier when she could have anybody."

In England, Vivien had become known for shamelessly cursing and uttering profanities in public, but this tendency of hers came as a total surprise to the Americans with whom she now worked in Hollywood.

In the middle of one of Vivien's lessons with Price, she received a call from Selznick's office. The producer wanted both Larry and Vivien to report to his office at ten o'clock the following morning.

Two weeks previously, Larry had rented a house for Vivien and himself at 510 North Crescent Drive in Hollywood.

Once in his office, "the adulterers" learned that on the previous day, gossip maven Louella Parsons had called and pointedly asked Selznick if Larry and Vivien were living together at their rented house. Selznick denied it.

He told the lovers that the reason he did not cast Paulette Goddard as Scarlett was because of her on-going affair with Charlie Chaplin. "They say they're married, but Paulette couldn't produce a marriage license. Even Gable and Carole Lombard are pretending to live in different houses. I'm investing my left testicle in *Gone With the Wind*, and I don't want a scandal about Scarlett and Heathcliff breaking in the press when I've already shot half the film."

"What do you suggest we do, Mr. Selznick?" Larry asked.

"Until your divorces come through, I'm asking that you be discreet," Selznick said. "I don't want you seen in public cooing over each other. As for you, Larry, I've arranged for you to live temporarily in a house I've rented for Leslie Howard."

"But Leslie is a married man, and he's living there with his mistress," Larry protested.

"But Leslie is not cast as Scarlett O'Hara," Selznick said. "Vivien, as you must surely know by now, is going to be the most gossiped about and watched young actress in Hollywood."

Selznick also forbade Larry to come onto the set of *Gone With the Wind*, fearing some photographer would snap Vivien and Larry as a romantic duo.

Vivien and Larry caved in to Selznick's request, learning that he had rented a house for her at 520 North Camden Drive. He'd also arranged for his secretary, Sunny Alexander (who later changed her name to Sunny Lash) to live with Vivien.

"I'll be a prisoner with a guard?" Vivien asked.

"Yes, there will be a 24-hour security guard to keep the press at bay," Selznick said. "Larry can sneak in late at night, when Sunny will go to her room."

With their living arrangements secured this way, Vivien hated having to slip around in the middle of the night to meet her lover. She also dreaded her upcoming first meeting with Clark Gable.

Worried that Vivien had designs on Gable, Lombard the next day was Vivien's first visitor to the set of *Gone With the Wind*. Their meeting in Vivien's dressing room was chilly. Lombard was still fuming mad that she had not been cast as Scarlett O'Hara opposite her real life lover.

The outspoken Lombard seemed to want to diminish Gable's reputation as a means of preventing any possible liaison between Vivien and Gable. "He may be called the King of Hollywood," Lombard said, "but if he had one inch less, he'd be the Queen of Hollywood. And, lest you get your silly English schoolgirl hopes up, Clark is less than Mount Vesuvius under the sheets. He's a lousy lay. Just ask Joan Crawford."

"I will be no threat to your affair," Vivien assured her. "I hear Mr. Gable has false teeth and foul breath. I also hear that by eleven o'clock in the morning, he smells like a brewery."

"Clark has his faults, and god knows I've had better lovers," Lombard said. "William Powell, for instance. But there is no understanding the ways of love, and I love Clark and plan to marry him if I can keep him from vixens like you."

"Leslie Howard is more my type," Vivien said. "Like Scarlett O'Hara, I plan to pursue Ashley Wilkes. As for Rhett Butler, I have him to come home to every night. His name is Laurence Olivier."

"Listen, Miss Scarlett, everybody in Hollywood—not the general public—knows that you and Errol Flynn are wearing that English man out."

"I was unaware that my private life was the subject of such gossip," Vivien said.

"Are you kidding?" Lombard said. "At every party in Hollywood, you and Larry are the hottest topics."

"You should be grateful to me," Vivien said. "I've taken the pressure off you and Gable in the gossip columns."

Vivien perhaps was referring to Kirtley Baskette's exposé article about "Hollywood's Unmarried Husbands and Wives." Gable and Lombard were the prime examples cited, although the reporter named other unmarried couples living together, including Barbara Stanwyck and Robert Taylor, and Constance Bennett and Gilbert Roland.

Before leaving that day, Lombard had warmed considerably to Vivien, especially when Lombard learned that Vivien possessed a potty mouth almost as foul as her legendary one.

At the door to the dressing room, Lombard turned to say goodbye. Before she did, she reached into her purse. "I have a note to you. When you read it, I think you can forget all about Olivier and that older gentleman known as Leslie Howard. Who would want that one?"

After Lombard left, Vivien opened the note. It read:

Please meet me at two o'clock this morning at a location I will give you later in the day. It will be on a street in downtown Los Angeles. I want to sign you to an exclusive contract. Don't, repeat don't, sign with Selznick.

He's a dirty Jew and will fuck you over.
Howard Hughes

She was startled by the note, having just learned that the aviator was dating Olivia de Havilland and had even proposed marriage to her. Not only that, but he'd also proposed marriage to Joan Fontaine, Olivia's estranged sister.

By three o'clock that afternoon, a messenger arrived with another note from Hughes, giving the location in front of a building where Hughes wanted to have a rendezvous with her. A mysterious phone number was also enclosed.

As far as it is known, she tore up the note and did not respond to the offer.

Ironically, when Larry slipped in through the back door of her home to make love to her later that night, he told her of an incredible afternoon he'd spent.

"Howard Hughes, of all people, took Errol and me flying over Los Angeles," he said. "Later we went back to Errol's house and had a swim. *Au naturel*, of course. That Hughes is quite a man. He carries around an endowment that is larger than that of most universities."

The very next day, Scarlett O'Hara had been scheduled to meet Rhett Butler on the set of *Gone With the Wind*. MGM's publicity department had asked them to pose for stills dressed in costume.

Cukor claimed that Gable resented Vivien even before he met her. When Cukor had met with Gable to discuss his role as Rhett, the director said that his star had poured out his resentment.

"As far as I'm concerned, Vivien Leigh is a slut," Gable claimed. "She lets Olivier fuck her in the ass but she's a married woman with a kid—boy or girl—in London. Who cares? She's flaunting her affair with Olivier and getting away with it. Me and Carole get blasted all over the newspapers. We're mad as hell about this thing. Carole is doubly pissed because she would have made the greatest Scarlett O'Hara."

Billionaire and aviator, the notorious Howard Hughes, in 1938

Before leaving, Gable turned to Cukor. "I'm going to hate this fucking movie, and I want you to know that upfront. If I see that you, the so-called woman's director, is throwing the picture to Vivien, I walk."

"That won't happen," Cukor promised. "I'm too much of a professional to let that happen."

At the door as he was leaving, Gable

paused. "Everybody tells me Olivier likes both kinds of sugartits, male or female. It doesn't matter with him. But, of course, you would know more about that than I would." He turned and left.

On the set, as agreed on the occasion of their first meeting, Gable, who was fully aware of his star power, was kept waiting by Vivien for an entire hour.

"I couldn't make love to this dame if she were the most beautiful woman in the world," Gable told Howard Strickling of MGM publicity. "In fact, I might just walk off the picture and not come back."

No sooner had he said that than he smelled lilacs in spring and heard the rustle of silk.

"I quite agree, Mr. Gable," came a voice entering the set behind him. "If I were a man, I'd tell that Vivien Leigh to go straight back to England and fuck herself. Or else I'd throw her a good fuck myself to teach her who's boss."

Gable broke into laughter at meeting what he later called "this gutsy dame." For the time being at least, the tension between them was relieved, and they posed for some very dramatic stills which ran in newspapers across the country.

Later, after her meeting with Gable, Vivien told Olivia de Havilland, "I do not think Mr. Gable is too bright. Certainly not very responsive as an actor like Larry is."

Vivien astonished Gable during the first weeks of production. He had just assumed she was a proper English lady, but found out she had more in common with his lover, Carole Lombard, than she had with the Queen of England.

One afternoon she became annoyed when a malfunctioning lighting switch held up production. "What in bloody hell are they fucking around for?" Vivien shouted with Gable standing nearby. "My god damn makeup's running in this blasted heat. California is a fucking desert, fit for habitation only by rattlesnakes."

For her scenes with Gable, Vivien never showed up on time, and he demanded punctuality. "Olivier's whore is keeping me waiting once again," he said to Cukor. "Doesn't that bitch know I'm the King of Hollywood?"

"Now, now, my darling," Cukor told him. "Would you like me to go down on you like I did in 1928 and relieve some of your tension? I still remember that night."

Furious, Gable stormed off the set. He later told Leslie Howard and others, "That fucking queen's gone too far. I don't think I can stand to work another day with him as director."

Emanuel Levy, the biographer of Cukor, claims, "Cukor knew of Gable's days as a hustler in the Hollywood gay circuit when the actor first arrived in Los Angeles. One of these sexual encounters was with William Haines, an

343

actor who later became Cukor's friend and designer."

Cukor's very presence reminded the macho actor of his dubious past. To his co-workers, Gable constantly referred to Selznick as "the Jewboy" and to Cukor as "that faggot."

Gable became particularly infuriated when he heard that Anderson Lawler, the on-again, off-again lover of Gary Cooper, had attended one of Cukor's Sunday afternoon gatherings. As reported to Gable, Lawler had said, "Oh, George is directing one of Billy's old tricks." Whereas the reference to "Billy" was about Haines, the reference to "Billy's old trick" was about Gable himself, and as such, "Rhett Butler" was mortified.

During his early career, when Gable was "gay for pay" (before the term was invented) in the late 1920s, he had let Haines service him for twenty dollars, good pay back then, before Haines passed him on to Cukor himself.

From the set of *Gone With the Wind*, Gable called Haines and threatened him with physical violence if he didn't stop telling tales about the actor's early days trying to break into Hollywood.

Joan Crawford, who had endured as Gable's on-again, off-again lover, was still fuming about her loss of the role of Scarlett when she spoke privately. She claimed, "Clark hated making *Gone With the Wind*. He absolutely detested George Cukor, who was a discreet homosexual. George, bless him, was my favorite director. But Clark could not stand working with him. To make matters worse, George constantly referred to Clark as 'dear' on the set. But he called everybody that, male or female. Clark also resented an English girl taking the part of Scarlett. I tried to talk him out of some of his resentments, but he was a very stubborn man. He had the upper hand in Hollywood at that time. He had power and knew how to use it. I feared George's days were numbered as the director of *Gone With the Wind*."

One day Gable in exasperation told Vivien, "I just can't play this god damn Rhett Butler. He's not my kind of guy."

"On the contrary, sir," Vivien shot back. "I think you fit the role perfectly. After all, like Rhett, you have a way of looking at women as if they are naked."

Under Cukor's direction, Gable was finding the role of Rhett more and more uncomfortable. Tensions flared between Cukor and Gable, and this only increased Vivien's nervousness.

Gable continued to complain about every costume he was fitted for, and, finally, demanded that his own tailor, Eddie Schmidt, be brought in to design the Rhett Butler outfits. Selznick gave in to Gable's demands.

To make matters worse on the almost unbearably tense set, Selznick every day sent changes of dialogue to his actors, including Vivien, at the last minute.

"Selznick constantly appeared on the set and interfered with Cukor's direction," Vivien said. "The producer felt his director was going too slow, languishing over parlor scenes and not getting the bigger picture. He also didn't like my breasts, finding them a little too meager for his tastes. He even bought fuller bras for me."

Selznick seemed obsessed with mammaries, especially those of Scarlett O'Hara. As Vivien remembered, she went through a series of more than two dozen brassieres from wardrobe. Overseeing the action was Selznick smoking a giant cigar. "More pointed!" he yelled at the wardrobe mistress. "Lower the left nipple!" he shouted.

Finally, in desperation, Vivien asked for some privacy, disappearing into her dressing room and locking the door. She emerged thirty minutes later.

Selznick immediately welcomed her back on the set and checked out her *décolletage*. "See how much better you look now?" he said to her.

"It's just plain me," she told Selznick. "*Fiddle-dee-dee*, at last you've found a pair of tits to your liking. You're definitely a breast man, Mr. Selznick."

The opening shot on *Gone With the Wind* was of a very young Scarlett flirting with the Tarleton twins on the front porch of Twelve Oaks. The twins were played by Fred Crane and George Reeves, the latter eventually becoming famous on TV as Superman.

Selznick had grave doubts when he first saw the rushes of Vivien as Scarlett. Something wasn't quite right with her characterization, but he couldn't pinpoint it. Over the following six months he would order the porch scene re-shot several times. The scene on the veranda, in fact, became both the first and final one shot for *Gone With the Wind*.

In the final take, Vivien looked much older and very haggard, with dark circles under her eyes. The exhaustion of making *Gone With the Wind* clearly showed on her face. In desperation, Selznick went back to the first version, and that was the scene shown around the world.

During the course of the shoot, Gable learned that he was a

MOVIE SCENES WE LOVE, VIGNETTES WE REMEMBER:
During Reconstruction, Scarlett O'Hara hits "the New Atlanta" with Mammy as her chaperone.

free man at long last. After a five-minute hearing, a California District Judge, William Orr, granted the divorce after hearing Ria Langham Gable's testimony that her husband had deserted her in October of 1935. Gable did not show up in court, but had agreed to a settlement reportedly around $300,000, which he borrowed from MGM as an advance against future earnings.

Shortly thereafter, when a break came in filming, he slipped off to a remote location where he married Lombard in the sleepy little town of Kingman, Arizona.

Returning from his brief honeymoon, Gable greeted Vivien with a smile. Whereas his marital situation had at last been straightened out, hers had not, and she almost resented him for that.

She also resented Larry for languishing around Hollywood after the filming of *Wuthering Heights*. And although he was officially looking for his next meal ticket, he was nonetheless enjoying himself immensely with Errol Flynn.

When he sneaked in to see Vivien late at night, Larry seemed tanned and rested, having spent the day around Flynn's pool. Vivien surely must have wondered what was going on between her prospective husband and Flynn. On the set of *Gone With the Wind*, Olivia de Havilland had related many tall tales about the swashbuckling star. Cukor, too, had dozens of details about the escapades of Flynn.

At one point, Vivien, in front of Sunny Lash, told Larry, "I fear Flynn will completely corrupt you before you leave Hollywood."

"My sweet little tiny baby girl," Larry said. "It is impossible to corrupt the corrupted."

That was not very reassuring to Vivien's ears.

***

Both Vivien and Olivia de Havilland witnessed the big blow-up between Cukor and Gable. When Cukor did not like any of the dance scenes with Vivien and Gable during the film's depiction of a fund-raising bazaar in Atlanta, Gable signaled the musicians to stop playing. Dressed in her "widow's weeds," Vivien stood by silently.

"Fuck this!" Gable said. "I want to be directed by a man—not a fairy!" He walked off the set.

Embarrassed and humiliated in front of cast and crew, Cukor also walked off the set, heading in another direction.

Lee Garmes, one of the cinematographers, also witnessed the outburst. "It was obvious to all of us that Cukor was finished that day. There is no way he would have gone on with the picture after that."

Russell Birdwell, the publicist, spotted Gable leaving the Metro lot in his

346

Dusenberg roadster. He rushed over to see what was the matter.

"Tell Selznick I'm not reporting back to work until he fires Cukor and gets another director." He drove off.

True to his word, Gable remained gone for a week and refused to answer his telephone. Rumors circulated throughout Hollywood that Selznick had fired Gable, not Cukor. There was an even bigger rumor that Selznick had pulled the plug on *Gone With the Wind*.

Despite Cukor's standing as one of Selznick's best friends, Cukor was called in to be fired. Ironically, within his endless memos, Selznick never left any clue that he fired Cukor because Gable would not let him direct him.

Of course, Gable was certainly a factor in Cukor's downfall, but there were other more pressing reasons. Selznick did not like the rushes he'd seen of *Gone With the Wind*. When confronted with this, Cukor blamed the poor script. Previously, he'd delivered an ultimatum to Selznick that unless the script was improved, he, too, would walk off the picture.

Perhaps that was the final straw for Selznick. "I'm sorry, George," was all he could say. Selznick didn't actually fire Cukor that day, but the next morning he ordered Henry Ginsberg, his general manager and hatchetman, to do the dirty deed.

Selznick told Ginsberg, "George is just too fussy. He doesn't get the grand scope of *Gone With the Wind*. He is more concerned that the petticoats be made of genuine Val lace than he is of the overall storyline."

Vivien and Olivia were still wearing their widow's black mourning dresses, their costumes for the bazaar scene, when they heard the news that Cukor had been sacked. They immediately rushed to Selznick's office, finding the harried producer surviving on a mixture of thyroid tablets, Benzedrine, and sleeping pills.

Both Olivia and Vivien demanded that Selznick rehire Cukor. But the producer remained adamant. "Please, please ladies," he told them. "Vivien, you must remember you're cast in a role that any actress on earth would fuck Quasimodo to win. As for you, Olivia, you are a very expensive trinket I purchased with my last dime from Jack Warner, that

A Charity Fundraiser in the Old South
The movie scene that ended George Cukor's involvement in GWTW.

347

walking piece of shit. You've got to excuse me. I've got to find another director for *Gone With the Wind*." He dismissed both of them from his office.

Howard Strickling of MGM publicity said, "Clark wasn't the sole reason Cukor was fired. But Clark's dim view of Cukor contributed to the director's sacking. Clark complained to me all the time about Cukor. They weren't getting along at all. He wanted Victor Fleming to direct, claiming he would put some guts into the picture. Clark was very spunky. Of course, there was that personal thing."

Strickling, of course, didn't explain, but over the years the conflict between Gable and Cukor became legendary and was referred to as "the pansy thing."

Cukor later said, "Clark is a liar to say I was just a woman's director. Pure nonsense, and my screen credits prove that. He accused me of throwing the picture to Scarlett. That was very naïve of him. If the script dictated it, I put the emphasis on Scarlett. When the script shifted to Rhett Butler, so did I. Gable has no self-confidence in himself as an actor. He's a very insecure man, and was very nervous about every scene I directed him in. He's got serious problems, some of which are sexual. *I should know*."

***

As if Vivien didn't have enough troubles on the set, she came home to find an irritated Larry, who told her that even with her here in Hollywood, he could not tolerate another night in California.

After his completion of *Wuthering Heights*, there were no more film offers. His role as Heathcliff, of course, had not come to the attention of the film world, including directors. That acclaim lay in his future.

"It's better not to smudge my reputation just hanging around," Larry said. "Besides, when *Gone With the Wind* is released and we're married, I'm going to be known as Mr. Scarlett O'Hara. We'll miss each other but I signed a deal to return to Broadway to star in *No Time for Comedy* opposite Katharine Cornell."

Sitting in the living room was Sunny Lash, Vivien's roommate. She would later claim that, "Vivien just exploded that night. I'd never seen anything like it. She picked up any object she could and began throwing that missile at Larry. She was completely crazed."

"I don't remember all the vile things she said to him, but she was deranged," Sunny claimed. The biggest accusation was that he was afraid that she was going to become a bigger movie star than he was."

"You failed in pictures, you bloody, untalented fool," she shouted at him. "You failed in stage play after stage play. But even before the release of *Gone*

With the Wind, there is talk that I'm going to become the biggest movie star in the world. No thanks to you, you ungrateful louse. You're a parasite sucking my blood. I don't want to ever see you again. No, I will not marry you."

Lash claimed that within ten minutes, while Larry was packing, Vivien underwent a total transformation. By the time he was heading for the door, she ran after him.

"You can't leave me now," she pleaded with him. "What will I do? There is no one to stand by me now that George is fired. I'm facing an unknown director. Don't you care, even a little bit?"

Lash reported that Larry's face was ashen as he looked at Vivien with loathing.

"Without you by my side to protect me, what's going to happen to me?"

"Frankly, my dear, I don't give a damn." He turned his back on her and, with suitcase in hand, headed into the California night.

Two Yankee redheads and a blonde: Hopefuls for the role of Scandalous Scarlett in
GONE WITH THE WIND
Would movie history have been different?
And would Rhett (or Larry) have told any of THEM that he didn't give a damn?

| Susan Hayward | Lucille Ball | Lana Turner |

350

CHAPTER NINE

In late March, 1939, the moment Larry arrived in New York, after his abrupt departure from Los Angeles, he telephoned Vivien for a reconciliation. Her flare-up and attack on him, followed by her plea for forgiveness, and then a reconciliation, would be a pattern they'd follow for the rest of their troubled, turbulent marriage.

While he was in New York performing on Broadway, he agreed to wear a carnation in his underwear during every performance and then send it to her in each letter. In turn, she had agreed to send him a pair of her "knickers."

Often heated telephone calls would be followed by long letters. In one, he complained about what he considered an extravagantly expensive cost of $105 for one of their long distance calls. Many times she argued over the phone with him. Each of them usually followed the argument with a letter.

Viv,
Oh my darling little loveling I do adore you so. You're so original. The way you make absolutely no attempt to hide your darling feelings is so adorable! I hope you've noticed what a healthy regard I have for your anger!
Larry

Vivien learned that it had been David O. Selznick who had personally intervened with arrangements for Larry to appear with Katharine Cornell in New York, and Vivien resented her producer deeply for his interference in her private life. Larry's play, *No Time for Comedy,* was being produced by a company controlled by Selznick. Vivien impatiently waited for the end of *Gone With the Wind's* filming so that she'd be out from under his control. Then she was abruptly reminded by Sunny Lash that she'd signed a seven-year contract. "I'll be an old lady before I escape this bondage," Vivien said. "I've plunged down a rabbit hole!"

Years later, Vivien said, "Selznick lived in constant fear of a scandal breaking. That's why he wanted Larry out of town."

Early one morning in New York City, Larry was awakened by a phone call from Sunny in Los Angeles. Half asleep, he heard the dreaded news. Vivien had taken an overdose of sedatives, and Sunny had discovered her staggering around naked and tripping over the furniture. Sunny managed to get her into the shower where she turned on the cold water to revive her. Vivien then collapsed in Sunny's arms.

Larry wanted to rush at once to the West Coast, but Sunny called later that morning, reporting that Vivien had recovered.

He immediately sat down and wrote his beloved:

"Darling baby oh sweet little tiny baby girl, I do love you so. O how terribly touching you are. I do adore you Vivien my darling little girl. O but I ought to be sooooo cross with you. Urrrgh Urrrgh! How dare you take four pills like that you hysterical little ninny (and I know perfectly well you knew people would get alarmed and ring me up and put the fear of God into your poor old Larry at five o'clock in the morning). Urrrgh! Bend over—yes, take your drawers down—no, lift your skirt up—now then: —Smack! Smack! Smack! -!-!-!-!-!-!-!!!!! Yes—Eleven!! Naughty poooossey. Now you come here and I'll kiss it and make it better—Oh my Vivling. Poor Sunny was demented. I'm afraid you lead your loving ones one hell of a dance and that's terribly naughty. You're awfully spoilt yes you are, and it's all because you're so pretty. Ah poor pussey that's enough isn't it? Hey? Oh my dear true love I do adore you and love you so put on a brave front. True blood, stout hearts and grey herrings and pretty pussies and Larry's carnations, and beloved, O beloved Vivlings, don't give way in front of the common herd like this."

Vivien managed to pull herself together and report to the set of *Gone With the Wind* on Monday morning where, as before, she was required to work sixteen hours a day under great mental and physical distress.

There were temperamental fits and bouts of hysteria. She told Ona Munson, "Beware of what you want, for you will surely get it. I wanted to play Scarlett O'Hara, but now I don't want to hear that girl's name mentioned to me ever again. With all the publicity I'm getting, I fear I'll be tainted with the Scarlett legend for the rest of my life."

That was a sentiment she'd continually express again and again.

"Worse things can happen to a working gal," Munson told her, embracing her and holding her in her arms. Vivien snuggled her head into Munson's breasts and felt more comfort than she had since Larry had last embraced her.

Later that afternoon, Vivien confided to Munson that she might be entering into one of her "states" and explained to the actress what that meant.

At that time, Vivien's undiagnosed mental and physical illnesses had not been determined, either her manic depression or her oncoming tuberculosis. Abandoning her usual good manners, she was no longer polite with Selznick and sometimes expressed her resentment at his interference in both the production and his personal interpretation of how she played her role as Scarlett.

One afternoon, Selznick found her crying and trembling on the set of *Gone With the Wind*. He feared for his production if she had a collapse and immediately cabled Larry in New York, fearing he'd made a mistake in sending him away and leaving Vivien to cope on her own. He told his staff, "I did not know this but Vivien is on the verge of a nervous breakdown. She's certainly giving me one. The most temperamental actress I've ever worked with."

That emergency passed, but Selznick followed with an urgent plea for Larry to come at once to the West Coast. "Vivien is on the verge of collapse. Her condition seems to grow worse by the day. Come at once."

Cornell and Guthrie McClintic kindly released Larry from dress rehearsals, allowing him to retrace his now familiar route west, an interconnected series of night flights and refueling stopovers. In Amarillo, Texas, he cabled her with his anticipated arrival time in Burbank, where he hoped he'd have "two glorious days and two even more glorious nights" to spend with her.

Before leaving New York, he'd shoved a letter into his pocket. It turned out to be from his sister Sybille. Other than talking about their father's death, it contained a strange statement. "You know, Kim [her nickname for Larry], I believe that if you and Jill hadn't married, maybe she and I would one day have had a thundering love affair!"

In her nondescript Plymouth, Sunny retrieved Larry at the airport in Burbank at four in the afternoon. Rumpled and tired, he emerged from the airplane in dark glasses, with a hat pulled down over his face.

Sunny drove him to the house she occupied in Beverly Hills with Vivien, who was waiting inside. Sunny had stocked the larder with delicacies that included bottles of Mumm's Extra Dry and Beluga caviar.

"Larry's stay with Vivien was brief," Sunny later recalled. "She greeted him with hysteria like some soldier long feared dead in the war and miraculously returned to life. They were either fucking or fighting during Larry's entire time on the coast. Vivien sometimes could be heard weeping hysterically, with Larry trying to comfort her. Both of their lives were in confusion. These were two very emotional but smart people. Each of them seemed to know that with the release of *Wuthering Heights* and *Gone With the Wind*, they would be on the dawn of world fame. But neither of them seemed conditioned enough to brace themselves for the inevitable, Vivien especially. At times she looked so delicate I feared a strong wind would blow her right out to sea."

"But when I saw those two say good-bye to each other before Larry's departure, I, too, wished that I was in love," Sunny said.

En route to the airport, Larry confided to her, "The fucking was worth putting up with all the fights." There was a long delay at the Burbank airport before the departure of his flight to Indianapolis.

In this Midwestern city, *No Time for Comedy* was launching its out-of-town tryouts en route to Broadway.

On a refueling stop at Albuquerque, he cabled her:

O WHAT A JOYOUS LITTLE RESPITE OUR DEARLING LITTLE FLYING VISIT WAS MY ANGEL—THE JOY OF IT WILL LAST FOR WEEKS. MY LIFE IS PERCHED ON YOUR DARLING LOVE.

Sunny returned to her shared home after depositing Larry at the Burbank airport, she found Vivien eating a plate of California avocados, which had become her favorite food, and smoking incessantly. "I delivered your hunk safely."

"I'll miss him," Vivien said. "I'd much rather get fucked by Larry than open up for Leslie Howard's dick."

S.N. Behrman's play, *No Time for Comedy*, opened on Broadway at the Ethel Barrymore Theatre April 17, 1939, and would run for 179 performances. Katharine Cornell was cast as Linda Paige, with Larry playing Gaylord Esterbrook, each of them under the direction of Cornell's gay husband, Guthrie McClintic.

Screen rights to the play were immediately acquired by Hollywood for a 1940 release, the Cornell and Olivier roles recast with Rosalind Russell and James Stewart. The plot concerned an actress who tries to keep her playwright husband from taking himself too seriously. Both the play and movie were smoothly executed but rather artificial.

The Broadway play drew mostly favorable notices, each of them focusing on Katharine Cornell. *The New York Post* defined Larry as "a sort of indifferent understudy of Alfred Lunt," but other reviews were kinder.

The New York critics nominated Larry as best actor in a Broadway play, but he lost the honor, which went to Maurice Evans for his portrayal of Hamlet. In the category of best performance for the 1938-39 season, Larry tied with Katharine Hepburn, who won for *The Philadelphia Story*.

Two days after his opening, Vivien wrote Larry a long love letter which no longer exists. Along with it, she sent him another pair of her soiled knickers. She told Sunny, "I made sure they were quite discolored." Later he wrote her back that, "I kissed them once and kissed them again and again. The smell was intoxicating."

During the run of the play, Larry was contacted by Jill with news about Tarquin, a boy growing up without his father. Jill delivered an ultimatum with two options: If he demanded an immediate divorce, she would designate Vivien as co-respondent. But if he opted to delay the divorce for another year, she would charge him only with the lesser, and less scandalous, charge of desertion.

Larry forwarded Jill's letter to Vivien, which prompted her to write Leigh in London once again, pleading for a divorce.

In New York, when *Wuthering Heights* opened, the press began treating Larry like a matinee idol, asserting that he evoked John Barrymore in the 1920s. Elliott Arnold in a June, 1939 interview in *The New York Telegraph* wrote, "Mr. Olivier is quite without question the matinee idol these summer days. First he sends many women into a mild nervous breakdown in the motion picture *Wuthering Heights* and now he is sending them into some other dream world with his performance in the stage comedy at the Barrymore."

What Arnold didn't print but told his editor was: "That Olivier faggot is attracting almost as many young men around the stage door as he is young girls. Word has gotten out that he likes beautiful boys, and they offer themselves to him, along with the beautiful girls, every night after curtain, some rather blatantly. The stage manager told me that many of these guys send nude pictures of themselves to Olivier."

Larry was often blunt to the press in New York, telling Bosley Crowther of *The New York Times*, "I have no use at all for motion pictures. The screen demands much more literalness than the stage. This is due partly to the fact that living actors are able to establish a personal communion with their audiences which the screen cannot achieve."

Larry quickly grew tired of the masses

(top photo) Katharine Cornell with Laurence Olivier on Broadway in 1939 in *No Time for Comedy*
(lower photo) Evidence of Cornell's fame: The Dec 26, 1932 cover of *Time.*

355

gathering outside his stage door. Finally he delivered an ultimatum. "I will not sign any more autographs."

This, obviously, did not endear him to his previously adoring fans.

In a phone conversation, Larry told Vivien that he'd agreed with Cornell and McClintic to extend his run in *No Time for Comedy*, and that he would not be returning to Hollywood right away. Reacting, she burst into hysterical denunciations, which would have far-reaching implications during the concluding months of *Gone With the Wind*.

Exhausted from her heavy work load and the unending pressure, she blamed Larry for all her maladies.

After she slammed down the phone, he immediately wrote to her:

"O God how dreadful—half an hour of absolute madness again. What is happening to us pussey? Hey? Something's gone so wrong and it only becomes apparent on the phone. O darling dear I am so sorry we're getting so horribly spoilt. It's just insanity, that's all. . .I'm always reproached with having a gay time and I'm not having any such thing. . . On the phone when it costs a fortune—you willfully misunderstand and distort what I've said and construe it all in the best way to keep up the quarrel longest. O baby we're getting so depressed we must try not to . . . It feels that I have learned to expect 'trouble' somehow, and I find myself rising from my cave, with smoke coming out of my nostrils before my cue. So please forgive me my dear one."

Sunny feared that Vivien would alienate Larry. At Selznick's office, Sunny dashed off a letter to him in New York. "Vivien misses you so much she cries herself to sleep every night. Her heart is breaking. Hurry back!"

***

Two views of director
Victor Fleming
(lower photo)
on the set with Vivien Leigh
as a scarlet version of Scarlett

Vivien's first meeting with the new director of *Gone With the Wind*, Victor Fleming, was a disaster. He immediately nicknamed her Fiddle-dee-dee. "I know you're a prim and proper English lady," he told her, "but as Scarlett O'Hara you've got to show some bosom regardless of what Mammy told you. You're not playing Queen Victoria, you know, but a Southern belle, a real vixen."

"Oh, God, not another tit man," she told Fleming. "Just like Selznick." In front of cast and crew, she ripped the bodice of her dress, revealing her entire breasts. "Is this enough tit for you, Fleming?" She stormed off the set, retreating to her dressing room until the end of the day.

When Vivien and Fleming reported to work the next day, both of them resumed shooting *Gone With the Wind*, as if no words had been exchanged between them.

The previous night, Vivien had revealed her plight to Larry in a letter. "I hate film acting," she wrote. "Hate! Hate! Hate! I will never make another movie again. I get nothing from Fleming and still turn to George at night. Fleming may be Gable's hunting, shooting, fucking, and drinking mate, but I literally can't stand to be in his presence."

Nervous and insecure, she visited Cukor's house every night. There, the director prepared her for the scene or scenes she'd be in the following day. "After I left the picture," Cukor said, "Vivien would come over to my house and I'd run over the scenes with her, doing some moonlighting. She didn't mind going behind Fleming's back—she hated him—but she felt somehow she might be betraying Olivia. That is, until Vivien learned that Olivia was also seeing me on the side."

Fleming didn't get along with Selznick either. On his first day at work, he told the producer, "The script for this Southern melodrama is full of shit. Bring in some more of your script doctors if you want me to shoot this turkey."

In contrast to Selznick and Vivien, Gable got along fabulously with Fleming, who had recently directed him in *Test Pilot*.

Gable told Selznick that Fleming was "my kind of man. A womanizer, he's seduced everybody from Norma Shearer to Clara Bow. A big game hunter, he also raced cars and was a photographer for the Signal Corps during World War I."

Producer Arthur Freed once said, "Gable owes everything, even his personality, to Vic. He modeled himself on him."

Before coming over to take charge of the *Gone With the Wind* set, Fleming had directed Judy Garland in *The Wizard of Oz*. Before leaving the Oz set, he'd nixed a song called "Over the Rainbow."

Even though she looked like a delicate piece of porcelain, Vivien stood up to Fleming, especially when he wanted to direct her in a scene that was different

It was a man's world:
Clark Gable in 1939

from what Cukor had coached her in the night before. "She was like a fierce tigress," Gable recalled. "She disagreed with almost everything Fleming said. He was giving me good direction."

"Scarlett is a terrible bitch," Vivien said to Fleming.

"That should not be too hard for you then," Fleming said sarcastically. "Now go back in front of the camera and make Scarlett more bitchy in the scene like I told you."

"But George told me only last night to make the character softer," she protested.

"Just who is directing this fucking picture?" Fleming shouted at her. "Me, a real man, or some flamer like Cukor?"

"I will play it like George told me," she said defiantly.

"Cukor is advising you all wrong," he said.

"I will not play it like you say," she said. "Your suggestions are moronic."

Infuriated at her, he took the script and hurled it in her face. "You can stick the script up your royal British ass." Then he barged off the set.

Leslie Howard later claimed that Fleming "was stark raving mad and was shooting up on something. When he couldn't take it any more, he'd retreat to his bungalow and inject God only knows what into his bloodstream. Like Vivien herself, Fleming was on the verge of a nervous breakdown. The other day when I asked him how he wanted to play a scene, he just stared into space and didn't say a word. At the rate we're going, I don't think *Gone With the Wind* will ever be made."

***

Gable went over to Fleming's house that night and, over many a drink, persuaded the director to return to work the following morning and cope with Vivien for the good of the picture.

The jug-eared actor told Fleming that only that day he'd seen an array of publicity stills of MGM beauties in the entrance to the studio. They'd been arranged by the publicity department to greet visitors. "I've had every one of them," he bragged to Fleming. "All except one, and that's Vivien Leigh. Like Scarlett O'Hara, I think what the bitch needs is a good fuck, and I'm the man to do it. For me, this is the first time that the girl isn't sure that she wants me from the minute she sets eyes on me, both on the screen as Rhett Butler and off the screen as Clark Gable."

"I agree with you," Fleming said. "Fuck hell out of the bitch. The filly needs to be broken in, and you can do it, Clark, I know you can."

"You're the director," Gable told him. "I don't usually ask ladies if I can screw them. I just take them."

At this point, the picture grows dim, and versions differ remarkably.

In 2009, journalist Peter Evans recalled a dinner party that had been hosted during the mid-60s at the home of actor Sir John Mills. Among the guests were Noël Coward, Richard Attenborough, Jack Hawkins, and David Lean. His dinner companion was Vivien. He noted that "the beauty that was Scarlett had faded, along with her career."

At one point, Vivien asked Evans if "I make you nervous?" He admitted that she did.

"Clark Gable claimed the same thing when I first met him just before they started filming *Gone With the Wind*," she said. "But I relaxed him. He got over it. He turned out to be just another movie actor who wouldn't take 'no' for an answer. The trouble was, Clark Gable was Rhett Butler and Rhett Butler was Clark Gable."

He pressed her for more details, wondering if she meant the scene in the movie where Rhett Butler forces himself on Scarlett and carries her up the stairs to rape her. Scarlett wakes up the next morning stretching luxuriantly, and with a smile on her face.

When pressed, Vivien said she was recalling "the time Mr. Gable tried to rape me. He was a method actor long before they invented the method." She related this in a rather matter-of-fact tone. "Gable probably got overheated watching me being squeezed into Scarlett's sixteen-inch corset."

She would provide no more details, but George Cukor, Leslie Howard, Sunny Lash, and Ona Munson all confirmed that Vivien had told them the same story.

"Under the threat of death" [Cukor's words], "Sunny, Leslie, and Ona were called to Selznick's office. He warned them if word of this gets out, we're finished. I'll probably have to shut down *Gone With the Wind*."

Of course, the rape story was too tantalizing to be kept a secret for long. It made the gossip circuit in Hollywood.

From most reports, it can be assumed that the alleged attack took place in Vivien's dressing room. When Gable truly wouldn't take no for an answer, Vivien, or so it is said, scratched one side of his face.

Fleming had to restrict his cameras to filming only the good side until MGM's doctors and the makeup department could conceal the evidence.

"After that little flare-up from our English queen," Fleming said, "Clark Gable gave Miss Leigh wide berth. Someone told me the bitch had to have dick every day. She certainly wasn't getting it from Olivier, who was probably in New York screwing around with chorus boys on Broadway. So who did Vivien turn to to satisfy her voracious sexual appetite? I would have plugged her, but I'm sure both Gable and I would have been too much man for her. Ashley Wilkes, of course. She turned to Ashley Wilkes."

Although Vivien and Gable clashed frequently, she got on reasonably well with Leslie Howard. She chastised him only once when he didn't know his lines. "This picture means a lot to me," she told him, "although it's obvious to me that you don't give a shit about it."

He stayed up half the night learning the dialogue for the following day, only to have Vivien forget her lines late that morning. "I was not cross with her," he recalled. "Oh, no, I was not unpleasant. 'Never mind dear,' I told her. 'Take your time.'"

Vivien wasn't the only one on the set conducting an adulterous affair. Leslie had a wife but was actually having an affair with the beautiful, red-haired Violette Cunningham, who was his production assistant. Vivien had met her, but the two women were rather chilly with each other.

"Vivien was a cuckoo bird," Leslie later recalled. "But god damn attractive and alluring. I came across her one day when she and Ona Munson and some others were playing a game called 'Killing Babies.' The object of the game was to see which person could come up with the most creative way to kill an infant. Vivien always won."

One cold February afternoon, Vivien found Leslie sitting by himself at the far side of the set. He was wearing his Confederate uniform. He stood up and modeled it for her. "Don't I look like a fairy doorman at the Beverly Wilshire?"

A sudden rainburst drove them inside her dressing room where, "I found him in a state of utter despair," she'd later tell Cukor. "I fear everybody is neglecting Leslie. He'd show up on some days to work, but he would not be in any scene. That sadist, Fleming, nevertheless insisted that he show up."

In her dressing room, she lent him a sympathetic ear. "The whole picture is about *coitus interruptus* in which Scarlett continues to go to bed with the wrong man because I, as Ashley Wilkes, won't give her a tumble. The idea that you're so fascinated by a slender, middle-aged, and rather effete gentleman of leisure that you spurn the husky Rhett Butler is a bit of a stretch."

After that afternoon, Leslie and Vivien began to spend as much time together as they could. Apparently, for the next two weeks, he envisioned some legal work that his mistress, Cunningham, needed to perform in the offices of his lawyers in Los Angeles.

In a highly self-edited note, Vivien wrote Larry that "Leslie is grief-stricken over his mother. She's suffered a heart attack. He's a great patriot and fears that England at any minute will go to war with Germany."

"Here I am sitting around on a Hollywood set fighting the Civil War for the Americans—and losing," Leslie told Vivien. "If war breaks out with Germany, I plan to desert the Confederate army," he confided. "They can have me killed off earlier in the picture."

One afternoon when he wasn't needed on the set, Leslie drank heavily. He seemed deeply disturbed and in a confessional mood. Very matter of factly, he told her, "I'm a British spy. I think both you and Larry should see the War Office about becoming spies, too."

"I'm no Mata Hari," she protested. "Leave that to Garbo."

"You don't have to be Mata Hari," he said. "I can arrange for you and Larry to talk to someone. I'm sure the War Office might find a useful role for each of you. You know that war is inevitable. Here's a chance for both of you to do something for the country we love."

"A spy?" she said. "The idea is outrageous, but I'm warming to it. Larry and I are very strong patriots. We'd give our all for England."

Sometimes, somehow on those long, terribly frustrating late spring afternoons between takes, Leslie and Vivien bonded.

Sunny Lash remembered that she walked in on them in Vivien's dressing room when they'd forgotten to lock the door. "They were having sex. Vivien was down on her knees committing fellatio on Leslie, and he was in his full Confederate uniform. Leslie seemed awfully embarrassed and broke from Vivien, rushing to her small bathroom. She didn't seem in the least embarrassed."

When Leslie emerged from the bathroom and hastily left, Sunny confronted Vivien. "I can't believe what I saw."

"Why not?" Vivien asked. "Seeing is believing."

"But Larry . . . ? Sunny said. "You love him so."

"I'm sure he understands that on occasion I will need a temporary replacement for him," Vivien said. "For me, a day without cock is a day in hell. I'm sure Larry in New York takes his forbidden pleasures. I don't really want to know about them."

After that day, Leslie and Vivien had nothing to conceal from Sunny. A few sleepovers were arranged.

"I remember getting up one Saturday morning and preparing breakfast for myself," Sunny said. "I was shocked when Leslie emerged from Vivien's bedroom in his undershorts. I gave him my breakfast when Vivien came in to join us."

"You didn't see any of this," Leslie warned Sunny.

"I won't be calling Parsons and Hopper if that is what you mean," Sunny told him. "I'm the pinnacle of discretion. That's why Mr. Selznick hired me."

One night when Vivien and Sunny were alone, Vivien told her, "In the movie, Scarlett never got Ashley Wilkes. But in real life, Vivien Leigh gets her man. I've been planning to seduce Leslie ever since I saw him in *Outward Bound*. He looks like a handsomer version of Leigh when I first met him in Devon. But Leslie is a hell of a lot better in the sack than Leigh ever was."

"When Leslie learned that his wife was on the way to Hollywood, he dropped out with Vivien," Sunny claimed. "With a wife and a mistress in tow already, Ashley was a bit busy."

Leslie had married Ruth Martin in 1916, and they had two children, a boy and a girl.

In England, Leslie told David Niven that he had not chased after Vivien, but she had gone after him. "She was desperate for Larry but threw herself at me. I was just a substitute."

"She had to have sex, whether it was with the man she loved or not," Niven claimed.

Douglas Fairbanks Jr. weighed in with his opinion. "Larry and Vivien back then seemed constantly impatient to get the trivia of everyday life over with so they could rush madly back to bed. Vivien was extremely libidinous."

Years later Fairbanks claimed, "Vivien was madly in love with Larry, and wanted only him. But when she couldn't get him, she found sex—not love—elsewhere. Early in her career, she was able to distinguish between sex and love. Larry also knew the difference. Just ask me. I, of all people, should know that."

With Leslie occupied with a wife and mistress, Vivien longed for Larry even more. A daring plan was conceived for them to meet for a rendezvous in the center of the United States, America's great heartland.

***

Desperate to see each other, Larry took a fifteen-hour flight from New York to Kansas City, Kansas, where he checked into the Hotel Meulbach to spend just one night with Vivien who arrived two hours later.

As she would later blatantly tell Selznick, "Larry met me in the hotel lobby, and we went upstairs where we fucked and we fucked and we fucked until it was time for us to go. I took it in all three holes and begged for more."

That's exactly how she described this romantic weekend rendezvous, graphic and to the point. Her bluntness shocked Selznick, who did not shock easily.

Back in Hollywood, Vivien resumed her role as Scarlett O'Hara. In a pattern she had established during the first weeks of shooting, she continued to lose weight, and, if anything, increased her chain smoking. At home, Sunny tried to get her to eat more, but she had little interest in food. Her nights were restless, and often she got by with only three hours of sleep.

362

Ona Munson had only a minor role and wasn't needed in many scenes, but she came to the set every day to comfort Vivien. She seemed to be the only one capable of getting Vivien to eat something. When Vivien became too tense and broke into crying jags, Munson was there to hold her and give her comfort and courage to go on.

"That Ona is after our Miss Scarlett," Hattie McDaniel told Clark Gable who spread the word around. Perhaps he believed that if Vivien were a card-carrying lesbian, it would explain her rejection of him.

One morning when Sunny heard noises coming from Vivien's bedroom, she suspected that the star had invited Leslie over for another sleepover. To her surprise, both Munson and Vivien appeared in the kitchen wearing robes. "I asked no questions," Sunny said. "I long ago learned working for Selznick that one must overlook a lot. It was their own business what they were doing. Both of them were big girls, especially Ona. I knew that Vivien loved men too much to be a real lesbian. Frankly, I think Ona was a sexual opportunist moving in on a very distraught young actress who was coming to pieces. I didn't like her very much for that."

"I was not ignorant of such affairs," Sunny claimed. "David's wife, Irene Mayer Selznick, was also a lesbian and engaged in a sometimes affair with Katharine Hepburn. David found out about that. I could write a book about all the things going on in Hollywood, but no one would publish it."

Munson took Vivien to at least three parties where all the guests were women. At one such party, Vivien and Munson met Mercedes de Acosta, the screenwriter and international beauty who had been the lover of both Greta Garbo and Marlene Dietrich. Born in New York City in 1893 to a Cuban father and a Spanish mother who claimed lineage to Spain's Dukes of Alba, De Acosta was usually credited with more emotional and sexual involvements with high-profile lesbian and bisexual women in Hollywood than any other woman of her generation. When Munson went into the kitchen to get drinks for them, De Acosta told Vivien, "Miss Munson's eyes are very sad. Her eyes are her most vivid feature. They touch me deeply."

Here Lies the Heart
(Top and center photos):
Two views of Ona
Munson
(lower photo):
Mercedes De Acosta

Both Vivien and Munson must have known their fling would be brief. Vivien was sent home that night in

363

a taxicab, and Munson and De Acosta became lovers. In a letter that later surfaced, Munson wrote De Acosta, "I long to hold you in my arms and pour my love into you."

Munson and Vivien continued to be friends. In one letter to Vivien, circa 1946, Munson wrote: "With Mercedes I shared the deepest spiritual moments that life can bring to a human being. Together we created an entity so close it was as if we had conceived and borne a child. I wish I could have shared that with you."

In February of 1955, Vivien cried when a friend called to tell her that Munson, at the age of 44, had committed suicide with an overdose of barbiturates in her apartment in New York City. A note found next to her deathbed read, "This is the only way I know to be free again. Please don't follow me."

Vivien turned to Larry for comfort. "There are nights, dear heart, when I'm tempted to follow in Ona's footsteps."

When he returned to Hollywood after the war, David Niven learned about Vivien's involvements with both Leslie and Munson. "I'm not surprised," he told Selznick and two associates. "After living with Errol Flynn, I became used to bisexuality in Hollywood. I guess poor Vivien in her despair gave in to it too. Larry certainly did years ago, way back when. He once propositioned me, but I turned him down. I told him I wanted friendship and loyalty from him, not sex."

***

Vivien wasn't the only one suffering through the agonies of making *Gone With the Wind*. Victor Fleming also appeared to be coming unglued.

Tensions continued to mount daily between Fleming and Selznick. It didn't help that Fleming was violently anti-Semitic, constantly calling Selznick "the dirty Jew." Foul-mouthed and blunt, Fleming often read one of Selznick's rewrites from the night before and told him, "Your rewrites are no fucking good." At one point he accused Selznick of "sabotaging *Gone With the Wind*."

Gable, however, remained Fleming's loyal friend. At one point, Fleming confided to Gable that, "I came within a hair of committing suicide this morning by driving over a cliff on the way to work."

One morning when Fleming didn't show up on the set, Gable went to his MGM bungalow to find out what was wrong. He found Fleming collapsed on the floor. Apparently, he'd spent the night in his bungalow. There were three empty whiskey bottles beside his body. At first Gable thought he'd died, but when he detected breathing he called Selznick, who had Fleming rushed to the hospital, where the director was checked in under an assumed name.

Selznick did not want the press to learn that tough guy Fleming had suffered a nervous breakdown. "I thought your friend had more balls than that," Selznick later told Gable. "My God, he's as delicately strung as Vivien."

While Fleming recuperated at his Malibu house, Selznick brought in Sam Wood, who had recently directed *Goodbye, Mr. Chips* with Oscar-winning Robert Donat. Although in *Gone With the Wind*'s final credits, Fleming was acknowledged as the film's director, the contributions of Sam Wood were enormous, as were those of Cukor. Both Vivien and Olivia resented Wood, and Gable remained maniacally loyal to Fleming.

As a former assistant director to Cecil B. DeMille, Wood had mastered the art of the movie spectacular, and he'd dealt with such greats as Gloria Swanson and Rudolph Valentino, even the Marx Brothers.

Years later, in the mid-1950s, during the height of the Cold War, the most famous of the Marx brothers, Groucho, called Wood a "fascist," based on his later testimony before the House Un-American Activities Committee.

In his emergency role as substitute and uncredited director, the first scenes Wood shot were of Scarlett and Ashley embracing at the lumber mill at war's end and Belle Watling approaching Melanie on the hospital steps. Wood began directing on May 1, but on May 15 Fleming surprisingly returned to the set. In the words of one cameraman, "Fleming was like Cagney sneering at rookie cops."

To take some of the pressure off the hardly recovered Fleming, Selznick retained Wood. Gable demanded that Fleming direct him in his scenes, but Wood directed Vivien in such scenes as when she tears down the draperies and makes a fashionable gown of them. Sometimes the stars would work with Fleming in the morning, Wood in the afternoon. Throughout the chaos, both Vivien and Olivia continued to rely on Cukor for directorial advice.

Although Fleming was just one of three directors during the filming of *Gone With the Wind*, he received sole on-screen credit and walked away with an Oscar for Best Director. Ironically, in his receipt of the Academy Award, he beat out Wood for *Goodbye, Mr. Chips* and William Wyler for *Wuthering Heights*.

There was no love lost between Wood and Fleming. "That fucker Fleming took credit for my work," Wood claimed. "In fairness, the Oscar should have been shared by three directors, including that pansy Cukor."

When major shooting on *Gone With the Wind* ended, and Vivien had some time off, she went to tell Olivia goodbye. "She'd lost so much weight," Olivia recalled. "She was so diminished by overwork. Completely depleted. Her whole personality had been altered by playing Scarlett O'Hara. She gave something to that film that I don't think

Director #3:
Sam Wood

365

she ever got back."

Two nights before, a very distraught Vivien had called Olivia. "Aren't you afraid that *Gone With the Wind* will flop after this super buildup?"

"No, just the opposite," Olivia said. "Only today I talked to George. In spite of his getting fired, he still thinks *Gone With the Wind* will be the biggest film ever to come out of Hollywood. He also warned me that as actresses we'll never escape the curse of being identified as Scarlett O'Hara and Melanie Wilkes."

***

Vivien owed Selznick one more picture before the year was over, and she wanted her role to be the second Mrs. Maxim de Winter in the producer's upcoming film, *Rebecca*. It was scheduled for direction by Alfred Hitchcock, the first picture he was to helm after signing a seven-year contract with Selznick's private production company.

The story was based on Daphne du Maurier's Gothic novel set within a grand and ghostly stately home in England. "I can just see myself playing the second Mrs. de Winter who replaces Rebecca as the mistress of Manderley," Vivien told Sunny.

Selznick had already warned Sunny that other actresses were vying for the role, including Joan Fontaine, Geraldine Fitzgerald, Anne Baxter, Susan Hayward, Virginia Mayo, Loretta Young, and even Lana Turner. Sunny didn't want Vivien to be disappointed, so she alerted her to this formidable arsenal of carnivorous actresses waiting in the wings.

"Fiddle-dee-dee," Vivien said. "I faced 1,400 other actresses or would-be actresses for the role of Scarlett O'Hara."

The date was June 27, 1939, the last day of shooting on the set of *Gone With the Wind*. Vivien walked from one sound stage to another, leaving the role of Scarlett behind to film a test for *Rebecca*. Her journey took only ten minutes, but the roles were miles apart.

At the end of the test, Vivien knew that it had not gone well for her. Without the benefit of any rehearsal or preparation, she realized she had not crossed that vast chasm between the tempestuous Scarlett O'Hara and the timid heroine of du Maurier's novel. She conveyed that in a note to Selznick and asked him to be understanding and arrange another screen test for her with Larry at their offices in New York. Sunny told her that Selznick had agreed to that.

At that point, Selznick did not want to anger Vivien, because he might need her for retakes on *Gone With the Wind*, and he definitely wanted her to show up for the December premiere in Atlanta.

Larry had won the role of Maxim de Winter after Ronald Colman had turned it down. The English actor felt that the woman's role was stronger than the male part. Selznick then offered it to William Powell, who demanded $100,000, which was more than Selznick wanted to pay. He and Hitchcock finally agreed on Larry, who Selznick's brother, Myron, said would do the part for only $30,000.

Selznick and Hitchcock watched Vivien's screen test together. "A horror," the portly Hitchcock said. "She's playing Scarlett O'Hara, not Rebecca. She's too eager. Much too aggressive. Our heroine has to be more passive, more virginal."

"After the American public sees Vivien as Scarlett, they can never accept her as the mousey Mrs. de Winter," Selznick said. "The movie-goers of America like to see their stars typecast."

Even after Cukor was fired, Selznick and the director remained friends. "I showed the tests to George," Selznick said. "He didn't say anything during the screening except for some loud guffaws at Vivien's attempt to become Mrs. de Winter."

Since a break had come in her schedule, Vivien flew immediately to New York, wanting to see Larry in his last performance in *No Time for Comedy*.

At the airport at Newark, New Jersey, "Scarlett O'Hara" was besieged by reporters and photographers with blinding flashbulbs. Facing the public again, she came to realize she was the most talked about woman star in America, even before the release of *Gone With the Wind*.

Selznick had warned these "illicit lovers" not to stay in the same hotel. For weekends, Katharine Cornell graciously offered the pair the use of her country home at Sneden's Landing, on the Hudson River.

Vivien was so desperate to see Larry that she couldn't wait for nightfall. Columnist Radie Harris accompanied Vivien to the matinee, arriving just as the curtain was going up.

At intermission Vivien, along with Harris, went backstage to Larry's dressing room. The columnist witnessed the long-delayed reunion. "They clung to each other as if they were never going to see each other again," Harris said. "'Really, darlings,' I told them, 'you are going to see each other after the next act.'"

"How long a wait is that?" Vivien asked.

Joan Fontaine as the very demure
Mrs. de Winter in *Rebecca*

"About forty minutes, Puss," Larry said, sitting down to check his make-up. He looked at her and smiled. "I'm worth the wait."

"That you are," Vivien said, kissing him passionately one more time before taking her seat out front.

In spite of Selznick's warning that utmost secrecy had to be maintained in New York about their relationship, the news was out. The story broke not in New York City but in the *Syracuse Herald* under the headline VIVIEN LEIGH'S ROMANCE GIVES JITTERS TO GONE WITH THE WIND DIRECTORS.

It didn't help matters that Samuel Goldwyn was advertising *Wuthering Heights* with a caption—"I am Heathcliff. I love a woman who belongs to another by law."

One New York paper was more discreet, claiming "Miss Scarlett O'Hara was seen with her new boyfriend," without naming Olivier. Another paper referred to Larry as "Vivien's good friend."

On the third day of their reunion, Larry and Vivien went to a studio where Selznick had arranged for them to do a screen test for the roles of Mr. and Mrs. de Winter. This time, Vivien had prepared for the part. She thought the screen test "had gone wonderfully." On the other hand, Larry wasn't so sure.

Shipped to the West Coast, the test was viewed by Selznick in his private offices in the presence of Sunny, who had flown back to the West Coast after accompanying Vivien on the plane to New York.

Selznick told Sunny, "You talk of all this sexual chemistry between these two lovebirds. Amazingly, it doesn't show up on the screen. Olivier delivers his role perfectly, but Vivien would be hopelessly miscast in *Rebecca*. I think I'll delay flashing the news to them. Let them enjoy their little holiday."

On July 11, 1939 Larry and Vivien sailed on the *Ile de France* heading for England. As Vivien recalled, a band on the pier was playing "*Should auld acquaintance be forgot . . .*"

Aboard the vessel, they were very discreet, booking separate cabins under assumed names. "Just by chance," they happened to meet on deck.

The ship's captain had instructed baggage personnel to label Vivien's luggage simply as "Madame X."

Five days at sea brought them closer than they had ever been before, and they relished the time away from America, longing for their homeland, which both of them feared was in great peril from Hitler's Germany.

In spite of the disappointing screen tests, Vivien remained confident she could persuade Selznick to cast her in *Rebecca*. "After what I did for him in *Gone With the Wind*, Selznick wouldn't dare turn me down," she told Larry.

"Selznick would dare do anything," Larry warned her.

"With positive thinking, I willed myself into the role of Scarlett O'Hara," she said. "I'll do the same thing for *Rebecca*." She leaned over from a chaise longue on the deck and kissed him, even though they were supposed to be discreet. "You're looking at your second wife both on and off the screen."

During the transatlantic crossing, Vivien and Larry plotted to approach their respective spouses again with a final plea for a divorce. "That way, Selznick will stop worrying about a scandal," she said. "One that might interfere with the profits of *Gone With the Wind*. Once our divorce papers are in our pockets, he can cast me opposite you in *Rebecca* without fear of unwanted headlines."

"Once we're back in England," Vivien promised him, "our lives will be dreamlike. Our spouses will agree to divorce us. We'll see our children. We'll set up housekeeping at Durham Cottage. Nothing . . . nothing can ever go wrong between us again."

Larry may have seemed to share her sentiments, but he was not in love hopelessly, blindly, the way she was. His more cynical attitude was revealed in a letter Larry sent to Noël Coward, who kept it.

That letter fell into the hands of Coward's longtime lover, Graham Payn, who didn't mind showing it to some friends in the theater, perhaps to discredit Larry, of whom Payn had always been jealous.

"Noël, your baby boy's coming home. I'm now an established Shakespearean actor and a Hollywood movie star, first class. Viv and I make mad love, and you know what that is like from me, but we quarrel too, sometimes for hours. A marriage to her is probably doomed to failure but I plan to marry her anyway. What the bloody hell! We're sometimes sadistic with each other, sometimes loving and kind. I fear Vivien will go stark raving bonkers one day. Viv represents danger. She cannot satisfy all my desires, and wants more sex than I can provide. She is DANGER! PASSION! AN INTRIGUING RIDDLE! I am going to open the door marked Vivien Leigh and walk down the steps behind that door into her waiting arms. I fear it will lead to a stairway to a dark gulf.
Love and kisses.
Larry."

***

After disembarking in Plymouth, Larry and Vivien discovered a vastly different country from the one they had left. As war clouds loomed over their homeland, the English were building air raid shelters, filling sandbags, and manufacturing and distributing pig snout gas masks.

After its long abandonment, Durham Cottage seemed cramped after

California. There was a forlorn feeling in the air. Vivien gave parties for her friends, but the mood was somber. It was as if Londoners, including their friends, were preparing for war against Nazi troops. Headlines screamed: FRANCE MOBILISES.

When Vivien went out to enjoy her courtyard, she spotted barrage balloons hanging over London. On August 9, 1939, London was plunged into its first trial "blackout."

Some of their friends joked about all these preparations, claiming, "It's just Chamberlain's way of scaring off Hitler. Nothing's going to happen."

That opinion was not shared by Leigh Holman when Vivien knocked on his door. For one brief moment, he didn't seem to recognize her. The woman standing on his doorstep was not the vivacious Scarlett O'Hara pictured in the paper, but a tired and demoralized actress who had lost a lot of weight. She wore almost no makeup, and the lines of exhaustion showed on her face, lit only by threatening skies over London.

"I know I must be unrecognizable," she told him," coming into their living room. "It's from overwork. *Gone With the Wind* was hell."

Suzanne was out with her nanny, and Leigh invited her to wait until the girl returned home.

"Once again I must ask you for a divorce," she said.

"I was hoping you might change your mind," he said. "I really can't get into this divorce thing right now. There's too much going on here. Unlike some of my fellow countrymen, I believe war is inevitable. I'm preparing. I'm even talking seriously about a possible school for Suzanne in Canada."

She urged a divorce again.

He was dismissive. "When I get around to it. It's all such foolishness. I may petition for divorce, but I also might change my mind. I reserve that right."

At that point Suzanne and the nanny arrived. All Vivien could remember about that reunion was that her young daughter didn't seem to know her. Life had gone on without her mother.

Leigh and the nanny seemed to be doing a fine job of parenting in her absence. After only a few short moments of idle talk, Suzanne asked to be excused. She had played hard and wanted to lie down in her bedroom.

Vivien made an ungraceful exit from the place she'd once called home.

Larry took a taxi to St. John's Wood, an exclusive district in northwest London, where Jill had moved with Tarquin. Here he had a reunion with his wife and "the stranger," his three-year-old son.

When Tarquin was excused, Jill and Larry talked seriously of divorce. He had always been rather tight with his money, and now he feared Jill was going to "ransom" him for alimony. She believed that he was going to become a big and highly paid film star like Robert Donat. For the price of his divorce, she wanted very generous alimony and "huge sums" set aside for Tarquin.

He pleaded with her that he was far from rich and asked her to be reasonable.

"It is you, not me, who is being unreasonable," she told him. "I've talked to my solicitor, and he claims my rights should be protected, after the scandalous way you've conducted our marriage."

As he was leaving, she told him, "You will have your divorce. But you must agree to take care of Tarquin and me for life. Otherwise, I won't permit it."

When he got home, Vivien was waiting. "How did it go with Tarquin?" she asked.

"Awkward," he said. "How did it go with Suzanne?"

"Awkward," she said.

He explained Jill's demands for divorce, citing her requests as "exorbitant."

Vivien was impatient with him and precipitated an argument. "Bloody hell! Give the bitch what she wants and be done with it. After *Gone With the Wind* is released, I'll be drawing so much money I can look after both of us."

"I didn't fall in love with you looking for some woman to support me. I won't hear such talk." In fury he stormed out of the house.

Rapidly moving into one of her "states," she screamed at him in the streets, not caring if the neighbors heard. "Where are you going?" she shouted at him. "Over to one of your boy friends?"

Larry spent the night with Glen Byam Shaw. But, to make up for their fight, he invited her the next day for a brief holiday in France. "Let's call it a pre-honeymoon. Forgive me, darling, the tensions over this divorce are unbearable at times."

In France they did relax for the first time, and Vivien's glow began to return to her face, the color added by the sun of the Côte d'Azur.

Upon their return to London, they made one final call on their former families, but nothing had changed from before.

Sailing back to America on the *Île de France*, each of them agreed that their spouses were obstinate. "Leigh is a stubborn old mule, and Jill would see me bankrupt," Larry told her.

The westbound transit to New York wasn't as pleasant or private as its eastbound counterpart. Vivien's mother, Gertrude, had decided to travel to New York with them.

The news that arrived by cable aboard ship suggested that tensions between England and Germany had eased. A poll taken on August 31 showed that only one Briton in five anticipated war, far fewer than a similar poll conducted eighteen months before. There was renewed hope throughout the British Empire.

"Soon we'll be back in the California sun making a film together, like we used to do for Korda," Vivien said.

Unknown to either of them, cables from Selznick were on the way to the ship's communications center. It would change their life. On August 18, 1939, two cables arrived from Selznick—one for Vivien, another for Larry.

To Vivien, he wrote: "I regret telling you we are finally convinced you are as wrong for the role in *Rebecca* as the role would be for you. Hitchcock feels even more strongly on the question than I do. I am positive you would be bitterly criticized and your career, which is now off to such a tremendous start with Scarlett, would be materially damaged."

To Larry, he wrote: "Vivien's anxiety to play the role has, in my opinion, been largely, if not entirely, due to her desire to do a picture with you."

Aside from the bad news over the casting of *Rebecca*, a more momentous event was about to happen within three or so weeks. Their beloved England would declare war on Nazi Germany.

When *Gone With the Wind* would finally open in December of 1939, the first line uttered by Scarlett O'Hara would have a horrific topicality.

"Everyone is talking about war, war, war."

***

Two views of Mr. de Winter (Olivier) and his 2nd wife (Fontaine) in *Rebecca*

Back in Hollywood, Vivien was still miffed that she did not get the role of Mrs. de Winter in *Rebecca*, the part going to Joan Fontaine. Impulsively she invited her rival, along with her bisexual husband, Brian Aherne, for cocktails at their rented villa on Crescent Drive. It was one of those "let-us-be-friends" invitations.

Fontaine hesitated to accept but decided to be gracious, since she would soon be filming with Larry. She didn't want the kind of tension with him that had existed between Merle Oberon and him.

In her memoirs, Fontaine claimed that the invitation was Vivien's revenge on her. "The maid showed Brian and I to the pool where we waited alone in the garden for an hour. Eventually, Larry and Vivien sauntered, arm in arm, across the lawn from the house. They offered no apology. I don't know whether they'd deliberately given us the wrong hour; we left without finding out. Vivien and I were to cross swords again in 1965."

At one point Aherne had to excuse himself to go to the bathroom. When he was out of earshot, Larry asked Fontaine: "When you went hunting for a husband, couldn't you have done better than that?"

A Gothic tale, *Rebecca*, scheduled for a 1940 release, was a psychological thriller casting Larry as Maxim de Winter, with Fontaine as his second wife. Judith Anderson was typecast as the late Rebecca's lesbian housekeeper, Mrs. Danvers.

A strong supporting cast, perhaps the finest of the year, included George Sanders, Nigel Bruce, Reginald Denny, C. Aubrey Smith, Gladys Cooper, Florence Bates, Leo G. Carroll, and Melville Cooper. Hitchcock, of course, made his customary cameo appearance.

The voiceover that begins the film became a movie legend: "Last night I dreamt I went to Manderley again . . ."

Selznick had paid $50,000 for screen rights to the Daphne du Maurier novel, the same amount he'd shelled out for *Gone With the Wind*. He had originally conceived it as a vehicle for Carole Lombard, with Ronald Colman as Maxim. Leslie Howard was also considered for the lead.

On the first day of the shooting of *Rebecca*, Hitchcock privately told Fontaine something she already knew.

"Olivier didn't want you in the part" the director said. "He wanted Vivien and claimed she was the only actress in Hollywood who could play the role the way it should be played."

"It was Hitch's intention that I should hardly be friends with Laurence Olivier after that, though I hope I didn't show it on the set."

During filming, when Larry would blow a take, he'd shout, "Bloody fucking hell."

Hitchcock felt he had to caution him. "I say Larry old boy, do be careful. Joan is just a new bride."

"Yes," Larry said sarcastically, "I've met her new husband if that's what he's called."

"I had to keep Fontaine in her place so she would play this frightened young woman," Hitchcock said. "I constantly

A Gothic lament from *Rebecca:*

"Last night, I dreamt I went to Manderley again."

reminded her how much Olivier hated her. On several occasions I threatened to fire her and replace her with Vivien Leigh."

Throughout the shoot, Olivier showed his utter disdain for Fontaine. She later thanked him for that. "His resentment made me feel so dreadfully intimidated that I was believable in my portrayal."

Larry did not get strong direction from Hitchcock, and Selznick was not pleased with Larry's performance. Selznick told Hitchcock, "Olivier's pauses are ungodly slow and the most deliberate reactions I have ever seen. He acts as though he were deciding whether or not to run for president instead of whether or not to give a ball."

Toward the end of the film, Larry shocked Hitchcock by telling him, "Frankly, I'm glad you didn't cast Vivien as my wife in the film. At times she annoys me. She's like a clinging vine hanging on to me. I'm not that much of a demonstrative man. I don't believe in a constant display of touchy, feely affection."

Mostly he got along with Hitchcock, though he complained that his character, especially "the haunted quality, the mystery element, was thinly written." Larry and Hitchcock would never work together again. "I detest Olivier," Hitchcock later told Selznick. "He seems to possess that which I do not—good looks and sexual self-assurance."

(top photo) Rebecca's author, Dame Daphne du Maurier.

(lower photo) Mrs. Danvers (Dame Judith Anderson) terrorizing "the 2nd Mrs. de Winter" (Joan Fontaine)

Larry later issued a comment on Hitchcock's directorial style. "He treats us like pawns in his own personal chess game, where he's made up all the rules."

Critic Pauline Kael called *Rebecca* "magnificent romantic-Gothic corn . . . one of Olivier's rare poor performances."

Rebecca won the Oscar as Best Picture of the Year, beating out such contenders as *The Letter*, *The Philadelphia Story*, and *The Grapes of Wrath*. Larry lost the Best Actor Oscar to James Stewart in *The Philadelphia Story*, and Fontaine lost to Ginger Rogers in *Kitty Foyle*.

Jane Darwell beat out Judith Anderson, winning for her interpretation of Ma Joad in *The Grapes of Wrath*. Hitchcock lost the Best Director Oscar to John Ford for *The Grapes of Wrath*.

In an ironic touch, a decade later, on November 6, 1950, Vivien finally got to appear as the second Mrs. de Winter opposite Larry, but it was for the Lux Radio Theater.

***

It was a tranquil, sunny Sunday morning on September 3, 1939 off the coast of Catalina Island. Back in Hollywood, Vivien and Larry had accepted a weekend invitation to go sailing on the yacht of Douglas Fairbanks Jr.

Other guests included their close friend, David Niven, Fairbanks' new wife, Mary Lee, Vivien's mother Gertrude, and British character actors Nigel Bruce and Robert Coote, who would become famous in the role of Colonel Hugh Pickering in the long-running original Broadway production of *My Fair Lady*.

Anxious for news from his homeland, Niven turned on the radio early Sunday morning to listen to Neville Chamberlain. The other guests on the yacht gathered around the set to hear the prime minister announce to the world that Nazi Germany had ignored Britain's ultimatum to withdraw forces from invaded Poland.

Larry and Vivien listened intently and in silence as Chamberlain announced, "I have to tell you now that no such understanding has been received and that consequently this country is at war with Germany."

Vivien burst into tears, and Gertrude comforted her. Both Larry and Vivien were concerned for the safety of Suzanne and Tarquin. "Our lives are blighted through and through," Larry told Niven and Fairbanks. "Our careers, our hopes, our dreams."

The disgraced British Prime Minister, Neville Chamberlain, shortly before his betrayal by Adolf Hitler

To break the dour mood, Fairbanks brought out bottles of champagne and proposed a toast to Britain's ultimate triumph over Hitler's armies.

Most of the party of expatriates got drunk, Larry excessively so, which was unusual for him. Niven behaved outrageously, going water-skiing in a dinner jacket.

Larry got into a speedboat attached to the yacht and began to weave in and out of the other vessels moored at Emerald Bay, one of which belonged to

Vivien and Larry (4th and 5th from left) yachting off Catalina Island in September, 1939.

375

"look-alike" Ronald Colman.

"You're finished, each last one of you!" he shouted, fervently and theatrically to the yachties on their decks. "You're relics. Bloody *relics*!"

Fairbanks later recalled that Larry "looked like some Cassandra predicting doom in his bathing trunks."

After his drunken tour, Larry returned to the Fairbanks yacht where he vomited on deck before falling asleep in the sun on a chaise longue.

Fearing trouble, Fairbanks directed his captain to leave Emerald Bay.

Calls went out to the harbor patrol, whose chief was informed that Ronald Colman was drunk and menacing his fellow boatmen.

A ship-to-shore radio blasted across the bay, demanding that Colman apologize to the boat owners. "You must apologize, Mr. Colman, for your insulting behavior."

By the time the announcement was made, Larry was sleeping off his drunk on the open sea.

Back on shore the following day, Larry called Colman to apologize. "You would never have made such a disgusting spectacle of yourself like the drunken fool I was."

"All is forgiven," Colman said. "News of our country at war drove you only momentarily insane."

As a reserve officer in a Highland Regiment, Niven told them that he would soon be returning to England. Larry met with his friend over drinks and dinner, telling him of his desire to join the Army. Filming the last scenes of *Rebecca* for Hitchcock seemed less important than ever.

Niven became the first major British officer to leave Hollywood, rushing back to his homeland, where in time he served honorably with the Rifle Brigade.

Larry, in uniform, preparing for WWII

Larry attended Niven's elaborate send-off on September 30, a lavish party thrown by Samuel Goldwyn, who had hired a band of Scottish pipers and drummers, even a stripper. The alcohol flowed and was consumed by Coote, Cary Grant, George Sanders, Brian Aherne, and even Larry himself.

Niven would later tell Larry, "I had come to believe the studio's ludicrous publicity about me. I think I was saved from being a total shit by the war. Going to war was the only unselfish thing I have ever done for humanity."

Impulsively Larry decided that he'd rather be an RAF pilot than a soldier in the British army.

He began to take flying lessons at a small airport in San Fernando Valley. Even Vivien took flying lessons, although such a delicate creature hardly qualified as RAF pilot material.

Larry and Vivien contacted Alfred Duff Cooper of the Ministry of Information in London who told them that the government wanted them to stay in Hollywood for the moment and "continue what you are doing." Rather mysteriously, he added, "a special agent" would be contacting them. He did suggest that both of them could begin immediately to sponsor charity events to aid the British war effort.

They carried out that mission for Britain with zest and courage. At one point in Toronto they appeared in one afternoon at eight different cinemas to help raise funds for their homeland. A few weeks prior to this trip, Vivien and Larry had visited Canada once before to find a haven for their children.

Gertrude, who was staying with Vivien and Larry, told them she planned to return at once to take care of Suzanne and possibly plan an evacuation of Vivien's daughter to Canada to ride out the war. Leigh had been called up for military service, and proper care had to be provided for Suzanne.

Both Larry and Vivien grew impatient waiting for some special assignments from their government. They went so far as to contact Lord Lothian, the British ambassador in Washington. "Keep making movies," he told them. "If all our English actors return to England, American actors will portray us with ghastly accents, wearing monocles and spats. Whatever you do, don't violate the neutrality act. If you can influence screenwriters to give their films a pro-British stance, so much the better. Enough of those caricatures of Englishmen who appeared in American movies in the 1930s."

Not knowing of these instructions from Lord Lothian, many people in Britain attacked Vivien and Larry for being expatriates living in luxury in Hollywood, while England faced the Blitz and severe rationing. In the British press, the expatriate colony in Hollywood was referred to as " The Gone With the Wind Brigade."

The London press continued to ask embarrassing questions. "Why isn't Laurence Olivier over here fighting for his country? Why isn't he with his son? Why is Vivien Leigh not in London caring for her daughter?"

Vivien told the Los Angeles columnist Radie Harris, "If and when Larry goes, I must go with him. I couldn't bear the agonizing suspense of another separation."

"Most of Hollywood was on the English side," Larry recalled. "But there were many artists who were sympathetic to Germany. There were embarrassments—for example, Charles Laughton found himself working for the German director William Dieterle in *The Hunchback of Notre Dame*."

In the meantime, the Selznick office was calling Vivien daily about the

December premiere of *Gone With the Wind*. Irene Mayer Selznick, along with her husband, David O. Selznick, and Jock Whitney had attended a sneak preview.

The applause had been enormous, and word spread rapidly. *Gone With the Wind* was a sensation, and almost overnight Vivien had become one of the leading film actresses of the world. No English actress had ever achieved such fame.

At that time, not much was known about Vivien so the public began to assume that she was virtually playing herself as Scarlett O'Hara. "Vivien Leigh and Scarlett O'Hara, to much of the world, became interlocked," she said. "I would never escape her curse, a curse that began before the film's official premiere."

Right before she went to bed one night with Larry, Selznick called her. "I hear all this shit talk about you and Larry planning to return to England. Are you out of your fucking mind? Remember, you're under exclusive contract to me. Keep your ass where it is. By the end of the war, and with you in Hollywood, I'll make you the biggest female star in history."

"I'll think about it tomorrow, Mr. Selznick," she said before gently putting down the phone.

***

Vivien told both Larry and George Cukor that "I feel no satisfaction from having played Scarlett O'Hara. As you both know, I coveted the role ever since I read the book. But the toll it's taken on me wasn't worth it. I feel playing Scarlett has been very destructive to my body and my mental condition. Twice I came very close to a nervous breakdown like Victor Fleming himself. Had it not been for Ona Munson, I might have gone out of my mind."

"George Cukor stood by me," Vivien said. "Larry was in New York doing God knows what."

She also confided that when Selznick had called her back for retakes, Olivia de Havilland had walked right past her, later claiming she didn't recognize Vivien. She reached for Larry's hand. "Please, please tell me I haven't changed that much."

"You look as beautiful as ever," Larry assured her.

At the wrap party, a very nervous Selznick approached Vivien. He had money on the brain. "This film is going to cost me $4,250,000—maybe a lot more, and I have exactly $20,000 in the bank."

Noting her $25,000 salary, Vivien said, "You certainly didn't spend it on me."

In its edited form, the final cut of *Gone With the Wind* would run for three hours and 40 minutes.

Selznick confided that $5,000 of his dwindling bank account went to pay a fine for breaching the Production Code. "I triumphed over the Joseph Breen censors," he claimed. The word 'damn' cost me that much money."

In Gable's closing line in *Gone With the Wind*—"Frankly, my dear, I don't give a damn"—the word "frankly" was written in by Sidney Howard and added to Margaret Mitchell's original text.

***

The world premiere of *Gone With the Wind* took place on December 15, 1939 at Loew's Grand Theatre in Atlanta, Georgia. "Sherman's March through Georgia would be nothing compared to Selznick's," wrote Kay Brown, the producer's "Girl Friday."

The whole city was turned into one giant advertisement for *Gone With the Wind*. Georgia governor E.D. Rivers declared a statewide holiday.

Many of the sightseers paraded around in Confederate uniforms or else clothes worn by their grandparents during the Civil War. On almost every street corner in downtown Atlanta the sounds of "Dixie" could be heard. The façade of Loew's Grand Theatre had been transformed into a *faux* Twelve Oaks.

In Atlanta, it was estimated that some 300,000 people turned out for the event, many of them lining the seven-mile route that the stars took from the airport to the Georgian Terrace Hotel.

Selznick chartered a plane from L.A. for the transport of Vivien, Larry, Olivia de Havilland, and himself to Atlanta. Leslie Howard was not available. As a true British patriot, he had returned to England to aid his country in its war against the Nazis.

There was a reason Gable and

Nostalgia and fan worship in the New South: Two views of the Atlanta premiere of *Gone With the Wind*

Lombard were not on the special plane. A drunken Fleming had discovered a press release that named Cukor and Wood as the other two directors of *Gone With the Wind*. After that, Fleming refused to go to Atlanta. Gable sided with him, and also refused passage on Selznick's special *Gone With the Wind* plane.

Selznick, along with Vivien and Olivia, almost died in the plane before landing in Atlanta. Shortly before landing, to avoid the unexpected but rapidly approaching granite dome of the Atlanta region's Stone Mountain, the pilot swerved at the last minute, sending the frail Vivien falling into the aisle with Larry tumbling down on top of her. No bones were broken.

Upon their own (separate) arrival in Atlanta, Gable and Lombard were driven from the airfield along a flag-decked Peachtree Street that was lined, six feet deep, with thousands of cheering fans. Arriving at the entrance to the hotel, they were astonished to be met by the governors of five Southern states.

Prolonging the opening festivities, shortly thereafter, Larry and Vivien also arrived by limousine to meet hordes of welcoming crowds, clamoring for autographs. Once Larry's car door was opened, a nine-year-old aspiring young actress from Thomasville, Georgia, Joanne Woodward, jumped into the car and sat on his lap. (Years later, in 1979, when Woodward worked with Olivier on a TV production of *Come Back, Little Sheba*, Olivier remembered her doing it.)

Actually Selznick didn't want Larry to accompany Vivien to Atlanta. He continued to be worried that the press might blow this "adulterous affair" into a scandal that would damage Vivien's reputation. Actually, word was already out.

A passion for protocol on opening night: (*left to right*) Clark Gable, Margaret Mitchell, and Vivien Leigh

The affair of Larry and Vivien received its major airing in a December, 1939 issue of *Photoplay* in an article by Ruth Waterbury. She wrote of "the high tumultuous romance that laughs at careers, hurdles the conventions, loses its head along with its heart, and laughs for the exhilarating joy of such wildness."

Hattie McDaniel, in her words, wanted to arrive, along with Vivien and Larry, "like a queen in Atlanta, but the white folks had other thoughts about my grand entrance." William B. Hartsfield, the mayor of Atlanta, even refused to allow her likeness to be used at the theater advertising *Gone With the Wind*, even though she was one of the major stars.

380

Later back in Hollywood, Hattie complained to Vivien, "I guess I don't even exist."

"Never worry," Vivien said. "You will have immortalized yourself on the screen. *Gone With the Wind* will be shown one thousand years from now."

When Vivien met Margaret Mitchell, the Atlanta author told her that her most favorite working title was *Ba! Ba! Black Sheep*, but she also considered *Not in Our Stars*, *Bugles Sang True*, *Tote the Weary Load*, and *Tomorrow Is Another Day*.

"I'm glad you decided on *Gone With the Wind*," Vivien told her. "Also I heard you originally called my character Patsy O'Hara. Scarlett is so much better. I've always thought of myself as a scarlet woman."

At the premiere, klieg lights shone down on Gable and the celebrities at Loew's. "This is Margaret Mitchell's night," Gable proclaimed, "and Atlanta's night. I want to see the picture just as you see it. Please, Atlanta, allow me to see *Gone With the Wind* tonight just as a spectator."

At the end of the showing, Vivien complained to Larry that sitting through such a long movie "is hard on one's ass."

Dressed in their costumes from *Gone With the Wind*, Vivien (accompanied by Larry), Clark Gable, and Olivia de Havilland made their entrance into the post-premiere Junior League Ball that night. Gable danced with the mayor's daughter, and she swooned and fainted in his arms.

Although Hattie McDaniel faced problems of segregation, it is not true that all blacks were excluded from the cotillion ball. A prominent Atlanta preacher, Martin Luther King Sr., was invited. The black community had urged him to boycott the festivities because none of the other black actors, such as Hattie or Butterfly McQueen, was allowed to attend. Ignoring their advice, the preacher showed up at the ball with his "date," his son, Martin Luther King Jr.

At the premiere, Margaret Mitchell thanked everybody on behalf "of me and my poor Scarlett." The following morning she gave a farewell breakfast for the cast at the Atlanta Riding Club.

The next stop before New York was in Washington, where Franklin and Eleanor Roosevelt declined an invitation to attend the premiere, but had a special White House screening. As Mrs. Roosevelt was later to tell Margaret Mitchell, her husband slept through most of the picture. When she woke him up at the end, he said, "No movie has a right to be that long."

After the New York premiere, Larry and Vivien flew to Los Angeles for the West Coast premiere of *Gone With the Wind* two days after Christmas in 1939. The movie attracted a galaxy of stars to the Fox Cathay Circle Theater, and was released in time for *Gone With the Wind* to qualify for the 1939 Oscar sweepstakes.

On the night of the Oscars, February 20, 1940, at the Ambassador Hotel in Los Angeles, Bob Hope was master of ceremonies for the first time. In his opening monologue, he referred to the event as "a benefit for David Selznick."

That night, *Gone With the Wind* swept the Academy Awards. Vivien was named Best Actress of the Year, the award presented to her by Spencer Tracy.

Rumors still persist that backstage Tracy propositioned Vivien. "I'm a hell of a lot better in the sack than my old buddy, Rhett Butler," he reportedly said. "I can't screw you right now. I just left my hospital bed suffering from strep throat."

She backed away from him in horror. "Bloody hell! Don't get near me."

To win her prize, Vivien beat out Bette Davis in *Dark Victory*, Greta Garbo in *Ninotchka*, and Greer Garson in *Goodbye, Mr. Chips*.

Larry lost his bid for an Oscar for his role as Heathcliff in *Wuthering Heights*, losing to another British actor, Robert Donat, for *Goodbye, Mr. Chips*, in which he played a shy British schoolmaster.

Olivia was nominated for Best Supporting Actress, pitting her against Hattie McDaniel's Mammy in the same picture. Usually two actresses competing for the Oscar in the same picture cancel each other out, but not in this case. Hattie became the first black ever to win an Oscar, and, of course, Olivia was disappointed as she'd worked so hard to bring Melanie to the screen.

Victor Fleming won as Best Director, although that Oscar should have been shared with George Cukor and Sam Wood. Sidney Howard won for Best Screenwriter, but he was no longer around. Before the event, he had been run over and killed by a tractor on his farm in Tyringham, Massachusetts.

Viennese-born Max Steiner, who had fled the Nazis in his native Austria,

Vivien Leigh with George Cukor at his house during the filming of GWTW

wrote the memorable musical score for *Gone With the Wind*, although he did not win an Oscar, an oversight the Academy has never lived down.

Even though Hattie won an Oscar, she had to endure attacks from the black community until her dying day. She was charged with perpetuating Hollywood racism in her depiction of stereotypical blacks on the screen.

At one point Vivien invited Hattie for lunch. "I just had a phone call from Butterly McQueen," Hattie said. "That little pickaninny is out of her mind."

"She told me what a sell-out I was to my race," Hattie said. "I told her what in hell did she think she'd done playing Miss Prissy. Mammy has already forgotten more than Prissy will ever know. At least Butterfly refused to eat watermelon on camera for Fleming. 'I'm no field nigger,' she told Fleming."

Of all the reviews of *Gone With the Wind*, Vivien's favorite was from Frank Nugent of *The New York Times*. "Miss Leigh is so perfectly designed for the part by art and nature that any other actress in the role would be inconceivable."

Although it eventually evolved into America's most beloved film, *Gone With the Wind* drew the ire of the Legion of Decency, a hardcore conservative wing of the Catholic Church, its members finding it "morally objectionable," supposedly because of how Scarlett had lusted after Ashley, a then-married man.

On July 25, 1940, in Czechoslovakia, a high-ranking Nazi official marched into MGM's branch office in Prague, where a copy of *Gone With the Wind* had been shipped three months earlier for subtitling. At gunpoint the copy was seized and sent to Josef Goebbels in Berlin where he arranged a special viewing for Adolf Hitler and other high-ranking Nazis. Reportedly, Hitler liked the movie but refused to have it released for showing to the German public, for reasons known only to himself.

Over the years, *Gone With the Wind* has come in for some critical brickbats, notably from the chief book critic for *Punch* in London, Roger Lewis:

"Vivien is best known for Gone With the Wind, *which must be the most cumbersome and crappy film ever made. The repetitive 'Tara theme' by Max Steiner is enough to induce the dry heaves; the photography by Ernest Haller, and the design by William Cameron Menzies, is lurid to the point of pain; the greens are greener, the reds are redder, the sunsets more preposterously orange, than any pigment outside the paint pots of Walt Disney. Did the technician at the Technicolor lab have one too many? But this aside, what's very horrible is the character of Scarlett. She's the apotheosis of the self-willed, petulant, possessive wee miss, who wants the privileges normally accorded men—she wants to dominate—but, then again, she's seeking that strong, devil-may-care fellow who'll slap her around—who'll dominate her. I can't do better than quote Noël Coward on the subject. 'Ah, me! The ladies. God bless them. What silly cunts they make of themselves.'"*

Margaret Mitchell's *Gone With the Wind* does not die, still selling almost 50,000 hard copies a year and some 250,000 paperback copies annually. In all, it has sold 25 million copies in 27 languages worldwide.

Years later, for those lucky enough to have heard it, Larry eventually got to interpret a radio version of the role of Rhett Butler opposite Vivien's Scarlett O'Hara. For a fee of five thousand pounds, the two stars worked for two days recording an adaptation of *Gone With the Wind* for an Australian radio broadcast, as produced by Harry Alan Towers.

Although her words were more or less identical to the words Vivien had, perhaps insincerely, uttered in the 1939 film version to her nemesis, Clark Gable, they had special meaning when delivered, years later, to Larry:

LARRY: I'm going to Charleston, back where I belong.
VIVIEN: Please, please, take me with you.
LARRY: No, I'm through with everything here. I want peace. I want to see if somewhere there isn't something left in life of charm and grace. Do you know what I'm talking about?
VIVIEN: No, I only know that I love you.
LARRY: That's your misfortune.
VIVIEN: Oh, Rhett, Rhett, Rhett. But if you go, where shall I go?
LARRY: Frankly, my dear, I don't give a damn!

Vivien for the rest of her life would never escape her association with the legend of Scarlett O'Hara. To her regret, in many situations, she was forever introduced as Scarlett O'Hara instead of as Vivien Leigh. "I really don't think much of my role," she told Rex Harrison.

"But the Oscar, dear girl, you won it," Harrison said.

"Oh, that," she said. "I use it as a doorstop."

***

Vivien was eager to work with Larry again after the premiere cycles of *Gone With the Wind*. Two scripts held out especially strong possibilities. George Cukor was getting ready to direct *Pride and Prejudice*, although he would later drop out.

Mervyn LeRoy
Director of *Waterloo Bridge*

Also in pre-production was a remake of *Waterloo Bridge*, a 1931 James Whale film that had starred Mae Clarke, Douglass Montgomery, and Bette Davis.

Under the terms of her contract, Vivien owed Selznick one more picture that year. After losing *Rebecca*, she focused on the upcoming *Pride and Prejudice*, based on Jane Austen's novel.

Larry was assigned to star in it,

although *Waterloo Bridge* had originally been written with him in mind.

Selznick had decided he could make more money by lending Vivien and Larry out for two different films instead of producing one movie that starred both of them.

Vivien was announced as the female lead in *Waterloo Bridge*. Myron Selznick told Vivien that she'd be appearing opposite Robert Taylor, with whom she'd made *A Yank at Oxford*.

Vivien begged Louis B. Mayer to replace her in *Waterloo Bridge* and let her take the female lead opposite Larry in *Pride and Prejudice*. "Replace me with Joan Crawford," Vivien urged. "She would be much better playing a whore than I would."

"My mind is made up," Mayer told her. "I'm keeping you in the picture with Bob. As for *Pride and Prejudice*, I've just signed Greer Garson this morning."

Until he permanently settled on the combination of Garson with Larry, Mayer had previously toyed with the idea of teaming Gable with Vivien in *Pride and Prejudice*, hoping that they'd recapture the flame of Scarlett O'Hara and Rhett Butler. Gable absolutely hated the idea.

With little choice in the matter, Vivien reunited with Taylor for *Waterloo Bridge*, even though the flame that had briefly flickered between them had long ago died. By now, the bisexual actor was spending his nights with either Howard Hughes or Barbara Stanwyck.

In *Waterloo Bridge,* Taylor and Vivien were backed up with a stellar cast, including C. Aubrey Smith, Virginia Field, and Maria Ouspenskaya. The unsmiling Lucile Watson—one of Hollywood's most indomitable mothers of the 1930s and 40s—

Vivien Leigh in *Waterloo Bridge* (*lower photo*) with Robert Taylor

385

stole every scene she was in. Playing an archetypal and fiercely protective matriarch, she was cool as ice as she tries to separate her son (Taylor) from a *fiancée* with a sordid past (Vivien).

On the first day of the shoot of *Waterloo Bridge*, Vivien made her objections known to the director, Mervyn LeRoy. "The part was written for Larry. Throwing Taylor into the mix was a horrible case of miscasting."

"Thanks for your confidence, Miss Scarlett," LeRoy remarked sarcastically.

He later told Cukor something he already knew. "Leigh is one of the best actresses I've ever worked with, but I've never met a woman, even a cheap hooker, who talks as dirty as she does."

Actually, in spite of her objections, *Waterloo Bridge* became one of Vivien's best films. She brilliantly played the ballet dancer who, disillusioned after learning of the possible death of her lover, becomes a streetwalker.

Photographed in romantic close-ups, her face looked stunningly beautiful on screen. Bosley Crowther of *The New York Times* even suggested that she might be the finest screen actress of her day.

Mervin LeRoy was one of the most technically accomplished directors she'd ever worked with. "I will not bruise your beauty," he told her, "even when you're trying to pick up tricks at the rail station."

Taylor, MGM's leading star, except for Clark Gable, was shocked when he saw that Louis B. Mayer had given Vivien top billing in the wake of her success in *Gone With the Wind*.

On viewing the film years later, one critic claimed it was "as if Anna Karenina had fallen under the wheels of *A Streetcar Named Desire*."

***

WATERLOO BRIDGE: For sensitive, embittered women, love, shame, and suicide are the only options.

Back in the 1930s, Irving Thalberg at MGM had originally conceived *Pride and Prejudice* as a vehicle for Clark Gable and Thalberg's wife, Norma Shearer. But the producer's death ended that plan. Mayer revived it and ultimately decided that Larry should play the lead. After reading the script by Aldous Huxley, Larry agreed to it but urged Mayer to cast Vivien as the female lead.

Larry was disappointed to learn that Mayer had placed Greer Garson in the role, his former girlfriend from London.

Edna May Oliver and Mary Boland had also signed to appear, along with that marvelous old character actor Edmund Gwenn, who had starred with Jill Esmond in *The Skin Game* and Vivien in *A Yank at Oxford*.

Directed by Robert Z. Leonard, *Pride and Prejudice* was Jane Austen's witty classic of manners and mores in late 18th-century England. Published in 1813, the novel had taken sixteen years to write. In the film, Garson's other sisters were played by Maureen O'Sullivan, Ann Rutherford, Marsha Hunt, and Heather Angel.

Leonard had directed Garbo in her first American screen test, but he was known mainly as the husband, between 1918 and 1925, of silent screen star, Mae Murray, Erich von Stroheim's "Merry Widow" herself.

Larry was very upset that Greer's name preceded his as the star of the film. He told the director, "I invented Greer, and now she gets star billing over me." In the wake of that complaint, many of the posters were revised so that, indeed, he received top billing.

"During the making of *Pride and Prejudice*, Vivien became insanely jealous of Garson," Leonard said. "Apparently, a few years back in London, Olivier had pounded Garson, and Vivien knew about this. She practically tried to make me a spy on the set, reporting any romantic overtures going on between Garson and Olivier. I kept telling Vivien 'nothing is happening.' Maybe she believed me.

A silver screen comedy of manners adapted from Jane Austen's 18th-century novel

(*center photo*): Olivier as Darcy ever-so-stylishly courting Greer Garson in her portrayal of Elizabeth Bennet.

(*lower photo*) A quintet of sisters neurotically competing for husbands

Actually, Olivier and Garson were extremely affectionate on the set, cooing like lovebirds in front of the crew. Maybe Vivien had reason to be jealous."

Larry hated his role, calling Darcy an "unattractive looking prig." He also claimed, "Darling Greer got it all wrong. She was supposed to be the down-to-earth one among her idiotic sisters. But Greer played her as the most affected and silly of the lot."

Most movie critics did not agree with Larry's dismal assessment of Garson's performance. The actress gave a quick-witted, confident performance that was the very opposite of silly.

"Olivier was just jealous—that's all," Leonard said.

***

"Of course, I knew Laurence Olivier and Danny Kaye were having a long-term affair. So did all of London. So did their wives. Why is America always the last to know?"

--Dame Peggy Ashcroft

In his own words, Danny Kaye's first venture into London in 1938 was "a disaster." Before his gig in England, a previous engagement had also been a disaster. He'd been hired by Sally Rand, a fan dancer with one of the biggest busts in the world of burlesque, as a schtickster providing comic relief between the various stages of her act. At the time, her celebrity rivaled that of Gypsy Rose Lee as America's most famous stripper.

In those days, strippers didn't show strategic zones. One of Kaye's duties  involved keeping Rands breasts and genitals provocatively concealed behind a fluttering medley of fans. When confronted onstage with a gigantic bluebottle blowfly which was buzzing around during her act, Danny swatted at the insect with one of Rand's fans, thus exposing one of the stripper's breasts. The police promptly arrested her, and the act was closed down.

Kaye then got a job in New Jersey working for Nick Long, a low-rent comedian of his day. Long and Kaye, billed as Nick Long & Co., worked for two months for Abe Lyman, one of America's favorite band leaders in the Big Band Era. Danny was allowed to sing two songs, including "Minnie the Moocher," which he sang in a radically different style from that of the performer who had made it a virtual signature song, Cab Calloway. Kaye also sang "Dinah," which he pronounced as Deenah, or Dena,

"Fan Dancer"
Sally Rand

388

a name that he'd select for his only child with his wife-to-be, Sylvia Fine, in the years ahead.

Henry Sherek, one of the great British impresarios of the time, had come to America to search for cabaret artists. He'd been impressed with Kaye, less so with Long, and booked their act into the Dorchester Lounge at one of London's premier hotels. The club attracted *chic* London on its opening night, including a devastatingly handsome Laurence Olivier, looking impressive in his Savile Row tuxedo, and his mistress, Vivien Leigh, whose emerald green gown seemingly made her eyes sparkle.

Against the backdrop of the Art Deco architectural glory of the sophisticated lounge, Vivien and Larry watched Kaye "go down in flames" [his words].

Amazingly, both Vivien and Larry applauded wildly, but as they recalled they seemed to be the only members of the audience doing so. Londoners, perhaps, were in no mood for levity that night from what was viewed as a second-rate Jewish comedian imported from America.

Kaye and Long opened their act at the Dorchester during September of 1938, during the peak of the Munich crisis, when the umbrella-carrying British prime minister, Neville Chamberlain, virtually abandoned Czechoslovakia to the Nazis. Chamberlain had persuaded Hitler to sign the Munich Agreement. The dictator later ridiculed and trivialized Chamberlain. "He seemed like a nice little man, so I gave him my autograph."

Vivien and Larry were so enchanted with Kaye, for reasons never fully explained, that they came back to his dressing room to congratulate him and to booster his courage. He embraced both of them, saying, "It was my fault. I was too loud for the saloon. I died the death."

"No, you didn't," Larry claimed. "You were fresh and original. As for the audience, they were snobs."

"You are great," Vivien assured him, "just great." She may not have felt that. At that time in her relationship, Vivien was trying to please Larry and virtually go along with every one of his pronouncements.

Larry even dropped into the Dorchester the following morning to have a "proper English breakfast" with the comedian. Kaye showed him a review by Richard Richards in London's *Sunday Pictorial*. "Danny Kaye's impact on the sophisticated Dorchester crowd was like that of a ping pong on a rhinoceros's hide."

Danny Kaye

389

Larry took his hand and squeezed it. "Both Viv and I have received far more devastating reviews than that. Welcome to show business."

Even though Vivien and Larry had busy schedules, they took time out to escort Kaye to some of their favorite sights in London and even invited him for dinner.

One night at the Dorchester Lounge, Vivien and Larry introduced Kaye to Noël Coward. Coward later told his party of friends that he could not understand why Larry "was socializing with this cheap vaudevillian and second-rate stooge." Rather sarcastically Coward added, "Maybe Larry is attracted to Kaye's unruly shock of red hair. But, of course, you can only do so much with that in bed."

Kaye had been booked at the Dorchester for a seven-week stint. But as audiences grew thinner and more hostile, the event was terminated after only three weeks. Along with that went Kaye's salary of 40 pounds a week.

Larry had become so impressed with Kaye that he drove the comedian to his next gig in Larry's native Surrey, the historic town of Guildford. During Kaye's show, Larry applauded loudly and laughed heartily. The Guildford patrons, far less snobbish than those at the Dorchester, also seemed to take to Kaye.

Late that night, Larry and Kaye ordered steak-and-kidney pie and lager in a local pub, where Kaye spoke in a Scottish brogue and claimed he was a Welshman born in Brooklyn whose real name was "Kaminsky." The bartender looked completely puzzled.

In an unheated room, cold and clammy, Larry and Kaye spent their first night together in a small bedroom above the bar.

It has never been documented and cannot be proved, but it appears this was the first time the two men engaged in sex. It would be the first of many nights to come in far more luxurious circumstances.

When Larry told Danny good-bye, as the comedian headed back to America, he promised Kaye that sooner than later he'd be seeing him again in Hollywood. Both performers warmly embraced. Larry told Kaye, "You'll return to London one day, and I'm sure when you do you'll become the toast of the town."

In this case Larry turned out to be a prophet. But before that could happen, World War II had to be fought.

***

Larry must have had second thoughts about a relationship with Kaye. The comedian was not among the first people Larry contacted upon his return to California in 1939 to film *Wuthering Heights*. When Myron Selznick called

390

Larry and invited him to a party at his home, Larry learned that Kaye would be among the guests.

During the months Larry had been in Hollywood filming *Wuthering Heights*, Kaye had made several attempts to contact him. But he didn't return Kaye's calls. Impulsively, perhaps out of delayed guilt, he finally called him and told him he was looking forward to meeting him again at the upcoming Selznick party.

Larry perhaps excused himself from not contacting Kaye earlier because in the meantime the comedian had married his childhood friend, Sylvia Fine, a lyricist.

As host, Myron later recalled that it was "instant chemistry, a combustion, when I introduced Larry to Kaye." Apparently, he was unaware that Kaye had met Vivien and Larry during his London engagement.

Both Vivien and Larry were introduced to Fine, but there was hardly any chemistry there. Larry pointedly ignored Kaye's new wife. Vivien was respectful, but had far more intriguing people at the Selznick party to talk to.

Myron later claimed, "No two men could be as different as Larry Olivier and Danny Kaye. But they seem to adore each other. Vivien worked the room but Kaye and Larry huddled together all evening, ignoring Fine and Vivien and my other guests. I had invited Larry to show him off as my hot client, and he seemed to have no interest at all in meeting a lot of important people in Hollywood. Later in the evening when I walked out on my terrace to smoke a cigar, I saw these two guys in a huddle. They were having an intense talk, very animated. Jokingly, I called out to them, 'Get a room, guys.'"

Before the evening was over, Kaye was calling Larry by his pet names of "Lala," which he in time changed to "Lally."

Near the end of the party, Kaye invited Larry and Vivien to a late-night club in Los Angeles where he said he was going to try out some material. It was obvious that Larry didn't want Vivien to go along with them, reminding her that she had an early morning call at the studio, "where you have to look fresh as the morning dew."

Sylvia Fine Kaye
(1913-1987)

The more sophisticated Sylvia, who knew of her young husband's proclivities, bowed out and said she'd get a ride home with a young Robert Steele, whom Kaye had introduced as "my facilitator."

What little is known about the very private life of Kaye and Larry would come from this very "facilitator" when Kaye fired him in the late 50s for some unknown reason.

Seeking revenge and left with no money, Steele

tried to peddle his story of Larry and Kaye to *Confidential* magazine, which turned it down, perhaps in fear of libel.

Steele lived in a one-bedroom cottage in the rear of a house occupied by Sylvia Fine and Danny Kaye on San Ysidro Drive in Beverly Hills. As Steele revealed in his *Confidential* proposal, one of his duties was having sex with the comedian, or else arranging liaisons for him with willing young men who were paid for their services.

Sylvia was well aware of her young husband's nocturnal adventures, and had no objection, as she conducted discreet lesbian affairs herself.

According to Steele's claims, Larry and Kaye arrived at the cottage around five o'clock in the morning after they'd returned from the club where Kaye had performed. "Danny told me to get lost after I brought them some ice water. When I came into their room, both men were getting undressed. I retired to the courtyard where I fell asleep as I'd had a lot to drink at Myron's party. I woke up around seven o'clock. I heard Olivier on the phone having a fight with somebody—perhaps Miss Scarlett herself. I don't know."

"Later Danny had me fix breakfast for Olivier and himself, and I was then ordered to drive Olivier home since he didn't have to report to the studio that day," Steele said. "He became much friendlier to me as the years went by, but on that morning he was cold and distant, as if embarrassed that I was in on his little secret."

"When I returned to Danny's house, I was told to go into his study," Steele said. "Danny was there and he handed me a letter from a realtor. The house next door to his had become available, and he wanted to see if he could rent it for Olivier and Miss Scarlett."

"The very next day, Kaye signed the papers for the rental, and I helped Miss Leigh and Olivier move in," Steele said.

The house was just off Benedict Canyon above the Beverly Hills Hotel. Nearby was Pickfair, the abode of Mary Pickford and her husband, Buddy Rogers. Fred Astaire was also a neighbor. As the days went by, both Larry and Kaye spent a lot of time together, filling in the gaps in each other's lives, relating what had gone before.

"Kaye had been a 'toomler' on the Catskill borscht circuit, while Larry had appeared in Shakespeare plays in London," Myron Selznick said. "Before meeting each other, the only thing they had in common was repressed homosexuality."

The son of Ukrainian immigrants, the Kaminsky family came to America seeking the *golden medina* or "the golden land." Their son grew into a gangly young boy with an outrageous shock of uncontrollable bright red hair. He hardly looked like a star when he told his parents he wanted to perform on the stage.

Breaking into show business, Kaye took the long way there, including ignominious stints hustling chocolate malts to lovesick teenagers in a drugstore, even work as a dental assistant holding bowls for patients to spit out blood.

Word of Kaye's intimate link with Larry spread through the cocktail party chatter of Hollywood. The combination of Danny Kaye and Laurence Olivier struck some as incredulous, especially since Larry had Miss Scarlett O'Hara waiting in his boudoir.

Over the years, literally hundreds of people have weighed in with their comments about the affair, ranging from Ralph Richardson to George Cukor.

One writer said that Larry and Kaye were as different as "chalk and cheese—here was Laurence Olivier a man's man and the greatest Shakespearean actor of his day, as contrasted with Danny Kaye, a fast-talking Borscht Belt comedian, the epitome of wholesome American family entertainment. Not to mention their respective marriages."

With Larry and Vivien next door, Steele, on Kaye's instruction, became their virtual errand boy, even shopping for their groceries or preparing an evening meal for them. Kaye and Sylvia were often guests. On some nights Dame May Whitty showed up to train Vivien's voice in case a decision was made to go on tour in America with *Romeo and Juliet*.

A gate connected the back gardens of the two properties. In addition to his main house, Kaye also had a guest cottage in back. According to Steele, "On most nights, Larry came through that gate to visit Danny in the cottage where I lived. During his visits, I made myself scarce."

"Danny told me that as long as Olivier was in town, I wouldn't have access to Danny for sex," Steele said. "'You'll have to make do with Minnie,' he told me."

"Who's that?" Steele asked.

"As 'many' fingers as you can get around it," Kaye said, laughing at his own joke. "He had a streak of cruelty in him."

"For the rest of his time in Hollywood, Larry came over to see Danny, usually at night, but often in the afternoon," Steele said. "Although I'm not sure, it appeared to me that between Danny and Miss Leigh, Olivier was being worn to a frazzle. He didn't seem all that oversexed. Both Danny and Miss Leigh were pressing more sexual demands on Larry than he cared for, and, believe it or not, I felt sorry for the guy. Too much of a good thing."

"On one of two occasions when Larry came by and Danny was called away, I more or less made myself available to Larry," Steele said. "But he didn't go for it. I guess it was Danny Kaye or no one, except Scarlett, of course."

Interviewed at her home in Thousand Oaks shortly before her death, the blonde bombshell of the 40s, Virginia Mayo, had starred with Kaye in several movies. "I remember Bob Steele, a great swell guy, although Danny abused him a lot. I knew that Danny was gay, even back in those days, although we didn't call it gay then. Whenever I talked with Danny off camera, I found Larry Olivier was his favorite subject. He bragged about Olivier's accomplishments all day, and carried on like Olivier was the greatest thing since sliced bread. The long separation the two men endured during the war was hard on Danny. He seemed impatient for the war to end so he could be reunited with his beloved."

Although Mayo was not completely informed about Kaye's relationship with Larry, she was very aware that Kaye, a total bisexual, was having an affair with actress Eve Arden.

"Eve often would come to the movie set where Danny was working and disappear with him into his dressing room," Mayo said. "I think Sylvia knew all about this affair and may have encouraged it for all I know. Even though Danny and Eve were longtime lovers, I really believe that Danny would have dropped Eve in a minute if Olivier miraculously returned from wartime England for a reappearance in Hollywood. Danny told me he couldn't wait for that day to happen."

As it was later revealed, Larry was a temple of mental health compared at the time to both Kaye and Vivien.

Steele claimed that Kaye was subject to wild mood swings and mental instability over the years. "In the beginning of their relationship, Danny concealed from Larry how crazy he was."

"I first discovered how nutty Danny was when I signed on with him," Steele said. "Early one rainy morning, I woke up and found him standing nude over my bed. At first I thought he wanted sex. But he told me to get my ass out of bed and go feed the crows. At first I thought he was joking—after all, he was a comedian, but he turned out to be deadly serious. There was bird seed resting on the kitchen table. He actually sent me out buck naked into his backyard with bird seed. After that night I realized that my boss and sometimes lover was a bit of a sicko. But life was good, and so was the money, so I was determined to hang in for the duration."

Virginia Mayo.

"Sometimes Danny wasn't very funny at all, but deadly serious," Steele said. "One drunken night he said, 'Vivien has a parlor game. I played it with Larry and the bitch last night. The game is to see who can come up with the most ingenious way to kill an infant.'"

"That sounds pretty gruesome," Steele said.

"I wanted to do her one better," Kaye said. "Sometimes at night I like to conjure up ways to kill Vivien Leigh."

"He also demanded that I come up with ways to kill Leigh," Steele said. "I didn't want to play the game, so I stumbled, trying to conjure up a plot. When I suggested damaging the brakes on her car, he slapped my face and called me an idiot. My mind grabbed at anything, finally suggesting that when Larry wasn't there we release a nest of baby rattlers in her bedroom. 'Death will be instant,' I told Danny."

"He came up with an even more frightening scheme," Steele claimed. "Three nights before, he'd seen up close and personal Vivien as she'd entered into one of her 'states,' denouncing both Danny and Olivier."

"The best way to get rid of Vivien would involve being with her when she enters one of her states," Danny told me. "Not when Larry is around, of course. She becomes a lunatic. I've been told by a psychiatrist that there are ways to induce a person in that state to suicide. Yes, that's it. I think I know how to drive her to suicide, but the conditions have to be right."

"I'll never know for sure, and I don't know if Danny ever acted on it, but he claimed he did on more than one occasion. 'I almost drove her over the edge one night,' he told me years later. I believed him. His mind could conjure up ways to make people laugh, but he had the dark side of genius too. A lot of people don't know how really devious he was."

"In spite of dark shadows, there were many lighter moments," Steele said.

"I remember both Olivier and Danny lying in the concealed courtyard of the cottage sunning themselves," Steele said. "They were completely nude. Through the open window of my kitchen where I was preparing lunch for them, I could overhear their conversation. Those two were actually talking about what Danny called symmetricals—or leg falsies. Both of them were discussing the merits of giving themselves more shapely legs in the tights they wore. Olivier claimed he'd done that when appearing on stage. I know for a fact that when Danny made *The Court Jester* in 1956, he wore leg falsies to give himself more shapely legs. I should know. I helped him put them on."

Danny Kaye in
The Court Jester (1956)

Like Vivien's, Danny's mood could change within minutes. Many of his closest friends were well aware of his manic depressions. Jack Warner Jr. claimed, "He was the most depressed, dejected person in the world."

Larry told Kaye, "With Vivien and me, it is love or hate, no gray zone," Larry said. "At times I feel she possesses the power to destroy me."

"You must never marry her," Kaye warned him.

"I never will," Larry said. "That is a solemn promise to you."

"In the few times I ever talked to Olivier, I got the impression that he wanted to run away from both Danny and Miss Leigh," Steele said. "In very different ways, each of those two were an albatross for Olivier."

Steele also claimed that on two different occasions, Kaye became almost suicidal. "One was when he learned that Larry had sneaked off and married Miss Scarlett. Kaye had urged him never to do that, warning him that marriage to her would be a life of heartbreak and misery for him. The other time occurred during the summer of 1940, when Larry had to leave California to go on tour with *Romeo and Juliet*, starring none other than Miss Leigh herself."

"Over the years, especially after the war, I had a front-row seat watching the relationship between Olivier and Danny grow, change, self-destruct at times, rejuvenate, blossom anew, and eventually wither between Danny and Olivier," Steele said. "One night in London, Danny told me that Olivier had the night before claimed that 'he loves me more than he ever loved Vivien.' Of course, I don't know if Olivier actually said that, but Danny definitely thought it was true."

The editors at *Confidential* wanted to know if Danny really loved Sylvia—they did have a daughter together. Steele's answer was not direct: "Danny is a total sadist as far as his marriage is concerned. Sylvia is a total masochist."

Kaye's most serious biographer, Martin Gottfried, the author of *Nobody's Fool*, claimed Kaye was "frequently morose, sometimes even nasty—someone who found it difficult to maintain relationships with men or women. He was a sad, detached man, emotionally insulated from all who knew him."

Larry was the exception, different from all his other relationships. "Both of those guys were relatively cold and distant from other people, even their wives," Steele claimed. "But they seemed to blossom when they were around each other. They could sit and talk for hours, each of them sharing their darkest secrets. I often eavesdropped as they made revelations to each other—dark thoughts they had."

"Without Sylvia, I would be nothing," Kaye was reported to have said. "I'm a wife-made man. Yet I hate her at times. I have an unhappy marriage but that is just beginning. But I never plan to leave her. People are already saying, 'There is a Fine head on my shoulders.' They know that Sylvia Fine is the power behind me."

In the last years of her life, Sylvia was writing her memoirs, *Fine and Danny*, about her life with Danny Kaye for Knopf Publishers. Her editors wanted her to include at least two or three chapters about her husband and Larry. But she never finished the memoirs, so it is not known what her final decision was on that subject.

Over the years, Vivien weighed in with many comments, spoken off the record to friends. Occasionally when going through one of her "states," she would confront Larry about his homosexuality, often citing Kaye as his lover. At one such party at George Cukor's home, attended by such gay men as William Haines and Anderson Lawler, Vivien screamed at Larry. "Go to your lover. You like making love to Danny Kaye more than you like making love to me."

"Kaye was the most repressed innate homosexual I ever met, and I met them all," said Haines.

When both Noël Coward and Ralph Richardson confronted Larry about the rumored affair with Kaye, Larry had a pat answer. "Danny fits the classic profile of the unhappy clown. All of us know how unhappy clowns are when they're not performing. But I know and understand this man. When I'm with him, I know how to push the right buttons. The trouble is that little Danny Kaminski, born in Brooklyn in 1913, doesn't really know Danny Kaye at all."

Further allegations of a lengthy affair were made by Sarah Miles, Larry's co-star in *Lady Caroline Lamb* and *Term of Trial*.

Larry's third wife, Joan Plowright, seemed to remain rather ambivalent on the subject. Reportedly, she once said, "I have always resented the comments that it was I who was the home-wrecker in Larry's marriage to Vivien Leigh. Danny Kaye was attached to Larry far earlier than I was."

However, in a BBC radio program, *The Archive Hour*, broadcast on May 19, 2007, Plowright denied the story of the affair totally.

While some biographers, without any firsthand knowledge, have dismissed rumors of an affair with Kaye, author Donald Spoto has weighed in heavily on the subject, acknowledging that such a long-term love relationship existed.

Larry, "knight of the realm, embodiment of England, great Shakespearean actor, and movie star, was saddled with self-loathing, chronic guilt over failed relationships, and sexual ambivalence," Spoto claimed. He also made the claim that Larry's affair with Kaye drove Larry to "suicidal thoughts."

Arguably, culture critic Michael Bronski, a fan of the star since his childhood, is the world's leading expert on Danny Kaye. At Harvard University, he once presented his conclusion about Kaye and the connections between gay culture and Jewish culture in the 1950s.

"I identified with Kaye because he was not a butch man and because he was very expressive," Bronski said. "He was a slightly effeminate blond man with fluttery hands and silly grin. I identified with him as being 'queer.' His songs, quick, funny, patter songs were incredibly gay—the Fairy Pipers sung in falsetto, the mad queen hat designer who shrieks with chic. In his movies Kaye was just as queenly and flighty in them as he was on his records."

"He was sometimes so effeminate that it was hard for us to see it any other way," Bronski claimed. "In *The Kid from Brooklyn*, he even flirts with other men. Kaye succeeded in a time and place where it was not acceptable to be gay or too Jewish in mainstream entertainment. He perfected the character of the non-masculine man and then used that to make fun of, ridicule the idea of butch masculinity. Think Jerry Lewis, Woody Allen."

"Danny Kaye is part of gay history," Bronski said, "whether he slept with men or not. And I think there is more than enough evidence to suggest that he did. Kaye looks and sounds like a gay man."

"Another culture critic, Roland Pedersen, said, "Danny Kaye and Laurence Olivier provided the *anima* and *animus* in each other. Olivier was masculine, struggling with his feminine side; Kaye was feminine struggling with a masculinity he never really found."

***

Even as Vivien and Larry waited out the months before their joint divorces came through, the white heat of the passion they'd shared during the late thirties had cooled. It was not a dying ember, but their passion—not their love for each other—burned on a much lower flame than before.

Their new friend, writer Garson Kanin, had a chance to observe Vivien and Larry close up. He was sharing a house in Beverly Hills with Larry. At times, Kanin used to expound on his theory that the white heat of passion within any relationship lasts no more than eighteen months, if that. "Larry and Vivien had long passed that point even before they got married," Kanin claimed. "At least their mad passion for each other had lasted longer than most. Some couples hardly make it through the night."

"Since the press was referring to Larry and Vivien as Romeo and Juliet, I urged them to take advantage of that reputation and set up a road tour for *Romeo and Juliet*," Cukor said. "I told them they could really cash in, and I pointed out there would be plenty of alimony payments in their future. I also told them I felt Larry would eventually be in the military, and Vivien might need a nest egg in war-torn London to see her through the dark years."

"Even as I urged that, I knew in my heart that they were fairytale lovers no more," Cukor said.

CHAPTER TEN

Finally, Jill Esmond and Leigh Holman agreed to divorce their errant spouses. On January 5, 1940 Vivien learned that Sub-Lt. Leigh Holman, RNVR, Ramsgate, had petitioned for a divorce from his wife, Vivian Mary Holman. Larry was named as correspondent. A judge granted the divorce in February.

Esmond followed suit, petitioning for a divorce from Larry after he'd agreed to a financial settlement. She named Vivien as correspondent.

Leigh retained custody of Suzanne, and Jill kept Tarquin. In the view of their friends, both in America and London, Larry and Vivien didn't want custody of either of their children.

"We will never settle down," Vivien told George Cukor. "Larry and I are wandering souls, not put on this Earth to remain in one place. Bringing up children is for the middle class."

"You're sounding more like Marie Antoinette every day," Cukor said jokingly.

With his divorce behind him, and marriage to Vivien looming, Larry confessed to Cukor another big problem. "Vivien right now is a bigger star than I am, and I am . . . very, very envious. I don't know how that is going to affect our relationship."

Larry was experiencing not only jealousy of Vivien, but a conflict in his romance with her.

Cukor had become Larry's confidante in matters homosexual. "Between Danny and Vivien, I'm exhausted morning, noon, and evening. At least I've given up masturbation."

While filming *Pride and Prejudice* and *Waterloo Bridge*, Larry and Vivien were plotting on their separate sets to mount their own stage production of *Romeo and Juliet* to tour America.

Thanks to their recent movies, they had a combined savings of $60,000, a respectable sum in the early 1940s.

Warner Brothers agreed to match Olivier's investment since they wanted to star him in another film—this one on the life of Disraeli.

"In a fit of madness," as David O. Selznick later said, "I agreed to release Vivien so she could play Juliet to Olivier's Romeo."

Selznick and Louis B. Mayer had conspired to keep Vivien and Larry from working together, either in *Waterloo Bridge* or *Pride and Prejudice*.

Their contracts allowed them to do a stage play, and Cukor came up with what he claimed would be the perfect play, *Romeo and Juliet*. "You are America's reigning sweethearts of the moment, and here's your chance to clean up," he assured them. "The lines at the box office will stretch around the block. Not only that, *Romeo and Juliet* could be a triumph in the theater for both of you. People will talk about it for years. You could also show America that two talented actors like you guys can do more than play Heathcliff and Scarlett O'Hara."

Vivien had her doubts, fearing she wasn't ready to take on the role of Juliet. "By the time an actress has mastered the lines, she's too old to play the part," she said.

Larry told Vivien, "The world has seen, of all things, Sarah Bernhardt play Juliet in her seventies and on one leg. Katharine Cornell, of course, played Juliet when she was far too old for it. But you are perfect, young and beautiful, the way Juliet should be presented on stage."

Larry himself was thirty-two, not a sixteen-year-old Romeo. Before he accepted a major role, he always contacted Ralph Richardson, his mentor, for advice. Larry had written him about whether he should produce *Romeo and Juliet*. Finally, after many war-time delays, a brief reply arrived from Richardson. "*Romeo and Juliet* is a bit too luxurious for wartime."

At the time, the road to Verona was hardly Richardson's major concern. He was already on active duty in the Fleet Air Arm. "Ralphie may be right," Larry told Vivien, "but we've sunk our bloody fortune into *Romeo and Juliet*; we've made commitments, and we've got to see it through."

Rehearsals and casting were concluded in Hollywood while Larry was still filming *Pride and Prejudice*. A tour was being set up that would begin in San Francisco, go on to Chicago, then open in New York for a long run, ending perhaps in Washington, D.C.

For the production, Larry took on so many responsibilities that it would lead to his near collapse. He was not only starring in *Romeo and Juliet*, he was also producing and directing it.

He hired Thoda Cocroft to do publicity for the tour. In *Great Names and How They Are Made*, Cocroft wrote of the impression Vivien made. "Her naïveté and her wisdom, her warm beauty that could instantly freeze if Olivier were criticized, her juvenility and her matronly dignity paradoxically combined to give this slip of a girl a refreshing wine-and-water personality. The screen fails to register her utter delicacy and daintiness, the changing colours of her eyes, the transparent quality of her skin, the most beautiful skin I have ever seen."

"Larry was very gallant directing Vivien," said Cocroft, "calling her 'sweetheart, do it this way. No, darling, pause with your line instead of blurting it out too much. Remember, it is poetry.'"

Larry signed Edmond O'Brien to play Mercutio and Alexander Knox to be Friar Lawrence.

The aging English character actress, Dame May Whitty, was asked to play the pivotal role of the Nurse, but she turned it down. "I'm much too old to tour," she said. "But it is so tempting. I've known all the great Juliets of the English stage, and I'm convinced Vivien will be the shining light of all of them."

Later, however, when her husband, Ben Webster, was cast as Montague, Whitty signed on as the Nurse, although Larry secretly wanted Edith Evans, who was trapped in England.

Before leaving Hollywood, Vivien and Larry threw a party for their friends at their house on San Ysidro Drive, inviting Danny Kaye and his wife, Sylvia Fine. Larry also invited Gladys Cooper, who had recently appeared with him in *Rebecca*. Her escort was her stepson, Jack Merivale, a twenty-three-year-old English actor known to both Larry and Vivien. Not spectacularly talented, Merivale had appeared onstage with both Vivien and Larry in England, although they had never taken particular notice of him before.

Observing him keenly at her party, Vivien urged Larry to cast him in *Romeo and Juliet*.

"Larry wanted to cast me as Paris," Merivale claimed. "I couldn't do it the way Larry wanted, so I suggested John Buckmaster, my stepbrother. I noticed a deep frown cross Larry's face. He obviously knew that John and Vivien had been lovers. I did not know that at the time." Finally, Larry asked Merivale to play Balthasar and to be his understudy as Romeo.

(Merivale's greatest role lay in Vivien's future. After Larry divorced Vivien to marry Joan Plowright, Merivale would become her longest surviving lover, even though he was somewhat of a gigolo.)

John Herman Merivale, later called Jack, had been born in Toronto in 1917, the son of Philip Merivale, the English actor. His stepmother was Gladys Cooper, and he was educated for the most part at Oxford.

Jack Merivale

401

He made his acting debut at the age of 15 when James Whale cast him in the role of the newsboy in his film *The Invisible Man*. Whale also took the opportunity to seduce the rather handsome teenager. He made his stage debut at the age of 21 when he was an understudy in *A Midsummer Night's Dream*. "That is where I first met Vivien," he said, "but she didn't even know I existed at the time."

"Jack worshipped the boards that Vivien trod on at the theater," claimed Dame May Whitty. "She adopted him like a surrogate brother or son. He was gorgeous, but timid. Some women, of course, are won over by that quality. He was a bit younger than Vivien and madly in love with her. I think he was also in love with Larry. He virtually worshipped both of them. But I think it was Larry who got to sample Jack's charms first."

Early in his life, Merivale was sharp enough to realize that he had much to gain by attaching himself to either or both members of a famous couple.

Before Vivien entered Jack Merivale's life as "Jack's longest-running engagement," there was (*top photo*) Jan Sterling and (*lower photo*) Nina Foch

His future mistress, Nina Foch, once said, "Jack would hustle men or women, it didn't matter to him. He was ambitious and knew he needed a meal ticket in life. He didn't expect to become rich in the theater, so he attached himself to those who had already arrived—Jan Sterling, myself, Larry Olivier, and ultimately Vivien Leigh, his longest running engagement."

Even though Merivale was cast in a minor role in *Romeo and Juliet*, Larry cracked down hard on him, warning him he had to work more on his fencing.

But as the rehearsals deepened, Larry and Merivale grew closer and closer, as members of the cast noticed. "Jack started out as the actor who did nothing right and went on to become perfection itself, at least in Larry's eyes," Whitty said. "He came to adore the boy, and it was obvious to me that Vivien's green eyes were becoming even greener."

"At one point," Whitty said, "Vivien became so exasperated she walked off the stage, but not before telling Larry in front of the cast, 'If you don't like the way I'm performing Juliet, let Jack do it. I'm sure in

402

your eyes he'd make the perfect Juliet.'"

The Canadian actor, Alexander Knox, accidentally learned of another backstage affair. A handsome young bisexual actor, Cornel Wilde, was descended from Hungarian Jewish parents.

Studying to be a doctor, he became a skilled swordsman as a hobby. He qualified for the United States fencing team prior to the 1936 Summer Olympics, but resigned from the team to take a role in the theater instead.

Larry hired him as a fencing teacher to help him in his role of *Romeo and Juliet*. In addition, Larry offered him the role of Tybalt. It was his performance as Tybalt that netted Wilde a contract in Hollywood.

Wilde and Larry were seen working on fencing scenes in a Hollywood gym, wearing only jock straps which left them bare-assed, according to Scott Markin, the manager. "Those two guys even showered together and looked really cozy, but a lot of crap like that happens in my gym."

When Larry became ill at the end of one rehearsal, Wilde fulfilled an earlier dream and became "Dr. Wilde" to the ailing actor. He even administered injections of some sort to allow Larry to rehearse the following evening, although his Romeo that day was hardly his most athletic performance.

"Merivale detested Wilde and made disparaging remarks about him," Knox said. "Both Wilde and Merivale vied for Olivier's attention, and our great director seemed in his glory with Vivien waiting in the wings. O'Brien and I often joked that Larry was taking 'director's privilege.' You know, the old casting couch routine."

"I began to fence with Larry way back when we did *Romeo and Juliet*," Wilde later said. "The fights I find most dangerous are those involving swords, spears, and lances, especially if the combats are on horseback. I have been hurt several times in swordfights, generally because my opponent had to learn fencing for the first time in his life and then memorized a difficult routine which had to be done at considerable speed to look good. I have been pierced and cut many times on various parts of my body."

"Larry was the first actor who nicked me," Wilde said. "In Hollywood, he didn't want us to wear protection when practicing

Two views of Cornel Wilde
(*lower photo*) in *Naked Prey* (1966)

403

fencing. He told me he wanted to study the fencer's body nude in motion as we dueled, and I agreed to that, providing we'd go easy. We fenced more like a slow-motion ballet than a clashing duel."

"I was fluent in Italian, French, German, and Russian," Wilde said. "He told me he wanted me to go either to Hollywood or London with him and make him proficient in all those languages, so he could perform Shakespeare in each of the countries using the native language. Larry told me his dream one day was to perform Romeo in Italian in Verona. That never happened, of course, but Vivien liked me to speak to her in Italian, French, or German, not Russian, of course. She had a marvelous gift for language."

Never a modest man, Wilde later in life was quite blunt. "I had what it took to become a romantic lead in the 1940s. Virile good looks, so they said. A well-developed physique. A very generous endowment, a gift from God. And that thing critics called a smoldering intensity. If I had to lie on a few casting couches to get my start in the early 40s, so be it."

Was he referring to Larry?

At the time Wilde became involved with Larry, he had been married to actress Patricia Knight since 1937. "Having a girlfriend in Olivier's case, or a wife in Wilde's case, didn't stop those two," O'Brien alleged.

At the time of Wilde's death in 1989, he was writing his autobiography, *My Very Wilde Life*. He planned to include a chapter on Larry.

Cast in swashbuckling roles, Wilde became Hollywood's "king of Beefcake Bondage." In *At Sword's Point* (1952), he appeared bound and stripped to the waist in a torture chamber where his torso was burned with a hot iron. In *California Conquest*, also in 1952, he was again stripped to the waist and bound to a tree, where he was lashed across the chest with a whip. Sadists went to see his movies with a raincoat to hold over their laps, even on a sunny day.

"After we learned our roles [in Romeo and Juliet]," O'Brien said rather cynically, "our motley crew headed north to San Francisco and the Geary Theater. Most of us were alone, but Larry was traveling with a virtual harem—Vivien Leigh in the front, with Cornel Wilde and Jack Merivale for the rear action, no pun intended."

***

In San Francisco, hundreds of fans mobbed Larry and Vivien at the rail station with the banner WELCOME LAURENCE OLIVIER AND VIVIEN LEIGH.

Even though their divorces had not been granted, the press agent announced: SEE REAL LOVERS MAKE LOVE IN PERSON.

When she saw that promotion, Vivien said, "I hope they don't expect Larry and me to fuck on stage."

At the Fairmont Hotel, both Vivien and Larry were besieged by fans. Vivien told the press, "Our love affair has been simply the most divine fairytale, hasn't it?"

When O'Brien read that, he told Alexander Knox, "Their love affair is a fairytale all right. I'm convinced either of them would fuck anything in pants that came along."

Unlike his London interpretation of Romeo, directed by John Gielgud back in 1935, Larry's American Romeo was more lyrical, more romantic. "That's because I'm in love," he told O'Brien.

O'Brien listened politely, not breathing a word of it. Later he told Knox, "Romeo told me he's in love. But perhaps not with Juliet."

Larry was somewhat bitter that the critics in San Francisco preferred Vivien's Juliet to his Romeo. That may have been because of his exhaustion on opening night. He was supposed to leap over a wall, but couldn't make it. On stage he was left dangling by his fingertips.

Too exhausted by overwork, he failed to make the leap and found himself hanging there "helplessly by the fingers, kicking and scratching, gasping, sweating, entirely unable to move in an upward direction." Finally, the stage manager took pity on him and doused the lights.

Appearing nearby in *The Man Who Came To Dinner*, the critic Alexander Woollcott made a curtain speech every night, proclaiming the Olivier production of *Romeo and Juliet* "the greatest ever presented of Shakespeare's work." He had not seen the play.

EXCLUSIVE!
Laurence Olivier and Vivien Leigh in "Romeo and Juliet"

In San Francisco, Olivia de Havilland, who had such fond memories of Vivien, flew in with her *beau du jour*, James Stewart. Both came backstage to congratulate Larry and Vivien on a "brilliant performance," although Stewart was seen dozing off in the first act.

On another night, Clark Gable, on a surprise visit to San Francisco, dropped in to congratulate Vivien on her performance as Juliet. "I don't know a God damn thing about Shakespeare," he told her, kissing her with his foul, whiskey-tainted breath. "All I know is he was a faggot, but your words as Juliet sounded like beautiful music to my big ears."

Poster issued by San Francisco's Geary Theater for the Olivier's 1940 production of *Romeo & Juliet*

"Welcome, Rhett Butler," she said, embracing him in a pretend warmth she didn't feel but masked.

"I brought along a little mule-kick," he said, putting a quart of Kentucky bourbon down on her dressing table. "How about joining me?" he asked.

"Don't mind if I do," she said. "Pour me a glass and don't be stingy, darling." She looked back at the door, as if expecting someone else. "Is Carole with you?" she asked.

"She's tied up in Hollywood," Gable said. "Tonight I brought another film goddess. We've been working together." He leaned out the door and whistled. "Coast clear."

Within the minute, a very glamorously dressed Lana Turner was in Vivien's dressing room.

"Oh, Miss Leigh," Turner gushed, "I loved you so much as Scarlett O'Hara. I don't know what possessed me to try out for the role myself. I would have fucked up that picture big time."

"I'm sure you would make a divine Scarlett," Vivien graciously said. "At least you're young enough to look sixteen in the opening sequence."

"My love scenes with Lana would have been terrific," Gable said. 'Unlike certain parties, Lana really digs a he-man like me."

"I'm certain she does," Vivien said.

"You lost out on your big chance," Gable told her, "and I have to warn you. I don't go back to women who turn me down on the first go-around."

"I turned you down because I'm in love with another," Vivien said.

"Hell, I'm in love with another woman," Gable said, "but that doesn't mean I don't enjoy fucking Lana." He motioned for the blonde star to come and sit on his lap.

"I'd love to talk over old times," Vivien said, "but I have a dinner date with Larry. Let me leave first and face all the cameramen and screaming fans. I don't think it wise for you and Lana to be photographed and have your pictures splashed all over the front page."

"Carole Lombard would be seriously pissed," Turner said.

"More than that, I bet she'd cut off your left nipple," Vivien said. "And then what would half the men in the world do for nourishment?"

"Oh, Miss Leigh, how you talk."

"She looked at her watch. "Our chat is over..." Vivien said, getting up and reaching for her rain jacket. "Clark, give me another bolt of that God damn fucking mule kick before I have to face those raging fans."

***

Although Vivien and Larry didn't know it at the time, San Francisco would be the highlight of their tour. On the sixty-hour train ride on the Santa Fe Railway east to Chicago, Vivien was ill for most of the trip, running a fever. She was not used to touring on this magnitude as she crossed the great American wastelands.

Larry offered her what comfort he could, dining at night in the railway car with both Wilde and Merivale. Neither actor had warmed to each other, and each vied for Larry's attention.

Arriving at Union Station in Chicago, Vivien and Larry were greeted with a banner welcoming them. She appeared pale and weak as she disembarked. To Larry's fury, nearly all the fans waiting to greet them had come to see Scarlett O'Hara in the flesh. Police had to clear their way to a limousine waiting to take them to the Ambassador Hotel beside Lake Michigan.

The next day, they arrived at the vast and echoing theater, finding it could hold 3,500 people and was geared mostly for concerts. An elaborate revolving stage confronted them, and it malfunctioned for most of the play's run.

Vivien's growing distaste for her overly exuberant fans solidified in Chicago. She'd later refer to the American brand of adoration as "the rape of worship. They come at you. They want a piece of you. They try to grab your hair, a piece of your clothing. They terrify me."

The critiques in Chicago were not as enthusiastic as in San Francisco, one reviewer suggesting that the production should be called *Jumpeo and Juliet*. Some members of the press claimed "the audience didn't come to hear Shakespeare, they came to see Heathcliff and Scarlett O'Hara."

In spite of Dame May Whitty's training, Vivien's voice remained weak and didn't carry to the balcony.

In Chicago, Wilde recalled that Vivien "became gloomy and threw some irrational tantrums, often attacking Larry. He had to cancel two performances, and we had no understudy for her, so the theater went black. But on other occasions, she tried to bolster Larry's sagging spirits. He became lifeless on stage after reading critical reviews. She told him the Chicago critics wouldn't recognize dog shit if they stepped in it."

"Larry began to drink, and I often drank with him," Wilde said. "We became very close, very confidential. Vivien became aware of our growing friendship, and she resented me for it. One night before curtain, she told me, 'If you think you'll take Larry from me, forget it! That will never happen.' I thought the attack completely unprovoked, as I had no real intention of coming between them. I think she resented Larry hanging out with his men friends and not devoting every offstage moment to her."

"During the run of the play," Knox claimed, "Vivien seemed to undergo a personality change. She was gracious to us at first but shut herself off and seemed rather hostile toward the end of the run in Chicago. Of course, things were going real bad for her, and there were obvious conflicts with Olivier. When she left by the stage door, autograph seekers hounded her every night, pulling at her clothes, even her hair. 'Fuck off!' she'd yell at them. 'All of you, go fuck yourselves!'"

Also performing in Chicago was a fast-rising star, Gene Kelly, the actor/dancer. He was on tour with *One for the Money*, which had been booked in the Selwyn Theatre.

Young Kelly found himself hanging out with some of the biggest names in show business, including Katharine Cornell and her husband, Guthrie McClintic. They also introduced him to Orson Welles who was in Chicago doing his magic act along with excerpts from the George Arliss piece, *The Green Goddess*. After each evening's end of their respective performances, Kelly usually pre-arranged a meeting with John Barrymore, who was playing at the Harris Theatre next door to the Selwyn.

By the time Kelly arrived at whatever bar they'd agreed upon for a rendezvous at eleven, he found that Barrymore was usually so drunk he had to escort him to his hotel and put him to bed.

(top photo) John Barrymore and (lower photo) Gene Kelly

For Kelly, the highlight of his Chicago gig was the night he went to see *Romeo and Juliet*, accompanied by McClintic and Cornell. Backstage, Cornell introduced him to the famous lovers. "I was really awed meeting the couple," Kelly said. "We hugged and kissed and embraced several times, so much that I thought they might be suggesting a three-way. But nothing like that happened, although we agreed to meet again in Hollywood. We were an unlikely trio."

Kelly claimed that "my touchy-feely with Vivien and Larry was tinged with just a hint of sexual allure, I mean, from both of them. Their reputation had preceded them to Chicago. But all we did on the first night was to greet each other warmly, with the promise of a friendship yet to come."

"The next night, Larry called me," Kelly said. "He'd heard from McClintic that I was meeting Barrymore every night, and he told me, 'I've met him before in London, but I am most anxious to pay my respects to him once again before it's too late.' Larry had already heard about Barrymore's alcoholism and his declining health."

Vivien did not go but Larry accompanied Kelly that night for a reunion with Barrymore, who did not recall him. "Hello, young man, you're meeting the stag at twilight," Barrymore said to Larry.

After the exchange of admiration and congratulations, Barrymore said, "I see you've been bitten by the Hollywood bug. It ruined me, but I made two and a half million dollars in ten years. Spent it all. My lavish lifestyle was blamed."

Barrymore insisted on another drink, which Larry ordered for him. "I could tell by the shock on your face when you saw me how much I've changed since London. Many people say it's what the years do to a man. In my case it's what Jack boy here has done to the years."

He invited Larry and Vivien to come and see his show, *My Dear Children*, at the Selwyn. "A nurse awaits me backstage. I have to take eye drops. In fact I do right now." He reached into his coat pocket and removed his eye drops. "The doc tells me my eyes are congested, whatever in the fuck that means."

Larry had almost nothing to say to Barrymore except repeat endlessly what a marvelous actor he was, as he later confessed. "I listened in fascination at what was coming from that once-golden throat of his."

"If I did *Hamlet* today, I would be both the prince and Falstaff too," Barrymore said. "Many fans are coming two or three times to see me perform in this dumb play. They're not coming to see the play but hoping that I will die on stage so they can witness that."

"You will never die," Larry assured him. "You're immortal."

"Don't kid a kidder," Barrymore said. "The stage door keeper told the press that I faithfully show up every night at eight . . . dead or alive."

Barrymore insisted that Larry stay and drink with him, but he sent Kelly on an errand. "Tonight I fancy a high yaller gal, and I want the best," he told Kelly. "Get me one and put her in my suite at the Sherman. Tell her I never pay more than twenty."

One hour later when Larry helped Barrymore to his suite, Kelly was waiting with a beautiful mulatto woman.

She was ordered to wait in Barrymore's bedroom, and Kelly slipped her the twenty. It was obvious to both Larry and Kelly that Barrymore was about to pass out.

"Come here, my boy," Barrymore said to Larry. "I want to kiss your mouth. In so doing, I pass my blessings on to you. The kiss from the fading actor of yesterday, the greatest of his generation, to the bright young star of tomorrow."

Larry started to take leave, but Barrymore held him back. "Don't try to drown yourself in liquor like I've done. You don't drown, you float."

Larry along with Kelly headed toward the door. Looking carefully at Barrymore for what he knew would be the last time, Larry whispered to him, "Good night, sweet Prince." He kissed Barrymore gently on the lips and left quickly.

On the street below, Larry broke down in tears.

The Great Profile drew his last breath on May 29, 1942.

***

Romeo and Juliet opened at the 51st Street Theater in New York City on May 9, 1940 and closed on June 8, 1940.

Larry read the reviews the following morning and sobbed. In New York their *Romeo and Juliet* was called almost everything from "pretentious" to "arrogant."

One critic called it "the worst *Romeo and Juliet* ever," another claiming that "Olivier talks like he's brushing his teeth." "Incomprehensible" was another word used, giving way to "hollow." Brooks Atkinson of *The New York Times* wrote, "Much scenery—no play."

John Mason Brown of the *New York Post* found that Larry "gulped down his lines as if they were so many bad oysters." Andrew Pollock of the *Journal-American* found that Larry "suggested the general romantic attitude of a window cleaner."

Critic John Anderson claimed that, "Instead of *Romeo and Juliet*, the play should be called *Laurence and Vivien*, and let it go at that."

Larry cried out, "Here I am, in uttermost misery, sweating, flinging myself painfully around, tearing my soul to bits and being paid with shrieks of mocking laughter."

Vivien took the attacks more stoically, perhaps because she had made out better than he did in the reviews.

After breakfast, he went to the box office and was gratified to see lines forming around the block.

The stage manager rushed out and told him patrons weren't buying tickets, but demanding a refund. Furious and outraged, Larry headed for the box office and began distributing the cash to the prospective members of the audience himself. When some of the would-be ticket holders saw that it was Heathcliff himself, they left in embarrassment and decided to see the play regardless of the critical attacks.

Even friends or acquaintances backstage in New York had veiled reactions. Typical remarks came from Samuel Goldwyn, who appeared with his beautifully dressed wife, Frances. He shook Larry's hand. "You're still Olivier," he said. "As for you, Vivien, you're still as beautiful as you were in

Gone With The Wind."

"We have painfully learned," Vivien told Noël Coward, "that there is a backlash from being celebrated for our roles as Heathcliff and Scarlett O'Hara. Personally, I think the critics were just sharpening their axes for these snobbish British movie stars, namely, Larry and me."

Later, Coward told Jack Wilson, "I think they are trying to bring back the early days of their love affair. *Romeo and Juliet* is but a failed attempt to convince each other they are still smitten. Like their own *Romeo and Juliet*, I predict their upcoming marriage will end in tragedy."

Actress Ruth Gordon came to see the performance, noting that "where Romeo's privates bulged under his tights swung two distracting golden tassels. If Shakespeare had seen the show, I bet even he would have been distracted."

While suffering through their doomed tour, Vivien assembled "bundles for Britain." Larry flew planes with pontoon-style floats. The murky Hudson River was his splash-down strip. He was still trying to log enough hours to get into Britain's Fleet Air Arm with an active commission.

Larry and Vivien, though two of the most famous movie stars in the world, found themselves broke, their losses amounting to $100,000. They immediately left their expensive hotel suite and moved into Cornell's house at Sneden's Landing on the Hudson. The final performances were sliced to only three dozen.

"We were *persona non grata* in the theater world," Larry said. "Only Alfred Lunt and Lynn Fontanne invited us to dinner."

On another outing they attended a war relief ball in New York to be greeted by Coward. "Darlings, how brave of you to come," he said.

***

After *Romeo and Juliet* closed, Merivale was reached by phone in upstate New York, where he was rehearsing for a summer stock production. Vivien sounded urgent.

"Her voice was strange," the actor later recalled. "But she told me it was imperative that I visit with them at Sneden's Landing."

He accepted, taking the train to Cornell's home where he found both Vivien and Larry very tipsy from martinis.

He was eager to hear what emergency had summoned him to their side. But nothing seemed amiss. Larry sat in an armchair reading a flight manual, and Vivien invited him for a game of Chinker Chess. "Chinker Chess" was her nickname for Chinese checkers.

When he won the first round, she exploded in fury. "How dare you come

411

between us? You're trying to break up our upcoming marriage. We've been lovers for years, and you want to destroy our happiness."

Having never seen Vivien in such a state, Merivale was furious. Larry sat in his armchair, continuing to read as if nothing had ever happened.

"You don't play fair and square," she said when he won the game. "You cheated."

"I did nothing of the sort," Merivale said. "I would never do that."

"You're a liar." She stood up and tossed the game off the table and onto the carpet. "That's the only way you'll get ahead in life—by cheating. You're not coming between me and Larry—and that's that! I won't have it."

Deeply offended, Merivale planned to leave at once but there wasn't a train until morning. Larry insisted he stay.

"She has these outbursts of anger," Larry privately told him. "Don't take them seriously. By morning she will have forgotten all about them."

Merivale left on the early train the next morning. His real role in the lives of Larry and Vivien lay far in the future.

At the time Larry and Vivien worked with him, Merivale was getting ready to marry the blonde American actress, Jan Sterling, in 1941.

A child of wealth, Sterling had studied acting at the Fay Compton School in London before returning to America to make her Broadway debut. Merivale took her backstage in New York to meet Larry and Vivien. He'd be married to her until 1948. In the years following his 1941 marriage, however, he put his career on hold, opting for wartime service with both the British and Canadian air forces. After the war, in 1946, he resumed his career with a starring role in Oscar Wilde's *Lady Windermere's Fan*.

In 1948, shortly after her divorce from Merivale, Sterling went on to marry an even more famous actor, Paul Douglas.

Biographers have cited Vivien's act of hostility toward Merivale as an example of her oncoming mental instability. Merivale may not have cheated at Chinese checkers, but he was cheating in the ways of love.

To advance himself in the theater, he'd been having sex with Larry, and somehow Vivien found out about it. For Merivale, it was probably a move toward career advancement and not based on a sexual desire, as he genuinely seemed attracted to women.

"As a member of the cast of *Romeo and Juliet*, Vivien may have been the last to find out about Merivale and Larry," O'Brien claimed. "I was astonished to hear that she planned to get married in August. When Vivien accused Merivale of trying to break up her relationship—all of us heard about that—she may have known of which she spoke."

Years later, Vivien tried to explain her outburst to Merivale, claiming "perhaps I saw him as a danger." She didn't explain what the danger was. It could have been the fling he was having with her husband-to-be, although it may have been the mutual sexual attraction they had for each other.

***

In 1940, under threat of attack from German U-boats, Tarquin and Suzanne made the dangerous crossing aboard the ship, *Scythia*, following a route along the North Atlantic via Iceland to Newfoundland. To Gertrude's shock and dismay, she found herself traveling on that same vessel with Jill Esmond and her son, Tarquin. Tarquin and Suzanne socialized with each other, but Gertrude remained aloof from Jill throughout the entire trip.

Because of wartime currency controls, adults were allowed to export only ten pounds from England, and five pounds for each of the children who accompanied them. Jill planned to settle in California, where she hoped to find work in films.

In New York, Jill and Tarquin moved into a small apartment on 20 West 72nd Street, rooming with an out-of-work actress, Jessica Tandy. A lesbian, Jill slept in the same small bed with Tandy. The gossip along Broadway was that they were lovers, but no smoking gun has emerged.

Jill's hair had turned gray, and Tandy urged her to dye it auburn so she might be cast in more roles. She followed that advice and managed to get minor work, often on radio.

An embarrassment would occasionally arise, as Tandy and Jill often competed for the same roles.

Jill was not completely shunned by the theatrical friends of Larry and Vivien. Lynn Fontanne and Alfred Lunt invited her to dinner. Even Charlie Chaplin called to make a date for dinner.

Allegedly, Chaplin had an unusual request to make to Jill. He wanted to arrange for Jill to put on a private "show" for him with one of his girlfriends, in which he could voyeuristically take pleasure. She politely turned down The Little Tramp.

In New York, Larry and Vivien had an embarrassing and awkward rendezvous with the spurned Jill and her son Tarquin. In time, Vivien would become friends with both Tarquin and Jill. But at the time, Jill recorded in her diary that Vivien had such a beautiful face, but she feared it was "just a mask and her eyes were hard and cruel."

At the close of *Romeo and Juliet*, Larry returned with Vivien to the West Coast. Before he left, he paid a farewell visit to Jill. After soliciting promises that he would send money, she had a final request.

She wanted him to take Tarquin into the bathroom and urinate and to show him what a grown man's penis looked like.

As reported in his future memoirs, Tarquin cried that night. "Daddy has male organs, and I only have flies," he sobbed to his mother.

Months later in Hollywood, Tarquin would urge his mother to marry the lackluster Alexander Knox. Jill had found him a "bore," but young Tarquin was impressed that Knox owned a racing car.

The summer of 1941 found Jill and Tarquin living next door to Jill's former lover, Joan Crawford. In her diary, Jill recorded what a wonderful mother Crawford was to her adopted daughter Christina. Jill seemed sad that she couldn't give Tarquin all the many advantages Christina enjoyed.

At her new home in Brentwood, Jill, along with her son, lived with Ella Voysey, who was separated from her husband, Robert Donat.

When she returned to England, Jill would take up with her friend, Joy Pearce. The two of them occupied a modest semi-detached house in Wimbledon, in South London, living quietly together for many years. Her neighbors did not know that she had once been married to the fabled Laurence Olivier.

Back during the war years in Hollywood, Jill had appeared in such popular films as *Random Harvest* (1942) and *The White Cliffs of Dover* (1944). Emlyn Williams cast her in his Broadway play, *The Morning Star* (1942), a play notable for being the acting debut of Gregory Peck.

She was offered fewer and fewer roles as time went by, and she made her farewell film appearance in 1955 in *A Man Called Peter*. However, she appeared as Eleanor of Aquitaine in the late 1950s TV series, *The Adventures of Robin Hood*.

In later years, she expressed bitterness at times toward Larry. "I sacrificed my career only to be discarded by him," she said. Larry and Jill did stay in touch after their divorce, mainly because of their mutual concern for Tarquin.

In July of 1967, she attended Vivien's memorial service. "I don't know why I went, but she had been a part of my life for so very long, I felt an urge to attend. At the end of the service, I turned to go. To my surprise, I found that at some time during the service Larry had stepped up behind me in this very large church filled with hundreds of people. It was a coincidence. I greeted him warmly. He appeared not to recognize me, and then said, 'Vivien led a short life, but a full one.' Then he kissed my cheek, turned, and walked away."

More than twenty years later, proud of her status as a survivor of the many ironies of her life, Jill attended Larry's memorial service at Westminster Abbey in October of 1989. She was frail and had to be pushed in a wheelchair.

"It's funny after all that time how I can still love him so much," she told Tarquin.

On a windy summer day, July 28, 1990, at the age of 82, Jill Esmond Moore Olivier "passed into heaven," in the words of her pastor.

***

EMMA:	*What are those bells?*
LORD NELSON:	*Have you forgotten what night this is? Last of 1799.*
	Eight bells for the old year and eight for the new.
	Happy New Year, darling.
EMMA:	*Happy New Year.*
LORD NELSON:	*The dawn of a new century.*
EMMA:	*1800. How strange it sounds.*

From his base in New York during the summer of 1940, Larry received a call from Alexander Korda's wartime base in Hollywood. "Have you ever heard of Admiral Horatio Nelson, and what do you know about him and Emma Hamilton?"

"Well, he confronted Napoléon's navy in the decisive Battle of Trafalgar, and he was incredibly neurotic," Larry said. "He also had the most extraordinarily girlish mouth. If you're making a movie of him, an actor would have to paint his lips rose."

"And the woman?" Korda asked.

"A dance hall girl and courtesan," Larry said. "Eventually the mistress to Admiral Nelson."

"You've got it right," Korda said, except we've got to make Nelson more patriotic than neurotic. I'm calling the picture *The Enchantress*. I want you as Lord Nelson, Vivien as Emma."

"Not a bad idea," Larry said. "After Romeo, I need to appear on-screen as a conquering hero."

When Vivien returned from shopping, Larry said in a mock Cockney accent, "How would you like to play Lord Nelson's piece?"

She understood the question at once. "An actress never goes wrong playing a slut."

Screen Guide magazine stated the case for Vivien after her return to Hollywood.

"Jealousy over the fact that a foreigner won Hollywood's prize role of 1939 has not faded. Indeed, it has become a two-headed monster menacing Vivien Leigh. First, the ghost of Scarlett shadows her so that people can't resist comparing her every role with one even she may never equal or surpass; second, producers, given such a good thing, are tempted to type her in Scarlett-like parts—as Lon Chaney Jr. was typed after playing Lenny in *Of Mice and Men*."

"Being a wise lady, Vivien won't discuss the subject," the magazine claimed. "But she would hardly be human if she failed to sense Hollywood's jealous delight when she and Olivier were less than triumphant on the stage in *Romeo and Juliet*. And there is no doubt that more than one critic will see their latest picture, based on the life of Lord Nelson and Emma Hamilton, with an axe in hand instead of a pencil."

Although their friend, Radie Harris, would lie in her column by implying that Larry and Vivien were living in separate quarters, when they returned to Hollywood after their disastrous run of *Romeo and Juliet*, they moved into a rented house at 9560 Cedar Brook Drive, off Coldwater Canyon. The abode had once been the home of poet, satirist, and screenwriter Dorothy Parker. To help with the rent, Garson Kanin lived in the small poolhouse out back.

Vivien found the house gloomy, with darkening shadows creeping down the canyon every day at four o'clock. But its next tenant, Olivia de Havilland, claimed, "I loved the house. Two great love affairs took place here." Ironically, the second of the two love affairs de Havilland referred to was Parker's acerbic marriage to her gay collaborator, Alan Campbell, who spent more time bedding men than his wife.

Larry continued with his flight training at Clover Field. Previously, his instructor, Cecil Smallwood, had taught many A-list celebrities to fly, including both Katharine Hepburn and Olivia de Havilland herself, who often flew with her beau, Jimmy Stewart.

Later, Olivia observed, "No matter what airport we landed in, Larry would also descend from the air, no doubt sideswiping some plane with his wing. If he joins the RAF, England has lost the war. One day Jimmy and I had trouble landing in Monterey because Larry—that grand pilot—had destroyed part of the landing field."

In exasperation and tired of worrying, Vivien asked him, "Will your bones be in the right place on our wedding day? I doubt it."

When Korda discovered that Larry had been taking flying lessons, he strongly objected. "I hear you're the worst pilot on two continents," the producer told him. "If you have an accident and my insurance company hears you were taking flying lessons, I'm fucked. I want you to stay alive, at least until the end of the Nelson picture."

Finally, Korda relented when he saw how stubborn Larry was about continuing flying lessons. "Okay, but let's keep the insurance people in the dark. Perhaps we should retitle the film *The Flying Nelson*."

Before filming began on *Lady Hamilton*, Korda warned his stars that an isolationist Congress, particularly the anti-Roosevelt contingent, might attack them for making such a pro-British movie.

"The Man Himself [a reference to Winston Churchill] wants us to make a propaganda film but disguise it so people won't know what they're watching but will leave the theater with sympathy for dear old England," Korda said.

"I hear it's going to be called *The Enchantress*," Vivien said. "I know you have cast Larry in the lead, but what role will I play?"

"You're a wicked girl," Korda said, laughing. "A wicked sense of humor. The picture is now called *Lady Hamilton*."

For its American release, Korda later retitled it *That Hamilton Woman*.

Since Larry and Vivien were broke after *Romeo and Juliet*, Korda agreed to pay half their salaries in advance.

Emma Hamilton and Lord Nelson were engaged in an adulterous relationship. So were Larry and Vivien at the time. Far from being accused of propagandizing for Britain, Korda was accused of being an apologist for adultery.

On hearing that Larry and Vivien were going to play adulterers on the screen, it was inevitable that Hollywood reporters would call it "type casting."

In Hollywood, where Korda had been sent by Churchill to make propaganda films for the British, he encountered a very different Vivien and Larry. They were no longer "the starry-eyed kids" he worked with on *Fire Over England*. Both of them were far more cynical, especially of each other.

When Vivien disappeared into the powder room, Larry confessed his concerns to Korda, telling him, "I fear that in this picture, the role of Emma will far overshadow that of Lord Nelson. It is so ungentlemanly of me, but I must tell you the truth. I'm jealous of Vivien. After losing the Oscar for *Wuthering Heights*, I was furious at her for winning for Scarlett. I know that sounds insanely jealous."

He claimed that on the way home from Oscar night, they rode in the rear of a limousine. "I grabbed her Oscar from her. It was all I could do to hold myself back. I wanted to hit her face with it and ruin her beauty."

"Dear boy, I will have to warn you: Don't make this confession to anyone else," Korda said. "Of course, I will have to tell Merle."

Waiting for the script of *Lady Hamilton* to be finished by Walter Reisch and R.C. Sherriff, Larry and Vivien decided they would get married as soon as their divorce decrees were granted.

On August 9, 1940, Vivien was informed of her decree absolute, meaning she was free to remarry. It took until August 28 for Larry's divorce

Is It Love or Is It Propaganda? Emma Hamilton (Leigh) with Lord Nelson (Olivier)

from Jill to become final.

Wanting to keep their upcoming marriage a secret, Larry and Vivien confided in their close friends, Ronald and Benita Colman. Benita even agreed to purchase the ring, and Ronald himself arranged for the wedding to take place at his partner's San Ysidro Ranch in the Montecito Hills above Santa Barbara. Later Ronald would arrange for them to take a brief honeymoon aboard his yacht, the *Dragoon*.

After a three-day waiting period for the registration to take effect, Larry and Vivien were ready to drive 100 miles to the Santa Barbara ranch. They needed a best man, and their tenant, Garson Kanin, was called in for active duty.

Their maid told Larry that Kanin had gone to see Katharine Hepburn at home. During the past few months, the writer had been involved in a *faux* romance with her, which was choreographed after Howard Hughes flew out of her life and before Spencer Tracy landed.

Larry called Kanin to pitch the idea of being his best man.

When the call came in for Kanin, he was pitching his own idea, a script for Hepburn based on the life of Julia Dent Grant, the wife of general and later

president Ulysses S. Grant. Kanin had tentatively entitled his screenplay simply, *Mrs. Grant*.

Larry asked Kanin to return home immediately to the complex in Beverly Hills. It was all very hush-hush.

With profound apologies to Hepburn for his hasty departure, Kanin left, but got a ticket for speeding because he drove so fast in response to the phone call. Once he reached the house, he found Larry and Vivien dressed for a wedding. Their own. It seemed that Ronald Colman and his wife, Benita, had arranged for them to get married that very night.

"Couldn't you have waited a little longer after your divorce?" an exasperated Kanin asked Larry. "I was just pitching a film to Hepburn that would have won her an Oscar—that is, if she is still speaking to me. I also have other plans for Hepburn. In other words, if you guys had waited, it might have been a double wedding."

"Oh fiddle-faddle," Vivien said in her Miss Scarlett voice. "We want you to be best man. Let's get going."

"Who's going to be your maid of honor?" Kanin asked. "Dame May Whitty?"

"We haven't thought about that," Vivien said.

In a flash, Kanin proposed Hepburn as matron of

Two views of Katharine Hepburn. *(top photo)* with Garson Kanin

honor and the couple agreed.

Larry and his bride-to-be, dressed formally in their wedding finery, piled into the back seat of Kanin's car as he drove back to Hepburn's house. She had gone to bed, and she sleepily opened the door attired in a night gown. He quickly explained the situation and asked her to be matron of honor, telling her that Vivien and Larry were already waiting, fully dressed, in his car. "All right," she said, but she demanded to take a shower first.

"C'mon, Kate," he implored. "Time for baths later. Besides, haven't you already had eight showers today?"

Hepburn took that final shower after all, but was fully dressed and in Kanin's car in just ten minutes. The first part of the trip went reasonably well, as Hepburn assured them that they would soon dethrone the Lunts and the Barrymores and become the new king and queen of theater, both on Broadway and in London. The couple, soon to be universally known as the Oliviers, liked that a lot. What they didn't like was when Hepburn said, "I adore how the two of you have been lovers for years while married to other people."

After that, the atmosphere in the car soured. Kanin got lost, and Larry and Vivien began to fight bitterly over directions.

"Before Garson and I knew it, Lord Nelson and his Lady Hamilton (aka Miss Scarlett O'Hara) were fighting bitterly," Hepburn later said. "Neither one of them would give in. I didn't give this marriage much of a chance."

As Kanin later recalled, "They were scrapping all the way. Larry was tough as hell, and Vivien was as sharp-tongued as a Times Square tart."

Larry became so upset with Vivien at one point that he demanded that Kanin stop the car. He got out and told Kanin to drive on. "I'm not marrying that bitch. Have the wedding without me."

Hepburn got out of the car too, and after about thirty minutes managed to persuade Larry to get back into the rear seat with Vivien and to continue north for their upcoming nuptials.

They arrived an hour and a half late. To keep the minister, Judge Harsh, there, Ronald Colman had been plying him with whiskey. By then, Harsh was completely sloshed.

Even though they'd arrived late, Larry learned they had to wait until the stroke of midnight before his divorce decree would be final. He wanted to be married in the living room, but Vivien demanded the rose-covered terrace.

Kanin later said, "There was something in the night air I was allergic to. I had history's worst case of hay fever and coughed all through the ceremony."

The judge pronounced her name "Lay" and called him "Oliver." Although he asked Larry if he'd take Vivien as his lawful wedded wife, he forgot to propose a similar question to Vivien. Benita had purchased the wedding ring for Olivier as a means of maintaining secrecy, but Kanin as best man forgot to produce it. It seemed that everybody forgot about the ring, until razor-sharp Hepburn called for it.

After Judge Harsh drunkenly pronounced the Oliviers man and wife, he shouted, "Bingo!"

Following the ceremony, in the very early hours of the morning, Kanin and Hepburn drove the newlyweds to San Pedro, where Colman's schooner, *Dragoon*, was waiting to take them on a brief honeymoon to Catalina Island.

Hepburn and Kanin came aboard, where they enjoyed two bottles of champagne and caviar arranged by the Colmans. After kissing the Oliviers good-bye, Hepburn stood on the pier with Kanin watching them and the schooner disappear into the dawn. It could have been a scene from the upcoming *Lady Hamilton*.

Delivering Hepburn back to her doorstep, Kanin in the early morning sun grabbed her and kissed her passionately. "How about you running off with me and getting married next week?"

"We'll be too busy getting *Mrs. Grant* ready to show Mr. Mayer," she said before gently closing the door in his face.

At the last minute, Hepburn pulled the plug on *Mrs. Grant*. When she pulled out, Kanin could not convince Louis B. Mayer to produce the film. Kanin lost in another way. He was out the door. Spencer Tracy had walked in.

"All those stories about our illicit relationship in the press are now over," said Vivien when she heard a long-delayed broadcast of their secret wedding in Santa Barbara. "All that is left to write now is 'they lived happily ever after.'"

Larry looked skeptical. "But what comes *after* they lived happily ever after?"

***

"I'm seriously pissed off," said a drunken Louella Parsons when she heard about the Oliviers' marriage and realized that she'd missed a big scoop.

In her morning column, she wrote: "In looking back over the years, it is amazing to realize how many great love stories between two great stars have gone on the rocks or have had tragic consequences."

For once, Parsons got it right.

***

Back in Hollywood, Vivien called on Hepburn to thank her for standing in as matron of honor.

Vivien repeated what Larry had already told the Colmans. "Larry and I listened to every broadcast for news of our marriage. Apparently, we were so secretive nobody found out, not even Louella and Hedda. Larry had to disguise his voice and call a radio station to alert the sluggards to this big news development."

"You wanted them to find out and tail us, didn't you?" Hepburn asked, a bit perplexed. She was an actress who didn't want any of her secrets known, and with good reason.

From the beginning, Hepburn seemed to view Vivien as a wounded bird that she could nurse back to health. Sitting in her garden after the wedding, Hepburn told Vivien, "My birth sign is Scorpio, and they eat themselves up and burn themselves out. I swing between happiness and misery. I say what I think and am prepared to accept the consequences of my actions. I think in some ways we are very much alike."

Around Vivien, Hepburn often pontificated. "Both you and I have wild hearts. A wild heart cannot settle down with one person. I know that is a strange thing to say to a bride recently married, but marriage can kill romance. You and I are artists, and an artist must be free to follow her whims. I suggest your marriage be one of loyalty, a deep and abiding friendship. It is foolish for a romantic couple like you and Larry to follow the morals of a middle-class couple from Kansas. Both of you seem to want to devour life, whole chunks of it. Don't let some traditional sense of values hold you back in your development."

"Oh, Kate," Vivien said. "You are such a darling. Thanks for the advice, which seems so practical and so full of Kate Hepburn wisdom. From now on, we'll be best friends. Please tell me that is all right."

As Humphrey Bogart might say, it was the beginning of a beautiful, long-standing friendship. Hepburn wanted to make it far more romantic than Vivien preferred, but somehow they worked out a compromise.

"I'll be a steadfast ship through the night, a guiding light steering you into the right port," Hepburn said.

"How does Larry fit into our arrangement?" Vivien asked.

"What does it matter?" Hepburn asked. "Men always manage to intrude in the bonding rituals between women. Somehow, some way, these devils sneak in under the crack in the door. They are best ignored, except when we need them, which is rare indeed."

***

It was years after his marriage that it was revealed that Larry was a foreign agent working for British interests in America. What wasn't known is that Vivien was also a secret agent. Actually they had volunteered their services when England declared war on Poland. When nothing came of that, they issued yet another appeal to London to see if any "roles" might be found for them in whatever capacity.

While still in New York performing in the ill-fated *Romeo and Juliet*, Larry had placed a personal call to his friend, Alfred Duff Cooper, who was Minister of Information in London. Such calls to England were virtually impossible at the time, but he got through.

Duff Cooper was married to the celebrated beauty, Lady Diana Manners, and Vivien and Larry had entertained them on occasion.

Larry explained that at the age of thirty-three, he was beyond enlistment age, but wanted "to do something for our beloved, beleaguered England."

Cooper told him, "We have a very important role for you to fill while in America. Korda will explain everything."

Korda was in Hollywood, and Larry and Vivien were going from New York to the West Coast to meet him.

Larry received an emergency cable from Duff Cooper in London: THINK BETTER WHERE YOU ARE STOP KORDA GOING THERE.

Korda had been given instructions to set up offices in Washington, Los Angeles, and New York. These offices would be a camouflage and a "cover" for British agents operating in the United States, which at the time was a neutral country. "A movie studio would be an ideal cover to mask intelligence operations," Winston Churchill had told Korda.

Korda was prepared to take all risks, including the fact that he might be a victim of a planned assassination within the United States. Undercover German agents, taking their orders directly from Berlin, of course, were also operating in the United States.

Alfred Duff Cooper
British Minister of Information,
with his wife,
Lady Diana Manners.

Nazi activity, as Korda admitted, may have been far more extensive in America before Pearl Harbor than ever assumed. Even J. Edgar Hoover of the FBI did not know the full extent of German foreign agents operating within the U.S.

At all costs, Korda was ordered by British Intelligence to avoid the scrutiny of the FBI and the United States Senate.

Before departing for America, Korda spent countless hours being briefed by the SOE and the men of MI6, the British intelligence-gathering agencies.

Established in 1940, the "Special Operations

Executive" (SOE) was often called "The Baker Street Irregulars" or "Churchill's Secret Army." The prime minister established SOE with orders to "set Europe ablaze." Churchill himself called SOE "The Ministry of Ungentlemanly Warfare." At its peak, SOE employed some 13,000 recruits, conducting more than a million worldwide secret operations.

Korda had been recruited by the British Secret Intelligence Service. Sir Claude Dansey, deputy head of MI6, was his main contact, and MI6 officers were ordered to acquire film-making skills as a cover for their secretive spying. Korda was well connected. He worked in secret with the Office of Strategic Services (later the CIA), an agency that had been set up by his own lawyer, William Donovan.

During Korda's final meeting with Churchill, the prime minister, perhaps as an afterthought, added, "In some capacity, perhaps as a courier, use Miss Leigh and Mr. Olivier. They are such good actors they could pull off any subterfuge. No one would believe that Scarlett O'Hara was a British spy, not in a million years."

As declassified documents have revealed, Korda was one of the major British spies working in the United States before that country's entry into World War II. Actually, he'd been recruited as a secret agent as early as 1933.

It started when he cultivated a friendship with Robert Vansittart, a well-positioned member of Britain's foreign office in London. As it was later revealed, Vansittart secretly organized his own intelligence-gathering agency outside of the official British intelligence service, which had been penetrated by German spies after Hitler assumed power in 1933.

Korda proved a valuable contact for Vansittart. The producer still had many important business and social contacts not only in his native Hungary but in Germany and Austria as well.

During the 1930s, he made frequent visits to the heartland of Europe, ostensibly for reasons involving filmmaking deals. In return for these services, Vansittart arranged loans to Korda for his London Films which occasionally suffered financial reverses, particularly in 1936.

Korda played an even more important role after England declared war on Germany in 1939. At great risk to his life, he flew from the United States to England nearly thirty times with important intelligence data gathered in the United States.

Korda evolved into a vital link for the British

Sir Robert Vansittart

A senior British diplomat before and during World War II, and hardliner staunchly opposing the appeasement of Hitler's Germany

Secret Service in their counterespionage work against the Nazis. Vansittart later said that the information Korda transmitted was especially critical during that 27-month period when England virtually stood alone against Nazi Germany. The United States was officially neutral, and many American isolationists wanted to keep it that way.

For months, Korda's offices in New York, L.A., and Washington D.C. were a front for the illegal activities of SOE and MI6. Reports from America were sent to Electra House (EH) in London for processing. SOE's London headquarters were identified by the building in which they were was housed.

SOE wanted to help win the war against the Axis, and it employed virtually anybody who could aid the cause. Known homosexuals weren't welcomed in the military but the door was open at SOE if these men could be of use. Bad conduct records or even criminal files in the armed forces were not a strike against a potential SOE member.

Even anti-British nationalists and communists were employed. Such a motley crew could have been considered a security risk, but there is no known case of an SOE agent going over to the enemy.

Five days later, Larry made a private call to Korda, volunteering to work in any capacity for his network of spies. His role for Korda, along with that of Vivien, would be outlined in a face-to-face meeting with Korda in Hollywood. Both Noël Coward and David Niven had urged Larry to join the secret service as an agent.

It is believed that Coward, who worked for British naval intelligence during the war, was the one who had recommended Larry to Churchill as a candidate for the secret service. Vivien's name was added later. "Churchill wanted people who could move freely around the world, and the theatrical appearances of both Larry and Vivien gave them a mobility—in essence, a cover," Coward claimed.

Back in Hollywood, Vivien and Larry met Korda in his rented home in Bel Air. Here Korda received not only movie stars, but couriers from his intelligence services. Merle Oberon was nowhere to be seen.

Risking imprisonment and even assassination by the Nazis, Larry became an agent for the SOE in 1940.

At the time, prior to its own entry into World War II, America didn't tolerate foreign agents, including those from Britain. Both Larry and Korda, even Vivien, were playing dangerous games.

"If Nazi agents knew the full extent of the activities of Vivien and Larry, I'm sure they would have gone after them," Korda said. "Goebbels would have seen to that."

Although many of his fellow countrymen bitterly criticized Larry for remaining in Hollywood with Vivien during the Blitz, both of them were engaged as spies. "I was a regular Mata Hari," Vivien once told George Cukor after the war.

By remaining in Hollywood, Larry and Vivien were doing more for the British war effort than they'd have accomplished in England, but they were nonetheless vilified in the London press, along with another Englishman, Cary Grant, as war profiteers. "They are making thousands and thousands of dollars, living in great luxury, while their fellow Britons are living on limited rations and facing nightly aerial bombardments," one editorial writer in London claimed.

Robert Donat and Michael Redgrave were singled out for particular praise and called "real troupers" for going around England touring in great plays for meager salaries to keep the tradition of British theater alive and to entertain a war-weary people.

Ralph Richardson received special praise for entering the military service as well. At one point, a boycott was urged, suggesting that "the people of Britain should no longer go to movies starring Heathcliff or Scarlett O'Hara."

Unaware of what they were doing for Britain, the British Consul in Los Angeles even called Larry and Vivien in for a stern lecture, chastising them for not doing enough for the British War Relief. He pointed out that many of their friends, such as Basil Rathbone, were "working tirelessly for our cause." Rathbone had been made president of the British War Relief Association on the West Coast, raising large sums of money to aid a war-torn Britain.

The distinguished actor Sir Cedric Hardwicke and Cary Grant were major contributors. Grant, in fact, donated his salary from two movies, *The Philadelphia Story* and *Arsenic and Old Lace*, to aid Britain. Ronald Colman, Herbert Marshall, and Brian Aherne were cited as shining examples for Vivien and Larry to emulate. Before leaving the office of the British Consul, Vivien and Larry promised to work much harder for war relief. Of course, they did not inform the consul about their illegal activities.

In Birmingham, England, one editorial writer said, "We have a word to describe Vivien Leigh and Laurence Olivier—and it's a bit stronger than 'deserter.' Miss Leigh and Mr. Olivier should be banned from England, never to set foot in their Mother Country again. Let the palm trees shelter them forever."

The German consul in Los Angeles used these attacks on British actors in Hollywood to embarrass stars such as Larry. The Germans distributed hundreds of copies of a

Cary Grant in
Arsenic and Old Lace

425

London newspaper story headlined: COME HOME, YOU SHIRKERS.

Lord Lothian, the British ambassador in Washington, publicly called such attacks on British expatriates "undesirable . . . harmful to our cause."

He urged British movie stars working in Hollywood to remain there and to counter anti-British propaganda put out by German interests. He requested a private meeting with a few stars in Washington, and Sir Cedric Hardwicke, Cary Grant, and Larry agreed to fly there.

Regrettably, Nazi agents in Hollywood somehow learned of their upcoming flight.

***

It was arranged that the actors would fly to Washington on a private plane kept at a hangar in Burbank. The night of their intended flight, Samuel Goldwyn, an ardent anti-Nazi, alerted Korda that the aircraft carrying these patriotic Britons may have been tampered with and possibly might crash before it reached Kansas.

How Goldwyn came to possess this information is not known. He did have security agents working for him, however, as he feared for his life since he was a prominent Jewish producer in Hollywood who frequently expressed his loathing of Hitler.

Goldwyn placed a call to Howard Hughes, requesting that his henchmen check out the private plane the Englishmen were planning to fly to Washington. The aviator came to the rescue, instructing the engineers at his aircraft factory to examine the plane the actors were going to fly. Indeed, the Hughes' technicians found that the aircraft had been tampered with by unknown forces who had access to it. Hughes very generously offered one of his own private aircraft to the actors.

When Vivien, already in an extremely agitated state, learned of the dangers associated with the flight, she absolutely refused to allow Larry to go to Washington. If he didn't give in to her, she threatened to leave him. Finally, she persuaded him to remain behind when she claimed she'd commit suicide if he didn't submit to her wishes.

To capitalize off his loan of a plane to the actors, Hughes dispatched his public relations agent, really his pimp, Johnny Meyer, to meet with Vivien. When she agreed to see Meyer privately, he told her that Hughes was willing to buy out her contract and make her "a sweetheart deal," if she would agree to meet with him privately one night at a villa in the Hollywood Hills.

Hollywood gossip about that possible rendezvous became prevalent. Columnist James Bacon published a not-so-veiled comment: "What aviator is flying over Tara?"

When confronted, Vivien denied ever having met Hughes. Meyer claimed that she lied, and that he personally delivered her for a meeting with Hughes that lasted six hours. That is not beyond the realm of possibility. Meyer, incidentally, was the pimp who originally hauled Errol Flynn to a private villa where Hughes waited inside.

Whatever transpired between Vivien and Hughes, if anything, may never be known. What is known is that Hughes considered negotiating with David O. Selznick to buy out her contract, with the intention of configuring Vivien as an exclusive property of his own. The setup would be equivalent to the agreement he had with Jack Buetel and Jane Russell, stars of his notorious film *The Outlaw*.

Katharine Hepburn also revealed to George Cukor that Hughes wanted to put Vivien under exclusive contract. The aviator/movie producer had no interest in Larry whatsoever, telling associates that "I consider him a pretentious bore on screen."

Cary Grant was Hughes's closest friend, and he wanted to protect him and secure his safety. Hughes took personal charge of the plane lent to Grant, who was joined by Hardwicke on the flight to Washington. The ambassador instructed them to organize and endorse an aggressive and ongoing roster of charity events, both as a means of raising money for the British war effort and to offset German propaganda in the Hollywood community. This policy of Lord Lothian was eventually communicated to other British agents operating in California.

Although it seemed a daunting task, the actors were asked discreetly to insert British propaganda into films whenever they had the power to do so, perhaps in the form of private meetings with writers sympathetic to the UK who were producing screenplays.

In the closing months of 1940, Vivien and Larry became more social than ever before. They seemed the embodiment of England in pre-war Hollywood, and were highly desirable as party guests. Larry was somewhat wooden, but Vivien was a vivacious guest with a sparkling wit and great beauty.

No one at the parties they were attending knew that they were secretly spying on not only their hosts but on the other guests as well. They were particularly interested in reporting to Korda

When Hollywood columnist James Bacon surmised, in print, "What Aviator is flying over Tara?", could he have been referring to *(top photo)* Howard Hughes?

which stars had pro-Nazi sympathies.

Korda had compiled a list of movie-industry stars suspected of having Nazi connections. The list was topped by Wallace Beery, Victor McLaglen, Errol Flynn, Gary Cooper, and Walt Disney. Vivien and Larry were shocked to find Flynn, Cooper, and Disney on the list.

Cary Grant and Larry also suspected producer Winfield Sheehan, former head of 20th Century Fox, of having Nazi sympathies. They interpreted his relationship with George Gyssling as "highly questionable."

Gyssling was the German Consul General for the Los Angeles area, and his headquarters were suspected of being the "center for Nazi activities on the West Coast."

In his improbable role as a spy, episodes seemingly coming from a movie script, Larry never revealed very much about what he actually did in Hollywood in 1940. His role for the SOE has to be pieced together from snippets of information provided by others.

After the war, Larry downplayed his work for the secret service, and wouldn't discuss Vivien's part at all.

Niven, in rebuttal, claimed that Larry had a far more important role than he'd admit in applying pressure on people of high influence within the American government. "Larry worked diligently to defeat German interests in America, the full scope of which may never be known," Niven said. "If Nazi agents were on to him, I think they would have targeted him for assassination, and I think they did on at least two different occasions."

Party-goers at night, Larry and Vivien became money raisers during the day. The first person Larry solicited for funds was Clark Gable. Although the "King of Hollywood" was still in debt to Louis B. Mayer for paying off his divorce from his second wife, Gable agreed to contribute "whatever is left in my pockets. Carole will help out, too," he promised.

Korda received a tip that Barbara Hutton, the Woolworth heiress who planned to marry Cary Grant, was under investigation by the FBI. Her code name was "Red Rose."

When Korda presented this evidence to Vivien and Larry, they were dumbfounded. "Of all the actors in Hollywood, Cary is the best thing that ever happened to Britain," Larry claimed.

Nonetheless, Grant too came under FBI surveillance, and Korda instructed Larry and Vivien to socialize with Hutton and Grant to learn more about their activities and sympathies.

Vivien and Larry discovered that both Hutton and Grant were doing more for British War Relief than almost anyone else in Hollywood.

Although Larry reported to Korda, Grant worked with Sir William Stephenson, the head of British Security Co-ordination in the U.S.

Stephenson, who died in 1989, was a friend of both Franklin D. Roosevelt and Winston Churchill.

Author Roy Moseley, years later, contacted Stephenson who admitted that he had worked with Grant in identifying spheres of Nazi influence in the Greater Los Angeles area.

Hutton wielded her checkbook more generously than most Americans. She, of course, had a fatter checkbook to wield. In time, she would contribute millions to the war effort, even sending an anonymous check for $1 million to General Charles de Gaulle's Free French movement.

Grant was the biggest fundraiser in Hollywood, turning over generous checks to the British War Relief Society.

After private dinners with Hutton and Grant, Vivien and Larry concluded that Hutton, and even Grant himself, were under suspicion only because of their friendship with the notorious Countess Dorothy di Frasso, who had been the lover of Gary Cooper in the early 1930s.

The countess was an intimate friend and confidante of Benito Mussolini and had even entertained Field Marshal Goering at her villa near Rome.

Larry concluded, and communicated to his superiors, that Hutton, and especially Grant, should be given a clean slate, at least insofar as their loyalties to Britain were concerned. Years later, Larry learned, however, that the FBI continued to pursue Grant and Hutton throughout the course of their marriage.

"Hoover assumed that birds of a feather flocked together," Larry said. "Through Barbara, Cary had some weird associations. Hutton knew and entertained many Nazis but was not sympathetic to Hitler. She appeared to be incredibly naïve about world politics."

Many of the neo-Nazi sympathies of which Hutton was suspected were based on false information. Even though the heiress planned to marry Grant in 1942, she was still enamored of a certain "German baron with pro-Hitler leanings."

The accusation was false and a reference to the dashing Baron Von Gramm, a national tennis hero in Germany. Although he was accused in the West of being a Nazi, it was discovered that not only had he expressed anti-Hitler views but had been arrested and sent to prison by the Gestapo in March of 1938. His imprisonment was partly based on the accusation that he had had homosexual relations with another male member of the German Davis Cup Team.

Through Hutton, Vivien and Larry met the

Too detached and self-involved to consciously collaborate?

Woolworth heiress Barbara Hutton with husband (#3 of 7), Cary Grant

429

American-born Countess Dorothy Taylor di Frasso, and were included on her guest list for parties, many of which "were of a somewhat lecherous nature," as claimed by David Niven, who had met her in the 1930s.

The countess seemed honored to include Vivien and Larry among her "special friends." Soon they were seen dining with the countess and her friends at such Los Angeles restaurants as Vendôme, a favorite of movie stars.

Although she never expressed any overt support of Hitler in their presence, di Frasso was definitely on the side of Mussolini, and she hoped Italy would emerge triumphant from the ashes of World War II. Although she numbered British friends among her associates, including Grant himself, she detested Winston Churchill. She rather outrageously maintained that Britain was only fighting World War II to hold onto its empire.

Larry and Vivien never defended Britain in her presence. Vivien said, "I can't abide war. Larry and I plan to sit out the war in America. Let our fellow Englishmen fight over there all they want." That was, of course, a deliberate lie.

The countess became so enchanted with Vivien and Larry that she invited them for a vacation in her rented hacienda in Mexico City, where Hutton and Grant would later go on a honeymoon.

On the dawn of America's entry into World War II, Mexico was like Lisbon in Europe, a haven for international spy rings, smugglers, and black market operators.

It was also a haven for the FBI, including volunteer members of the Hollywood community who served as "listeners." These listeners included actresses Rochelle Hudson and June Duprez, who had achieved success in Korda's 1940 film, *Thief of Bagdad*.

At the last minute, Larry called the countess and turned down her invitation to Mexico. The countess had enlarged her guest list to include several Hollywood stars, especially Gary Cooper, her former lover. The FBI had both Cooper and Countess di Frasso under surveillance.

Korda had warned Larry that he had received information that Larry's life might be in danger. Vivien's life might also be threatened by going south of the border. "The Nazis are on to you and Vivien," Korda claimed. "There's a plot to kill both of you."

No one ever accused Cooper of being a liberal. He voted once for Calvin Coolidge and twice for Herbert Hoover, the latter vote cast at

Countess Dorothy di Frasso out on the town with Gary Cooper

the beginning of America's long Depression.

"Coop" had been a founding member of the "Hollywood Hussars," a reactionary group with Fascist sympathies funded by William Randolph Hearst and claiming leading actor Victor McLaglen and character actor Ward Bond as members. In the years before the war, this Right Wing club paraded around at social events in fancy uniforms and practiced military drills.

Louis B. Mayer and others labeled the Hollywood Hussars as "Nazi Jew haters."

Korda concluded that this para-military organization was more interested in protecting the United States from the New Deal and the "red menace" than they were as a stalking horse for Nazism.

On the advice of his agent, Cooper later abandoned the Hussars but still behaved suspiciously. When Larry got to know him better, he reported that Cooper on occasion had dinner with the German consulate general in Los Angeles.

Cooper was also heavily criticized as being pro-Nazi when he visited Germany late in 1938 when it was politically incorrect to do so. Defending himself to Larry, Cooper claimed that the trip had actually been ordered by Franklin D. Roosevelt.

His father-in-law, Paul Shields, stepfather to Cooper's wife at the time [Veronica Balfe] was a liberal and an economic adviser to FDR. Shields was sent by Roosevelt to Berlin to investigate the German war machine and its financing. Because Cooper's movies were greatly admired by Josef Goebbels, the actor went along to open doors of the Nazi hierarchy that might have been closed to Shields visiting on his own.

Cooper told Larry that his isolationist view of America had been changed when he'd seen the mammoth Nazi build-up of its military machine in Berlin. "They'll be coming after us soon," Cooper said. "I didn't think that at first. But I do now."

Nonetheless, Cooper and McLaglen remained close friends, even though the character actor who won an Oscar for *The Informer* was practically a Nazi storm-trooper. McLaglen was also extremely anti-Semitic, as were many Americans of that time. On occasion, Cooper himself was known to express

Male flash mixed with something approaching Nazi sympathies
Action/adventure heroes Victor McLaglen *(top photo)* and Gary Cooper

anti-Semitic remarks.

Two skirt chasers, Cooper and Republican presidential nominee Wendell Wilkie, became great friends. A bitter opponent of the New Deal, Wilkie ran against Roosevelt in the race for the presidency in 1940.

In his report to Korda, Larry asserted that he did not believe Cooper had Nazi sympathies, despite his past associations with fascist friends, most of whom were connected with Di Frasso, and his involvement in right wing paramilitary groups.

"He is not pro-British, but he is pro-American, which means he is of no harm to us," Larry said. "A lot of his political views stem from McLaglen. I met him only once at a club. McLaglen may have been born in Kent, but he is to the right of Attila the Hun."

Although the pro-Nazi label tainted Cooper for years, Larry later claimed that the actor became outspoken against the isolationists in the U.S. and publicly warned in interviews about the danger of not preparing for war in Germany.

A super-American patriot, Cecil B. DeMille, somehow learned that Vivien and Larry were working undercover for the British secret service. Korda may have warned him that their lives were endangered. Jesse Lasky Jr., who worked for DeMille, claimed that the director very generously offered both Vivien and Larry security guards during their last two months in Hollywood. There were continued fears of an assassination attempt, and even fears of a possible kidnapping.

Unlike Cooper and Errol Flynn, who aroused suspicions, Jimmy Stewart was a true American patriot who supported Larry in his struggles to raise funds for Britain. Stewart believed that America would eventually be dragged into the war, and that it should more aggressively prepare for the oncoming hostilities.

Anti-war activists became aware of the activity of the Oliviers and of Korda. Heads of various studios were sent letters asking them to boycott any film cast with Larry and Vivien or produced by Korda. According to whatever reports are available, the Germans wanted the Oliviers out of California, if not out of the picture industry completely.

"Not just the Germans, but many Americans held the British in contempt," Larry said. "The Irish for example. And there were many German immigrants living in America. I didn't stage any pro-Britain rallies in Milwaukee."

He later admitted that he feared that his life was in danger in America. "I would have liked to have had all the Nazi buggers shot."

***

432

People who compile lists of the various lovers of both male and female movie stars often include a surprising duo, Walt Disney and Vivien Leigh. The creator of Mickey Mouse screwing around with Scarlett O'Hara? A romantic link seems preposterous, but the rumors stemmed from Korda's belief that Walt Disney was aiding German causes in America. When he'd seen *Gone With the Wind*, he'd sent Vivien a fan letter.

With Larry's approval, she called Disney and accepted his invitation to dinner, which turned into a series of three "dates."

Disney always claimed that he'd been a Republican ever since his boyhood, when a pack of Irish kids, whose fathers worked for the local Democratic political machine, held him down and coated his testicles with hot tar.

Korda had received reports that Disney was an admirer of both Hitler and Mussolini, and that he'd attended Bund meetings of Nazi sympathizers in Los Angeles.

Further suspicions were aroused when Disney extended an invitation to Leni Riefenstahl to tour his studio during her visit to California. Reported to be the mistress of Hitler, she had made the most effective propaganda film in cinematic history, *Triumph of the Will (Triumph des Willens)*. Released in 1935, it chronicled the 1934 Nazi Party Congress in Nuremberg, glorifying Hitler and his ideals for the Third Reich.

After her visit, Riefenstahl pronounced Disney "the greatest personage in American films." The pair had hugged and kissed away from the camera.

Vivien later reported to Korda, "Disney made no sexual overtures to me—he seemed asexual, in fact—and I learned almost nothing. Of course, Mickey Mouse is one great big liar. He told me that he didn't even know who

(left photo) Walt Disney around 1940.
(central figure in right-hand photo) Nazi filmmaker and propaganda genius
Leni Riefenstahl in August of 1936

433

Riefenstahl was when she visited his studio, other than being a German actress who made mountain films for UFA.

Disney's claim that he did not know who Riefenstahl was is laughable. His *Snow White and the Seven Dwarfs* had lost out to her Nazi propaganda film, *Olympia*, winning first prize at the International Moving Picture Festival in Venice in 1938. He just had to know who she was. Other than Hal Roach, producer of the *Our Gang* comedies, Disney was the only notable who welcomed her to Hollywood.

Even if he didn't know who she was, Disney could have found out by reading the morning newspapers. He faithfully read *Variety*, in which the Hollywood Anti-Nazi League called for the movie industry to boycott "Hitler's puppet."

After her limited exposure, Vivien could not determine whether Disney was pro-Nazi or not. "He will do nothing for the British cause," she assured Korda. "His position is 'let 'em fight their own wars over in Europe.'"

Her final opinion of Disney was that "he is a hopeless reactionary. He told me that he found the institution of slavery, as depicted in *Gone With the Wind*, rather benign."

"If Southerners abused their slaves, why would such characters as Mammy still stick with the O'Hara family when they were free to go?" Disney asked Vivien.

In her final report, Vivien wrote: "I do not think Disney is secretly funding any pro-German groups. Personally, I don't think he wants to be caught funding any political groups at this time. He doesn't want to lose any Mickey Mouse fans, either in Germany or anywhere else. However, he does have a sharp political knife in his pants and will probably later on use it to slash the left wing if he has a chance. But I think his interests are political concerns solely confined to the Roosevelt haters in America. His main reason for opposing the current war is that it has cut off his lucrative German market. Larry and I have heard rumors that he is also a homosexual."

***

Korda ordered Larry to befriend Tyrone Power, arguably the leading matinee idol in Hollywood in 1940, directly competing with Errol Flynn and Robert Taylor. "It would be great if we could get a big box office draw like Tyrone Power appearing for us at charity events."

Johnny Meyer, Howard Hughes's pimp, was the best source of information about Power's involvement with Larry. Hughes had ordered Meyer to keep him completely abreast of what was going on.

Noël Coward had already enjoyed the passionate embrace of Power before Larry ever met him. "Count yourself lucky," Coward told Larry. "He's extraordinarily handsome, and he's not stingy with his charms. He once told me that he doesn't like to frustrate people. 'I feel horny all the time and I'll oblige them.' Those were his exact words. He also said that 'most people are just curious. I allow them to satisfy their curiosity.'"

Smitty Hanson, Power's long-time "trick," claimed his "master" was basically homosexual who "married girls from time to time, or had affairs with them."

Because of their mutual interest in the theater, Larry had far more in common with Power than he did with Flynn. On their first meeting around a pool, Power confided, "For anyone truly interested in the theater like us, it's a tragedy to be born beautiful."

A fan magazine had recently written, "Tyrone Power is actually as good looking as Robert Taylor is supposed to be."

As Larry was soon to learn that day, Power was the fourth in a famous acting dynasty stretching back to the 18th century. Larry was immediately attracted by his bright smile and flashing white teeth.

Hanson claimed that Power told him that he and Larry went to bed on the first night they met. "We were very compatible in bed," Power reportedly said. "We liked to do the same things. We were a perfect match."

Larry became involved with Power in early December of 1940, earning the movie idol's promise that he could be counted on to aid in British War Relief. "I can even do a song-and-dance routine," Power assured Larry.

Three views of bisexual heartthrob Tyrone Power
"The handsomest man in Hollywood"

However, Korda presented Larry with some very disconcerting news. Power had recently been placed on the J. Edgar Hoover's FBI surveillance list.

The actor was suspected of having pro-Nazi affiliations, and Larry was asked to investigate. Having known Power for only a short time, Larry was shocked by these revelations. "He seems like an American patriot and has even volunteered to help us," Larry told Korda.

In one of those strange coincidences that happen in life, Power had invited both Larry and Vivien to a house party he was throwing for Manuel Ávila Camacho, who had been elected president of Mexico on December 1, 1940. His brother, Maximino Ávila Camacho, was Power's house guest. Power had bonded with Maximino after meeting him in Mexico City at a party thrown by the Countess Dorothy di Frasso.

Notorious for his carousing and womanizing, Maximino was a four-star general in Mexico's revolutionary forces and was the political boss of his home state of Puebla.

After seeing Power and Maximino together, Larry concluded that Power was more attracted to the Mexican's male flash and machismo than he was to his right wing politics.

At the party, Larry met Annabella, Power's French wife. She introduced him to Alfredo Ignacio Padilla, a member of Maximino's staff. Alfredo later slipped Larry his telephone number and requested a private luncheon meeting in Larry's hotel suite the following day.

Larry called Korda that night and asked him if he should show up. "By all means," Korda said. "Alfredo works for us. He's on our payroll. See what he has to say."

At their luncheon, Larry concluded that Alfredo seemed to be on many payrolls. Not only was he getting a check from Maximino and from British interests in Mexico, but he was also on the payroll of Maximino's brother. As president of Mexico, Manuel wanted to know what his wilder brother was doing at all times.

Mid-war Presidential Summit
Franklin D. Roosevelt dining with
Mexican President
Manuel Ávila Camacho

Before the end of the meal, Larry learned some astonishing news. Maximino was working for the Nazis, who were lobbying to have Mexico switch its alliance to the Axis powers. Hitler's long-term plan was to secure safe ports along the western coast of Mexico for a possible German and Japanese invasion of California.

Alfredo warned that Maximino was a member of the National Synarchists,

436

an organization created in 1937 by the Nazis, working in conjunction with the Japanese and the Spanish Falange. Their goal was to create a military force in Mexico directed at the United States.

Larry had just begun to learn what he could of these activities south of the border, with the intention of reporting them to Korda, when he and Vivien decided to leave.

Months later in England, Larry read that all danger of Mexico going over to the side of the Axis had ended on May 22, 1942, when Maximino's brother, Manuel, declared war on Germany. Two of Mexico's ships carrying vital oil supplies had been destroyed by German submarines operating in the Gulf of Mexico, close to the port of New Orleans.

Before he left America to endure the war in England, Larry reported to Korda that Power was under FBI surveillance not because of any threat he represented to Britain or the United States, but because of his "poor choice of friends. He fraternizes with the Di Frasso crowd, many of whom are Fascists. Power is a good-time guy and a great partygoer. I also think he has one big crush on Maximino. You know, nearly all those great womanizers like Maximino want a little boy ass on the side. A sort of murky Don Juan complex."

Larry advised Korda not to waste time and money worrying about Power's involvement with the Nazis. Larry's advice proved sound. After America entered the war on the side of the Allies, Power served in the Marine Corps in World War II as a pilot and saw action in the South Pacific.

In the post-war years, the bond between Larry and Power would grow stronger. Whenever he could, Power was a presence at Larry's opening nights in the theater.

On one occasion, Larry and Vivien entertained Power and his wife, Linda Christian, at Notley Abbey; on two other occasions Larry and Power had Notley to themselves without their spouses.

***

Korda told Larry and Vivien, now that he was back in what he called "bloody California," that he was taking an awful beating in the British press. Fleet Street viewed him as a virtual deserter who had fled to sunshine and palm trees to escape the nightly bombardment, the Blitz, compliments of the Luftwaffe.

"How can I defend myself?" Korda asked Vivien and Larry. "I can't say that Churchill virtually ordered me to Hollywood to continue British film production and to make propaganda. Also Churchill wants to earn American dollars desperately needed for Britain's war effort."

437

The producer told his stars of *Lady Hamilton* that their film should not be overtly propagandistic, like those coming out of Berlin. "Churchill wants us to depict a patriotic viewpoint, but in a subtle way," Korda claimed.

Even though the final cut was blatantly jingoistic, *Lady Hamilton* (aka *That Hamilton Woman*) became a success both in Britain and the United States, even in Russia.

Churchill had insisted that a speech he personally wrote be inserted into the script. In the speech, Nelson pleads with the Lords of the Admiralty not to trust Napoléon's offer of peace.

Delivered from Larry's mouth, the moving speech read in part: "Napoléon can never be master of the world until he has smashed us up—and believe me, gentlemen, he means to be master of the world. You cannot make peace with dictators, you have to destroy them."

It was obvious that Lord Nelson was really talking about Hitler, not Bonaparte.

The supporting cast, among others, included Gladys Cooper as the icy cold Lady Nelson and Alan Mowbray as Sir William Hamilton, Emma's husband and the British ambassador to Naples.

Henry Wilcoxon, cast as Nelson's right-hand man, Capt. Thomas Hardy, said, "During the shoot, I never had an affair with Viv at any time. Good god, Larry was an old friend of mine, and I was newly married and happily married myself. But in Viv's case, if circumstances had been different, I definitely would have made an exception to my rule regarding on-stage romances. To this day I have always felt that I would have been a better match for Viv than Larry was. Our personalities and our senses of humor meshed far better. I mean, Larry was always taking himself so seriously in those days."

Vincent Korda, brilliantly talented in his own way, re-created the Battle of Trafalgar in miniature, which he supervised in a rowboat.

During the filming of *Lady Hamilton*, Vivien wrote several letters to the ex-husband she had recently divorced, Leigh Holman. In one she complained about the United States, claiming it was a country "which I never had the slightest wish to come to, and cannot grow to like."

Korda told Merle Oberon, who told everybody, that Vivien and Larry were living in "the limelight of a faded love affair." Many English actors wanted to bask in the California sun, making good money, and not having to endure the deprivations of war-time England. But Larry and Vivien wanted to return to England.

Korda at times noted that Larry and Vivien seemed bored with each other, or even antagonistic. It was easy to provoke an argument between the two of them.

At one point, critical of Vivien in a scene, Larry said, "You'll never win your second Oscar playing Lady Hamilton like that."

"At least I have a first Oscar," she shot back.

"Except for her sudden flare-ups, Vivien worshipped Larry for the most part," Korda claimed. "But at times he didn't seem to want that. He was a very restless man, growing increasingly impatient during the short weeks we shot *Lady Hamilton*. He wanted to be back in England no doubt. Even though he'd just married Vivien, he also wanted his freedom."

"During the shoot, Vivien was drinking far too much," Korda said. "Larry was often cold and aloof from her. It was obvious he was seeing somebody else. Danny Kaye often came to the set. There were a lot of rumors about Kaye and Larry at the time. Vivien seemed aware of what was going on, but was overly polite to Kaye, who, no doubt, was after her man."

During the final week of the shoot, Korda pitched the idea of another propaganda film to the Oliviers. This movie would be based on a real incident. The civilized world was shocked on Friday, the 13th of September in 1940. The 11,000-ton ocean liner, *City of Benares*, was sunk by Nazi U-boats. Torpedoed during gale force winds, the ship was carrying British children to safety in America or Canada. The Nazis sunk the vessel, killing 258 passengers, most of them children. Only 13 children were known to survive.

Korda wanted Larry to play the ship's captain, with a role written in for Vivien as the supervising nurse aboard the ill-fated vessel.

The sinking of the *City of Benares* left Vivien and Larry thankful that their own children had already made it safely to Canada and the United States.

Both Vivien and Larry expressed an interest in doing the script. But the attack on Pearl Harbor radically changed their plans. The story of the sinking of the *City of Benares* never made it to the screen as a Korda production.

When Larry saw the final cut of *Lady Hamilton* with Vivien, he turned to her and looked more than a little annoyed. "I am furious. You stole the god damn picture right out from under me."

"All's fair in love and war," she said in her delicate voice.

"You're a scene stealer from hell," he told her. "Just for that, I am going to deny you sex for one entire month."

"*Fiddle-dee-dee*," she said. "I'll get it from someone else. Like you are already doing." She then rose to

Things that drove British filmmakers in the 40s crazy: Joe Breen, Hollywood censor, demanding rewrites because of the Nelson/Hamilton adultery

her feet and stormed out of the screening room.

Korda sat with Merle Oberon in the seat behind the Oliviers. When they'd left the screening room, he said, loud enough for the small audience to hear, "Now you've been an eyewitness to another day in the life of America's new dream couple."

More trouble lay ahead. Joe Breen, the Hollywood censor, refused to grant Korda the Production Code Seal of Approval, since *That Hamilton Woman* condoned adultery.

A compromise was reached when Larry went back to the studio and filmed a scene where Lord Nelson laments his errant ways. After getting the seal of approval from the Breen office, Korda cut that scene for the film's international release.

Lady Hamilton or *That Hamilton Woman* enjoyed worldwide success, even in such places as Leningrad, then under Nazi aerial bombardment.

Lady Hamilton was Winston Churchill's favorite film. In Flora Fraser's *Emma, Lady Hamilton*, she makes the astonishing claim that Churchill watched it more than a hundred times. Other seemingly more reliable figures claim the prime minister watched it five to eleven times.

In the late 1980s, Larry, deep into his dotage and suffering severe illness, agreed to allow some journalists to interview him. At that point in his marriage he was calling Joan Plowright "Vivien." Every December like a ritual he sat through a screening of *Lady Hamilton*.

He told the journalists, "Vivien and I were really in love when I played Admiral Nelson and she played my mistress, Emma. Our love was the real thing. Everything else in life, before or after Vivien, was merely the mock."

***

As Louis B. Mayer counted up his take for releasing *Gone With the Wind* through MGM, he decided to throw a party at his home honoring both Vivien and Larry. He'd heard rumors that they planned to return to England instead of staying in America to capitalize off the fame the roles of Scarlett O'Hara and Heathcliff had brought to them.

Vivien Leigh as the 18th-century courtesan Emma Hamilton

The party at the Mayer mansion

began with perfection, but ended in embarrassments. As defined in the press in the party's aftermath, Vivien "had never looked more beautiful," in the words of Louella Parsons. In the opinion of Hedda Hopper, "Larry Olivier wouldn't even have to blow in my ear, and I would follow him anywhere."

Mayer had hired a small, tuxedo-clad orchestra to play for those who wanted to dance. Vivien had already told Mayer how much she and Larry had liked Gene Kelly when they'd met in Chicago. "You've found your answer to Fred Astaire," Larry said. "Gene is much handsomer and far more virile than Astaire."

"I have some reservations," Mayer said. "I'm thinking of loaning him to Harry Cohn at Columbia for a musical with Rita Hayworth. But Kelly's a little too short for Rita."

"Don't worry," Vivien assured him. "Gene will rise to the occasion."

Later in the evening, Mayer asked Kelly if he'd dance with Vivien. "It would please her," Mayer told him. "Olivier told me she's been very depressed lately. He has even talked to psychiatrists about her."

"Okay, I will ask Miss Scarlett O'Hara to the dance floor," Kelly promised.

A half hour later the small orchestra began to play a foxtrot. Kelly rose from his own table and crossed the floor to where Mayer was seated between Vivien and Larry.

Sipping champagne, Vivien didn't look depressed at all. She was clearly drunk, but Kelly decided to chance it. "Miss O'Hara, may I have this dance?"

She spun around. He detected a small frown. Perhaps he should have called her Mrs. Olivier or Miss Leigh.

"The only thing left for me in Hollywood is to dance with Gene Kelly," she said, rising on unsteady feet and knocking down her chair.

As fellow dancers saw Kelly and Vivien coming onto the floor, they backed away, taking their seats to take in the action drama unfolding in front of them.

As he placed his hand on her back, she still seemed unsteady on her feet. "We were bobbing back and forth, not really dancing," he recalled. "All eyes were on us. I feared she'd collapse in my arms if I made her head spin too much. Right from our first step, I knew our dance would be a failure. She simply couldn't follow me. I was a bit high myself."

"In one of the most embarrassing moments of my life, one which I later regretted, I told her, 'Let's sit this one out.' It was a cruel and thoughtless thing for me to do, especially to someone as lovely and gracious as Miss Leigh. I hated myself for saying that to her. The shock, the pain, the rejection on her beautiful face made me feel like a worm."

"Somehow I managed to steer her back to her chair, now placed upright,"

Kelly said. "Mayer was still there, blowing dragon smoke. He had not only witnessed the failure of my invitation to a dance, but Olivier had stormed out on him."

"I found out later that Mayer and Olivier had gotten into a furious argument about his returning to England," Kelly said. "Perhaps Olivier had had one too many as well. He'd rejected Mayer's request to remain in Hollywood and had left the party."

"Very stupidly, I asked Mayer where Olivier was," Kelly said. "I felt he was needed to protect Vivien in her condition."

"Mr. Olivier has left my home," Mayer said, "perhaps never to return. Danny Kaye volunteered to drive him home."

"I thanked Vivien, nodded at Mayer, and hurried back to Betsy," Kelly said.

He was referring to his wife, Betsy Blair.

"From where I sat across the room, I saw one of Mayer's servants escort Vivien out of the room," Kelly said. "No doubt he was taking her home."

"I woke up feeling like shit the next day," Kelly said. "I knew I'd treated Vivien like the rotten pig I was. Impulsively I got dressed, stopped at a florist for some flowers, and rang her bell. A secretary came to the door. When she saw who it was, she welcomed me."

"I found Vivien sitting in her garden sobbing," Kelly said. "Even in her condition, she was willing to see me. Right away I apologized. I assumed she was crying because of my horrible treatment of her. That wasn't the case."

In the course of the morning, she revealed that she was upset because Larry had gone away to Palm Springs with Danny Kaye, leaving her alone in the house.

"Oh, Gene, oh, Gene," Vivien said, reaching for him. "I'm so desperately alone. Make up some excuse for Betsy and spend the day with me." She gripped his arm in a tight squeeze. "I'm coming unglued."

The next day when his landlord, the author, Stanley Haggart, arrived at Kelly's house with a plumber, the dancer showed the plumber the way to the bathroom. He asked Stanley to meet him outside in the garden.

"You're not going to believe this," Kelly said. "Yesterday I fucked Scarlett O'Hara."

***

The America First Committee, its members charged with keeping the United States out of World War II, asked the isolationist senators in Washington to investigate, among others, Larry and Korda.

All this British espionage activity had attracted not only the attention of the FBI, but that of the isolationists in the U.S. Senate, especially Senator Gerald Nye.

Nye represented North Dakota in the U.S. Senate from 1925 to 1945. He had an unexplained loathing for Larry, who had somehow earned his greatest hostility. Between 1935 and 1937 Nye was instrumental in the development and adoption of the Neutrality Acts. He also helped to establish the America First Committee with the intention of mobilizing anti-war sentiments in America.

He told his staff, "If it's the last thing I do, I'll see to it that that puppet and mouthpiece of imperial Britain, Laurence Olivier, is denied a visa to enter America ever again. Korda may go to jail."

Senator Nye charged that Hollywood, especially with the release of *That Hamilton Woman*, was turning out films designed to "drug the reason of the American people, set aflame their emotions, turn their hatred into a blaze, and fill them with fear that Hitler will come over here and capture them."

He cited Larry's speeches in *That Hamilton Woman* as the most blatant example of the many instances of British propaganda. He ordered a list of the names of studio executives who had collaborated. When the list was presented to him, he assumed that a majority of the names it contained were Jewish. He referred to Hollywood as "a raging volcano of war fever."

In spite of such anti-Nazi films as Chaplin's *The Great Dictator*, Hollywood actually turned out very few anti-Nazi films in the months before Pearl Harbor. At the request of the Germans, some studios had caved in and fired "non-Aryan" employees. At the time, Hollywood studios feared the loss of revenue from their lucrative European markets.

As the days passed, Senator Nye seemed less concerned with investigating the Hollywood film industry and more interested in investigating *That Hamilton Woman* and its sponsors. Vivien, Larry, and Korda feared they might be deported as foreign agents.

In his investigation, Senator Nye referred to *That Hamilton Woman* as Exhibit A. He very accurately was on to Korda, accusing him of indulging in espionage in California and functioning as a propaganda tool for Britain, and citing Korda as a foreign agent in violation of Federal law that called for the registration of all foreign agents.

Nye also demanded proof that Larry's famous scene—"You have to destroy dictators, wipe them out"—be justified historically. Korda had no evidence that the speech

American Gothic:
Gerald Nye, Republican Senator
(1925-1945) from
North Dakota

443

that Churchill has personally written had ever been uttered by Lord Nelson.

The German ambassador filed a protest with Nye that "Jews and British agents" were taking over Hollywood. He claimed that films were being turned into propaganda whose purpose was to lure America into an unwanted war.

Senator Nye became convinced that the German charges were accurate, and he announced that the Senate Committee on Foreign Relations would investigate British agents in the movie business. In fact, Larry and Korda were informed that Senator Nye's office would soon be sending out subpoenas to them to testify in Washington.

"We're going to be lynched for sure," Larry told Vivien.

Korda, not Vivien or Larry, was the first to be subpoenaed for an appearance before the committee scheduled for December 12, 1941.

But on December 7, based on the Japanese attack on Pearl Harbor, the United States found itself at war with both Japan and Germany. Nye's hearings were no longer relevant.

America had joined the battle allied with Britain. Korda, Larry, and Vivien were no longer foreign agents, but allies united against a common enemy.

Even after the attack on Pearl Harbor, Nye said, "This is just what Britain and the likes of Korda and Olivier planned for us. They were in cahoots with that traitor, Franklin D. Roosevelt."

***

Things got tense after Pearl Harbor, when Korda asked Larry to once again investigate Errol Flynn's Nazi sympathies. According to the British secret service, Flynn had been recruited in 1933 by Dr. Hermann Friedrich Erben, a member of Hitler's Gestapo.

Larry called Flynn and wanted to get together. Flynn invited Larry on a yachting trip to Catalina Island "to meet some of my mates." Larry bowed out at the last minute because he and Vivien had decided to return to England.

Charges that Errol Flynn was pro-Nazi would have to wait for exposure in the years to come.

David Niven also learned that Larry's life in California may have been endangered. But he dismissed all charges that his friend and former housemate, Flynn, was involved in any pro-Nazi activities or would ever collude with plot to do harm to Larry. It is not known whether Niven was defending a friend or telling the truth.

Vivien and Larry knew they were doing important espionage work in Hollywood, but the allure of returning to war-torn England was overpowering.

Now married and with no screen or stage commitments, Vivien urged Larry to return home at once. After all of his pathetic attempts to learn to fly an airplane, he at long last earned his "civilian wings."

From their salaries on *That Hamilton Woman*, Vivien and Larry took home only a modest amount of dollars. The bulk of their salaries was left behind to support Tarquin and Suzanne during the war. "We took just enough for our immediate survival," Vivien later said.

Larry confronted Korda and told him that he would continue to work for the secret service, but what he really wanted to do was to return home and enlist. "Like David Niven, I want to fight the war where it is happening."

Korda could not convince the stubborn actor to change his mind. But he told him that he was to go first to Lisbon for the first lap of his journey home. A top secret document would be delivered to him, which Larry would then personally transport to England.

In Hollywood on the Sunday before Christmas of 1940, Dame May Whitty came by for a farewell visit. "My beloved Juliet." She looked up at the threatening sky. "All of Hollywood is weeping raindrops for you, my dear ones."

Some eighty friends showed up at their home for a final farewell. They included Douglas Fairbanks Jr., Gladys Cooper, and Greer Garson.

The lavish party, including live entertainment, champagne, and caviar, was paid for by Danny Kaye. Later that night, he reportedly told Larry, "You leaving Hollywood is like taking a dagger and plunging it into my heart."

***

Stopping off briefly in New York before their embarkation for Lisbon, Larry and Vivien attended a party for them given by Alfred Lunt and Lynn Fontanne. At the Lunts, Vivien and Larry encountered Jack Merivale, whom Vivien had previously kicked out of Katharine Cornell's country house.

The tensions between them were over. When Merivale got Vivien alone in a corner, he whispered in her ear, "I'm madly in love with you, and that will always be so."

She looked at him with her sparkling green eyes and her Cheshire cat smile. "Catch me later."

After the party, Larry and Vivien were delivered to the port of Jersey City where they were scheduled to sail on the *Excambion* to Lisbon in neutral Portugal. The date was December 26, 1940.

Only one reporter saw them off, unlike past arrivals and departures when they'd been mobbed. The world was at war, and the mood was somber.

Vivien told the journalist, "London is hell now, I know that," she said. "Not the safest place to be. But it's my home, and Larry and I are going back to defend it. I just can't see storm-troopers marching through Piccadilly

445

Circus."

A cable was handed to Larry before he walked up the gangplank. Thinking it was from a well-wishing fan, he put it in his pocket and didn't think any more about it.

Two days at sea had passed before he opened the cable. The warning in the anonymous communication was dire.

"A Nazi agent is aboard your ship," the note read. "He plans to kill you at sea. Beware. Maybe he also plans to kill Miss Leigh. I'm not in a position to tell you how I know this, but trust no one. I am German but a great fan of you and your wife. Save yourself!"

CHAPTER 11

The Oliviers had just celebrated Christmas, 1940, in New York when they set sail the next day for the port of neutral Lisbon.

At quayside, Larry's last words to reporters were, "We won't be back until the war's over."

Before she left America, Vivien answered a reporter's final question. "Why are you leaving Hollywood? You're a big star now."

"Larry and I are going back to England, because it is our home."

The *Excambion* was an American freighter and passenger liner only one-eighth the tonnage of the *Queen Mary*. The captain was an American citizen born in Hamburg, and most members of the crew he'd selected were Germans sympathetic to Hitler.

The chief engineer and chief steward were German. The ship's doctor, an American, confided to Vivien and Larry that most of the crew and passengers were members of the pro-Hitler American Bund.

Fairly fluent in German, Vivien confirmed that for herself, based on what she overheard from what the passengers and crew said to each other.

Sometimes Larry and Vivien would stand on deck looking out at the endless sea, as if expecting the periscope of a German submarine to surface. Larry wrote that "Vivien endured the most apprehensive voyage I have ever known."

Years later when Vivien made *Ship of Fools*, the plot of that movie brought back her nightmarish voyage from New York to Lisbon.

Throughout the ocean crossing of the *Excambion*, Vivien lived in constant fear the vessel would fall into Nazi hands. "Everybody seemed to be speaking German, not English. We felt alienated and alone. We were certain there were Nazi spies aboard, one of whom had orders to kill us."

"If we're not killed," Vivien complained to Larry, "we may be taken prisoner by some marauding German U-boat. God knows what will happen to us then."

U-boats at the time were boarding non-German vessels and carting off all non-German citizens to a fate unknown.

On the following day, a Sunday, the ship's radio received a bulletin that London had suffered its second Great Fire, the most severe rain of Luftwaffe bombs since the beginning of World War II.

With the Battle of the Atlantic raging, it was probably the most dangerous time in the history of the war to cross the ocean by ship. Every month, transatlantic shipping lost an average of some 300,000 tons.

"This drama needs both of our former co-stars," said Larry. "Definitely Erich von Stroheim with support by Conrad Veidt."

Larry later admitted "I was paranoid, but perhaps for a good reason. Maybe not the captain, but one of his Nazi underlings could easily have sent a signal to a nearby German U-boat to come and arrest us. What a coup that would have been for Josef Goebbels."

"We stayed inside our cabin most of the time," Vivien said. "One passenger, a dead-ringer for Peter Lorre, kept his eye on us throughout that terrible trip."

Like a cloak-and-dagger mystery, the Lorre clone trailed them any time they went outside their cabin.

Larry and Vivien were at sea on New Year's Eve when the captain toasted crew and passengers with *DEUTSCHLAND ÜBER ALLES*. Of the two dozen passengers, more than three-quarters of them responded to the captain with a "Heil Hitler."

For a dinner companion, Larry and Vivien sought out a US naval lieutenant who wore pilot's wings.

After the war, Larry admitted to David Niven that he believed that Nazi agents were aboard the *Excambion*, with at least one of them instructed to kill him, perhaps shove him overboard. "Vivien and I avoided the railings."

Niven agreed with Larry's assessment that Goebbels would have won a propaganda victory based on the arrest or assassination of the Oliviers. "It would have sent a Nazi signal to the world that no Englishman was safe," Niven said. "Look what they did to Leslie Howard, to Glenn Miller. Goebbels would have been delighted to have killed figures the Allies loved. Hitler personally ordered that Clark Gable be either shot down or taken prisoner and brought to Berlin in chains for 'fun and games.'"

Larry wrote that when he arrived in Lisbon with Vivien, he found the city "rammed with spies as a pomegranate is with pips. There was a Mata Hari behind every palm tree. Behind every pillar in our hotel, men would pause, say something in an undertone, and move casually on."

***

The hit movie of the week in Lisbon was *Wuthering Heights*.

The Oliviers were ordered to wait outside Lisbon in the swanky Estoril Palacio, a hotbed of spies and international intrigue during World War II. The elegant bar displayed the Union Jack, the Stars and Stripes, and the Nazi swastika, since Portugal, officially at least, was a neutral country.

Larry became so alarmed that he went to the Air Commodore, the Air Attaché for the British Embassy who provided him with a pistol and taught him how to use it.

The commodore warned Larry that "Lisbon is the most dangerous city in Europe if you've been targeted by the Nazis."

Then the commodore revealed that eight of the crew members aboard their ship had been arrested on espionage charges. "They were indeed Hitler's agents."

At the hotel, Larry and Vivien refused to go down to the dining room, staying in their room and ordering from room service. When there was a knock, Larry concealed himself behind the door to make sure it was a waiter or a maid.

On the afternoon of the second day, a call came into their room. They had a guest downstairs waiting to be shown upstairs to their suite. "A Mrs. Violet, to see you," the front desk said.

Violet was the password for their mysterious visitor. When Larry opened the door, he encountered a well-dressed, rather masculine woman. He invited "Mrs. Violet" into their suite.

Vivien cowered by the sofa, looking apprehensive. Introductions were hurried.

Strangely dressed in women's clothes, their guest introduced himself as Dudley Wrangel Clarke, a Brigadier (i.e., Brigadier General) in the British Army. In time Vivien and Larry would realize what a remarkable James Bond type of creature this man was. He would become

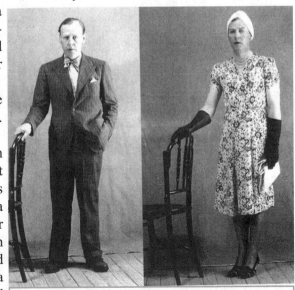

"Close your eyes, dear, and think of England."
Brigadier General Dudley Wrangel Clarke ("Mrs. Violet")
in and out of drag

responsible for some of the grand deceptions of World War II. One of the deceptions he organized, code-named Operation Copperhead, had recruited a look-a-like who resembled the British General Bernard Montgomery. The look-a-like had been deployed to the Mediterranean region to distract the Germans away from Montgomery's actual location on the English Channel.

Clarke also created the First United States Army Group, a fictitious brigade based in Southeast England. The deception had been designed to fool Hitler into thinking the Allies were going to invade France at Pas-de-Calais, and not at the Normandy beaches.

Despite the woman's attire he was wearing, Clarke was terse and business-like with the Oliviers, warning them that the diplomatic packet he was turning over to them contained information so dangerous it could topple the monarchy. They were to deliver the pouch to Bristol, where the British secret service would make contact with them and retrieve it.

At the door in his high heels, Clarke wished them "God speed on your journey." Then he left, shutting the door behind him.

Larry turned to Vivien, "Had I not married you, I would have proposed to Mrs. Violet."

"You bugger," she said, tossing a pillow from the sofa at him. After a sleepless night, Larry picked up the ringing phone the next morning to learn that two seats had become available on a dangerous flight from Lisbon to Bristol.

With the secret pouch strapped to Larry's body, he looked like he'd put on extra weight as a limousine carried them to the airport for their flight. No flights were going into London at the time.

In amazement, Larry passed both Lufthansa and B.O.A.C. aircraft parked side by side. Departure times were not communicated to passengers, who had to arrive hours before a flight and wait restlessly for takeoffs to be approved. As the Oliviers, in disguise, unobtrusively made their way to the plane, a photographer suddenly appeared in front of them for a candid snapshot.

It was suspected that Lufthansa agents working at the airport cabled Berlin when Larry and Vivien departed from the Sintra Airport, near Lisbon, aboard a twin-engined Portuguese Dakota.

It was a seven-hour flight between Sintra and Bristol, where it was understood that they'd turn over their secret documents to a contact yet to be named. Larry remembered the flight as "nightmarish."

He would claim that a Luftwaffe plane had taken off from La Coruña airport in northwestern Spain, and had trailed them for part of the flight. It was later revealed that Josef Goebbels had known they were aboard the flight, and had perhaps ordered that their plane be shot down.

Why the plane's mission was aborted at the last minute remains one of the many enigmas of World War II. Apparently, two major Nazi agents were aboard the Olivier's flight, Englishmen who were traitors and were returning to Britain for sabotage.

Goebbels may have made a decision that his agents landing safely in England was more important than killing the Oliviers. Thanks to their status as high-profile stars, they could be easily assassinated another day.

As the plane began its descent to Whitchurch Airfield outside Bristol, two members of the crew rushed into the blacked-out passenger cabin for fire extinguishers. The second pilot in command had fired a recognition signal to air control in Bristol but had forgotten to open a window to allow for its escape. The cockpit was in flames as the plane set down in the middle of an air attack. The city of Bristol was under Luftwaffe aerial bombardment.

The aircraft landed haphazardly and with many swerves and bumps at the airport. It came narrowly close to being bombed. "Welcome to dear old England, Puss," Larry said to Vivien.

They had been told that in November alone, some 4,560 British civilians had been killed in Luftwaffe air raids.

As Vivien stepped off the plane, her ears were assaulted by the wail of sirens, her nose assailed by the dust of bombings. "Oh, to be back at Tara before war broke out," she whispered to Larry.

Rushing off the plane, they ran to the passengers' lounge, which offered little protection—or none if a bomb hit. As Luftwaffe bombs rained down around them, soldiers manning anti-aircraft guns lit up the night sky.

Hotel rooms were scarce in war-crowded Bristol, and the Oliviers were put in a hotel that had been previously bombed. One entire wall was missing. Still in their clothes, they cuddled in blankets and rode out the night.

After New York, which still maintained a certain gaiety, Vivien and Larry experienced "a dead city" in Bristol on this bitter January night. A flapping tarpaulin did little to keep out the night winds.

At three that morning, there was a loud knock on their door. It was an army sergeant with a message for Larry. He was to be prepared to leave the hotel in two hours. He would be met downstairs, and was to carry with him the documents he'd been given in Lisbon.

***

At an army camp outside Bristol, a lieutenant delivered Larry to a large tent and instructed him to go inside. "Your breakfast will arrive soon," the lieutenant said.

Inside, still dressed in his underwear, Prince George, Duke of Kent, await-ed him. The handsome, dashing member of the British royal family was the fourth son of George V and Mary of Teck. His father was the eldest surviving son of Edward VII and Queen Alexandra.

Larry bowed before him, as the prince welcomed him. "Your Royal Highness," Larry said.

"I hope this won't be the last time Heathcliff kneels before me in my underwear."

The remark in all its flippant informality both shocked and intrigued Larry.

Prince George, Duke of Kent
(The Celebrity Seducer)

The reputation of the notorious prince had preceded him. For some eighteen years, he'd been the lover of Noël Coward, as Larry knew so well. Although married to Princess Marina of Greece, his second cousin, he had continued a long string of romances with both men and women, from socialites to Hollywood celebrities.

Some of his conquests included Fred Astaire, the African-American cabaret singer Florence Mills; socialite Margaret Whigham (later Duchess of Argyll); musical star Jessie Matthews, and banking heiress Poppy Baring.

He'd had sexual liaisons with his distant cousin Louis Ferdinand, Prince of Prussia, and even the traitor and art historian Anthony Blunt. Larry wondered if he were the latest celebrity who'd be added to the Duke's list of conquests.

He watched as the Duke dressed slowly, a striptease in reverse. "I hear you have something for me," the Duke said.

"Safely carried from Lisbon in a concealed pouch," Larry said.

"Now it's your turn to undress in front of me," the Duke said.

Larry removed his jacket and unbuttoned his shirt.

"Here, I'll help you," the Duke said,

Their closets were filled with secrets:
Edward, Prince of Wales *(left)* with his
brother, Prince George *(right)* on a visit
to Vancouver in 1927

452

moving over to unfasten the last of Larry's shirt buttons. He reached inside for the pouch and also felt Larry's chest. "Thank you for bringing these documents to England," he said. "They are highly sensitive, and we'll have to deliver them unopened to the man himself."

Larry knew he was referring to Winston Churchill.

The pouched removed, Larry stood before the Duke, his shirt unbuttoned.

The Duke reached for Larry and held him in his arms as he planted a deep, long, and probing kiss on his mouth. Perhaps the Duke would have gone further, but they were interrupted by the lieutenant delivering breakfast.

After breakfast, the Duke told Larry he had to leave at once for London. Before he left, each of them wrote out points of contact for each other.

At the doorway to his tent, the Duke hesitated. "I really don't want to leave you. I feel I've made a very special friend this morning." He reached out his arms to Larry. "Come here for one final goodbye until we meet again, which will be sooner than later."

The contents of the diplomatic pouch that Larry turned over to the Duke of Kent that morning will perhaps never be known. Churchill reportedly burned the documents after reading the highly classified information.

It was rumored at the time that the diplomatic pouch Larry carried contained details relating to the alleged Nazi connections of Wallis Simpson who had married King Edward VIII, the Duke of Kent's older brother, who had become the Duke of Windsor after his abdication. The king had abdicated the throne in December of 1936 "to marry the woman I love," the notorious twice-divorced American, Wallis Warfield Simpson, which was followed by a constitutional crisis.

The Duchess was known to harbor pro-German sympathies, and was believed to be passing secrets to a leading Nazi with whom she was thought to have had an affair. The FBI was also investigating her, and found out that the high Nazi official was none other than Joachim von Ribbentrop, formerly the German ambassador to Britain before Hitler promoted him to the post of

Princess Marina of Greece and Denmark (*left*) became HRH the Duchess of Kent after her 1934 marriage to George, Duke of Kent (*right*)

453

Germany's Foreign Minister during the war.

The full report, somehow compiled by Dudley Clarke and transported to Lisbon by way of Madrid, also revealed the details of the indiscreet 1937 visit by the Duke and Duchess of Windsor to Germany, at which time they arrived as the personal guests of Adolf Hitler. It was during the context of that visit that Hitler promised to restore the Duke to the throne of England after the subjugation of Britain.

It was alleged that during the summer of 1940 the Duke, voluntarily in exile in Spain, engaged in treasonous talks with the Nazis and expressed his willingness to defect into the German camp.

In August of 1940, Churchill had dispatched the Duke and his notorious American-born Duchess to The Bahamas where he would rule as governor. He was sent to this backwater of the British Empire as a means of lessening the embarrassment he might cause because of his pro-Nazi sentiments during the war.

Before he was shunted out of the way to the Americas, however, the Duke was "outed" by Lord Caldecote, [Minister for the Coordination of Defense from 1936-1939, and by 1940, Lord Chancellor of Britain] who informed Churchill that "[The Duke of Windsor] is well known to be pro-Nazi and he may become a center of intrigue."

The Duchess had met von Ribbentrop when he was the German ambassador in London, and it was believed that after his wartime recall to Berlin, she had remained in constant contact with him, continually leaking British secrets to the Nazis.

After the war, the Duke of Windsor was never given another official appointment and spent the remainder of his life in retirement and in what was referred to as "voluntary exile."

***

Both Larry and Vivien had not slept for two nights as they journeyed by train from Bristol to London's Paddington Station. Two reporters awaited their arrival. "We feel we've stayed away long enough," Larry told the journalists. "We've come back to do our small part in helping England win this horrid war," Vivien said.

I remember the day we arrived back in Durham Cottage," Larry said. "Because of nearby Blitz bombing, two of our ceilings had collapsed. Still in our overcoats, Vivien and I sat in our living room and cried and cried before getting on with it. Getting on with it at that moment meant finishing off a bottle."

One morning, Vivien by herself went to Little Stanhope Street in Mayfair where she'd lived with Leigh. Their former home was in ruins, a victim of the Blitz. She let out a muffled little scream and walked away. At the time, Leigh was away serving on a naval base, and Suzanne was safely in Vancouver.

Once they fixed up their battered cottage, they resumed a rather austere social life, in contrast to the gaiety of their pre-war parties. They visited Ursula Jeans and Roger Livesey in King's Langley, a historic town 21 miles northwest of London in Hertfordshire.

Jeans later recalled that Vivien was experiencing "enormous emotional strains in her marriage. Even after her great success in Hollywood, she was terrified that she would never equal the acting ability of Larry, whom she regarded as the greatest stage actor on earth."

"I will never match his achievements," she told Jeans.

"But, dear, you don't have to," Jeans said. "No actress could have played Scarlett O'Hara like you did."

"*Fiddle-dee-dee,*" she said, dismissing her role. "I want to be acclaimed as a great classical actress. But my light voice and even my personality don't seem to work on the stage like it does in film."

"Then become the greatest film star of all time," Jeans advised. "Garbo is *finis.*"

"No, I don't like films," Vivien said. "I want to work with Larry on stage. We'll do *Antony and Cleopatra*, even *Titus Andronicus*, definitely *Macbeth* and *Coriolanus.*"

Fellow actor John Mills invited them on January 6, 1941 to his wedding to Mary Hayley Bell. Mills was in the Royal Engineers, and Larry's brother Dickie was an RNVR officer.

"The great parts in this war drama have been grabbed by others," Larry said. "We don't even have good supporting roles."

Jack Hawkins, now in the Royal Welsh Fusiliers, arrived at Durham to tell Larry, "You *are* a silly bugger—*really.*" Hawkins at the time seemed to be gloating over his role within the British military and, without saying so, pointing out Larry's lack of enrollment.

"I never really liked Hawkins," Larry once told John Gielgud, "although we remain great friends."

"Don't you see the contradiction in that declaration?" Gielgud asked him.

Ralph Richardson met with Vivien and Larry in London to talk over Larry's plans to become a pilot. Lady Richardson remembered the occasion: "They were so enchanting, so obviously in love. Their love affair was no longer a secret."

When Leigh Holman returned to London for a brief visit, Vivien agreed to see him at Durham Cottage. Larry wasn't at home that day. Leigh recalled the experience in a letter to Hamish Hamilton. "Vivien was a dream of beauty, but a little tired and too thin."

Hamilton showed the affectionate letter to Vivien when she visited him at his home in Sussex. "Leigh will never love another woman," he told her. "He'll go to his grave faithful and loving you. But now that I see how happy you and Larry are together, I wish you well. Forgive me my original bitterness toward you when you broke from Leigh."

After Vivien and Larry made their cottage livable, they set out to do their part for the war effort. Larry told a reporter he wanted to join the Royal Air Force, and even though it would mean a separation from Larry, Vivien claimed that she wanted to be a nurse in Egypt. The RAF did not accept Larry, and Vivien was turned down as a possible nurse in North Africa.

After a thorough medical examination, it was discovered that Larry had a damaged nerve in his inner ear, disqualifying him for the R.A.F.

When both Larry and Vivien were rejected in their bid for a more active role in the British war effort, they had second thoughts about their homecoming. "Maybe we're merely chasing windmills across the plains of La Mancha," Larry told Vivien.

Finally, Larry's assignment in the Fleet Air Arm came in, thanks to the influence of Richardson. During his weeks of training, he had to move out of London.

He would be sent first to Lee-on-Solent, a small seaside town in Hampshire, five miles west of Portsmouth. After training, he would be transferred to RAF Worthy Down, a Royal Air Force station near Winchester.

Vivien insisted on moving out of Durham Cottage and renting a place near his base. He protested and they fought bitterly. "I need my space," he claimed. "I won't be a good companion. I will be exhausted every night, and I need to concentrate on my work and rest the other time. It will be very grueling."

In spite of his objections, she insisted on coming with him, claiming, "I will provide a cozy home for you to come to at night."

Larry had one compelling reason he didn't want to be with Vivien during training. He was seeing someone else.

As Richardson said, "Viv and Larry had a great romance, in full bloom in the late 1930s. But this was wartime. A grim reality had set in. The bloom was off the rose. It would not bloom again."

Before leaving London, Larry received a call from the Duke of Kent. "Your dossier was delivered safely to Whitehall," the Duke said. "You really must be rewarded. I'm here in a suite at the Dorchester. Please come over right away. Tell your beautiful wife you have a secret mission to carry out for the government."

It is believed that Larry's months-long affair with the Duke of Kent began that night.

Mired in the rubble, death, and destruction of wartime London, Vivien sank deeper and deeper into depression. Privately she told friends that she at times regretted her decision to leave California. "I was the Queen of Hollywood," she told Ursula Jeans, "and, like Queen Christina, I abdicated my throne."

"In Viv's wildest fantasies," said John Gielgud, "she saw herself as Joan of Arc leading Britain to victory over the Huns. But in reality there wasn't much for her to do. It became perfectly clear to her that England could win the war without either Larry or herself, especially when the Yanks arrived on our shores."

Vivien often roamed the West End, looking at the theaters that had been shut down or bombed. Sometimes wearing a large hat with the collar of her cloth coat turned up, she walked through the rubble of London, remembering streets and landmarks of her life that were destroyed in the Blitz.

She frequently wandered back to her beloved Mayfair, where she'd lived with Leigh and Suzanne while struggling to break into the theater. "It's our house on Little Stanhope Street that's *Gone With the Wind*," she told Noël Coward. "There is nothing now. Somehow I feel that bombed-out house is the symbol of my life. I often stand at the corner of Pitt's Head Mews and look down the street at the ruin. I feel I'm that wreck every morning when I wake up."

"You've come a long way, Scarlett, since antebellum Tara."
A London neighborhood after one of the Luftwaffe's bombing raids

"Cheer up, duckie," Coward said in a mock Cockney accent, which he did brilliantly. "One day bluebirds will fly again over the White Cliffs of Dover."

"The bacon I cook for Larry in the morning is rancid," she wrote Gertrude in Canada. "There's no place in London with heat. How I wish all of us could be lying in the sun of California, plucking a ripened orange from a nearby tree. Larry and I have taken to wearing long underwear—it's very unbecoming, very unromantic. How can you have sexual fantasies about a man in long underwear?"

At their home, when they had the time, Vivien tried to restore some of their pre-war gaiety, inviting John Mills and his new bride, Rex Harrison and Lilli Palmer, even David Niven and his new wife, Primula.

To enliven the atmosphere of London at war, Robert Helpmann showed up one night in a leopard skin jock strap in which he'd placed a tiny kitten, greatly enlarging his genital pouch.

Vivien feared that if she didn't get a theatrical job soon, she'd be drafted as a factory worker in a munitions plant.

She might not have been sought out in London casting circles, but the Theatre Guild in New York wanted her to play in *Caesar and Cleopatra* with Sir Cedric Hardwicke. Of course, that would mean crossing the dangerous Atlantic again. There was also the problem of being under contract to David O. Selznick.

Larry still wanted to be a pilot, although Vivien taunted him during one of her "states." "You'll just kill yourself. Let's face it: you can't even fly a kite."

Not accepting the diagnosis of one ear specialist, he went to five others in London, although appointments were hard to come by. "There is one advantage in being a movie star," he told Richardson. "You can always get bumped to the head of the queue."

Finally, he found a specialist who reversed the Admiralty's decision and agreed to admit him into the Fleet Air Arm, the aviation branch of the Navy. It was hardly the RAF, but at least he'd be a pilot and get to wear an impressive uniform.

Before that commission came in, he found himself with three unscheduled, relatively listless months in London. Fortunately, two film roles emerged.

***

Larry was cast in a cameo role in a propaganda film, *49th Parallel,* which was renamed *The Invaders* for distribution in the United States.

The director, Michael Powell, was said to be "horribly full of himself," but he worked smoothly with Larry. In the film, Larry was cast as a gentle

French-Canadian trapper called "Johnnie." The French/Canadian accent he adopted was called "Clouseau-esque."

Larry later claimed he had learned "something about the economy and directness of film acting from my days in Hollywood."

Launched in April of 1940, *49th Parallel* took eighteen months to complete. Most of it was shot in England, except for two expeditions to Canada.

Britain's Ministry of Information financed this episodic adventure drama for only $100,000, and, surprisingly, it became one of the best of the anti-Nazi propaganda films.

Several major stars, working for half their usual fee, agreed to appear in the drama. Many of Larry's friends were cast, notably Leslie Howard and Raymond Massey. Also included among the actors was the talented character actor Finlay Currie. The noted British composer, Ralph Vaughan Williams, composed its musical score.

At first it was announced that Larry would be teamed once again with the expatriate German actress Elisabeth Bergner, with whom he'd made the ill-fated *As You Like It.*

The plot required that some of the scenes be shot within the Hutterite community near Winnipeg. With religious and cultural roots extending back to the Protestant Reformation in the Austrian district of the Tyrol during the 16th century, the strictly pacifist Hutterites led an austere but communal lifestyle, similar to the Amish and Mennonites, with rigid moral codes.

Bergner can still be seen in some long shots. Filming with the archly conservative Hutterites in Canada, she was spotted by a local woman painting her nails and smoking. The Hutterite became so incensed she attacked Bergner who resigned from the film that day. The picture was deep into production when Bergner at the last minute "defected."

Taking over for Bergner was a South African-born Glynis Johns, whose husky voice was part flaky, part sexy. She would add her charm to a whole series of British and American post-war movies, including a co-starring role with Danny Kaye during his finest hour, *The Court Jester* (1956).

Yorkshire-born Eric Portman was cast as a brutal Nazi, Lieutenant Hirth. Known mainly as a stage actor, he delivered one of his most brilliant performances.

When praised for his acting in the film, he

HAMLET HITS THE NORTH WOODS Laurence Olivier playing a French-Canadian trapper at war with the Nazi invaders of Canada in *49th Parallel*

459

said, "Acting is like masturbation—one either does it or one doesn't but one never talks about it." Portman, a homosexual, was very infatuated with Larry, but his dream of seduction never came true.

The 49th Parallel, of course, functions as the U.S./Canadian border, and was noteworthy at the time as the world's longest undefended border between two nations. One of the purposes of the film involved influencing public opinion in the still-neutral United States. Powell said, "I hoped it might scare the pants off the Americans and bring them into the war."

Screenwriter Emeric Pressburger, a Hungarian Jew who had been a journalist in Hungary and Germany, was the screenwriter. He said, "Goebbels considered himself an expert on propaganda, but I thought I'd show him a thing or two."

In this WWII movie, Nazi survivors of a German U-boat sunk in Hudson Bay attempt to evade capture by traveling across enemy terrain (i.e., Canada) to safety in the then-neutral United States.

The film turned out to be immensely popular with British audiences.

Even though he'd been cast into a minor role, reviewers claimed that Larry had never been so ruggedly handsome and dashing on the screen, particularly when he is depicted singing joyfully in the bathtub.

***

Between film assignments, Larry frequently saw Glen Byam Shaw and his other male friends in the theater. His relationship with Shaw had settled into a deep friendship, with Larry calling him "Glennie," in the way that Noël Coward had become "Noëlie."

Shaw later revealed that he thought Larry was "torn between two worlds, feeling he should come home at night to an increasingly demanding Vivien, yet at the same time wanting to be involved with his close and personal male friends." It was a conflict that would be with him throughout his days.

Larry and Vivien moved out of London to the more tranquil village of Fulmer in Buckinghamshire, so they would be close to Denham Studios where Larry was to make his next film. In the wake of their departure, actor Robert Newton leased their Durham Cottage in London's Chelsea district.

The house outside London had been recommended to them by Noël Coward, its previous occupant. "If only the walls could talk," Larry said. "What scandalous stories they would tell."

For his next "quickie," Larry was cast in the British propaganda film, *The Demi-Paradise*, in which he had to fake a Russian accent. He feared his early experiment with a Russian accent made him sound too effeminate, so he came up with an accent of his own invention.

460

"*The Demi-Paradise* was made to get the British to cuddle up to the Russians, who, for the time at least, were on our side," Larry said.

A crew-cut Larry played Ivan Dimitrievitch Kouznetsoff, a Soviet engineer sent over to liaise with technicians responsible for British shipbuilding. "I played it like a male *Ninotchka*," he said, recalling the 1939 Greta Garbo hit.

Larry bonded once again with the director Anthony Asquith, whom Larry still affectionately called Puffin. "Puffin was the excellent, experienced, and very charming director he always was," said Larry.

He was cast opposite Penelope Dudley Ward as his leading lady, but it was veteran actress Margaret Rutherford, playing Rowena Ventnor, who stole every scene she was in.

The Demi-Paradise was released in England in 1943, but its opening in the United States was delayed until the end of the war when Universal Pictures renamed it *Adventure for Two*.

William Whitebait in *The Nation* referred to Larry's performance as "dazzling," and *Variety* claimed that the film put Larry "in the top rank of British actors." Bosley Crowther of *The New York Times* took a dimmer view, judging Larry's role as a "ponderous caricature," and calling the picture itself "a limp and dampish hand across the sea."

***

At long last, Larry's assignment as a naval aviator came in. He and Vivien prepared to leave at once, heading toward the West Country.

He'd asked her to remain behind in London, but she insisted on going with him. Although the newspapers and their friends still reported how madly in love they were, they had in fact been lovers for years and he didn't feel the need to be with her every night of his life.

In mid-April of 1941, he headed for Lee-on-Solent in Hampshire to undergo a three-week conversion course, in which he'd be taught to adapt his private flying lessons in California to British planes.

Larry, now an Acting Sub Lieutenant with the R.N.V.R., with Vivien and her stray cat, Tissy, in tow, set out like a gypsy caravan in two cars.

She steered her old car which actually had to be towed all the way to Hampshire since it needed repairs after sitting idle so long in London.

Larry led the "caravan" in his Invicta automobile "with its chromium entrails bursting through the bonnet." On the way, the radiator of the Invicta bubbled and boiled on every hill.

She found a small Victorian house which was named "Forakers." She set up housekeeping in the sparsely furnished place with some treasures she'd brought from Durham Cottage, including a small painting by Boudin and an Aubusson carpet.

To her horror, she was going in and out of her "states" more frequently. After three weeks, Larry was transferred from Lee-on-Solent to Warsash, a town on Hampshire's coast. That meant an hour's ride back home every night on his motorcycle, a German-made B.M.W. twin-cylinder.

On some nights Vivien wouldn't speak to him but locked herself away in the downstairs bedroom. On other evenings, she was welcoming and gracious, having prepared him a warm supper with the limited rations available. "We ate a lot of cabbage, I remember," Larry said.

She detested the drafty Victorian house they'd rented in Warsash so she and Larry, along with Tissy, found a more intimate bungalow outside Worthy Down. For the transfer, they activated their caravan once again.

Even though Larry was hardly a first-rate pilot, he was assigned a job of training air gunners and running a training camp for teenage members of the Air Training Corps. Churchill had ordered this based on the possibility that the war might drag on until around 1950, with the understanding that Britain would eventually need replacement flyers for the RAF.

"The average age of my Air Scouts is twelve," Larry told Richardson.

Larry later became a flight instructor to older but very inexperienced pilots. He told Richardson, "The blokes I teach are mainly lorry drivers, butchers of innards, and the suet-brained who start the day with two pints of lager under their belts."

In addition to the recruiting speeches Larry made during the war, he also delivered propaganda broadcasts and staged charity events featuring entertainment, with himself as the main attraction.

In a propaganda speech he delivered to an audience at London's Royal Albert Hall, news clips on the BBC sounded Churchillian as Larry shouted: "We will attack! We will smite our foes! We will conquer the evil Nazi empire!"

After reading in the paper details about Hermann Goering's wardrobe, Larry strode onto the local airfield wearing red leather boots lined with mink. "A bit ostentatious, wouldn't you say?" fellow actor Robert Douglas asked when he saw Larry.

The crew nicknamed Larry "The Red Baron."

Douglas, the actor who had replaced Larry years before in *Theatre Royal* after he broke his ankle, also served with him at Worthy Down. The two actors bonded and shared memories of Hollywood, even discussing their mutual friend Errol Flynn, whose embrace each of them had enjoyed.

Douglas later commented on Larry's growing impatience about seeing some action in the war. "He wanted to go into battle, not train some blokes in an old Swordfish that should have been retired long ago. Larry's Swordfish didn't take off into the sky. It staggered upwards into the blue."

In one of Larry's demonstration flights, a groundsman signaled that the chocks, which were hidden from the pilot's view, had each been pulled away from the wheels. But when Larry revved the engine and released the brakes on his antiquated Blackburn Shark, it swung around on a 180-degree spin, crashing nose-to-nose into the aircraft immediately to its left.

Larry had never gotten along with the commanding officer. On the first day he reported to duty, the C.O. had greeted him with, "I don't think you look one damn bit like Lord Nelson."

After crashing two planes, the C.O. took an even dimmer view "of my worst pilot. Not just the worst, but the worst in the history of British naval aviation."

His C.O. filed a report: "Lawrence (sic) Olivier never got off the ground and managed to destroy two of our aircraft. I need to put a lid on the simmering pot called Olivier. I suggest you cancel his leave for one month as punishment for his carelessness."

The C.O. later wrote to his superiors. "Olivier has taken to calling his fellow airmen 'darling,' each and every one of them. Perhaps this is a theatrical conceit—you know, *actors*—but I feel some of our crew will misinterpret his remark and view it as a homosexual solicitation. What shall I do?"

The command from headquarters came back: TELL OLIVIER TO CEASE AND DESIST WITH DARLING.

Vivien wrote Leigh Holman with this bit of news: "In Larry's new role, he is but an understudy for a British warrior. The RAF is defending our coastline. Larry is costing the government money by wrecking our aircraft. We are definitely in the backwash of the war, but perhaps we'll survive while others are sacrificing their lives for England."

During one of her darkest moments of despair, Vivien also wrote Katharine Hepburn, whose romantic interest in her had never ceased. "Our Europe is dying. It will not come alive

"[Larry was] more effective and less dangerous as a moralebooster than as a pilot"

Two views of Larry teaching young RAF recruits

463

again in our time. The only hope for theater and the screen now resides in America."

As the war ground along, Larry admitted he began to feel like a "shirker," and wondered if he were in uniform merely for the sake of "keeping up appearances."

"Maybe I should have stuck to the job I knew . . . acting," he told Vivien. "Perhaps I would have been better off pursuing the same course I'd followed for nearly two decades."

Near the end of his military service, Larry volunteered to pilot Walruses, a small flying boat built to be catapulted from battleships. His request was granted, but there would be a three-month delay.

His life as a Walrus pilot never happened. Just before he was scheduled for duty, the British military informed him that this particular type of plane had been abandoned. "There goes my last hope of getting into combat," he lamented to Vivien.

With his career as a pilot coming to an end, he decided to devote his full time to acting. For the next eighteen months he would take on the greatest challenge of his entire career. He would both direct and star in a color film version of *Henry V*.

As the weeks had dragged on, Vivien had grown increasingly restless. She finally announced to Larry, "I am not a housewife. It was wrong for me to try to become one. I belong on the stage. I must return to the theater, and you must help me. You owe it to me after all the dirty laundry I've washed, ruining my paws, and all the horrid meals I've cooked for you."

***

There is little doubt that Larry was mesmerized by the charismatic Prince George, Duke of Kent. He'd always lived in the shadow of his more famous brother, the Prince of Wales, who became King Edward VIII very briefly, before settling into his lifetime role as the Duke of Windsor.

Although the two royal princes were close, the younger brother was also jealous of his older sibling. In his heyday in the 1920s, the Prince of Wales drew more romantic fan mail than Rudolph Valentino, the Sheik of Hollywood.

Prince George did manage to attract the spotlight from his brother when he married Princess Marina in 1934, making her the Duchess of Kent.

The Royal Family hoped that the marriage would dispel rumors spread about the Duke's sexual life. His closeted existence sometimes led to blackmail, as when he indiscreetly wrote love letters to a male prostitute in Paris. The contents of those letters were pornographic.

464

Larry's relationship with the Duke of Kent has only been revealed with leaks from secret reports, more from the American side than from the British. During World War II, American agents worked in Britain, gathering data on key figures among their ally, just as the British secret service spied on persons of influence in America. It is believed that the file the British secret service accumulated on the Duke of Kent was either destroyed or hidden in the deepest vault of some dungeon.

Aside from investigating agents from both the United States and Britain, the romantic liaisons between the Duke and Larry were known to some of their friends, including Glen Byam Shaw, Denys Blakelock, Noël Coward, and Ralph Richardson. Dame Peggy Ashcroft may also have found out about it, but, as far as it is known, Vivien was kept out of the loop.

After the war, Danny Kaye also became privy to the affair of Larry with the Duke of Kent. Ironically, the bisexual Kaye was conducting an affair with Marina, the widowed Duchess of Kent at the same time he was continuing his romance with Larry.

Larry and the Duke of Kent may have seen each other as many as eighteen to twenty times between the time they met in Bristol and the time the Duke was killed.

As a patriotic Englishman, Larry was presumably shocked by the pro-German stance of the Duke of Kent, although that did not deter his interest. Reportedly, the Duke told Larry, "Every drop of my blood is German."

Strongly anti-Semitic, the Duke before the war had been quoted as saying, "Nazism is the best solution to undercut the Socialists in Britain who want to topple the monarchy."

Originally, he claimed that Hitler had prevented the spread of communism to Germany and, perhaps, to Britain itself.

Both the Prince of Wales and Prince George may have been more anti-Russian than pro-Nazi. George V's cousin and the godfather of the Duke of Kent, Czar Nicholas, was murdered along with his family by the Bolsheviks at Ekaterinburg. Thanks partly to that atrocity, each of the young princes developed a lifelong fear and dread of a communist takeover, a fear which moved each of them closer into the German camp.

The Duke of Kent's pro-German stance became even more pronounced when he met in 1933 with Baron Wilhelm de Ropp in London, who placed a swastika wreath on the cenotaph to the war dead.

The Baron spent long hours with the young prince and later reported to Josef Goebbels in Berlin. "Prince George is definitely in our camp."

Before Larry and the Duke could move into a deeper and more meaningful relationship, a tragic event occurred.

On August 25, 1942, the Duke, along with eleven other passengers, took off in a Sunderland "flying boat" from Invergordon in Scotland, en route to a refueling stop in Iceland with a final destination designated as Newfoundland in Canada.

In circumstances never yet explained, and even though the plane was piloted by one of the RAF's best pilots, it crashed near Dunbreath in Caithness shortly after takeoff. The Duke was killed instantly.

The death of the young prince has been the subject of rumors and speculation that refuse to die even to this day. Baron von Hoyningen-Huene, the German ambassador to Lisbon, filed a report to Berlin that the Duke's flying boat had been sabotaged "to eliminate this friend of Germany."

Although once favored by Churchill, the Duke had appeared on his enemy list. The Duke was outspoken about his political views. He wanted Churchill to make peace with Hitler so that the Nazis could dedicate their full military force to the destruction of Russia. Secretly, the Duke wanted the monarchy restored in Russia.

Whether the British government was deliberately involved in the sabotage of the plane has never been revealed. Such an audacious act by the government would have had to be approved by the Prime Minister himself. Churchill, it was reported, viewed the Duke of Kent as a "menace" to Britain's struggle against the Nazis.

The Duchess of Kent, known before her marriage as Princess Marina of Greece and Denmark, had given birth to their third child, Prince Michael of Kent, only six weeks before the Duke's fatal air crash in Scotland. His body was on display in St. George's Chapel at Windsor Castle. Noël Coward, in attendance at the funeral, sobbed so loudly that security had to remove him from the church.

The Duke was later buried behind Queen Victoria's mausoleum at Frogmore, outside Windsor.

After the Duke's death, Larry, or so it is believed, was drilled extensively by the British secret service about his relationship with the Duke. Because of that association, Larry was viewed as a high risk agent, and apparently was never used by the government for any further covert operation in the wake of the Duke's death.

Vivien, however, was considered "untainted" and may have been unaware of the drama swirling around her husband.

The F.B.I., however, was very suspicious of Vivien, but not because of any pro-German slant. J. Edgar Hoover viewed Vivien as a possible danger after the war, because of her association with the "Bolshevik-loving" Clare Sheridan, her sculptor friend. Hoover instructed his agents to keep an eye on Vivien, especially if she ventured into the Soviet Union or into any of the Eastern European countries that had come under Soviet domination.

In 2004, Jeffrey Corrick, the American playwright, dramatized the Duke of Kent's drug addictions and bisexuality in a stage presentation. A year before, in Stephen Poliakoff's 2003 television broadcast, "Prince Georgie" is portrayed as "sensitive, intelligent, and artistic:" code words for gay.

Queen Victoria's mausoleum and the Duke of Kent's tomb can only be viewed one day a year at Frogmore. On the first anniversary of the Duke's death, Denys Blakelock drove Larry to Windsor, where he placed a single rose on the fallen prince's tomb.

As reported by Blakelock, Larry kneeled at the grave and said, "Good night, sweet prince," the same *Hamlet*-inspired words he'd said to John Barrymore in Chicago.

Later, Blakelock claimed that after the gravesite visit, en route back to London, Larry told him, "Had Prince George become King of England, not one German bomb would have fallen on our beloved country."

Whether these words were actually spoken by Larry or not will never be known. In theatrical circles, Blakelock was known as a "drama queen."

***

Bored with idleness, Vivien sought work at the Old Vic with Tyrone Guthrie, asserting that she'd even appear in a minor role. He turned her down, fearful that her star status would upset the balance of his productions. "Audiences would flock to see Scarlett O'Hara in the flesh, not our play. Sorry."

She had such a burning desire to return to the stage that in spite of her seven-year contract with Selznick, she told theatrical producer Hugh Beaumont, "Binkie, darling, I'd rather be Edith Evans any day than Garbo."

Knowing how desperate she was to work again, Larry suggested that she try out for the role of Jennifer Dubedat in *The Doctor's Dilemma* by George Bernard Shaw. She did not like the play. "It's cold blooded," she said. "It questions the value of the artist to society." But he persuaded her to do it anyway.

She wanted to play Cleopatra in the major film that director Gabriel Pascal was planning. But when she called Pascal, he told her that the playwright, Shaw, had reserved casting approval exclusively for himself.

That made up Vivien's mind. She decided to

Vivien Leigh in 1941 playing Jennifer Dubedat in G.B. Shaw's *The Doctor's Dilemma* give an outstanding performance as Jennifer Dubedat, which would bring her to the attention of Shaw.

With Binkie Beaumont in charge, *The Doctor's Dilemma* moved forward. Her contract demanded that she agree to a long road tour through the provinces before opening at the Haymarket.

The play was helmed by Irene Hentschel, one of the few female stage directors in the West End. The Irish actor, Cycil Cusack, played the artist and womanizer Louis Dubedat, with Vivien cast as his cuckolded, long-suffering wife.

The play's first preview was scheduled for Manchester in September of 1941. From there the troupe continued to Edinburgh, where they launched a six-month tour during one of the coldest winters in recent British history. Vivien played such cities as Leicester, Blackpool, Liverpool, Leeds, and Glasgow. At one point, she wrote both Larry and Leigh Holman, "Will this tour ever end? Will we ever come to London?"

In Edinburgh, the society photographer Cecil Beaton saw the play and went backstage to congratulate Vivien. In his diary, he wrote, "Vivien is almost incredibly lovely. She is madly in love with her husband, who adores her, and is convinced he is a much greater person than she is. The adulation of her beauty leaves her cold."

Beaton also complimented Vivien upon not having her character spoiled by her tremendous fame. But he found her performance as Jennifer "monotonous."

Vivien's weight dropped, her nervous agitation increased, and she grew thinner and thinner as she faced six long and grueling months touring with *The Doctor's Dilemma*. Nearly every day she read reports of death and destruction, including the loss of many friends of her youth. In unheated rooms, her coughing grew worse and would sometimes interfere with her performance.

Finally, when she felt she could tour no more, *The Doctor's Dilemma* opened in London at the Haymarket on March 4, 1942 to mostly rave reviews.

In contrast to London's wartime austerity, when many women were seen on the streets dressed as men, Vivien stood out, in all her Edwardian splendor, evoking a more glorious age for London. She was bewitching in her velvet scarlet dress and high lace collars, a vision of ruffles and bows with beguiling, long-brimmed, veiled hats.

Critics thought Vivien's portrayal of Jennifer was just as Shaw had created and described her: "She has something of the grace and romance of a wild creature, with a good deal of the elegance and dignity of a fine lady."

After the play's London opening, Vivien journeyed after each evening performance in a blackout train from the Haymarket to the house she shared with Larry in Warsash. If she thought she'd have time with Larry, it didn't happen. Totally exhausted, he'd be asleep when she arrived home. Conversely, when he left early the next morning, riding his motorcycle to the aerodrome, she was asleep.

Two weeks into the play's London run, her co-star, Cycil Cusack, fell sick, flubbing his lines and going into a total blank as an actor. In desperation, he began to recite lines from another play, *Playboy of the Western World*. This caused Vivien to stumble over her lines, and the curtain mercifully fell. For the next act, Cusack's understudy, Geoffrey Edwards, took over.

Cusack was replaced with the devastatingly handsome and charming Peter Glenville, who had been hired by Beaumont to fill in for a salary of ten pounds a week. Glenville had performed as the play's loveable rake many times before, and knew the role perfectly.

Born the same year as Vivien (1913), Glenville was the adopted son of two actors, Shaun Glenville and Dorothy (Dolly) Ward. His mother became famous, treading the boards on the music hall and variety circuit. Both Winston Churchill and David Lloyd George "adored" Dolly. On stage she was known for her English rose looks and her red-gold tresses.

During Glennville's involvement in the play, Larry managed to slip into London to catch one of the performances, and then came backstage to embrace Vivien and tell Glenville he'd given a magnificent performance.

It was obvious to Vivien that her husband was mesmerized by the stunning Glenville, who sported a goatee beard and mustache for the role. "You look thoroughly amoral," Larry told him.

"It's the role I'm playing," Glenville responded. "I'm actually immoral."

"My kind of fellow," Larry said, warming to the actor.

"It was an instant friendship," Beaumont recalled. "Not since Danny Kaye had Larry been so drawn to another actor." Beaumont, apparently, was unaware of Larry's relationship with the Duke of Kent.

Glenville claimed, "When I first met Vivien she seemed, if anything, almost too much in command of herself, of her beauty, and of her success. At that time she reigned in London not perhaps so much as an actress but as a dazzling woman. Although she was dainty and frail she had an iron determination and seemed to have no weaknesses. Her looks were startling, the charm was feline and

Matinee-handsome Peter Glenville, who became a well-known film director, was often mistaken for Tyrone Power. He had affairs with both Danny Kaye and Larry Olivier. Here's he's shown emoting with Vivien Leigh in G.B. Shaw's *The Doctor's Dilemma*

irresistible, the wit sharp, and her practical commonsense and her ability to entrance, entertain, and even to manage and organize every group of people she encountered would have done credit to an ambassadress."

Suddenly in February of 1943, Glenville became ill with yellow jaundice. John Gielgud was called in to take over the role, because Glenville's understudy also had become ill. Gielgud later complained to Shaw, "I am far too old for the role, but it's a part."

When Gielgud replaced the ailing Glenville, he began what he would later call "a deep friendship and even deeper affection for Vivien."

During his time with her, he told friends, "Poor Viv is often quite ill. Her health seems to grow worse. She suffers the most horrendous bouts of depression. I fear that in the years ahead, her condition will only become worse. She seems to have the sexual appetite of a rabbit in heat. After the theater, and I know this for a fact, she's been known to pick up servicemen on the street." Privately Gielgud told his gay friends, "But so have I. As the kettle, I can't call the pot black."

When Britt Perdue, PFC, returned home to Columbia, South Carolina, he told his friends and family that "Scarlett O'Hara picked me up in a pub. We did it in a blacked-out park right on a wooden bench." No one believed him, but he might have been telling the truth.

Vivien became particularly incensed and threatened to leave Larry when she learned that he'd slipped into London one night and spent all his time with Glenville, not even telling her he was in town.

"Larry showed up whenever he could," Glenville told another of his lovers, author Stanley Mills Haggart. "Larry even bathed me when I was too weak to sit up in a bathtub," Glenville claimed.

Vivien urged Beaumont to arrange a meeting for the two of them with George Bernard Shaw, ostensibly to discuss *The Doctor's Dilemma*, although she secretly was seeking his approval to play Cleopatra in the upcoming movie by Pascal.

"I must warn you to be on your guard," Beaumont told her. "Most

Director Peter Glenville (*left*) with author Stanley Haggart (*right*) at their shared cottage retreat in Essex, which was often visited by Larry Olivier.

photo © Darwin Porter

470

actresses fall in love with him, at least those who want coveted roles in his plays."

"Have no fear," she said, "I can resist his red beard. In general, I don't seduce vegetarians."

Beaumont and Vivien arrived at the Irish Bard's flat at Whitehall Court in London.

Shaw had not yet seen Vivien's performance of his play at the Haymarket. He had attended only rehearsals. "If Shaw agrees," Beaumont told her, "he'll let you play his Cleopatra in my movie."

Beaumont recalled that from the moment she met Shaw, Vivien did not act like herself, "but more like a Persian kitten. She never mentioned the role of Cleopatra to Shaw, but throughout our tea she *became* Cleopatra in front of him."

Of course, Shaw was aware of what she was doing. At the end of the tea, he told her, "You're the only actress in the West End who can pull off the role of my Cleopatra." Vivien was modest for a while, asking Shaw if he thought she was really up for such a role.

"You're up for it," Shaw said. "And you know you are or you wouldn't have come here. Your role-playing is wasted on me. Save it for the camera."

Shaw then continued his dialogue with Vivien. "You're a fine figure of a girl, the right physical type for the role. Up until now the actresses who have coveted the role of a teenage Cleopatra were giantesses over fifty...You are the Mrs. Pat Campbell of this age," a reference to his lover of fifty years earlier, an actress known for getting every role she sought.

At the doorway to his flat, Shaw pinched Vivien on the butt and wet-mouth kissed her. "Don't worry about playing Cleopatra. The part is fool-proof."

While Vivien was flirting with Shaw about playing his Cleopatra on film, another offer came in from Selznick, who still had her under contract. He wanted to star her in *Jane Eyre*. To entice her to return to Hollywood, he suggested that Jane as a child be played by her daughter Suzanne. Vivien turned down the role. *Jane Eyre* reached the screen with Joan Fontaine in the lead instead.

The Doctor's Dilemma was a hit, running for thirteen months, a record for a Shaw play in the West End.

It closed in April of 1943 after taking in some £300,000 at the box office. "There is much more money to be made in Shaw than in Shakespeare," Beaumont said.

***

Fleeing from Fascist Italy, movie producer Filippo del Giudice wanted to show the British government what a loyal subject he was. After making the propagandistic *In Which We Serve*, with Noël Coward, he approached the Ministry of Information in London, promising to "make the greatest British propaganda film of all time," *Henry V*.

Del Giudice wanted to star Larry as *Henry V*, but when he proposed the idea to him, Larry was reluctant. But eventually, even though he had never interpreted Henry V as a sympathetic character, the play's spirited call to arms dovetailed neatly with England's wartime identity as a nation fighting for its survival. Eventually, Larry became convinced he could play the part but was leery of directing it too.

He learned that William Wyler, who had directed him in *Wuthering Heights*, was staying at Claridge's Hotel in London. He'd been stationed in Britain in 1943 with the American forces—"oversexed, overfed, and over here."

He had detested Wyler as his director during the making of *Wuthering Heights*, but had eventually come to respect him. Wyler flatly turned him down. "I don't know nothin' 'bout birthin' Shakespeare," Wyler said.

It was Wyler who threw the challenge back at him. "Olivier," he said, "direct the damn thing yourself. You can do it, boy. I know you can."

Wyler didn't completely convince him that day, and Larry "shopped" the position to one or two more directors before finally taking Wyler's advice and signing on to direct it himself.

Making such an epic film was a daunting challenge. The first hurdle was to find some 650 able-bodied young men in an England at war. He'd also need 150 horses.

Since Ireland had remained neutral throughout World War II, and its towns and fields were filled with able-bodied and otherwise unemployed men, Larry decided to film in that country, which he'd pretend was actually France.

At the age of thirty-seven, Larry shouldered the biggest artistic challenge of his career. He'd not only have to star in the film with his "pudding-basin haircut," but he'd have to oversee an army of extras and some of the brightest stars in Britain, plus the new technology of Technicolor battling the unreliable weather of Ireland.

He'd been given a budget of some $2 million to film the most expensive production in the history of British cinema.

There were countless problems: Chain mail armor was unavailable, so Larry hired Irish women to fake chain mail by using gray wool. During the filming of a medieval battle scene, Larry halted production as a group of British fighters appeared overhead and within camera range, attacking a formation of Luftwaffe aircraft heading toward London to bomb it.

Winston Churchill himself censored the script so that the English king would not appear in an unfavorable light. One scene that was axed from Shakespeare's script involved Henry hanging a friend of his as an example of his iron-fisted military justice.

Larry had originally wanted Stewart Granger for a role, but the handsome actor was otherwise occupied. Nonetheless, Larry rounded up a talented array of actors, including his old friend, Leslie Banks, along with Robert Newton, Robert Helpmann, and Leo Genn.

The actress Renée Asherson (later the widow of Robert Donat) was brought in to play Katherine, the French princess. Vivien had thought she was going to do the role and wardrobe had already fitted her for her costumes. Asherson later claimed, "The only way I got the part was that Vivien and I were the same size, and I could fit into her wardrobe."

A cable arrived from David O. Selznick, to whom Vivien was under contract. He warned her that the role was far too small for a star of her stature and refused to allow her to do it.

Larry intervened and once again tried to get Selznick to change his mind. "I offered him your tits and my balls," Larry said, "but the bastard still turned us down."

John Gielgud asked Larry to cast him as "The Chorus" in the movie, but Larry rejected the idea, suggesting that he play the effete King of France instead. Gielgud turned down that role.

In lieu of using stuntmen, Larry personally demonstrated the techniques he was looking for during preparations for action scenes to the "soldiers," at one point jumping out of a tree onto the horse-riding back of an Irish taxi driver cast as a member of the French army. Larry fractured his shoulder in the process. Later, he had an accident with a run-

Three views of Laurence Olivier as Henry V, appropriately heroic and victorious against the enemies of England in 1415 at Agincourt

away horse that ran into the camera that was filming it, cutting Larry's lip and leaving a lifetime scar.

The first Technicolor movie ever made of a Shakespeare play, the film also had the longest title—*The Chronicle History of King Henry the Fift with his Battell Fought at Agincourt in France.*

Upon its release in 1945, *Henry V* was a critical success in both England and America. Although too "arty" for some audiences, it finally made a profit by 1949. Some critics hailed it as the best film since Orson Welles' *Citizen Kane.*

Ernest Betts, writing in *The People*, said, "Laurence Olivier produces, directs, and stars in *Henry V.* He deserves credit for undertaking the most ambitious film of our time. But it is also the most difficult, annoying, beautiful, boring, exciting, wordy, baffling picture yet made. It has a sort of damnable excellence."

In 1946, Larry won the Best Actor award from the New York Film Critics, and went on to carry home a special Oscar for outstanding achievement as an actor, producer, and director.

The influential director/producer Tyrone Guthrie asked the British Admiralty to release Larry and Ralph Richardson from military service as a means of allowing them to restore the reputation of the bombed out Old Vic. The naval commanders seemed only too willing to let them go, considering the number of British planes both actors had wrecked.

Larry's commanding officer gave him some caustic parting advice. "In this war the object has been for you and Richardson to destroy enemy aircraft, not British planes."

***

As the war dragged on, Vivien grew more and more despondent as she watched Greer Garson emerge as one of the leading ladies of Hollywood, virtually becoming The Queen of MGM. "With Selznick's guidance, it could have been me, and I could have done it so much better than Garson," Vivien told Larry.

With Larry virtually absent from her life, thanks to *Henry V* absorbing all of his time, Vivien wanted a job. When an offer came in from Hugh ("Binkie") Beaumont to entertain Allied troops in North Africa, she eagerly joined his troupe in a production called *Spring Party.* She told Beaumont, "I want to bring the real Scarlett O'Hara to the British and Yank forces."

The tour was now feasible because on May 12, 1943, the last organized Axis army force in North Africa had surrendered. The Allies had killed, wounded, or captured about 350,000 Axis soldiers, setting the stage for the

Allied invasion of Italy.

The director of the show, John Gielgud, persuaded the Canadian-born comedienne Beatrice Lillie to sign on as Vivien's co-star. Hailed in the press as "the funniest woman in the world," she was known offstage as Lady Peel because of her 1920 marriage to Sir Robert Peel. He had died in 1934, and their son had been killed in military action in 1942.

"Bea," as she was known, admitted she was *Every Other Inch a Lady* (the title of her autobiography). Through Noël Coward, Vivien had already met Bea, and was familiar with the star's notorious lesbian affairs with such actresses as Tallulah Bankhead, Eva Le Gallienne, and Judith Anderson.

Bea had been entertaining troops long before Vivien. She was a great believer in the theory, "the show must go on." In fact, she was entertaining troops when she learned that her son had been killed. Refusing to postpone her performance, she told the stage manager, "I will cry tomorrow."

Dorothy Dickson, an American-born but London-based theater actress and singer, was also in the cast with her husband, Carl Hyson (*né* Heisen*)*. Dorothy became a celebrated ballroom dancer, enjoying the peak of her popularity after World War I.

Vivien had met her when she co-starred with Ivor Novello in *Careless Rapture*. During her early days on the London stage, Dickson had become friends with another future celebrity—and a future centenarian—Elizabeth Bowes-Lyon. Later, of course, she became the wife of the man who became King George VI, and eventually, after the ascent to the throne of her daughter, Elizabeth II, as Elizabeth, the Queen Mother. Dickson's friendship with Bowes-Lyon lasted until Dickson's death at the age of 102.

For comic relief, Leslie Henson joined the cast. Popular as a music hall comedian, he was famous for his bulging eyes, malleable face, and raspy voice. Along with Basil Dean, Henson had formed the Entertainments National Service Association (nicknamed ENSA), which entertained British troops at war. ENSA was the sponsor of the show starring Vivien and Bea.

Before embarking on the tour, Henson, as himself, had appeared with Larry in *The Demi-Paradise*.

From England the plane flew to neutral Lisbon before going on to British-controlled Gibraltar.

Vivien sent a cable to Larry in Ireland where he'd rented the estate of Lord and Lady Powerscourt, 30 miles from Dublin. "HENRY WILL CONQUER."

After its debut in Gibraltar, the troupe launched a tour which would take them first to Morocco and then on to Algeria, Tunisia, Libya, and Egypt, encompassing the entire sweep of war-torn North Africa where the Nazis had once maintained formidable strongholds. Under horrid conditions, with temperatures sometimes reaching 120°F in the shade, the troupe stuck it out.

At times they didn't even have wash water. Bea later confessed, "Often Vivien and I had to take a whore's bath. The mosquitoes sucked our blood, and we learned all about squat toilets."

Vivien's weight continued to drop throughout the tour, until at the end of the tortuous jaunt she was almost skeletal.

Her act consisted of recitation, including scenes from Clemence Dane's *Plymouth Hoe*. She alternated that with a recitation of Lewis Carroll's *You Are Old, Father William*. Backstage she'd quickly change into a crinoline Scarlett O'Hara dress and perform a mocking satire of her role as a Southern belle in *Gone With The Wind*.

Regrettably, when confronted with an audience of ten thousand battle-weary troops, Vivien often couldn't be heard. But these rugged men didn't seem to care. They yelled and applauded her rare beauty encased in a flowing dress of patterned garden flowers and a picture hat, as she sweltered under the heat and lights.

During Larry's absence from Vivien, who had by now arrived in Algiers, he wrote "Pussy Love" letters to her, and she replied claiming that she'd die with "joooy" when she saw him in the flesh.

In Algiers, Vivien claimed "I went looking for Charles Boyer but landed General Dwight D. Eisenhower instead." She was referring, of course, to the sultry 1938 film, *Algiers*, that had starred Boyer and Hedy Lamarr.

Franklin D. Roosevelt had appointed Eisenhower as Commanding General of the European Theater of Operations in 1942, with a base in London. That same year, Roosevelt also designated Eisenhower as Supreme Commander of Allied Forces of the North African Theater of Operations. In December of 1943 Eisenhower would be named Supreme Allied Commander in Europe.

That night after the show, Eisenhower invited Vivien for a private dinner in his villa. "He asked many questions about Hollywood and told me that Clark Gable and Carole Lombard had been his favorite movie stars during the 1930s," Vivien recalled.

At the end of the evening, he revealed that she had been approved by the British government as a courier for secret documents.

He told her that he was turning over a pouch of secret documents so sensitive that their exposure could lead

Two views of Bea Lillie
"The funniest woman
in the world"

476

to several deaths. The documents were so dangerous that they could be read only by heads of state, in this case, Winston Churchill, King George VI, or Roosevelt.

"Guard these documents with your life," Eisenhower instructed her, and she promised the general faithfully that she would. During her next stop, in Tunisia, she would be approached by a messenger who would deliver the documents to the king, where copies would then be transported to Washington, D.C. for Roosevelt's eyes only. At no point was she ever to open the diplomatic pouch.

"It is best that you not know what's in that pouch," he told her.

Ever the gentleman, Eisenhower kissed her good night on the cheek, which she turned into a full kiss on the mouth. "If he'd asked me, I would have said yes," she told Bea. "After all, he was Supreme Commander. But I'd heard rumors that he was impotent, so I didn't press myself onto him."

Vivien told Bea that she found Ike "a charming, handsome, and a gracious man, a product of the golden wheat fields of America. Unlike Roosevelt, Ike actually sat through all of *Gone With the Wind* and didn't fall asleep. He did tell me that he was happy that 'the Yankees won the war, defeating Johnny Reb.'"

A subsequent stop was the ancient city of Constantine, Algeria's third-largest city and a strategic Allied base for their North Africa campaign.

Here Vivien would perform before U.S. General James (Jimmy) Doolittle, an American aviation pioneer. He had become one of the greatest military heroes in the West, as the leader of the first retaliatory aid raid on the Japanese homeland in the wake of their December 7, 1941 sneak attack on Pearl Harbor.

Carl Andrew Spaatz, nicknamed "Tooey," was another American hero who congratulated Vivien on her act. He became the first Chief of Staff of the United States Air Force.

Bea later told friends that in Constantine Vivien met "a gorgeous specimen of male flesh, a man who looked like Hitler's fantasy of a Nazi soldier, but who turned out to have grown up in Saffron-Walden in East Anglia. Vivien did not sleep alone that night."

The headquarters of the Eighth Army was in a small nearby town variously known as Bougie, Béjaïa, Bejaya, or Bgayet, depending on the language of its various occupants throughout the centuries. Set to perform there, Vivien learned that Alec Guinness was serving with the British

General (later, U.S. President) Dwight D. Eisenhower

navy at the nearby port of Njidjelli (also known as Djidjelli). She asked an army officer to deliver the actor a note requesting his presence at the *Spring Party* show in Bougie.

Having no transportation, Guinness and fellow officer and fellow actor Peter Bull hitched the sixty miles to rendezvous with Vivien.

After the show, and after more than a few shots of whiskey, Vivien learned that the two naval men had no ride back to their base. She charmed a starry-eyed admiral into lending his vehicle. Commandeering the car, she drove Guinness and Bull back to their ship in time.

Guinness didn't want her to drive back alone through the desert, so he hired a young Arab man to accompany her. She didn't get back until morning. She told Bea that, "He demanded that I stop every ten miles so he could fuck me."

Beginning with her appearance in *The Doctor's Dilemma* at the Haymarket, Vivien was now embarked on a course of having sex with strange men. As a sign of her mental deterioration, this pattern would remain a factor throughout the rest of her life. Her obsessive drive for sex led her into one potentially dangerous situation after another.

Midway through the tour, tragic news reached Vivien. On June 2, 1943, Leslie Howard had died in a KLM/BOAC flight from Lisbon to Bristol, England. His aircraft had been shot down by a German Junkers-88 over the Bay of Biscay. His death evoked memories of what might have happened to Larry and herself when they were carrying documents from Lisbon back to England.

There were rumors that the Nazis believed that Winston Churchill, who had been in Algiers, was on board. In his autobiography, Churchill expressed that a mistake about his activities might have cost Howard his life.

Subsequent research does not verify Churchill's belief. Other authors have concluded that the Germans wanted to shoot down the plane specifically as a means of killing Howard himself. His intelligence-gathering activities had come to their attention. It is also believed that the Nazis wanted to demoralize Britain with the loss of one of its most outspoken and patriotic public figures.

The Nazi High Command knew the whereabouts of Churchill at the time of the attack on Howard's plane. Also, they were hardly naïve enough to believe that the prime minister would be traveling alone aboard an unescort-ed and unarmed civilian aircraft during wartime when both the secrecy and the air power of the British government were at his disposal.

It is believed today that the order to liquidate Howard came directly from Josef Goebbels. He had already denounced the actor as "the most dangerous propagandist in the British service."

"My beloved Ashley Wilkes, the love of Scarlett's life, is now shark meat," Vivien rather indelicately told Bea.

Fighting a depression sparked by the death of her co-star in *Gone With the Wind*, Vivien said, "One by one, we'll fall away. Clark Gable and Hattie McDaniel will die first, then me. Butterfly McQueen is such a mean little devil, she'll live many years. Of all the major stars of this movie, I predict Olivia de Havilland will outlive everybody, even the younger supporting players like Evelyn Keyes. Olivia is a steel magnolia in spite of that sweet Melanie façade she portrayed on the screen."

Despite her gloom, Vivien found Tunis the highlight of her trip. Along with Bea and Dorothy Dickson, Vivien occupied a suite within a villa recently vacated by the retreating Nazi general, Hans-Jürgen von Arnhim, who had been placed in command of the Afrika-Corps after the departure of Field General Erwin ("The Desert Fox") Rommel in North Africa.

"I slept in this Nazi's bed," Vivien later said. "The sheets were still warm." The general had stayed at the villa before the humiliating defeat of his Afrika Korps at Cap Bon.

At three o'clock in the morning, as had been pre-arranged by Eisenhower's headquarters, a messenger was cleared for entrance into Vivien's suite. "This is exactly how Ike told me it would happen," she told Bea.

The messenger turned out to be a British airman born in Rutland. He had very little to say after a few pleasantries and quickly departed from the suite with the pouch of documents tucked away in his briefcase for King George VI. She never knew what information the secret documents contained.

Later, it was speculated that the documents contained clandestine proposals from some members of the German High Command. Fearful of losing the war, based on their defeat in North Africa, they were willing to sue for peace with England for a conditional surrender that would avoid a military occupation of Germany. In exchange for leniency from the West, the Germans proposed their withdrawal from occupied Western Europe and a concentration of their forces on the Soviet Union instead.

If the names of these Nazi officers had ever been discovered, they would have been executed by the Gestapo. But whereas this contervention of Hitler's wishes was never discovered, a year later, another group of

King George VI (ruled 1936-1952) was the brother of the forced-to-abdicate King Edward VIII, and the father of Queen Elizabeth II

Nazi officers conspiring against Hitler were discovered and tortured to death.

In the resort of Hamamet, near Tunis, Vivien's troupe performed before King George VI, who that very day had knighted British General Sir Bernard Montgomery. The Command Performance was staged within Air Marshal Sir Arthur Coningham's villa. The audience of sixty consisted mainly of British officers.

Vivien later had fond memories of that moonlit night and the perfect weather—"except for the heat." "The King never stuttered once the whole time," she recalled. "He stayed up until 1:30 in the morning talking to us."

"He said he liked my act very much, but suggested that next time I include his favorite poem," Vivien said. He was referring to *The White Cliffs of Dover* by Alice Duer Miller, who had died in 1942.

Not one word was exchanged between King George and Vivien about the secret diplomatic pouch she'd delivered to his aide.

Regrettably, Bea had eaten a green salad that evening, erroneously believing that it was safe. Soon after, she came down with an attack of dysentery. "I kept performing the next day and the day beyond, but I planned an exit strategy from the stage in case of an emergency. Backstage, the door to the toilet was kept open and vacant for me."

The troupe's next stop was near Tripoli, in Libya. Their show was presented in its most dramatic setting yet, the ruins of a Roman amphitheater in Leptis Magna in the midst of desert sand dunes.

In spite of the rather high tone of Vivien's recitations, her act went over with airmen, sailors, and soldiers, both American and British. She'd gotten only one bad review and that was from a British officer, Patrick Kinross, who called her recitations "sentimental" and "pathetic."

On June 28, 1943, the troupe flew into Cairo, a center of WWII intrigue and espionage, evocative of Lisbon. Bea and Vivien were lodged in a suite at a bastion of British colonialism, the legendary Shepheard's Hotel. Dickson was going to share the suite with them, but at the last minute Bea asked her not to.

"Poor Vivien," Dickson later recalled. "I think Miss Lillie had seduction on her mind. It was no secret among the performers that Bea had nursed a crush on Vivien all through the tour."

When Leslie Henson returned to London, he spread the rumor of a Leigh/Lillie romantic liaison. "Vivien was the pursued, Bea the pursuer," he claimed. "I don't think Vivien cared for Bea in that way, but gave in to her demands. Isn't that an example of a mercy fuck?"

At Suez, Vivien gave two performances, one on a ship, which she compared to living in a Turkish bath. "We had parties every night and lavish spreads of goodies of every sort of deliciousness," she wrote to Gertrude and

Suzanne in Canada. "In both Alexandria and Cairo, the war did not seem to exist."

In Cairo the British ambassador, Sir Miles Lampson, threw an elegant dinner party for them on July 2, "at which Bea Lillie practically depleted our whisky supply," he later recalled.

The British troupe of entertainers, including Vivien, left the ambassador's party as dawn was breaking over the ancient city. Vivien had spent most of the evening talking to Prince and Princess Aly Khan.

The following night Vivien was "taken by a handsome soldier from Yorkshire" [Bea Lillie's words] to see the Sphinx and the Pyramids. She told Lillie that she was going to play Cleopatra in Pascal's film upon her return to England.

From Cairo they flew back to Tripoli where on July 10 they learned about the Allied invasion of Sicily.

The troupe ended their tour when they flew to Gibraltar, where Vivien rested up. Her assigned escort turned out to be the actor Anthony Quayle, whom she already knew. He was the Aide-de-Camp to the military governor of the colony and was at the peak of his suntanned handsomeness. He had divorced his actress wife, Hermione Hannen, two years before and was still a free agent.

Quayle later confessed to his very intimate friend Alec Guinness that he'd seduced Vivien. "She was up for grabs, easy pickings."

He later explained why he didn't follow up on the seduction. "I think she would have fallen for me and forgotten all about Larry if I had pursued her. But I feared that the imperiousness in Vivien, if it ever got fully within its orbit, would have led either to our quarreling and estrangement, or else I'd become her courtier."

In a touch of irony, Quayle would later enjoy intimate relationships with both the bisexual Guinness, who would appear in several films with him, and with Larry with whom he'd be associated professionally, especially from 1948 to 1956 when he directed the Shakespeare Memorial Theatre in Stratford-upon-Avon.

In Gibraltar, Vivien once again shared quarters with Bea and Dorothy Dickson. In yet another touch of irony, Quayle would marry Dickson's daughter, Dorothy Hyson, in 1947.

While in Gibraltar, Vivien also had a reunion with Noël Coward who had sailed in on the HMS *Charybdis* from Plymouth.

He invited her aboard for lunch, followed by tea later that afternoon at the Rock Hotel. "We both talked over old times and our future careers after the war," Vivien recalled. "Many, many questions about Larry. Too many if you ask me."

Coward told her, jokingly or not, that "there were so many pretty sailors aboard the *Charybdis* he didn't know which one to seduce first." He was later very saddened to learn that ship had been sunk off the Channel Islands in October of 1943.

As war-weary Britain neared the summer of 1943, there was hope in the air when Vivien and her troupe reached Plymouth. She found an optimism that she and Larry had not observed when they'd landed in Bristol during an air raid in 1941.

Her good mood faded when she was forced to strip down by a "very burly lesbian who inspected every inch of my body for lice."

Larry was still filming *Henry V* in Ireland, and she was anxious for a reunion. As she entered the bleak airport terminal at Plymouth, she was handed a cable.

Thinking it was from Larry, she tore it open. It was from the Hungarian producer and director, Gabriel Pascal.

WELCOME BACK FROM CAIRO, YOUR MAJESTY. YOU WILL NOW REIGN AS QUEEN OF EGYPT.

Vivien reigns as "The Serpent of the Nile."

482

CHAPTER 12

At the end of the summer of 1943, a very exhausted Larry and Vivien came together in their temporary home at Old Prestwick, Gerrards Cross, in Buckinghamshire. Vivien had just completed the most grueling and debilitating tour of her life, and Larry was on the verge of a nervous breakdown after bringing *Henry V* to the screen. Even so, Vivien demanded love-making, but he claimed that "all my energy has been sapped."

When her dear friend, Oswald Frewen, came to visit her, she related her marital woes to him. "Larry didn't fuck me until my fourth night back," she lamented. "On a scale of one to ten, I'd give his performance a minus two."

Impulsively, he pulled her to him and kissed her. "Guess I'll have to do the job for the bloke. Larry's exhausted. I'm very well rested. As you no doubt noticed as I held you in my arms, I'm 'up' for the job."

"Oh, Oswald, haven't you gotten over that crush you had on me?" she asked.

"Not at all." He revealed that he'd written his best male friend, Leigh Holman, out of his will and had bequeathed his beloved home, The Sheephouse, to Vivien in case of his death. Of course, his remarriage in June of 1945 would end that commitment.

Ironically, both Vivien and Larry, in *Caesar and Cleopatra*, and in *Henry V*, respectively, were not only appearing in two rare (for the time) Technicolor films with lavish sets, but two of the most expensive productions ever shot in Britain.

To star in *Caesar and Cleopatra*, Vivien had to get permission from David O. Selznick. After much bickering, he agreed to let her perform in the Pascal film for a fee of 50,000 pounds.

Before the film was wrapped, it would end up costing 1.3 million pounds, about five and a half million in 1944 U.S. dollars.

When George Bernard Shaw heard that Pascal "was spending money like a drunken sailor," he predicted the movie would cost a million pounds. In his frantic search for authenticity, and even in the middle of a world war, Pascal had shipped in sands from the Sahara Desert, as one example of his extravagance.

Pascal secured the money from the great producer, J. Arthur Rank, a former North Country flour miller.

When he met Vivien after her tour of North Africa, Pascal admitted to his associates, "Frankly, I'm disappointed. Her beauty is not as striking as it was, and she looks pale and even a bit sickly. Also, perhaps because of all those dust storms, her voice is weaker than before. She seems to be suffering from dehydration. But I'm going through with my commitment to her."

Vivien began coughing on the first day of the shoot and would continue to do so throughout the filming. The sets were unheated, and she was portraying a young Cleopatra in very skimpy costumes.

Pascal had cast an array of some of the most talented actors in England in supporting roles, including Flora Robson as Ftatateeta. Michael Rennie and Leo Genn were also cast, as was Felix Aylmer.

Many actresses who would go on to become household names were also hired, including a very young Jean Simmons as the harpist. Kay Kendall, who played an uncredited slave girl, would later marry Vivien's friend Rex Harrison.

As a magnificently magisterial Pothinus, Francis L. Sullivan didn't mind letting his Nero-like gut take up half the screen.

Renée Asherson, who had appeared with Larry in *Henry V*, was also cast, as was Russell Thorndike, the brother of Dame Sybil Thorndike. He would also appear with Larry in minor priest roles in *Hamlet* (1948) and *Richard III* (1955).

Stewart Granger had been cast in the third lead as the tanned Sicilian dilettante Apollodorus. Some critics have suggested that Granger was never more sexily alluring than when he was darting about the sets of *Caesar and Cleopatra* while half dressed in a red tunic.

George Bernard Shaw had wanted John Gielgud to play Caesar, and Gielgud met with Pascal to discuss his interpretation of the role. After meeting with Pascal, Gielgud told Vivien, "I detest the man. I would never work with him."

Weeks before shooting began, she learned from Pascal that Claude Rains had been cast as Caesar. She may have blanched in embarrassment, as she'd known his former wife, Isabel Jeans, intimately.

Although born in London in 1889, Rains had become an American citizen. Rains told Vivien, "I was not particularly eager to do a play by Shaw. You know, I turned down the role of Professor Higgins in *Pygmalion* (1938).

In an amusing coincidence, Rains, back when he was an acting teacher at the Royal Academy, had taught a young and eager student, John Gielgud, "how to act."

"While Bette [a reference to Bette Davis] and I were making *Now, Voyager* (1942), she told me to tell you that she would have made a far better Scarlett O'Hara than you were."

"You tell Bette that she can go on eating her heart out," Vivien said.

The Allies hit the beaches of Normandy on June 6, 1944, and the road to Berlin was far away, but the people of Britain began to see a possible end to history's most horrendous conflict.

Shooting on *Caesar and Cleopatra* began on June 12, 1944. The film was to be shot in four months, but dragged on for nearly a year.

In spite of the invasion of France, Hitler continued the Luftwaffe's air raids on England. When the sirens went on, cast and crew had to rush to a shelter. One V-1 flying bomb fell only 150 yards from Pascal's offices, shattering his windows but not seriously damaging the building itself.

***

Vivien was eager to resume her relationship with Granger, which had been so brief when they'd appeared on stage together.

At the most convenient time, she invited him to her dressing room, where she signaled to him that she was readily available to take up where they'd left off on their brief fling. But he seemed to have lost all sexual interest in her.

He talked mostly of how he detested the direction of Pascal. "He wants me to play an effeminate version of Apollodorous. I think Shaw meant for Apollodorous to be queer. Me, of all people. You know, I'm the last man on the British stage who could play it queer."

She smiled politely, having already been informed that he was engaged in a torrid affair with his best friend, Michael Wilding, who would later go on to marry Elizabeth Taylor in an ill-fated union.

Rebuffed, Vivien dismissed Granger from her dressing room. She became even more furious at him when she learned that he was having an affair with the much younger and also beautiful Deborah Kerr. Vivien had met Kerr, a potential rival, when both of them had been represented by John Gliddon.

At the time of his affair with Kerr, Granger was married to Elspeth March, who was pregnant with his child.

To make Vivien even more jealous, she learned that Granger had gone out on a date with aspiring actress Glynis Johns, who had long nourished a girlhood crush on the dashing star.

Even more upsetting to Vivien was the news that Granger had fallen madly in love with Kerr and was seeing her every night after work.

Word traveled fast across the set, the cast hearing of Granger's romantic liaisons. Having been rejected by him, Vivien became exceedingly difficult on the set. She spoke to him in what he called her "waspish voice."

One afternoon when he'd forgotten his lines, she called out to him in front of cast and crew. "Why don't you try and concentrate more on your work and less on Deborah Kerr?"

At that point, Granger knew his secret was out. "I went white with shock and red with fury," he recalled in his memoirs.

He shouted back at Vivien. "You're a total shit to embarrass me like that. What bad taste! What a bitch!" He marched off in his red toga to his dressing room.

With a wife at home, a beautiful mistress on the side, and "Scarlett O'Hara" giving him a come-hither look, Granger was entranced by Jean Simmons, who had been born in 1929. (Vivien, in contrast, had been born in 1913.) "She was very, very young," he later said, "and I waited a few years to marry her. I had to fight off Howard Hughes."

In one of the many ironies associated with Vivien, she would later learn that her husband, Larry, was having an affair with Simmons when they filmed *Hamlet* (1948) together. "Granger got her, even Larry got her," Vivien said. "I guess I'm last year's old pair of boots. But, let me tell you, men all over the world still desire Scarlett O'Hara."

What Granger left out of his autobiography, *Sparks Fly Upward*, was that he also fell in love with Jean Simmons on the set of *Caesar and Cleopatra*. He doesn't even mention that she was in the picture, because the young actress was not quite sixteen at the time and definitely "jail bait."

Even though he didn't write about it, Granger told Wilding and other cronies, "I took her virginity. Between Jean and Deborah, I had nothing left for Vivien. I rejected her and went for the younger stuff. But don't all men do that?"

In later life, Simmons claimed she understood Vivien's feeling "when both Larry and Stewart went for me, a much younger woman. But I've lived long enough to walk in her shoes. Every actress has to face the fact that there are younger, more beautiful girls right behind you. Once you've gone beyond the vanity of the business, you'll take on the tough roles."

One day, watching Granger do a take, Vivien turned to Pascal. "Even if he can't act, he's got grand piano teeth." Observing Granger in another scene the following day, she made yet another comment on an actor she'd begun to loathe. "In that scene you just shot with Granger, his red cocktail dress was lifted by the breeze. I could detect no bulge in his red scarlet panties. Has he been castrated?"

A 17-year-old Roger Moore, later of James Bond 007 fame, cast as a Roman soldier, appeared uncredited in the film.

Robson later claimed that Vivien was planning to seduce the teenage Moore, perhaps as an act of revenge against Granger.

She told Robson that "Roger has the most beautiful legs I've ever seen on a man. Larry's legs are too skinny. Roger looks better in his toga holding a spear than Granger does."

After an explosion on the set one afternoon, Robson suggested she see a doctor. "No, I won't," Vivien said. "I absolutely refuse. The darkness will pass and dawn will come. But on some nights I wonder if there will ever be a morning."

Vivien was very tired and nervous on the day of the shoot when she had to rush across a slippery marble floor and flog a rather tubby Nubian slave. In doing so, she fell.

Granger was on the set that day and heard her screech. "I'll never forget it," he recalled.

"It was only days later that I learned what had happened," Granger recalled. "What might have been one of the most gifted boys on the planet, the son of Vivien Leigh and Laurence Olivier, was not to be. Could you imagine the young man that those two might have spawned? He might not only have been the most beautiful man in England, but one of the most talented. Alas, it was not to be."

***

"Two days later she miscarried, and she never forgave Pascal for forcing her to do this scene which could have been shot with a double," Robson claimed.

Vivien detested Pascal so much she tried to get the producer, Rank, to hire another director, but he refused.

After visiting her in the hospital, Robson later said, "She was a caged lioness whose cub had been taken from her."

Larry rushed to the hospital but arrived late. After he inquired about the status of Vivien, he demanded to see the fetus before going to her room. Inspecting it, he said, "It's perfectly formed. I thought at this point it might be a glob. But it has a penis. It would have been a boy." He then visited Vivien's room but found that she'd been heavily sedated and had passed out.

When Frewen came to visit her, she made a startling confession to him. "I don't think the boy was Larry's. "We had a long, dry spell in our relationship."

"Then who's the daddy?" Frewen asked.

"I don't really know," she said. "He could be someone I met casually— perhaps a Yankee. I remember on more than one occasion I didn't exercise caution like I should."

She revealed to Frewen that she'd suffered her first miscarriage in September of 1942.

"Would that have been Larry's kid, too?" Frewen asked.

"Don't ask me questions known only to God himself," she snapped at him.

In the wake of her miscarriage, Vivien began to attack Larry, her fury growing more venomous. For weeks she'd been saving newspaper and magazine articles about them, story after story claiming that they were England's most romantic couple since the Duke and Duchess of Windsor.

"That pair is a sham, and so are we," she shouted at Larry. "The Duke's a queer, and his precious Duchess is a lesbian. One article claims that the public vicariously feeds off stories of our love affair to escape wartime gloom. We're also called the royals of the theater. How very charming. If anyone wants to know what gloom is, try living with the great Henry V himself." She picked up some magazine articles resting on a table and tossed them into the burning fireplace."

"How symbolic," he said. "You're burning the pages of our passion. You surely don't expect me to love you after this disgraceful performance."

"I'm sure that your love, such as it is, is reserved for others," she said, practically spitting out her words to him the way he'd uttered his dialogue to Merle Oberon on the set of *Wuthering Heights*. "Where is Danny Kaye now that you need him? I'm sure that you write him every day."

He looked at her in dismay.

"You want to fuck me?" she screeched out to him like a harridan. "Answer me, you small-dicked ham."

He didn't say a word.

"I asked you if you wanted to fuck me," she shouted even louder. "Well, you can go and fuck yourself."

"Did you ever see a play called *The Taming of the Shrew*?" he headed for his coat. "I won't be back tonight."

When he returned at ten o'clock the following morning, the living room looked as if one of Hitler's flying V-1 bombs had exploded inside. She'd broken some of her most precious treasures, which she had painstakingly gathered in antique markets.

When he came into her room, he found her sleeping peacefully. Hearing him, she slowly woke up and looked at him with loving eyes. "Oh, darling," she said, "you've come back to me. I had the most awful nightmare last night. In my dream you were making love to Greer Garson, and I was lying naked and unattended on the bed beside you."

When Larry did come home to Vivien, and often he didn't, he never knew what to expect from her moods. At times she seemed locked in some deep despair from which there was no key to escape. On occasion he found her weeping uncontrollably and unaccountably. On her worst night, she lacerated him severely, trying to destroy his confidence both as a man and as an actor.

He told Richardson, "After attacking me all night, she then demands that I fuck her. That's about as much fun as Churchill would have crawling into bed for sex with Hitler. On some nights, there would be an inexplicable meta-morphosis. I'd come home and she'd look fetching, purring like a kitten. The fire would be blazing at the hearth, and a beautifully prepared dinner would be waiting."

Her miscarriage delayed production on *Caesar and Cleopatra* for five weeks. Returning to work, Vivien told Pascal, "After a long journey through a dark tunnel, you finally see the light at the end of that tunnel."

When Robert Lowell, the American poet, heard she'd said that, he didn't agree, as he, too, suffered from a manic depressive condition. "What she said about that light at the end of the tunnel might be true, but it's beaming from an oncoming train."

"Back to work, Vivien was in a very delicate state," Rains said. "The smallest detail could set her off. One afternoon she didn't like the way I delivered a line and slapped my face. In return, I smiled graciously at her and said I would do it right next time. She seemed on the verge of hysteria. But I'm used to hysterical actresses. I've worked with Bette Davis."

"When I was shooting the banquet scene, Vivien had a complete breakdown in front of cast and crew," Pascal claimed. "When she confronted me, she seemed demon possessed. I saw it in her eyes. She was reckless, a woman who would stop at nothing to destroy anything in her pathway. She lashed out at me, at everybody, especially a helpless creature from wardrobe. Larry may wake up one night with Vivien standing over him with a butcher knife ready to plunge it into his heart. How can he love her? Fear her, yes, love her, no. She can turn on you in a second like a cobra. I'm sick and tired of reading all that crap about England's most romantic couple."

In spite of all the big names involved, and the lavish, costly production, *Caesar and Cleopatra* when it opened in 1945 was pronounced "a stinker." It virtually ended Pascal's career, but had no lasting detrimental effect on Vivien's career.

In *The Observer*, Caroline Lejeune wrote: "There was more of Cleopatra in her Scarlett O'Hara than in this pale elf."

When Vivien read a particularly bad review she blamed Pascal for casting Claude Rains, whom she accused of ruining the picture. "You should have cast Larry," she told Pascal. "Makeup could have aged him. He's the only actor in England who can play Caesar the way it should be portrayed. Someday I'll

489

play Cleopatra opposite Larry's Caesar."

Vivien's most loyal fans, those who had fallen in love with her as Scarlett O'Hara, stood by her side. The most devoted of her fans interpreted her performance as a luminous "kitten queen."

Pascal arranged for Shaw to see the film in a private screening. He didn't think Rains ruined the picture. "He was the best thing in it," Shaw claimed. "It was Miss Leigh who ruined the picture. She flubbed every scene. My words, coming out of her pretty mouth, were ever so wrong. The best thing for her at this point in her career is to star in a sequel to *Gone With the Wind*."

***

Larry was stunned by how quickly Vivien had recovered from her miscarriage. When he'd gone to see her after a sedated night, she was sitting up in bed eating a soft-boiled egg and toast.

"*All's Well That Ends Well*," she said, borrowing from Shakespeare. "My heart is in the theater, not the nursery."

"Rather heartless of you," he said, "coming from that pretty mouth of yours. Are you rehearsing for your next role as Clytemnestra?" He was, of course, referring to Agamemnon's Clytemnestra in the Aeschylus tragedy—"a male strength of heart."

"I'm a free man," he told her. "The Sea Lords have untied the noose around my neck."

He was referring to the Admiralty, which had discharged him upon request. He claimed their action was done "with a speediness and lack of reluctance—positively hurtful. How eager they were to rid themselves of Ralphie and me."

"Ralphie" (Ralph Richardson) had approached Larry with an enticing proposal, to restore the Old Vic to its pre-war glory. The theater itself had become the victim of one of Hitler's bombs that had rained down during the Blitz.

Founded in 1818, the Old Vic was as close as England came to having a National Theatre. Churchill wanted to see "the glory of the British theater restored," and he gave the project his blessing. "With Richardson and Olivier, the Old Vic can't lose."

Only later did Larry find out that his participation had originally been offered to John Gielgud, who turned it down. "Larry and I competing on stage at the Old Vic would be a disaster," Gielgud predicted. "I don't relish the idea at all." He warned Richardson that he would have to become a referee. Instead of being a referee, Richardson would be the one who'd end up competing with Larry.

Richardson's first wife, Muriel Hewitt, had died in 1942 at the age of 35, having succumbed to *encephalitis lethargica*. The actor had married Meriel Forbes in 1944, who had been his mistress during the final years of his wife's illness. Larry sensed a lighter step in his longtime comrade, "a more flippant air."

This latest incarnation of the Old Vic would be housed in the New Theatre on St. Martin's Lane. For Larry, it would mark his return to the stage of the West End after an absence of six years.

In addition to Richardson and Larry, John Burrell would participate in the re-launch. At least a decade younger than Larry and Richardson, Burrell would function as a non-acting director. Before joining the Old Vic, he'd scored a big hit with Shaw's *Heartbreak House*, starring Robert Donat, Edith Evans, Isabel Jeans, and Deborah Kerr.

Don't worry about Burrell," Richardson told Larry. "He will play Lepidus to our Antony and Octavius."

The third big name in the Old Vic's touring company was Dame Sybil Thorndike. It was during these appearances with the Old Vic that Dame Sybil established her claim as England's foremost stage actress.

Along with Nicholas (Beau) Hannen, Larry invited his dear friend George Relph, who was married to actress Mercia Swinburne (not the sister of the more famous Nora Swinburne, as so often reported).

Relph, a stage actor from Northumbria, had appeared in silent pictures beginning in 1916. He still walked with a limp from a gunshot wound in his leg while serving in the British Armed Forces during World War I.

Mercia and George became lifelong friends of both Vivien and Larry, and acted in plays with the company, including its 1948 tour of Australia and New Zealand.

Relph was joined by another Old Vic veteran, Harcourt Williams. Joyce Redman was also one of the lead actresses, along with another young woman, Margaret Leighton, whom Richardson and Larry had selected from the stable of actors associated with the Birmingham Rep. Of course, Miss Leighton would be headed for major stardom in the years ahead.

The pay scale was low. Larry's contract, a long-term agreement with stipulations that lasted for five years, called for a salary of forty pounds a week (around $150).

Richardson arrived for rehearsals at the National Gallery Exhibition Hall while Hitler's V-1 bombs were raining down on London during the Luftwaffe's dying attempt to hold onto the crumbling Nazi empire.

Richardson told Larry, "Don't take yourself too seriously. You are career obsessed. I just saw Vivien. She told me she finds her marriage disappointing. You'd better do something, you old sod, or you'll lose your pretty one. Buy her a beautiful home in the country. She loves to decorate and restore. That

491

will occupy her mind."

Richardson wanted to reintroduce himself to London audiences with Henrik Ibsen's *Peer Gynt*, in which Larry would have only a brief appearance at the end, in the minor role of Button Moulder.

"I know I was on the stage for only ten minutes," Larry later said, "but I wanted to leave audiences with my unearthly glow. I had but a short time but I established the aura of this sinister figure and left an impact. Of course, it was Ralphie's showcase."

Peer Gynt opened at the New Theatre on August 31, 1944, and ran for 83 performances.

For his own showcase, Larry chose Shaw's *Arms and the Man*, in which he'd have equal roles with Richardson. With only six theaters still left open in the West End, Olivier and Richardson retreated to Manchester for tryouts.

In the beginning, Larry said he "detested" the priggish character, Sergius Saranoff, that he was playing. "He's pompous, cowardly, and egomaniacal." The reviews were dismal, and Larry regretted having chosen the Shaw play for his comeback. "I was a flop as a pilot, and now I'm a flop as an actor," Larry told Richardson.

When Tyrone Guthrie came to Manchester for the performance, he had only slight praise for Larry's role. "Don't you love Sergius?" Guthrie asked.

"Love that stooge? God, Tony, if you weren't so tall I'd hit you, if I could reach you."

"Well, of course, if you can't love him, you'll never be any good in playing him, will you?" Guthrie asked.

Larry said that that offhand remark changed his entire outlook for how to portray a character. It was amazing that such advice hadn't already occurred to him.

From that night on, audiences saw a new Sergius as performed by Larry. At the London opening on September 5, 1944, he awed audiences by his entrance in a white uniform, his head adorned with a rakish pillbox hat. His style of mustache had last been seen on the villains of the silent screen. At his heel-clicking best. Larry transformed Sergius from a burlesque buffoon into a self-assured *braggadocio*-studded rogue with a slight edge of disarming warmth.

His performance on his comeback night was called "a museum of invention" and a "joyous travesty."

Arms and the Man would be followed by Larry's most challenging part to date, *Richard III*, a role that nearly drove him to suicide.

***

"I bet you'll hate it when we get there," Larry told Vivien as he drove to Notley Abbey to inspect the real estate, including 70 acres of grounds. He'd taken Richardson's advice and interested Vivien in the possibility of their having a country house in which to live and relax and also to entertain their friends as weekend guests.

The landscape was frozen along the roadside, as Larry steered the car through the ancient town of Aylesbury in Buckinghamshire to Long Grendon, some fifty miles north of London. "It's a memorial to kings named Henry, even the one I just played," he said. "Henry V endowed the abbey for Augustinian canons, although it was built in the time of Henry II. That swine, Henry VIII, closed it. "It's living history, Puss, and it could be ours."

Turning into Notley Abbey, he drove past trees with spidery branches waiting to bloom again. A little bridge spanned the River Thame (a tributary of the larger and better-known River Thames), bringing them to the massive oaken front door of the abbey. Mullioned windows pierced the gray stone. Together with Larry she climbed to the 16th-century central tower where she surveyed this wreck of a property, a ghost of another day.

In all its winter gloom, it was a monument to days gone by, looking like it had emerged intact from the pages of a Daphne du Maurier novel.

In the distance she saw abandoned poultry houses where no eggs had been laid in anyone's memory. Adjoining the abbey was a six-car garage and a bleak-looking bailiff's bungalow.

At that point he steered her to four greenhouses where he promised her she could grow flowers all year round.

Having walked through cold, drafty rooms, she looked out onto a gloomy landscape of tangled gardens, burst water pipes, and mounds of garbage not picked up in years. From one mound of debris emerged one of the largest rats she'd ever seen.

Back in the main hallway, Larry surveyed all that he could see. "I'm the Lord of this domain, and you are My Lady Fair. Welcome, Puss, to your new home. Notley Abbey."

"Bloody hell!" she shouted at him. "I'll never darken this door again."

That night when she returned to London, she woke up while having a nightmare. Later she told Larry that she had dreamed that she'd drowned in the dark, murky waters of the River Thame.

***

For his first starring role back in the West End, Larry felt very competitive and wanted to outshine Richardson's performance in *Peer Gynt*. After mulling it over through many a sleepless night, he set upon the Prince of Evil,

493

the twisted, misshapen Richard III. The actor, Donald Wolfit, had delivered a recent memorable performance as Richard, so Larry would have to face inevitable comparisons.

He decided to move ahead with his plan, not only recognizing what a daunting challenge the role was but aware that failure could seriously derail his participation in the post-war theater scene in England.

"I was terrified as I rehearsed my lines with Vivien and Garson Kanin," Larry told critic Kenneth Tynan years later. "I thought of Jed Harris, that ghoul of Broadway who had tortured me all through *The Green Bay Tree*. I thought of the Big Bad Wolf."

"I experimented with makeup, especially a big nose," Larry said. "Time and time again, I regretted my decision to undertake the role. Tyrone Guthrie told me I had to love my character. How could anyone of sane mind love Richard III?"

A phenomenal success, *Richard III* opened at the New Theatre on September 13, 1944 and ran until April 11, 1945.

As opening night loomed, Larry went into a panic mood.

In a suite at Claridge's, he'd worked on his lines with Kanin until four o'clock in the morning, and still couldn't remember all of them. "I've been off the stage for so long I've forgotten how to remember."

"His makeup was so hideous it frightened even me, his friend," Kanin recalled. "He'd spent hours on the make-up alone, especially on that mammoth nose evoking some wolf in the forest smelling out his supper. He'd enlarged his lower lip and even placed a wart to accentuate a hollow cheek. Instead of eyes, he had long slits, the embodiment of evil itself."

When John Mills came backstage before curtain time, he found Larry on the verge of a nervous breakdown, evoking one of Vivien's "states." He ushered Mills into the room and slammed the door. "I can't go on," Larry told him with tears in his eyes. "I just can't propel myself onto that stage tonight to face the failure of my life."

"Steady, old boy," Mills told him. As if to impart his own energy into Larry, he held him in a tight embrace. "You'll not only go on tonight, you'll deliver the performance of your lifetime. Years from now, people will talk about this night and heap praise on you."

Larry didn't believe him. At one point, Larry's face reflected a growing turbulence, almost suggesting violence to come. "It's that bastard Richardson," Larry charged. "He set me up for this so he can destroy my career. With me out of the way, Richardson will have only the Big Sis, Gielgud, to wipe out. Then Ralphie boy can become the reigning actor of the British stage."

Mills later said, "I practically had to drag him to the wings where he was

494

to make his entrance. I then returned to my seat. When his cue came, a stage-hand had to push him out there, or so I heard. But once he faced an audience of hundreds, his adrenaline started pumping."

"All I remember was emerging from shadows with my lupine nose," Larry said. "My heart was beating so loudly I thought it would rip itself from my flesh. I was frightened, so very frightened, the way an instinctive animal feels when it faces the man it knows is going to slaughter it and devour its flesh. It was terrible, oh, so terrible, and even worse than that."

"As I had waited to go on, a poisonous spider was eating my stomach walls, definitely not a butterfly," Larry said.

The opening night audience was stunned by both his appearance and his voice. His lank black hair became blood red by the time it reached his shoulders, the wig crowning a satanic-looking face. He described his own thin reed of a voice as a "mixture of honey and razor blades. I spoke with the speed of a viper's tongue but my words were perfectly understood even in the back row."

"Suddenly, I found myself playing my character," he said. "If not loving Richard III, I understood him."

He spoke his first lines:

"Now is the winter of our discontent. Made glorious summer by this sun of York."

His words came out like whip-lashes, as he waved his rubber-encased shriveled left hand at the front rows.

Vivien sat in the opening night audience. Of all people, she knew how he'd struggled and even battled with himself over the role. She later told John Gielgud, "There was magic on the stage. He was no longer the actor, Laurence Olivier, but the king, Richard III. I sat mesmerized throughout the performance. At the final curtain, I didn't just applaud with my hands, I applauded with my heart."

One of his most sophisticated critics, Noël Coward, who knew every inch of Larry, delivered his own judgment. "I think he gave the greatest male performance I have seen in the theatre. He is far and away the greatest actor we have."

Writer Jesse L. Lasky Jr. said, "In the truly great performances, there is something that every member of the audience can recognize in himself: cravings, longings, ambitions, self-justifications, even defeats. The stage is an enlargement of the

Laurence Olivier as the complex, evil, and regal Richard III

visceral weaknesses—it's only a matter of degree. Olivier's Richard was a presentation of a complex nature stunted by his own appetites."

If an actor can become the toast of London, Larry became just that the night the reviews for *Richard III* came out of Fleet Street. In *The Observer*, J.C. Trewin wrote: "Olivier's Richard gives to every speech a fine new glint. His diction flexible and swift—often mill-race swift—is bred of a racing brain. If outwardly, he is a limping panther, there is no lameness in his mind. There is no attempt to force excitement. From the first the actor, dark-haired, evilly debonair, pale of cheek, has Richard's measure, whether as a sea-green corrupter or as scarlet sin."

Sitting in the audience that night was a seventeen-year-old Kenneth Tynan, about to go up to Oxford. He would become one of the most important critics in Larry's future and his future lover. Even at that age, he had the ability to write a penetrating review and he did, claiming that "Olivier's Richard eats into the memory like acid into metal."

James Agate described Larry's voice that night in the most poetic terms: "His high shimmering tenor has not the oak-cleaving quality; it is a wind that gets between your ribs. If this Richard is not Shakespeare's, it is very definitely Mr. Olivier's, and I do not propose to forget its mounting verve and sustained excitement."

Recognizing that Larry had ended his own fifteen-year reign as the world's greatest Shakespearean actor, Gielgud laid down the sword so to speak. He presented Larry with his most treasured possession, the sword that Edmund Kean had carried as Richard III and which had been passed on to the great Henry Irving when he'd first starred in the role in 1877.

Before that opening night, Donald Wolfit had been hailed as "the definitive Richard III." But after Larry's appearance, actress Hermione Gingold said it all: "Olivier was a *tour de force*; Wolfit is forced to tour."

At the close of *Richard III*, Larry's most enthusiastic fans were calling him "the world's greatest living actor." At that moment of his highest acclaim, he was just thirty-seven years old.

On closing night, Larry said, "As *Richard III* came to an end, I think I had actually fallen in love with the hunchback."

Cecil Beaton, who had become a friend of Vivien's, reacted to that remark. "I think what he said is true. When he started falling in love with the characters he played, he began to fall out of love with Vivien, long before he could admit that to himself. His love for dear, sweet Vivien was flagging long before most people thought it would, even Vivien herself."

***

496

Vivien and Larry had heard that Tallulah Bankhead on Broadway had scored a blockbuster hit in Thornton Wilder's *The Skin of Our Teeth*. Tallulah had played Sabina, allegorically representing "The Eternal Feminine." She never ages as she goes through the millennia in the archetypal guise of women ranging from a housemaid to a beauty queen.

"Sabina is a great role for me," Vivien told Larry, persuading him not only to acquire the British rights but to direct her in it. "I can be a comedienne. My public will forget all about Scarlett O'Hara when they see me as Sabina."

On Broadway, Elia Kazan, who would later direct Vivien, helmed not only Bankhead but a young and beautiful aspiring actor, Montgomery Clift.

Vivien's hopes were dashed when David O. Selznick, who still had her under contract, threatened legal action. He'd originally granted her a twelve-week leave of absence, but Vivien had dragged that out for months longer.

From Los Angeles, the producer had his attorneys threaten to bring an injunction against Vivien. Selznick hired one of London's most distinguished barristers to represent his interests. Sir Walter Monckton had been the legal adviser to Edward VIII at the time of his abdication.

At the Chancery Division of the English High Court in London, Sir Valentine Homes, Vivien's barrister, claimed that as a married woman she was under obligation to the national service regulations. Under such an agreement, Vivien might have to find work, perhaps in a munitions factory.

A fan of Scarlett O'Hara, the judge ruled in her favor, finding it preferable that she work on the stage and not become a blue collar factory worker. "I can just see myself as Rosie the Riveter," Vivien told Larry.

The headline in *The Daily Mail* blared: VIVIEN LEIGH MIGHT BE A CHAR.

Actually the judge ruled that he couldn't see Selznick suffering "any appreciable damage" if Vivien appeared in *The Skin of Our Teeth*. Vivien never made another film for Selznick, and legal challenges against her from Hollywood faded.

Though temporarily freed of Selznick, Vivien had not fulfilled her obligations to Alexander Korda, who was in charge of Metro-Goldwyn-Mayer productions in Great Britain.

Perhaps owing to mental deterioration, Vivien "became the most impossible actress to work with in the British Empire," Korda said. He, too, threatened her with legal action, after she turned down three literary properties, beginning with Enid Bagnold's *Lottie Dundass*, which Korda had acquired from Myron Selznick for $40,000.

The Bagnold property was a strange story of an actress who aspired to greatness but was unable to perform because of a weak heart.

In *The Old Wives' Tale*, a novel by Arnold Bennett, Vivien would be playing one of the Baines sisters and would have to age in a setting that stretched from 1840 to 1905.

Thomas Hardy's *Far from the Madding Crowd* was a worthy property and had been a success since its publication in 1874. Korda wanted Vivien to play Bathsheba Everdene, a proud and somewhat vain young beauty. In the script, Bathsheba is pursued by three suitors. Vivien would have been ideal as Bathsheba, but she claimed, "I hate the role."

"Vivien acted as if contracts didn't mean a bloody damn thing," Larry said. "She wanted to do *The Skin of Our Teeth* on stage—and that was that."

Because he planned to retire at the end of 1945, Korda decided not to pursue action in court against Vivien because of the services she'd performed for Britain during the war.

Eventually Korda made a deal with MGM. Instead of Vivien, the studio would get two pictures from Deborah Kerr, who was ready, willing, and able to do each of them.

In *The Skin of Our Teeth*, Vivien had a strong back-up support, including Cecil Parker cast as Mr. Antrobus; Joan Young as Mrs. Antrobus, and Ena Burrill as the Antrobus daughter. The role of the son was cast last. Larry's

Vivien Leigh ("a green-eyed lioness waiting to devour her prey") playing Sabina in the London stage version of *The Skin of Our Teeth*.

friends, George Relph and Mercia Swinburne, suggested a young actor, Terence Morgan, whom they affectionately called "Terry."

Larry had caught Morgan's performance in the West End in a production of *There Shall Be No Night*, and told Richardson, "I want to work with that young man some day. I couldn't take my eyes off him."

Mercia introduced Larry to the devastatingly handsome young man, and Larry signaled his immediate approval. They soon became "Larry & Terry."

The actor had come from Lewisham in southeast London, having been born there in December of 1921.

Even though the Old Vic was notorious for its low pay scale, Morgan claimed that the pay was the best he'd ever known. He'd once worked for a pound a week as a clerk in an insurance firm before winning a scholarship at RADA. He'd also served in the British Army.

"Larry seemed enchanted with Morgan and invited him to his dressing room where they

498

must have talked for two hours," Mercia said. "Without trying him out, Larry impulsively offered him the role of Cain in *The Skin of Our Teeth*. When Morgan met Vivien, she also became enchanted with him."

"I knew Larry very well, and I was familiar with his sexual opportunism," Relph said. "As a man of the theater, I understood such things. I'd heard stories about Vivien. Before the run of *Skin*, I suspected that young Terry would get to know both of these stars intimately. I was right."

"Terry virtually became Larry's boy, and a jealous Vivien also had a lean and hungry look in her eye, like a green-eyed lioness waiting to capture her next prey," Relph said. "Terry was flattered by the attention of these two great stars, and for such a young man he seemed adept at playing one against the other."

To complicate matters, Morgan also began dating another member of the cast, Georgina Jumel. At times there seemed to be more drama going on off stage than onstage.

At last Vivien was free to go on tour with *The Skin of Our Teeth*, launching the play in Edinburgh in April of 1945. Most members of the preview audience were baffled by the play, not really understanding it.

V-E Day, May 8, found Vivien performing in Blackpool, the play's final stop before its opening in the West End.

Unlike viewers in theater-loving London or Edinburgh, the more literal audience of the North Country didn't seem to understand the play at all. At its end, they booed both it and Vivien. Some of them had "burned up a month's ration of precious petrol to see Scarlett O'Hara in the flesh," and were bitterly disappointed.

Sitting in a matinee audience, Jack Merivale "adored" Vivien and "liked" the play, although the woman sitting next to him called it "muck."

Backstage, Vivien had an unexpected visitor. Merivale rushed into her dressing room and hugged her tightly, planting a deep, penetrating kiss on her lips. "Oh, darling, I've missed you," he said. "This war has gone on forever. Every day away from you is a day in hell."

After she broke from him, she stepped back and appraised him carefully. He looked more virile and handsomer than ever. "The Royal Canadian Air Force seems to have been good to you. How's your marriage to Jan Sterling going?"

"It's not a serious marriage," he told her. "We never really see each other. It's you I love. If you'd ever leave Larry, I'd leave Jan in a second. As it is, we're practically separated now."

After the show, she invited him back to her suite for a drink. He told her he wanted to return to the stage once he was released from military service.

He also brought her up on all the news, including a report from his stepmother, Gladys Cooper, who he said was doing fine. He also reported that his stepsister had married the actor, Robert Morley, "although God only knows why."

They talked until about three o'clock in the morning when he popped the question. "Do I really have to return to my room?"

With her Cheshire cat smile, she became Scarlett O'Hara again. "I owe you something," she said, "considering that you had to give up your fledgling career to defend Britain in its hour of need."

His leave had been scheduled to end at 6pm the following evening, and with the understanding that there wasn't any particular rush, both of them slept until around 11am.

She awoke in his arms, and her smile evoked Scarlett when she woke up on screen after Rhett Butler had raped her. She told Merivale what men liked to hear, "When God was handing out the jewels, he was kinder to you than to most men."

Over breakfast, he prophetically told her, "One day when you leave Larry, and that day will come eventually, I want to wake up in your arms every morning for the rest of my life."

"That day will never come, but you're entitled to your fantasies," she told him, leaning over to kiss him on the nose.

He would remember "that perfect evening in Blackpool" with Vivien. Actually the night wasn't quite perfect. At one point, she'd locked herself in the bathroom, and he heard her coughing without an interruption for almost ten minutes.

When he suggested she should see a doctor about that cough, she dismissed the idea. "*Fiddle-dee-dee*," she said, "It's this smog. Breathing it could kill anyone."

Before he left to return to the R.A.F. station, he held her in his arms and kissed her once again. "Regardless of how long I have to wait, I'll be there for you. Without you, I'm trying to find some semblance of a life, but it's hollow. After last night I know you, and you alone, are what I've been waiting for so very long."

***

On May 16, 1945, in the wake of Germany's surrender, Londoners were in a mood to celebrate when many of them attended the opening night of *The Skin of Our Teeth*.

When Vivien walked onstage, she made the opening night audience forget all about Scarlett O'Hara. This was a new and unfamiliar Vivien in a carmine-colored wig and a skirt that made her look like a dancing girl who'd just jumped out of a birthday cake, according to the observations of one viewer.

Unavailable in the weeks immediately following V-E Day, her fishnet nylon tights had to be shipped in from New York.

As the curtain was drawn, John Gielgud, keeping a promise to her, was the first to go backstage to congratulate her on her brilliant performance. "I'll tell Tallulah to eat her heart out," Gielgud said. "You've found a dimension in Sabina that Tallulah never found. She was too busy playing it for comedy."

Following in Gielgud's footsteps were Lady Ralph Richardson and Oswald Frewen, along with a parade of friends and admirers.

When Agate had arrived ten minutes late, and after the curtain had gone up, a furious Larry attacked him, slapping his face. He warned Vivien backstage what he'd done and told her to expect "the most venomous review of your career."

But Agate, ignoring the attack from an outraged director, gave Vivien a good review and didn't even mention that he'd been struck by Larry. Agate weighed in, "Through it all, lovely to look at, flitted and fluttered Miss Leigh's hired girl, Sabina, an enchanting piece of nonsense-cum-allure, half dabchick and half dragonfly."

Even a young Kenneth Tynan, who in the future would write devastating reviews of Vivien, praised her opening night at the Phoenix Theatre. "Miss Leigh's particular brand of frail, unfelt *coquetterie* fits the part like an elbow-length glove. She executes all the accepted repertoire of femininity—vapid eyelash-fluttering, mock-unconcern, plain silliness—with convulsive effect and yet always with her brows slightly arched in affected boredom."

Larry told her that he'd be arriving late at the opening night cast party and had arranged for Vivien to be accompanied by Ena Burrill, who had played the Antrobus daughter in *The Skin of Our Teeth*.

At the party, Larry was an hour late. As Vivien was talking with John Vickers, who had taken photographs for the production, he looked at the newly arriving guests. "Those are the two handsomest men in the West End," he said.

Vivien's eyes darted to the door as Larry, along with Terry Morgan, made a spectacular entrance to be greeted by dozens of well wishers, including Hugh ("Binkie") Beaumont.

Vickers did not leave her side, but stood by her as her green eyes watched young Morgan and Larry working the room, accepting congratulations.

"You'd think the star of the bloody show—linked arm in arm with Larry—should be making the rounds," Vivien said to Vickers.

It was almost an hour before Larry—still with Morgan—walked over to her. "You were absolutely brilliant," he told his wife. "Your Sabina will dazzle audiences for at least the next three years."

"How nice of you to notice," she said sarcastically.

Morgan had played the son in *The Skin of Our Teeth*, but she had not excessively noticed him until she saw Larry's interest in him.

She turned to Morgan, dazzling him with her charm, including her enticing smile. "Would you be a dear and accompany *the star* of the show to the bar for a well-deserved glass of bubbly?"

"I'd love to escort you, Miss Leigh," he said.

She possessively linked her arm with his, as Larry looked on with a bewildered expression. Snuggling up to him, she told him, "It is said that Montgomery Clift, who played your role on Broadway, is devastatingly handsome. But I suspect he is no competition for you. You were divine tonight, and I predict you'll have an amazing future on the stage. Already people are referring to you as the *young* Laurence Olivier of tomorrow."

With Morgan by her side, she glided through the room accepting congratulations.

Thornton Wilder had come to London but didn't stay for the opening night of his play. He saw her as Sabina but only in a dress rehearsal with no audience. Vivien was dead before he expressed his opinion of her in the role.

"The fates and the graces bestowed on Vivien Leigh a rare endowment for the art of acting—great beauty, an enchanting nature, lively imagination and observation, and the skill with which to project them. But they withheld one major gift—a voice of wide range and resonance."

***

"I finally had to give in on Notley," Vivien said. "Larry fancied himself a country squire, and he claimed he was destined to play that role. I long ago learned it is counter-productive in life to argue with another man's fantasy."

"In time, Notley Abbey became the symbol of our fame and glamour, the happiness of our marriage—that is, the press agent's dream of the supposed happiness of our wedded bliss," Vivien said.

Notley would take all of their savings, and a lot more of their future earnings. But Vivien went from hating it to loving it, perhaps even more so than Larry did.

After much persuasion, he'd won her over, claiming "Notley is our destiny. We will live here until the Grim Reaper comes for us. For me, it will be like having an ongoing affair with the past. Its atmosphere, its memories drench me in a kind of mesmeric power."

When she needed him the most, he announced that he was off with the Old Vic Company to entertain Allied troops on the continent.

Night after night, Vivien did everything she could and took every medication, trying to prevent herself from coughing on stage. For the most part, she

502

succeeded, but sometimes one of her coughing fits would last for about an hour. She was growing weaker and weaker.

Surprisingly, Larry had ignored signs of her oncoming illness and frequent coughing. She was either bone tired or else overly stimulated, bouncing back and forth like a ball, but he didn't seem particularly alarmed. He dismissed the signs, claiming "I get exhausted myself, then wake up the next morning feeling ready to go at it."

While he was touring, Vivien's condition worsened, and her weight loss continued. She began to smoke even more than before and became very dependent on bottles of wine.

Without writing to Larry, she consulted two specialists in London, one of whom advised her to go to a spa in Switzerland for a rest cure. Another suggested that she head for the Highlands of Scotland.

Both of the doctors came up with the same diagnosis of a tubercular infection in her right lung. Each of them gave the same medical advice. "You must leave the stage and go somewhere to recuperate." One doctor suggested she take a leave of nine months, the other doctor advising a year or more.

The Skin of Our Teeth was forced to close in July, 1945, after 78 performances. She was too weak to perform and checked into University College Hospital for a six-week stay.

Aboard a troop ship at Tilbury, Larry in a British army uniform had hooked up with Richardson and sixty-five members of the Old Vic for a multi-play tour of the Continent.

Larry and Richardson launched this victory tour, stopping off in Brussels, Antwerp, Belsen, Hamburg, and, finally, Paris. The tour lasted six weeks, and from Larry, Vivien received three dozen letters, some of which he addressed as "Most Adorable." The Old Vic troupe dazzled the continent with *Arms and the Man*, *Richard III*, and *Peer Gynt*.

In Hamburg, the old Staatliche Schauspielhaus had survived Allied bombs, and they played in that theater to enthusiastic audiences. At this state theater, Larry per-

Two views of Terence Morgan

formed his memorable *Richard III.*

The next stop in Germany was Belsen, site of the notorious concentration camp. Larry turned down an invitation to visit the camp. After her visit, Sybil Thorndike told Larry, "I'll never get over what I saw today. *Never!*"

The town was filled with 500 British and French soldiers charged with supervising the liberation of the concentration camp where 40,000 barely alive men and women, many suffering from typhus, were discovered along with 10,000 corpses.

In one note to Vivien from Belgium, Larry claimed, "My genital life has made no manifestation whatever since I've been away—most peculiar? It knows who it belongs to, doesn't it, hey? It just can't rise without you, that's what."

While Vivien was stricken, Larry was being fêted in Paris and seemed to be on the guest list of every aristocrat.

On the final week of his tour in Paris, Larry dined with Alfred Lunt and Lynn Fontanne, who told him they'd just seen Vivien in London. "She is seriously, even dangerously, ill," Fontanne told Larry. "You must rush back to be at her side."

"I think you should take her to our beautiful Arizona," Lunt told hm. "She'll recover from TB there."

Larry was shocked at the news and was eager to hurry back to London. Vivien had written to him, citing the doctors' opinions, but the mail had gone astray in chaotic post-war Europe.

When Vivien began to spit blood and cough for long stretches at a time, she decided to enter the hospital to have her lungs more carefully examined, especially the right one.

In Paris, the Old Vic troupe appeared at *La Comédie Française*, the first foreign company to perform in the National Theatre of France. Larry received a standing ovation.

One of the strangest incidents in the life of Larry occurred after he returned to his hotel in Paris. As he was writing a letter to Vivien, he heard a noise outside his window.

When he went to investigate, he spotted a drunken Richardson scaling the drainpipe. "Get down you bloody fool before you kill yourself," Larry shouted at him.

Richardson obeyed him, descending to the ground before taking the elevator to Larry's room. "He came into my room and picked me up like a baby and carried me to the balcony where he held me over the edge of the railing, a sixty-foot drop."

"Ralphie," I said to him in my gentlest of voices, not wanting to agitate him. "Don't you think you'd better put me back on *terra firma*? You might

504

drop me. It'd look terrible in the morning papers if you killed me."

Finally, as if mulling it over, Richardson carried him back into the suite and dropped him on the sofa. "I truly believe that Richardson in his stupor wanted to kill me," Larry later claimed.

The next morning over a cup of tea, Larry confronted Richardson, "You really wanted to kill me last night, didn't you?"

"Yes, how foolish of me," Richardson admitted. "But it was your fault as much as it was mine."

Larry was stunned. Why was he, the victim, at fault?

As improbable as it seemed, Richardson was a man who could not control his temper or his impulses. Once, he knocked down his friend Alec Guinness and badly injured him, not because of anything the actor had done, but "because I was in a foul mood." Richardson's brother once shot a fellow soldier in France during World War I because he didn't like "what he'd said to me."

Richardson later admitted to John Gielgud, "I did try to kill Larry, but his only sin was being so good in *Richard III*. It was just a drunken impulse I had—we all have them. It lasted for only a second or two, but I came very close to tossing him over that balcony to his certain death."

"I really can't believe my ears," Gielgud said, "Yet I also believe you're telling me the truth. If I ever see you sitting out front when I'm performing, I'll definitely give the role only a fourth of my power."

Larry came back on the day of Vivien's release from the hospital and took her for a vacation in Scotland. While resting in a hotel there, both of them heard the news over the radio.

After two atomic bombs were dropped on their country, the Japanese were suing for peace. The date was August 15, 1945. A BBC bulletin that night claimed that General Douglas MacArthur had, in essence, become the "new Emperor of Japan."

Dame Sybil said, "More than any woman I know, Viv was desperately in love with her husband. But it seemed an all-consuming, possessive love. It was a love of extremes, combined with a devotion that could quickly turn into a denunciation of everything he was trying to do in the theater, a mockery and a belittling of his achievements. Ultimately, I think he viewed her as a patient, not a wife and lover."

***

Instead of Vivien, Larry had his mind on the second season (1945-46) for the Old Vic. He and Richardson agreed to present four plays, including *Henry IV, Part I* and *Henry IV, Part II*. Later in the same season, to be presented as a double bill, would be Sophacles' *Oedipus*, and *The Critic*.

"I'm lacerated by work," Larry told his confidants in the autumn of 1945. He had to learn four widely varying parts, plus thousands of difficult lines of prose and poetry.

In *Henry IV, Part I*, Larry would be cast as Hotspur, Richardson as Falstaff. The role of Hotspur had rarely been shouldered by a star actor until Larry opted to perform the part.

The critic of *The Sunday Times*, James Agate, had always been contemptuous of the Hotspur role, dismissing it as little more "than a trumpet solo and, in the Pluck bright honour speech, a coach-horn tootle."

But Larry, donning a carrot-red wig, decided to make far more of the role. He also elaborately made himself up for the role. Even Richardson admitted that Larry "could do makeup better than Lon Chaney. The dear boy was born to the greasepaint."

Larry invented a stammer for Hotspur, which even Agate labeled "a stroke of genius."

Sitting in the opening night audience was John Mills. On his left sat a large, balding man. When Larry appeared in his red wig, the man called out in a loud voice, "Oh, here's old Ginger again!"

For the rest of his life, John sent Larry a telegram on every one of his opening nights, saying, "Oh, here's old Ginger again!"

Theater-goers of the time felt that Larry as Hotspur made one of the most dramatic exits in the London theater. With his dying breath, Hotspur spoke to Prince Hal who had stabbed him. "Oh, Harry, thou hast robbed me of my youth."

On stage, Larry clutched at his throat in an impossible attempt to stem the flow of the gushing "blood" oozing between his dying fingers. In death, he falls down two steps and collapses on the floor, the sound of his armor echoing through the galleries.

The audience was held spellbound as Richardson's Falstaff hauls him offstage by his heels, with Larry's face bumping painfully along the floor.

That night, Dame Sybil Thorndike complimented Margaret Leighton's performance as Lady Hotspur to Larry. Not knowing that Leighton was directly behind the curtain, Larry said, "That Leighton girl is a fucking parrot!" Although Leighton would become a close friend of Vivien's, she found Larry "less than enchanting."

Henry IV, Part I opened at the New Theatre on September 26, 1945, and would run for 69 performances.

In *Henry IV, Part II*, Richardson would again play Falstaff, but Larry would take the role of Justice Shallow, perhaps to show his versatility. Part II opened on October 3, 1945 and ran until April 13, 1946.

In an amazing feat, Larry would go from the stuttering, vainglorious

Hotspur to the lecherous old Justice Shallow.

Under a white wig and with a goatee, the sharp-nosed, spinsterly lecher that was Shallow emerged on the stage. When he spoke, it was in a comically disdainful accent.

As the old country justice, Shallow, Larry wore more makeup than ever, even for *Richard III*. "My magic lies in makeup," he said.

Richardson was furious at Larry for turning Shallow into a bee-keeper and comically swatting a bee during many of Richardson's big moments as Falstaff.

Agate found Larry's Justice Shallow the perfect country judge "peering through eyes purging thick amber and plumtree gum, tapering nose exploring chinlessness—the perfect jigsaw of old."

***

After presenting both parts of *Henry IV*, Larry and Richardson decided on a double bill, *Oedipus*, the Athenian tragedy by Sophocles in translation by W.B. Yeats, and *The Critic*, a satire by Richard Brinsley Sheridan first staged at the Drury Lane Theatre in 1779.

In the far lesser-known *The Critic*, misadventures arise when the author, "Mr. Puff," invites Sir Fretful Plagiary and two theater critics to a rehearsal of his play, *The Spanish Armada*, Sheridan's parody of the then-fashionable tragic drama.

"I could really sink myself deep into the Greek tragedy without reservation, secure in the anticipation of the joyous gaiety that was to follow," Larry said.

Larry decided to accept Tyrone Guthrie's offer to direct him in Sophocles' *Oedipus*, as the patricidal, incestuous king. "It will be my most challenging role to date, even more so than *Richard III*," he told Vivien.

Feeling the one-act play not long enough for the evening, he chose to also present *The Critic*, Sheridan's satire on actors, producers, and aesthetes, even audiences, in the 18th century.

That decision led to a break in the relationship between Guthrie and Larry. The director not only opposed adding *The Critic* to the bill, but mocked Larry's film, *Henry V*, as "vulgar." After resigning, Guthrie headed for Broadway.

James Agate, theatre critic for
The Sunday Times

Larry arranged to have two directors from the Old Vic, Miles Malleson and Michael Saint-Denis, take over for Guthrie.

In just twenty minutes, Larry had to leave the stage as the tragic Oedipus, eyes streaming with blood, and return as the foppish, silly Mr. Puff. Critics called the double bill "Oedipuff."

On May 20, 1946, *Oedipus* and *The Critic* would jointly open at the New Theatre, running for 15 performances.

Larry recalled his feeling on opening night. "The joy of being an actor on that night was completely intoxicating. There are some occasions when you stand in the wings and cannot wait to get in front of the audience, and that was one of those moments. You can smell the excitement, feel the adrenaline coursing—like being drunk on spring water."

The highlight of Larry's *Oedipus* was the blood-curdling scream at the end of the performance, both offstage and onstage. It was called "unearthly."

In a talk with John Mortimer, Larry revealed how he created the off-stage howl of agony, as he plucks out his eyes. "I thought of trapped foxes screaming when their paws are caught in the deadly teeth of a trap. I remembered how ermine are caught in the Arctic. The hunters put down salt, and the luckless ermine comes to lick it. His tongue freezes to the ice. He must wait there in sheer agony until the hunter comes and clubs the poor creature to death."

The stern critic of the British theater, John Mason Brown, lost his reserve when he saw *Oedipus*. "It pulls lightning down from the sky," he wrote, "Olivier's Theban king is godlike in appearance. It is one of those performances where blood and electricity are somehow mixed."

To relieve the audience after sitting through the horror of *Oedipus*, Larry appeared as "Puff" in *The Critic*, and did so in his most charming way. In one 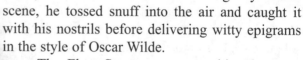 scene, he tossed snuff into the air and caught it with his nostrils before delivering witty epigrams in the style of Oscar Wilde.

The Fleet Street press gave him the most laudatory reviews of his career. "It was a milestone in English theatrical history," one reviewer wrote. "As long as one member of that audience is still alive, they'll be talking about Mr. Olivier's premiere night, starring in two plays."

Mr. Puff, if nothing else, gave Larry a chance to show off his stage acrobatics as no other role had ever done. When asked why he wanted to perform such daring feats, he said, "What is theater if not excitement?"

Margaret Leighton

As Mr. Puff, Larry devised an exciting and

dangerous exit as he was flown offstage on a painted cloud. "It was a moment of terror," he recalled. However, he continued with this "living dread" every night, performing the same reckless feat of daring.

He allowed himself to be hoisted into the flies of a painted cloud. One night the rope for his descent, taken off its cleat, gave way in his hands. To save himself from a 30-foot fall, he clung desperately to a thin wire that supported the painted cloud. He hung there precariously until stage hands rescued him.

If he hadn't been rescued, the drop would have landed him into a sea of battleships, representing the Spanish Armada, whose jagged, upward-facing edges were fashioned from plywood.

Richardson was furious on opening night, as the applause for Larry lasted longer than his ovation. "Why in hell is the bastard doing this to me?" Richardson asked the baffled stage manager. "At times I hate him. Then I see him, and he charms me once again."

Outside, some 3,000 screaming fans closed down St. Martin's Lane. Young girls screamed *WE WANT LARRY! WE WANT LARRY! WE WANT LARRY!* He'd become more than just a matinee idol; he'd evolved into a kind of God.

Reminiscent of 1940 on Broadway, crowds of fans, almost equally divided by gender, waited to ambush him at the stage door. He was often hoisted onto the top of his car where he waved and blew kisses to his fans.

Watching the acclaim one night, Richardson said, "Mr. Olivier has now arrived, after many a false dawn. He is the reigning king of the West End. There will be no actor who will top him in this generation, including myself."

***

"A remarkable change occurred in Larry because of Vivien's illness," Dame Sybil said to Richardson and others. "He is becoming the greatest actor in the world, and he's determined to carry on, following the heady path of his professional good fortune. He is going to help Vivien in any

Two views of Larry Olivier as Oedipus. "A performance where blood and electricity are somehow mixed."

way he can, but he will not be dragged down by her. Her inconsistency of behavior ultimately has become irritating to him."

"She is still very beautiful, and he appreciates her for aesthetic reasons more than sexual," Dame Sybil claimed. "As Larry confessed to me one time, he wants white heat in his love affairs. Now that passion's fire burns on a low ebb with Vivien, he turns to others. But he is loyal to her. He always comes back to her, but obviously he doesn't love her as he did when they made *Fire Over England*. It is humanly impossible to maintain that kind of fierce passion."

After a rest cure in Scotland, Larry installed Vivien at Notley Abbey in the spring of 1945, where, even though ill and in need of rest, she took on the mammoth job of restoring the property and furnishing its twenty-two rooms on their very limited budget.

Lady Sibyl Colefax, a society hostess skilled in the restoration of England's historic houses, helped Vivien with an overall design for Notley.

On his salary of 60 pounds a week from the Old Vic, Larry was facing serious financial problems. The court had ordered him to pay 3,500 pounds a year in alimony to maintain Jill and Tarquin. To beef up his thin purse, he was getting minor royalties from the release of his film, *Henry V*.

To aid with the grounds, Larry's brother Gerard ("Dickie") Olivier, had moved into Notley's bungalow along with his wife Hester. Under his direction, the grounds began to come alive again. He even trained the ivy to grow up the stone walls of the old manor. Trees needed to be planted, and the riverfront had to be cleared along the Thame. Larry had put his beloved Dickie through agricultural college after the rubber plantation in India had failed.

Even though physically fragile, Vivien supervised the restoration of the abbey, aided by Dickie. Larry was gone for most of the time, except for brief visits on the weekends.

Every night at the New Theatre, Larry had to brave fans, ripping the buttons from his coat or grabbing at his jacket. The police managed to fend them off. The most aggressive of the homosexuals reached for his crotch.

"It was a scene that belonged more to Hollywood than staid old London," Richardson said, "but Larry boy brought a new kind of passionate involvement to the stars of the West End."

In her illness, Vivien lived up to critic Beverley Nichols' appraisal of her in *The Skin of Our Teeth*. He'd called her "sparkling as a diamond." Even in recovery, in the wake of two miscarriages, she was battling depression and facing her worst bout of tuberculosis, but her spirit remained almost invincible. Two nurses were installed at Notley Abbey to care for her, and every two weeks, a specialist arrived in an attempt to control her tuberculosis. Despite these developments, Noël Coward claimed, "She has a body like a swan's down and the constitution of a G.I. on leave."

Vivien's most nightmarish fear was that Larry was going to use his power as her husband to force her into a sanatorium. She confided to Dame Sybil that she would consider divorcing him so he would no longer have power of attorney over her.

Even though, according to "official" reports that she was recovering at Notley Abbey, something began to eat away at Vivien. "Her extraordinary deteriorating had begun," claimed Dame Sybil, who'd gone to visit her at Notley.

Vivien's bedroom was the first to be restored, along with new plumbing and bathrooms as well as the kitchen and dining room. As soon as the abbey became livable, she began to invite a series of distinguished guests, although Larry might have preferred to rest and recover on the weekends.

The only guest that he consistently invited was Terry Morgan, with whom he continued to be fascinated.

On most Sundays, Larry would go for long walks in the country with Morgan. Vivien wanted to come along, but he would not hear of that. "You're far too weak, Puss," he said, as he headed out the door with Morgan to explore his newly acquired acres.

Dame Sybil said, "That beautiful boy Terry was the apple of Larry's eye, and we at the Old Vic knew what that meant. Most of Larry's boys came and went fairly quickly, but Terry stayed around far longer than most. Larry really helped his career a whole lot."

David Fairweather, who had become the full-time press representative for the Oliviers, claimed that "Vivien extended invitations to an endless court of friends and admirers. She ruled over this distinguished bunch with far more regal bearing than the actual Queen of England, who was a bit dowdy. Larry actually wanted to retreat to Notley to rest up, but found that it was always party time, with Vivien at the center of around-the-clock activities. And she was supposed to be recuperating."

At Notley you might find Katharine Hepburn out weeding the rose garden or Marlene Dietrich in the kitchen preparing her famous omelette. Orson Welles and Rex Harrison might be in the living room having an argument.

Harrison recalled one night when he was at Notley with only Larry, Vivien and the servants. "She was the perfect hostess, so loving and attentive. But on this particular night she started to sob inconsolably. There was nothing I could do for her. I'll remember forever the look on Larry's face. He just stood there looking on hopelessly. By morning she'd recovered."

In spite of Larry's objection, Vivien continued to invite "the adored ones" for weekend house parties, including Douglas and Mary Lee Fairbanks, John Gielgud and his *beau du jour*, Noël Coward and his *beau du jour*, Michael and

Rachel Redgrave, and John and Mary Mills.

Cocktails began at their cottage in Chelsea, after which each tipsy guest piled into a car for the 90-minute caravan drive to Buckinghamshire.

When guests arrived, the abbey was ablaze with lights, with fires crackling in every hall. She'd arranged fresh flowers throughout, and selected the menus and the wines. Servants were on duty day and night over the weekends, but were given weekdays off.

It was often three o'clock in the morning when an elaborate four-course dinner was served. Almost manically, Vivien insisted that no guest go to bed before the dawn.

Even after a long day, and even if it were five o'clock in the morning, Vivien insisted that her house guests join her in games of charades and canasta. Larry always refused and went to bed.

"The draperies, the bed sheets, and even the toilet paper were in the same color," Katharine Hepburn said. "When I came back to California, Laura Harding and I searched all over Los Angeles until we found an outlet for magenta toilet paper. I became addicted to it because of Vivien."

"She ran Notley Abbey like an elegant five-star hotel," said Gielgud. "The press called them the most beautiful couple in the British theater, and Vivien reigned like a queen at Notley, where the guests slept on silk sheets and wiped their bums on toilet paper that matched the bathroom tiles. Lunch and dinner could be ordered any time a guest wanted it, day or night."

In the morning, Vivien took her guests on a tour of the grounds and gardens, especially her stunning garden of white roses. She even showed her guests her favorite cows—namely, Cleopatra, Ophelia, Sabina, and Titania. John Mills asked, "Where is Scarlett O'Hara?"

"No cow of mine will ever be called that," she snapped back.

The ghosts of Scarlett O'Hara and Heathcliff, so it is said, still haunt the hallways and nine bedrooms of Notley Abbey, even in its commercial role today of a wedding and catering facility. *Photo courtesy of Bijou Wedding Venues, Ltd.*

For almost four months, when not giving parties, Vivien rested upstairs in a four-poster bed rescued from the set of *Gone With the Wind*.

One afternoon Dame Sybil came for another visit to Notley. Vivien had requested that she bring Terry Morgan, who seemed only too eager to go along. Once at Notley, Dame Sybil retreated with a script to memorize, while Vivien entertained Morgan in her rose garden.

"They were so terribly fond

of each other they seemed like lovers," Dame Sybil told her friends at the Old Vic. "Terry didn't want me to tell Larry he visited Notley that day."

"Vivien Leigh has become Marie Antoinette at her Petit Trianon, far removed from the intrigue at the Court of Versailles—in this case the London theater world," Dame Sybil said.

When the actress Ena Burrill planned to drive up to see Vivien, Morgan asked to come along. When Burrill arrived, she feared she should have asked permission to bring Morgan along, but later claimed that Vivien seemed "besotted" with the dashing young man.

After that visit, Morgan visited Notley on at least nine different occasions. He arrived on his own when he knew Larry wouldn't be there.

To complicate matters in his life, he was also falling in love with Georgina Jumel, whom he'd later marry, the union lasting for 58 years until his death in 2005.

When the cynical Noël Coward heard of this, he told friends, "That darling boy must be so exhausted I don't know how he has any energy left for the Old Vic. He certainly knows how to advance himself in the theater. How long will it take before he gets around to Johnnie and me?" He was referring, of course, to John Gielgud.

Vivien's recovery was rapid, and her doctor, a specialist, thought that if she'd be careful, she could go to New York with Larry where he was set to appear in three productions. The doctor warned her, "At any time, however, you are subject to a relapse. You must give up smoking and drinking." She would not listen to that mandate, however.

Nearly all their friends who loved them were also sophisticated and articulate observers of what was going on in their lives. Not only their friends, but their critics weighed in with various opinions over the years, right or wrong.

Ena Burrill had become a *confidante* of Vivien, but she was also sharply observant of her. "You can love someone and not approve of the way your friend leads her life. I'm not faulting either one of them, but it was clear to me that Larry had decided to wrap Vivien in cotton wool and place her on the back shelf of his priorities. He'd become obsessed with his roles at the Old Vic, and with Terry Morgan as well."

"Vivien was a woman Larry once adored," claimed Burrill. "He had moved on. I'm not saying he had abandoned Vivien to her fate, but by 1945 Larry was marching to a different drum beat. While resting with her in Scotland, Vivien said that he was not so interested in her recuperation as in spending his time agonizing over missing early rehearsals at the Old Vic. The plays seemed to absorb his every waking thought."

Peter Glenville, who would later direct Larry in *Becket* and *Term of Trial*, said, "Vivien Leigh was the only woman Larry ever loved. Larry Olivier was

513

the only man Vivien ever loved. Sex was not love to them. Sex was something you did like eating a dinner when you're hungry. What made the show exciting was when their sexual desires focused on the same young man—take Terry Morgan for example."

Vivien went into a horrible bout of manic depression when she received a particularly nasty note from critic James Agate. He mailed her one of his *Ego* volumes of memoirs with a note: "Hurry up and get well or people will think Larry thrives in your *absence*. He is becoming a great actor!"

During one of her "states," she struck back at Agate with a piece of malicious gossip she'd heard from Coward. "I'm told that Mr. Agate, our darling drama critic for the esteemed *Sunday Times*, demands that his catamites urinate into a whisky glass reserved for the finest of Scotch," she said. "He then knocks back the savory golden brew in one big swallow, not even taking time to savor it. However, before the offering from one of his boys, he asks the child to down four pints of lager. After his libation, he then rushes forth to review a play. Would you say that makes him full of piss and vinegar?"

Roger Lewis, who wrote an acclaimed biography of Peter Sellers, issued the most colorful description of Vivien's physical and mental condition. "Call it consumption, an infection of the lymphatic system, an immunodeficiency disorder, a combination of genetic, hormonal, or uterine abnormalities; label her a manic-depressive psychotic and squirt her full of anti-depressant drugs; give her two or three blasts of electro-convulsive therapy per week to induce such brain seizures she's sexually excited by a pop-up toaster; tot up her fevers and chills and monitor her intake of gin and tobacco; what she was dying slowly from was a broken heart, and nobody can convince me otherwise. She became vituperative and unmanageable because she wanted to claim Olivier's love exclusively."

"Both Vivien and Larry would wallow in the glow of world approval that soon turned to idolatry," said Burrill. "They would share stage triumphs together. They would issue public declarations of love. But at Notley they were sleeping with some of their guests instead of each other. To the world they kept up appearances until they could no longer pull off that act."

CHAPTER THIRTEEN

In April of 1946, when spring was bursting out at Notley Abbey, Larry granted Vivien permission to go to New York with him "just for the ride." They would be joined by members of the Old Vic Company for a six-week season on Broadway. Vivien felt she was able to make the trip, although she feared a relapse, as the doctors had warned her.

Funds were extremely low, but they checked into the St. Regis Hotel anyway, finding a garden of flowers. "I feel like I've been transplanted to Kew Gardens," she said. Some of the flowers came from the garden of Helen Hayes.

The suite for Larry and Vivien had been arranged by Ruth Gordon and Garson Kanin, who invited them to the Stork Club on their first free night. After the deprivations of wartime Britain, Vivien was amazed as she perused the menu. "This must have been the same menu that Nero served at one of his Roman orgies."

It was a time for renewal of old friendships, mostly Katharine Cornell, Guthrie McClintic, Alfred Lunt and Lynn Fontanne, and George Cukor who was in town with what Vivien called "the most gorgeous young man I've ever seen in my life."

The homosexual director had met young Marlon Brando, and was urging him to give up his dreams of a Broadway career in favor of movie stardom in Hollywood.

While Larry was performing on Broadway, Vivien often went with friends to other Broadway shows.

She was so delighted with Kanin's comedy hit, *Born Yesterday*, that she urged Larry to bring it to London for the following season. He agreed with her and would produce *Born Yesterday* that winter.

Kanin found Vivien increasingly restless and "almost eager to pick a quarrel with anybody. Here was a talented young actress at the peak of her power but without work. She was a mere hanger-on who came to New York as part of Larry's luggage."

Larry could hardly pay for his suite at the St. Regis, as he was pulling in less than two hundred dollars a week, but Vivien demanded—and got—a new mink coat.

"Darling," she said, "I was out with Tallulah Bankhead last night, who tried to go down on me in the back of a taxi. She let me feel her new mink which she got from playing Sabina. She made fun of my cloth coat, suggesting that I robbed it off the back of a Polish refugee."

Virtually every seat at the Century Theatre was sold for the performances of the Old Vic. Some 30,000 potential theater-goers were turned away at the box office.

At the end of the week, the best of Broadway tickets went for under $4.00 but scalpers could get as much as $50 from fans wanting to see Larry perform.

He opened on May 1, 1946, playing one of his favorite characters, Astrov, in *Uncle Vanya,* for eight performances. The play was followed by *Henry IV, Part I* (eighteen performances) and *Henry IV, Part II* (nine performances). He finished the season on Broadway with the "double feature" that incorporated *Oedipus* and *The Critic,* opening on May 20 and closing June 15.

Although the competition was stiff, the New York Theater Critics voted Larry the best actor of the 1945-46 season. He faced such daunting talent as Walter Huston, Raymond Massey, Alfred Lunt, Maurice Evans, and Oscar Homolka.

In New York, Vivien received guests like a queen at court. One caller identified himself by saying, "Would you like to meet an old sod who thinks you are the world's most enchanting creature?" It was W. Somerset Maugham, who insisted on speaking to her in French.

Larry had changed his opinion about working in the movies. To pay for the ever-mounting expenses at Notley Abbey, he wanted work in films.

But David O. Selznick had successfully established a boycott of his acting talents because of his animosity "about that rebellious bitch, Vivien Leigh." Other producers agreed not to hire Larry.

***

Cornell and McClintic invited Larry and Vivien to attend a dinner for Marlon Brando, the most promising young actor on Broadway except for Montgomery Clift. Vivien declined because she felt ill, but the actress Mildred Natwick joined Larry and Marlon for a late-night supper with Cornell and McClintic.

Years later, Natwick would claim that she saw an attraction developing between Marlon and Larry "right before my eyes." She also noted that it was taking place in front of McClintic. It is not known if Larry at that point was

516

aware of McClintic's own romantic interest in Marlon.

"I'd even heard rumors that Larry had had a brief fling with Guthrie when he was appearing with Katharine in that silly play, *No Time for Comedy*," Natwick said.

"I really believe that if Larry did know about Guthrie's interest in young Marlon, it would not have made the slightest difference to him," Mildred later claimed. "He was of the school of 'All's fair in love and war.' John Gielgud slept with Larry on several occasions, so it was said. He once told me that whenever Larry spotted a handsome actor, especially one in green tights, he went after him with an unusual determination—and most often got his man."

"I remember only bits and pieces of the dialogue between Larry and Marlon when I visited the Cornell home," Natwick said. "Larry was complaining that he and Vivien were regarded as mere *arrivistes* by the American press."

"Sometimes autograph seekers mistake me for Maurice Evans," Larry said. "I'm considered a movie star. I don't think Americans are aware of my career on the stage."

Mildred remembered Marlon asking Larry why he wore so much perfume. "I know it's gilding the lily," Larry said, "but I sweat a lot in crowds and under lights. I like to smell kissable at all times. You wear no cologne at all?"

"Just my natural smell," Marlon said. "Sometimes I don't even take a shower, much less a bath. I just throw a glob of spit into the air and run under it."

"Larry laughed and it was obvious to me that he was both attracted and repulsed by Marlon's vulgarity," Natwick claimed. "Marlon's crude sexual animalism mesmerized Larry. I don't want to say that Larry had his tongue out panting for Marlon that night, but seduction was obviously on Larry's brain."

Larry suggested to Marlon that in "just a few short months, and I predict this, you'll be followed everywhere by autograph hound dogs. Once I was standing at a latrine at the Plaza Hotel, and the man next to me used that inopportune moment to request an autograph. I rather testily told him that his dick wasn't long

"I remember it well..."

Mildred Natwick *(top photo)* remembers the affect of a young Marlon Brando *(lower photo)* on Larry

enough for me to write Laurence Olivier. I buttoned up and walked out as grandly as I could."

According to Mildred, Marlon laughed at this. He told Larry, "If one of those hound dogs comes up to me, I'll tell him he'll get his autograph if he'll show me his ass. I'll write 'Marlon' on one buttock, 'Brando' on the other."

Before the night ended, at least according to Mildred, "Marlon and Larry were exploding off each other. There was a great chemistry between them, even though they were from entirely different sides of the ocean. Different worlds, really. Before midnight when I went home, Kate, Guthrie, and I could have been invisible ghosts. Larry had eyes only for Marlon—and Marlon only for him. Romeo had met his Juliet in an unlikely form."

Three days later, when Mildred once again encountered Larry, he told her, "I am the happiest man alive."

"Strong comments coming from a man who in the past had been so unhappy that he'd contemplated suicide," Mildred said.

"Our love is triumphant," Larry told her. "In Marlon, I have found what I've been seeking but never came across in all my life. Vivien will have to understand. I'm moving Marlon in with us."

Those plans, alas, did not materialize, at least not immediately. After less than a month, Marlon abandoned Larry, giving him the same treatment he'd given such luminaries as Clifford Odets and Leonard Bernstein.

"One morning, he was lying nude under the sheets with Larry," Mildred said, "and the next day he was gone from the bed. Marlon dumped Larry to resume his one-night stands."

The full story of Marlon and Larry, catalyzed by the ongoing presence of Vivien and a film version of *A Streetcar Named Desire*, hadn't yet evolved. "Marlon merely put Larry on hold until some future date," Mildred said.

Marlon later confided to Stella Adler and Bobby Lewis, as well as others, that he'd been with Larry "merely to listen to the sound of his voice." He told his friends that Larry himself had admitted to "imitating absolutely and unashamedly" such stars as Ronald Colman, Alfred Lunt, and John Barrymore. He did caution Marlon, however, that "imitation is good provided you don't mold yourself around that one actor you admire—that you don't merely imitate. In your case, I just know you'll allow your own conception of a character to develop. Make it your own!"

Adler once said that she was amazed at the future comparisons others would make between Marlon and Larry. The debate would rage for decades, and it's still going on: "Who was the greatest English-speaking actor of the 20th century?"

John Gielgud, years later, found comparisons between Marlon and his friend, Larry, "odious. How can you compare a young man who appeared on the stage for the last time in 1948 at the age of twenty-three with a gifted performer who first walked on the stage at the age of ten, and who would later define theater as we know it today?"

Gielgud was practically alone in deriding comparisons. William Redfield, in his *Letters From an Actor*, wrote: "Ironically enough, Laurence Olivier is less gifted than Marlon Brando. But Olivier is the definitive actor of the 20th century. Why? Because he wanted to be."

Tennessee Williams himself pronounced Marlon "the greatest living actor ever . . . greater than Olivier."

As amazing as it seems, considering what different characters and actors they were, Larry and Marlon were sometimes up for the same role. In one of the ironies of Hollywood, it was Larry, not Marlon, who was the first choice to play Don Corleone in *The Godfather*. In yet another irony, on the night of March 27, 1973, in Los Angeles, Marlon would find himself competing with Larry for an Oscar for the best actor of the year, Marlon for his role in *The Godfather*, Larry for his star turn in *Sleuth*.

The Olivier/Brando coupling was too good a story not to make its way to London. In 1949, at a party attended by Vivien, the British theater critic, Kenneth Tynan, confronted the emotionally unstable actress. Although not wanting to cause her even more pain than she was experiencing because of her personal demons, he became a little bitchy after a few drinks. He told her all that he knew of her husband's affair. Vivien listened politely, then said, "Oh, my. What fiddle-faddle! If that's true, I only hope that poor Larry knew what to do. Marlon Brando. I must try him myself one day!"

With that pronouncement, she turned on her heel and walked away. All Tynan saw was the curve of her back as she graciously made her way across a crowded London living room to greet the just-arriving Noël Coward and his partner, Jack Wilson. Both of these men already knew what Vivien didn't know.

What Marlon Brando was like in bed.

***

When their brief run came to an end in New York, Larry, suffering from a torn Achilles tendon, flew to Boston. From there, he limped onto the stage at Tufts College in Medford to accept an honorary degree as "the real interpreter of Shakespeare in our age."

When the other members of the Old Vic company flew back to London, Larry and Vivien stayed on to attend the American premiere of *Henry V*. On June 19, 1946, when their attendance at that event was completed, and with the intention of returning to Britain, they boarded a Pan American Clipper flight, which well might have been their last journey on earth.

In a four-engine Lockheed Constellation, Larry and Vivien took off from New York's La Guardia airport at 5pm, heading for London with stopovers scheduled in Newfoundland and Shannon. The plane carried fifty-two passengers, ten of whom were members of the crew. The vessel itself was the fastest airliner making the Atlantic crossing at the time.

At the last minute, Anthony Eden, the former British foreign minister, cancelled his reservation.

Vivien was the first to notice something wrong. She let out a scream that mirrored Larry's fatal screech of agony in *Oedipus*. She rose from her seat, and, as she did, the other passengers broke out in panic, rushing to peer out the windows to discover a wing of the plane on fire. The emergency lights suddenly went on at 5:30pm.

One woman shouted that the plane was going down. What had happened was deadly serious. A shaft from one of the starboard engines to the cabin pressurizer had broken free from its holding and was banging around in the intense winds outside. It set fire to the clipper's hydraulic fluid.

When the engine caught fire, the pilot turned back as he knew the plane would crash at sea. Desperately searching for a landing field, he saw the flames melting the engine, which then fell off, plunging to earth.

Finally, the pilot spotted Windham Field at Willimantic, Connecticut. Passengers were warned to brace themselves for an emergency landing on this small field. Since the pilot couldn't lower the wheels, the plane had to face the landing strip for the inevitable belly-scraping skid.

At 6:10pm, the pilot had notified air control that the Lockheed Constellation was coming in for an emergency landing, warning to clear any plane from the runway. Hitting the ground, the plane skidded along for nearly a half a mile, metal meeting concrete. It finally came to a stop, tipping over like a one-wing bird.

Larry later said, "I owe my life to the brave pilot, Captain Samuel Miller. I was so grateful to him I impulsively kissed him on the lips, which seemed to shock the dear boy. I think he would rather have kissed Vivien."

The landing field was 25 miles east of Hartford. Reporters rushed to the scene of the emergency when they heard Larry and Vivien were aboard. The Associated Press sent a bulletin across America. OLIVIER & WIFE SURVIVE NEAR FATAL AIR CRASH. A subsequent headline (see illustration) gave Vivien equal billing.

When Vivien heard the initial report in the airline terminal, she turned to Larry. "We've got to do something about my billing. Have I been away from America so long that I've become 'the wife?' Don't they remember? I was Scarlett O'Hara!"

After such a fright, both Larry and Vivien considered sailing back to Southampton, but changed their mind when they found they had exactly $17.46 between them. They took the next plane to London, and now that the Luftwaffe was not shooting down planes flying from the United States to England, it was a smooth flight all the way.

***

Storm clouds were coming, but Vivien and Larry enjoyed the last tranquil summer of their lives in 1946 at Notley Abbey, with him playing the Grand Squire and she presiding as his Ladyship.

At Notley, Vivien found she could relate to Tarquin better than Suzanne. Now a teenager, her daughter was viewed by Vivien "as a bit awkward." Unfortunately, she did not inherit her mother's beauty. "She takes after Leigh's side of the family," Vivien told her mother, Gertrude, who agreed, even though she adored and doted on Suzanne.

Larry's close friend, the theatrical agent Laurence Evans, claimed that "those in the theater world came to view an invitation to Notley on par with

Laurence Olivier and Vivien Leigh Escape Crash Landing of Airplane

New York, June 19. (AP)—A giant four-engined Pan-American Clipper made an emergency landing on a field near Willimantic, Conn.. at 5:10 p. m. (cdt) Tuesday—little more than an hour after leaving LaGuardia field on a scheduled transatlantic flight.

Forty-two passengers — including the British actor, Laurence Olivier, and his wife, Vivien Leigh—escaped injury, Pan-American said.

The plane radioed back to the field a few minutes after takeoff at 5 p. m. that engine trouble had developed and it was returning to New York.

Next word from the crew came after the landing on Windham field, near Willimantic. The company said passengers were being transferred by bus to Hartford, 25 miles distant.

Olivier and his wife were returning to London after a six weeks engagement in New York with the "Old Vic" repertoire company.

Other members of the cast left earlier in the week but Olivier and Miss Leigh remained for the premiere of the actor's British-made film "Henry V."

Capt. Leo Carroll of the Connecticut state police said that one engine of the giant plane "fell off" while the plane was over the town of Plainfield about 30 miles from Willimantic. He quoted observers as saying a portion of the wing was on fire when the pilot made the landing.

The airfield, Carroll said, was too small to permit a wheel landing and the pilot was forced to pancake.

"That fellow did a remarkable job," Carroll said, "in bringing down that big ship on three engines so that none of its 43 passengers and 10 crew members were injured."

an invitation to spend the weekend at either Windsor Castle or Sandringham."

Cecil Beaton was a frequent visitor, and Alexander Korda and Tyrone Guthrie came to call. Vivien was very forgiving in compiling her guest list, sometimes inviting luminaries from the stage who had made unkind remarks about Larry, notably Margaret Leighton and Alec Guinness.

On occasion, before dinner, Robert Helpmann would deliver a brilliant impersonation of Dame Edith Evans that brought the guests to the point of laughing hysteria.

On a visit to Notley, Lord Cottesloe remembered Larry fleeing from what he assumed was a field of bulls. "The dear chap likes to think of himself as a gentleman farmer. It was a field of steers."

Even David O. Selznick, their past legal challenges buried, paid one visit to Vivien and Larry at Notley. However he later complained that the cuisine "tasted like wartime deprivations."

Before David's arrival in post-war London, they had received a cable from his brother, Myron Selznick. "DAVID WANTS YOU BOTH TO STAR IN CYRANO DE BERGERAC. VIVIEN AS ROXANNE. SALARY? $100,000 FOR EACH OF YOU."

"SIGN US UP," was the immediate response signed "Larry & Viv." At long last Larry had an answer to his monetary problems.

After David's return to Hollywood, Myron sent another cable to Vivien and Larry, telling them that regrettably, Cyrano had been postponed "indefinitely."

"We were so horribly disappointed we cried," Vivien told Bea Lillie when she called to inquire about them.

Months later, Larry from London called Vivien at Notley. "I just heard that Jose Ferrer, a Puerto Rican of all things, is going to play Cyrano. Hollywood remains inhabited with idiots. What do they know about casting?"

Later, he was even more mortified when he heard a broadcast from Hollywood that Ferrer had won the Oscar for his 1950 performance. "The role turned Ferrer into an overnight movie star," Larry said. "It belonged to me. First Ralphie stole it from me on the stage, and now Ferrer stole it from me on the screen."

***

Throughout most of 1946, Vivien went without showing any signs of mental deterioration, but physically, she was in a weak and delicate condition, and would remain so for the rest of her life. She saw her husband drowning in expenses from alimony and the astronomical cost of restoring and operating Notley Abbey.

She wanted to help out and, to do so, the husband-and-wife team came up with the idea of reviving her highly popular *The Skin of Our Teeth*.

Once again, he would be the director and she would, of course, be his star.

Both Vivien and Larry wanted Terry Morgan to repeat his role as the son. Each of them had continued to see Terry privately, each enjoying an intimate relationship with him. He was a frequent guest at Notley, and Larry also saw him privately in London.

"Don't try to convince me otherwise," Gielgud told Coward. "Viv and Larry are sharing that divine creature. And he still has time to service his intended, Miss Georgina Jumel. I pray there's something left for poor Jumel on their wedding night. What does that dear boy have? I'm dying to find out."

Perhaps out of jealousy, Noël Coward, when drunk, often made catty remarks about Morgan. "The child is a virile husband to Vivien and a submitting wife to Larry. Like they said of Caesar, a wife to every man and a husband to every woman."

Right before opening night, September 11, 1946, Vivien went into one of her "states." George Devine was playing Antrobus, and she got along with him fairly well. But before Esther Somers went on stage as Mrs. Antrobus, Vivien told her, "You can't act at all."

On that same opening night, Larry confided in Cecil Beaton, claiming that, "I've never had so much trouble with not just any actor, but *anybody*. Vivien was at her most horrid."

When queenish Beaton repeated this gossip to Vivien, she retorted, "Isn't Larry just darling?"

At London's Piccadilly Theatre, *The Skin of Our Teeth* would run for 109 performances.

***

"I was but a wee laddie when I played Lear," Larry said. "The king is an old, old monarch."

In London, Larry at the age of thirty-nine told his backers at the Old Vic that he wanted to play King Lear. "A mite young for the part," Richardson said. Actually Richardson coveted the role for himself, but had already requested to star as Cyrano de Bergerac.

"I outfoxed that cunning old sod, Ralphie, who really wanted Lear," Larry said. "Since he stole Cyrano from me, I got back at the bugger. I robbed him of Lear as an act of pure villainy."

"I didn't really want to do Lear at first—I wanted to prevent Ralphie from doing it," Larry said. "Too late. I had signed on to play the stupid old fart."

"When you've the strength for it, you're too young; when you've the age, you're too old," Larry said. "It's a bugger, isn't it?"

Alec Guinness signed on as the "Fool." For the role, Laurence Evans had negotiated a salary for Guinness, his client, of 35 pounds a week.

Piers Paul Read, the authorized biographer of Guinness, claimed that the actor's attitude toward Larry "was a mixture of admiration and dislike. Olivier was just what Alec did not want to be—an actor who was merely an actor—technically brilliant but humanly shallow."

To the public, Guinness presented a different view, claiming that Larry was so popular he could have won an election as Prime Minister.

Larry told Coward, "I don't think much of Guinness as an actor. He's very limited in his range. Jealous as a queen of me."

Familiar actors such as Margaret Leighton, Pamela Brown, George Relph, and Joyce Redman gave Larry as Lear full support.

"Lear was easier to play than Romeo, a character who spends the entire evening searching for sympathy," Larry said. "But then, anyone who lets an erection rule his life doesn't deserve much sympathy, does he?"

Unlike previous Lears, Larry played the blustery old monarch like a comical and rather witty grandfather.

Years later, at the age of seventy-five, Larry would reprise the role of Lear, giving an even greater performance.

King Lear opened on September 24, 1946 at London's New Theatre and ran for 42 performances, followed by a seven-night run beginning on November 25 at the Théâtre des Champs-Elysées in Paris.

In his diary, Coward claimed, "Larry's performance as Lear ranks with his *Richard III* as being unequivocally great." James Agate pronounced Larry "a

comedian by instinct and a tragedian by art." When Agate asked him why his voice was better than ever, Larry told him, "I practiced by shouting at the cows at Notley."

J.C. Trewin of the *Observer* called it "the best Lear yet." Yet Beverley Baxter of the *Evening Standard* maintained that Lear floored Larry "almost as completely as though he were a British heavyweight." Kenneth Tynan called it "moderate Lear."

Tynan, who would later fall in love with Larry, wasn't infatuated with Larry when he saw *King Lear*. The critic found that as Lear, Larry "has no intrinsic majesty; he always fights shy of pathos; and he cannot play old men without letting his jaw sag and his eye wander archly in magpie fashion—in short, without being funny."

After each night's performance of Lear, Larry would be greeted with pandemonium outside the theater, not equaled until The Beatles came along. The police liter-

Young Larry playing old King Lear

524

ally had to carry him to his car, moving at a snail's pace through his fans, mostly kiss-blowing women who seemed to want a piece of him. On many a night, the fans struck the constables in their attempts to get to their beloved. And all this adulation for an actor playing an ancient crone.

Once again, many male fans, most of them presumably gay, also turned out to greet Larry. Word of his bisexuality had already spread through the "lavender circles" of London. As one gay fan said, "In spite of Scarlett, we know in our hearts that he's one of us."

At one point, Vivien's nerves were shattered. She sobbed in Gertrude's arms. "Once he was the Prince of Players. Now he's been crowned the King of British Theatre. That means I'm the queen. I'm not adequate for the position. I don't have the strength and stamina to be his proper queen."

Both Larry and Vivien had reached the point in their careers where they attracted unwanted attention from psychotic stalkers. Herbert Wanbon, age 28, was the most notorious case. Larry had once befriended him and given him a walk-on part at the Old Vic, but later fired him for incompetence.

Twice outside the theater, he attempted to assault Larry, yanking at his clothing, but was restrained by bobbies.

Wanbon then plotted to assault Vivien as the Oliviers' Rolls Royce pulled up at Durham Cottage. He leaped from the bushes, grabbing Vivien and shoving his tongue down her delicate throat.

Larry struck at the assailant, breaking a finger as he did. The police were called and the attacker arrested, later being sentenced to six months in prison for the assault.

When Larry appeared as King Lear in the production in Paris, he kept his bandaged hand concealed in his stage costume.

***

In his capacity as a West End producer, Larry cast Yolande Donlan, an American actress, to play the not-so-dumb blonde role, Billie Dawn, in the London stage production of *Born Yesterday*. Of course, Judy Holliday in the screen version would win an Oscar, beating out heavy favorites Bette Davis for *All About Eve* and Gloria Swanson for *Sunset Blvd.*

Vivien graciously entertained Yolande at Durham Cottage in Chelsea, along with Judith Anderson, Noël Coward, and Mary Martin. Donlan was impressed with Vivien's perfection as a hostess and the elegant appointments of Georgian silver, Battersea enamel candelabra, and hand-painted plates from Quimper.

Born Yesterday opened in London at the Garrick Theatre on February 1, 1947 and ran for a year. Once it was up and running successfully, Larry, both as an actor and producer, was open to other offers. He wanted to keep busy with work and not anchor down at Notley, mostly because of Vivien's swift mood shifts.

"I still visited with Larry and Viv, but most often on separate occasions," Coward said. "By 1948 they were very far apart, virtually living in different worlds. Larry was the busiest man in London. His appearances at Notley became rarer."

In London, Filippo Del Giudice, who had collected the money to produce *Henry V*, invited Larry to lunch at his Park Lane suite. There, he pitched the idea of doing another Shakespeare play together.

"You could be the greatest of all Hamlets, and your performance would be immortalized on the screen forever," Del Giudice asserted.

Larry promised to mull it over and call Del Giudice in Switzerland, where the producer would be for the next three weeks.

In retrospect, Larry would have preferred to perform in *Macbeth* instead of in *Hamlet* but Orson Welles had just done the film *Macbeth* (1948) and was working on *The Tragedy of Othello: The Moor of Venice* (1952).

Larry immediately called Vivien, "Dear Filippo wants me not only to co-produce *Hamlet* with him, but to star in it and direct it."

"What glorious news," Vivien said. "Once again, like at Elsinore, I will be your Ophelia."

He didn't respond to that.

Blonde American bombshell Yolande Donlan

Under Larry's supervision, she starred in the London stage version of *Born Yesterday* a year after Judy Holliday opened in an equivalent stage production in New York.

In his dressing room, in front of his lover, Terry Morgan, Larry lamented turning forty. "I'm too old to play Hamlet," he said, "but I'm doing it anyway. In 1936, when I was 29, I was at the peak of my beauty. Now I'm getting a bit jowlier. More thick of chin. Time races by like a rushing stream in the mountains."

He confided to Morgan, "I think after *Hamlet* I will give up acting. In the future I'll either be a producer or director, definitely not an actor. Acting is for silly little boys; a director's job calls for a man."

Morgan urged Larry to dye his hair blond. "You will be so much sexier that way," Terry claimed. "Besides, Hollywood loves blondes of any sex. And you will look younger."

"All right, I'll go blond, you little bugger," he told Morgan. "But I refuse to let any other actor in the film go blond. I want to stand out in those long shots. As for you, my sweet child, I want you to play Laertes."

"Sign me on," Morgan said.

That night, Larry called Del Giudice in Switzerland. "I'm your Hamlet," he told the producer.

"With balls of brass, I set out to do the drama of a man who could not make up his mind," Larry told Morgan. "My friend and enemy, Ralph Richardson, needs to be shown up a bit. He's walking around with his nose high in the air. I might even win a bloody Oscar for my screen Hamlet from those jackals in Hollywood."

The industrialist and film producer, J. Arthur Rank, a devout Methodist, was known for "his deep pockets and short arms," his employees said. His tight-fisted offer to Larry for *Hamlet* was ten thousand U.S. dollars.

Rank wrote Larry a letter of warning. "I have heard your incestuous theories about Hamlet and his mother. They are not mine. It is imperative that at

no point in this film you present a sexual link between Hamlet and his mother. This is not a film about incest. You have already played Oedipus on the stage. You do not need to repeat the role here."

Larry set about casting the film. The biggest problem was telling Vivien that he didn't want her to be Ophelia. He knew she would be disappointed, but Rank personally had told him that Vivien was "long beyond playing a convincing Ophelia on the stage."

That night after dinner he delivered the blow.

"Puss, you must understand. At thirty-three years old, you're far too old to play Ophelia."

"But at forty years of age, you're not too old to play the Prince of Denmark," she shouted at him. "Talk about a double standard in the theater. I'll never forgive you for denying me the role of Ophelia. Never!"

After he turned her down for the role, she told him, "If you want sex, don't come to my bed. Get it somewhere else, which I'm sure you're already doing."

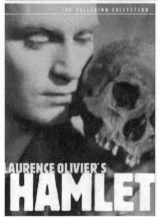

He took her advice.

"I agreed with Larry's assessment," said Cecil Beaton. "Vivien was wrong for Ophelia. Her dearest friends constantly told her how beautiful she was, but her ill health had aged her very badly and

Laurence Olivier as the tormented, indecisive, and incestuously provocative Prince of Denmark

very prematurely. She would never again have that wonderful glow and sparkle she had in the late 30s and early 40s."

Knowing how close Morgan was to Larry, she attempted to win him over to her side, wanting to destroy his friendship with her husband. Meeting with Morgan privately, she told him that Larry was "the most insensitive man I've ever known. I lost the role of Roxanne, and I had my heart set on that part, not to mention the $100,000. Then Larry stabbed me in the heart by denying me Ophelia. With makeup I could be convincing as Ophelia. After all, she was in her late teens, and you tell me I look more beautiful than I ever did. You did tell me that, didn't you, dear heart?"

Claire Bloom, a future lover of Larry's, auditioned for the role of Ophelia but was also turned down.

For the role of Ophelia, Larry selected Jean Simmons, a demure British beauty who was seventeen years old—"jail bait" as her future husband, Stewart Granger, who'd already seduced her, claimed. Her interpretation of Ophelia was a star-making part, and she was nominated for a Best Supporting Actress Oscar. She asked Larry, "What's an Oscar?"

"I made her a star," Larry claimed.

"He also made her," said Morgan. "I was a mite jealous."

By the end of 1950, Simmons was the number four box office attraction, American or British, in English cinema.

Larry had urged her to perfect her craft on the stage. Instead, she followed hunky Granger to Hollywood where she married him. For a time the couple lived with newly married Elizabeth Taylor and Michael Wilding.

"I chose this darling girl, Jean Simmons, because her beauty evokes your beauty when we did *Hamlet* at Elsinore," Larry told Vivien.

"What part can I now play?" Vivien asked. "Some old hag. Maybe one of the witches from *Macbeth*." She stormed out of the room.

In this movie I want to make it perfectly clear that Hamlet knows what is under Ophelia's skirt," Larry told Simmons.

J. Arthur Rank

"That's up to you to find out," Simmons provocatively answered him. She had become much more experienced since becoming Granger's lover.

She recalled she was shocked when Vivien arrived on the set. "I had known her when she played Cleopatra. But on this particular day she must have been in another one of her states. She came up to me and said, 'Well, you teenage twat, you aren't satisfied with Granger. You want Larry too. You're welcome to him. I hope he can get it up for you. Living with Larry has convinced me that the male sex organ is one of most unreliable of all human organs.'"

A letter Vivien wrote to a friend during the filming of *Hamlet* now rests among Larry's correspondence at the British Library. "Goddamn Larry is fucking his Ophelia—I'm losing him to a bloody child. I was barely out of my teens when Larry started fucking me." She was referring, of course, to Simmons.

Some biographers have concluded that Vivien wrongly accused Larry of having an affair with Simmons. But she told cast members Eileen Herlie and Felix Aylmer that Larry had seduced her, adding "I wasn't a virgin." This was too tantalizing a story for these actors to keep to themselves.

Near the end of her life, Simmons was asked why she let a middle-aged man, Larry himself, seduce her, especially when she had such a good-looking man as Stewart Granger falling madly in love with her. Without blinking, she said, "You don't say no to his Lordship."

In Larry's desperate search for an actress to play Queen Gertrude, he offered Vivien the role of Hamlet's mother.

She looked stunned. No sooner had he done that, than he realized what a mistake it had been. She tore into him and attempted to scratch his face, but he restrained her.

For a brief time, he flirted with casting Mercia Swinburne, the wife of his old friend George Relph, as Gertrude. In a letter to Swinburne, Larry wrote of the "Oedipus complex," suggesting that her role should be a "wonderfully glamorous mummy to Hamlet."

In the end, Swinburne lost the role, the part of Queen Gertrude going to Eileen Herlie, who was actually thirteen years younger than Larry. Not only that, she was younger than Vivien.

Herlie would repeat her role of Gertrude in the 1964 film production of *Hamlet* starring Richard Burton.

Larry was careful in his stage costumes, rejecting three outfits until he settled on a timeless doublet and hosiery for the dashing young prince.

In his capacity as the film's producer, Larry hired William Walton to create the music and Roger Furse to design the sets, as they had done for him in *Henry V*.

Larry had developed a feud "with those Technicolor sons of bitches" during the making of *Henry V*, so he determined that *Hamlet* would be shot in black and white. "I will never do a bloody film again with those Technicolor assholes," Larry claimed.

"We're not going to make a film as long as *Gone With the Wind*," Larry told Vivien. "I will cut the Bard's text." He set to work at once, simplifying the plot and killing off such famous characters as Rosencrantz and Guildenstern, even Fortinbras, the Prince of Norway.

Harcourt Williams, a member of The Old Vic, called Larry a "curious blend of humility and arrogance, seriousness and comicality. At the board of governors, he would be as somber as a funeral director, and only five minutes later he'd be telling the most ribald of stories."

Ignoring Rank's commands, Larry played up the Oedipal overtones of Shakespeare's drama by having Hamlet kiss his mother lovingly on the lips. This certainly attracted the attention of the critics, including film scholar Jack Jorgens. "Hamlet's scenes with the queen in her low-cut gowns are virtually love scenes."

When Richardson heard of this, he said, "The poor dear has always been hung up on his Mummy. He not only calls Vivien Mummy on occasion, but once told me he'd much rather be her son than her husband."

Cast member Peter Cushing always remembered Larry's aggressive directorial style in *Hamlet*. During the course of the filming, he lost three of his front teeth because of abscess poisoning. Back on the set with false teeth, his speech was altered somewhat.

Larry immediately noticed that. "You are afraid of spitting at people," Larry said to Cushing. "I had the same problem with Merle Oberon when we were filming *Wuthering Heights*. Drown me! It will be a glorious death so long as we can hear what you're saying."

Larry stuck his face three inches from Cushing's lips and demanded he deliver his lines.

Cushing recalled that after that encounter, the problems of shooting *Hamlet* increased. "Larry became a bloody dictator. He had no patience with us if we didn't get it right the first time. At one point when I questioned him, he snapped back at me, 'Do it my way, goddamnit! Don't you dare argue with me.'"

Although Del Giudice had been Hamlet's guardian angel, Rank sacked him before shooting ended. As one writer put it, "Never again was the cocky little Italian to pull a cinematic rabbit from his Borsolino. He retreated to a Roman monastery where he died a forgotten figure."

In an interview with Margaret Gardner, writing for *Screen Guide*, Larry said: "I think I will not get through *Hamlet* alive. First I fell off a rostrum and injured my leg. Just when that was beginning to heal, a certain dolly rode over my foot, and after I had let out a yell of pain—with some justification, I believe—the cameraman got so flustered, he backtracked again over the same foot, and I ended up in bed for a week. Two broken bones. To complete my bad luck cycle, I was stabbed in a dueling scene."

He was referring to a rehearsal with Morgan involving a dueling scene. He'd instructed him to show more rage in battle with him, and had directed Morgan to point the sword directly at his face. Larry promised that he'd jump back in time. Distracted, he forgot his timing, and Morgan plunged the sword directly at him, almost putting out his right eye. He didn't blame Morgan, however, since the young actor did exactly what he'd told him to do.

During the filming, Larry was surrounded by three handsome young actors on the set who each adored him. His assistant was Anthony Bushell, an Oxford-educated actor who also appeared in an uncredited bit part. Larry cast Anthony Quayle as Marcellus and Morgan as Laertes, son of Polonius.

"Larry spent more time in his dressing room at various times with those lovely boys than he did with the rest of the cast—that is, except for Simmons," Herlie said. "He adored her. I decided that Larry was nothing but a hound dog in heat."

"He might no longer be king of his castle at Notley, but he was king on the set of *Hamlet*," Herlie said. "He ran the show, and all the actors were anxious to do his bidding."

Basil Sydney, who appeared memorably as Claudius in the film, agreed with Herlie. During the production, he made several nasty cracks to other cast members about Larry's alleged "philandering." Perhaps Sydney was jealous; after all, he'd played the title role of *Hamlet* way back in 1923.

"I think a lot of this whoring around had everything to do with Larry turning forty," Noël Coward said. "It does that to men, you know, even a stately old sod like me."

"What's the matter with me?" Larry asked Richardson who dropped in on the set for a visit. "I have a beautiful but temperamental wife and critical acclaim throughout the world. I'm appearing in a major production and surrounded by young actors who think I'm the greatest thing since V-E Day. But I'm miserable. Why?"

"Old cockie," Richardson said, "your trouble is that you haven't been knighted by the King like I have. When that day comes, all your problems will vanish. I've always called you Laurence. But if you're knighted, I promise to address you on all occasions as Sir Laurence, and I'll drop the old cockie bit."

Larry's saga of the two Tonys who adored him: (*top photo*) Larry's theatrical assistant, Anthony Bushell, and (*lower photo*) Anthony Quayle, cast as Marcellus to Olivier's Hamlet

***

Vivien had passed the summer of 1946 in a kind of tranquil state, but as she later confessed to Richardson, "The summer of 1947 was a time of great turbulence for me. I feel I'm in the twilight of my life. I had a

531

vision the other night of my upcoming death. I am going to die in the summer of 1955."

Larry was consumed by guilt, especially when she accused him of "driving me mad" for not letting her play Ophelia. Without her knowing it, he went behind her back and persuaded Korda to offer Vivien the lead in Leo Tolstoy's *Anna Karenina*.

Richardson had already signed to play Count Karenin. Korda agreed but was frank when he told Larry, "Neither Ralph nor Vivien is suited for their roles."

Korda's original plan was to cast Larry as Count Vronsky. Vivien later admitted, "With Larry at my side, we could have made a great film."

At first, she bitterly rejected the offer. "Like bloody hell, I'll play *Anna Karenina*. Every critic in the world will compare me to Greta Garbo's performance." Garbo had filmed *Anna Karenina* in 1935.

It took a lot of persuading on Larry's part before Vivien accepted the role. She owed Korda a picture. Filming was set to begin in May of 1947 at Shepperton Studios in Surrey. Larry was already underway with *Hamlet* being shot at Denham Film Studios, in Buckinghamshire.

When Vivien first read the script of *Anna Karenina*, she impishly said to Korda, "Do you think I would be believable as a woman who leaves her dull husband and child to run off and launch an affair with a dashing, handsome young man?"

Korda had contracted Cecil Beaton for the design of Vivien's elaborate costumes for the film. "We went together to Paris to shop for fabrics which had come on the market," he said. "She objected to almost every one of my selections, finally caving in. I've never known her to be so irascible."

"Most of her rage was directed at Larry," Beaton said, claiming that she'd kicked him out of her bed.

"He's crawling between the covers of virtually every actor on the set of *Hamlet*, and also that teen tart, Jean Simmons," Vivien said.

"Could you name these gentlemen for me?" the gossipy Beaton asked her.

Two views of Vivien Leigh in *Anna Karenina*.
(*top photo* with Kieron Moore as Count Vronsky)

"I can and I will," she said, "Terry Morgan. Quayle. Bushell, those two Tonys. He's seducing more people who work for him than Darryl F. Zanuck in Hollywood. His next movie should be *Caligula*."

"He's just going through a middle-aged crisis," Beaton assured her. "Men do that around the time they turn forty. It's not the sex. He just wants to prove to himself that he's still alluring to either gender—that's all. When he gets that out of his system, he'll come running back to you."

"I can't wait," she said sarcastically.

Depending on her mood, Vivien on some days claimed she desperately wanted Larry to come back to her. On other days, she said, "Frankly, dear, I don't give a damn."

As Vivien "became more of a harridan" [Larry's words], he stopped coming back home to her. He slept over at Denham, often with one of the handsome young actors on *Hamlet*.

She placed so many harassing phone calls to him at all hours of the morning that he switched off his phone at Denham and wouldn't speak to her for days at a time. "Her idea of loving is suffocation," he told Morgan. "I do not find her sexually exciting. I want my freedom. "I once thought of Notley Abbey as my refuge from the cares of the world. Now I find that my work is a refuge from Notley. Sometimes I dread entering the grounds of that ghostly old place."

Vivien continued to entertain at Notley. On some occasions, Larry would show up. Perhaps to infuriate him, one night she invited Stewart Granger, Jean Simmons, Terry Morgan, Tony Bushell, and Tony Quayle, all to the same party. She also called Robert Helpmann and asked him to "come by to give me moral support."

"Sometimes Viv was the perfect lady, the perfect hostess," said Helpmann. "But, like me, she had a ribald side. When Vivien and Quayle were sitting at the piano at Notley, singing scatological songs, I noticed that she was actually feeling his crotch."

Playing her lover in *Anna Karenina* was Kieron Moore, who at the age of twenty-two was "hailed as the most promising young actor in British films."

She was introduced to Moore, who ironically had made his London stage debut as Heathcliff in a production of *Wuthering Heights*.

The director, Julien Duvivier, later claimed that Vivien and Moore had an affair. But after two weeks, his fling with Vivien came to an end. He also felt he was failing in the role of Count Vronsky and at one point asked Korda if he could be replaced in the role. The producer rejected "such an outlandish request."

"As Vivien was filming *Anna Karenina*, I think she went over the edge," said Bea Lillie. "Not only had she lost the roles of Ophelia and Roxanne, she

533

met only indifference from Larry. He was attracting more handsome young men than she was. And then there was that brief fling he had with that teenager . . . that Jean Simmons. Larry was an old man trying to recapture his youth. Darling Viv felt rejected by the world and betrayed by Larry. She would never really forgive him."

When her new friend, Margaret Leighton, called on her on the set of *Anna Karenina*, Vivien sobbed in her arms. "He's abandoned me for all his other lovers."

Gertrude came to comfort her, and Vivien broke down and couldn't finish the shoot for the day. "Something terrible is happening to me. I know it," Vivien said. "There is no turning back. I can't tell you the spells that overcome me. I wander the streets. I do unspeakable things."

Sobbing, Gertrude begged her to seek both medical and psychiatric help.

"Never! Never!" Vivien shouted at her mother. "Now get out. I don't want you here."

On the set of *Anna Karenina*, Vivien was in a nervous state, locked into a feud with director Julien Duvivier. "The man is a total asshole," she told Beaton, who was handling costumes for the film. "His direction is moronic."

"Vivien didn't like anything," Beaton recalled. "She even attacked me for the elegant gloves I'd selected for her, claiming they were too small. I shot back, 'The gloves were designed for a woman, not someone with the paws of a grizzly bear.'"

Duvivier, a French director who had made *Pépé Le Moko* with Jean Gabin, claimed that Vivien was not listening or following his directions, because she was tuned to Larry, who was privately directing her.

"Duvivier and I hated each other on sight," she told Larry. "You will have to direct me through the film at night, the way George guided me through my role as Scarlett O'Hara."

Later, Beaton's friendship with Vivien almost ended when she learned that he was in constant touch with Garbo, who wanted to know how this newer version of *Anna Karenina* was going. After sitting through the rushes, he assured Garbo that Vivien "was absolutely horrid" in the film.

As the filming progressed, Beaton softened his position, claiming that Vivien's Anna "is sympathetic and has great character and style. Vronsky is a disaster. Where is Larry now that we need him?"

Another offer came in from MGM to cast Vivien in *Young Bess*. She confronted Larry with the news. "At least Hollywood thinks I'm perfect to play *Young Bess*."

He later read the cable and pointed out to her that she was being offered the role of the mature Queen Catherine, not the title role. Ironically when the film was later made in 1953, Deborah Kerr was cast as Catherine. The role of

"Young Bess" went to Jean Simmons, Larry's Ophelia.

One afternoon, an unexpected call came in from Larry at the very moment Vivien was feuding with her director.

She picked up the phone to hear him say, "From now on, your Ladyship, you can refer to me as Sir Laurence."

***

In his diary, on July 8, 1947, Larry had made this notation: "Buckingham Palace, 10:15." Underneath he'd drawn a picture of a sword. This was the day he was to be knighted.

He'd spent most of the night with Anthony Bushell, his assistant.

In fact, as he made his way to the palace, he was attired in Bushell's braid-trimmed morning coat. Richardson had lent him his waistcoat. "I'm going to be the blondest knight in the realm," he told Bushell.

The youngest actor to be so honored, Larry was to become a "Knight Bachelor of the Empire." A precedent had already been established by thespian Henry Irving who, in 1895, was the first British actor to be knighted, "for services to the stage."

Larry's bisexuality, apparently well known to the royal family, did not prevent him from being granted the honor of knighthood.

Coward had told Larry, "I would have long ago been knighted had I not been a homosexual." He was later knighted, but he was practically on his deathbed when that belated honor occurred.

Not only Coward was denied a knighthood because of his homosexuality, so was John Gielgud. After he received the honor, Larry wrote Gielgud a personal note, apologizing that he had been knighted and Gielgud had not. "You of all actors are a Knight of the Theatre if not of the Realm." Like Coward, Gielgud was also knighted later on.

Bubbling with joy, pretend or otherwise, Beaton barged into Vivien's dressing room the day before Larry was to be knighted. "I told her how thrilled I was at Sir Laurence's good fortune. Staring back at me in the mirror was a face of fury. The next day she didn't even want to go to Buckingham Palace for the honors, but Korda shut down the set and insisted that she go."

Larry had practically a nervous breakdown when Sir Ralph Richardson had been knighted, and he was overlooked.

Morgan later claimed that "Larry acted violently, practically destroying his dressing room when he learned that Richardson had been knighted and now must be addressed as Sir Ralph. In desperation, Larry fell on the floor sobbing."

"I should have been the fucking knight!" Larry had shouted angrily.

He later learned that his divorce from Jill Esmond and his remarriage to Vivien had damaged his selection as a candidate on the "Honours List."

Larry later said, "Deeply fond of Ralphie as I was, I was unable to stop the cracked record from grinding around in my head: I've done every bit as much as he has; look how I've carried the flag abroad, the American road, Hollywood pictures, and an even fuller record in the classics, *and* there was a little film called *Henry V*. If only we could have been done together, that would have been fine."

When the press had asked Larry's dresser why his boss was overlooked, he said, "My guv'nor would never accept a knighthood. He'd only take something bigger!"

Larry later told Vivien, "The King doesn't like me, and the silly old Queen Mother is crazy about Ralphie. She's told everybody. 'I positively adored him in *Q Planes*.' No mention of my performance, of course. You know, she was born with a tail. The doctor had to clip it off."

Although still chilly to Larry because of the loss of the Ophelia role, Vivien dressed simply for Larry's ceremony, appearing in "that little black dress" popularized by Coco Chanel. She decided not to wear jewelry. "With a face as beautiful as mine, adored around the globe, why should I adorn the lily?"

"Oh, my God, I saw her in stark black with no adornment when she was leaving for the palace," Beaton claimed. "She looked like she was dressed for the funeral of an only child. I begged her to wear jewelry but she dismissed me."

At the end of the ceremony at the palace, Vivien sourly informed Larry, "I think granting knighthoods is an anachronistic and ridiculous tradition. After all, this is the 20th century."

She left the palace arm in arm with him, for the benefit of the photographers. "I must skip lunch today," she told him. "I'm due on the set." She was referring to *Anna Karenina*.

He knew that wasn't true because he'd talked to Korda that morning, and he'd closed down the film for the day. He didn't bother to ask Vivien where she was going that afternoon.

Beaton attended a dinner party celebrating Larry's investiture. Richardson, Korda, and, of course, Vivien were also guests. "Vivien seemed to hold a grudge against Larry," Beaton claimed. "He'd become a Knight, and she had not become a Dame."

In the middle of the dinner, she abruptly stood up. "Bloody hell! Lady Olivier is no fucking lady." Without announcing where she was going, she left the building.

When Larry departed for the studio the next morning, she still hadn't come home. He called Korda and learned she'd already reported for work. "But we can't shoot her face today. She looks haggard."

***

"My fondness for Mr. Kieron Moore lasted no longer than frozen ice cream in an oven," Vivien told Julien Duvivier. As the weeks progressed, she grew increasingly impatient with Moore's acting.

By the time they sat with Korda before her first-time view of the first cut of *Anna Karenina*, she was polite but hardly familiar. At the end of the screening, she bluntly told Moore, "You lack the charisma or drive for top stardom. Only a few of us can pull that off."

Moore, who died in France in 2007, later claimed, "Those were the most devastating words ever spoken to me, though probably true." Interviewed shortly before his death, he said, "Isn't it ironic? I'm remembered more for my biggest failure, *Anna Karenina*, than for anything else."

Vivien was one of the most adept people in London's theatrical world at hiding her true feelings, but at times, it appeared she had no control over her emotions and her fierce honesty would burst forth, although she never liked to cause pain to anyone.

"The premiere was a disaster," Moore recalled. "I knew I was going to my own hanging. Vivien didn't fare much better. She later said, 'That bastard Richardson. He stole the picture out from under us.'"

For the most part, *Anna Karenina* opened to bad critiques in both Britain and America. Many reviewers found Vivien's performance "lifeless." Her prediction came true. Nearly every reviewer cited Garbo's "superior and most sensitive" 1935 performance in the same role.

When she found out that Larry had gotten the part for her, she lashed into him. "You knew I'd fail in the role, you dirty bastard. You did this to sabotage me. You want me to fail so you can be Sir Larry, greatest actor on the planet."

She completely exploded when Larry, over a morning cup of tea, read James Agate's appraisal of *Hamlet* in *Time* magazine. "In its subtlety, variety, vividness, and control, Olivier's performance is one of the most beautiful ever put on film."

On hearing this, she shouted at him, "You ham!" She picked up her cup of tea and tossed it at him. Fortunately, it had cooled and didn't burn his face. She ran upstairs to her room and locked herself in for the rest of the day and night.

After all the cuts and the inevitable fights with Rank, the final running time for *Hamlet* was two hours, thirty-five minutes, though Rank would have preferred only two hours.

A very lovely young princess, Elizabeth, saw both *Hamlet* and *Anna*

537

Karenina while accompanied by her dashing, handsome new prince, Philip. She was overheard telling two of her aides, "*Hamlet* was as thrilling a moment on the screen as *Anna Karenina* was a disappointment."

Larry was 41 when *Hamlet* was released, Herlie only 28, but makeup had aged her enough to be believable as his mother.

He became the first actor to ever direct himself in an Oscar-winning performance, and *Hamlet* became the first non-American film to win the Oscar for Best Picture.

He did not win an Academy Award for Best Director, the Oscar going to John Huston for *The Treasure of Sierra Madre*. Ronald Reagan remained "forever furious" that he did not get cast in the Sierra Madre film.

Regardless of the era, there is always an embarrassment on Oscar night, and this time the focus was on Ethel Barrymore. Without knowing the final results, the Academy committee had assumed that Larry would win the Oscar for Best Actor. Ethel was selected because her brother, John Barrymore, had played *Hamlet* in 1922 in a memorable performance.

Prior to the presentation, Ethel had told a journalist, "I saw Olivier's *Hamlet*, and I didn't like it. It's a shaved down version, badly cut, with some of the memorable speeches removed. Jack was so much better. His performance remains the definitive one. Olivier struggled up the mountain but fell off before reaching the top."

On the night of the awards, when Ethel announced the Oscar winner, she was visibly shaken and did not completely conceal her disappointment, although as a consummate actress, she could have if she'd chosen to. Ethel was enraged that Larry had cut out the characters of Rosencrantz and Guildenstern. She shocked audiences at the end of her announcement, saying, "I didn't sound *too* Sonny Tufts, did I?"

The reference was to a notorious radio incident when the MC was handed the names of his "distinguished" guests for the program. In bewildered disbelief, he loudly and questioningly exclaimed, "*SONNY TUFTS?!?*"

Larry treasured a telegraphed review of *Hamlet* from Richardson. OLD COCKIE, YOU SHOWED US MORTALS HOW HAMLET SHOULD BE PLAYED.

Larry had recorded his own speech patterns as the voice of Hamlet's father and then played the recording back at a reduced speed. This gave the ghostly voice its macabre quality.

In America, many critics attributed the voice of the ghost to John Gielgud. Larry did sound a bit like his longtime rival.

He didn't want to appear in any more Shakespeare plays with Gielgud. However, Gielgud was allowed to play the ghost in productions of *Hamlet* with Richard Burton and Richard Chamberlain.

Because he was tied up with a commitment to perform in London in a play with Vivien, Larry did not attend the Academy Award presentations, in which he won for Best Picture and Best Actor.

"With the omissions, the mutilations, the mistakes, this is very likely the most exciting and most alive production of *Hamlet* you will ever see on the screen," wrote Pauline Kael.

The movie even today is shown in film studies courses. One scholar, J. Lawrence Guntner, claimed that its style "owes much to German Expressionism and to *film noir*: the cavernous sets featuring narrow winding stairwells correspond to the labyrinths of Hamlet's psyche."

Not all critics came to worship at Larry's princely throne. In New York, John Mason Brown wrote, "To sacrifice great language, to have innuendo dispensed with, and to lose key characters, speeches, and scenes merely because so much time is wasted getting the actors from one part of the castle to another, is to be a *Hamlet* dislocated by being on location."

"He doesn't look young. He looks like a middle-aged man with a furrowed brow and a Jean Harlow dye job," wrote one reviewer in Los Angeles.

Two weeks after Larry won the Oscar, Vivien was still filled with despair over the public reception of *Anna Karenina*. "Now that Larry is the most celebrated person on earth," she told Morgan, "I feel I've been reduced to consort status."

He tried to reassure her, predicting that in her next film she, too, would "carry home an Oscar as a companion to keep Scarlett O'Hara company."

***

Back in Hollywood, Samuel Goldwyn released Danny Kaye's latest film, *A Song Is Born*, to lackluster business. The movie garnered only $2.4 million at the box office, and Goldwyn told co-star Virginia Mayo, "I don't plan to renew the pansy's contract."

"He's so talented," Mayo said. "One would think that audiences would want to flock to his movies. Why not?"

"Because nobody wants to fuck Danny Kaye."

Goldwyn's assessment of Kaye's sex appeal would be exploded the moment the comedian's plane set down in London.

GREAT MOMENTS IN THE BRITISH THEATRE

An advertisement for the lineup of plays presented by the Old Vic Theatre Company during its 1945-1946 Season

540

Chapter Fourteen

In 1948, Val Parnell, a fast-talking carnival spieler in Savile Row finery, booked the American comedian, Danny Kaye, into London's Palladium, the greatest variety theater in the world. At the time, it was one of the biggest gigs of Kaye's career. Kaye had broken from his wife Sylvia and was struggling to make it on his own without her show business savvy.

"Mickey Rooney was a bust at the Palladium," Parnell had told Kaye. Let's see if London is ready for you the second time around."

From America, Kaye cabled Larry that he was on his way and that he'd be appearing, beginning February 2, 1948, as part of a six-week engagement. He'd be on stage with the Skyrockets Orchestra conducted by Woolf Phillips.

Other stars who eventually followed Kaye to this vast theater on Argyll Street for gigs of their own included Judy Garland, campy Carmen Miranda, and emotionally troubled Betty Hutton. The king and his royal family visited once a year for a Command Performance.

Installed in a suite at the Savoy, Kaye immediately telephoned Larry. "Sir Laurence, I'm back."

"Your shining knight is on his way there," Larry told him.

At their reunion, Kaye rushed into Larry's arms, pouring out his fear of the London opening, his breakup (once again) with his wife Sylvia, and his departure from the studios of Samuel Goldwyn. Larry, too, poured out his problems, including financial woes. He also admitted his failure as a husband. "I'm not the man she wants me to be."

Both men took comfort in each other. "We bonded," Kaye once said, "as never before. We both pledged it would be a lifetime commitment."

There was no recording device to fully inform us about what transpired when Larry entered Kaye's suite, where he would remain for a long weekend. A room service waiter the next morning reported being received by Kaye in his underwear who called to Larry within the suite's bedroom to "come and get it."

Larry was with Kaye on opening night at the Palladium, reassuring him at every turn. "I came near to having a nervous breakdown," Kaye later admitted. "Larry was my rock."

The morning papers raved about Kaye, calling him everything from a superb artist to "a sort of schizoid kid who appeals to the lunatic fringe in all of us." During the days and nights that followed, Danny Kaye fever swept over London. He was like a contagious disease. His act was an astonishing success.

After seeing Kaye perform, Larry told a journalist. "Only two minutes into his act, Danny exploded that myth that Londoners have tired of the personal appearances of Hollywood stars. It's true that Rooney didn't connect with our audiences over here, but Danny did. To me, he is the most exciting, the most vital, and the most entertaining of any performer in London today."

Larry never tired of seeing his lover perform his Tchaikovsky showstopper, which he'd premiered back in 1941 in the Broadway hit, *Lady in the Dark*. In just thirty-eight seconds, Kaye could rattle off the clearly enunciated names of fifty-four Russian composers, a verbal tongue twister no one could equal.

One night after Kaye's show at the Palladium, Larry was in the star's dressing room as he was changing into his street clothes in preparation for leaving. There was a knock on the door although Kaye had told the stage manager he would receive no visitors in the dressing room, only backstage.

With a sense of anger, Larry opened the door to discover the cigar-puffing Great Man himself, Winston Churchill, who was then the leader of His Majesty's Opposition. "A Knight of the Realm," Churchill said to Larry, entering without being invited. He'd come to congratulate Kaye on his show. "It seems you're the most popular man in Britain. I fear one day you'll run against me for some office. No doubt prime minister when I make my comeback."

During their brief chat, with Larry listening in, Churchill told Kaye that he was "going to steal one or two of your bits—as show people say—for my own act. I studied your act very carefully, and there are a couple of things I could use to enhance my own performance. None of the zany stuff but catch my 'act' the next time I speak. That turning your back to the audience and then turning around again and pausing before you spoke," Churchill said. "You could have heard a pin drop. You had the audience spellbound. Everyone was anxious to see what you were going to say or do next."

"I heard you visited my dear friend Franklin just a few short years ago," Churchill said to Kaye, referring, of course, to the late U.S. President Franklin D. Roosevelt. "And what did you teach him? Poor man, I miss him so."

"This sounds insane but I crawled around his wheelchair and succeeded in getting him to bark like a dog," Kaye said. "He wanted to talk to his dog Fala."

After thanking Kaye once more and congratulating Larry on his recent honor, the fabled WWII leader departed.

Churchill was not alone in visiting Kaye's dressing room. Even members of the royal family showed up. Kaye's most loyal fan was Princess Margaret, then only seventeen years old. She went time and time again to see his show, going backstage to congratulate him personally.

She even brought her sister, Princess Elizabeth, to see the show. On February 26, 1948, King George VI and his wife, Queen Elizabeth, showed up with Princess Elizabeth and her husband, Prince Philip, whom she'd married less than a year before.

Princess Margaret was completely mesmerized by Kaye, finding "his zanyish antics like something from another world. She sang his songs, mimicked his patter, and even imitated his dance steps," said her biographer, Theo Aronson.

Breaking with protocol, Princess Margaret even invited Kaye to dinner at Buckingham Palace. She also invited Kaye, accompanied by Larry, to Clarence House where they were surprised to encounter Prince Philip. The future Queen of England presumably was home in bed. Vivien was not invited.

"We sat on the floor, even Princess Margaret and the Duke of Edinburgh, drinking champagne all night and listening to phonograph records until five in the morning," Larry said. He was shocked to hear Kaye calling Margaret "honey."

A Kaye/Margaret romance was whispered about. In the book *Elizabeth and Philip*, authors Charles Higham and Roy Moseley claimed that "Princess Margaret became romantically attached to Kaye, fascinated by his copper hair, handsome face, and lithe figure. At first, the King and Queen were amused by the friendship, and charmed by it."

When his wife, Sylvia, made up with Kaye and came to London, she was amazed at how much he knew about meeting royalty. "He instructed me to curtsy first and then to talk, when meeting royalty," said Sylvia. "He also told me who should be addressed as 'Ma'am' or 'Your Royal Highness.' When I asked him how he'd learned all that, he told me from Larry—he's a knight, you know. From

Two views of HRH Princess Margaret Rose of York (aka Princess Margaret, Countess of Snowdon) (1930-2002; Rest in Peace)

now on, I want you to address him as Sir Laurence."

"Like hell I will," Sylvia said. "When I see him again, I'll come up to him and say, 'Larry, how's it hanging, kid?'"

"You're a Jew; you're short; you're too bosomy, and you've got a long nose and protruding ears," Kaye told her. "I don't think I can take a low-rent gal from New York's Bowery to Buckingham Palace."

Even though Sylvia was back guiding Kaye's career, rumors still circulated throughout London society that Britain's teenage Princess Margaret had fallen hopelessly in love with an American entertainer twice her age.

Since Larry was seen late at night with both Kaye and Princess Margaret, the most scurrilous rumor was that they were involved in a *ménage à trois*. Though widely gossiped about at the time, this rumor has never been proven one way or the other. Vivien, however, believed it was true and repeated the accusation to Peter Finch, Margaret Leighton, and Noël Coward, among others.

"I loved Vivien dearly, but she gained no sympathy telling people that Larry was cheating on her with Kaye and, horror of horrors, with Princess Margaret herself," Coward said. "Precious Viv was locked in a deep affair with Peter Finch, so she kept her own nights busy even if Larry didn't come home."

Kaye and Margaret were seen dancing together late at night. Their romance became so public that the Lord Chamberlain's office became involved. He demanded that a line, "Even Princess Margaret goes out with Danny Kaye" be censored in the London production of *Call Me Madam*.

As if a three-way wasn't salacious enough, Cecil Beaton compounded the rumors by reporting that Princess Margaret, Danny Kaye, Larry, and John

Photographer, set desinger, and major-league gossip Cecil Beaton

Profumo were having orgies at night. According to Beaton, it took all three men to satisfy the princess.

Beaton spread this rumor when he saw Profumo, Kaye, Larry, and Princess Margaret dining in London at the Café de Paris, sharing champagne, caviar, and dancing late at night. The Princess was also having an affair with Profumo, the rich descendant of a Lombard banking family and a rising star in the Conservative Party. He would later be involved in a sex scandal that "shook the British Empire."

The bisexual Kaye also launched an affair with Princess Marina, Duchess of Kent, the widow of the Duke of Kent who had been

544

Larry's lover.

When he wasn't staying with Larry and Vivien at Notley Abbey, Kaye was with Princess Marina at Coppins, the former Buckinghamshire farmhouse that the Duke of Kent had inherited from his aunt, Princess Victoria. *[Editor's note: Princess Victoria (1840 – 1901) was the eldest child of Queen Victoria of the United Kingdom and Prince Albert of Saxe-Coburg and Gotha.]*

Princess Margaret and Princess Marina, according to rumors, were said to have had a "catfight" over Kaye.

"This little stand-up comic was in his glorious heyday in 1948," Noël Coward later told Anne Baxter. "Here he was with England's greatest actor and two royal princesses vying for his off-stage attention, and tickets hard to come by at the Palladium for each and every one of his performances."

Gradually, Princess Margaret's continued interest in Kaye disturbed her parents. "There was something grotesquely improbable in the thought that she might even want to marry him," claimed Higham and Moseley in their biography on the royal family. "The entire matter threatened to erupt into a scandal."

Buckingham Palace made it clear that "Princess Margaret's prince was going to remain a frog."

It took Princess Margaret three years to break off her relationship with Kaye. Palace insiders claimed that the Kaye/Margaret Rose romance was such an unlikely mating that it wasn't to be taken too seriously. Even Princess Elizabeth allegedly said, "It's a mere infatuation."

When Margaret's parents, King George VI and his Queen, began to hear reports about the intimate nature of the relationship, the Queen ordered Margaret to end her friendship.

Buckingham Palace announced that Princess Margaret was leaving on a tour of the continent. It was hoped that this would squelch rumors about Kaye and her. The palace also privately "invited" Kaye not to make any more public visits to London.

Kaye might not be able to visit Buckingham Palace, but the door to Notley Abbey was always open to him, much to Vivien's regret.

"He comes and goes whenever he wants to," Vivien told Noël Coward. "He doesn't even ring up. He just appears on the doorstep. At least when Kaye's in town, Larry is forced to give up his male harem."

On a visit to Notley, Coward had a chance to observe Kaye with Larry. "The two of them are stand-up comedians, Larry trying to outdo Kaye as a comedian. At one luncheon, Larry actually took a cheesecake and smashed it into his own face. At night we were entertained by the road show act of 'Danny & Larry.' I told them they should take their act on a motor trip through the provinces."

The renewal of Larry's romance with Kaye was short lived. Vivien and Larry were joining the Old Vic Theatre Company on a tour "Down Under," with months-long stage shows scheduled in Australia and New Zealand.

At Durham Cottage in London, just before their departure, Kaye hosted the final farewell buffet supper for Larry and the newly designated Lady Olivier.

To keep Larry in her life, Vivien was learning to tolerate Kaye. She later told Margaret Leighton, "Larry and I had been feuding for weeks, but we decided to make up. Kaye was our house guest. Larry insisted he sleep in one of the guest bedrooms. After making love, Larry and I went to sleep together in the nude, of course."

"When I woke up the next morning, I found a nude Kaye in bed with us. We certainly didn't have a three-way that morning. I rose and reached for my robe. With what dignity I could manage, I asked him when he wanted his breakfast. Larry was sleeping peacefully. God knows what happened between them when I went downstairs."

She admitted that Larry and Kaye spent the rest of the afternoon together, the comedian seeking advice on how to present himself at the Palladium. "I remember his exact words," Vivien said.

"I want to be less Jewish on stage," Kaye told Larry. "Let's face it: Londoners don't like Jews. But, then, in all fairness, who in the world does? I want to be a white one in spite of my Jewishness."

"But, dear boy," Larry told him, "I love the Jews. Always have, always will."

"Did Kaye actually use the words 'a white one?'" Leighton asked.

"Those were his exact words," Vivien said. "Perhaps Larry can get directions from Kaye if he ever decides to play Shylock on stage."

At Durham Cottage that final night, Kaye cooked most of the dishes himself, revealing he was a master of Chinese cuisine. He not only was a great chef but afterward Kaye entertained the event's 70 or so guests who included Ralph Richardson and Noël Coward.

At the end of the evening, Larry excused himself to accompany Kaye back to the hotel in his Rolls-Royce. "Don't wait up for me," Larry warned Vivien.

"Lala [Kaye's nickname for Larry] and I might have a nightcap," Kaye said.

Larry arrived back at Durham Cottage as dawn was breaking over London.

The love lives of Laurence Olivier, Danny Kaye, and Vivien Leigh were complicated enough in London, but before 1948 came to an end they would be the subject of worldwide scandalous gossip, most of it true.

***

For the Old Vic, Vivien and Larry agreed to embark on the most ambitious tour of their lives, bringing three plays to Down Under. They included *The School for Scandal, Richard III,* and *The Skin of Our Teeth.*

The British Council announced that the Old Vic was sponsoring the tour as a gesture to show Commonwealth unity in the post-war years. An unannounced motive was also to make some much-needed money. Before the tour of Australia and New Zealand came to an end, Vivien and Larry would travel 30,000 miles.

At the time of their embarkation for Australia, Sir Laurence and Lady Olivier were hailed as "Theatre Royals" in Britain, occupying a position claimed in America only by the Barrymores (Ethel, Lionel, and John) and Alfred Lunt and Lynn Fontanne.

In front of popping flashbulbs and movie news cameras, their sendoff from London's Euston Station was treated like the departure of the King and Queen. Even the station master turned out in a ceremonial top hat and tails.

Departing from Euston Station on Valentine's Day, February 14, 1948, Vivien had her arm entwined with Larry's. "They looked like the perfect lovers," one reporter wrote.

When Larry saw a copy of the article, he said, "Looks can be deceiving."

On his departure, Samuel Goldwyn cabled Larry: WHY ARE YOU, THE GREATEST ACTOR IN THE WORLD, TAKING A TOURING COMPANY TO AUSTRALIA OF ALL PLACES?"

They docked at Fremantle, Australia on March 14, having sailed aboard the *SS Corinthic* which departed from Liverpool. One reporter asked Larry what he most wanted to see in Australia. "A lake of black swans," he replied.

Terence Morgan and his new wife, Georgina Jumel, went along. Larry and Vivien still expressed "adoration for our Terry," but frankly their fickle interest was about to shift elsewhere, allowing the once sought after young actor to enter into a successful and long-enduring relationship with his wife.

Also on tour, George Relph said, "Viv and Larry returned Terry to Jumel. I always wondered if she knew what had been going on."

Relph's wife, Mercia Swinburne, was also part of the company, as was Peter Cushing and his wife, Helen Beck. Larry called them "My dear boys and girls," paying them fifteen pounds a week when they were in rehearsal and thirty pounds a week when they were performing.

"When they got to Australia, it was as if Princess Elizabeth and Prince Philip had arrived," Relph said. "Viv and Larry were treated like royalty. Their marriage might be falling apart, but the Aussies didn't know that. Sir Laurence

547

and Lady Olivier were fêted wherever they went. Mobs turned out to greet them."

"Regardless of their private conflicts, Larry and Viv kept up appearances through it all," Relph said. "They may have felt like shit but they didn't show it. She was in frail health and mentally unstable. He would also suffer a series of health problems—his throat, his foot, his knee, even a very complicated operation."

They arrived in Perth where Vivien found that the mosquitoes "are flying elephants." Not only that, but she had to face temperatures of 100°F at mid-day. She agreed with travel writer Cynthia Nolan's assessment that Perth was "an overgrown country town . . . grimy, dishevelled, noisy."

The Old Vic troupe opened *The School for Scandal* on March 20 at the Capitol Theatre in Perth, with Larry cast as Sir Peter Teazle with Vivien playing Lady Teazle. In spite of the weather, the entire 2,280-seat theatre was filled to capacity. Under Cecil Beaton's heavily brocaded costumes and period wigs, Sir Peter and Lady Teazle sweated out the performances to thunderous applauses. Larry had selected Sheridan's 18th-century comedy to launch the tour.

All her costumes were by Cecil Beaton, who chose to work in such colors as toad, newt, mushroom, cinnamon, grape, and mustard, with lime green selected for her ball gown.

Beaton's assistant, Marton Battersby, who worked the costumes for Vivien, said, "I have the impression that Lady Olivier has fought hard to climb to the top of the tree and can't stop climbing even when she's reached the pinnacle. A woman of such determination was ideally cast as Scarlett O'Hara."

Sometimes at night in a pub, Larry joined cast members, amusing them with his impersonation of a rather effeminate John Gielgud and even stuttering King George VI, a performance he would not give in England. "The 1-1-1 last time I saw you, you weren't b-b-b-blond."

In Adelaide they had never seen such mass devotion. Some 100 fans at 4am slept out in front of the theater, in spite of a rain storm, so that they would be the first in line to purchase tickets.

Larry had selected an alternating double bill, both *Richard III* and *The Skin of Our Teeth,* great showcases for each of their talents. Suffering one of his worst cases of gout, he tried to be an actor, director, and manager of the troupe, while accepting social engagements and public speaking appearances. In Adelaide, he was forced to walk with a cane.

Night after night, they were besieged by autograph-seeking mobs, one crowd estimated at 8,000. They were buried under an avalanche of fan mail. Everyone seemingly wanted to touch them.

With an exception or two, most of the Old Vic cast members expressed their "love" for Vivien and their "respect" for Sir Laurence.

In Adelaide, cast members began to understand Vivien's personality much better, as related by author Garry O'Connor. "Working from instincts and emotions, she could always switch moods dangerously and unexpectedly. Those who got on with her, or worked with her, while acknowledging her great sense of fun, were always conscious of how carefully they needed to treat her. Suddenly, if she misunderstood something, she could turn and become very frightening. Her expression would harden quite inexplicably, her eyes would change colour."

During an eight-week stay in Melbourne, they performed all three plays even though exhausted from their schedules.

Of course, not all their receptions were enthusiastic. The theater critic for the newspaper in Melbourne claimed, "We have better Richard IIIs right here in Melbourne." In a challenge to that critic, Larry ordered a search and found that there were no professional actors working in Melbourne.

In public Larry seemed overcome "with the glitter of our social position," but in private tensions flared between them. Morgan and his wife Jumel were often assigned rooms next to Larry and Vivien.

"Through cardboard thin walls, we often heard them fighting for hours," Morgan said. "Vivien did most of the haranguing, yet she seemed to be at her most charming when she was in my presence."

In Melbourne, a fan confronted Larry as he was leaving the theater after performing *Richard III*. "Tell me, Sir Laurence. About that stoop of yours. Was it a childhood accident?"

Larry wrote to John Burrell at the Old Vic, claiming he found the locals "piss-elegant and nervously smug at first. As we reach more sophisticated cities such as Melbourne, the fans became progressively less enthusiastic, seemingly inclined to sit back saying, 'All right, then show us.'"

Everyone agreed that Morgan was the handsomest actor in the cast, but he was increasingly involved with his wife Jumel. Vivien's attention turned to another minor actor, Dan Cunningham. Except for public appearances, she was seen more with him than Larry. The other cast members commented on Cunningham's "constant attention to Vivien."

At first Larry viewed Cunningham as Vivien's "frivolity, a harmless infatuation." He told George Relph, "The boy keeps her amused so I can get on with the business of this company."

One day Relph asked Larry, "Do you think Dan is actually shagging her?"

Larry's reply shocked Relph. "Oh well, Vivien deserves a good fuck now and then."

She told Cunningham, who back in London spread the news, that "my love for Larry is doomed. We are merely posing as great lovers, because our public expects it of us. We are actors and it's easy to look adoringly into each other's eyes for the camera. His knighthood has made us an institution. In *Fire Over England*, we were on fire but that was a long time ago. Our fire for each other has drowned in its myth. Larry even had me put up a DO NOT DISTURB sign on my dressing room door to convince the cast he was still fucking me."

He injured his right knee during a savagely realistic duel in *Richard III*, causing harm to his cartilage. More injuries to his leg were to come.

Like royals, in Sydney, Vivien and Larry had to attend dozens of social functions and make public appearances where they were asked to give speeches. Larry told a reporter, "We are but two walking corpses."

Prime Minister Ben Chifley told Vivien that *Gone With the Wind* was his favorite all-time movie. "I personally want to welcome Miss Scarlett O'Hara to Australia."

In a very delicate way, she corrected him. "I'm Lady Olivier now."

One newspaper critic in Sydney admitted that he did not understand *The Skin of Our Teeth* "but the sight of Scarlett O'Hara on stage was really something."

At the second performance of *Richard III* in Sydney, in an episode crucial to the plot, Larry overdid his whip attack on Dan Cunningham's Richmond, perhaps seeking revenge upon the actor for being Vivien's latest infatuation.

In Sydney on July 3, while performing *Richard III*, Larry suffered one of the worst accidents of his accident-prone stage career. He slipped and fell on his right knee, ripping the cartilage and causing "the worst pain of my life." After seeking medical treatment, he performed the rest of his engagement on a crutch using it as a stage prop. Unknown to his audience, he was often on morphine.

"I was forced to wear crutches for my final performances of *Richard III*," Larry said. "When I had to shout, 'My kingdom for a horse!' I feared mocking laughter. But the audience was polite."

One night he lashed out at George Cooper, playing a minor role of Brackenbury, and broke the crutch over the actor's back. In way of apology, he told Cooper backstage, "Great theater demands realism."

On July 15, he received stunning news from Lord Esher, chairman of the Old Vic Governors. Richardson, John Burrell, and Larry himself, he was told, were no longer in control of the Old Vic. The board needed actors who could devote themselves full time to running the Old Vic, unlike Larry and Richardson, who were frequently accepting outside assignments. Richardson was in Hollywood filming *The Heiress* with Olivia de Havilland when he received the news he'd been fired.

Tyrone Guthrie had led the charge against the "tripartite directorship," maintaining that the world was calling the company "Olivier's Old Vic," which was inappropriate for a National Theater. He also said, "It is very, very unwise to have the Old Vic run by two actor-knights," although he did not explain why this was so.

When that letter arrived in July from the Old Vic, Larry faced two performances, both a matinee and evening show of *Richard III*. Although he was devastated by the news, Larry knew that his fans from Down Under had lined up since before dawn to see his appearances that day. "When things go wrong," he said, "it's typical of the body to jump on the bandwagon."

From Hollywood, Richardson cabled Larry: OFF WITH THEIR HEADS!

Burrell's wife, Margaret, later called Guthrie "the rogue elephant who kicked the whole thing down."

In London, Guthrie fired right back at her, claiming, as reported by the press, that "Larry and Ralphie want to have their cake and eat it too. Instead of paying attention to the Old Vic, which is their responsibility, they pursue outside engagements. They are Old Vic actors-managers in name only, in essence, absentee landlords."

Larry called the action of the governors "murder most foul. I sacrificed a fortune by turning down Hollywood movies to work for a shilling or two for the Old Vic."

He protested to the entire troupe of the Old Vic players that the governors of the company treated him "more shabbily than I've ever been handled in my life."

In retaliation, he decided to move forward to present plays under the banner of Laurence Olivier Productions. He told Vivien that he'd recruit and even steal the most talented actors away from Old Vic.

After a series of blistering letters to the governors, he finally won their commitment to a final season in London where he agreed to present *Richard III, The School for Scandal,* and *Antigone.*

Before leaving Sydney, both Larry and Vivien were invited to the Mercury Theatre Club in a glass factory, where plays were presented at lunchtime to the factory workers. All performances were usually packed, although every play had to be condensed down to one hour so that the factory workers could punch the time clock at one that afternoon.

They'd accepted an invitation to see a young actor, Peter Finch, perform as the comic, cunning hero in Molière's *Le Malade Imaginaire.* Larry had sat mesmerized by the performance of the tall, handsome, dark-haired actor and eagerly came backstage to greet the thirty-two year old, whom he found "compelling, especially his penetrating blue eyes, his intelligent and alert responses, and his ruggedly masculine features."

Finch was so honored to meet Larry that he threw his arms around him and kissed him on both cheeks, before apologizing for "getting so carried away."

He reached to shake Vivien's hands. "What?" she said. "No kiss for me." Finch gently kissed both of her porcelain cheeks.

"With the two greatest stars in the world sitting out there watching me, I was a wee bit nervous," Finch told them. "I was afraid I'd forget every line."

"I was witness to that meeting," said a jealous Terence Morgan. "In theatrical circles, it almost became a historical meeting. That opportunistic Aussie fart, Mr. Finch, stood only six inches from Larry's face. I thought he was getting ready to kiss him. Finch was practically rubbing his dick up against Larry. Vivien didn't mind. She seemed to have the hots for this country boy too. It didn't take me long to realize that I just might have been replaced that hot afternoon as the golden boy of the Oliviers."

In Finch, Larry saw a buoyant, devil-may-care kind of rugged individual, whom he would also encounter in Richard Burton. Finch's physical presence was intense, especially by his habit of standing so close you could smell his breath.

Born in London in 1916, Finch was a remarkable young man with an incredible intensity for life and a brilliant talent as an actor. He was the illegitimate son of a Scotsman, Major Wentworth Edward Dallas Campbell, an army officer in the Poona Horse Regiment. Enduring a tumbleweed childhood, young Finch traveled from England to France and on to India before settling in Australia.

He broke into show business as a straight man to a stand-up comedian, and he eventually formed Peter Finch's Mercury Theatre Company, touring Queensland and New South Wales. During World War II, he'd been a gunner in the Australian Army, serving with the North African Troops.

It was easy for Finch's young disciple, Trader Faulkner, to understand his mentor's attraction to Larry. "I'm heterosexual," Faulkner claimed, "but I could see Sir Laurence's enormous attraction for both men and women, a charismatic personality. In his elaborate makeup as *Richard III*, he impressed me as a bluebottle fly in color, but like a scorpion underneath. When he walked about, there was something lethal in his movements. Even off stage he gave the feeling that he wasn't a person to go too near. He created an illusion of physical danger."

Faulkner, who had trained at the Mercury Theatre in Sydney under Finch, also impressed Larry with his acting talent. In 1950 Faulkner moved to London and launched a career in films, theater, and television. Larry hired him in 1955 for a season with Vivien and him at Stratford-upon-Avon.

It has been suggested that Larry was not only sexually attracted to Finch, but somehow in the handsome young actor saw a mirror of himself at the end of the 1930s when he had cut a more dashing, romantic figure.

"I think Larry felt that if he could possess Finch, some of his brashness and virility would wear off on him," said actor Harcourt Williams. "Broken and bent by his health and his increasing problems with Vivien, Larry seemed to turn to Finch as a source to renew his own vitality, in the same way a middle-aged man turns to a younger woman for what's called a renewal."

Like Larry, Vivien was sexually attracted to Finch from the first day they met," said Williams. "No doubt she envisioned him as a strikingly handsome young courtier in her future, far more worldly wise than Terence Morgan."

She told Williams, "Peter has that kind of passion that drew me to Larry back in 1936. There is a lust for life in him that I find most appealing in an actor. He must be a demon in bed."

Many accounts claim that Larry told Finch, "If you ever come to London, look me up."

But the reality was far more intimate than that. Larry and Vivien invited Finch and his wife, Tamara Tchinarova, a Russian ballerina, to dinner after their show. Over a late night supper, they solidified their deal, Larry promising to find work for Finch as an actor in London, either at the Old Vic or in one of his productions.

Tamara was more or less left out of the excitement. She remembered her husband coming together with Larry and Vivien as a "lovefest."

Finch told Larry and Vivien that he had long planned to come to London, along with Tamara, of course, and he eagerly awaited his next reunion with the Oliviers.

Outside the restaurant, a taxi was hailed for Larry and Vivien. Both actors shook Tamara's hand and told her how delighted they were to meet her.

But she couldn't help but notice that both Vivien and Larry gave her husband a rather passionate kiss on the lips.

As he would later recall, "both kisses held out much promise to me," Finch said. "I couldn't wait to get to London and be with them again. But had I not met them, had I not come into their life, so much heartbreak could have been avoided."

***

The Old Vic troupe arrived in Brisbane for its tropical rainy season. Vivien appeared in a Jacmar headscarf inscribed in Afrikaans. She and Larry enjoyed a picnic lunch on Bishop Island and a swim in the warm water.

They invited Morgan and Cunningham to go with them. At a secluded spot, it was Larry who suggested they remove their bathing suits. "Since Sir Laurence was already familiar with the nether regions of Vivien and Terry

Morgan, I think his real desire was to check me out, which he did repeatedly, although he was clever about it, not dwelling too long on my jewels but getting an eye full," claimed Cunningham. "I knew that sooner or later I would end up on his casting couch like so many other hopeful young actors. In the theater, a struggling actor has to do what a struggling actor has to do."

Brisbane wanted to see Larry perform in *Richard III*, but he complained that it was too difficult to transport the props needed to put on a production. Instead he chose to present *The School for Scandal* to local audiences.

Theater critics shot back, claiming that Vivien was "always the hornet, buzzing in and out of her husband's periwig." Another critic lamented that "not once, during the entire performance, did the virile dynamic of Sir Laurence assert itself."

Vivien lost more weight and became more fragile than ever. They had chosen to take the eleven-hour flight to New Zealand aboard a cargo plane carrying the Old Vic scenery. At one point Vivien couldn't breathe, and she was slowly suffocating. The pilot descended to a lower altitude, and his co-pilot fitted her with an oxygen mask which was what she was still wearing when they touched down in Auckland.

In Auckland, Prime Minister Walter Nash asked Larry to address the New Zealand Parliament, although he expected some disturbances from the Maori minority. During his introduction of Larry to the Members of Parliament, Nash said, "When people look at Vivien Leigh, they are inclined to forget her famous husband."

Although stunned by such an introduction, Larry rose to the occasion. "I have become so accustomed to seeing faces falling about three yards when I appear anywhere alone that I am forever reminded of my wife's appeal. But I know how they feel. When I think of Vivien Leigh, I find it impossible to think of anyone else."

When *The School for Scandal* opened in Auckland for seventeen performances, some 33,000 fans viewed it. Although they appreciated the adulation, Vivien and Larry backstage faced declining energy, frayed nerves, and exploding tempers.

Vivien had misplaced the red shoes she wore as Lady Teazle, and told Larry she wouldn't go on that night unless she wore those same shoes. That outrageous demand was more than he could handle. In front of the cast, he slapped her face, real hard. "Go out on that stage, you god damn bitch!" he shouted at her.

She struck him back in the face with all the power her frail body could muster. "Don't you dare hit me again, you fucking bastard!"

"Don't you dare call me a bastard," he shot back at all, raising his voice. He looked around at the astonished cast. "We all know who is one, don't *we*?"

In a pair of black pumps, Vivien, ever the trouper, emerged on stage in a floor-length brocaded gown, compliments of Cecil Beaton, and from all reports delivered a brilliant performance.

As the tour wore on, the ambitious sexual opportunist, Cunningham, later said, "It became increasingly difficult for the Oliviers to keep up an appearance of wedded bliss."

In Christchurch, to present an illusion that "this old married couple was still having hot sex" [Cunningham's words], they created a scandal at the United Services Hotel. The local papers reported that they rejected a room with two single beds in favor of one with a double bed.

One journalist wrote that Larry confirmed this with a "coy blush—'yes, that's what we are old fashioned enough to prefer.'" Standing by his side, Vivien was said to have "purred."

In New Zealand, Larry and Vivien gave forty-nine performances in such towns as Wellington and Dunedin. One local newspaper reporter wrote that "until the arrival of the Oliviers, entertainment in our lovely little country meant sports and watching an American movie."

Larry went on stage one night and gave his smooth performance, but he was in so much pain he could hardly walk. The following morning he consulted with two doctors, who told him he needed immediate surgery.

On October 10, 1948, after their last show in Wellington, he entered the hospital where Dr. Kennedy Elliot removed the ruptured cartilage from his leg.

At long last Larry and Vivien were going home, returning on the *Corinthic* bound for London. Each of them had booked different staterooms.

He could not bend his leg, which was encased in plaster, so he was trussed up in a canvas tarp and swung onto the ship's deck, to the delight of photographers covering their departure.

Vivien Leigh as Cleopatra

"Up, up, and up I soared into the sky, smoothly floating over the side of the ship and gently down, as delicately as if upon an angel's wing. I landed sweetly upon the topmost deck." On the sail back, Larry admitted that "I couldn't offer Vivien much life."

The entire troupe was aware that Dan Cunningham was making frequent visits to Vivien's cabin. In his *Confessions*, Larry wrote, "I pleaded with her not, *please*, to make her flirtation with one young man in the company so obvious to the rest of them; I really couldn't see that it was justified that I should be so humiliated."

While Larry was locked away for most of the journey and often in great pain, Vivien launched a shipboard romance with Yorkshire-born Cunningham. His desire was to become a great classical actor. "I easily succumbed to the charms of Lady Olivier," he later recalled. "A woman that beautiful should not be neglected by her husband, although, admittedly, Sir Laurence was in bad shape."

A member of the Old Vic company, Cunningham had been cast in Jean Anouilh's *Antigone* with Vivien and Larry, which was set to open in London in February of 1949. As he later recalled, "During rehearsals on the ship for *Antigone*, Vivien virtually signaled to Sir Laurence and the rest of the cast that we were having an affair. I wanted to be more discreet, but then I relaxed about it. I figured that any couple who had been married as long as the Oliviers had already worked out a compromise on their sharing of various young men, most often actors. I'd heard all the stories."

One day Sir Laurence invited me to his cabin," Cunningham claimed. "He said he wanted to discuss my career in theater. I felt he really wanted to proposition me, perhaps as an act of revenge against Vivien. But he didn't seem to have the courage, and I wasn't going to make the first move."

Larry continued to have an interest in the young actor, and would cast him in 1955 in the film version of *Richard III*.

During the trip Larry's knee bled painfully and swelled under the cast. The ship's doctor sliced the plaster off and gave him a clean one. Larry had a great fear that gangrene would set in. He told Vivien, "I may spend the rest of my life acting in a wheelchair like Lionel Barrymore."

In his *Confessions*, he wrote: "Somehow, somewhere on this tour, I knew that Vivien was lost to me. I, half jokingly, would say at odd moments after we got back home, 'I *lorst* you in Australia.'"

In *Antigone*, Vivien would play Antigone, Larry was the Chorus, and George Relph played Creon. The supporting cast included Terence Morgan, Cunningham, and Mercia Swinburne. As critic James Agate sarcastically remarked, in private, "at least Vivien knows her three male stars as David knew Bathsheba."

Author Francis Beckett said, "Neither of the Oliviers felt like going through the scandal of another divorce. But sexually, they were bored with each other. She wanted far more sex than he did—she complained rather cuttingly about it, and he reacted by removing himself yet further from her. She also suspected his sexual ambivalence, the amount of time he seemed to want to spend with attractive young men. The intimacy with Vivien was disappearing along with sex, and their conversations were increasingly confined to work. 'We never *converse*,' Olivier confided to a friend, 'we only *confer*.'"

Facing a long, boring, and dreary month at sea, Vivien stayed in her stateroom reading a lot. Her sessions were interrupted any time Cunningham wanted to visit her.

In the middle of the sail, Vivien read a play that Cecil Beaton had sent to her. It was called *A Streetcar Named Desire* by Tennessee Williams, who had scored such a great success on Broadway with *The Glass Menagerie*.

That night she told Larry. "I am Blanche DuBois, and, like that poor wretched soul, I expected to be confined to a mental asylum one day."

At long last, the *Corinthic* docked at Tilbury, in Essex, southeast England, on November 16, 1948. They'd been away for months and had given 180 performances in front of some 300,000 fans.

For their labors, Larry and Vivien had earned 100 pounds a week in salary and came home with a bonus of 5,000 pounds each.

The rest of the cast, including Morgan, received a bonus of 60 pounds. "That hardly covered my expenses," he said to Larry.

"My partnership with Vivien must be preserved regardless of our sexual dalliances," he told Ralph Richardson. "We have worked too long and too hard to establish it. We must put up a public mask to deceive the world."

The post-war London they came home to was being rapidly rebuilt. But it was more than the city that had changed. After that exhausting tour of the Antipodes, Vivien and Larry, along with their legendary marriage, would never be the same again.

The best of their years were behind them.

***

Vivien's infatuation with Cunningham seemed to end the moment their ship reached England. "She soon discarded him," said Harcourt Williams. "Bigger game awaited her. Marlon Brando. Peter Finch. Richard Burton. The sad thing about Vivien was that Sir Laurence often got to these hunks before poor Vivien did."

Back at Durham Cottage they unloaded their Australian cache of boomerangs, aborigines' knives, and stuffed koala bears.

Even though he'd been fired, Larry faced a final six-month season at the Old Vic, after which he'd be dismissed. Back from Australia, Larry fulfilled his final commitment to the Old Vic, staging in London, *Richard III* again, Sophocles' *Antigone*, and *The School for Scandal*, also again.

When it became widely known that his involvement with the Old Vic was coming to an end, he found himself deluged with offers. The first offer presented to him was from the Royal Opera House in Cairo, Egypt, who wanted both Vivien and Larry "to appear in any production, your choice." Intrigued by the proposal, he was forced to reject it. For some reason, he delayed his response to Cairo for an entire month.

"We've had a terrible drubbing here with one thing and another; illness, Vivien very nearly killing herself falling down stairs, my old knee effusing, flu, and God knows what. Vivien and I have been away for the better part of a year and are anxious not to stir again for a time because we got homesick."

The first of the plays to open in London was *The School for Scandal*. "We knew Sheridan's words so well at this point we could recite them backwards," Vivien said.

The School for Scandal marked the first time Larry had ever appeared on the London stage with Vivien. Opening January 20, 1949, their first night was both an artistic and social triumph.

That opening night is still remembered as one of the great social events in English theater, with celebrities being disgorged from their Rolls-Royces, including Sir Ralph Richardson and his wife Meriel Forbes. Margaret Leighton arrived, as did Lady Hardwicke (Sir Cedric was in Hollywood). Honored guests included Richard Attenborough and Sir Alexander Korda.

David Niven showed up with his new wife, Hjördis. Margot Fonteyn arrived on the arm of Robert Helpmann looking ever so gay. Terence Rattigan appeared "with a young friend."

Princess Elizabeth showed up on the arm of Prince Philip, and Princess Margaret was escorted by Lord Porchester.

Le Tout Londres took its seats in the audience as the curtain went up on a glittering production of *The School for Scandal*.

The fans saw not a dashing Romeo but Larry with a "drawn cheek, gray hair, and the frog of age in his throat." In contrast, Vivien was radiantly beautiful in Cecil Beaton's elaborate costumes.

Beaton learned painfully that Sir Laurence and Lady Olivier could extend love but could also withdraw it. Beaton thought his costumes and sets for *The School for Scandal* were the highlight of his career.

He went backstage to praise Vivien on her performance. As he recorded in his diary, "She did not turn around to greet me. I kept up a hollow form of flattery, filled with green room jargon, in praise of her performance and appearance. Vivien's eyes of steel now stared at herself as she rubbed a slime of dirty cold cream, a blending of rouge, eye black, and white foundation over her face. Not one word did she say about my contribution to the evening."

"In Larry's dressing room, I let forth an avalanche of praise but he did not respond."

Beaton spent the rest of his life reviling them and telling indiscreet stories about their private lives. Much of the private life of the Oliviers is known today because Beaton "turned over every stone to learn about their latest scandals to broadcast to everyone in the West End theatrical circles," according to Noël Coward.

Tensions had arisen between the Oliviers and Beaton. At one time Larry said, "The only time he shows up is when he hears a journalist is there with a photographer from one of the papers."

Beaton complained to Garbo that "Olivier, and you of all people have had your problems with *that one*, bombards me with requests for new costumes and alterations to the set."

To Beaton's dismay, the Oliviers never forgave him for being "too busy" to take an active part in *The School for Scandal*. "They are both out of my life forever," wrote Beaton in his diaries, *The Strenuous Years*.

Actually he wrote that just for public consumption. He did meet again for lunch with the Oliviers in April of 1950. The next day, he wrote Garbo once again: "I didn't like her. Oh dear no, she has lost her looks, very fat in the face."

Although Beaton and Larry had once claimed "a rich jewel of friendship," Larry managed to omit Beaton's name from his memoirs.

After seeing *The School for Scandal*, John Gielgud came backstage to congratulate Vivien in her dressing room. Later, all he could remember was "the intoxicating scent, almost funereal, of lilies, roses, tulips, carnations, even black orchids."

Prince Philip invited Larry and Vivien to join his party—which included Princess Margaret and Lord Porchester—at a ring-side table at the Café de Paris for a late supper. Larry and Vivien eagerly accepted, as they were always great "royalists."

Vivien's reviews for *The School for Scandal* in the role of Lady Teazle, which she'd always disliked, were mostly positive. But the words of one critic puzzled her. He called her "negatively perfect."

Leonard Mosley interpreted Vivien' performance as "a little too Scarlett O'Hara." Other critics were more enthusiastic, calling her "a ravishing minx" or a "fetching cream-fed kitten."

Cecil Wilson maintained that she had "all the prettiness of a doll with the fascination of a demon."

***

Only six days later, still at the New Theatre, Larry opened *Richard III*, appearing with two of Vivien's former "*beaux*," Terence Morgan and Dan Cunningham.

Four years had gone by since Larry had stunned West End audiences with *Richard III*, and he did it again, perhaps playing the role more forcefully than before, electrifying theater-goers.

Richard III was producer John Burrell's swan song as an Old Vic director. Vivien played Lady Anne, a part she "detested," although she performed well in the role, "a brilliant contrast to her Dresden china Lady Teazle," in the words of one critic.

Critic Alan Dent, who edited the film versions of both *Henry V* and *Hamlet*, gave the most memorable review of Larry's performance as *Richard III*. "His range of expression is extraordinary, even for him, his eyes are Machiavellian, his nose is a sinister sonnet of Baudelaire, and his hands in their scarlet gloves are quick and shrewd. He lives the life of Richard with an almost alarming gusto, and he dies the death horribly—like an earthworm cut in two."

When he saw Vivien perform as Lady Anne, Dent wrote: "Here is Vivien Leigh giving this feckless and be-wimpled bobby-soxer more strength and compulsion than I suspected were in either Lady Anne or Miss Leigh."

When Beaton didn't go backstage to greet Larry and Vivien after a performance of *Richard III*, he wrote Garbo: "I heard the Oliviers were absolutely furious with me for going to *Richard III* and not going round to congratulate them afterwards. I guess they just found an excuse to put me in the pan or double boiler."

The third play in Larry's 1949 swan song trilogy to the Old Vic was *Antigone*.

In London, as Vivien prepared to star in *Antigone* with Larry, much of her time was consumed with lobbying to play Blanche DuBois in the London production of *A Streetcar Named Desire*. Nothing since the role of Scarlett O'Hara had tantalized her more than a decade before had she wanted to portray a character as much.

"I could be that delicate moth from the Old South, clinging to the memories of a past gone with the wind," she said. "For my public, it might answer the often-asked question, What Ever Happened to Scarlett O'Hara?"

Antigone was to some degree a female counterpart of *Oedipus*. "I want to do something comparable to his *Oedipus*," Vivien told Dame Edith Evans.

In a phone call to Dame Sybil Thorndike, Vivien said, "Please come and see me, darling. I'm playing a tragic target of the gods."

Larry tried to dissuade Vivien from starring in *Antigone*, feeling she did not have "the emotional and vocal power to pull it off." He finally gave in to her and worked tirelessly to improve her stage voice, lowering it by an octave.

Larry passed on the role of Creon, giving it to his friend, George Relph, instead. Relph played the tyrant who forces the outlawed princess into poverty.

Antigone opened at the New Theatre in London on February 10, 1949,

560

with Vivien in the lead, backed up by Larry as the Chorus. As before *tout* London descended on the theater,. As one newspaper report had it, "all the Knights and Dames in the Empire showed up."

On opening night, even before the final curtain, Vivien confronted Larry backstage before taking another curtain call. "I'm a hit," she told him, "and you thought I couldn't do it."

Writing in the *Observer*, Ivor Brown noted Vivien's "new and strong vocal range, a fanatical force of character. It is a most notable achievement and surmounts expectation."

As always, Vivien had her critics, notably T.C. Worsley who claimed that her role "does require an emotional intensity and a fanaticism which Miss Leigh does not command." Larry defended Vivien, calling her critics "frivolous, untutored, and blasphemous."

The ink on the papers from Fleet Street, carrying mainly rave reviews for her performance in *Antigone*, had hardly dried, when Vivien told Larry, "At long last I have buried the ghost of Scarlett O'Hara."

In Australia, his fellow actors in the theater had many opinions or labels for Peter Finch. He was called "a wild man," or even "a remarkably sensitive bisexual." "Maverick," "loner," and "nomad" were words often used. One writer called him "a curious mixture of sensitivity, erudition, and candour."

He also had an earthy streak, bordering on the vulgar. He told his stage manager in Sydney, "I'm going to London to become an asshole buddy of Sir Laurence Olivier."

Finch and his wife, Tamara, had arrived in England in November of 1948, finding a cheap flat in Notting Hill Gate.

"Flowers arrived at our Chelsea flat, and Larry called inviting Tamara and me for a drink at their home in Chelsea," Finch said. "We had drinks and Larry and Vivien had to dash off somewhere. Larry did agree to put me in touch with his agent, Cecil Tennant."

"And that was that," Finch recalled. "My hopes of becoming his Golden Boy like Terence Morgan were dashed when I left their cottage that night in Chelsea."

Far from forgetting Finch, Larry called him and told him that he was sending Tennant, his managing director—technically Finch's new agent as well— by his house with a script for a play called *Daphne Laureola* by James Bridie. He asked Finch to study the play and report the following Tuesday to Wyndham's Theatre for an audition for the first production of Laurence Olivier Productions (L.O.P.).

L.O.P., as it came to be called, had been set up by Larry with his longtime friend, Tennant. Both men persuaded Sir Alexander Korda to sit on the board, along with designer Roger Furse and Larry's intimate friend, Anthony

Bushell.

Arriving on time at the cold, dark theater, Finch stood on the stage, a thirty-three-year-old Australian trying to impersonate a twenty-year-old Pole.

In the black abyss out there sat Larry, Vivien, Dame Edith Evans, James Bridie, and the play's director, Murray Macdonald. After Finch's audition, there was a long pause. Unknown to him, Dame Edith, the star of the play, was conferring with her bosses and giving her approval. Finally, a voice called out from the dark. "Peter, the part is yours." It was Larry.

Backstage, Dame Edith confronted Finch. "As Ernest Piaste, you must fall hopelessly in love with me as the dipsomaniac Lady Pitts. Look at my ugly face, young man. Can you pull off such a stunt? In love with me?"

"I love you already," Finch said, kissing her on the lips.

An instant friendship was born.

By the time the play opened, Tamara had given birth to a daughter, Anita, and Larry and Vivien became the girl's godparents.

Vivien attended the glittering opening night of *Daphne Laureola* on March 22, 1949. Even before the reviews emerged from Fleet Street, there was talk in the star-studded audience that "another Olivier has emerged."

Later that evening, after the successful opening performance, Vivien came backstage and asked Finch to escort her to a party at the home of set designer Roger Furse. The guest list included John Mills, Emlyn Williams, Sir Alexander Korda, and Joseph Cotten who had, back in 1941, scored such a big hit in Orson Welles' *Citizen Kane*.

Vivien told Finch that Larry was detained giving interviews and that he'd arrive late for the opening night party.

"With Vivien looking regal and elegant, also beautiful at my side, I was the highlight of the Furse party until the arrival of Larry with a dashing Tyrone Power at his side," Finch said. "Throughout the night, I seemed to be Vivien's date. Power, who was probably the most gorgeous man on the planet at that time, was clearly Sir Laurence's boyfriend. They made that rather obvious. Vivien, bless her, pretended not to notice."

The party lasted until dawn, in time for the remaining guests to read the reviews. *The Daily Telegraph* claimed "Peter Finch as the Pole makes a name in a night." Other reviewers cited his "fire and romanticism," or his "quicksilver acting."

"After hugging and embracing me," Finch said, "Larry kissed Vivien and asked me to escort her home. Then he disappeared out the door with Tyrone Power, headed for God knows where."

"At the door to her home, Vivien kissed me tenderly on the lips," Finch said. Before disappearing inside, she whispered in my ear, "That was just a preview of coming attractions."

Daphne Laureola would run until February of 1950. Finch's role in the life of the Oliviers would have a six-year engagement.

After Power left town, Larry called Finch for a private dinner at a home in Hampstead Heath. Finch told Tamara he was going to a business dinner with the board of Laurence Olivier Productions. When he reached the house, he discovered that he was the only guest. A servant had prepared dinner, before discreetly leaving for the night.

"I never knew who owned the house," Finch later recalled. "Larry didn't tell me."

"Larry seduced me that night," Finch later confessed to Dame Edith, who had long ago become aware of Larry's homosexuality. "She became my Mother Confessor throughout the run of the play. I loved that woman. Dame Edith could be cold and aloof, but when she opened her heart to you, she could be the warmest person on earth."

After Finch's night with Larry, Tennant arrived two days later with a five-year contract with Laurence Olivier Productions, beginning at thirty pounds a week, with raises promised in the future.

Tennant had previously told Finch he was living on the "wrong side of the park" and had secured a flat for him in the center of the theater district at Burleigh Mansion off St. Martin's Lane.

"I felt like King of the World," Finch later claimed. "I had a beautiful talented wife in Tamara, and I was a gleam in the eye of the world's greatest actor. What could possibly be missing from my life? I soon discovered what was missing. Miss Vivien Leigh kept her promise to me, and she was appearing in a theater close to mine. How convenient for us."

***

Daphne Laureola was successful, playing for a year in the West End and making Finch known to a wide circle of admirers. Its success inspired Larry, through his Laurence Olivier Productions, to take a four-year lease on London's St. James's Theatre, which had been constructed in 1835, evoking the gilt and scarlet upholstery of a more opulent era. Vivien had nostalgic memories of the theater, having triumphed in *The Mask of Virtue* there.

It was a cold and threatening day in London, with storm clouds brewing over the city. The trees were in bud in Hyde Park. But at Durham Cottage more clouds were on the horizon. Larry was sitting on the porch of their small winter garden having a drink.

Vivien emerged abruptly. He looked at her, seeing an expression on her face he'd never witnessed before. Without any formality, she announced calmly to him, "I don't love you any more."

Startled, shocked, and unable to speak at first, he finally was able to mouth some words. "Is there another man?"

"No, that's not the reason," she said. "I still love you, but it is the love a sister has for her big brother. It is not the love a woman has for a man."

He later recalled, "I felt I had been condemned to a slow death. I almost thought my ears had deceived me," he said.

As she went on, he wrote, "The central force of my life, my heart, in fact, had been removed by the world's most skillful surgeon. It left me agasp but not gasping; it was as if I had been rendered forever still inside, like a fish in a refrigerator."

Later, as the long tedious months of the stage version of *Streetcar* went on, he later recalled, "Brother and sister—*ho, hum*. Somewhat to my surprise, occasional acts of incest were not discouraged."

Before that night ended, Larry and Vivien entered into a pact together. They agreed to carry on as if their relationship were still intact. "The world must never find out," Vivien said. "We must go on being the romantic couple, Sir Laurence and Lady Olivier that the world adores."

"Ralphie told me I should have kicked Vivien out that very night," Larry later confessed. "But I couldn't bring myself to do it. Perhaps I had become the victim of our own myth."

In his *Confessions*, Olivier admitted, more so than most men would, that he could not satisfy Vivien's desires. "One cannot be more than one kind of athlete at a time," he claimed, "and often the most magnificent boxers, wrestlers, champions proved to be disappointing upon the removal of that revered jock strap."

At one point, John Mills said, "Vivien wanted to punish Larry, to make him suffer as much as she'd suffered. But Larry, being Larry, remained rather detached. However, he did say that he once, in a desperate attempt to hold onto their marriage, tried to 'fuck love back into our existence."

At this point in their relationship, Vivien and Larry decided not to inform their children of their moving away from each other.

Tarquin, Larry's son, would come to visit Larry and Vivien. She seemed to relate to him as if he were her own child. On one occasion, Larry, perhaps remembering his own days as a schoolboy, issued a warning to Tarquin, who related it in his memoirs of his father.

"You've been warned about bigger boys and taking advantage," Larry said. "Seldom happens but it might. You're small for your age and the youngest in school and you'll be wearing bum freezers. Unfair somehow."

"One's loss of love must be endured like a fall from grace that occurs in every man's life," Larry told John Mills, who had become his best friend. "It must be faced with fortitude, stiff British upper lip and all that."

Garry O'Connor, in writing a two-part biography of Larry for the BBC, came to this conclusion: "The union of Laurence Olivier and Vivien Leigh was the 'marriage for love' of its time. But were he and Vivien truly married, or had both contracted themselves to passion instead, loving love itself and being in love with love—conditions they needed in order to act successfully—more than with one another?"

He claimed that passion as a basis for their marriage was "really only the patterns for infidelity." He noted that what entranced people about Vivien was that she remained unobtainable. "Paradoxically, to possess her meant to lose her."

In the late spring and early summer of 1949, Vivien's mental state deteriorated rapidly, Larry never knowing from day to day what mood she was going to be in.

"She was the worst I've ever seen," Dame Sybil Thorndike said. "Larry was most depressed, owing to her condition and his own personal struggles."

Sometimes tensions between Vivien and Larry at Durham Cottage reached a boiling point. In one of her "states," she seemed to welcome a confrontation, even violence. Their domestic fighting continued even when they went for a rest at Notley Abbey.

One night she entered his room at Notley and began to denounce him. He dragged her back to her own room. He later recorded the event. "Before hitting the bed she struck the outside corner of her left eyebrow on the corner of her marble bedside table top, opening up a wound half an inch from her temple and half an inch from her eye."

Three weeks went by and she seemed rather demure, covering her injury with makeup for the stage. He often didn't sleep at Notley, preferring to seek comfort elsewhere. But one night had been particularly troubling. Normally fastidious, she'd thrown her plate of food on the floor and had denounced him, claiming that she was a far better actress than he was an actor. She stormed upstairs and shut herself away, presumably for the night.

At Notley, around three o'clock that morning, he was suddenly awakened. She was standing over him, slashing his face with a wet, stinging towel.

Bolting up, he grabbed her by her wrists, wringing the towel from her delicate hand. He dragged her toward the stairwell and on to her room.

She seemed to sense he was going to toss her down that stairwell where she'd once fallen and broken her wrist. She screamed at him, "No, no, it'll kill me. Don't do it!"

Even if such an impulse had occurred to him, evocative of that balcony scene with Richardson in Paris, he pulled back, coming to his senses. He tossed her onto the bed in her room, this time avoiding injuring her.

He bolted his door that night. The next day he called a locksmith. Any nights he slept over at Notley after that, he firmly locked his door.

***

Vivien was performing in *Antigone* at the New Theatre, with Finch appearing in *Daphne Laureola* at Wyndham. Its stage door was opposite the back of the New Theatre. Finch could dart over for a "quickie" visit with Vivien before or after the show.

She confided in Dame Edith, "Like so many affairs between actors, it began in the dressing room and became something more, so much more. Of course, I'm married, and Peter is married, so it's a sometimes thing. The title of my memoirs will be *Back Street*."

Cecil Beaton was one of the first to hear of the Finch/Leigh affair. He

immediately spread the word, even telling critic James Agate, who sarcastically remarked at a party, "It seems that young Finch is replacing Larry both on stage and in the boudoir."

Larry and Vivien virtually paraded Finch in front of their guests at Notley, including Orson Welles. "I could not help but notice that Peter did not have his own room," Welles said. "He slept either in Larry's bedroom or with Vivien, perhaps playing musical chairs before the night ended." Finch was part of a guest list that also included Irene Mayer Selznick; Tennessee Williams; Tennessee's lover, Frank Merlo; and Rex Harrison.

Tennessee had a peculiar take on the Notley household. "I think Larry is dangling Vivien in front of Peter, perhaps other men, so he can seduce the studs himself."

Oddly enough, he was echoing one of the themes of his future movie, *Suddenly, Last Summer* (1959), starring Katharine Hepburn, Elizabeth Taylor, and Montgomery Clift.

TROUPERS IN THE DIFFICULT ART OF ENGLISH RESTORATION COMEDY

Two views of Vivien Leigh playing Lady Teazle in
The School for Scandal. Lower photo: John Gielgud (far left) and Laurence Oliver (far right)

Author Anthony Holden made an astonishing claim about the Finch/Vivien romance. "If Olivier later believed that he had in some way 'encouraged' Vivien's affair with Finch, without quite understanding why, it may be because he wanted his wife to be reminded, through the younger man, of the Olivier with whom she had first fallen in love. He may also have felt that surrogate excitement, not uncommon among some married men, in another man's enjoyment of his wife. As long as the liaison remained discreet, it could even prove useful to his colder, more calculating self in keeping Vivien on an even keel."

Larry told his agent, Cecil Tennant, "I can't blame Peter Finch for taking Vivien from me. After all, all he's doing is what I did to Leigh Holman years ago."

Shortly before Finch's death, he was asked about his involvement with the Oliviers. He didn't answer specifically, but said, "A high libido and a sense of life's absurdities can breed queer bedfellows, and in the good old public days when I was getting launched in London theater, I landed up in some pretty queer situations."

"I've loved many a dollybird—my three wives, Maxine Audley, Shirley Bassey, Kay Kendall, Mai Zetterling, a Sabena Air Lines stewardess, a German princess, the daughter of an African chieftain, a professor of Greek, many prostitutes, lots of starlets. Of them all, Vivien Leigh had the style and wit to match her beauty."

***

"I'm looking for Elysian Fields."
—**Blanche DuBois in *A Streetcar Named Desire***

"Larry's first mistake was getting involved with A Streetcar Named Desire. His second was letting Vivien get involved. It led to the final collapse of the Olivier-Leigh marriage."
—**Producer Saul Colin**

"Deliberate cruelty is not forgivable. It is the one unforgivable thing in my opinion, and it is the one thing of which I have never, never been guilty."
—**Blanche DuBois**

Larry finally agreed to read the Tennessee Williams play, *A Streetcar Named Desire*. Putting it down, he told Vivien the drama was repulsive. "What are we dealing with here? Homosexuality? Nymphomania? Insanity? Incestuous rape? Have you ever heard of the Lord Chamberlain? Unlike Broadway, stage morals are still censored in Britain. Have you forgotten that?"

Larry was right. *Streetcar* would even be denounced in the House of Commons as "low and repugnant." The Public Morality Council called it "lewd and salacious."

An official of the Royal Household, the Lord Chamberlain had licensed plays in England since 1737. Licensing actually meant censoring them. Such a policy was abolished in Britain in 1968.

The Lord Chamberlain later decreed that on stage Blanche could not reveal to the audience that she'd learned that her young husband had been the lover of an older gentleman.

"Dear boy, the great man of the British theater, I must override your objections to *Streetcar*," Vivien said to Larry. "Bloody hell! This is the stage role of the decade for an actress. You must not stand in my way. I've given you the limelight long enough. I never thought in my lifetime I would find a role to equal Scarlett O'Hara. At long last I have, and cannot allow your pettiness to block me. I will immortalize myself in this role, especially when I scheme my way to do it on the screen."

Her friend, Alan Dent, tried to get her to turn down the role. "It's not for you to play one of Tennessee Williams' walking and wandering casebooks, sluts, inconstant nymphs, the victims of men who could be sadistic and even cannibalistic."

A Streetcar Named Desire had opened on Broadway on December 3, 1947 to rave reviews. It had starred Jessica Tandy, Jill Esmond's longtime friend, in the pivotal role of Blanche DuBois. The play had made an overnight sensation of its young male star, Marlon Brando, who was hailed on stage as "lightning on legs."

Vivien still exerted control over Larry, and he agreed to direct her in *A Streetcar Named Desire*, opening at the Aldwych Theatre in London on October 11, 1949.

Although a bit leery of the subject matter of *Streetcar*, Hugh (Binkie) Beaumont had negotiated with its produc-

Ratcheting up the sexual tension: Marlon Brando

er in New York, Irene Mayer Selznick, former wife of David O. Selznick and the daughter of Louis B. Mayer. Irene was relishing the biggest achievement of her career when she produced *Streetcar*.

"I am doing this play not because I want to but because Vivien demands that I do it," Larry told Beaumont. "As you know, Blanche DuBois is led off to the madhouse at the end of the play. There is a strong possibility that Vivien as Blanche will be driven into total madness. I warned her of the risk of her scheme to play Blanche. At first I was going to say her 'mad scheme,' but I censored that tongue of mine at the last second."

As he signed on to direct *Streetcar*, Larry became convinced that this was Vivien's last chance to erase the haunting ghost of Scarlett O'Hara. Whenever her role in *Gone With the Wind* was brought up, Vivien in the late 40s and early 50s had taken to saying, "Damn you, Scarlett O'Hara."

"I thought, if her critics have one grain of fairness, they will give her credit now for being an actress and not go on forever letting their judgments be distorted by her beauty and Hollywood stardom as Scarlett O'Hara."

In May of 1949, Irene lured Tennessee from Rome to meet her in London to watch Vivien in two Old Vic performances, *The School for Scandal* and *Antigone*. "Let's see how David's beloved Scarlett O'Hara is holding up after all this passage of time," Irene said. "David told me she's quite mad, at least part of the time. Cecil Beaton informed me she's aged dreadfully."

"If Beaton is not being his queenly self, then the aging part would be perfect for Blanche DuBois," Tennessee said.

He liked Vivien's performance in *The School for Scandal* but thought she "is not really good in *Antigone*."

Nevertheless, in a letter to his close friend, Donald Windham, he claimed that "she might make a good Blanche, more for her off-stage personality than for what she does in repertory."

Meeting backstage after each performance, Tennessee found Vivien delightful, noticing that she paid as much attention

Southern, Gothic, Theatrical, and High-drama

(*Top photo*) Tennessee Williams in Key West
(*Lower photo, left to right*) Frank Merlo, Elia Kazan, Tennessee Williams, and Charles Feldman

569

to his lover, Frank Merlo, as she did to him, which he thought was exceedingly kind and gracious on her part. She liked them so much she invited both of them to Notley Abbey where they would be joined by Larry.

Tennessee's visit to Notley did not get off to a good start, as he and Frank arrived late. "Sir Laurence had gone to bed," Tennessee later said. *"Quelle insulte!"*

He also noted that the other visitor at Notley, Danny Kaye, was "extremely quiet," which was uncharacteristic for the comedian. Unknown to Tennessee at the time, Vivien, Larry, and Kaye had become embroiled in a catfight before the playwright's arrival.

She had demanded that Larry choose between Kaye and her. Insults were hurled for an hour or so, with no resolution. At breakfast the next morning, she seemed to have withdrawn her ultimatum and was charming and gracious to her guests, especially Merlo. She was polite but cool to Kaye.

When Tennessee returned to New York, he told his agent, Audrey Wood, that he suspected Kaye and Larry had become lovers. "Not on your life," Wood said. "Larry could have his pick of the most beautiful men in the British and American theater. Why would he choose Danny Kaye? I know for a fact that when Kaye wants sex with a young man, either in New York or Los Angeles, he pays for it."

Tennessee seemed adamant. "I know the ways of the human heart better than you, dear lady. Sir Laurence and Danny Kaye are lovers."

At dinner on their second night at Notley, Larry presided like a country squire, directing his conversation to Tennessee or Kaye, and virtually ignoring Frank and Vivien.

"Vivien was very nice," Merlo recalled. "She included me in the conversation. After dinner, Kaye and Olivier excused themselves and went upstairs. Vivien looked disdainfully at their backs. Tenn retired to the library to write some letters, and Vivien invited me to go for a moonlit walk in her gardens."

"Outside in the night air, she told me that she sympathized with me for living with such a great artist."

"Tennessee must torment you at times the way Larry torments me," she told Merlo. "Having a relationship with Tennessee or Sir Laurence must be something to endure. For causing us so much pain, we should get back at them. The bungalow is empty tonight. Do you like girls just a little bit?"

"I love women, but not in bed," Merlo told her.

"Has the whole world turned gay?" she asked. "What are we poor girls to do?"

"Perhaps not hang out with men in the theater," he said. "Men who like to paint their faces and dress up in costumes every night are not the straightest arrows."

"That I have found to be true," she said. "At least Tennessee is open about his homosexuality. Larry likes to keep his secrets buried."

Her sudden sexual interest in Merlo may have stemmed from the fact that before dinner Tennessee had confided in her that, in part, he'd based the character of Stanley Kowalski on Merlo.

Later that night, Merlo told Tennessee that Vivien had come on to him. "Don't flatter yourself," he said. "She's just getting back at Sir Laurence who this very minute is probably in his bedroom plugging that red-haired comedian, whose art form has always escaped me."

When Tennessee came down for breakfast on the morning of his departure, he found that only Vivien and a house servant were up. Sir Laurence, Kaye, and Merlo were still in bed.

"It was our first real discussion of the character of Blanche," Tennessee recalled. "I told her that Blanche was a demonic creature, the size of her feeling too great for her to continue to live without the escape to madness."

"I fear you have given me the blueprint to my own life," she told the playwright.

She appeared shocked when Tennessee told her, "You were not my first choice for Blanche. I actually took the script to Garbo and asked her to return to the screen as Blanche."

"I could never play such an involved and complicated person," Garbo had informed him. "I am too direct and masculine. I couldn't bear to tell lies and see things around corners like that girl."

"Garbo told you the truth," Vivien said. "If you want to bring the best Blanche DuBois on the planet to the screen, you're looking at her."

After a weekend at Notley, Tennessee returned to Key West where he told Truman Capote, "Larry Olivier is a great actor in that he preserves the myth of his long-faded romance with Vivien and brilliantly conceals his private unhappiness. Their romance died a long time ago, and only the ghosts of a love lost remains."

When a journalist once asked Tennessee his opinion of Vivien, he responded: "There may have been, in her time, as beautiful a lady, but if there was, I never encountered her. Her social behavior was a bit unpredictable owing to the nervous torment that I am afraid she always had to live with. She realized that I lived with the same nervous torment. When she was not tormented, she was capable of the most discreet and exquisite kindness."

Privately, Irene Mayer Selznick met with Larry. She didn't want either Vivien or Tennessee to attend their meeting. "I have an idea I want you to incorporate into the British version of *Streetcar*. Gadge absolutely rejected it for Broadway." She was referring, of course, to Elia Kazan.

"I'm all ears," Larry said.

"To help goad Blanche into madness, I want Stanley Kowalski to rape her . . . by suggestion of course. After resisting him, I want her to begin to respond and dig her fingers into his back. He gets to her and she welcomes his love-making. But at a brutal moment, I want him to pull away from her and leave her gasping for breath and unsatisfied. I want him to stand up, with his cock put away, naturally, and laugh at her savagely, a final humiliation that will tip her over the top into pure madness."

He looked at her strangely, his face paralyzed with agony and dread. "Oh, dear, dear woman, I can't do that. It would destroy me and destroy Vivien. You see, once, in a rage, I did the very same thing to her. I can't live that moment again . . . ever!"

***

Before taking on the complicated role of Blanche DuBois, Vivien announced to Larry that she was going on a short vacation in Switzerland. She told him she'd be the guest of Collette Harrison (*née* Thomas), who had divorced Rex Harrison in 1942.

Collette was having an affair with the handsome, very masculine Robert Capa, arguably the finest photojournalist of the 20th century. He'd covered the first wave of Allied landings on Omaha Beach on D-Day, and before that, the Spanish Civil War. His glamorous reputation had preceded him. Capa was a friend and confidante of such men as Ernest Hemingway, John Steinbeck, and director John Huston. Capa was also known for seducing some of his era's most celebrated women, Ingrid Bergman being just one of them.

From the moment Vivien arrived in Klosters, Capa had eyes only for her. His fling with Collette had been "just one of many," and the relationship was hardly intense.

Author Peter Viertel, who would famously be married to Deborah Kerr, was also at Klosters with his girlfriend of the moment, Bettina Graziani.

Bettina later told Capa's biographer, Alex Kershaw, author of *Blood and Champagne*, that "Vivien fell for Robert's charms one evening. She was alone and fragile. She came down and Capa started to drink with her and then they danced—Russian dances. He was incredible, so much fun. I don't think it lasted long with her. I don't know if he had a life with any woman that lasted very long."

Back in London, a depressed Vivien told Bea Lillie, "I fell madly in love with Robert Capa but he dumped me and moved on to his next conquest. Such a pity! So far, he has been the only man in the world with enough stamina to satisfy me sexually."

***

Back from her holiday in Switzerland, Vivien began to rehearse Tennessee's play. It was announced in the newspapers that Laurence Olivier Productions would open *A Streetcar Named Desire* on October 11, 1949 at the Aldwych Theatre in London, with Vivien cast as Blanche DuBois, the tragic heroine of Tennessee Williams' drama. Bonar Colleano was cast as Stanley Kowalski. Renée Asherson starred as Stella, which Kim Hunter had played to such acclaim in New York. Previously, Asherson had appeared with Larry in *Henry V.*

Amazingly, Larry was still smitten with Terry Morgan and had offered him the role of Stanley Kowalski, although he would have been completely miscast. Morgan turned down the choice part.

Vivien had not seen Jessica Tandy's Blanche on Broadway, so she developed her own characterization. "I came to understand Blanche and ultimately love her," she told Ursula Jeans. "Blanche lives in her own dream world which is far preferable than the nightmare of reality."

Attending the first week of rehearsals, Irene Selznick did not like Vivien's interpretation of Blanche. The producer had perhaps been indoctrinated by the countless performances she'd watched of Jessica Tandy emoting as Blanche.

Larry later told Richardson, "Directing *Streetcar* was humiliating for me. Irene Selznick is destroying my creativity. She is demanding that I present an exact replica of her Broadway hit. She reminded me, of course, that *Streetcar* ran on Broadway for years."

At one point, Larry confronted Irene, telling her that, "In Britain, Vivien and I are known as the King and Queen of the West End."

She shot back, "That's nothing. In Hollywood, my father, Louis B. Mayer, is an Emperor."

When Larry was asked if playing Blanche every night was driving Vivien mad, he said, "Acting great parts devours you. It's a dangerous game."

"I wonder if Blanche's madness is contagious," Irene asked Larry during rehearsals. "I hope Tennessee's play doesn't drive your girl over the cliff."

"It's a risk Vivien wants to take," Larry told her. "As you can see for yourself, she has the shaky emotional equilibrium of Blanche and she brings to life her delusionary colorations and deceits. The problem is, she can't turn off Blanche when she goes home. At times, she seems to become Blanche in real life. Playing Blanche seems to trigger bouts of hysteria and depression."

Years later, Larry had second thoughts about casting Vivien in *Streetcar*. "She was too much affected by the part she played. It had a great deal to do with playing Blanche DuBois and being ill in the same way."

The critics piled attack upon attack on Vivien for starring in *Streetcar* and

573

on Tennessee for writing it. All she would say was, "Of course, it's not a drawing room comedy." One reviewer in town from Leeds headlined his critique: SCARLETT O'HARA DROWNS IN A CESSPOOL.

A woman who arranged flower shows in Chelsea told the press, "It's sordid, a perfectly awful play that gets even more horrid every time I see it."

The London newspapers played up the "sex sensationalism" of *Streetcar*, and Vivien noted that on many a night, the audience flocking to see her as Blanche was "like a pack of apes waiting to scc mc gct raped. I feel as if I've been bulldozed and can't believe I have to go through a gut-wrenching performance of Blanche every night."

After watching Vivien on stage, Kenneth Tynan continued his life-long assault on her, claiming that Larry's casting of her in the role had been a mistake. "Why not call it *A Vehicle for Vivien*. She plays Blanche like a bored nymphomaniac, a Hedda Gabler of the gin palaces."

During the London heyday of *Streetcar,* Larry had rebuffed Tynan's latest sexual solicitations. Perhaps to strike back at Larry, Tynan wrote that "*A Streetcar Named Desire* is a good play scarred by unsympathetic and clumsy direction." He and Larry were soon back together again.

Novelist and playwright J.B. Priestley on the BBC likened Vivien's performance to that of a bearded woman in a circus. He also said that Vivien's audiences were mostly men who on other nights might be catching a nudie girlie show at the Windmill.

Noël Coward, after seeing *Streetcar* in October of 1949, wrote: "Vivien magnificent; audiences sordid, theatre beastly."

When Dame Edith Evans saw the play, Vivien confided to her that it was hard "to shake off Blanche after playing her. I do not have the self-control and artistic discipline to bury Blanche once the curtain has gone down. Isn't playing Blanche like flirting with suicide?"

Dame Edith told her that "actors can shake off their roles faster than actresses."

In an interview with David Lewin, Vivien said, "I challenge any woman to be able to accept the scene when Blanche's face is held pitilessly under a naked light bulb and she is asked to contemplate what she will look like when her beauty has gone. Blanche is a woman with everything stripped away. She is a tragic figure and I understand her. But playing her has tipped me into madness."

John Gielgud delayed going to see her in *Streetcar*, because he'd heard the play was "loathsome." When he came backstage to congratulate her on a brilliant performance, he found her sobbing and shaking. Her lips trembled. "I fear she was near a nervous breakdown. I held her in my arms and let her have a good cry. Her demons were on parade that night. But were they really her demons? Perhaps they were straight from New Orleans and from the psyche of Blanche DuBois herself?"

During the time of Vivien's greatest emotional distress, she played Blanche night after night for eight grueling months, enduring attacks from critics who asked, "What is Scarlett O'Hara doing in this garbage?" Tennessee's play was also dismissed as "not fit for human consumption."

After the curtain came down on Blanche every night, Vivien's alcohol consumption reached new highs, alarming Larry who could do nothing about it.

Some nights when Finch returned home to Tamara, his wife, Vivien walked through the streets of London's Soho district, where she encountered prostitutes. She was immediately recognized and often chatted with the girls "trolling the Dilly," a reference to streetwalking at Piccadilly Circus.

Many of these working women were fans of hers, and some told her that their clients had taken them to see *Streetcar*.

One young girl from Leeds claimed that Marlene Dietrich walked these same streets and had picked her up for sex, giving her 20 pounds. "That's more than any client has ever paid me," she told Vivien. "But I bet you could make even more than that."

In pursuit of a prostitute, many a john on the make did not recognize this trampish-looking woman as Lady Olivier. It was rumored, but never proven, that in one of her "states" she went back to a client's room for sexual intercourse. If so, she was repeating her performance as the ballerina turned prostitute in *Waterloo Bridge*.

At times she was seized by a bout of amnesial depression. She would disappear after the evening's show, often with a coterie of young actors eager for her company. She'd return very late to her home in Chelsea, with almost no recall about what had occurred that night.

The most notorious occurrence came one night after the curtain had gone down on *Streetcar*. She was invited to join the cast of another play for a late-night party in a London flat.

Other cast members noted, and later gossiped about, her encounter with a young Welsh actor. When he invited her to go back to his flat, she willingly agreed.

The details of that evening are missing, but he later told friends that she was talking aimlessly, making no sense in her conversation. He later

Richard Burton
"I was once a homosexual,
but it didn't take."

claimed he thought she was drunk. But at his flat that night, he realized that she was "off her rocker."

Richard Burton later told Emlyn Williams that, "Vivien wanted me to reenact her on-stage rape by Stanley Kowalski in *Streetcar*. I obliged, stripping off her clothes and getting into it, although I was a bit plastered myself."

At three o'clock that morning, policemen found Vivien wandering the streets of Soho in a mink coat and looking deranged. Recognizing her, the policemen brought her home to Durham Cottage and to the safety of Larry who put her to bed.

The next morning he quizzed her about her activities, and she claimed she did not remember.

Burton showed up at the stage door the next evening, and Vivien seemed relatively well adjusted. She willingly went out for a late supper with him. As he recalled, "This time she raped me. I did not resist."

In 1949, Burton was in London appearing at the Globe Theatre in Christopher Fry's period comedy, *The Lady's Not for Burning*, starring John Gielgud, who also directed it, and Claire Bloom.

As a brash young man, Burton couldn't keep this seduction to himself, and he spread the word. The gossip made the rounds among London theatrical circles, and soon Larry heard of it. He called Burton and asked to meet him for dinner one night.

"Before the evening was over, I seduced Sir Laurence himself," Burton claimed. "In those days all the stately homos of Britain were after me—John Gielgud, Noël Coward, Emlyn Williams. What else could I do? You don't reject such distinguished personages in the theater if you are a struggling actor wanting to get ahead."

Soon both Vivien and Larry were inviting Burton to Notley.

Burton would later brag to friends, "Sir Laurence and Lady Olivier were soon to learn that there's more than enough of me to go around."

Spencer Tracy had signed with director George Cukor to film *Edward, My Son,* a talky, stagy drama in which brash, rags-to-riches Tracy pampers his son, failing to instill within him a sense of responsibility. Although she rejected a co-starring role in *Edward, My Son*, Katharine Hepburn agreed to fly to London on a separate flight to join Tracy during part of the filming in 1949. Because the story was set in

How to Cope with Your Hosts when they invite you for a weekend in their English country manor

Spencer Tracy and Katharine Hepburn--Show-biz buddies with secrets to conceal

Britain, the studio decided to film it at an authentic locale instead of trying to re-create the sets on a Hollywood sound stage. Tracy had accepted an invitation to stay at Notley Abbey. For appearances' sake, Hepburn booked a suite for herself in London at Claridge's.

Privately, Hepburn had told George Cukor, who had signed to direct *Edward, My Son*, that the role of the alcoholic wife was not for her. Consequently, he cast Deborah Kerr in the part instead. Hepburn also told Cukor that he'd badly miscast Tracy as the ruthless, self-made British millionaire.

Most days, while Tracy was on the set filming, Hepburn hung out at the British Museum and in curio shops, but mainly she poked around London, discovering its secret alleys and hidden mews.

Each night, when he returned from the set, Tracy was more and more despondent, realizing after only the first week of shooting, that he was wrong for the role of a pompous rags-to-riches British tycoon. Robert Morley had written the play, and it had been a big hit in London, with the portly actor/writer himself as the star.

Hepburn spent her first week in London at Claridge's, but accepted a weekend invitation to visit Notley Abbey and the Oliviers. She'd seen the Oliviers on and off for a number of years, their friendship developing casually after she'd been matron of honor at their hasty wedding. Hepburn had long ago forgiven Leigh for taking the role of Scarlett O'Hara in *Gone With the Wind*.

When Hepburn had first arrived at Notley with Tracy on a Friday night, their reunion with the Oliviers had been triumphant. Larry and Vivien made a stunningly handsome couple and seemed very much in love. Vivien was the perfect hostess, having filled the drafty old mansion with flowers and having ordered the staff to keep the fireplaces blazing because oil was still in short supply in post-war England.

It was so cold for a Californian like Tracy that he didn't even take off his overcoat. Hepburn didn't mind the cold—in fact, welcomed "the bracing air of the place."

Wisely assuming that Tracy and Hepburn no longer slept together, Vivien had assigned different bedchambers to her honored guests.

Tracy drank too much on their first dinner together, and staggered off to bed early to read detective stories. Hepburn followed shortly afterward.

About an hour later, she heard Vivien screaming at Larry. She couldn't make out all the words, but Hepburn quickly realized that something was seriously wrong with the marriage.

She had forgotten that Vivien and Larry were the world's greatest theatrical couple. That "perfect evening" and the "perfect couple" had been staged for her benefit and for Tracy. But it had been just that—a stage play. They were perfect in their roles.

But what Hepburn heard that night might have made Vivien and Larry the ideal stars for Edward Albee's *Who's Afraid of Virginia Wolff?*, a play that wouldn't be produced until more than a decade later.

The following morning, Larry and Vivien hardly spoke to each other. Vivien directed her conversation at Hepburn, and Larry concentrated on Tracy. Larry had arranged for them to attend a special screening of *Hamlet* in London. Neither Hepburn nor Tracy had seen the film, since they rarely attended movie theaters—and never together. Larry, of course, had just recently won the Oscar as Best Actor for his portrayal of *Hamlet*, and the film had garnered the Oscar for best picture.

Tracy complained about the shortage of hot water in England, and Hepburn countered that she loved it, having taken cold showers all her life. As Tracy headed for the studio and Larry left for a luncheon in London, Vivien invited Hepburn for a walk along the banks of the murky and fast-flowing Thame.

Vivien had bundled herself up heavily. When Hepburn suggested biking or a game of tennis later in the day, Vivien had to refuse. It was only then that Hepburn became aware that Vivien, in spite of the beauty of her porcelain skin, was a woman in physical torment. As the Thame rushed by, Vivien confessed that she was very seriously ill, having recently suffered one of her worst attacks of tuberculosis. She said that she felt very debilitated and could only hold herself together for a few hours at a time before she had to retreat to her bed.

Ever the caretaker, Hepburn offered to help, but Vivien said that there was nothing she could do. As the days went by, Hepburn began to realize—and she confided this to both Cukor and to Tracy—that Vivien was not only physically ill but mentally ill as well, suffering from some undiagnosed form of manic-depression.

Mother Confessor takes charge: Katharine Hepburn

In a confidential moment one night when they were alone in his library, Larry confessed to Hepburn that Vivien had run, two weeks previously, screaming into the night from Notley. "When I caught up with her, I found her completely nude. She scratched at my face, and threatened to kill me. I had to use brute force to get her back into the house before she died of pneumonia."

Hepburn had already noted the rapid mood swings in Vivien. One night at Notley Abbey,

578

she'd be the perfect hostess, telling them about how the manor had been endowed by Henry V himself. Her charm, wit, and beauty glowed by the open fireplaces. On other evenings, she came to dinner morose and melancholy, wearing no makeup and appearing in a sloppy dress, unlike the well-tailored gowns she wore most evenings.

Regardless of Vivien's condition, Larry was always charming, ignoring his wife when she was quiet, sullen, or withdrawn, and including her in the conversation when she was her "normal" self. Mostly, Larry concentrated his attention on Tracy, wanting to talk more about acting styles than his reluctant guest did.

On the following weekend when Hepburn arrived with Tracy, Vivien and Larry introduced them to Richard Burton. His reputation had preceded him. Hepburn said that she'd heard that the handsome young Welshman was "the newest and brightest light in the West End—tell me, is it true?"

"I plead guilty," Burton immodestly said.

Tracy said, "No matter how good you are, boy, you will never beat me as an actor."

"Don't I know that?" Burton said.

Hepburn found Burton "robust and very masculine," as she later reported to Cukor. "He seemed filled with an inner fire. He's unpretentious and I love his frankness."

After a dinner in which Burton heaped lavish praise on Tracy's acting, the quartet retired from the dining room for more drinking. Hepburn preferred to sip a sherry instead of Scotch.

Despondent over his miscast role in *Edward, My Son*, Tracy, with great effort, rose from an overstuffed armchair and announced his retreat upstairs to his cold bedchamber. Vivien had her maid deliver him a hot water bottle.

Hepburn, too, turned in early, leaving the Oliviers in the living room talking to Burton. She felt largely excluded from all this gossip about the British theatre. As she was leaving, Burton was entertaining his hosts with a story about how John Gielgud had made a pass at him the first night they'd met.

An hour later, as Hepburn was propped up in bed reading, she heard Larry come up the steps. He must have seen her light on from under the door, as he called out "good night" to her. He shared the room next to her. She was mildly perturbed that she could hear virtually every sound coming from his room, as the walls seemed paper-thin.

Unable to sleep, she got up an hour later and went downstairs to get some water. She was only mildly surprised to see Burton on the sofa with Vivien. "It looked like he was going for her tonsils," she told Cukor. "He was all over her."

Later in the evening, as she was to report, she heard double footsteps com-

579

ing up the stairs. She figured that Sir Laurence and Lady Olivier had long ago worked out their frequent changes of sexual partners, in much the same way that she and Tracy had.

Hepburn just assumed that the randy young actor had retired to bed with Vivien for the rest of the night. Later, Hepburn was awakened around two o'clock that morning. From the sound of voices next door, Burton was entering Larry's bedroom. Burton seemed drunk and was talking in a loud voice.

Larry tried to get him to speak more softly. The two men were talking with great animation, and at one point, they got into an argument. It was quickly settled. Then, in a loud voice, Burton called out, "That, my dear Sir Laurence, is what we call a 'blunt instrument' in Wales." It was designed to give the greatest pleasure to man, woman, or beast in the field."

There were no more voices, although Hepburn heard the sounds of rhythmic squeaking coming from the bedsprings. It seemed that Burton was the lover in charge of the action, Larry the willing recipient.

As Hepburn would later recount to Cukor, "Those Welsh boys have stamina. As a houseguest, I must say that Burton believes in sharing his favors with his hosts."

"Surely you've known for years that Larry is gay," Cukor said. "I'll let you in on a secret. All English actors are gay. That's why they're better than American actors. English actors are more in touch with both their male and female sides."

Vivien Leigh as Blanche DuBois
in the London Stage Production of
A Streetcar Named Desire

Cecil Beaton, who seemed to know whenever a cockroach walked in front of a theater in the West End, continued to stay abreast of Vivien's affairs with Finch and Burton. "I just hope that Vivien is sharing Finch and Burton with Larry."

"My darlings," Beaton told many a gay theatrical party, "Burton and Finch are merely the flame of the candle. Miss Leigh does more one-night stands than a Soho tart."

"I hear she's going to Hollywood to star opposite Marlon Brando," Beaton said. "I predict by the second night Brando will be enjoying Lady Olivier's charms.

Years later, a journalist took a dare and asked a slightly drunk Burton about those rumors of his homosexuality, specifically about his widely reported liaisons

580

with the Oliviers. "Perhaps most actors are latent homosexuals, and we cover it with drink," Burton confessed. "I was once a homosexual, but it didn't take."

"This is strictly off the record," Burton said, "but the truth is I fell more for Larry than Vivien. She was a bit crazy, but Larry knew what he wanted from me and went for it. Both of us had stage voices ideally suited for romantic utterances in one's ear."

***

After 326 exhausting performances of *Streetcar* on the London stage, Vivien joined Alexander Korda on his yacht for a sail along the Mediterranean.

It was during this trip that a rumor was spread that Vivien had gotten involved with a "sensitive" seventeen-year-old beach boy she'd met on the sands at Cannes. Korda privately told friends, "I think Vivien was just reenacting a scene from *Streetcar* in which Blanche gets involved with such a young boy."

***

Although devoting most of his time to producing plays, Larry was deluged with offers for acting roles. He later recalled that at various times he was asked to play such characters as Shakespeare himself in a play—also Leonardo da Vinci, Lord Byron, and even Manet.

In 1949, after the success of *Daphne Laureola*, Larry took a chance and optioned Jean Anouilh's new play, *Romeo et Jeanette*, which was retitled *Fading Mansions*.

The play did not survive its translation into English. Somehow the constantly repeated "*je suis cocu*" sounded better in French than the English-language equivalent, "I'm a cuckold." Directed by Anthony Bushell, *Fading Mansions* flopped, with an Irish actress, Siobhan McKenna, in the lead. It ran for only two weeks.

Two views of an *Über*-Diva:
Jennifer Jones

(Lower photo) with
Laurence Olivier in *Carrie* (1952)

In November of 1949 Larry was casting Christopher Fry's *Venus Observed*, but he took time out to fly to Philadelphia in December to see Garson Kanin's ill-fated *The Rat Race*. Larry had done well with *Born Yesterday* in London, and was eager to see this latest play of his friend. Larry wrongly predicted that *The Rat Race* would be a great hit on Broadway.

Back in London, he turned his attention to launching *Venus Observed*, Fry's first play since his more celebrated *The Lady's Not for Burning*.

Vivien told Fry she would not play Perpetua in *Venus Observed*. "The part calls for a younger, unknown actress, not a person that autograph hounds call out nightly, 'Scarlett, sign this, duckie.'" Heather Stannard ended up playing Perpetua.

Larry told Fry, "Your play has an autumnal sadness to it." Larry appeared in the play as the Duke of Altair, a middle-aged gent who decides to marry one of the trio of women he'd loved when he was young. As the debonair *roué*, the Duke learns that as regards his three former mistresses, his own son is the rival for "my lady of choice."

"It took me a long time to find the green umbrella," Larry told Vivien. He was referring to stage slang for just the right prop required to interpret a plot—the beard and pince-nez in *Uncle Vanya*, the stammer of the "w" as Hotspur.

He launched his season in January of 1950 with *Venus Observed*, both directing and starring in it. Opening on January 18, 1950, the play ran for seven months at the St. James's Theatre, "but did not earn its keep," as Larry put it.

T.C. Worsley called the production "a real mess. Olivier's part called for nothing but an easy command and a negligent air. Sir Laurence supplies them both."

In the crypt of the church where Finch's baby, Anita, was being christened, Larry pitched another script, *The Damascus Blade*, to the actor.

Larry defined *The Damascus Blade* as "a promising piece" by a new author, Bridget

Two views of director Elia Kazan with Vivien Leigh.

Lower photo: Directing the film version of *Streetcar*. *Center figure*: Kim Hunter.

Boland. He cast both John Mills, his best friend, and Finch, his lover, as the leads, sending them on a tour from Edinburgh to Glasgow in the spring of 1950.

"Audiences positively hated the play," Larry recalled. It was so bad it closed on the road. Neither Larry nor Mills wanted to face the London critics. Only Finch, secure in his role, asked to take it into the West End.

After the failure of *The Damascus Blade*, Larry, never one to give up, plunged into *Captain Carvallo*, a modern comedy, by Dennis Cannan. Once again he cast Finch in the lead role. "There's nothing like him since I caused a sensation in the West End," Larry told Noël Coward.

"How is he under the sheets?"

"That's for me to know and you to find out," Larry said.

In *Captain Carvallo*, Larry cast Diana Wynyard as the female lead.

At every opportunity he escaped for a rendezvous with Finch. "I find him to be utterly enchanting," he told Glen Byam Shaw, an enchantment of yesterday.

Dame Sybil Thorndike said, "Finch and Larry were seen everywhere together; in a huddle at the theater, having a cozy luncheon, pubbing at night."

Vivien had departed earlier for Hollywood to film *A Streetcar Named Desire* with Marlon Brando. That gave Larry the chance to see Finch whenever he chose at Durham Cottage. He told his wife, Tamara, "We're into rehearsals running late at night."

Opening on August 9, 1950 at the St. James's Theatre, *Captain Carvallo* would make no profit either. The loss of all this revenue inspired Larry "to take the best offer out there. It was a film called *Carrie*. Though I had reservations about the script, I went for it. Financial necessity and all that rot."

***

In 1949 Larry needed money, and he turned to Hollywood to get it. Income tax in Britain had become paralyzing. In 1949, he ended up with an income of only 1,091 pounds.

In reaction, he opted to channel his expenses through his production company, Laurence Olivier Productions, a financial decision which allowed him to drink his favorite champagne, Taittinger & Krug (1943), and to purchase a new Bentley outfitted with the same upholstery supplied to the king. But because of overspending, especially on too lavish stage presentations, the coffers of L.O.P. had run dry. "With this Labour Government," he'd told Vivien, "we'll always be strapped for cash because of the U.K.'s high taxes. Do I hear the siren call of Hollywood?"

After directing Larry in *Wuthering Heights* and vowing "I'll never work with Olivier again," William Wyler had asked Larry to consider the lead in *Carrie*, based on Theodore Dreiser's *Sister Carrie*. His co-star would be Jennifer Jones, who was famously married at the time to David O. Selznick.

Desperate for cash, Larry signed on. "We're running up a deficit," he'd told Vivien. "Let Hollywood foot the bill. It will be a pleasure to snoot old monsters."

Because of commitments to L.O.P., Larry had to remain behind in London when Vivien returned to the United States after a long absence.

He was genuinely worried if she had the stamina to make the film version of *Streetcar*. She'd gone into one of her "states" in the closing days of the stage version. An understudy, Betty Ann Davies, went on as Blanche, much to the disappointment of audiences, even though she was a well-respected actress.

For playing Blanche, Vivien received $100,000, the highest salary ever paid to an English actress at the time. In contrast, Marlon Brando, her co-star, was given $75,000.

"I absolutely refuse to have Vivien Leigh play Blanche DuBois," Elia Kazan had told Charles Feldman, the film's executive producer. "If you don't give it to Jessica Tandy, I'm walking. You saw Tandy as Blanche on Broadway. She was stunning."

Jack Warner wanted Olivia de Havilland because of her box office clout, but her salary demands were too excessive for the studio chief. There was a certain irony here, in that "Melanie" in *Gone With the Wind* might have taken the role from Vivien, the way she'd made off with Scarlett's desire, Ashley Wilkes.

Other actresses had also been considered for the role before Vivien. Anne Baxter claimed that she was once offered the screen version of Blanche DuBois. "I was a bit young, not that faded. I won the part of Eve Harrington, so that time in my life was not entirely wasted." She was referring to her Oscar-nominated role in *All About Eve* (1950), which, thanks to how her nomination split the votes of the Oscar committee, was one of the factors that cost Bette Davis a well-deserved Academy Award.

Finally, Kazan caved in and agreed to accept Vivien in the role. Stopping off in New York en route to California, she called Kazan, who was studying the script of *Streetcar*, and organizing his transit to Hollywood to direct her in the film. She knew he'd had reservations about casting her, and she desperately wanted to see if she could break through to him.

She was driven to his home in Newtown, Connecticut, where she stayed with him. He immediately told her she could call him "Gadge." "You'll hear Marlon calling me that and the rest of the New York cast of *Streetcar*." He warned her that some members of the Broadway cast, not just Brando, but

Kim Hunter and Karl Malden, might resent her playing Blanche, since each of them wanted Tandy to repeat her Broadway triumph on film.

"My first mission will be to de-Larry you," Kazan told Vivien. "I'm the director now. Forget his direction of you as Blanche DuBois in England. From now on, I will mold you into Gadge's Blanche."

"Is that mold into Blanche or bitch?" she asked.

In the short time they spent together, she and Kazan became intimate. She even discussed her marital woes with him. "Larry cannot face the truth. He wants to continue pretending we're the young lovers we were in 1939."

Kazan suggested that she file for divorce. "The two of you are destroying each other. You're destroying yourself. Forget about him. Save yourself."

She looked horrified at the suggestion. "I will never leave Larry!" she said adamantly. "Never! Never! I will *never* grant him a divorce."

"I did take Vivien to bed during her time with me," Kazan later told Tennessee Williams and his lover, Frank Merlo. "It took very little persuasion. She wasn't getting much at the time from Olivier. It was okay. There's a certain thrill in fucking Scarlett O'Hara. But, frankly, I found Marilyn Monroe much better in the hay."

That's what Kazan said in private. What he said in public was, "Vivien is full of grace, most intelligent, and clever enough not to say all she thinks."

After leaving Kazan, Vivien decided to take the train to California, stopping off in Wisconsin to visit Alfred Lunt and Lynn Fontanne.

In Tennessee's play, Blanche was married to a young homosexual who committed suicide. She bluntly asked Fontanne, "What is it like in real life to be married to a homosexual?"

Fontanne was momentarily taken back by the impertinent question. Regaining her composure, she told Vivien, "My dear, *you* should know more about that than I do."

Both Fontanne and Vivien agreed that they'd rather their husbands be involved with a man instead of another woman. "It's less threatening that way," Fontanne said. "After all, he's getting something we can't give him."

Vivien agreed, although she'd later change her mind because of Danny Kaye's increasing involvement in Larry's life.

***

She was greeted with a Hollywood headline, "SCARLETT O'HARA'S BACK IN TOWN" as Vivien, after an absence of more than a decade, returned to the scene of her former glory. When facing overly deferential reporters, calling her Lady Olivier, she shocked journalists with the statement, "Her Ladyship is fucking bored with such formality and prefers to be known as

585

Miss Vivien Leigh."

Charles Feldman arranged for the Oliviers to take the same Coldwater Canyon house, with its egg-shaped pool, where they'd stayed when they made *Lady Hamilton*. Vivien set about making it more intimate and homelike for Larry's return to Hollywood.

On the Warners' lot, she was given the former dressing room of Bette Davis, who had departed after the disastrous box office returns of *Beyond the Forest*. There was a certain irony here. Had William Wyler directed *Streetcar* as originally planned, he'd have preferred Davis as the actress to play Blanche. Consequently, she ended up losing both of the roles that brought Vivien Oscars, beginning with Scarlett O'Hara.

Tennessee met Vivien in Hollywood, where he complained of censorship from the Breen office, which refused to allow the word "homosexual" to be even mentioned in relation to Blanche's dead husband or her promiscuity with military men. The Breen office also wanted to eliminate the suggestion that Blanche, prior to her arrival on the doorstep of Stanley and Stella in New Orleans, had been sexually involved with a seventeen-year-old boy.

A key reference within the Broadway stage version was the line, "I came into a room and found my young husband with an older man who had been his friend for years."

Broadway audiences clearly understood within that line the implication of homosexuality. But for the film version, the line was rewritten. Movie audiences heard, "He wasn't like other people."

Vivien's dear friend, Robert Helpmann, was also in Los Angeles at the time, and Tennessee sometimes joined them on their forays to the clubs of Hollywood. During this, the pre-Stonewall era, gay bars didn't exist as such, but there were many taverns where those seeking same-sex intimacies with a stranger could achieve that aim.

"We were looking for tricks," Tennessee said, "and Robert knew how to maneuver. If Vivien and I couldn't pick up something on our own, he could. Many of the men in this bar were bisexuals, and it wasn't difficult finding a handsome young man who'd want to fuck Scarlett O'Hara. The homosexual men in these bars loved Vivien and crowded around her. Larry might not desire her, but she soon learned that dozens of handsome young men wanted to be with her. Unlike her, Robert and I often had to pay."

"California has the most delicious men on the planet," Robert claimed. "These hunks come here to break into the movies, and the pick-ups are easy to come by."

Helpmann told Tennessee, "Vivien is certainly getting into her character of Blanche. She's picking up young guys like her character, a sort of Method acting approach."

She had strangers in her bed, but Los Angeles itself was a stranger to her. The city had changed, and in her opinion, for the worse. A horrible yellow blanket of smog lay over Greater Los Angeles, stinging her eyes and intensifying her coughing spasms.

When Kazan heard that Vivien at night was frequenting gay bars, he made a confession to her. "Until I met Tennessee I'd never been close to a homosexual. I was so square that I would still ask myself who does what to whom when faggots bed together. I made up my mind to find out, so I double-dated with Tennessee in the company of a young lady, one couple to each of his twin beds, and my curiosity was satisfied."

***

"I can't stand the cunt!" Marlon shouted at Kazan after the first three days of shooting *A Streetcar Named Desire*. "Miss Vivien Leigh. Miss Scarlett O'Hara. Now Lady Olivier. 'Good morning, Mr. Brando.'" He imitated her accent perfectly. "'Good afternoon, Mr. Brando.' She'll suffocate me with her politeness. I can't wait for the rape scene!"

"If the censors will allow it," Kazan cautioned.

The first time Marlon sat down to talk to Vivien, he found a vulnerable character, not the "prissy English bitch" he'd envisioned. She reached out and gently touched his hand, as she spoke of the first time she'd read *A Streetcar Named Desire* in 1948. "I was touched by the haunting quality of Blanche," she said. "The play seemed to speak to a woman inside myself who lives within my own heart. Blanche DuBois is the *animus* of my own being."

That remark seemed to win Marlon to her side. After that, and until the end of the eight-week shoot, he became almost inseparable from her.

He was full of questions about how she'd fared in the London stage production of *Streetcar*, which had been directed by her husband. He was also anxious to learn details of the feuds Larry endured with Irene Selznick and Tennessee Williams over cuts to the script.

One Saturday morning, he drove her into the desert so she could breathe the fresh air. She'd had a struggle with tuberculosis and was having a hard time breathing in Los Angeles. "It's been ten years since Larry and I were in this city. Now there's this bloody smog. You're used to it. I'm not. It fills my lungs with poison."

He told her he knew of an inn thirty miles away that was outside the smog's radius. She could rest there for the weekend.

"When I first came to Los Angeles to play Scarlett," she said, "I remember oranges everywhere. Now those orange trees have vanished like my virginity. Housing developments galore!"

587

"From what I was told, you and Larry had to live as secret lovers the last time you were in Hollywood," he said. "Now you are the married Sir Laurence and Lady Olivier. The King and Queen of the London theater."

"It's a respectability I don't deserve, and a social responsibility from the throne I don't want. As you'll get to know me, and I hope you will, there is nothing respectable about me. In London, I pick up taxi drivers and fuck them."

Startled, he looked at her. Had he heard right? Did she actually say that?

"Don't be surprised," she said. "I'm just as whorish as Blanche DuBois was, taking on all those soldiers at that army base."

She paused, lighting her own cigarette, as if remembering something he'd just said. "Forgive me, but you just referred to my husband as 'Larry.' Do you know my husband, Sir Laurence?"

"I met him a few years ago in New York when he came to see me in a play," he said. "I was very honored."

"I won't bother to ask you how well you knew Sir Laurence," she said, sucking the smoke deeply into her tainted lungs.

"It's just as well, because I won't tell you."

"Growing up in the theater, I am used to such things. I never quiz Larry about his private life. His first wife was a lesbian, you know. When he's with Richard Burton, Danny Kaye, Noël Coward, I ask no questions. Larry asks no questions of me either. We are only Sir Laurence and Lady Olivier in front of the press. When our pictures aren't being taken, we lead completely separate lives."

"If I ever get married, and I don't plan to, I will demand from my woman that I go on leading my separate life."

Driving through the desert with Vivien, Marlon arrived at a wayside motel that seemed to evoke that dreary place she'd seen in *The Petrified Forest* with Bette Davis, Humphrey Bogart, and her friend and lover, Leslie Howard, her beloved Ashley Wilkes in *Gone With the Wind*.

They registered at the inn as "Petticoat Blossom" and "Durango Canyon." Inside the best room, Vivien began to remove her clothing to take a shower. "Do you know," she said to him in the stifling heat of the desert bedroom, "I am part of the world's most beautiful, the world's most talented, the world's most admired, the world's most successful, and the world's most adored couple? If the world only knew the truth. Why don't you rape me like Stanley Kowalski raped Blanche DuBois?"

"An invitation I can't resist," he said, moving toward her.

After sex, he told her, "I can't believe I've slept with Scarlett O'Hara. Rhett Butler's woman. You won't be the first woman that Clark Gable and I have shared.

"Trust me, Clark Gable never got into my pantaloons."

***

Marlon's relationship with Vivien would have gone unrecorded had he not confided in both Charles Feldman, the producer of *Streetcar*, and its director, Kazan. The story of Marlon and Vivien was just too hot for these two men to keep to themselves. When Frank Merlo, Tennessee's lover, arrived with the playwright on the set of *Streetcar*, both Kazan and Feldman shared the news about Marlon's sexual adventure with the two men, who were each anxious to hear (and eventually repeat) the latest gossip.

Tennessee and Frank were also eager to learn about Vivien's first meeting with Marlon. The playwright had predicted "fireworks." Kazan related the story of how Marlon had arrived at the Green Room of Warner Brothers on a buttercup-yellow motorcycle. He wore a tight-fitting Halloween orange T-shirt that showed off his muscles. But instead of his usual dirty blue jeans, he was clad in a pair of elephant brown slacks for the occasion. Later, Vivien remarked to her dining companion, Kazan, "I was surprised when he came into the dining room in shoes. I fully expected to see his bare feet."

As Marlon approached Vivien's table, he overheard an argument she was having with Kazan. She was demanding that she play Blanche the way her husband had directed her in London, and Kazan wanted her to do the role the way he'd directed Jessica Tandy on Broadway.

Not wanting to become part of the argument, Marlon shook Vivien's hand and wandered over to join Feldman at another table. At the time, Feldman had the most notorious black book in Hollywood, and Marlon wanted his producer to fix him up with only the hottest names on the list of available starlets.

After Marlon's hasty departure, Vivien told Kazan, "I find him offensively rude. But it may be just the kind of Stanley vs. Blanche hostility that will play well before the camera."

"Before this movie began, I knew that Jack Warner had paired a gazelle with a wild boar," Kazan said. "But we're going to make a great film, and both you and Marlon are going to walk off with Oscars. His first, your second. Surely you want a brother to go with that lonely statue you won for Scarlett. *Gone With the Wind* was a long time ago. It's time you set Hollywood on its ass once again. With Marlon you can do it. I know you two are not matched socially, but in this case, talent will be the great leveler."

"But he mumbles," she protested. "I too have been accused of lack of projection on stage. It seems that no one can hear me in the upper tiers in those cheap seats."

"Marlon mumbles," Kazan said, "but believe it or not he can also speak with articulation." Catching Marlon's eyes at Feldman's table, Kazan summoned him over again. Marlon came over and sat next to Kazan. "I've got to get back to Charlie. He and I are in hot negotiations over my pussy line-up."

She pretended she didn't hear him, feeling that he was deliberately trying to shock her.

Jokingly, Kazan claimed that after *Streetcar* was finished, he planned to take on a film version of *Henry V* as his next creative venture. Patting Marlon's hand, he urged him to give a quick audition in front of her.

Without being asked again, Marlon launched into a perfect imitation of Olivier doing *Henry V*. He must have gone on for ten minutes before getting up from table and excusing himself once again.

"Now eat your fucking meal," were his departing words.

"I'm shocked, truly shocked," she said when he'd departed. "If I'd closed my eyes, I could have sworn that that voice was coming from Larry himself."

"He's good," Kazan said. He looked at her as if he wanted her to forgive Marlon for his rudeness. Sensing his request, she brushed such a thought aside, "Oh, *fiddle-dee-dee*, I can handle Mr. Brando." Her eyes had narrowed and she looked like she did when uttering her famous, "I'll never go hungry again" speech from *Gone With the Wind*. "Before *Streetcar* is wrapped, it'll be Lady Olivier who will shock Mr. Brando."

***

After an eleven-year absence, Larry returned to Hollywood to make *Carrie* with William Wyler. He had to have an American accent and show the decline of a gentleman who had become a Bowery wino. Larry told Vivien, "We'll repeat our successes like you in *Gone With the Wind* and me in *Wuthering Heights*.

In Hollywood, Vivien's seventeen-year-old daughter, Suzanne Holman, stayed with them for a while, the first time she'd ever lived in the same place with them. She remembered the awful fights, which she termed "theatrically pitched," that took place behind closed doors. But at the time she said she was not aware that their marriage was on the rocks.

On the first day of the shoot, Wyler admitted to Larry, "You weren't my first choice to play George Hurstwood. Cary Grant turned it down."

"This tragedy of a man's downfall and decay somehow mirrors my own life with Vivien," Larry told Wyler, "but I don't quite know how."

"My two stars, Larry and Jennifer Jones, hated each other on sight," Wyler later confessed. "They didn't feud, but they made their loathing of each other apparent. I think David O. Selznick had poisoned Jennifer against the Oliviers. After all, David had boycotted Larry for two full years when Larry was seeking work in Hollywood, and he had even brought legal action against Vivien."

Larry told friends that Jennifer "was really being a cunt every day on the set."

When she heard that, she bitchily responded, "I dreaded a love scene with him. I never knew where his mouth had been the night before. Stories of his homosexuality have preceded him."

"I guess Mrs. Selznick bloody well fucking doesn't know anything about anything," Larry told Vivien. "No soul. A dumb animal with a human brain."

Because of the matrimonial musical chairs of show business, Larry would be sharing close-ups with the newest wife of the man whose ex-wife had produced Larry's current wife's current vehicle.

In Hollywood, his friend Spencer Tracy privately worked with Larry to prepare him for the toughness of his role as Hurstwood.

During the shooting of *Carrie*, Larry heard stories of how Vivien had caroused with Tennessee and Helpmann. He went to talk over her episodes with Tracy.

"It's the drinking," Tracy said. "It happens to me too often. I go off on a bender and can't remember what I did the night before, or even the weeks before. There's nothing wrong with Vivien's mind. It's just the sauce. Get her off the booze and you'll see a tremendous change in her."

It is an arguable point whether Vivien had become an alcoholic at this point. She did not drink as much as Tracy. She told Marlon, "I like to drink enough to stay high all day. It gives me courage. I'm a better actress when I drink."

It is estimated that, beginning at lunch, she consumed at least a dozen gin martinis before 8pm, switching to champagne later in the evening.

While Vivien was often away with Katharine Hepburn, Tracy told Larry, "I think Kate is absolutely falling for Vivien, but I've told her how hopeless it is. Oh, she may get her in bed once or twice, but that's about it. She likes to pursue these romantic fantasies—it's not for the sex, it's for the drama of it all."

Deep into production on *Carrie*, Jones told Wyler and Larry that she was pregnant and would have to be strapped in with corsets for full figure scenes. Wyler was furious that she had misled him. After the picture, she lost the baby and claimed that "all those corsets were to blame."

One night at a party thrown by William Wyler, Larry went to find Vivien, discovering her stark naked balancing on a wrought-iron rail. He rescued her and brought her home, but she'd left the party screaming at him, much to the consternation of other guests.

***

591

In a note to Wally Cox, his friend and lover in New York, Marlon at the beginning of the shoot of *Streetcar* had written that, "Scarlett O'Hara has fabulous tits and a tight ass even at her age. I want to fuck her so much I walk around the set with a perpetual hard-on."

Cox was away and didn't read the letter until Marlon had already seduced Vivien.

In his memoirs, Marlon claimed, "Like Blanche, she [meaning Vivien] slept with almost everybody and was beginning to dissolve mentally and to fray at the ends physically." He also falsely claimed that, "I might have given her a tumble if it hadn't been for Larry Olivier. I liked him too much to invade his chicken coop."

In spite of the five million dollars Random House had given him for his autobiography, Marlon wasn't being entirely candid. He not only invaded the Oliviers' chicken coop, he anchored there for a while as the chief rooster.

Day by day on the set, Kazan had seen the burgeoning flirtation between Vivien and Marlon unfold before his eyes. "Vivien's wild sexual craziness, her flirtatiousness, her faded Southern belle appearance turned Marlon on."

When not before the cameras, Kazan saw them constantly sitting with each other and smoking cigarettes. Sometimes Marlon would sing "Songs My Mother Taught Me" (the title of his autobiography). Vivien's two favorite songs from Marlon's mother-fueled repertoire were "Don't Fence Me In" and "Streets of Laredo," two odd choices for her.

Even Kazan was shocked to see exactly how Larry intruded into the romance—and hardly as a jealous husband. In fact, he didn't seem jealous at all. "All Sir Larry wanted was a piece of the action. Or, should I put that differently? A piece of Marlon's ass."

One afternoon, Larry invaded the set. He'd been working that day, shooting *Carrie*. Vivien was telling Marlon, "Like Blanche, I'm a pathetic creature. An artist too sensitive for her own good. Too vulnerable. I am destructible. The world will soon do me in, I fear." Blowing out smoke, she looked at Marlon in a new light. "Perhaps, for all I know, you will be my executioner. I may at this very moment be talking to a reincarnated version of Marie Antoinette's guillotine ghoul."

"No, not that. Anything but that."

At that point Larry intruded, hugging Marlon into a tight embrace he'd not known since their last night in New York together.

Their reunion was followed by an invitation to dinner at their home that night and a midnight swim. It would be the beginning of many dinners and many swims in the elegant Coldwater Canyon house where four years later Feldman would introduce Senator John F. Kennedy to by then-a-star Marilyn

Monroe.

Although he'd lived briefly with Kazan in a house nearby, and had "permanent quarters" with his agent Jay Kanter and roommate Tony Curtis, Marlon moved in with the Oliviers that night.

The Oliviers occupied separate bedrooms in the mansion. Larry turned in first and was soon followed by Marlon. Vivien later told Kazan, "Sometimes I'd see a light on in Larry's bedroom, and I just assumed that he and Marlon were doing whatever two men do when they go to bed together. I've never really understood that kind of love. But I must say this for Marlon. When it comes to couples, he's an equal-opportunity seducer. On many a night he rose from Larry's bed and joined me in mine. I never sleep. All my nights are sleepless. Sometimes he would find me in Charlie's garden wandering around like Ophelia in a see-through nightgown."

Another house guest who'd just arrived from London, actor David Niven, remembered walking into the garden to discover "Brando and Larry swimming naked in the pool. Larry was kissing Brando. Or maybe it was the other way around. I turned my back to them and went back inside to join Vivien. I'm sure she knew what was going on, but she made no mention of it. Nor did I. One must be sophisticated about such matters in life."

Niven later recalled that he felt that both Larry and Vivien "were hopelessly in love with Brando. My God, he was so handsome I could have fallen for him myself, and I'm hopelessly straight. Marlon Brando was adorable. So unlike Stanley Kowalski that he was playing on the screen, he was so gentle, so kind. Of course, I saw only his gentler side. But from the sounds coming from Larry's bedroom, I also knew that Brando could be a brute."

Niven very accurately predicted that the so-called romance between the Oliviers and Marlon would not last beyond the shooting of *Streetcar*. The actor did think that his friend Larry was "walking on thin ice in combining an affair with Marlon and the very jealous Danny Kaye. All Hollywood at the time was talking about Brando's romance with the Oliviers. There was no way in hell that Kaye couldn't have heard about it."

Even so, Kaye, along with Sylvia Fine, went along with his original plan to throw a grand party for the Oliviers in the ballroom of the Beverly Hills Hotel. The Kayes had worked desperately to trim their guest list to one hundred and fifty. Jack Warner claimed, "If someone didn't get an invitation to this bash, they either left town or turned off their lights at eight o'clock."

Without a specific invitation for him, the Oliviers invited Marlon to join them for the event. Larry even lent Marlon one of his tuxedos to wear for the occasion. Unknown to Marlon at the time, Kaye was deeply in love with Larry.

Passing through the lobby leading to the ballroom, Marlon spotted

Marilyn Monroe in plunging *décolletage*. A fellow male guest was introducing her to Errol Flynn. Marlon merely winked surreptitiously at her and walked on. Later, Marilyn would report that Flynn not only seduced her that night, but played "You Are My Sunshine" on his piano using only his erect penis to hit the ebony and ivory keys.

At the head of the reception line, and under glittering Austrian chandeliers, Kaye embraced both Larry and Vivien, holding his hug with Larry longer.

On seeing Marlon, Kaye looked shocked, staring first at Marlon and then at Larry with a "how could you?" look. Suddenly, Kaye slapped Marlon. It was no stage slap but one using all the power and force in his body.

Marlon was a boxer and could have clobbered Kaye. He chose not to. "Like your hair color," Marlon said to Kaye before turning and walking away.

Kaye just stood there staring in defiance as he left. He'd dyed his hair bright red—almost orange—for a movie.

Vivien saved the night by linking her arm with Kaye and, pretending a pride she didn't feel, grandly entered the ballroom where the elite of Hollywood was watching. Nearly everybody at that point knew that Kaye and Larry had been having a prolonged affair, and her fellow guests wanted to see how Vivien pulled off the evening.

"She was brilliant," Feldman later said. "What theatrics, entering the ballroom on the arm of her rival. She was gracious throughout the evening. No one could believe that she knew of the affair and secretly detested Danny Kaye. As for Marlon, I'm sure he found companionship later that night."

At the party Larry spotted a stunning blonde. When she went to the women's room, he asked her agent, Johnny Hyde, "Who's the blonde? Very sexy."

She's one of my newest starlets," he said. "Marilyn Monroe."

The following morning, neither of the Oliviers found Marlon in their beds. Later, Vivien discovered a note addressed to both of them on their breakfast table in the Feldman garden. Larry seemed to know the contents.

The note from Marlon read: "Dear Vivien and Larry. Thank you for your hospitality. You were both wonderful to me. I will treasure my memory of you always. But it is time to move on now, and I'm heading back to New York to resume my life. My regret is never having gotten to know either of you. But, then, I have always depended upon the kindness of strangers."

***

When *A Streetcar Named Desire* was wrapped, Kazan threw a party for his cast members, including Tennessee Williams, who showed up with some beefy unknown actor. Vivien arrived accompanied by Larry, but they sat apart. Kim Hunter was one of the guests of honor, and even Jack Warner stopped by for a brief appearance. Karl Malden showed up with his wife Mona. He later claimed, "I think I was the only one in the cast who genuinely hated Vivien."

At the party, Mona remembered sitting between Vivien and her former lover, John Buckmaster, at table. "They hardly acknowledged Mona," Malden said. "They traded bizarre non-sequiturs all evening. We later read that Buckmaster had been arrested running down Fifth Avenue in New York stark naked."

A scandal erupted at the party, according to a slanderous story that may have been apocryphal. The head waiter allegedly told Larry that his wife was in the men's room giving blow-jobs, and asked him to remove her from the premises. This story almost made the pages of *Confidential* but was suppressed only a day before publication. The editors of *Confidential* had enough witnesses to run with the story, but the magazine's lawyer nixed it before its press run.

When Vivien heard the story, she adamantly denied it. When she encountered Lana Turner the next week at another party, the blonde goddess told Vivien, "The same story was spread about me. Only I was in this nightclub in Harlem taking on every black dick presented to my succulent little mouth. Welcome to Hollywood, honey."

While Vivien left with Kazan for New Orleans for some final shooting, Kaye practically took over Larry's life.

Kaye told his wife, Sylvia Fine, that Larry had confided in him that "Vivien's sexual demands in time became burdensome and now repugnant." Fine couldn't resist spreading the news. She and Kaye at this point in their lives were pursuing their independent sexual agendas. She told her husband, "I'd rather you be with a man like Olivier than some street hustler."

After *Carrie* was filmed, Kaye and Larry flew to Jamaica where they stayed with Noël Coward at his home near Port Maria and Ocho Rios. At an all-male party, both Larry and Kaye performed in drag.

Two views of screen goddess Lana Turner

Relaying details of her tabloid horrors to Vivien Leigh

"Welcome to Hollywood, honey."

Someone snapped a photograph of the duo and sent it to Vivien. In one photograph Kaye had dressed as the groom, Larry the bride, before they performed a dance duet in front of Coward's gay friends.

In Hollywood, after seeing the final cut of *Streetcar*, Kazan said, "After sitting through Vivien's performance as Blanche, I have my doubts. I should have gone with my first instincts and given the role to Geraldine Page or Julie Harris, either of whom could have played it better."

Later, however, after Vivien won an Academy Award, Kazan claimed, "She deserved her Oscar. She would have crawled over broken glass if she thought it would help her performance."

Oddly enough, in his memoirs, Tennessee made no mention of Vivien as Blanche either on the London stage or in Hollywood's film version. The photo editor of the book, however, did run a picture of Marlon and Vivien interacting together in the screen adaptation.

With *Carrie*, Larry faced a disappointment at the box office. His role is often cited as one of his screen mistakes, when, in fact, it is one of his most evocative roles.

In the *Sunday Times*, Dilys Powell cited Larry's acting as "a triumph of autumnal sensibility." Pauline Kael wrote that Larry gave one of his finest screen performances, although "Kahn" in *Variety* wrote that Larry gave "a mostly thankless performance. He never quite fits the role."

Both Larry and Vivien moved cautiously into the 1950s, which would be the scene of great triumphs and great failures. "It was the decade of our discontent," Vivien told Bea Lillie. "We would both find new people to love, but nothing would ever top the emotions we felt in the late 1930s."

Of the tumultuous decade, Larry would later write: "I had not the faintest inkling of how life would have taken me and shaken me like a rat before the 50s came to a close."

CHAPTER FIFTEEN

With their Hollywood commitments behind them, Vivien and Larry were homesick for England. They decided to return at once, but she told him that she was in no condition to endure a long flight back to England, so they decided on an ocean voyage.

No transatlantic liner was available, so Larry and Vivien, along with three other passengers, boarded a small freighter, filled with 40,000 cotton bales, 40,000 crates of apples, and 10,000 cans of sardines. It sailed from San Francisco through the Panama Canal and on to England.

After the thrill and excitement of Hollywood, Larry felt that a long ride across the Atlantic on the freighter would be good for both of them. The trip turned into a disaster.

During the five-week cruise back to England, Larry mainly read plays, deciding what would be their choices for their next starring roles at the Festival of Britain. They briefly considered a double bill, debating the production of George Bernard Shaw's comedy, *Caesar and Cleopatra*, with the intention of alternating it with a production of Shakespeare's tragedy, *Antony and Cleopatra*.

"The idea of combining a comedy with a tragedy appealed to us," Larry said. But they discarded the idea as too ambitious. However, once in London, Roger Furse, their business partner, proposed the same idea. Somewhat reluctantly, they went along with this daring theatrical concept and adventure.

On the freighter, Larry also began to despair about "my graying—I am no longer suitable to play Romeo, or many other parts. I am having a midlife crisis."

Admitting that he and Vivien were hardly a honeymoon couple any more, he claimed that "the stark reality of our company plunged us both into depressions." He also said that "the idea of suicide had its attraction, and I found myself more and more drawn to the ship's rail and the fascination of the foam sweeping by."

As for Vivien, he recalled, "She was sinking deeper into depression. I knew she'd never really come back."

During the trip, she read all the works of F. Scott Fitzgerald, deciding she'd like to star in *Tender Is the Night*, based on his novel. She was bitterly disappointed when she read that David O. Selznick had cast his wife, Jennifer Jones, in the part. "That bitch will ruin the picture to judge from her acting in your *Carrie*," Vivien told Larry.

Back in London at Durham Cottage, Vivien and Larry led more or less separate lives. She focused most of her romantic attention on Finch, while Larry pursued his own agenda. No questions were asked.

During the rehearsals of the two Cleopatras, cast members noticed that Vivien would suddenly attack Larry, as when he accidentally stained one of her Cleopatra costumes with fake stage blood. On another occasion, as they were taking their stage bows, he forgot to turn and bow to her.

She ran off the stage and slammed her dressing room door. When he came to apologize, she opened the door and began throwing flowers at him, even the vase. But the next day she was telling cast members, "I married a theatrical genius."

G.B. Shaw's *Caesar and Cleopatra* opened on May 10, 1951. Opening night at the St. James's Theatre was a gala event for the two plays which would run for four months. The stage for the show was constructed on a rotating platform—one side had an Egyptian backdrop, the other a Roman background.

Larry didn't like the role of Shakespeare's Antony, calling it "the strumpet's food." Vivien claimed that during her preparations for Shakespeare's interpretation of (the older) Cleopatra, "I applied makeup like Marlene Dietrich."

Kenneth Tynan, who had not yet connected with Larry on a personal level, chose the occasion to issue his most notorious attack on Vivien. At the age of twenty-four, he was the drama critic of *The Spectator*. Perhaps to make a name for himself, he launched a brutal attack on Vivien's interpretation of the two Cleopatras, asserting that her acting diminished Larry's. "How obsequiously Sir Laurence seems to play along with her. Blunting his iron precision, leveling away his towering authority, he meets her halfway."

He never stopped attacking her acting, claiming she was overrated. "She keeps threatening Sir Laurence's greatness."

Tynan wrote that Vivien "picked at her Cleopatras with the daintiness of a debutante called upon to dismember a stag."

Maxine Audley, an actress in the play, claimed that after he read Tynan's attack, "Larry threatened to knock Tynan's block off."

Cecil Beaton attended *Antony and Cleopatra*. He later told Lady Juliet Duff, "I was most disappointed. I cannot but think that she must have deteriorated, because her voice was quite phony. I was never once moved and could not understand what she was saying as Larry has taught her to put on a fake voice to disguise her own little birdlike pipe. It is not a success."

Amazingly, Tynan "hero-worshipped" Larry. When Larry became intimately involved with Tynan, he frequently invited him to Notley.

Robert Helpmann later said, "This was sadistic on Larry's part. Not only was he sleeping with Tynan under her roof, she had to welcome him and be a gracious hostess to him, even though one of his reviews led her to have a nervous breakdown."

Coward later called Tynan "a little bitch. He knows Viv's marriage to Larry has cooled, and they are keeping it going to maintain their partnership in the theater. But now Tynan is not content to call Vivien 'a parasite of the species,' but he wants to undermine what relationship remains between Vivien and Larry by sleeping with Larry at Notley. How humiliating this must be for her."

Churchill came to see the show, as he'd become mesmerized by Vivien. To celebrate Larry's birthday, Churchill invited them to a private dinner party. Larry maintained that "the elder statesman has always nourished a crush on Vivien." Instead of giving Larry a birthday gift, he gave one of his paintings to Vivien. It was a still life of two white roses in a crystal vase. She hung it in her bedroom as a treasured heirloom.

"By jove," Churchill said to Larry, "Vivien's a clinker!"

In a letter to her husband, Clementine Churchill wrote, "I heard that both you and Olivier are in love with Vivien Leigh."

It is believed that Larry was instrumental in securing, through the intervention of Churchill, a knighthood for John Gielgud, in spite of his known homosexuality. That honor occurred in June, 1953. But four months later, a drunken Gielgud was arrested in a public men's toilet on a charge of solicitation.

"Johnny," according to Hugh (Binkie) Beaumont, "went to pieces and contemplated suicide.

Beaumont was staging *A Day by the Sea*, Gielgud's next theatrical venture. He called a meeting at his house in Great North Street, which he shared with John Perry, Gielgud's former lover. Larry and Vivien were invited, along with Glen Byam Shaw, Angela Baddeley, Ralph Richardson, and his wife, Meriel Forbes. Beaumont pointedly asked each of them if Gielgud should open on schedule. Every actor there, except Larry, said he should.

Vivien predicted that "Johnny will get a standing ovation," but Larry dissented. He told his friends, "I think production should be delayed three or four months until this scandal dies down."

Maxine Audley

"To the surprise of everyone there," Richardson claimed, "Vivien turned on Larry. She was furious and accused him of being insanely jealous and trying to wreck Johnny's career. Larry's sole negative vote was overridden."

Sheridan Morley, Gielgud's official biographer, thought Vivien was right. "Olivier saw the chance to do his old rival down."

Beaumont also weighed in. "Had Johnny bowed out, like Larry suggested, his career might have been over."

When Gielgud heard of this gathering, he told friends, "I have always liked Vivien better than Larry."

On opening night in Liverpool, when Dame Sybil Thorndike had to virtually pull Gielgud from the wings onto the stage, he was greeted with a standing ovation.

On June 25, 1951, for *Night of 100 Stars*, the annual benefit show, Danny Kaye prevailed on Vivien and Larry to perform in a comic number called "Three Juvenile Delinquents." The audience applauded loudly. Whenever Kaye was in London, Larry went to live with him.

When the Cleopatras ended their run in London, Larry had made arrangements to take both plays to New York for a limited engagement at Billy Rose's Zeigfeld Theatre.

On the transatlantic *Mauritania*, the Oliviers brought a twenty-seven ton stage design for the two Cleopatras for the opening.

"We're bringing to New York not only Cleopatra's barge, but a revolving stage, even the bloody Sphinx," Larry told reporters.

On the sail to New York, Larry noticed that more and more Vivien was acting like a frightened little girl, turning to him for protection. He felt strong and fatherly toward her, or as he later described it, "a reliable, comforting teddy bear."

Two views of Edmund Purdom (top photo) filling in for the body (but not the singing voice) of Mario Lanza in *The Student Prince* (1954), and (lower photo) as a gunslinger in a spaghetti western

Gertrude Lawrence had lent them her New York apartment for the run of the play. She was obviously in love with the color of gray. "These inhospitable tones made me feel like I was living in a brain cell," Larry said.

He often found Vivien lonely and depressed, sometimes crying for hours at a time. "I desperately tried to give her some comfort, but for some time she would be inconsolable," he said.

For most of the time, Vivien disguised her mental state except from Larry. With him, she completely exposed that "uncannily evil monster," as he called it. She was often in the grip of her manic depression, with what her husband viewed as "its deadly, ever-tightening spirals."

The gala opening night at the Ziegfeld on December 19, 1951 for *Caesar and Cleopatra* was the highlight of the theatrical season, drawing a dazzling array of stars.

David O. Selznick showed up with Jennifer Jones. Alfred Lunt was there with Lynn Fontanne. "Danny Kaye was arranging everything," Vivien said. "He shows up everywhere we go. After curtain that night I never saw much of Larry."

The opening night was attended by Ethel Merman, Ruth Gordon, John Steinbeck, Rosalind Russell, Margaret Truman, Cole Porter, and Sarah Churchill. It was also attended by Tyrone Power, who tried never to miss one of Larry's opening premieres. As Power made his way backstage, Kaye blocked him, falsely claiming that "Larry doesn't want to see you tonight."

"It was an act of jealousy on Kaye's part," said Robert Helpmann. "When Larry heard of this the next day, he chastised Danny and called Tyrone and apologized."

In New York the critics raved, with only one dissenting appraisal cast by a budding Kenneth Tynan for *Time* magazine. He wrote that she was "an *enfant terrible* auditioning to be a *femme fatale*."

Their performances even brought a good notice from the often skeptical Brooks Atkinson of *The New York Times*. "There has not been an *Antony and Cleopatra* to compare with this in New York in the last quarter of a century, and there have not been many productions of any Shakespearean play that approached this exalted quality. Miss Leigh is superb as Cleopatra."

The two Cleopatras ran one after the other as part of an alternating schedule for four months within Billy Rose's Ziegfeld Theater in New York. Larry told Vivien, "We have exonerated ourselves from our disastrous *Romeo and Juliet* in 1940."

Offstage during the run, Vivien appeared tense and nervous and would often break down in tears and retreat to her dressing room. However, once the curtain went up she became a trouper, concealing her manic-depressive crises from the audience.

However, she'd often make indiscreet remarks, telling one journalist, "I have a husband and I have lovers. Like Sarah Bernhardt."

Peter Cushing found Larry "distant and remote. Knighthood had gone to his head."

Stewart Granger's wife, Elspeth March, played Ftatateeta, and Helpmann was cast as both Apollodorus and Octavius Caesar.

During the New York run of the two Cleopatras, Vivien developed a passionate crush on the handsome English actor Edmund Purdom. Although he appeared only in small roles in each of the Cleopatras, his talent and devastating good looks brought him to the attention of Hollywood agents, who came backstage to make various pitches to him to go to Hollywood.

His fame today derives mainly for two roles where he filled in for other actors, notably the 1954 MGM musical *The Student Prince*, originally intended for Mario Lanza, and the 1954 production of *The Egyptian*, the picture from which Marlon Brando had bolted.

Forgetting about Peter Finch momentarily, Vivien became so mesmerized by Purdom in New York that she invited him to return with Larry and her to London.

"I thought she was suggesting that I live with Larry and her as their boy," Purdom recalled in an interview he gave in Rome during the filming of one of his "sword-and-sandal" epics. "That wasn't exactly my scene."

After he left Vivien and the Cleopatras, he made his way to Hollywood where he'd more or less been promised the leading male role in the 1952 film *My Cousin Rachel*. "At the last minute, I lost the part to Richard Burton."

"I was so broke I couldn't pay the doctor's bill when our baby was born," he said. He was married at the time to the ex-ballerina, Anita Phillips. "I had no money for bus fare to even go to the hospital to see my wife and daughter. I had to walk from studio to studio looking for a job. Anita and I were evicted for non-payment of rent."

In desperation he wrote to Vivien. "She was so kind," he said. "Even though I'd walked out on her in New York, she wired us desperately needed funds. I'd turned down her overtures of making our relationship permanent, but she forgave me. We did have a brief affair. It was more her idea than mine."

During his roller-coaster career, the bisexual Purdom later became the lover of Tyrone Power, and even married the actor's ex-wife Linda Christian, the most famous of his four wives.

Although he turned down a veiled offer to become "the boy" of the Oliviers, Purdom later changed his mind about being kept. In between and during marriages, he was "sponsored" by "men with millions" in Rome who were drawn to his fading movie fame and his striking dark good looks and his dimpled cheeks.

While Vivien was pursing Purdom, Larry had eyes for the actress, Maxine Audley, who was in the cast. Vivien had known her from the time she'd appeared with her in the 1948 adaptation of *Anna Karenina*.

Vivien had a double reason to dislike Audley. Not only was she pursuing her husband, but Vivien had heard rumors that Audley had seduced Peter Finch when they'd both acted at the St. James's in the 1951 production of *Othello*, starring Orson Welles.

At first Vivien had been the epitome of graciousness to Audley, even sending her spring flowers when she contracted the measles in London.

Audley, who played Charmian in both productions of the two Cleopatras, later said, "During the run it appeared that Vivien and Larry loathed each other. I saw nothing wrong in going after Larry since she left the theater every night with Purdom. Of course, I had to steal Larry away from Danny Kaye who monopolized most of his nights."

While in New York, Larry and Vivien learned about the death of King George VI. Like the monarchist he was, Larry presided at the New York memorial ceremony.

Unable to attend the Oscar ceremonies in Hollywood, where she won an Academy Award for *A Streetcar Named Desire* in March of 1952, Vivien asked her husband's former mistress, Greer Garson, to accept the award there for her.

When word spread among Broadway's young actors that Larry was working out every morning at Pilate's Universal Gymnasium on Eighth Avenue, attendance at the gym increased. The manager said, "The actors were practically shoving it in Olivier's face, asking him to take a lick. But so far as I know, he never took up with one of them."

For a holiday break after the exhausting schedule of work in New York, Larry and Vivien flew to Jamaica to stay with Noël Coward.

While Vivien went wandering into Port Antonio one afternoon with Coward's maid, Larry had a long talk with Coward, pouring out the troubles in his marriage.

Larry admitted to him, "I feel trapped. I know I'm responsible for her, but I don't want the burden—it's too great. I was once told to love the characters I played. I did that for years, but now I'm bored with them and acting in general. It's Vivien. She constantly brings me down to her level of depression, and I don't know how to escape from her."

Coward's advice was blunt: "Find another love and let Vivien drift. I know this sounds heartless, but she's tough. She'll survive. You're the one who's on the verge of a nervous breakdown. Divorce her!"

Returning from Jamaica, Vivien shocked her friends with the change in her appearance. "Long periods of illness and her new lifestyle caused a deterioration to her face that was remarkable," said Margaret Leighton. "Her excesses of behavior, her crumbling marriage, her one-night stands, her emotional entanglements with Finch, and others, had seriously damaged her. She would never really recover."

"He is our greatest actor," wrote one journalist in Britain. "What is he doing appearing in such an unworthy trifle as Captain MacHeath in the movie version of *The Beggar's Opera?*" Christopher Fry had adapted the film script from the 18th century comic opera by John Gay.

The noted stage director Peter Brook made his movie debut in this film. He was called the most gifted stage director of his generation. When the twenty-seven-year-old "wonder boy" signed on the project, Larry agreed to go along. However, from the beginning they disagreed on almost everything, Larry referring to the relationship as "oil and water."

The first day of rehearsals got off to a bad start, when Brook informed Larry, "I would have preferred Richard Burton as MacHeath."

Early praise for Larry's singing voice, a light baritone, caused him to believe that he was "a miracle mixture of Caruso and Chaliapin." The reference, of course, was to Enrico Caruso of Italy and Fodor Ivanovich Chaliapin, the Russian opera singer known for his expressive bass voice.

"This was my first role as a singing actor," Larry said. "But the unhappy result was that the sounds that I made were not up to the general standard of the music. I just hope and pray that my personal flop in *The Beggar's Opera* will be the worst that I shall ever disenjoy."

Larry wanted realism in the role and performed his own stunts. In one scene he rode his horse so hard it died of a heart attack.

After its release, *The Beggar's Opera* was a "flop of embarrassing proportions," in Larry's words. *The Monthly Film Bulletin* charged that Larry lacked "the swagger, the roistering, that MacHeath requires."

But not all reviews were negative. A.H. Weiler in *The New York Times* wrote, "Abetted by the racy dialogue supplied by both Gay and Fry, Sir Laurence is, alternately, a reckless daredevil, a wily but manly lover and a fearless, brooding adventurer. It is a characterization that he endows with genuine abandon, stature and feeling."

Gay's comic opera did a lot better when it was turned into the Bertolt Brecht-Kurt Weill variation, *The Threepenny Opera.*

***

While Vivien spent as much time as she could at night with Finch, Larry developed what he later told co-producer Herbert Wilcox, "a case of *Leadinglady-itis.*"

He became entranced with the 22-year-old actress Dorothy Tutin, who was cast as Polly Peacham in *The Beggar's Opera.*

This Londoner captivated Larry with her unusual looks, her deep brown eyes, husky voice, wistful smile, and sense of humor. She was also a very talented stage and film actress. The press called her "one of the most enchanting, accomplished, and intelligent leading ladies of the post-war British stage."

Trader Faulkner, the Australian actor who had appeared on stage in Sydney with Larry in *Richard III,* was dating Tutin when he flew to Bermuda to shoot a film in 1952. "When I returned, she was Olivier's," Faulkner said. "I think he was her first lover."

Vivien heard about the affair when Tutin's mother phoned her. "When are you going to divorce Sir Laurence and let him go free to marry my beautiful, talented—and *young*—daughter Dorothy?"

"Frankly, I don't care who Sir Laurence is fucking so long as it's not me." She slammed down the phone. Forever afterward Vivien called Tutin "That Dot Tut."

At one point Larry was actually considering marriage to Tutin.

When Bette Davis appeared with Tutin in the made-for-television movie, *Murder With Mirrors*, based on the Agatha Christie novel, she bluntly asked Tutin, "What is it like to fuck Sir Laurence?"

Although their affair had long ended, Larry was instrumental in getting Tutin cast in the Emmy-winning TV production of Shakespeare's *King Lear*.

Beginning with Tutin, most of the affairs throughout the rest of Larry's life were with women, only occasionally with a man. He called his affair with Tutin and subsequent romantic links "my tender venturings into the blessed unction of sex."

Occasionally, Larry ran into Angela Baddeley. His crush on her was a faded page in his history, as was his affair with her husband, Glen Byam Shaw.

She later recalled Larry's condition at the time of her reunion with him in Stratford-upon-Avon. "I'd never seen him in such despair, mainly over Vivien, but he had other worries too," Baddeley recalled. "He was very despondent and felt he was responsible for driving Vivien insane. He didn't know how to cope with her. He told me he was no longer in love with her, but harbored a great affection for her. 'It is impossible to go on loving a woman who has turned both of our lives into a third-rate drama that should never have been presented,' he told me."

"Larry got drunk that night and cried," she said. "I felt really sorry for him. He seemed consumed by an overwhelming guilt."

He admitted to her that "I've reached rock bottom. I might be hailed as the greatest actor in the world, but I'm broke. My marriage is all but over; my last two films failed, I haven't had a real success on the stage in four years. My wife—at least I think she's my wife—has to bring home the bacon. She's gone to Ceylon to film *Elephant Walk*. With Peter Finch, of course. Originally I was offered the role of the plantation manager as a vehicle for Viv and me. But she preferred Peter instead."

"Not only that," he said, "but I'm still paying alimony to Jill Esmond, and I have to maintain Tarquin, of course. My God, it wasn't even a marriage. She was then and has always been a lesbian."

Esmond had obtained a court order, forcing him to increase his annual allotment of 3,500 pounds by another 750 pounds.

"I lost money on Finch in *The Happy Time*, and on Orson Welles in *Othello*," Larry said. "I'm also about to lose Notley. Vivien and I are thinking of selling our beloved old place."

"My brother Dickie's hooked up with a girl, Hester Capel-Dunn, that I think he's been fucking since she was thirteen," Larry said. "He finally became engaged to this young woman. She is seventeen now, Dickie forty-eight."

"I think Larry was fighting for his own survival," Baddeley said. "The solution was painfully obvious. He had to cut Vivien off, let her fend for herself."

***

Irving Asher, a Hollywood producer, had flown to meet Larry and Vivien in London to try to interest them in his upcoming film, *Elephant Walk*, part of which would be shot in Ceylon.

In a nutshell, it was the story of an English tea grower and his wife on their plantation. The plantation foreman has an affair with the wife of the owner. Asher wanted to cast the Oliviers as the married couple.

Because of prior commitments, Larry was forced to turn down the offer, even though he really needed the money.

He had grave reservations about Vivien going to Ceylon in late January, 1953, to film *Elephant Walk*. She told him she was going to star in the movie regardless of what he thought.

(top photo) Movie poster, focusing on the final cut of *Elephant Walk*, starring Elizabeth Taylor after Vivien dropped out after a nervous breakdown

(lower photo) Vivien Leigh with Peter Finch in an original scene, later cut, wherein Vivien played, however briefly, the starring female lead.

She was signed for $150,000 to appear in the film, the highest salary ever for her. The first scenes would be shot in Ceylon where the blistering heat was viewed as intolerable.

Ironically for *Elephant Walk,* Vivien was almost reunited with her former co-stars from *Gone With the Wind* and *A Streetcar Named Desire*. However, both Clark Gable and Marlon Brando turned down the script. Ralph Richardson and Claude Rains had also been considered for roles in the movie, but each of these actors had also turned down the script.

Dana Andrews had been cast as one of the two male leads, but the role of the other actor was still open. When Asher asked both Vivien and Larry for the recommendation of a British actor, both of them, almost simultaneously, said, "Peter Finch."

Larry took Asher to an Old Vic matinée to see Finch perform as Monsieur Beaujolais in *The Italian Straw Hat*. On Larry's recommendation, Asher decided to hire Finch. "I was a little worried about some aspects of his face, but I liked the fact that he wasn't a pretty guy."

One night in January of 1953, there was a knock on the door of the house that Finch shared with his wife Tamara. It was Vivien at one o'clock in the morning.

She was "starkers under her mink," in the words of one writer.

Finch remembered that she was almost in hysterics, telling him that he'd been selected to play one of the three leads in the upcoming *Elephant Walk*. Finch quickly reviewed his current stage offers—none of which appealed to him—and told Vivien he'd love to co-star in the film with her.

"I'm going back to the world of my birth and on to Ceylon where Sinbad the Sailor played out his adventures," Vivien told Larry.

A reluctant Larry drove them to the airport to see them off. Standing on the tarmac as the plane was about to depart, he told Finch, "Take care of her."

Finch possessively put his arm around Vivien. "Don't worry. I will."

Larry saw them off at the airport with a sense of foreboding. "As the plane began to move gently forward, they both looked back at me through the window, Peter making a gallant effort to look the assuringly protective friend, and, she, with a little smile of infinite sweetness, blowing me a sad little kiss."

He returned to Notley where he later claimed he felt more love for his old abbey than for his wife. "I began to think it was inhuman, immoral to love a thing more than a person. But the love of my life had been extracted like some rotten tooth."

Still afraid of planes, Vivien held tightly to Peter's hand during the flight of the Comet, remembering her near-fatal crash in Connecticut. The Comet could fly to India in a quarter of the time it used to take.

She was somewhat of a clairvoyant, telling Finch, "This plane is going to crash. I just know it." He tried to calm her fears.

Actually she turned out to be right. The following night after Vivien and Finch had exited, the plane, as part of another flight, crashed. The next Comet flight also crashed. After the second crash, that particular aircraft was permanently retired from service.

Once in Ceylon, she met her director William Dieterle. She was also introduced to her co-star, Dana Andrews. Having arrived in Ceylon previous to her arrival, he was drunk. One night she agreed to have dinner with him, which turned into an alleged wrestling match.

"He tried to rape me," she told Finch. "The drunken bastard. He told me, 'I hear you'll fuck anyone, and I've got the biggest dick in Hollywood.'"

Niven had heard this story in Hollywood and weeks later confronted Andrews. "That's a total lie. I did no such thing. In fact, it was Vivien who came on to me. When I wouldn't do her, she attacked me and became hysterical. She called me an old stick-in-the-mud. Several nights later she seemed to forget about our little encounter. She invited me to go with her and Finch for a night of heavy drinking. You know I'm not a man to turn down a drink, but that wild pair was a bit much for me. I coiled up with a beautiful teenage Ceylon gal for the night—and that was that."

From the very beginning, Vivien clashed with Dieterle. She reported to work wearing a wig she positioned an inch below her hair line. When he called for her hairdresser to make adjustments, she denounced him.

One scene called for Vivien to appear on horseback. When she couldn't hear Dieterle, he shouted his direction at her. That scared the horse which in turn frightened her.

A grip helped her down from the horse. She confronted Dieterle, telling him, "I'm off the picture if you look at me one more time. I absolutely forbid you to look at me."

"How in the fuck am I supposed to direct this picture when this insane bitch refuses to allow me to look at her?" Dieterle asked in a phone call to Asher.

Another day on the set, she encountered a young Singhalese native who had been ordered to bring cold drinks to the cast, whose members were sweltering in the heat. When he asked Vivien if she wanted lemonade, she started screaming. Finch rushed to her side. "Make him go away," she shouted. "He has black eyes. Indian black. I can't stand black eyes."

Finch later surmised she was recalling some traumatic event in her childhood when an attendant, perhaps a male, may have sexually abused her when she was less than five years old.

Regrettably, one of the first scenes she filmed involved a defanged but gigantic anaconda wrapped around her neck. She became so unnerved by the reptile so close to her that she began reciting the dialogue of Blanche DuBois in *A Streetcar Named Desire*.

Dieterle was horrified.

In Ceylon, she was unable to sleep, wandering along the secluded coves and beaches of the island at night, wearing either a see-through nightgown or, in some instances, completely naked.

Dieterle was severely disappointed when he saw the rushes. He bluntly told her, "You photograph like a tired old lady. Your acting is wooden like a zombie."

"Fuck you!" she shouted at him. "What did you think I'd look like? Scarlett O'Hara in that opening scene in *Gone With the Wind*? Well, I'm not young any more. I was born in 1913."

Vivien presented Dieterle with dialogue that she claimed had been rewritten the night before by the scriptwriter. He found it irrational, later discovering that she'd written it herself.

John von Kotze, the Technicolor technician on *Elephant Walk*, claimed that his assistant, a man named only as "George," once returned to the bedroom which they shared. "He was shaking," von Kotze said. "He claimed that Vivien had almost tried to rape him. George, by the way, is bald, fat, and sixty-four, if a day."

The next day, von Kotze casually mentioned George to Vivien. She didn't recall anything about the incident the night before. "The only George I knew," she said, "was King George VI," she said.

Ultimately, most of her attention became focused on Finch. She followed him around day and night, often referring to him as Larry. Finch tried in vain to conceal from the director and the crew that she was on the verge of a nervous breakdown.

Finch spoke privately to a few friends after his return to London, describing his ordeal while locked in a hotel suite in Ceylon with Vivien. "Half the time she was proud and bold, wanting to show Larry she could survive without him. The other time she attacked him for letting her go to Ceylon. At one point she claimed that he had forced her to make the film so he could spend her $150,000 on one of his moronic vanity projects in the theater. When I got back to London, our affair had been made public. Friends of Larry's attacked me. But I was Vivien's protector. Did they want her to wind up in the clutches of some beastly grip or get gang-raped one night?"

After Finch divorced Tamara in 1959, he married Yolande Turner the same year. He told his second wife many stories about working with Vivien on what he came to call "Elephant Shit."

In her own memoirs, Yolande described "how utterly impossible Vivien became, drinking heavily straight out of the bottle, tearing her clothes off and running around the streets and their garden naked, throwing dangerous objects at her best friends, or through windows and at passing cars. She had gone over."

[When Finch married Yolande, she was a 25-year-old South African actress. With her he had a son and daughter. But ultimately, his affair with the singer Shirley Bassey finally broke up their marriage.]

By the second week, word from Ceylon reached Larry that Vivien had become "impossible to work with." The producer of the film, Irving Asher, asked Larry if he could fly to Ceylon to help stabilize Vivien.

Heeding the request, Larry flew the long route to Ceylon, going through Paris, Rome, Beirut, and Bahrain to reach Ceylon.

Surprisingly, Vivien met him at the airport, although she was supposed to be in front of the cameras that day. When he suggested this to her, he was met with what he called "a blaze of rage that surprised even me."

When he arrived at the hotel in Kandy, he encountered Finch and became aware almost from the first hour that the actor's relationship with his wife had grown far more serious than it had been at Notley.

Amazingly, during Larry's brief visit to Ceylon, Vivien seemed in reasonable control. Except for a sudden harsh denunciation, "the old gal is holding up pretty well," he told Asher. "I must return to London to finish the final work on *The Beggar's Opera*." Embracing both Finch and Vivien at the airport, he began the long, circuitous air route back to London.

Once back home, Larry had dinner with Cecil Tennant, his friend and agent who would come to his rescue in the weeks to follow, as Vivien's condition continued to deteriorate.

"In many ways, the white heat of passion had diminished as we drove to Santa Barbara with Katharine Hepburn on that long ago night in 1940," Larry claimed. "By 1948 all real romantic love had ended. From then on, it was just a caretaker relationship. My first marriage was empty, a dark shell. My second marriage was a living nightmare. By marrying Vivien, I've taken the night train to hell."

In his *Confessions*, Larry used Victorian prose to describe the love affair of Finch and Vivien. "The two of them were hopelessly lost in the floodtide of the all-consuming passion to which, for the first time, they were giving enthusiastic license."

Maxine Audley, with whom Larry had had an affair, was also an intimate of Finch. "He was well known for his stud-like qualities," she once said. "Poor Larry didn't always get high marks for his performance in bed the way he did on the stage. In Finch, Vivien found a man whose passion was the equal of hers. Poor Peter was just putty in her hand. He was attracted to her glamour and reputation. She would call him and he'd come running like a little puppy to gulp down a plate of milk. What Peter didn't know was that Vivien had laced that creamy milk with just an aroma of arsenic."

***

After the shooting of the Ceylon segments was finished, Vivien and Finch, along with the film crew, were ordered to fly to Hollywood on March 4, 1953 to continue shooting the film's interior scenes.

Vivien had always had a fear of flying. To reach Los Angeles and the Paramount lot in Hollywood, involved a seventy-two hour trip. After take-off, she became hysterical and started screaming.

Finch was by her side and held her down when she jumped up and tried to tear off her clothes. The other passengers panicked when they realized that she was trying to jump out of the plane.

Vivien beat at the windows, as if trying to escape. She told Finch, "I'm going through the emergency door and parachuting down."

"But you don't have a parachute," Finch said, forcefully restraining her. He sat her down in her seat and made her take what he called "some knock-out pills."

Finally, when the plane landed in Burbank, Vivien was subdued and went in a studio limousine to a house that Finch had rented. She stayed there and slept with Finch until the arrival of Tamara and his daughter Anita.

George Cukor had offered Vivien the use of Spencer Tracy's cottage on the Cukor estate while the veteran actor was away making a motion picture.

Katharine Hepburn rushed to Vivien's side to inaugurate caretaker duties.

Cukor told his lover at the time, Jay Garon, that he believed that Hepburn was "taking advantage of poor Vivien and moving in like a sexual predator." While waiting for Tracy's return, Hepburn did spend time with Vivien and slept with her. At least she got Vivien on a healthier diet and took her on long walks in the Hollywood Hills, hoping to restore her health.

When Hepburn was called away, Sunny Lash stayed with Vivien briefly, as she'd done more than a decade and a half previously, during the filming of *Gone With the Wind*. Sunny was shocked when Vivien asked her to procure young men for her. "I don't do that," Sunny told her.

When Vivien presented her desires to Cukor, he was far more obliging. "For such matters, I refer to Scotty." He was referring to Scotty Bowers, the owner of Scotty's Gas Station at the corner of Van Ness and Hollywood Boulevard. Scotty was functioning as a sort of male madam, servicing the sexual needs of Hollywood celebrities.

Scotty employed some twenty handsome young men at this gas station, each of whom did more than pump gas. For ten or usually twenty dollars, they

611

would disappear into one of the back rooms with a client. More often, they did house calls. In his spare time, Scotty worked as a bartender at Hollywood parties.

Scotty also maintained links with a number of women who would make house calls at the homes of both men and women.

In Scotty's as yet unpublished manuscript, *Full Service*, he documents his encounter with Vivien at the Cukor home on Cordell Drive. He admitted that Vivien "fancied me—and I had the hots for her."

At the end of a dinner party at Cukor's, Vivien told Scotty, "Get your tight little ass back over here in half an hour, lover boy. I'll leave the gate unlocked."

Slipping back in to see her, he wrote that she "was a hot, hot lady, very sexual and very excitable. Once she got going, nothing could stop her passion from requiring full and complete satisfaction. That night we screwed as though the survival of the world depended on it. She could not control herself. She was loud. She would squeal and holler and laugh. She had orgasm after orgasm."

After Scotty had finally finished with her, she told him, "That was one of the best fucks I've ever had."

That night marked the beginning of an affair between Scotty and Vivien. When he wasn't available, he generously sent around "one of my best boys."

Vivien soon learned that Scotty was supplying boys to both Cukor and to her friend Tennessee Williams as well. She was rather shocked when she learned that Scotty also supplied girls, usually young models or aspirant actresses, to Katharine Hepburn.

But, as Scotty told Vivien, "If Hepburn finds a girl with only the slightest blemish on her, she sends her back."

***

Later in his life, Finch admitted, "I fell in love with Vivien and didn't plan to let Tamara stand in the way of our happiness. I didn't really know how sick Vivien was in the beginning, You see, I was too drunk to tell."

"When did you first come to realize how mentally ill Vivien was?" a reporter asked Finch.

"Vivien threw this big party for me in Hollywood," he said. "She wanted me to meet all the big shots she knew in the film colony. At the party were such guests as George Cukor, Stewart Granger, Jean Simmons, and David Niven. She even invited Clark Gable. But three hours into the party, Vivien emerged from an upstairs bedroom with a pair of scissors. It was like some psycho movie. She rushed down the stairs and raced toward Tamara. She was going to plunge the scissors into Tamara's heart. Within moments, I had restrained her, wrenching the scissors from her. She looked up at me in a daze. She suddenly came to her senses. Without saying a word to anyone, she fled the house."

Peter's friend, Trader Faulkner, wrote: "For Tamara, it was a cruel and unfair game, and Vivien was ruthless. She wanted Peter and she got him as she had wanted Olivier, and got him away from his first wife, Jill Esmond. Vivien was outrageous. Peter was not strong enough to handle Vivien or man enough to stand up to Olivier."

At one point Faulkner maintained that Finch himself had threatened suicide "to blot out the whole bloody business once and for all."

Faulkner later wrote that as part of her ongoing dramas with Finch, "Vivien tried to seduce Tamara. Vivien came on to Tamara very strongly, trying to force her into a lesbian relationship, but Tamara spurned her advances and fled the house."

When she reported this attack to Finch, he merely smiled. "Women do those things sometimes. I'd like to watch." He was drunk when he said that, but may have meant it.

Having heard about Vivien's ordeal during the airplane flight from Ceylon, Hollywood journalists were beating down Paramount's door, seeking an interview. The studio publicist agreed to have Vivien interviewed by Louella Parsons, Hollywood's reigning gossip maven at the time. She was subdued when she met Parsons, who found Vivien had "a kind of forced gaiety."

She told the columnist, "This is my last motion picture. Life is too short to work so hard."

After seeing Parsons, Vivien returned to her dressing room where she began to drink, not just in sips but gulps.

Her old friend, Sunny Lash, appeared on the scene and tried to calm her down, but Vivien slapped her face. "Get out!" she shouted at Sunny. By the time Vivien appeared on the set again, she was staggering.

She ran through the studio screaming FIRE! FIRE! FIRE! causing panic. She stumbled over a cable, falling to the floor. Finch caught up with her, cradling her in his arms. She turned to him, "Larry! Larry! Larry! You've come back."

Dieterle stood by, not knowing what to do. One of his assistants called the company doctor.

Sunny had put in a call to David Niven, who hurried to the studio. He came to her, taking her in his arms and telling Finch that he had the situation under control. Slowly he walked her out of the studio.

Someone later asked Finch if anyone called for the police when Vivien tried to create panic at Paramount.

"Hell no!" Finch said. "You don't arrest Scarlett O'Hara on her return to Hollywood, for God's sake. On the set the next day, Vivien didn't even remember the incident—or so she said."

Dieterle met with officials at Paramount. There was talk of junking the picture. There was also talk of getting another star—Elizabeth Taylor was suggested. The stunningly beautiful British star was under contract to MGM which had no current project for her. She was available for a very expensive loan-out.

Fearing it would be too costly to turn back at this point, especially with the location shots already filmed, Paramount decided to take a chance and go ahead with Vivien, even though they felt she would never hold up to see "The End" flash across the screen.

Irving Asher reported that Vivien called him at 2:30AM one morning and asked him to come over at once to see her. She was standing at the top of the stairs, wearing a see-through dressing gown. She took off the gown and slowly descended the steps completely nude.

"At the bottom of the steps, she took my hand and guided me into the television room," Asher said. "She asked me to sit down beside her. For two hours we sat and watched wavy lines on her TV set, since no stations were broadcasting at that ungodly hour."

"I finally told her I had to leave," he said. "As I was heading for the door, Peter Finch turned the key and walked into the main hallway. He'd either been out carousing or at home with his wife, Tamara. From the smell and looks of him, I felt he'd been whoring about. He was a known womanizer. Only a few people knew at the time he was bisexual. Maybe he'd met a young actor—who knows? Who really cares? A nude Vivien rushed into the hallway where she burst into tears and fell in his arms. 'Oh, darling,' she said, sobbing, 'you've come back to me.' I departed quickly as I saw him lift her up and head up the stairs with her."

In Hollywood, just when problems with Vivien were reaching the breaking point, Dana Andrews disappeared for three days on a wild binge. He'd just purchased a new Cadillac. But when he showed up after a long drunk, he didn't remember what had happened to his car.

"My God," Asher lamented to the officials at Paramount. "I've got an insane nymphomaniac and two drunken actors to work with."

***

At home, Tamara confronted her husband, demanding that Finch break up his affair with Vivien or else. She threatened to leave California and take their

614

daughter Anita with her. Giving in to her demand, Finch stayed home at nights.

For several days, he did not show up to be with Vivien. When he did, he told her of Tamara's demands. "It's got to end between us," he said.

Enraged, she started throwing things at him. "I didn't get to use those scissors on Tamara," she said. "So I'll use a butcher knife on you." When she headed toward the kitchen, he fled from the house.

Worried about Vivien, Finch slipped off the next day to see how she was. Using his key, he entered her house and went at once to her bedroom.

There he found Vivien and John Buckmaster, Gladys Cooper's son, crawling around naked on the floor. She looked up at him and flashed her smile. "Johnny and I are just trying to exorcise our demons." Quite unexpectedly, her old flame from the 1930s had come back into her life.

Finch left her house at once.

At the time he'd reunited with Vivien, Buckmaster had been in and out of three mental institutions. In New York police had arrested him after he'd attacked a woman on Madison Avenue and 67th Street at seven in the morning. Police gave chase and caught up with him, charging him with felonious assault and possession of two kitchen-type knives which he'd brandished before the woman.

Confined to the State Hospital for the Mentally Ill at King's Park, Long Island, Buckmaster was rescued by his stepbrother, John Merivale. It was a case of a future lover rescuing an old lover of Vivien's. Merivale took him back to England and put him in St. Andrew's Hospital in Northampton. But Buckmaster escaped.

When Merivale received an in-flight postcard, claiming he was returning to "the land of milk and honey," he knew he was heading for California. Once in Hollywood, he moved in with Vivien.

At one point, Buckmaster suggested that he and Vivien "fly out an upper window together in one running leap stark naked." Even in her deranged condition, she knew enough to turn down that suggestion.

During his short stay with Vivien, Buckmaster reportedly staged a Roman orgy. Someone had strolled along Santa Monica Boulevard, handing out invitations to attend "a private toga party at the home of Scarlett O'Hara. Dress code: bring your own sheet and don't wear any underwear."

No details remain of that event except for an article submitted to *Confidential* magazine that claimed that Vivien appeared at the orgy as Cleopatra, demanding to be "deflowered" by her sex slaves.

"Many a guy enjoyed Scarlett O'Hara that night until she mysteriously disappeared upstairs and locked the door," alleged one of the guests.

William Haines, a Sunday visitor to George Cukor's pool, remembered seeing a nude John Buckmaster with "an erection at full mast chasing a nude Scarlett O'Hara around the swimming hole."

Hearing reports of strange events occurring at Vivien's, including the arrival of Buckmaster, her friends, Stewart Granger and David Niven, went to investigate.

"We discovered Buckmaster barking madly himself," Niven said. "He was draped in a toga of toweling. I ordered Jimmy to get him out of the house and away from Vivien."

Niven stayed behind to look after Vivien as Granger drove Buckmaster back to his hotel, the notorious Garden of Allah where a coterie of actresses, at a late-night party, was urging the screen Tarzan, Johnny Weissmuller, to remove his bathing trunks.

Niven entered Vivien's bedroom. There he discovered her naked and sitting on a balustrade railing overlooking the garden. "What's the matter?" he asked in his most soothing voice.

"Oh, it's you," she said matter-of-factly, as if he'd merely gone downstairs to the kitchen and was returning. With misty eyes, she looked at him. "I'm in love."

"With whom, darling?" he asked her.

"Peter Finch. But it's not going well, and I plan to kill myself today."

He managed to get her to come inside.

Returning to Vivien's house, Granger prepared breakfast for Vivien. Into her scrambled eggs he placed the contents of a sleeping capsule.

Vivien Leigh with Peter Finch

When she confronted him, asking him why he and Niven weren't also eating, he told her, "We're not hungry."

She didn't believe him and ordered Niven to sample her eggs. He did just that and had soon passed out on the sofa, sleeping peacefully.

Granger recalled what happened next in his memoirs. "Suddenly she dropped the towel from around her body and walked into the garden. It was dawn now, and she said she was going to take a swim. Here I was at six in the morning sitting by a pool opposite a totally nude and utterly deranged stranger."

When Granger first submitted his memoirs, *Sparks Fly Upward*, it included a revelation which was later removed.

He claimed that during the time that he'd sat with a naked Vivien by the pool, she had demanded that he seduce her. "It's something I had done a long time ago," he'd written. "For old time's sake, I honored her request. Maybe I was just kidding myself, but I thought a good plugging might work better on Vivien than a sleeping pill. At least that's what I told myself when I performed the dastardly deed of taking advantage of her."

After the seduction, Granger called Vivien's doctor, who arrived with two nurses, "each more frightening than the next," he later recalled. The one with the hypodermic syringe said, "I know who you are. You're Scarlett O'Hara, aren't you?"

"I'm not," Vivien screamed at her. "I'm Blanche DuBois."

Granger carried Vivien up the stairs and held her down while a burly nurse administered the needle. "I fell across the bed, pinning Vivien underneath me and yelled at the terrified nurse to stick the needle in. As Vivien felt the point, she looked at me as if I had betrayed her. 'Oh, Jimmy, how could you? I thought you were my friend.'"

Granger's real name was James Stewart, which he'd changed for obvious reasons.

Granger and Niven felt ill-equipped to take care of her. Danny Kaye was in Hollywood at the time, and he was summoned to Vivien's house, where the two British actors informed him of her dire mental condition.

Larry was vacationing at the time in Ischia, and Kaye called him there, informing him of the tragic news. Vivien had suffered a total nervous breakdown, and her doctors wanted permission to commit her to a psychiatric hospital. Larry's okay was needed for that, but he refused, telling Kaye to "take care of Vivien until I get there."

One of the most ghoulish rumors—reported about Kaye's three-day stewardship of Vivien—was that he tried to goad her into suicide before Larry's arrival.

This was not the first time that such a charge had been raised against Kaye. A former assistant claimed that Kaye had thought of doing just such a thing.

Of course, these rumors were never verified, although months later, Vivien told Larry and others she thought they were true. "He wanted to get rid of me so he could have Larry all to himself," she told Cukor.

From Ischia, Larry made the long trip to Hollywood, taking three days to get there. He flew with Cecil Tennant.

Larry and Tennant arrived at New York's Idlewild Airport where Kaye met them with a limousine. They were taken to his suite at the Sherry-Netherland Hotel where they spent the night.

Then it was on to California. Arriving at the Burbank Airport, Larry and

617

Tennant were met by Niven who drove them to Vivien's house.

Larry went at once to her bedside, where Vivien was resting. On the plane to Los Angeles, he'd learned that twenty-one-year-old Elizabeth Taylor had replaced Vivien in the film.

When she saw Larry, she rather matter-of-factly told him, "You should not have come to Hollywood. I have Peter. I have room in my life for only one man."

"Right now Peter has a wife who loves him, and you have a husband who loves you, so we'll have to get on with what we have."

She seemed to think that made some kind of sense because she surprised him by agreeing with him. Her eyes had a far and distant gaze.

He offered to fetch a cup of tea and put her back into bed. Throughout the rest of the afternoon, he sat reading to her beside her bed.

That night, two nurses arrived to put her to sleep. Their technique involved wrapping her in cold, wet sheets, which they'd later remove, drying her gently before wrapping her once again in warm, dry bedclothes. This rather bizarre technique seemed to induce sleep in Vivien.

Finch came over to see Larry that night, and they hugged and kissed. Finch tried to explain himself. "I made the mistake of falling in love with her. Who wouldn't? She's magical. But I see how hopeless it is to love Vivien. She is beyond love at this point. That's why they sent for you, thinking you are the only one who could handle her."

"I'm not sure that is true but I think she also needs you in her life." He paused. "I need you too. Ever since I met you, I've loved you too. My love cannot be discounted."

"You mean . . . you're not angry?" Finch asked.

"Why should I be?" Larry said. "Love is too precious to throw away over a few misunderstandings. We'll work it out. Please sleep over tonight. I think Vivien needs all the loving support she can get."

Larry and Finch slept in the bedroom next to a heavily sedated Vivien who did not awaken until two o'clock the following day. By that time, Larry had called her English doctors who advised that Vivien should return home.

As Finch left for the studio, Kaye flew into Los Angeles. He'd talked repeatedly over the phone to Larry and came at once to see him. He was unaware that Larry had been with Finch.

Kaye had planned a return to New York in two days, where he promised to meet them when their plane from Burbank arrived. A stopover was planned in New York before their BOAC flight left for London the following day. "I'll take care of everything," Kaye promised Larry.

Although fearful of putting her on another flight to London, Larry heeded the advice of her English doctors and prepared to make this arduous final trip, beginning with the flight to New York.

That night in L.A., Vivien and Larry had an epic battle over Kaye, when she charged that he'd tried to kill her in Larry's absence. "How dare you say something so slanderous about a dear and trusted friend of ours, who is doing everything he can to save you." Larry slapped her face, a rare act of violence for him.

Niven drove Larry and Vivien to the airport at Burbank, where at least a dozen photographers were gathered, with their blaring flashbulbs.

As she was put on a stretcher and rolled to the ramp of a TWA Constellation flying to New York's La Guardia Airport, Larry shouted at them, "Get back. My wife is a very sick woman." Then, after embracing Niven, he boarded the plane.

Seated with Vivien in the aircraft, she looked at Larry with a faraway gaze. "Who in hell are you?" she asked.

After seeing her off, Niven, losing patience, no longer filtered his feelings with love and indulgence. He later told friends, "I have come to hate Vivien Leigh because she's destroying Larry, my dearest friend."

In the end, Paramount generously gave Vivien $130,000 of her pre-arranged $150,000 salary. For Elizabeth Taylor's loan-out during the completion of *Elephant Walk*, MGM received a fee of $100,000, most of which they kept since she was on salary.

In the final version of *Elephant Walk*, released to theaters, audiences saw Vivien only in distance shots filmed in Ceylon. These were far too expensive to reshoot with Taylor.

***

With a chauffeured limousine, Kaye met them at the airport in New York. Getting off the plane, Vivien was conscious and even smiled weakly at reporters and photographers. She leaned heavily into Larry for comfort and protection. Two nurses and Cecil Tennant closed ranks around her, guiding her across the tarmac into Kaye's limousine.

She spoke not a word to Kaye, and seemed resentful of his presence. Nonetheless, she got into his limo where the chauffeur drove them to the Long Island home of a friend of his. Here Vivien was sedated and left to sleep the night away to prepare for one more grueling flight, this time across the vast Atlantic Ocean to her homeland.

Both Kaye and Larry realized that to get her on an airplane back to England, she had to be sedated. A nurse appeared the next day with a very large hypodermic needle. Vivien had a horror of such needles. Seeing the nurse, she ran and tried to jump out her bedroom window.

Kaye grabbed her by her ankles, sending her tumbling to the floor.

Danny and Larry held her down, as she struggled against them, biting and scratching them. With her long nails, she aimed at Kaye's face, calling him "a faggot." He was bleeding but he held on to her. Larry joined in holding her down as the nurse punctured her skin with the needle.

Larry later claimed that the nurse was sadistic and had "a gleam in her eye" as she punctured the helpless, struggling Vivien.

As Larry so modestly stated in his *Confessions*, Vivien delivered screaming denunciations, paying "particular attention to my erotic impulses." What he meant to say, and didn't, was she denounced his love affair with Kaye. "Who's the fucker?" she screamed at Larry. "Who's the fuckee?"

In the same limousine, Kaye and Larry drove with her back to the airport where she had been booked to fly from Idlewild to London on a BOAC flight. En route to the airport, Kaye had wrapped her in a blanket. She was in the back seat, her body spread across the laps of both Larry and Kaye. Occupying the jump seat were two stern nurses. Tennant rode in the front seat with the driver.

By the time the limousine pulled into Idlewild, the sedation had worn off. Coming to, Vivien refused to be moved from the limo to the British airplane on a stretcher.

Larry tried to calm her. So did Kaye but she slapped his face.

Idlewild security police allowed the limo to be driven onto the tarmac. At the ramp to the waiting plane, Larry and Kaye visibly forced her out of the limo and onto the tarmac, supporting her frail, exhausted body.

Her final words shouted at Kaye, and overheard by attendants, were, "I hate you, you bloody cunt!"

Facing exploding flashbulbs, she screamed at the reporters and photographers. "Bloody hell, get out of here! You're scum! Dirty bastards! Let me alone."

Nurses virtually had to push her forward into the plane, handling her rather roughly.

Larry hugged and held Kaye in his arms for a final farewell, thanking him for all he'd done for Vivien. On the plane the nurses sedated her again for the long transatlantic flight.

Larry later recalled, "I asked myself where love had gone. Would it end with me sending Vivien off to that madhouse that Tennessee knew all too well was the fate of Blanche? Would it also be Vivien's fate?"

Aboard the plane to London she slept for ten hours, while a despondent Larry sat with Cecil Tennant, telling him, "I want to leave her and continue my life elsewhere, but I have so much guilt and feel responsible for her." Before the plane landed in London, Larry irrationally was blaming Finch for

Vivien's breakdown.

But later, when he met with Finch again, he was loving and supportive, having forgotten his outburst on the plane.

A reporter for the *Daily Mirror* described Vivien's arrival back in London: "For nineteen minutes the door of the airliner stood open and empty like a stage setting, and like a first night audience the crowd gathered and waited, apprehensive and silent. Inside, three doctors tried to persuade Vivien to leave the plane, bundled in blankets and under close escort. They failed. The actress, still pale and dark eyed, wanted to show England she could still be gay, happy, and vivacious. She appeared suddenly at the doorway with an armful of red roses and a jaunty little sou'wester hat and a gay smile. In that first moment of surprise we could hardly believe she was ill at all, until we looked more closely at the careful makeup and the worried face of her husband. Someone shouted, 'Welcome home, my lady!' and suddenly everybody cheered."

Larry watched with tears in his eyes as she was placed in an ambulance and hauled away to Netherne Hospital outside Coulsdon in Surrey. It specialized in the treatment of nervous disorders.

He was told that she would enter a period of isolation for at least three weeks, maybe more. From Notley, he placed a call to Niven. "Vivien's insane. I don't think she'll ever come back. Before, she just hovered on the brink of madness. Now she has descended completely into that dark state. Our dear Vivien is gone forever. The demon woman who lives inside her body today is not the Vivien we've known and loved."

At Netherne Hospital, the sedation of Vivien continued. Larry was told that she'd be asleep for three weeks, and that he could not visit her. He decided to finish his vacation in Ischia.

At this point, Larry deserted her in the hospital. He later expressed guilt for abandoning Vivien to those shock treatments. "I had to do it to save myself," he told Cecil Tennant. "I felt I was being driven mad myself."

In Ischia he hired a young bodyguard and personal trainer—called "a dead ringer for Sal Mineo." The boy accompanied him everywhere and slept in the same room with Larry at night. His tolerant hosts believed that Larry was having an affair with the beautiful Neapolitan boy.

A closeted gay, Garson Kanin had joined him on the trip. Away from their wives, both of them had taken up with "two Neapolitan gigolos," as Kanin later related to Cukor. "I happily settled for one that looked like he could play Rudolph Valentino in a picture of that star's life. We were two lucky fellows. When we grew bored with our choices, we changed partners."

The *Hollywood Reporter* took a dim view of that trip: "If you were supposed to be happily married and your wife became ill, would you park her in a nursing home and go off and finish your 'interrupted' vacation?" *Variety* reported that "The Laurence Oliviers were about to call it off when the breakdown brought them together."

Vivien's doctor at Netherne, who was giving her shock treatments, came up with a diagnosis. "She is suffering an evident manic-depressive condition which develops a marked increase in libido and indiscriminate sexual activity."

On April 11, 1953, Vivien was transferred to her familiar University Hospital, where she stayed eight days. Her illness and Larry's departure from England were widely reported in the press.

Opportunistic thieves broke into Durham Cottage in Chelsea and into Notley Abbey. All of Vivien's jewelry and her fur coats were stolen, even the Oscar she'd won for *A Streetcar Named Desire*.

At first, Vivien refused to be transferred from Netherne to University Hospital because the maid had brought her the wrong belt. Her maid had to go back to Chelsea to get the right belt before Vivien would get dressed to leave the mental institution.

On the way to the hospital, she attacked Larry for deserting her "in my hour of need and running off with some paramour in Italy. Thank God for dear Noël. He was all I had to hang on to at that dreadful time."

Coward visited her whenever he could and provided her with flowers and perfume. When she was installed at University, Coward was the first person she called. He remembered it as a "heart-break conversation, filled with tears." She delivered a vicious attack on Larry, claiming he wanted her to die.

On yet another day, Coward found her "calm and normal and really very sweet." Like a stern father, he gave her a lecture, making her promise not to "carry on like a mad adolescent of the twenties."

At University Hospital she was forced to receive electroconvulsive shock therapy. She was under a general anesthetic of sodium pentothal. The drug scoline was used as a muscle relaxant. After electrodes were applied to her temples, a Shotter-Rich electronarcosis machine sent six convulsions to her brain.

After treatments, Vivien told Coward, "I'm worse than before."

When Leigh Holman went to visit her in the hospital, he found her conscious but irrational. "She asked me to get her a vanity mirror, holding it up to her face."

"My face looks puffy," she said. "Get me my lipstick and some powder. I've got to get ready for the cameras. Any day I'll be returning to Hollywood to complete the filming of *Elephant Walk* with that darling man Peter Finch. He calls every day, urging me to divorce Larry and marry him. He's leaving Tamara, you know." Then she made an outrageous charge. "She once sexually attacked me."

Of course, it was Vivien, not Tamara, who was the sexual aggressor.

She asked Leigh to get her a hair-removal device.

Leigh learned that Gertrude, Vivien's mother, was on holiday in Paris; her father Ernest Hartley on a fishing trip in Ireland, and that Larry was "hiding out" in Ischia. Leigh told his ailing friend, Oswald Frewen, "What a world of memory-losers and liars!"

Tennant sent Larry a cable: AWAKENING IMMINENT. COME BACK QUICK.

But Larry did not receive the cable immediately since he was traveling, so his return to England was delayed.

Kanin and Larry had left Ischia because the press had discovered Larry's whereabouts. With their young companions, they had departed from Naples, traveling around the boot of Italy.

Back in London, Larry journeyed immediately to Vivien's bedside, where she chastised him for not being there when she came out of her long sedation.

She had once told Larry she no longer loved him. At the hospital, seeing her after her shock treatments, he came to realize that he no longer loved her, either. "Insofar as she was no longer the person I'd loved, I loved her that much less," he later said. "She was now more of a stranger to me than I could ever have imagined possible. Something had happened to her."

***

When he heard that Larry and Vivien were returning to Notley to start anew, Coward wrote in his diaries: "Apparently things have been bad and getting worse since 1948 or thereabouts. It is really discouraging to reflect how needlessly unhappy people make themselves and each other. They are now going to start afresh at Notley, which may work or may not. I shall be surprised if it does."

Back at Notley, Vivien didn't utter a word for three days and nights. One morning she woke up and told her maid, "I heard a nightingale sing last night. I viewed it as a sign of hope. We will win this war. Churchill will destroy Hitler and all his evil."

On hearing about this, Gertrude rushed to the aid of her daughter. Vivien was in such a state that she attacked one of Gertrude's breasts, as if to rip it off. Her mother was rushed to the hospital for emergency aid.

Tennant had a more calming effect on Vivien. With his clothes on, he slept in bed with her, his arms around her, while Larry went through a troubled night on a cot hastily placed beside her bed.

Gertrude stayed away for several days after the attack, but her love for Vivien drove her back to Notley again. Once again, she became Vivien's caretaker, though sometimes what her daughter said alarmed her.

One morning over breakfast, Vivien told Gertrude, "Every man I know, even strangers on the street, try to seduce Scarlett O'Hara. And often they do. I have a horrible problem. I fear I can't resist them."

As the days and weeks went by, Vivien, to the surprise of Larry himself, began to recover her mental health. She urged him to find some theatrical project for both of them.

At the time of Queen Elizabeth's coronation in 1953, Vivien and Larry decided to appear in Terence Rattigan's new comedy, *The Sleeping Prince*. Although Rattigan thought them miscast, he reluctantly gave in to their wishes to star in his play.

In September of 1953, Larry and Vivien took the show on a tour of the provincial capitals, stopping off in Brighton, Edinburgh, and Manchester, where they met great success.

On Vivien's 40th birthday, November 5, 1953, the play opened at London's Phoenix Theatre, and Princess Margaret attended. Vivien shocked some members of the audience with her strawberry blonde wig and Southern accent. One reviewer found that she seemed to be imitating Katharine Hepburn, mannerisms and all.

Backstage, Peter Finch arrived with his wife Tamara, and congratulations and kisses were exchanged. Without saying anything, Vivien communicated to Finch that she was ready, willing, and able to resume their affair. A mutual friend, actress Rachel Kempson (Lady Redgrave), often lent Vivien and Finch her studio for their sexual encounters.

Tamara later recalled, "I can't fight Vivien. It's like trying to fight the Queen of England."

Finch told Richard Burton, "Once you've slept with Vivien, you don't care about anybody else." On the surface, Burton went along with that, but obviously he did not agree.

Soon after their reunion, Finch was showing up again at Notley, spending weekends alone with both Larry and Vivien. She soon discovered that Finch had resumed his sexual relationship with Larry, but she said nothing, although she informed Gertrude of this.

"I understand, dear," Gertrude told her. "As you know, I had that problem with your father and Tommy. It's what men do when they're alone, I suppose."

As Finch told Cecil Tennant, "When I visit Notley, I'm one very busy actor. Sometimes I have to appear in Act I, Act II, and then repeat Act I—all in a matter of hours. They make tough men Down Under."

Larry both seemed devoted to Finch and jealous of him at the same time. Rex Harrison recalled a Christmas party at Notley when Finch was there. "Larry fired off some fireworks and aimed one right at Finch," Harrison claimed. "But at the last minute, he changed direction. I think he came very close for one moment to killing Finchie. I could see murder in Larry's eyes."

The Sleeping Prince ran for eight months, with Vivien missing only one performance. It closed on July 3, 1954.

Rattigan continued his fascination with the Oliviers by writing a screenplay called *The V.I.P.'s* (1963) about the relationships of Vivien, Larry, and Finch. The movie roles went to Elizabeth Taylor, Richard Burton, and Louis Jourdan.

***

Vivien would go for days being her kind, charming self, but then a bizarre pattern of behavior would emerge. When Kirk Douglas met her in 1954 during the annual *Night of 100 Stars*, he dined with Larry, Vivien, and the director Terence Young.

At one point in the dinner, as later related by Douglas, "She turned to Larry and said, 'Why don't you fuck me anymore?' Then she started coming on to me, very seductive, with Olivier sitting right there. At first, I didn't believe it. I felt uncomfortable. She was behaving like Blanche DuBois—sexual, bizarre."

In 1955, after the "frivolity" of *The Sleeping Prince*, Larry planned to return to Shakespeare. "I wanted to remind the world who I really am," he said. He agreed to produce, direct, and star in the film version of *Richard III*.

He knew the character so well, or, as he said it, "I'd played Richard III so often on stage, I'd let ham fat grow on my performance. I had to rid myself of this before the cameras got me."

He chose three knights—Cedric Hardwicke, Ralph Richardson, and John Gielgud—each a Bard-seasoned veteran, for the roles of King Edward IV, Buckingham, and the Duke of Clarence, respectively.

He later admitted, "I made a mistake casting Ralph Richardson as Buckingham. He wasn't oily enough. I should have gotten Orson Welles."

Vivien wanted to repeat her stage role as Lady Anne, but Larry bluntly told her, "I won't hear of it. I've cast Claire Bloom in the part. She resembles a *young* Vivien Leigh."

"Blanche DuBois abhorred deliberate cruelty," she told him, "and so do I."

Cast as Lady Anne, Claire Bloom had previously been chosen by Charlie Chaplin in 1952 to appear in

Claire Bloom with Laurence Olivier in the film version of Richard III.

625

his film *Limelight*, which catapulted her to stardom. A sophisticated, intelligent actress, she came from the North London suburb of Finchely and was some eighteen years younger than Larry.

She told Larry, "I would like to work in Hollywood but I don't want to live there. I'm too young to die."

After her affair with Larry, she married three times, two of them famously, to actor Rod Steiger and writer Philip Roth.

Bloom is one of the few actresses who has gone on record about an affair with Larry. She did so in her memoirs, *Leaving a Doll's House*, admitting that she was under his spell but "never remotely in love with him."

She found him "brimming with a false charm. Perhaps he was trying to show Vivien that he could still enjoy success with young girls." She admitted that she was flattered that he wanted to have an affair with her, considering that he was married to one of the world's most beautiful women.

She claimed their fling was brief and continued only for the duration of the filming of *Richard III*. "Then it was over—the classic situation of the young actress bedazzled by the attentions of her mature costar. It ended without rancor on either side."

Of course, during her affair, she was careful that her other lover, Richard Burton, did not find out.

Larry called his involvement with Bloom "an act of folly."

Alan Dent, who helped edit the text of *Richard III*'s screenplay, claimed Larry "combines the strength of Hercules with the ubiquity of Mercury." As one viewer said, "Olivier played Richard as "wickedly masculine yet seductively feminine, personifying an evil so outrageous that he can mock his own audacity."

His onscreen appearance was startling, as he'd made himself up with a limp and a padded humpback that evoked Charles Laughton in *The Hunchback of Notre-Dame*. He retained the deformed hang of his stage role, with his one dead eyelid, his hatchet nose, drooping shoulder, twisted, limping leg, and his silken black pageboy coiffure. He played Richard with lip-licking relish and a sardonic wit.

Six weeks of the shoot was in Spain, at which time Larry had his usual accident, as a stray arrow was shot into his leg. He endured the pain until the film sequence was finished before screaming in agony.

Before the film was wrapped, he would shoot 165 scenes in eleven weeks. In all, he would direct 70 actors in speaking roles plus nearly 600 extras.

At the end of the shoot, Larry embraced Cedric Hardwicke, who had received his knighthood in 1934. "You were George Bernard Shaw's favorite actor, and I'm sure the Bard would have singled you out for that same honor."

Hardwicke in the years to come was in failing health. All of his money was eaten up by hospital expenses incurred during his final illness. There was no money left to bury him, so Larry contributed generously to his funeral expenses.

The monthly *Film Bulletin* hailed *Richard III* as "the most exciting Shakespearean film ever made."

Even so, after its original release, *Richard III* did not make a profit in the U.S., effectively ending Larry's dream of filming Shakespeare again as a director. As regards Larry's ambitions for the filming of future Shakespearean plays, although he had been hailed as the "greatest Macbeth of the 20th Century," his performance as The Thane of Glamis and King of Scotland would never be captured on film as he could not raise the financing, especially in the wake of the untimely death of Alexander Korda.

Michael Todd, husband of Elizabeth Taylor, was willing to finance an Olivier film version of *Macbeth*, but he died in a plane crash.

Larry never again directed a Shakespearean film. He blamed it on "the actors' curse attached to that Scottish play."

For his role in the film version of *Richard III*, he was nominated for an Oscar as Best Actor of the year (1955). He competed against James Dean for *Giant*, Kirk Douglas for *Lust for Life*, and Rock Hudson for *Giant*, but lost to Yul Brynner for *The King and I*. Larry fared better at the British Film Academy, winning Best British Film and Best Actor awards.

***

Vivien wanted to keep working, and signed on for a part in a film called *The Deep Blue Sea* (1955) written by Terence Rattigan. She played a woman in love with a wild-living RAF pilot, as played by Kenneth More. It was only later that Alexander Korda told Vivien, "I really wanted Marlene Dietrich to play your role."

She saw very little of Larry, who was busy working on the film version of *Richard III*.

Directed by Anatole Litvak, *The Deep Blue Sea* also starred Eric Portman and Emlyn Williams. Vivien did not get on with More, who was usually affable, bright, and breezy, epito-

Two views of Vivien Leigh with
Kenneth More in
The Deep Blue Sea

627

mizing traditional English virtues of fortitude and fun. When he made this film with Vivien, he was one of the most popular film stars in Britain. Years later, when asked, Vivien responded, "Oh, Kenneth More, was he in that film?"

Some critics thought the plot "hit too close to home" for Vivien, as it was the story of a middle-aged woman who leaves her husband for another man. Rattigan later claimed, "Vivien couldn't bring herself to expose menopausal reality so that it could make her character believable."

Early in the shoot, Vivien learned that More had tried to get Litvak to replace Vivien with Dame Peggy Ashcroft. More was later uncharitable in his appraisal of Vivien: "I thought she was petulant, spoiled, overpraised, and overloved."

In a scene with Emlyn Williams, who played her husband, Vivien had to drive away with him in a car. On the third take, she asked him, "Wouldn't it be funny if we drove off now, and nobody ever saw us again?"

In some vague corner of her brain, Vivien might have felt that working with Larry again would give her a second chance at love. That didn't happen. At Stratford, they met only for lunch and that was to discuss the three plays they had agreed to do for the coming season—*Twelfth Night*, *Macbeth*, and *Titus Andronicus*.

She received fifty thousand pounds for her role in *The Deep Blue Sea*, Larry about the same for *Richard III*. But both of them planned to go to work for the upcoming season in Stratford-upon-Avon where each of them would be paid sixty pounds a week.

The season at the Shakespeare Memorial Theatre in Stratford opened on April 12, 1955 with *Twelfth Night*, directed by John Gielgud. Larry was reunited with Angela Baddeley, the object of his affection decades before, and with Maxine Audley, with whom he'd had an affair. "Old home week," Vivien called it.

Gielgud despaired in trying to direct the pair of them, Vivien listening more to Larry than to him. Larry played Malvolio in an anti-romantic mood.

"As Viola, Viv seemed trapped in some romantic comedy," Gielgud recalled. "But Larry played Malvolio as if cast in some psychological *film noir* drama." One writer claimed, "It was like combining a Wagner opera with a Strauss waltz."

On opening night, Larry's performance was generally praised, but Vivien was damned by faint praise. Critics suggested that she was "lovely to look at."

At Stratford, Finch joined Vivien in a rented room, while Larry fretted over the season's offerings.

In Stratford, Gielgud was still recovering from his arrest on a charge of homosexual solicitation. He noticed the unhappiness that Vivien's affair with

Finch was causing Larry. Sometimes in the middle of a rehearsal, Larry had stopped to say, "Bloody Finch! Bloody Finch." Yet when he saw Finch he'd place his arm around him and act like he was his lover.

At one point, Gielgud approached Vivien and suggested that it might be wiser if she let Finch go.

"What's the point?" she asked. "I don't love Larry anymore."

Companionship for Larry arrived in the person of his longtime lover, Glen Byam Shaw, who had signed to direct *Macbeth*, slated to open on June 5, 1955. For her direction, Vivien relied on Finch's coaching more than Shaw's. She still resented him for his affair with Larry, even though that event had begun before she'd met Larry.

Macbeth was not Larry's finest hour in the theater, with John Barber of the *Daily Express* claiming that "Olivier was a once great actor. But since his gleaming, viperfish *Richard III* and his fiery *Hamlet*, he has lost his way."

Kenneth Tynan came to see the production, claiming that in *Macbeth* "Olivier shakes hands with greatness here, but Vivien Leigh's Lady Macbeth is more niminy-piminy than thundery-blundery."

At Stratford, the longtime friend and frequent companion of the Oliviers, Anthony Quayle, recalled the insults that the Oliviers uttered to each other while reciting their lines. "Larry would spout the most marvelous poetry while hissing at Vivien, 'You shit, you shit! It was often a 'fuck you.' One day Vivien appeared with a swollen black eye. She claimed it was a mosquito bite but the cast knew he'd struck her."

The final production of the season was *Titus Andronicus*, directed by Peter Brook, with Vivien cast as Lavinia, Larry as Titus. Their familiar supporting players included Quayle, with whom both of them had been involved, and Maxine Audley, whose affair with Larry was a fast-fading memory at this point.

Quayle said he found it sad to see Vivien so ill and their marriage crumbling. "She wasn't very good in the part, but Larry as Titus was superb."

At one point, Quayle claimed that while Larry was performing as Titus, Vivien was cursing him "with the most terrible obscenities you can imagine. The audience couldn't hear her words. She had a piece of bloodied gauze tied over her mouth. But I could hear it, and it was all directed toward Larry. He didn't miss a beat of the Bard's poetic words."

Kenneth Tynan once again journeyed from London to Stratford to see *Titus Andronicus*. He was not impressed. "Vivien Leigh receives the news that she is about to be ravished on her husband's corpse with little more than the mild annoyance of one who would have preferred rubber," he wrote.

At the end of the season at Stratford, Vivien and Finch disappeared, showing up in Paris. When both of them returned to Notley, Larry invited Finch to come into the library for a man-to-man talk. Finch and Larry stayed in that library until three in the morning.

Finally, the large double doors of the library opened and there stood Vivien in a see-through negligee. "Well," she said, "is it decided? Which one of you is going to fuck me tonight?" Both Finch and Larry burst into laughter.

"I have an idea," Finch told them. "Let's all three of us crawl in the same big bed and see what happens."

***

Life began to move rapidly by for both Larry and Vivien. On January 23, 1956, they were notified that Alexander Korda had died of a heart attack at the age of 62. They also put Durham Cottage on the market, "Our lives are too large and it's too small," Larry said.

After a short holiday in Spain, Larry and Vivien returned to London. He'd warned her repeatedly that she had to protect his image. Even though he wanted out of the relationship, he agreed to take a small apartment with her at 54 Eaton Square in Belgravia.

In London, at Eaton Square, Vivien and Larry fought constantly. He tried to lock his door and keep her out, but she was uncontrollable. Gertrude was present one night when he lost control and violently pushed her away from him. She fell, seriously injuring her eye when it hit the corner of a marble-topped table. "I hate you! I hate you!" she screamed at him. "I want you dead."

Dr. Arthur Conachy, who had been treating Vivien since 1949, bluntly told Larry, "She is a hopeless schizophrenic. Her libido is out of control. She is picking up men indiscriminately, and she's confessed that to me. She's got to stop drinking."

Noël Coward came for a weekend at Notley and pitched to Vivien the idea of starring in his new comedy, *South Sea Bubble*, playing the role of Lady Alexandra Shotter. That night both Vivien and Larry read the play in the library while Coward retired upstairs with a young actor he was "auditioning," in much the same way he'd seduced Larry so long ago.

Vivien as Lady Shotter in Noël Coward's *South Sea Bubble*

Both Vivien and Larry thought Coward's play weak, but he suggested she do it anyway. "After all, it's from Noël, and the play does have its moments."

The original plan was to star Finch opposite Vivien. But one night at Notley, Larry and Finch had a showdown, and he agreed to leave Vivien behind.

Finch's friend, Trader Faulkner, explained what went

wrong. "Olivier had a position to uphold, and Peter and Vivien were liable to bring him into the limelight of the press in a way that could only be detrimental to all three."

The writer, Roger Lewis, suggested that one of Finch's "unwitting principal functions was to taunt, to degrade, to outrage; he was one of her stratagems to win her husband back (by making Olivier jealous), whilst, at the same time, his presence was allowing her to relive, after a fashion, the feelings of an exciting new romance. Finch was a reminder of happiness. She used him, when all is said and done, but he bore her no ill will."

After all the abuse, torment, passion, romance, pain, and wrecked lives, Finch made a final statement about his once beloved Vivien. "I remember her walking like an eager boy through the temples of Ceylon. I also remember the wind blowing through her hair at Notley. It was a scene straight from the film she did not make, *Wuthering Heights*. I will always see her hurrying through life as if to get the whole bloody thing over with."

During the first week of rehearsals, Vivien learned that her role in *South Sea Bubble* had originally been offered to Coward's friend, Gertrude Lawrence.

When *South Sea Bubble* opened at the Lyric Theatre on April 25, 1956, it received mainly bad reviews, but it was kept running by Vivien's box office clout. Player-goers, both foreign and domestic, still wanted to see Scarlett O'Hara in the flesh.

Before leaving Stratford, Vivien learned that Maxine Audley had become pregnant. Vivien told her, "I do long to have another baby, but I could never give up nine months of my life to bear a child."

While performing in *South Sea Bubble*, Vivien learned that she'd become pregnant again. Since she had had no sexual relations with Larry, she knew at once that the father was Finch. But then she couldn't be sure because in one of her "states," she'd also had unprotected sex with strange men.

When she told Larry about the upcoming child, he knew it was not his. She later recalled, "He seemed more excited about the upcoming arrival in London of Marilyn Monroe than he did about having another kid," she said.

He confided to both Richardson and Coward, "Soon we're going to have Baby Finch running around Notley."

On August 12, 1956 at Notley, a day after her last performance in *South Sea Bubble*, Vivien suffered her final miscarriage. Coward privately blamed her for "behaving irresponsibly in the first months of her pregnancy. She even danced wildly with Larry and Johnnie Mills rehearsing for *Night of 100 Stars*."

***

While appearing in the Shakespeare season at Stratford, Larry had received an offer to repeat his role in a Hollywood film adaptation of *The Sleeping Prince*. Milton Green, a photographer and Marilyn Monroe's Svengali at the time, had purchased the film rights from Rattigan and changed the title to *The Prince and the Showgirl*. He was fashioning it into a vehicle for Marilyn, who was at the peak of her career.

Fearing that Vivien would make a concerted bid for the role that was being groomed for Marilyn, and realizing that she was too old to play the role on-screen, Larry delayed informing her of his upcoming involvement in *The Prince and the Showgirl* until after Vivien had been cast in Coward's *South Sea Bubble*.

Larry had first met Marilyn when she was a starlet at Danny Kaye's party in Hollywood. He flew to New York for a second meeting to discuss the

Two views of Laurence Olivier and Marilyn Monroe in *The Prince and the Showgirl*

upcoming *The Prince and the Showgirl*. After that meeting, he claimed, "One thing was clear to me, I was going to fall most shatteringly in love with Marilyn. It was inescapable. I thought she was so adorable, so witty, such incredible fun and more physically attractive than anyone I could have imagined. I went home like a lamb reprieved from the slaughter just for now. Poor Vivien."

He'd predicted to his friends that "Marilyn and I will be wonderful in bed."

On July 14, 1956, a reporter for the *Daily Mirror* wrote: "Not since the arrival of the Spanish Armada has there been such excitement." Marilyn arrived with her husband, playwright Arthur Miller, at London's Heathrow Airport. Both Vivien and Larry turned out to welcome America's most famous couple.

Vivien later regretted the decision when she saw the morning papers. "I should never have posed next to a woman twelve years younger than me. It was more than the age. No woman should pose next to Marilyn."

To the press, Larry was asked his

opinion of Marilyn. "She has an extraordinary gift of being able to suggest one moment that she is the naughtiest little thing and the next that she's perfectly innocent."

Oswald Frewen, Larry's longtime friend, visited the set of *The Prince and the Showgirl* on several occasions. On his first day there, he said, "It was obvious to me that Larry had developed a crush on Marilyn. Marilyn's radar picked up on that. I knew it would be just a matter of days before they were fucking."

The actual seduction may have occurred when Marilyn stayed late on the set one afternoon to "go over a scene in my dressing room with Sir Laurence." Vivien had invited Arthur Miller to accompany her to a play in the West End.

Milton Green may have been the only person other than her coach, Paula Strasberg, to whom Marilyn confided the details of her rendezvous with Larry.

She told Green, "I've known some great men—John F. Kennedy, Arthur, and now Sir Laurence. But sometimes they are better in their public performances than in the show they put on in private."

Soon after their unsuccessful seduction, Larry soured on Marilyn. As he told Arthur Miller, "She does not care about who she keeps waiting, whose money she is spending. I also feel she's on the verge of a nervous breakdown. My patience has worn thin. We should place Vivien Leigh and Marilyn Monroe in the same insane asylum."

On the third week, when she showed up on the set after 11AM, he sharply rebuked Marilyn in front of the cast. "Why can't you get here on time, for fuck's sake?"

Pretending innocence, she said, "Oh, you have that word here in England, too."

Miller was of no help to Larry. The playwright had no control over his wife. Larry predicted that the Miller/Monroe marriage had only weeks left.

Frewen also escorted Vivien to the set one day, where Vivien talked briefly with Marilyn. "I saw you in *South Sea Bubble*," Marilyn told Vivien, adding no further comment. She turned to her vanity mirror and continued to work on her makeup. "When I was a little girl, my mother took me to see *Gone With the Wind*," Marilyn claimed. "Boy, did you fuck up in your decision as Scarlett. You turned down Rhett Butler for Ashley Wilkes. You must have been on something."

"I saw you in *Gentlemen Prefer Blondes*," Vivien said sarcastically. "Which role did you play?"

Marilyn went silent, as Vivien wished her luck on the picture and abruptly left the dressing room.

On the way out of the studio, she told Frewen, "The girl is rather vulgar and not the brightest bulb in the chandelier. In her scenes with Dame Sybil, she'll eat Marilyn as a starter."

Frewen later wrote, "Monroe had the brain of a *poussin* and one dress for day and evening: black & cut low."

After the filming ended, Larry went to see Marilyn and Miller off at the airport, but by then he had privately told Dame Sybil Thorndike, "I detested the little bleached blonde whore. She can act only when the camera is rolling. She has bad hygiene. She's a selfish little tart who fucked her way up the ladder. In front of the press, we put on a show for the cameras—and that's it. Monroe and I are finished. The picture is a disaster. Only in Hollywood would a two-bit hooker like Monroe get to act opposite Sir Laurence Olivier, and I say that in all modesty. Do you know what the silly cunt told me at one point? She said she'd like to play Lady Macbeth opposite me."

***

Vivien convinced Larry that they'd become an old-fashioned theatrical couple and needed to keep up with the changing times in drama. He agreed to go see John Osborne's *Look Back in Anger* at the Royal Court.

Backstage, Larry congratulated Osborne and even asked him if he'd write a role for him in his next play. The result was a play called *The Entertainer*.

Both Vivien and Larry read the finished work, and Larry immediately wanted to star as Archie Rice, a third-rate comedian who headlines a tacky music hall revue in some seedy resort town.

Vivien said the role of the wife would be ideal for her.

The next day Larry met with his producers, and together they decided not to offer Vivien the role. The role went to his sometimes lover, Dorothy Tutin, instead.

Vivien was devastated to lose the role to a younger actress. "The fate of all middle-aged actresses," she told Noël Coward.

Joan Plowright with Laurence Olivier during filming of *The Entertainer*

As rehearsals began, Larry went to Vivien at Notley and told her, "I've fallen in love with Dorothy. You can't condemn me. You once came to me and told me you were in love with Peter."

She did not respond but left that night for London.

When Tutin's mother finally realized that a messy divorce might damage her daughter's career, she asserted that marriage to Larry was too risky. She urged her daughter to pull out of *The Entertainer*, and she did.

Larry immediately replaced her with a young

actress named Joan Plowright. Osborne objected to the casting of Plowright, but Larry and the producers held firm. "Joan's acting represents a new generation of actors," Larry told Vivien, who sunk into a deep depression.

The Entertainer opened at London's Royal Court Theatre on April 10, 1957, running until May 11, when Larry left with Vivien to go on a tour of the Shakespeare Memorial Theatre Company with *Titus Andronicus*.

The tour began in Paris before descending into the countries behind the Iron Curtain. "It was a terrifying experience," Larry later claimed. "It marked the end of my marriage."

In Paris, Vivien launched a torrid affair with Jean-Pierre Aumont, the French actor whom she met at a celebrity party, and whom she'd spotted across a crowded restaurant decades previously. Their affair would accelerate when they both starred in *Tovarich* on Broadway in 1963.

When Larry learned of the fling, he shouted at her, "You are nothing but a real bitch, a sex-crazed maniac ruining other people's lives, including your own." He didn't seem to care if other cast members heard him denouncing Vivien.

David Barry was only a fourteen-year-old when he toured Europe with the Oliviers. He shared his memories of the famous pair in a memoir called *Flashback: An Actor's Life*. He claimed that "one minute Vivien was sweetness and light, and the next she became a screaming harridan as she publicly berated Sir Laurence."

Barry recalled that the director, Peter Brook, came down heavily on Vivien, criticizing her acting. "I saw her looking towards her Larry for support, but Olivier was staring at his feet, determined not to get involved. When the rehearsal ended, Vivien swept out, followed by Olivier, who resembled nothing more than a hen-pecked husband as he trailed in her wake. From outside the rehearsal room doors we heard the muffled start of a quarrel and Vivien's voice rising like a shrew as she berated him."

"Performing, Olivier had been mighty, a believably tragic Roman general, whose sudden laugh in the midst of horror sent shivers down everyone's spine," Barry claimed. "But as soon as the rehearsal ended, he became a small man in the presence of his wife. It was like watching a role reversal, as if she wanted to bring his actor's greatness down to size."

Vivien went from Belgrade to Warsaw, and was mobbed by fans, shouting, "Scarlett! Scarlett!" One afternoon in Belgrade, she disappeared. After hours of searching, members of the crew found her sitting nude in a public garden, weeping.

On the train ride between Belgrade and Warsaw, "Vivien just lost it," according to Maxine Audley. "Her rage exploded. She attacked passengers. She threatened to kill me. I had to hide in a compartment. Larry told me that night, 'It's the final straw. I'm leaving her.'"

***

Vivien had appeared with Larry for the last time. From now, she was on her own, as in February of 1958 when she signed to play Paola in Jean Giraudoux's *Duel of Angels*, staged at London's Apollo Theatre with a translation by Christopher Fry. Claire Bloom was cast opposite her as Lucile. After six months, Ann Todd took over for Bloom.

Bloom recalled that Vivien was aware of the affair she'd had with Larry when they'd filmed *Richard III*. "This was tactfully understood between us but never mentioned," Bloom said. "There was never any tension or rivalry between us. Vivien never showed me anything but the greatest kindness and affection."

Vivien was also aware that Todd had been another mistress of Larry. Unlike Bloom, Vivien detested Todd on sight, calling her a "cunt" loud enough for her to hear it.

An Anglo-French actor, Peter Wyngarde, was cast as Marcellus in *Duel of Angels*. Vivien found him fascinating. Staying with a family in Shanghai in 1941, Wyngarde had been captured by the Japanese at the time of their invasion of the little country.

He was sent to a concentration camp where on one occasion he had both his feet broken and had to spend two weeks in solitary confinement when he was caught carrying messages between the concentration camps.

During the run of *Duel of Angels*, Vivien was very attracted to Wyngarde. She seduced him. But early in the affair, she frightened him. He found her missing from her apartment and went outside only to find her running around

the gardens of Eaton Square with nothing on.

He put his jacket around her but she was discovered by a policeman. Once he recognized her as Scarlett O'Hara, the policeman didn't arrest her.

One time, Wyngarde found her "sobbing and out of control" at four o'clock in the morning. Friends of Wyngarde warned him that Vivien "might be more than you can handle." He drifted apart from her.

In later life, he had only praise for her. "She was a star in the real meaning of the word. She was visual,

Peter Wyngarde

Larry was oral. She had such intelligence, beauty, and style. She never left the stage door unless impeccably dressed. She was always amusing. And she was honest, totally and utterly honest. She was a woman, and yet always somehow a child."

Before appearing with Vivien, Wyngarde in 1956 had appeared on stage with Dame Peggy Ashcroft in *The Good Woman of Setzuan*. Around this same time he'd gone backstage to congratulate Alan Bates on his performance at the Royal Court Theatre. The two actors were mesmerized by each other, launching a decade-long love affair.

The homosexual Bates also starred with Larry and Joan Plowright in the movie version of *The Entertainer* (1960), which also featured Roger Livesey and a young Albert Finney. The movie was directed by Tony Richardson.

When *Duel of Angels* closed, Vivien decided to go on vacation with her daughter Suzanne and her former husband Leigh Holman, visiting the Lake District of England. Headlines read: "Vivien Leigh Reunites with Ex-Spouse."

Also in 1958, she picked up a paper to read a much-unwanted headline: "Olivier's Brother Dies." At the age of fifty-four, Larry's older brother, Dickie, died from leukemia.

Before 1958 ended, Vivien would read yet another headline: "Scarlett O'Hara Now Grandma." On December 4, Suzanne had a baby and named him Neville Leigh Farrington.

Back in England, Larry was a sensation in *The Entertainer* reviving it at London's Palace Theatre for a tour of the provinces, going to Glasgow, Edinburgh, Oxford, and Brighton, with Joan Plowright as his leading lady. She was much younger than Larry, having been born in 1929 at her parents' home in Lincolnshire.

Beginning in February of 1958, Plowright and Larry would appear on Broadway at the Royale Theater, playing *The Entertainer* for 97 performances.

When he returned to England, he did not visit Notley Abbey. Ensconced there, Vivien grew increasingly lonely. Two weeks later Larry called her and told her he'd prepared an advertisement for *Country Life* magazine. "I want to sell the property."

She agreed but added, "Our memories here are not for sale."

Feeling depressed, she sought work, and Noël Coward offered her the lead in his new comedy *Look After Lulu*, to be directed by Tony Richardson, with an opening set for London's Royal Court Theatre on July 29, 1959.

Suzanne Holman, her baby son Neville, and her mother, Vivien Leigh

Saddened by the loss of Larry and Notley, Vivien feverishly poured herself into the Coward play.

Meriel Forbes (Lady Richardson) co-starred in the play. She often comforted Vivien in her dressing room where she claimed she cried all the time.

She told Forbes that "Larry will always be my brilliant, shining, beautiful knight. But I've lost him just as surely as I have lost my youth."

But at curtain time, Forbes noted, Vivien was a real trouper. "You would never know that half an hour before she'd been weeping—immense control."

Even though the play got unfavorable reviews, Vivien still had enough box office clout to keep it running.

In the *Sunday Times*, critic Harold Hobson wrote, "The trouble is that Mr. Noël Coward is too witty and Miss Vivien Leigh is too beautiful. For a play like this, beauty and wit are as unnecessary as a peach melba at the North Pole."

One night in her dressing room, she received a very curt letter from Larry. He declared, "I am bored with the legend of the Oliviers."

On December 12, *Look After Lulu* closed. Another chapter in her life also ended, when news reached her that her father, Ernest Hartley, age 76, scheduled to be operated on, had died before the surgery. His health had grown steadily worse, and he left the world at seven on the morning of December 18.

***

Larry departed for California to star in *Spartacus*. Even though he was writing Plowright long love letters daily, as he had once done to Vivien, rumors reached London that Tony Curtis, also starring in *Spartacus* as a slave boy, and Larry were having a torrid affair.

Marlon Brando, the former roommate of Curtis, took delight in spreading this story. Curtis, in 2002, admitted that it was true but asked that the details not be published until after his death.

"Let's face it, at the time, I was the cutest boy in Hollywood," he said. "I sometimes engaged in mercy fucks with old-time stars, especially my idol, Cary Grant."

In Hollywood filming *Spartacus*, Larry wrote Vivien: "I am quite sure in my mind and heart that both are firmly made up not to return to our life together when I come back in June. In fact, I think it best that we do not see each other. It's time now that we dropped the legend that is being kept up for press and public, and before I return have some statement ready on the true state of affairs."

On receiving this letter, Vivien entered a nervous state, threatening suicide. Gertrude rushed to her aid. With Leigh accompanying her, she arranged for her daughter to undergo shock treatments.

Robert Helpmann remained Vivien's true and loyal friend, standing by her and spending weekends with her. He suggested a change of scenery was in order, and, using his influence, arranged for them to bring *Duel of Angels* to New York. It was set to open at the Helen Hayes Theatre on April 19, 1960, followed by a tour in Los Angeles, San Francisco, Denver, and Washington, D.C.

Vivien left for New York with Helpmann. Jack Merivale was also in the cast. He hadn't seen her in two years and was eager to work with her again and be a part of her life.

He was not immediately accepted into her inner circle until after five days had passed. After he rejected the advances of a homosexual man at the Hotel Plaza Bar, who had aggressively reached out and grabbed his ample crotch, Merivale retreated to the bar of the Sherry-Netherland Hotel. Vivien was dining with Helpmann, and both of them invited him to join them. From that time on, according to Helpmann, Vivien and Merivale became lovers. His own marriage had collapsed.

On opening night on April 19, 1960, Vivien received a telegram from Larry asking for a divorce. Peter Wyngarde, who was in the cast, claimed that Vivien was devastated but went on that night to deliver a brilliant performance.

In bed with Vivien later that evening, Merivale held her tenderly in his arms, assuring her that he loved her more than any man had ever loved her. "I will be with you forever until death do us part."

Although she kept sobbing, she responded to his warmth. "Don't ever leave me!" she pleaded with me.

The next morning, without Merivale knowing it, she wrote Larry asking him to change his mind and not divorce her. He cabled her: I'M IN LOVE WITH ANOTHER.

She didn't need to ask him who was the object of his affection.

On Larry's 53rd birthday, May 22, 1960 she issued her public statement in New York, which was read to the press by Helpmann.

Helpmann secretly detested Larry. He seemed only too glad to embarrass him, and he went on television with a public announce-

Two views of Vivien Leigh
with Warren Beatty in
The Roman Spring of Mrs. Stone

639

ment. "Lady Olivier wishes to say that Sir Laurence has asked her for a divorce in order to marry Miss Joan Plowright. She will naturally do whatever he wishes."

There was a feeding frenzy in the press, something Larry definitely wanted to avoid. "When I catch up with that queenie Helpmann, I'll bash his face in."

***

While Vivien was finishing *Duel of Angels*, she considered starring in a play about the life of Evita Perón, the former First Lady of Argentina, but the deal fell through.

After the tour of *Duel of Angels*, Vivien and Merivale stopped off in New York where Larry was appearing at the St. James Theatre in *Becket* with Anthony Quinn. Plowright was starring in *A Taste of Honey* at the Lyceum.

Vivien went backstage to congratulate Larry on his fine performance. Seeing her, he asked her to come inside his dressing room. Merivale had to stand outside.

"Puss, it's over!" he told her. "I belong to another. Let me go. Don't cling."

"I understand," she said, "and I will respect your wishes. I remember once when you were my dashing Romeo and I was your Juliet."

"That pair didn't end up too well, did they?"

"I guess not," she said, seemingly wanting to linger.

"Please go," he urged. "You're making me uncomfortable. Jack loves you. You're lucky to have him. What are your plans?" he asked.

"I'm going to make *The Roman Spring of Mrs. Stone*, Tennessee's play. It's about a fading actress whose husband has died, and she goes to live in Rome where she becomes the victim of gigolos. I originally turned down the role of the actress. The script was too cruel, too grotesque. But I've changed my mind."

***

During the making of *The Roman Spring of Mrs. Stone*, Vivien was introduced to Warren Beatty, miscast as the Italian gigolo. "I think there have been some casting couch sessions with Tennessee," she told Merivale.

Jose Quintero directed *The Roman Spring of Mrs. Stone*. His assistant, Charles Castle, later claimed that Vivien "felt she needed a light flirtatious relationship with Beatty to make their love scenes work in the movie."

The German actress and chanteuse, Lotte Lenya befriended Vivien during the shooting and became her confidante. "At first she disliked Beatty intensely, really didn't care for him at all, but he exerted a powerful charm and ended up seducing her."

Roy Moseley, who was there, did not agree, claiming that at the time, Vivien was involved with her chauffeur, the handsome, strapping Bernard Gilman.

Joan Collins, Beatty's girlfriend, signed on as an extra. Their relationship was winding down, as Beatty had eyes for other women.

Although Collins had seen her before, she'd never "officially" met Vivien. "I was thrilled finally to meet this icon, but when I did I was deeply disappointed," she said. "The powerful images of Scarlett O'Hara, Cleopatra, Lady Hamilton, and Sabina were still etched in my mind, and I was unprepared for this thin, quirky, paper-skinned lady, who chain-smoked and had ugly hands."

After *Roman Spring* was wrapped, Vivien, along with Merivale, came to New York. She called Larry to meet with him. He accepted her invitation only if she'd agree to dine in a public restaurant like Sardi's. He told her, "Joan will be there."

At the luncheon, Vivien was gracious to Plowright. Larry told Vivien that he planned to marry Plowright. Vivien smiled demurely.

It was alleged among the theatrical London elite that before she agreed to marry Larry, Plowright had insisted that he give up his long-term relationship with Danny Kaye. And whereas he hadn't been willing to do that for Vivien, he did for Plowright.

At Sardi's, Vivien toyed with her food and soon asked to be excused. She wished them all the happiness in the world before flying to Atlanta for the restaged premiere, in 1960, of *Gone With the Wind*, an event that was timed to roughly coincide with the Centenary of the Civil War itself. She and Olivia de Havilland were the only "star survivors."

Even though he was ill at the age of fifty-nine, David O. Selznick showed up, hugging and kissing her. Clark Gable had been invited, but he'd died of a heart attack the year before after finishing *The Misfits* with Marilyn Monroe. Leslie Howard, of course, had died in a plane crash during World War II.

When Vivien stepped off the plane, the first reporter's question was, "What do you think about Olivier's divorcing you?"

She said, "The story's over, gents."

Inside the terminal, the headline blared: SCARLETT O'HARA RETAKES ATLANTA.

Vivien was joined by Olivia, and they participated in the celebrations amid lots of Confederate flags. Vivien and Merivale had Southern fried chicken with okra and black-eyed peas at Aunt Fanny's Cabin before sneaking away for mint juleps.

At one of the celebrations, a cub reporter from the *Atlanta Constitution* asked Vivien, "What role did you play in *Gone With the Wind*?"

"Miss Prissy," Vivien shot back. "My famous line was, 'Miss Scarlett, Miss Scarlett, I don't know nothin' 'bout birth'in babies."

***

In London, Vivien was granted a divorce on the grounds of Larry's adultery with Joan Plowright. Roger Gage, Plowright's husband, was granted a divorce on the same grounds of Plowright's adultery with Larry.

Larry married Plowright on May 17, 1961 at Wilton, Connecticut. Immediately they set about trying to have a baby. As Plowright confided, "Larry insisted on employing the old method of holding me upside down on the bed so that 'none of the little buggers can escape.'"

Richard Kerr Olivier was born on December 3, 1961.

***

On the suggestion of Vivien's gay actor friend, Dirk Bogarde, she, along with Gertrude and Merivale, drove to look at Tickerage Mill in Blackboys, near Uckfield in Sussex. The Queen Anne style house had its own little river and a nearby lake. Set on 90 acres, it also contained a barn, near which the three of them enjoyed a picnic lunch they'd brought from London. That very day Vivien decided to purchase Tickerage as her country retreat.

But before she could really settle in, she agreed to go on a long, exhausting tour.

The tour departed on June 26, 1961 and returned to England on May 25, 1962. As part of the Old Vic Company, Helpmann directed Vivien in *Twelfth Night*, *Duel of Angels*, and *The Lady of the Camellias*.

Jose Greco,
dancer *extraordinaire*,
in *Ship of Fools*

In each play, Merivale was cast as her leading man, which brought their relationship much closer. He had to endure the anticipated critiques in the papers. "Miss Leigh's leading man is certainly no Olivier," was an often expressed opinion.

After her tour of South America, Australia, and New Zealand, a New York impresario, Abel Farbman, offered Vivien the lead in a musical version of the comedy *Tovarich*, the story of a Russian noble couple who are forced to work as a butler and chambermaid in a bourgeois French household. Cast opposite her was Jean-Pierre Aumont with whom she'd had a brief fling in Paris.

She began her rehearsals at Tickerage Mill, her new home, bringing in an instructor to help her with the singing and dancing.

One day without an invitation, Peter Finch appeared in the driveway at Tickerage. Vivien was working in her garden and rushed to greet him. With two failed marriages behind him, he held her in his arms. "I've decided to settle down and marry you. I can live with being called Mr. Vivien Leigh the rest of my life."

"I won't marry you!" she said. "But I'll throw you a mercy fuck."

"You're on, babe," Finch said.

After Finch left, Aumont arrived from Paris. Fortunately for him, Merivale was touring in a play. Vivien briefly moved the French actor into Tickerage.

He later claimed that going to sleep under the same roof with Vivien was out of the question. "She had eyes like Colette's favorite cat that changed from gray to mauve, and a little impudent nose. My exhaustion only made her laugh, since Vivien couldn't imagine anyone being tired in her presence even after the man had had sex with her three times in one night."

On November 2, 1962, Vivien flew to New York where Vivien and Aumont were set to open in *Tovarich* on March 18, 1963. She immediately began rehearsing her singing and dancing, which she had not mastered. She had to learn to speak with a Russian accent. Noël Coward watched her go through rehearsals. He advised her to drop out of the production. "You were crazy to have accepted this role. It's all wrong for you. The production is mediocre, the direction grotesque. You'll be laughed off the stage."

She withdrew from *Tovarich* but, almost as quickly, changed her mind and stuck with it through its many changes. Peter Glenville, her old friend and Larry's former flame, arrived to save the show. Finally, the musical opened and was a success, Vivien receiving a Tony award.

When Merivale arrived in New York, he found Vivien's nerves frayed. She was entering into one of her "stages." In the middle of the night he called Noël Coward and his lover,

Two views of Vivien Leigh in
Ship of Fools
(lower photo) cordially despising
but getting drunk with
Lee Marvin

Graham Payn, to come over at once. They arrived to discover a completely nude Vivien standing on a balcony over a dangerous drop. She was claiming that she could fly. Through the gentle, patient urging of Coward, she finally agreed to come in.

At show's end, Merivale arranged for her to be placed on a stretcher after giving her a strong dose of sedatives for the transatlantic flight. In London she was hospitalized in a clinic that specialized in mental disorders. She lay in bed there for three months trying to recover, before her doctor transferred her back to Tickerage where she had to have twenty-four hour supervision from nurses.

***

Vivien had one more great film in her, *Ship of Fools* (1965) for Columbia Pictures, produced and directed by Stanley Kramer. It was based on a celebrated novel by Katherine Anne Porter, who had originally wanted Katharine Hepburn in the role but happily settled for Vivien.

The film had a "Grand Hotel" type cast, including Simone Signoret, Jose Ferrer, Lee Marvin, Oskar Werner, Elizabeth Ashley, George Segal, and Jose Greco, the dancer.

The story takes place on an ocean liner in the 1930s, with passengers from every social class, sailing from Vera Cruz, Mexico, to Bremerhaven in Germany.

Tied up with a project in England, Merivale could not join her right away at her rented house in the Hollywood Hills at 8918 Thrasher Avenue

It was here at night that Vivien launched her final affair. It was with Greco, the Italian-born flamenco dancer and choreographer.

"Happiness always seemed to escape Vivien," Greco later recalled. "I tried to bring her some by loving her. We both knew it was merely a momentary passion. Sometimes she would drink too much and be filled with venom, but my loving could usually bring her out of her bad state."

"One of the highlights of the movie is when she performs a Charleston," Greco said. "I helped her make it camera ready, although she'd been in a Broadway musical. She told me that movie producers would no longer trust her in starring roles because of her mental condition."

"When I was staying with her before Merivale arrived in California, I remember Katharine Hepburn used to come by in the morning and take Vivien away for shock treatments," Greco said. "I dreaded to imagine what was happening to her at that clinic."

Vivien's co-star, Signoret, recalled that "From one moment to another, Vivien was either scintillating or desperate."

Both Merivale and Gertrude arrived in Hollywood to look after Vivien. Kramer had told them that for no apparent reason she would attack and insult other members of the cast or crew. In one crucial scene in the movie when a drunken Lee Marvin comes on to her, she is supposed to hit him in the face and on the head with the heel of her pump. She beat him so severely he had to be hospitalized.

At a Hollywood party Rosalind Russell threw for her, Vivien stood up and, in the words of her hostess, sang "the filthiest song I've ever heard in my life. It was about an anal queen who was always searching for bigger and bigger things to stuff up there where the sun don't shine."

Later, while going home from the Russell household, Vivien burst into screams. "I couldn't help myself. Now everybody will think I'm mad as a hatter."

"No, no," Merivale said, trying to comfort her. "You are not mad. A little ill—that's all."

During the filming of *Ship of Fools*, 20th Century Fox called Vivien asking her to fill in for Joan Crawford on the set of *Hush… Hush, Sweet Charlotte*. Bette Davis was the star.

Vivien turned it down, telling the press that, "I could just look at Joan Crawford's face at seven o'clock in the morning, but I couldn't possibly look at Bette Davis's."

Vivien was very disappointed to read what Larry had said about her to a journalist. "I had shared a life that had resembled nothing so much as an express lift skying me upwards and throwing me downwards in an insanely non-stop fashion."

***

After a reunion at Chichester in 1964, Vivien and Larry resumed their friendship, not their love affair. "We were past that," Larry told Noël Coward.

After four years of separation, Vivien and Larry met again. No one knows what words were exchanged between them, but after that meeting, they became friends and started seeing each other.

A maid remembered Larry showing up at Tickerage unexpectedly and calling out to Vivien "to come on down."

She was lingering in her bed-

Jack Merivale with Vivien Leigh in 1962

room to make herself extra beautiful for him. She'd prepared a special luncheon for him, and of course, she knew his favorite wine. The maid saw them walking hand in hand around the lake, and later going for a ride in Vivien's little row boat.

Their interlude was interrupted with a telephone call from Plowright, who demanded that Larry return to London to attend to urgent business.

He kissed Vivien good-bye and held her close. The next day she called John Gielgud, telling him, "I'm still hopelessly in love with Larry."

"Get over it, Viv darling," he told her. "He's moved on. He's got a family, a loving wife. He's more settled now. "You'd find him boring my dear. Trust me."

She told Merivale that she loved him very much "but I can never cut the cord with Larry. He was my first love. It wasn't Larry who betrayed me. It was Joan who turned him against me. We were once so happy. We caused each other such pain, but I want to remember only the happy years."

***

For her fifty-first birthday, Vivien impulsively returned to India, the country of her birth. She had not seen it since the 1920s. Merivale was in Hollywood working on a film.

She flew on this very long and arduous trip with Lady Alexandra Metcalf, the daughter of Lord Curzon, last viceroy of India.

In Nepal, the king lent her his private airplane. Wherever she went, fans shouted, "Look, it's Scarlett O'Hara."

She was impressed with the mystical atmosphere of India, as she flew over the Himalayas and the place of her birth. "I didn't know peaks were ever that tall," she said.

On the king's plane she also flew to Pokra for a close inspection of Mt. Everest. At Gwalior she was invited to stay in the Maharani's palace.

She arrived back in England in time to host a private luncheon for Winston Churchill about two months before he died. She'd always remember him with love.

She later told Merivale that, "The Great Man held my hand with tears in his eyes."

"Had you been born in another time, I would have made you my Clementine," he told her.

***

After her Broadway run in *Tovarich*, Helpmann directed her in another

646

play, *La Contessa*, which opened in England at Newcastle on April 6, 1965.

In a hideous red wig, Vivien played the notorious Marchesa Casati, who walked around with a leopard on a leash, who went on spending sprees, who bred wild animals, who raced cars, and who had numerous lovers.

Though ailing at the time and in very poor health, Larry with great difficulty made his way to Newcastle. Working with Vivien, he helped her sharpen her performance. But he wasn't satisfied with the final results.

He advised both Helpmann and Vivien not to take the play into London. "Kenneth Tynan won't be the only critic gunning for the two of you," Larry predicted.

Before she retired from the stage, there was one final play in Vivien. John Gielgud was both starring in and directing *Ivanov*, which opened at New York's Shubert Theatre on May 3, 1966.

In the role, Vivien played a Jewish wife who gave up everything for her man, in this case Gielgud as Ivanov.

Richard Watts Jr. of the *New York Post*, called her performance "nothing short of magnificent."

While performing in *Ivanov*, Vivien and Joan Fontaine exchanged apartments, Fontaine taking over her London residence. She later was furious when she learned that Vivien had moved her cat, "Poo," into her immaculate New York apartment. Vivien also refused to let Fontaine put her Alfa Romeo in her garage at Eaton Square. The two women ended up "hating each other for life."

Vivien may have had a premonition about her upcoming death, because she used the occasion to visit loving friends in New York who had known her for years.

Vivien once told Merivale that, "I plan to keep appearing on the stage until the day I die, even if they have to haul me out in a wheelchair."

In the last week of her life, she was reading a script sent to her by Edward Albee. Called *A Delicate Balance*, Albee and his producers had conceived it as a star vehicle for Michael Redgrave and Vivien.

***

On the night of July 7, 1967, her long-time friend and confidant, Roy Moseley, came to visit her and sat on the bed with her, holding her hand. She made a strange pronouncement, which had a certain finality to it, even though she was planning to return to the stage in the West End. It was obvious that she was regressing to another day, another time. Before he departed, she told him, "I'd rather lead a short life with Larry than a long life without him."

An hour later, Merivale kissed Vivien goodbye and left for his evening performance. He was appearing in *The Last of Mrs. Cheney* at the Yvonne

Arnaud Theatre in Guildford, Surrey, right outside London.

He called her during intermission from his dressing room. She said she was all right. "Don't worry about me, darling. Just hurry home."

Reaching their flat shortly after 11pm, he came into her bedroom to find her sleeping. He went to the kitchen to heat up a can of tomato soup.

After that, he went back to her bedroom and found her lying on the floor unconscious. Her body was still warm, but she'd stopped breathing. His attempt to resuscitate her failed. He immediately called a doctor who arrived shortly thereafter. After a quick examination, he told Merivale, "Miss Leigh is dead. She was my favorite actress."

At eight o'clock the following morning, Merivale called Larry at St. Thomas' Hospital, where he was recovering from an operation for prostate cancer.

When he learned the news, Larry let out a yelp of pain. In his terribly weakened state, he checked himself out of the hospital over his doctor's objections and slowly made his way to Eaton Square where Vivien's dead body had not been removed.

Merivale left him alone in the room with Vivien.

In his memoirs, Larry wrote, "I stood and prayed for forgiveness for all the evils that had sprung up between us."

He then looked at that "beautiful dead face" one last time.

After hugging Merivale, he left the apartment and walked out and looked up at a threatening sky over London. A reporter had heard that Vivien had had a heart attack. He rushed up to him. "Sir Laurence, what is the condition of Lady Olivier?"

With tears in his eyes, Larry turned to the reporter. "Lady Olivier entered immortality last night."

In Loving Memory

Laurence Olivier (1907-1989)
and Vivien Leigh (1913-1967)

With Respect, Admiration, and Affection

Rest in Peace

ABOUT DARWIN PORTER AND ROY MOSELEY

Darwin Porter has been fascinated by the Oliviers since his early 20s, when he first began collecting facts and anecdotes during his tenure as an entertainment columnist and bureau chief for *Knight Newspapers* and *The Miami Herald*.

Darwin sustained a 30-year writing partnership with Stanley Haggart, a Hollywood and London West End insider. Haggart was a companion of the famous British director, Peter Glenville, one of Larry Olivier's lovers and role models, and one of the hundreds of witnesses whose observations contributed to the percolating stewpot of insights into the motivations of Olivier and Leigh.

"Everyone who knew them," according to Darwin, "had anecdotes and points of view about the Oliviers. The challenge involved compiling them into a coherent overview of their personal histories and what made them tick."

Today, Darwin is one of the most prolific biographers in the world. His portraits of Paul Newman, Howard Hughes, Merv Griffin, Steve McQueen, Marlon Brando, Humphrey Bogart, Katharine Hepburn, and Michael Jackson have generated widespread reviews and animated radio and blogsite commentaries worldwide. Some of his biographies have been serialized to millions of readers in *The Sunday Times* of London and *The Mail on Sunday*.

He's also the co-author, with Danforth Prince, of *Blood Moon's Babylon Series*, Volumes One and Two, with others scheduled for release soon.

Darwin is also the well-known author of many past and present editions of *The Frommer Guides* (including the series' guides to London, England, Scotland, and Wales), a respected travel guidebook series presently administered by John Wiley & Sons Publishers.

650

Scheduled for upcoming release in 2011 are Darwin's *The Kennedys, All the Gossip Unfit to Print*, a rollicking overview of the peccadillos of America's most scandalous political clan; *Sinatra, The Boudoir Singer, All the Gossip Unfit to Print from the Glory Days of Ol' Blue Eyes,* about the 20th Century's most controversial and most politically connected singer; and a biography of FBI directors *J. Edgar Hoover and Clyde Tolson*, a story about celebrity worship, upper-echelon blackmail, and the dark side of the American saga.

When he's not traveling, Darwin lives with a menagerie of once-abandoned pets in a Victorian house in one of the outer boroughs of New York City.

***

Known in theatrical and film circles in both Hollywood and London, **Roy Moseley** is a distinguished biographer, having collaborated on best-selling books about Queen Elizabeth and Prince Philip, Merle Oberon, and Cary Grant. He also wrote the first major biography ever published of Sir Rex Harrison, and an intimate memoir of his intimate, decades-long association with Bette Davis.

For years, he was a close friend and confidant of Lord and Lady Olivier, sharing their secrets, tragedies, and triumphs. Much of the heretofore unpublished information he learned over his decades within their orbit is shared in this biography of the legendary pair, whose glamour and talent stunned the world.

An internationally recognized movie, television, and theater journalist, Roy has also known some of the major figures associated with the Oliviers, including Sir Noël Coward, Sir John Gielgud, and dozens of other luminaries of London's West End and the Hollywood Hills. Today, Roy lives and works in Los Angeles.

Currently, he is collaborating with Darwin Porter on a dual biography about the entertainment industry's most poisonous sibling rivalry: *Olivia de Havilland and Joan Fontaine--Twisted Sisters: To Each Her Own,* scheduled for release sometime in 2012.

BIBLIOGRAPHY

Alpert, Hollis. *Burton.* New York: Paper Jacks, Ltd., 1986.

Amburn, Ellis. *The Sexiest Man Alive—A Biography of Warren Beatty.* New York: Harper Collins, 2002.

Andersen, Christopher P. *A Star Is A Star, Is A Star, Is A Star!—The Lives and Loves of Susan Hayward.* New York: Doubleday & Company, Inc., 1980.

Arden, Eve. *Three Phases of Eve—Eve Arden—An Autobiography.* New York: St. Martin's Press, 1985.

Aumont, Jean-Pierre. *Sun and Shadow—An Autobiography.* New York: W.W. Norton & Company, Inc., 1977.

Barker, Felix. *The Oliviers.* Philadelphia: J.B. Lippincott Company, 1953.

Bartel, Pauline. *The Complete Gone With the Wind Trivia Book.* Texas: Taylor Publishing Company, 1989.

Beaton, Cecil. *Cecil Beaton—Memoirs of the 40's.* New York: McGraw-Hill Book Company, 1972.

Beckett, Francis. *Olivier.* London: Haus Publishing, 2005.

Beeman, Marsha Lynn. *Joan Fontaine—A Bio-Bibliography.* Connecticut: Greenwood Press, 1994.

Bemrose, Anna. *Robert Helpmann—A Servant of Art.* Queensland: University of Queensland Press, 2008.

Berg, A. Scott. *Goldwyn—A Biography.* New York: Alfred A. Knopf, 1989.

Bergman, Ingmar. *The Magic Lantern—An Autobiography.* New York: Viking, 1988.

Blakelock, Denys. *Round the Next Corner—An Intensely Personal Autobiography.* London: Victor Gollancz Ltd., 1967.

Bloom, Claire. *Leaving a Doll's House—A Memoir.* London: Little, Brown and Company,1996.

_____*Limelight and After—The Education of an Actress.* New York: Harper & Row, Publishers, 1982.

Bogarde, Dirk. *Snakes & Ladders—A Memoir.* New York: Holt, Rinchart, and Winston, 1978.

Bragg, Melvyn. *Richard Burton—A Life.* London: Little, Brown and Company, 1988.

Braun, Eric. *Deborah Kerr.* New York: St. Martin's Press, 1978.

Brett, David. *Errol Flynn—Satan's Angel.* London: Robson Books, 2000.

Brown, Jared. *The Fabulous Lunts—A Biography of Alfred Lunt and Lynn Fontanne.* New York: Antheneum, 1988.

Buckle, Richard. *Self Portrait With Friends—The Selected Diaries of Cecil Beaton 1922-1974.* New York: Times Books, 1979.

Buford, Kate. *Burt Lancaster—An American Life.* New York: Alfred A. Knopf, 2000.

Callow, Simon. *Charles Laughton—A Difficult Actor.* New York: Grove Press, 1987.

Capua, Michelangelo. *Vivien Leigh—A Biography.* North Carolina: McFarland & Company, Inc., 2003.

Castle, Charles. *Noël.* London: Abacus, 1972.

Cawthorne, Nigel. *Sex Lives of the Hollywood Goddesses 2.* Great Britain: Prion, 2004.

Chaplin, Charles. *My Autobiography—Charles Chaplin.* New York: Simon and Schuster, Inc. 1964.

Clark, Colin. *The Prince, The Showgirl and Me—Six Months on the Set with Marilyn and*

Olivier. New York: St. Martin's Press, 1996.

Coleman, Terry. *Olivier.* New York: Henry Holt and Company, 2005.

Collins, Joan. *Past Imperfect—An Autobiography.* New York: Simon and Schuster, 1984.

Connell, Brian. *Knight Errant—A Biography of Douglas Fairbanks, Jr.* New York: Doubleday & Company, Inc., 1955.

Considine, Shaun. *Bette & Joan—The Divine Feud.* London: Frederick Muller, 1989.

Conway, Michael, McGregor, Dion & Ricci, Mark. *The Films of Greta Garbo.* New Jersey: The Citadel Press, 1974.

Cottrell, John and Cashin, Fergus. *Laurence Olivier.* New Jersey: Prentice-Hall, Inc., 1975.

_____ *Richard Burton—Very Close Up.* New Jersey, Prentice Hall, Inc., 1971.

Coward, Noël. *Future Indefinite.* New York: Doubleday & Company, Inc., 1954.

_____*Present Indicative.* New York: Doubleday Doran and Company, Inc., 1937.

Croall, Jonathan. *Sybil Thorndike—A Star of Life.* London: Haus Books, 2008.

Curtis, James. *James Whale—A New World of Gods and Monsters.* London: Faber and Faber, 1998.

Curtis, Tony. *American Prince—A Memoir.* New York: Harmony Books, 2008.

_____*Tony Curtis—The Autobiography.* New York: William Morrow and Company, Inc., 1993.

Daniels, Robert L. *Laurence Olivier—Theater and Cinema.* California: A.S. Barnes & Company, Inc., 1980.

David, Lester & Robbins, Jhan. *Richard and Elizabeth.* London: W.H. Allen & Co. Ltd., 1979.

Davidson, Bill. *Spencer Tracy—Tragic Actor.* New York: Zebra Books, 1990.

De Acosta, Mercedes. *Here Lies the Heart—A Tale of My Life.* New York: Reynal & Company, 1960.

Devlin, Albert J. and Tischler, Nancy M. *The Selected Letters of Tennessee Williams— Volume 1, 1920-1945.* New York: A New Directions Books, 2000.

_____Volume 2, 1945-1957. 2004.

Douglas, Kirk. *The Ragman's Son.* New York: Simon and Schuster, 1988.

Dundy, Elaine. *Finch, Bloody Finch—A Life of Peter Finch.* New York: Holt, Rinehart and Winston, 1980.

Easton, Carol. *The Search for Sam Goldwyn.* New York: William Morrow and Company, Inc., 1976.

Edwards, Anne. *Vivien Leigh—A Biography.* New York: Simon & Schuster, 1977.

Eells, George. *Hedda and Louella.* New York: G.P. Putnam's Sons, 1972.

Fairbanks, Douglas, Jr. *Douglas Fairbanks, Jr.—The Salad Days—An Autobiography.* New York: Doubleday, 1988.

Fairweather, Virginia. *Cry God for Larry—An Intimate Memoir of Sir Laurence Olivier.* London: Calder & Boyars, 1969.

Falk, Quentin. *Anthony Hopkins—Too Good to Waste.* London: Columbus Books, 1989.

Faulkner, Trader. *Peter Finch—A Biography.* New York: Taplinger Publishing Company, 1979.

Finstad, Suzanne. *Warren Beatty—A Private Man.* New York: Harmony Books, 2005.

Flamini, Roland. *Scarlett, Rhett, and a Cast of Thousands—The Filming of Gone With the Wind.* New York: Collier Books, 1975.

Flynn, Errol. *My Wicked, Wicked Ways—The Autobiography of Errol Flynn.* New York: Cooper Square Press, 2003.

Fontaine, Joan. *No Bed of Roses—An Autobiography.* New York: William Morrow and Company, Inc., 1978.

Forbes, Bryan. *Dame Edith Evans—Ned's Girl.* Toronto: Little, Brown and Company, 1977.

Freedland, Michael. *Peter O'Toole—A Biography.* New York: St. Martin's Press, 1982.
____ *The Secret Life of Danny Kaye.* New York: St. Martin's Press, 1985.
____*The Two Lives of Errol Flynn.* New York: Bantam Books, Inc., 1980.
Garland, Patrick. *The Incomparable Rex—A Memoir of Rex Harrison in the 1980s.* New York: Fromm International, 2000.
Gielgud, John. *John Gielgud—Backward Glances.* New York: Limelight Editions, 1990.
____ *Early Stages—An Autobiography.* California: Mercury House, Incorporated,1974.
Godfrey, Lionel. *The Life and Crimes of Errol Flynn.* New York: St. Martin's Press, Inc., 1977.
Gordon, Ruth. *Ruth Gordon—An Open Book.* New York: Doubleday & Company, Inc., 1980
.____*Ruth Gordon—Myself Among Others.* New York: Atheneum, 1971.
Gottfried, Martin. *Arthur Miller—His Life and Work.* Massachusetts: Da Capo Press, 2003.
____ *Jed Harris—The Curse of Genius.* Boston: Little, Brown and Company, 1984.
____ *Nobody's Fool—Danny Kaye.* New York: Simon & Schuster, 1994.
Gourlay, Logan. *Olivier.* New York: Stein and Day,1974.
Granger, Stewart. *Sparks Fly Upward.* New York: G.P. Putnam's Sons, 1981.
Grobel, Lawrence. *The Hustons.* New York: Charles Scribner's Sons, 1989.
Guiles, Fred Lawrence. *The Last Word—Joan Crawford.* London: Pavilion Books Limited, 1995.
Guinness, Alec. *Blessings in Disguise.* New York: Alfred A. Knopf, 1986.
Guthrie, Tyrone. *A Life in the Theatre.* London: Columbus Books, 1959.
Harris, Jed. *A Dance on the High Wire—A Unique Memoir of the Theatre.* New York: Crown Publishers, Inc., 1979.
Harris, Radie. *Radie's World.* New York: G.P. Putnam's Sons, 1975.
Harrison, Rex. *Rex—An Autobiography.* New York: William Morris & Company, Inc., 1975.
____*Rex Harrison—A Damned Serious Business—My Life in Comedy.* New York: Bantam Books, 1991.
Haskell, Molly. *Frankly, My Dear—Gone With the Wind Revisited.* Connecticut: Yale University Press, 2009.
Hayman, Ronald. *Tennessee Williams—Everyone Else Is an Audience.* Connecticut: Yale University Press, 1993.
Heston, Charlton. *In the Arena—An Autobiography.* New York: Boulevard Books, 1997.
Heymann, David, C. *Liz.* New York: Carol Publishing Group, 1995.
____*Poor Little Rich Girl—The Life and Legend of Barbara Hutton.* New York: Random House, 1983.
Higham, Charles. *Errol Flynn—The Untold Story.* New York: Dell Publishing Co.,   Inc., 1980.
____*Merchant of Dreams—Louis B. Mayer, M.G.M., and the Secret Hollywood.* New York: Donald I. Fine, Inc., 1993.
____ *Orson Welles—The Rise and Fall of an American Genius.* New York: St. Martin's Press, 1985.
Higham, Charles & Moseley, Roy. *Cary Grant—The Lonely Heart.* Harcourt Brace Jovanovich, 1989.
____*Elizabeth & Philip.* Pan Books, 1992.
____*Princess Merle—The Romantic Life of Merle Oberon.* New York: Coward-McCann, Inc., 1983.
Hirsch, Foster. *Laurence Olivier.* Boston: Twayne Publishers, 1979.
Holden, Anthony. *Laurence Olivier—A Biography.* New York: Antheneum, 1988.
Hopper, Hedda & Brough, James. *The Whole Truth and Nothing But.* New York: Doubleday & Company, Inc., 1963.

Howard, Leslie Ruth. *A Quite Remarkable Father.* New York: Harcourt, Brace and Company, 1959.

Hudson, Richard and Lee, Raymond. *Gloria Swanson.* New York: Castle Books, 1970.

Hunter, Allan. *The Man and His Movies—Tony Curtis.* New York: St. Martin's Press, 1985.

Infield, Glenn B. *Leni Riefenstahl—The Fallen Film Goddess.* New York: Thomas Y. Crowell Company, 1976.

Jenkins, Graham. *Richard Burton—My Brother.* New York: Harper & Row, Publishers, 1988.

Kanin, Garson. *Hollywood.* New York: The Viking Press, 1974.

Kass, Judith M. *Olivia de Havilland.* New York: Pyramid Publications, 1976.

Kazan, Elia. *Elia Kazan—A Life.* New York: Alfred A Knopf, 1988.

Kershaw, Robert. *Blood and Champagne—The Life and Times of Robert Capa.* New York: St. Martin's Press, 2002.

Keyes, Evelyn. *Scarlett O'Hara's Younger Sister—My Lively Life In and Out of Hollywood.* New Jersey: Lyle Stuart Inc., 1977.

Kiernan, Thomas. *The Life of Laurence Olivier—Sir Larry.* New York: Times Books, 1981.

Kobler, John. *Damned in Paradise—The Life of John Barrymore.* New Jersey: American Book—Stratford Press, 1977.

Korda, Michael. *Charmed Lives—A Family Romance.* New York: Random House,1979.

Kulik, Karol. *Alexander Korda—The Man Who Could Work Miracles.* New York: Arlington House Publishers, 1975.

Laguardia, Robert & Arceri, Gene. *Red—The Tempestuous Life of Susan Hayward.* New York: Macmillan Publishing Company, 1985.

Lasky, Jesse L. Jr. and Silver, Pat. *Love Scene.* New York: Berkley Books, 1978.

Leaming, Barbara. *Orson Welles—A Biography.* New York: Viking, 1985.

Lesley, Cole. *The Life of Noël Coward.* New York: Penguin Books, 1976.

____*Remembered Laughter—The Life of Nöel Coward.* New York: Alfred A. Knopf, Inc., 1977.

Leslie, Anita. *Clare Sheridan—Her Tempestuous Life with Jennie Churchill, Mussolini, Lenin, Charlie Chaplin, Trotsky, Winston Churchill, and Others.* New York: Doubleday & Company, Inc., 1977.

Lillie, Beatrice. *An Autobiography by Beatrice Lillie—Every Other Inch a Lady.* New York: Dell Publishing Co., Inc., 1972.

Linet, Beverly. *Portrait of a Survivor—Susan Hayward.* New York: Berkley Books, 1981.

Lobenthal, Joel. *Tallulah!—The Life & Times of a Leading Lady.* New York: Regan Books, 2004.

Lord, Graham. *Niv—The Authorized Biography of David Niven.* New York: St. Martin's Press, 2003.

Lynn, Kenneth, S. *Charlie Chaplin and His Times.* New York: Simon & Schuster, 1997.

Madsen, Axel. *John Huston—A Biography.* New York: Doubleday & Company, Inc., 1978.

____*The Sewing Circle—Hollywood's Greatest Secret—Female Stars Who Loved Other Women.* New Jersey: Carol Publishing Group, 1995.

Manvell, Roger. *Chaplin.* Boston: Little, Brown and Company, 1974.

Marchant, William. *The Privilege of His Company—Noël Coward Remembered.* New York: The Bobbs-Merrill Company, Inc., 1975.

Marker, Lise-Lone & Marker, Frederick, J. *Ingmar Bergman—Four Decades in the Theater.* London: Cambridge University Press, 1982.

Marx, Arthur. *Goldwyn—A Biography of the Man Behind the Myth.* New York: W.W. Norton & Company, Inc., 1976.

Mason, James. *Before I Forget—An Autobiography.* London: Sphere Books Limited, 1981.

Massey, Raymond. *A Hundred Different Lives—An Autobiography.* Toronto: Little, Brown and Company, 1979.

Maxwell, Gilbert. *Tennessee Williams and Friends—An Informal Biography*. Ohio: The World Publishing Company, 1965.

Mayer Selznick, Irene. *A Private View*. New York: Alfred Knopf, 1983.

McCann, Graham. *Cary Grant—A Class Apart*. New York: Columbia University Press, 1996.

McClelland, Doug. *Susan Hayward—The Devine Bitch*. New York: Pinnacle Books, 1973.

McClintic, Guthrie. *Me and Kit*. Canada: Little Brown & Company Limited, 1955.

McGilligan, Patrick. *Alfred Hitchcock—A Life in Darkness and Light*. New York: Regan Books, 2003.

McNulty, Thomas. *The Life and Career—Errol Flynn*. North Carolina: McFarland & Company, Inc., 2004.

Miles, Sarah. *Serves Me Right*. London: Macmillan, 1994.

Miller, Arthur. *Timebends—A Life*. New York: Grove Press, 1987.

Mills, John. *Still Memories—An Autobiography in Photography*. London: Random House Group Limited, 2000.

____*Up In the Clouds, Gentlemen Please*. New York: Ticknor & Fields, 1981.

Molt, Cynthia Marylee. *Vivien Leigh—A Bio-Bibliography*. Connecticut: Greenwood Press, 1992.

Morella, Joe, and Epstein, Edward Z. *Paulette—The Adventurous Life of Paulette Goddard*. New York: St. Martin's Press, 1985.

Morley, Sheridan. *Gladys Cooper—A Biography*. New York: McGraw-Hill Book Company, 1979.

Moseley, Roy. *Bette Davis—An Intimate Memoir*. Dutton Adult, 1990

____*Evergreen—Victor Saville in His Own Words*. Illinois: Southern Illinois University Press, 2000.

____*Memories of the Oliviers—Vivien Leigh & Laurence Olivier & Joan Plowright*. 2006.

____*My Stars and Other Friends*. William Heinemann Ltd., 1982.

____*Rex Harrison—The First Biography*. Kent: New English Library, 1987.

____*Roger Moore—A Biography*. Kent: New English Library, Ltd., 1986.

Munn, Michael. *Kid from the Bronx—A Biography of Tony Curtis*. London: W. H. Allen, 1984.

____*Lord Larry—The Secret Life of Laurence Olivier*. London: Robson Books, 2007.

____*Richard Burton—Prince of Players*. New York: Skyhorse Publishing, 2008.

Munshower, Suzanne. *Warren Beatty—His Life, His Loves, His Work*. New York: Pinnacle Book, 1983.

Negri, Pola. *Memoirs of a Star*. New York: Doubleday & Company, Inc., 1970.

Niven, David. *Bring on the Empty Horses*. New York: G.P. Putnam's Sons, 1975.

____*The Moon's a Balloon*. London: Coronet Books, 1971.

O'Connor, Garry. *An Actor's Life—Ralph Richardson*. New York: Applause Books, 1997.

____*Darlings of the Gods—One Year in the Lives of Laurence Olivier and Vivien Leigh*. London: Hodder and Sloughton, 1984.

Olivier, Laurence. *Laurence Olivier—Confessions of An Actor—An Autobiography*. New York: Simon and Schuster, 1982.

____*Laurence Olivier—On Acting*. New York: Simon and Schuster, 1986.

Olivier, Richard. *Melting the Stone—A Journey Around My Father*. Connecticut: Spring Publications, Inc., 1996.

Olivier, Richard and Plowright, Joan. *Olivier at Work*. London: Nick Hern Books, 1989.

Olivier, Tarquin. *My Father Laurence Olivier*. Luton: Headline Book Publishing, 1992.

Paris, Barry. *Garbo*. New York: Alfred A. Knopf, Inc., 1994.

Parker, John. *Warren Beatty—The Last Great Lover of Hollywood*. New York: Carroll & Graf Publishers, Inc., 1993.

Payn, Graham with Day, Barry. *My Life with Noël Coward*. New York: Applause, 1994.

Payn, Graham and Morley, Sheridan. *The Noël Coward Diaries*. Toronto: Little, Brown and Company, 1982.

Peters, Margot. *Design for Living—Alfred Lunt and Lynn Fontanne—A Biography*. New York: Alfred A. Knopf, 2003.

Porter, Darwin. *Brando Unzipped*. New York: Blood Moon Productions, Ltd., 2005.

____*Hollywood Babylon—It's Back!* New York: Blood Moon Productions, Ltd., 2008.

____*Hollywood Babylon—Strikes Again!* New York: Blood Moon Productions, Ltd., 2010.

____*Humphrey Bogart—The Making of a Legend*. New York: Blood Moon Productions, Ltd., 2010.

____*Howard Hughes—Hell's Angel*. Blood Moon Productions, Ltd., 2010.

____*Katharine The Great*. New York: Blood Moon Productions, Ltd., 2004.

____*Paul Newman—The Man Behind the Baby Blues*. New York: Blood Moon Productions, Ltd., 2009.

____*The Secret Life of Humphrey Bogart—The Early Years (1899-1931)*. New York: Blood Moon Productions, Ltd., 2003.

Quirk, Lawrence, J. *Fasten Your Seat Belts—The Passionate Life of Bette Davis*. New York: William Morrow and Company, Inc., 1990.

____ *The Films of Gloria Swanson*. New Jersey: Citadel Press, 1984.

____*The Films of Robert Taylor*. New Jersey: Citadel Press, 1979.

____*The Films of Warren Beatty*. New York: Carol Publishing Group, 1990

Quirk, Lawrence, J. & Schoell, William. *Joan Crawford*. Kentucky: The University Press of Kentucky, 2002.

Rains, Sally Tippett. *The Making of a Masterpiece—The True Story of Margaret Mitchell's Classic Novel—Gone With the Wind*. California: Global Book Publishers, 2009.

Read, Piers Paul. *Alec Guinness—The Authorized Biography*. London: Simon & Schuster, 2003.

Redgrave, Michael. *In My Mind's Eye—An Autobiography*. London: Weidenfeld and Nicolson, 1983.

Salter, Elizabeth. *Helpmann—The Authorized Biography*. Sussex: Angus and Robertson, 1978.

Sands, Frederick, and Broman, Sven. *The Divine Garbo*. New York: Grosset & Dunlap, 1979.

Sellers, Robert. *Hellraisers—The Life and Inebriated Times of Richard Burton, Richard Harris, Peter O'Toole, and Oliver Reed*. New York: St. Martin's Press, 2008.

Selznick, David O. *Memo from David O. Selznick*. New York: The Viking Press, 1972.

Shavelson, Melville. *How to Succeed In Hollywood Without Really Trying—P.S.—You Can't!*. Georgia: BearManor Media, 2007.

Sikov, Ed. *Dark Victory—The Life of Bette Davis*. New York: Henry Holt and Company, 2007.

Signoret, Simone. *Nostalgia Isn't What It Used to Be*. London: Grafton Books,1986.

Singer, Kurt. *The Danny Kaye Story*. New York: Thomas Nelson & Sons, 1958.

Soister, John, T. *Conrad Veidt on Screen—A Comprehensive Illustrated Filmography*. North Carolina: McFarland & Company, Inc., 2002.

Spada, James. *More Than a Woman—An Intimate Biography of Bette Davis*. New York: Bantam Books, 1993.

Spoto, Donald.*The Dark Side of Genius—The Life of Alfred Hitchcock*. Toronto: Little, Brown and Company, 1983

.____*The Kindness of Strangers—The Life of Tennessee Williams.* Boston: Little, Brown and Company, 1985.

____ *Laurence Olivier—A Biography.* New York: Harper Collins Publishers, 1992.

____*Otherwise Engaged—The Life of Alan Bates.* Great Britain: Arrow Books, 2007.

Staggs, Sam. *When Blanche Met Brando.* New York: St. Martin's Press, 2005.

Steen, Mike. *A Look at Tennessee Williams.* New York: Hawthorn Books, Inc., 1969.

Stine, Whitney. *I'd Love to Kiss You—Conversations with Bette Davis.* New York: Simon & Schuster Inc., 1990.

Stumph, Charles and Ohmart, Ben. *The Smiling Girl on the Cardboard Moon—The Saga of Paulette Goddard.* New York: Writers Club Press, 2000.

Summers, Anthony. *Goddess—The Secret Lives of Marilyn Monroe.* London: Sphere Books Limited, 1985.

Swanson, Gloria. *Swanson on Swanson—An Autobiography.* New York: Random House, 1980.

Tabori, Paul. *Alexander Korda.* New York: Living Books, Inc., 1966.

Thomas, Bob. *Joan Crawford—A Biography.* New York: Simon and Schuster, 1978.

____*Selznick—The Man Who Produced Gone With the Wind.* California: New Millennium Press, 1970.

Thomas, Tony. *The Films of Olivia de Havilland.* New Jersey: Citadel Press, 1983.

Thomson, David. *Showman—The Life of David O. Selznick.* New York: Alfred A. Knopf, 1992.

Todd, Ann. *The Eighth Veil.* New York: G. P. Putnam's Sons, 1981.

Troyan, Michael. *A Rose for Mrs. Miniver—Greer Garson.* Kentucky: The University Press of Kentucky, 1999.

Tynan, Kathleen and Eban, Ernie. *Kenneth Tynan—Profiles.* New York: Random House, 1989.

Ustinov, Peter. *Dear Me.* Toronto: Little, Brown and Company, 1977.

Vickers, Hugo. *Cecil Beaton—A Biography.* Toronto: Little, Brown and Company, 1985.

____*Vivien Leigh.* London: Hamish Hamilton, 1988.

Walker, Alexander. *Garbo—A Portrait.* New York: Macmillan Publishing Co., Inc., 1980.

____*Vivien—The Life of Vivien Leigh.* New York: Weidenfelf & Nicolson, 1987.

Watts, Jill. *Hattie McDaniel—Black Ambition, White Hollywood.* New York: HarperCollins Books, 2005.

Wayne, Jane Ellen. *Crawford's Men.* New York: Prentice Hall Press, 1988.

____*Robert Taylor.* New York: Manor Books, Inc., 1973.

Welles, Orson & Bogdanovich, Peter. *This is Orson Welles.* New York: Harper Perennial, 1992.

Williams, Dakin, and Mead Shepherd. *Tennessee Williams—An Intimate Biography.* New York: Arbor House, 1983.

Williams, Tennessee. *Memoirs.* New York: Doubleday & Company, Inc., 1975.

____ *Tennessee Williams Letters to Donald Windham—1940-1965.* New York: Holt, Rinehart and Winston, 1976.

Wolfe, Donald H. *The Assassination of Marilyn Monroe.* London: Little, Brown and Company, 1998.

Woodhouse, Adrian. *Angus McBean—Face-Maker.* Surrey: Alma Books, 2006.

Zeffirelli, Franco. *Zeffirelli—An Autobiography.* New York: Weidenfeld & Nicolson, 1986.

Zierold, Norman. *Garbo.* New York: Stein and Day, 1969.

____ *The Hollywood Tycoons.* London: Hamish Hamilton, 1969.

Zolotow, Maurice. *Stagestruck—The Romance of Alfred Lunt and Lynn Fontanne.* New York: Harcourt, Brace & World, Inc., 1964.

INDEX

661

663

669

Guinan, Texas 84, 85

Guinness, Sir Alec 203, 251, 259, 260, 271, 477, 481, 505, 522, 523

Guntner, J. Lawrence 539

Guthrie, Sir Tyrone 203, 240, 249, 250, 252, 257, 259, 260, 271, 272, 282, 284, 287, 467, 474, 492, 494, 507, 522, 550, 551

Gwenn, Edmund 132, 387

Gyssling, George 428

Haggart, Stanley Mills 291, 442, 470

Haines, William 131, 132, 152, 329, 343, 344, 397, 615

Halburn, Roger 27

Haller, Ernest 383

Hamilton, Emma 415, 416, 417, 440

Hamilton, Hamish (aka "Jamie") 120, 311, 455

Hamlet 21, 25, 28, 89, 93, 137, 209, 210, 214, 224, 231, 245, 249, 250, 251, 257, 258, 259, 261, 279, 409, 467, 484, 526, 527, 528, 529, 530, 531, 532, 533, 537, 538, 539, 560, 578, 629

Hammond, Kay 86

Hannen, Hermione 481

Hannen, Nicholas (Beau) 491

Hanson, Smitty 435

Happy Hypocrite, The 215-216, 218, 220, 222

Happy Time, The 606

Harbord, Carl 219

Harding, Ann 74, 143

Harding, Laura 512

Hardwicke, Lady Cecil 558

Hardwicke, Sir Cedric 49, 141, 425, 426, 427, 458, 625, 626

Hardy, Captain Thomas 438

Hardy, Sally 210

Hardy, Thomas 498

Harlow, Jean 539

Harold 57, 60

Harris Theater (Chicago) 408

Harris, Jed 332, 494

Harris, Julie 596

Harris, Radie 377, 416

Harris, Robert 47, 48

Harrison, Collette Thomas 572

Harrison, Rex 252, 253, 254, 255, 262, 286, 289, 384, 458, 484, 511, 566, 572, 624

Harrow School, The 120

Harry Ransom Center (University of Texas at Austin) 327

Harsh, Judge 419

Hart-Davis, Rupert 26

Hartley, Ernest Richard 14, 15, 17, 37, 38, 39, 44, 118, 126, 212, 623, 638

Hartley, Gertrude Robinson Yackjee 15, 16, 17, 20, 22, 37, 39, 41, 44, 118, 122, 124, 126, 190, 214, 243, 261, 262, 273, 371, 375, 377, 413, 480, 521, 525, 534, 623, 624, 630, 638, 645

Hartsfield, William B. 380

Harvard University 397

Harvey, Frank 84

Harvey, Lilian 92, 93, 94

Havelock-Allen, Anthony 280

Hawkins, Jack 33, 73, 78, 109, 359, 455

Haye, Helen 132

Hayes, Helen 132, 210, 313

Haymarket Theatre, The (London) 468

Hayward, Susan 350, 366

Hayworth, Rita 305, 441

Heald, Father Geoffrey 8, 9, 10, 23, 26, 109

Hearst, William Randolph 88, 431

Heartbreak House 491

Hecht, Ben 298, 322

Heilige berg, Die (*The Holy Mountain*) 42

Heiress, The 550

Helen Hayes Theatre (NYC) 639

Helpmann, Robert 282, 283, 284, 458, 473, 522, 533, 558, 586, 591, 599, 601, 639, 642, 647

Hemingway, Ernest 572

Hennen, Nicholas 85

Henry II 493

Henry IV, Part I 505, 506, 516

Henry IV, Part II 505, 506, 516

Henry V 20, 231, 272, 464, 472, 473, 474, 482, 483, 484, 488, 493, 507, 510, 519, 526, 529, 536, 560, 573, 590

Henry VIII 32, 33, 49, 214

Henson, Leslie 475, 480

Hentschel, Irene 468

Hepburn, Audrey 221

Hepburn, Katharine 71, 88, 136, 147, 148, 149, 276, 283, 297, 313, 319, 320, 323, 332, 335, 336, 338, 354, 416, 418, 419, 421, 427, 463, 511, 512, 566,

BLOOD MOON PRODUCTIONS

Applying the tabloid standards of today
to the Tinseltown scandals of yesterday.

IT'S A TOUGH JOB, BUT SOMEBODY'S GOT TO DO IT!

Blood Moon Productions is a New York-based publishing enterprise dedicated to research-ing, salvaging, and indexing the oral histories of America's entertainment industry. Reorganized with its present name in 2004, Blood Moon originated in 1997 as The Georgia Literary Assn., a vehicle for the promotion of obscure writers from America's Deep South.

Blood Moon's authors, administration, and staff are associated with some of the writing, research, and editorial functions of THE FROMMER GUIDES, a subdivision of John Wiley & Sons, a respected name in travel publishing. Blood Moon also maintains a back list of at least 20 critically acclaimed biographies and film guides. Its titles are distributed within North America and Australia by the National Book Network (www.NBNBooks.com), within the U.K. by Turnaround (www.Turnaround-uk.com), and through secondary wholesalers and online everywhere.

Since 2004, Blood Moon has been awarded at least a dozen nationally recognized literary prizes. They've included both silver and bronze medals from the IPPY (Independent Publishers Assn.) Awards; four nominations and two Honorable Mentions for BOOK OF THE YEAR from Foreword Reviews; and Awards and Honorable Mentions from both the New England and the Hollywood Book Festivals.

For more about us, including free subscription to our scandalous weekly celebrity dish **(BLOOD MOON'S DIRTY LAUNDRY)** and access to a growing number of videotaped book trailers, click on **WWW.BLOODMOONPRODUCTIONS.COM** or refer to the pages which immediately follow.

Thanks for your interest, best wishes, and happy reading.

Danforth Prince, President
Blood Moon Productions, Ltd.

**Meet our affiliate,
The Georgia Literary Association**

Reading entertainment that you'd never have expected from the Deep South

688

GET READY FOR WHAT'S GOING TO ROCK THE COUNTRY JUST BEFORE JFK'S BIRTHDAY (I.E., MAY, 2011)

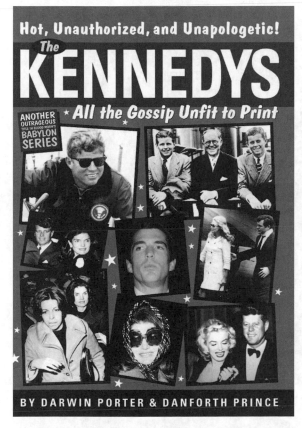

FROM THOSE WHO KNEW THEM:

THEIR POWER, THEIR PECCADILLOS, THEIR PORN.

OK, we appreciate their politics, but what about their sex lives? Read all about it in Volume 3 of Blood Moon's award-winning Babylon series, an inter-generational archive of embarrassments showcasing the libidinous indiscretions and extramarital romps of America's horniest political tribe.

Available in May, 2011
Hardcover, 425 pages
with hundreds of photos
7"x 10"
978-1-936003-17-4
$25.95

"So, with many hundreds of books about the Kennedys published over the years, you think you've heard all the deep dish, sizzling gossip and sexual intrigue surrounding America's royal family of politics and power? **Think again.** *This buzz-rich exposé, culled from decades of intense research by Kennedyphile Darwin Porter, carefully documents the mind-boggling chain of triumph and calamity that has dogged generations of a dynasty both idolized and reviled by a nation. Pick it up and you'll be hard-pressed to put it down."*

RICHARD LABONTÉ, BOOK MARKS AND Q SYNDICATE

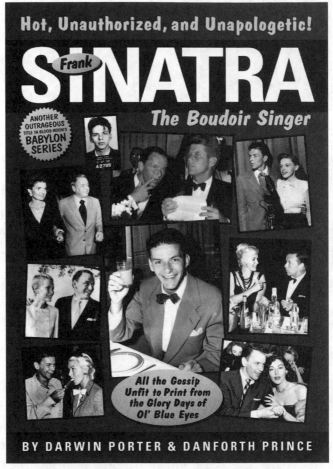

Humphrey Bogart

The Making of a Legend

by Darwin Porter

What Really Lay Under that Trench Coat?
The Secret of Bogie's Appeal
to Each New Generation.

He's Dead, but He Won't Lie Down!

Whereas Humphrey Bogart is always at the top of any list of the Entertainment Industry's most famous actors, very little is known about how he clawed his way to stardom from Broadway to Hollywood during Prohibition and the Jazz Age.

This radical expansion of one of Darwin Porter's pioneering biographies begins with Bogart's origins as the child of wealthy (morphine-addicted) parents in New York City, then examines the scandals, love affairs, breakthrough successes, and failures that launched Bogart on the road to becoming an American icon. Drawn from original interviews with friends and foes who knew a lot about what lay beneath his trenchcoat, this exposé covers Bogart's life from his birth in 1899 until his death in 1957. It includes details about behind-the-scenes dramas associated with three mysterious marriages, and films such as *The Petrified Forest, The Maltese Falcon, High Sierra,* and *Casablanca.* Read all about the debut and formative years of the actor who influenced many generations of filmgoers, laying Bogie's life bare in a style you've come to expect from Blood Moon Productions. Exposed with all their juicy details is what Bogie never told his fourth wife, Lauren Bacall, herself a screen legend.

This revelatory book is based on dusty unpublished memoirs, letters, diaries, and often personal interviews from the women—and the men—who adored him. There are also shocking allegations from colleagues, former friends, and jilted lovers who wanted the screen icon to burn in hell. All this and more, much more, in Darwin Porter's meticulously researched celebrity exposé.

HOWARD HUGHES
HELL'S ANGEL

by Darwin Porter

"The Aviator flew both ways. Porter's biography presents new allegations about Hughes' shady dealings with some of the biggest names of the 20th century."
New York Daily News

"Thanks to this bio of Howard Hughes, we'll never be able to look at the old pin-ups in quite the same way again."
The Times (London)

"Darwin Porter's access to film industry insiders and other Hughes confidants supplied him with the resources he needed to create a portrait of Hughes that both corroborates what other Hughes biographies have divulged, and go them one better."
Foreword Magazine

A DEMENTED BILLIONAIRE

From his reckless pursuit of love as a rich teenager to his final days as a demented fossil, Howard Hughes tasted the best and worst of the century he occupied. Along the way, he changed the worlds of aviation and entertainment forever. This biography reveals inside details about his destructive and usually scandalous associations with other Hollywood players.

Set amid descriptions of the unimaginable changes that affected America between Hughes's birth in 1905 and his death in 1976, this book gives an insider's perspective about what money can buy--and what it can't.

A BIG comprehensive hardcover,
832 pages, with photos, $32.95
ISBN 978-1-936003-13-6

PAUL NEWMAN

The Man Behind the Baby Blues
His Secret Life Exposed
by Darwin Porter

The most compelling biography of the iconic actor ever published

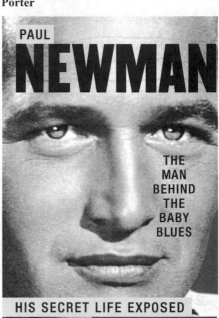

Drawn from firsthand interviews with insiders who knew Paul Newman intimately, and compiled over a period of nearly a half-century, this is the world's most honest and most revelatory biography about Hollywood's pre-eminent male sex symbol, with dozens of potentially shocking revelations.

Whereas the situations it exposes were widely known within Hollywood's inner circles, they've never before been revealed to the general public.

If you're a fan of Newman (and who do you know who isn't) you really should look at this book. It's a respectful but candid cornucopia of information about the sexual and emotional adventures of a young man on Broadway and in Hollywood.

One wonders how he ever managed to escape public scrutiny for so long...

A pioneering and posthumous biography of a charismatic icon of Tinseltown. His rule over the hearts of American moviegoers lasted for more than half a century--a potent, desirable, and ambiguous sex symbol, a former sailor from Shaker Heights, Ohio, who parlayed his ambisexual charm and extraordinary good looks into one of the most successful careers in Hollywood. It's all here, as recorded by celebrity chronicler Darwin Porter--the giddy heights and agonizing lows of a great American star.

Paul Newman, The Man Behind the Baby Blues
His Secret Life Exposed
ISBN 978-0-9786465-1-6 $26.95
Hardcover,   520 pages, with photos.

BLOOD MOON Productions, Ltd.

MERV GRIFFIN
A Life in the Closet

by Darwin Porter

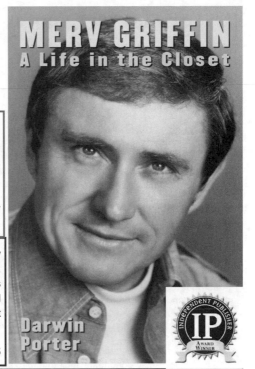

Merv Griffin, A Life in the Closet

Merv Griffin began his career as a Big Band singer, moved on to a failed career as a romantic hero in the movies, and eventually rewrote the rules of everything associated with the broadcasting industry. Along the way, he met and befriended virtually everyone who mattered, made billions operating casinos and developing jingles, contests, and word games. All of this while maintaining a male harem and a secret life as America's most famously closeted homosexual.

In this comprehensive biography--the first published since Merv's death in 2007--celebrity biographer Darwin Porter reveals the amazing details behind the richest, most successful, and in some way, the most notorious mogul in the history of America's entertainment industry.

Most of his viewers (they numbered 20 million per day) thought that **Merv Griffin**'s life was an ongoing series of chatty segués--amiable, seamless, uncontroversial. But things were far more complicated than viewers at the time ever thought. Here, from the writer who unzipped **Marlon Brando**, is the first post-mortem, unauthorized overview of the mysterious life of **the richest and most notorious man in television**

HOT, CONTROVERSIAL, & RIGOROUSLY RESEARCHED

HERE'S MERV! Hardcover, 566 pages with photos

ISBN 978-0-9786465-0-9 $26.95

695

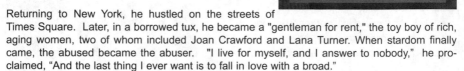

JACKO His Rise and Fall

THE SOCIAL AND SEXUAL HISTORY OF MICHAEL JACKSON

The most comprehensive and unbiased biography of the superstar ever published.

by Darwin Porter.

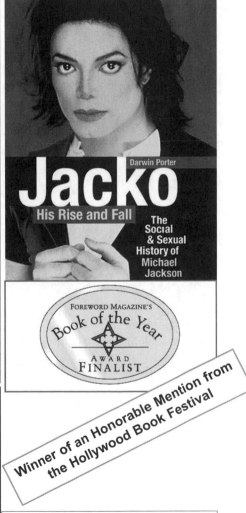

"This is the story of Peter Pan gone rotten. Don't stop till you get enough. Darwin Porter's biography of Michael Jackson is dangerously addictive."
The Sunday Observer

In this compelling glimpse of Jackson's life, Porter provides what many journalists have failed to produce in their writings about the pop star: A real person behind the headlines."
Foreword Magazine

"I'd have thought that there wasn't one single gossippy rock yet to be overturned in the microscopically scrutinized life of Michael Jackson, but Darwin Porter has proven me wrong. Definitely a page-turner. But don't turn the pages too quickly. Almost every one holds a fascinating revelation."
Books to Watch Out For

FOREWORD MAGAZINE'S
Book of the Year
AWARD
FINALIST

Winner of an Honorable Mention from the Hollywood Book Festival

The immediate notoriety of Michael Jackson faded with his trials. Since then, he's been defined as a musical luminary who rewrote the rules of America's entertainment industry. Read this biography for the real story of the circumstances and players who created the icon which the world will forever remember as "the gloved one," Michael Jackson.

ISBN 978-0-936003-10-5
Hardcover
600 indexed pages ©2009 $27.95

BRANDO UNZIPPED

by Darwin Porter

"Lurid, raunchy, perceptive, and certainly worth reading...One of the ten best show-biz biographies of the year."
The Sunday Times (London)

"*Brando Unzipped* is the definitive gossip guide to the late, great actor's life."
The New York Daily News

"Yummy. An irresistably flamboyant romp of a read."
Books to Watch Out For

"Astonishing. An extraordinarily detailed portrait of Brando that's as blunt, uncompromising, and X-rated as the man himself."
Women's Weekly

"This shocking new book is sparking a major reassessment of Brando's legacy as one of Hollywood's most macho lotharios."
Daily Express (London)

"As author Darwin Porter finds, it wasn't just the acting world Marlon Brando conquered. It was the actors, too."
Gay Times (London)

Hardcover, 625 indexed pages, with hundreds of photos.

ISBN 978-0-9748118-2-6.
$26.95

This "entertainingly outrageous" (FRONTIERS MAGAZINE) biography provides a definitive, blow-by-blow description of the "hot, provocative, and barely under control drama" that was the life of America's most famous Postwar actor.

Now in its fifth printing, with French, Portuguese, and Dutch editions available in Europe, this book was serialized by THE SUNDAY TIMES in the UK, and in other major Sunday supplements in mainland Europe and Australia

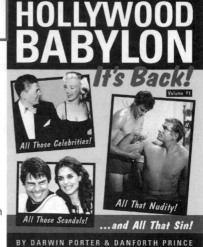

Wildly more outrageous than Volume One:

This is Volume Two of Blood Moon's Babylon Series

Hollywood Babylon

STRIKES AGAIN!

The Hollywood Babylon Series:

An overview of exhibitionism, sexuality, and sin
as filtered through 85 years of Hollywood indiscretion.

"These books will set the graves of Hollywood's cemeteries spinning"   **Daily Express**

"The Ultimate Guilty Pleasure"   **Shelf Awareness**

Hardcover, 380 pages, with hundreds of photos   ISBN 978-1-936003-12-9 $25.95

701

50 Years of Queer Cinema
500 of the Best GLBTQ Films Ever Made

**An indispensable reference source and gossip guide
for films about**

The Love that Dare Not Speak Its Name

As late as 1958, homosexuality couldn't even be mentioned in a movie, as proven by the elaborate lengths the producers of Tennessee Williams swampy *Cat on a Hot Tin Roof* took to evade the obvious fact that its hero, Paul Newman, was playing it gay. And in spite of the elaborate lengths its producers took to camouflage its lavender aspects, in-the-know viewers during the late 50s realized all along that Joe E. Brown was fully aware that Jack Lemmon wasn't a biological female ("nobody's perfect") in *Some Like it Hot* (1959).

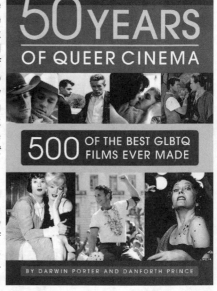

That kind of baroque subterfuge ended abruptly in 1960, when cinema emerged from its celluloid closet. With the release of *Boys in the Band* in 1970, gay cinema had come of age—It was queer and here to stay. Decades later came *Brokeback Mountain, Transamerica, Milk,* and hundreds of other gay-themed films.

This comprehensive anthology documents it all, bringing into focus a sweeping run-down of cinema's most intriguing Gay, Lesbian, Bisexual, Transgendered, and "Queer Questioning" films that deserves a home next to the DVD player as well as on the reference shelves of public libraries.   Crucial to the viability of this book is the fact that new DVD releases have made these films available to new generations of viewers for the first time since their original release.

More than just a dusty library reference, this book shamelessly spills 50 quasi-closeted years of Hollywood secrets—all of them in glorious Technicolor.

Winner of the New England Book Festival's "Best Gay Nonfiction title of 2010," this is a comprehensive paperback designed as a reference source for private homes and libraries.   524 pages, with 500 B&W photos
ISBN 978-1-936003-09-9 $24.95

HOLLYWOOD'S SILENT CLOSET

Orgiastic Excess in Pre-Code Hollywood

Hollywood's Silent Closet

An outrageously informative "info-novel" by Darwin Porter

An anthology of star-studded scandal from Tinseltown's very gay and very lavender past, it focuses on Hollywood's secrets from the 1920s, including the controversial backgrounds of the great lovers of the Silent Screen.

The first book of its kind, it's the most intimate and most realistic novel about sex, murder, blackmail, and degradation in early Hollywood ever written.

Valentino, Ramon Novarro, Charlie Chaplin, Fatty Arbuckle, Pola Negri, Mary Pickford, and many others figure into eyewitness accounts of the debauched excesses that went on behind closed doors. It also documents the often tragic endings of America's first screen idols, some of whom admitted to being more famous than the monarchs of England and Jesus Christ combined.

A banquet of information about the pansexual intrigues of Hollywood between 1919 and 1926 compiled from eye-witness interviews with men and women, all of them insiders, who flourished in its midst. Not for the timid, it names names and doesn't spare the guilty. If you believe, like Truman Capote, that the literary treatment of gossip will become the literature of the 21st century, then you will love *Hollywood's Silent Closet.* **THE PUBLIC NEVER KNEW!!!**

"Lush, luscious, and langorously decadent. A brilliant primer of *Who Was Who* in early Hollywood."

-Gay London Times

Softcover, 7" x 10" 746 pages 60 photos $24.95
ISBN 978-0-9668030-2-0

703

BLOOD MOON PRODUCTIONS ANNOUNCES THE RELEASE of the 75-minute documentary it filmed in May on the floor of America's world-famous and most important bookselling event, BEA 2010.

BOOK EXPO 2010: BLOOD MOON'S VIEW FROM THE FLOOR, represents history's first attempt to capture—close, in-your-face, uncensored, and personalized—the interactions, alliances, scandals, and dramas that explode for a small book publisher during a bookselling mega-event devoted to the marketing, pricing, and sale of its literary products.

Defined as both a documentary and an infomercial, the film was conceived as a publicity and promotion piece by Blood Moon's founder and president, Danforth Prince: "Book publishers operate in a state of barely controlled hysteria, especially in this economic climate," he said. "Within this film, we've captured some of the drama of how books are promoted and hawked at a highly competitive event where everyone from Barbra Streisand to the Duchess of York was shaking his or her bon-bon to sell something."

"At BEA 2010, enemies, competitors, and authors evoked Oscar night in Hollywood before the awards are announced," Prince continued. "This film is the first attempt to depict, on video, how a small press swims in the frantic, shark-infested waters of the book trade. It's a documentation of a specific moment in America's mercantile history, with implications for America's reading habits and how consumers will opt, sometimes through digitalization, to amuse and entertain themselves in the 21st century."

During the footage he shot from within and near his booth #3784 at BEA, Mr. Prince was assisted by members of Blood Moon's editorial staff, and directed by Polish-born Piotr Kajstura, winner of several filmmaking awards and grants for his work with, among others, the tourism board of South Carolina.

BOOK EXPO 2010, BLOOD MOON'S VIEW FROM THE FLOOR.
© Blood Moon Productions, Ltd. Available now, electronically and without charge, from the home page of **BloodMoonProductions.com**

WHAT BOOK-INDUSTRY CRITICS SAID ABOUT THIS FILM:

Blood Moon Productions, which specializes in books about Hollywood celebrity scandals of the past--many of which were hushed up at the time--offered a feature-length video on BookExpo America 2010, which aims to give "nonprofessional book people an insight into book fairs"--while highlighting some Blood Moon titles. The narrator is Blood Moon president Danforth Prince, who interviews, among others, Carole Stuart of Barricade Books, Philip Rafshoon, owner of Outwrite Bookstore and Coffeehouse, Atlanta, Ga., Graeme Aitkin of the Bookshop in Sydney, Australia, Eugene Schwartz of ForeWord Reviews, and a what seems like half of the staff of National Book Network, Blood Moon's distributor.

Shelf-Awareness.com August 3, 2010 (volume 2, issue #1247)